S0-EID-785

NATIONAL ELECTRICAL CODE®

REFERENCE BOOK

NATIONAL ELECTRICAL CODE®
REFERENCE BOOK

Second Edition

BASED ON THE 1978 CODE

J. D. GARLAND

Registered Professional Engineer

PRENTICE-HALL, INC.
Englewood Cliffs, New Jersey 07632

Library of Congress Cataloging in Publication Data

GARLAND, J D (date)
National electrical code reference book, based on the 1978 code.

Includes index.
1. Electric engineering—Insurance requirements.
I. Title.
TK260.G37 621.319'24'021 78–12447
ISBN 0–13–609313–2

®"NATIONAL ELECTRICAL CODE, NEC are trademarks of National Fire Protection Association, Inc., Boston, Massachusetts, for a triannual electrical publication. The terms NATIONAL ELECTRICAL CODE, NEC, as used herein means the triannual publication constituting the NATIONAL ELECTRICAL CODE and is used with permission of National Fire Protection Association, Inc."

Editorial/production supervision by Virginia Rubens
Manufacturing buyer: Gordon Osbourne

Printed in the United States of America
10 9 8 7 6 5 4 3 2 1

PRENTICE-HALL INTERNATIONAL, INC., *London*
PRENTICE-HALL OF AUSTRALIA PTY. LIMITED, *Sydney*
PRENTICE-HALL OF CANADA, LTD., *Toronto*
PRENTICE-HALL OF INDIA PRIVATE LIMITED, *New Delhi*
PRENTICE-HALL OF JAPAN, INC., *Tokyo*
PRENTICE-HALL OF SOUTHEAST ASIA PTE. LTD., *Singapore*
WHITEHALL BOOKS LIMITED, *Wellington, New Zealand*

Dedicated to my wife Mary, who undertook the prodigious and painstaking task of typing the entire manuscript for this work.

Contents

Preface

The second edition of the *National Electrical Code Reference Book* is based on the 1978 *National Electrical Code.* Numerous changes, additions and deletions have been made in the 1978 edition of the Code, and these are included in this edition. Among the more significant changes are: new rules governing ground fault protection; changes in requirements for installations on construction sites; new requirements for grounding of service equipment; a change in permissible use of nonmetallic boxes; new grounding requirements for appliances, tools, lighting fixtures and switch plates. There are new rules defining the extent of the hazardous areas around paint-spraying operations. Two wiring methods have been deleted, two added. A new Article—Agricultural Buildings—has been added.

The *National Electrical Code Reference Book* is for use as a reference guide for electricians, electrical contractors and inspectors, as well as a reference for vocational students and individuals making a study of the *National Electrical Code.* The book is not intended as a substitute for the Code. It is intended for use in conjunction with the Code, as an explanatory guide. The purpose is to expand upon and clarify Code rules through discussion, examples and illustrations.

The book represents some twenty years of Code study and research, including a number of years spent by the author with the Wisconsin Vocational System, as a full-time instructor in trade electricity. The book covers Chapters 1, 2, 3, 4, 5, and Article 600 of Chapter 6 of the 1978 *National Electrical Code.*

Chapter 1 covers the general requirements of Article 110, for electrical installations. Chapter 2 covers branch circuits, feeders, services, overcurrent protection, grounding, and a study of the method of calculating load and sizing services. Chapter 3 includes the general rules governing wiring, approved uses for the different types of conductors, and individual treatment of each of the 31 different wiring methods now approved for use. Chapter 4 is devoted to lighting, appliances, electric heating systems, motors, and transformers. Chapter 5 includes the rules and requirements for electrical installations in hazardous locations, garages, gas stations, theaters, and mobile homes. Article 600 of Chapter 6 covers the installation and wiring of electrical signs and outline lighting.

This book is comprised of approximately 1,500 Sections, including some 4,000 Code rules which are individually treated. The Code is covered in its entirety, with the exception of certain specialized sections (elevators, X-ray equipment, irrigation machines, swimming pools, community antenna systems) which are of interest only to a limited number of people in the electrical field.

A characteristic of Code reference books has been a tendency to overlook the necessity to impart to the reader an understanding and comprehension of the underlying aims and objectives behind individual rules. By providing such an overview, this reference book attempts to clarify and coordinate Code requirements in the mind of the reader. Considerable effort has been made to condense the more complicated rules into a compact listing which should provide easier understanding. The text is accompanied by numerous illustrations and examples which will serve to clarify further the intent of the rules. For example, under Article 430—Motors—the different basic requirements for motor circuits, which can otherwise be quite confusing, are here brought together into a composite picture by the illustrations (Figs. 439–446) which accompany the text.

A special feature of the book is a group of tables which list different items of electrical equipment and indicate the types (explosion-proof, dust-ignition-proof, etc.) permitted for installation in various categories of hazardous locations. Equipment is listed alphabetically for convenient reference. Use of these tables will eliminate the need to thumb through the pages of the Code when information is needed on specific requirements for equipment to be installed in a particular hazardous location.

For those engaged in class study of the Code, it is recommended that the rules be taken up in a systematic manner, progressing from one rule to the next, rather than attempting a random coverage of different rules from different parts of the Code. A systematic study of one part of the Code at a time will result in a fuller understanding of Code rules and requirements.

J. D. Garland

Chapter 1. General

ARTICLE 110 — REQUIREMENTS FOR ELECTRICAL INSTALLATIONS

A. General

110-1. Mandatory Rules and Explanatory Material

The word "shall," used with a rule, means that the requirement of the rule is mandatory; it *must* be complied with. "The conductors and equipment required or permitted by this Code shall be acceptable only when approved," etc.

In previous editions of the Code, the word "should" was used, in some cases, instead of "shall." Use of the word "should" indicated that the rule was not mandatory, but simply a recommendation. In the 1978 Code, the word "shall" is used exclusively.

110-2. Approval

All electrical installations must be approved. The Code definition of "approved" is "Acceptable to the authority having jurisdiction" (p. 70-4). In most cases, the "authority having jurisdiction" would be the inspector.

110-3. Examination, Installation, and Use of Equipment

(a) Examination

The Code does not provide detailed specifications for material and equipment. However, it is required that all equipment used in electrical installations be adequate and suitable for the intended use. This subsection provides guidelines for judging the equipment.

(b) Installation and Use

Any installation instructions supplied by the manufacturer and accompanying "listed" or "labeled" equipment shall be complied with when installing such equipment. Use of such equipment shall also comply with instructions. See definitions of "labeled" and "listed," p. 70-10 of the Code.

110-4. Voltages

"Voltage," as used in the Code, means circuit operating voltage.

110-5. Conductors

Circuit conductors shall be of copper, unless other metals are expressly permitted by the Code. Note that this rule refers to *circuit* conductors. Equipment grounding conductors may be of other metals.

110-6. Conductor Sizes

The American Wire Gage (AWG) is used throughout the Code for wire sizes.

110-7. Insulation Integrity

All wiring systems shall be free from stray grounds.

110-8. Wiring Methods

There are some 30 approved wiring methods, which are described in Articles 318 through 366.

General wiring requirements are set forth in Sections 300-1 through 310-61.

110-9. Interrupting Rating

Switches and circuit breakers must have a voltage rating at least equal to the circuit voltage. The interrupting rating must be high enough to handle the maximum short-circuit current of the circuit (see Section 230-98).

110-10. Circuit Impedance and Other Characteristics

Circuit breakers and fuses are "overcurrent protective devices."

Protective devices must be so constructed as to be capable of protecting equipment and conductors from damage should a short or ground occur in the circuit. On short circuit, the protective device must operate instantaneously. The protective device must also be capable of interrupting short-circuit currents without damage to itself. (See also Section 230-98.)

110-11. Deteriorating Agents

Certain types of conductor insulation are suitable only for dry locations. Other insulation types are approved for use in damp or wet, as well as dry locations.

Conductors exposed to corrosive fumes, gasoline, oil, grease, or other deteriorating substances must be either lead-covered or have special insulation approved for the conditions. See also Sections 310-7 and 310-8. Conductor insulation, in all cases, must be a type approved for the conditions of use.

110-12. Mechanical Execution of Work

The Code requires that electrical installations shall be executed in a "neat and workmanlike manner."

110-13. Mounting and Cooling of Equipment

(a) Mounting

All equipment must be firmly fastened. Wooden plugs in masonry, concrete, and brick do not provide a reliable footing for mounting screws and are not permitted. Metal expansion plugs are approved for this purpose.

(b) Cooling

Motors and other equipment that require a circulation of air for cooling must be so installed that an adequate supply of circulating air will be available to prevent overheating.

110-14. Electrical Connections

Splicing devices used with copper conductors shall be suitable for use with copper. Splicing devices used with aluminum conductors shall be suitable for use with aluminum.

Where dissimilar metals are in contact, a galvanic action will be set up when moisture is present. To avoid galvanic action, aluminum and copper conductors shall not be connected in a common splicing device.

(a) Terminals

Conductors may be connected to terminals by pressure connectors or solder lugs, or they may be spliced to flexible leads on the equipment.

For No. 10 or smaller conductors, wire binding screws may be used for terminal connections. Or studs and nuts may be used, provided they are equipped with upturned lugs or similar attachment.

(b) Splices

Solder may be used for making splices, provided the wires are firmly twisted together before soldering.

Splices may also be made by welding or brazing the conductors together. Or suitable splicing devices may be used for the purpose.

110-16. Working Space About Electric Equipment (600 volts or less nominal)

Clearances required around switchboards are illustrated in Fig. 354.

(a) Working Clearances

There are three cases considered:

1. Where there are exposed live parts on one side of a space and ungrounded parts on the other side.
2. Where there are exposed live parts on one side and grounded parts on the other (concrete, brick, tile walls are considered to be grounded parts).
3. Where there are exposed live parts on both sides.

Minimum clearances required are as follows:

	Voltage to Ground	
For case 1	0–150	3 ft
	151–600	3 ft
For case 2	0–150	3 ft
	151–600	3½ ft
For case 3	0–150	3 ft
	151–600	4 ft

(b) Clear Spaces

The clear spaces specified herein shall not be used for storage of any kind.

(c) Access and Entrance to Working Space

Working spaces, such as spaces behind a switchboard, shall be accessible from at least one side.

(d) Front Working Space

For live front switchboards, at least 3 ft of working space is required in front of the board.

(e) Illumination

(f) Headroom

Adequate illumination must be provided for working spaces around indoor switchboards, motor control centers, panelboards, and service equipment. A minimum headroom of 6 ft 3 in. is required in the working spaces.

Note: Service equipment and panelboards in "dwelling units," if rated 200 amps. or less, are exempted from these requirements.

110-17. Guarding of Live Parts (600 volts or less nominal)

The following are approved methods of guarding live parts of electrical equipment from accidental contact by persons:

1. By enclosing the live parts in a cabinet, box, etc.
2. By locating in a room accessible only to "qualified persons."
3. By locating behind a permanent partition or screen. An example would be a screened-in space in back of a switchboard having a locked door operable only by qualified persons.
4. By elevating at least 8 ft above the floor.

110-18. Arcing Parts

Electrical equipment likely to produce arcs or sparks shall not be located in the vicinity of combustible material.

110-19. Light and Power from Railway Conductors

Light and power circuits may not be taken from trolley wires having a ground return, except circuits for use by the electric railway company.

110-21. Marking

The manufacturer's name or trademark must appear on all electrical equipment. For certain equipment, such as motors and appliances, other information (volts, amps, watts, etc.) is also required to be furnished on the label by the manufacturer.

110-22. Identification of Disconnecting Means

Switches in a panel, or elsewhere, must be marked to show what equipment is controlled by the switch.

B. Over 600 Volts Nominal

110-30. General

The preceding sections under General also apply to circuits of over 600 volts. In addition to the general rules there are special rules for high-voltage circuits, which are set down in the sections following.

110-31. Enclosure for Electrical Installations

(a) Indoor Installations

Where accessible to "unqualified" persons, equipment shall be:

1. Metal-enclosed, or

2. Enclosed in a vault, or

3. In a locked area.

Where accessible to qualified persons only, the requirements of Sections 110-34, 710-32, and 710-33 apply.

(b) Outdoor Installations

Where accessible to "unqualified" persons, installations shall comply with the requirements of Article 225.

Where accessible to qualified persons only, the requirements of Sections 110-34, 710-32, and 710-33 apply.

(c) Metal-Enclosed Equipment Accessible to Unqualified Persons

Where equipment is metal enclosed, as in (a) above, any openings in the metal enclosure shall be so designed that any object inserted in the opening will be deflected from making contact with a live part.

If the bottom of the enclosure is less than 8 ft above the floor, the door or cover of the metal enclosure shall be kept locked.

110-32. Workspace About Equipment

Minimum clear vertical space required around exposed parts of high-voltage equipment is $6\frac{1}{2}$ ft. Minimum horizontal space required is 3 ft. Horizontal clearance shall in all cases be sufficient to permit at least a 90-degree opening of doors or hinged panels.

110-33. Entrance and Access to Workspace

(a) At least one entrance (at least 24 in. wide and at least $6\frac{1}{2}$ ft high) shall be provided for access to working spaces around high-voltage equipment.

For switchboards or control panels over 4 ft in width, two entrances are required—one at each end of the workspace.

(b) Where equipment is installed on platforms, balconies, etc., or in attics or roof spaces, *permanent* ladders are required.

110-34. Workspace and Guarding

(a) Working Space

Table 110-34(a) lists minimum clear working spaces required in *front* of high-voltage electrical equipment (switchboards, control panels, switches, circuit breakers, motor controllers, etc.).

There are three cases considered:

1. Where there are exposed live parts on one side of a space and ungrounded parts on the other side.
2. Where there are exposed live parts on one side and grounded parts on the other. (Concrete, brick, and tile walls are considered to be grounded parts.)
3. Where there are exposed live parts on both sides.

Minimum clear space required in front of live parts is as follows:

	Voltage to Ground	
For case 1	601–2,500	3 ft
	2,501–9,000	4 ft
	9,001–25,000	5 ft
	25,001–75,000	6 ft
	Above 75,000	8 ft
For case 2	601–2,500	4 ft
	2,501–9,000	5 ft
	9,001–25,000	6 ft
	25,001–75,000	8 ft
	Above 75,000	10 ft
For case 3	601–2,500	5 ft
	2,501–9,000	6 ft
	9,001–25,000	9 ft
	25,001–75,000	10 ft
	Above 75,000	12 ft

(b) Separation from Low-Potential Equipment

When low-voltage (600 volts or less) equipment is in a room or enclosure where there are exposed high-voltage live parts, the high-voltage equipment must be separated from the low-voltage equipment by a suitable partition, fence, or screen.

Note: If the room or enclosure is accessible only to qualified persons, a partition, etc., is not required provided the low-voltage equipment serves only equipment within the room or enclosure.

(c) Locked Rooms or Enclosures

The entrances to all buildings, rooms, or enclosures containing high-voltage exposed live parts must be kept locked, except where such entrances are under the constant observation of a qualified person.

(d) Illumination

Adequate illumination must be provided for all working spaces around electrical equipment.

(e) Elevation of Unguarded Live Parts

High-voltage live parts must be elevated above the floor not less than these distances:

For Voltages of:	
601–7,500	8 ft 6 in.
7,501–35,000	9 ft
Over 35,000	9 ft + .37 in. for each 1,000 volts above 35,000

Chapter 2. Wiring Design and Protection

ARTICLE 200 — USE AND IDENTIFICATION OF GROUNDED CONDUCTORS

200-1. Scope

Article 200 sets forth requirements for:

1. Identification of terminals.
2. Grounded conductors in premises wiring systems.
3. Identification of grounded conductors.

See definition of Premises Wiring System, p. 70-11 of the Code.

200-2. General

The Code requires that, for circuits used in premises wiring systems, one of the circuit conductors must be grounded.

This is the general rule. However, there are several exceptions to the rule, which permit ungrounded circuits to be used for premises wiring systems. The exceptions are noted in other sections of the Code, as follows:

1. Sections 210-10 and 215-7 permit ungrounded circuits to be used if tapped from a grounded circuit. Thus, a two-wire, 240-volt circuit may be tapped from the hot wires of a three-wire, 120/240-volt grounded circuit. The neutral need not be carried along with the tapped circuit. This rule is not intended to permit the use of such a tapped circuit as a service to a building. The rule applies only for circuits on a premises.
2. Section 250-3: Two-wire DC circuits operating at over 50, up to 300 volts, supplying only industrial equipment in limited areas, need not be grounded if equipped with a ground detector. (In all other cases, two-wire DC circuits of over 50 and up to 300 volts must be grounded.)

   Two-wire DC circuits of 0–50 volts do not require grounding.

Two-wire DC circuits of over 300 volts do not require grounding.

Two-wire DC systems derived from rectifiers supplied from a *grounded* AC system need not be grounded.

Two-wire DC fire protective systems, as specified in Article 760, part C, need not be grounded.

(The neutral of *all* three-wire DC systems supplying premises wiring must be grounded.)

3. Section 250-5 (see Fig. 234): AC circuits with voltage of over 150 to ground need not be grounded. A circuit would have a voltage of over 150 to ground if there were no conductor in the circuit having a voltage of 150 or less to *all other conductors* of the circuit. (See p. 70-14 of the Code for a definition of "voltage to ground.")

There are exceptions that require circuits of over 150 volts to ground to be grounded:

(1) A 480Y/277-V, three-phase, four-wire circuit. Here the voltage between each phase wire and neutral is over 150 volts (277). Nevertheless, the neutral must be grounded.

(2) A 240/120-V, three-phase delta-connected circuit, with the midpoint of one phase used as a neutral circuit conductor. Here the voltage between neutral and one of the phase wires is 208 V, which is over 150. Still the neutral must be grounded.

(3) AC systems of 1 kV and over supplying portable equipment shall be grounded. Where supplying other than portable equipment, AC systems of 1 kV and over *may* be grounded.

(4) When a service conductor is uninsulated, it must be grounded, regardless of voltage.

Indoor AC circuits of less than 50 volts supplied by a transformer need not be grounded if the transformer supply system is grounded, *and* 150 volts or less to ground. A bell-ringing circuit in a residence would be an example of such a circuit. Since the supply circuit is a grounded 120/240-volt circuit, with only 120 volts to ground, the bell-ringing circuit need not be grounded. (AC circuits of less than 50 volts, when run outdoors and overhead, must be grounded in all cases.)

Section 250-5 also permits circuits for industrial electric furnaces for melting, refining, and the like to be ungrounded.

Separately derived systems used exclusively for rectifiers supplying only adjustable-speed industrial drives need not be grounded.

4. Sections 250-7 and 503-13 permit ungrounded circuits for electric cranes operating over combustible fibers in Class III locations.

5. Section 517-63(b) *requires* that circuits in an anesthetizing location be *ungrounded.*

If a grounded conductor is required for a wiring system, the grounded conductor must be "identified" (colored white, etc.) according to Section 200-6.

For alternating current the foregoing rules indicate that, except for electric furnaces, certain cranes, separately derived systems for adjustable-speed industrial drives, and anesthetizing locations, all premises AC circuits of 50-150 volts to ground must be grounded.

200-3. Connection to Grounded System

If a premises wiring system has a grounded conductor, then the supply system to which it is connected (the power company lines, for instance) must also have a corresponding grounded conductor.

200-6. Means of Identifying Grounded Conductors

(a) For conductors No. 6 or smaller (except Type MI cable) the insulation or covering of the grounded conductor shall be white or natural gray. (There is an exception. Where it is assured that only "qualified" maintenance people will service an installation, the grounded conductor of *multiconductor cables* may be identified by white marking at outlets.) The individual wires of Type MI cable are uninsulated. The grounded conductor of Type MI cable must be identified by "distinctive marking" at terminations.

(b) For conductors larger than No. 6, the insulation of the grounded conductor need not be white or natural gray; but if not, the insulation on the grounded conductor must be painted or colored white at all boxes, terminals, and outlets.

(c) For flexible cords, the grounded conductor may have white or natural gray insulation, or braid. Or the cord may have a white or natural gray separator. Or there may be a tracer in the braid or marking on the outside of the cord. Finally, the grounded conductor may be a tinned conductor, the other wires being untinned. Any of these methods may be used to identify the grounded conductor of flexible cords.

200-7. Use of White or Natural Gray Color

This rule states, in effect, that no conductor except the grounded circuit conductor shall have a white or natural gray insulation. There are, however, four exceptions:

1. One black and one white wire may be used for a circuit with no neutral, if the white wire is painted the proper color at each outlet. For example, for a 240-volt two-wire ungrounded circuit a cable containing one white and one black wire could be used, but the white wire would have to be painted or colored black at each outlet.
2. A *cable* with one white and one black wire may be used for a switch leg. Here we have no neutral, only the "hot" wire both to and from the switch (the switched wire is always the "hot" wire). The only requirement here is that the white wire must be the one from the supply *to* the switch, and the black wire the return *from* the switch to the outlet (Fig. 210). Note that this exception applies only for cables; it does not apply for conductors run in raceways (conduit, EMT, etc.). For conductors in raceway, either both conductors must be black, or if there is a white conductor, the white conductor must be colored black at outlets.
3. Cords with an "identified" conductor may be used for plugging to ungrounded circuits.
4. AC circuits of less than 50 volts (such as a bell-ringing circuit taken from a bell-ringing transformer) are not usually grounded, but may nevertheless have a white wire.

200-9. Means of Identification of Terminals

The manufacturer is required to "identify" the terminal to which the grounded conductor is to be connected. For example, the screw shell of a lampholder must be connected to the grounded conductor. Therefore, the screw-shell terminal must be "identified." This is done by coating the terminal with a white metallic coating to distinguish it from the terminal for the "hot" wire, which would be a different color.

200-10. Identification of Terminals

(a) Device Terminals

"Identification" of terminals means marking the terminals in some way to show which terminal is to be connected to the grounded conductor, or in the case of a grounding device, such as a three-wire receptacle with one terminal

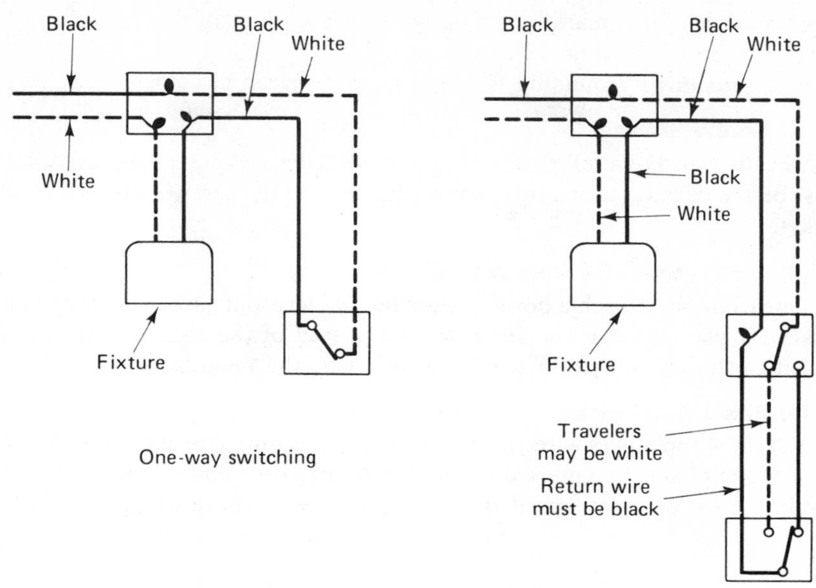

Fig. 210

Cable with white and black conductor may be used as a switch leg. White conductor must connect to "hot" supply conductor. White wire need not be colored black in junction box, or in switch (Sect. 200-7, Exception No. 2).

for grounding, the marking would show which terminal is to be connected to the *grounding wire.*

The general rule is that, if a device is provided with terminals for connecting to "more than one side of the circuit," then the terminals must be properly marked or "identified." There are exceptions, as follows:

The neutral terminals of a lighting panelboard need not be identified or marked, because in lighting panelboards the neutral conductor connection is clearly evident, being the solid bar in the panel.

Devices rated at over 30 amps. do not require identification of terminals, except for polarized plugs and receptacles. See subparagraph (b), following.

(b) Plugs, Receptacles, and Connectors

On *polarized* plugs and receptacles the terminal intended for connection to the grounded circuit conductor must be white in color.

The ordinary two-wire, parallel-blade attachment plug need not have terminal marking. Such marking would be useless in plugs of this type since the blades can be reversed at will.

The *equipment* grounding terminal must be green in color.

(c) Screw-Shells

The identified (white) terminal in screw-shell devices, such as lamp sockets, must be the one connected by the manufacturer to the screw-shell part of the socket.

(d) Screw-Shell Devices with Leads

One example of such a device would be a waterproof rubber-covered lamp socket for use out-of-doors. Here, the white lead of the socket is to be connected to the screw-shell of the lamp socket by the manufacturer.

(e) Fixed Appliances

For fixed appliances wired direct, the neutral terminal must be "identified." For fixed appliances connected by *field-installed* cords and plugs, the neutral terminal must be identified, if the cord has three or more wires.

ARTICLE 210 — BRANCH CIRCUITS

According to the Code definition, p. 70-5, a branch circuit is "the circuit conductors between the final overcurrent device protecting the circuit, and the outlet(s)." (A device such as a thermal cutout or motor overload protective device is not considered as the overcurrent device protecting the circuit.)

A premises wiring system can be thought of as consisting of three parts:

1. Service.
2. Feeders (and subfeeders).
3. Branch circuits.

Where there is a set of fuses or circuit breaker along the line, this is the point that separates one part of the wiring system from the other. As an example, a service runs to an entrance cabinet. Circuit breakers for feeders could be connected to the service. The circuit breakers mark the end point of the service. Connected to the load side of the circuit breakers are the feeders. Each feeder may be run to a distribution panel. Several circuit breakers may be connected to a feeder at its terminus in the distribution panel. Connected to the load side of these circuit breakers is another set of circuits which connect directly to lights, appliances, or motors. These circuits are branch circuits, because they are behind "the final overcurrent device"—the final circuit breaker in the line.

In some cases there may be no feeder, and the branch circuits connect directly to the service. This is frequently done in residential wiring. Several circuit breakers or sets of fuses are connected to the terminal end of the service. The circuits connected to the load side of these fuses or circuit breakers run directly to appliances, lighting, or other equipment. These circuits are branch circuits because they are "behind" the final overcurrent device along the line.

210-1. Scope

The provisions of Article 210 apply to branch circuits supplying:

(1) Lighting.

(2) Appliances.

(3) Combination lighting and appliance loads.

When motors are included in a branch circuit with lighting or appliances, the rules of Article 430 (Motor Circuits and Controllers) must be complied with, in addition to the rules of Article 210.

Most of the circuits in a household would come under the rules of Article 210. An individual circuit supplying only a motor, however, would come under the rules of Article 430 since this is a branch circuit supplying only a motor load. If the motor were on the same circuit with appliances, this would be a combination appliance and motor load, and the rules of Article 430 applying to the motor would have to be followed, as well as the rules of Article 210, for the appliances.

210-2. Other Articles for Specific-Purpose Branch Circuits

Branch circuits supplying equipment listed in this Section shall comply with the special rules governing the equipment, and also with the general rules of Article 210.

210-3. Classifications

A branch circuit is classified according to the maximum-sized fuse or circuit breaker setting permitted for protection of the circuit. The maximum-sized fuse or circuit breaker setting permitted depends, in turn, upon the kind of equipment connected to the circuit and the conductor size. For a full explanation of branch circuit classification, see Sections 210-23 and 210-24.

210-4. Multiwire Branch Circuits

This Section states, in effect, that the use of multiwire branch circuits is permitted. A multiwire circuit, regardless of number of conductors, is not a multiwire circuit unless it has a grounded neutral. Article 100, Definitions, defines a multiwire branch circuit as "a branch circuit consisting of two or more ungrounded conductors having a potential difference between them, and an identified grounded conductor having equal potential difference between it and each ungrounded conductor of the circuit and which is connected to the neutral conductor of the system."

A three-wire, 120/240-volt AC circuit is an example of a multiwire circuit. It has two ungrounded conductors, an identified grounded conductor (the neutral), and also equal potential difference (120 V) between the neutral and each of the ungrounded conductors. A 120/208-volt, three-phase, four-wire circuit is a multiwire circuit, having a grounded neutral and equal potential difference (120 V) between the neutral and each of the three ungrounded conductors.

A three-phase, three-wire circuit would not be a multiwire circuit since it has no identified grounded neutral conductor.

This Section does not exclude circuits that are not multiwire circuits. The purpose of the rule is to permit the use of multiwire circuits as well as other types.

A study of Exceptions No. 1 and No. 2 under this section will show that for multiwire *branch* circuits there are special rules for circuit protection. In some cases fuses are prohibited—only circuit breakers are permitted. To illustrate this point the following examples are given:

When a three-wire, 120/240-volt circuit serves 120 volt loads only, either fuses or a circuit breaker may be used for circuit protection.

When a three-wire, 120/240-volt circuit serves 240-volt as well as 120-volt individual outlets, the branch circuit protection must be a two (or three) pole circuit breaker. Fuses are not permitted.

When a three-wire, 120/240-volt circuit serves *one appliance only,* either fuses or a circuit breaker may be used for circuit protection. This would permit fuses as protection for an *individual* 120/240-volt range circuit, for example. If more than one range is on a 120/240-volt circuit, fuses are not permitted; a circuit breaker would be required for circuit protection (see Fig. 211).

210-5. Color Code for Branch Circuits

(a) Grounded Conductor

For branch circuits the grounded circuit conductor (neutral) must have a white or natural gray color. When there are two or more separate circuits, each

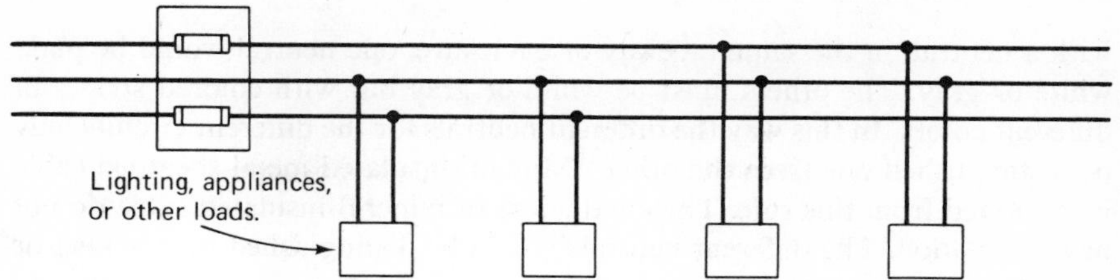

120/240 volt branch circuit supplying only 120 volt loads. Fuses may be used for circuit protection.

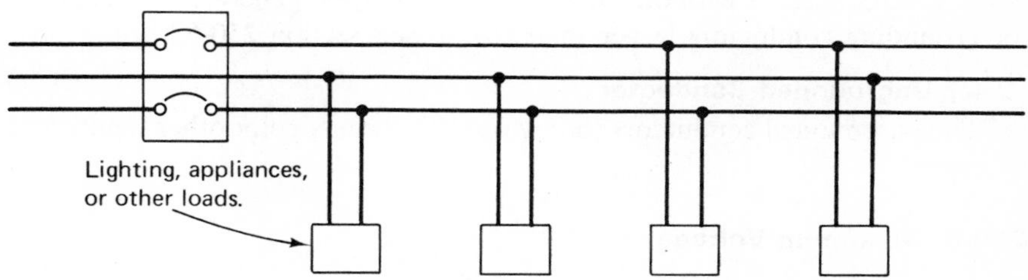

120/240 volt branch circuit supplying both 120 volt, and 240 volt loads. Fuses not permitted. Circuit breaker must be used for circuit protection.

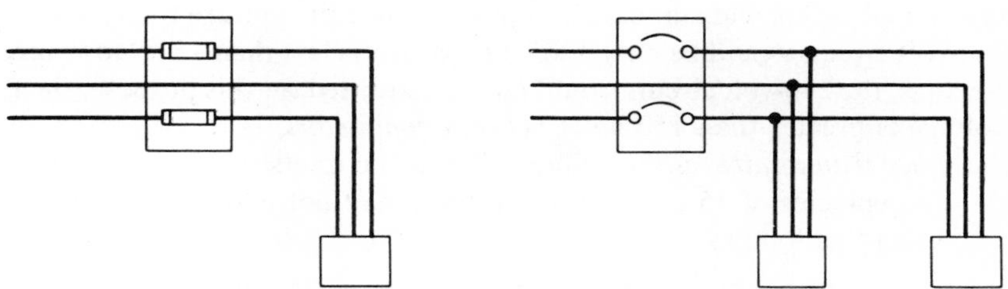

120/240 volt branch circuit supplying one appliance. Fuses may be used for circuit protection.

120/240 volt branch circuit supplying more than one appliance. Fuses not permitted. Circuit breaker must be used for circuit protection.

Fig. 211

Examples of requirements for circuit protection of multiwire branch circuits (Sect. 210-4).

with a neutral, in the same raceway or enclosure, one neutral would be plain white or gray. The others must be white or gray but with colored stripes of different colors. In this way the different neutrals for the different circuits may be distinguished one from the other. (Mineral-insulated metal-sheathed cable is exempted from this rule. The conductors of mineral-insulated cable do not have insulation. The different neutrals would be distinguished by marking or coloring the neutral terminals at all outlets.)

(b) Grounding Conductor

The "grounding conductor" is the one used for grounding equipment. The grounding conductor should not be confused with the "grounded circuit conductor" of subsection (a) above. The grounding conductor insulation must be either green, or green with one or more yellow stripes. [There is an exception for grounding conductors larger than No. 6. See Section 250-57(b).]

(c) Ungrounded Conductor

The ungrounded conductors (hot wires) may be any color other than white or green.

210-6. Maximum Voltage

(a) Voltage to Ground

This subsection permits a voltage *to ground* of up to 150 for branch circuits supplying lampholders, fixtures, and standard 15-amp. receptacles. This does not apply for "dwellings." Note that subsection (c), following, limits the voltage for such circuits *in dwellings* to 150 volts *between conductors.* Thus, for other than dwellings, the 240-volt legs of a 120/240-volt circuit may be used for lampholders and standard receptacles since the voltage to ground of the 240-volt circuit would be only 120 volts, which is less than 150. However, in dwellings, the 240-volt circuit would not be permitted for this purpose, since the voltage is greater than 150 volts *between conductors.*

For *other than residences* the voltage of branch circuits supplying lighting, standard receptacles of 15 amp. or less rating, may not exceed 150 volts to ground, except as follows:

1. For branch circuits supplying *mogul-base* screw-shell lamps in industrial establishments, the voltage may be as high as 300 to ground, provided the lighting fixtures are at least 8 ft above the floor, and are serviced by competent people. If fixtures are the "switched" type, the switch is required to be out of reach.
2. For branch circuits supplying only the ballast(s) for electric discharge lamps in industrial establishments, office buildings, schools, stores, and "commercial" areas of certain other buildings, such as hotels, the voltage may be as high as 300 to ground, provided the fixtures are perma-

nent or "fixed" (not portable), and are not the "switched" type. Fluorescent fixtures would come under this rule.

When screw-shell-type lampholders are used for electric discharge lamps, the fixtures must be at least 8 ft above the floor. For other than screw-shell types, height above the floor may be less than 8 ft.

3. For infrared industrial heating appliances, the voltage may be more than 150 to ground. Section 422-15 permits infrared lamps in industrial occupancies to be connected in series across circuits of more than 150 volts to ground. Some industrial infrared ovens are designed to operate on 440 or 480 volts, and this rule makes it possible to utilize this voltage for the lamps, with four 115-volt lamps connected in series across the circuit.

4. In railway properties the voltage may be more than 150 to ground.

(b) Voltage Between Conductors—Poles, Tunnels, and Similar Structures

For branch circuits supplying only the ballast(s) for electric discharge lamps mounted outside on poles at a height of at least 22 ft, or in tunnels at a height of at least 18 ft, the voltage *between conductors* may be as high as 500 volts.

(c) Voltage Between Conductors—Dwellings

Branch circuit voltage in dwellings may not exceed 150 volts *between conductors.*

Exceptions to this rule are circuits supplying:

1. Permanently connected appliances.

2. Portable and stationary appliances of over 1,380 watts.

3. Portable and stationary motor-operated appliances of $\frac{1}{4}$ hp or more.

For such appliances in dwellings, the voltage may be higher than 150 volts between conductors. Usually, in a residence (dwelling) the voltage would not be over 240, but there is nothing in the rule limiting the voltage of these appliances in dwellings.

"Permanently connected" appliances would include any appliance that is wired direct rather than connected by cord and plug. A hot plate wired direct would be a permanently connected appliance, and as such may operate at a voltage of over 150 between conductors. If connected by cord and plug, it would be a portable appliance, and may operate at a voltage above 150 only if rated at more than 1,380 watts.

Stationary appliances are appliances "not easily moved from one place to another in normal use" (but not fixed in place). This would include freestanding, plug-connected ranges, household refrigerators.

A portable appliance is one which can "easily be moved from one place to another in normal use." This would include such plug-connected appliances as portable heaters, toasters, plug-connected hot plates.

(d) Voltage Between Conductors—Medium-Base Lamps

Circuits supplying *medium-base* screw-shell lampholders are limited to 150 volts *between conductors.* This applies in all cases and *for all occupancies* except for (1) infrared lamps in industrial establishments, (2) railway properties. It will be noted that subsection (a) above permits higher voltage circuits to be used for medium-base screw-shell lampholders in these two cases (Exceptions No. 3 and No. 4). Other than for these two exceptions, medium-base lampholders are never permitted on 240-volt circuits, regardless of where installed.

210-7. Receptacles and Cord Connectors

All 15- and 20-amp. receptacles (except replacements as noted below) must be of the grounding type. A grounding path must be provided with the circuit feeding the receptacles. The grounding path may be the raceway (conduit, EMT, metal sheath of BX), or it may be a copper conductor.

The grounding terminal of receptacles is required to be grounded back to the service panel, but an exception is made when an existing circuit is extended for the installation of one or more new receptacles, and the existing circuit is without a grounding path back to the service entrance. In such cases the Code permits the added receptacle(s) to be grounded to a nearby *cold* water pipe, if such a pipe is available. This method of grounding is permitted only when receptacles are *added to an existing circuit without a grounding path.* All others must be grounded back to the service panel.

When nongrounding type receptacles are replaced, they shall be replaced with grounding-type receptacles, *if* a source of ground is available for grounding the new receptacles. If there is no means for grounding within the box, a nongrounding type receptacle must be used as the replacement.

If the wiring is a non-metal type such as Romex, and without a grounding wire, a nongrounding type receptacle is mandatory—*shall* be used as the replacement.

If the wiring is a metal-sheathed type of wiring—metal conduit, BX, etc. —or if a grounding wire is present in the box, this would be a ready grounding means, and a grounding-type receptacle, properly grounded, shall be used as the replacement.

When there are receptacles of different voltages on the same premises, the receptacles shall be of different design for the different voltages. For example, if there are both 120-volt and 240-volt receptacles, the 240-volt receptacles could be the polarized type, the 120-volt receptacles the parallel blade type. This would prevent plugging a 120-volt appliance to a 240-volt circuit. The same precaution should be taken to distinguish between AC and DC receptacles on the same premises.

210-8. Ground-Fault Circuit Protection

(a) In dwelling units, all 15- and 20-amp., 120-volt, single-phase receptacles installed in bathrooms and garages must have ground-fault protection. This applies for homes, apartments—all types of "dwelling units." (See definition of Dwelling Unit, p. 70-8 of the Code.)

For dwellings having "direct grade access," all 15- and 20-amp., 120-volt single-phase receptacles installed outdoors, *and* within reach of persons standing on the ground, must have ground-fault protection. The rule, as written, would definitely apply to private homes, or other living quarters having "outside" entrance doors at the first-floor level. It would not apply to apartment buildings where the entrances to the different apartments are from a hall or corridor, not directly from the outside.

Ground-fault protection is provided by installing a ground-fault interrupter in the circuit supplying the receptacles. When a ground occurs, the device opens the circuit. Ground-fault interrupters are set to operate on grounds of a few milliamps., and this provides effective protection for personnel when accidental contact is made with a "hot" wire.

(b) All 15- and 20-amp, 120-volt, single-phase receptacles on construction sites must have ground-fault protection. This applies for temporary receptacles, not permanent receptacles. An exception is made for receptacles on a generator of 5 kW or less, insulated from ground. These need not have ground-fault protection.

(The Code permits ground-fault protection for construction sites to be omitted, when a written procedure of inspection and testing is enforced, on the construction site. Permission to omit ground-fault protection must be granted by the "authority having jurisdiction.")

210-9. Circuits Derived from Autotransformers

Autotransformers are single-winding transformers, the single winding being common to both the primary and secondary circuits. To reduce the voltage, the primary is connected across the full winding, and the secondary across part of the winding. To boost the voltage, the primary circuit is connected across part of the winding, the secondary across the full winding.

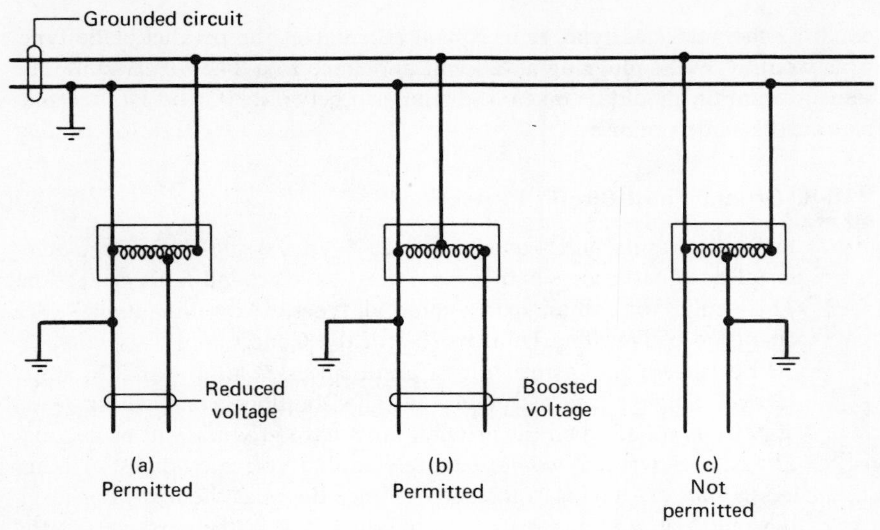

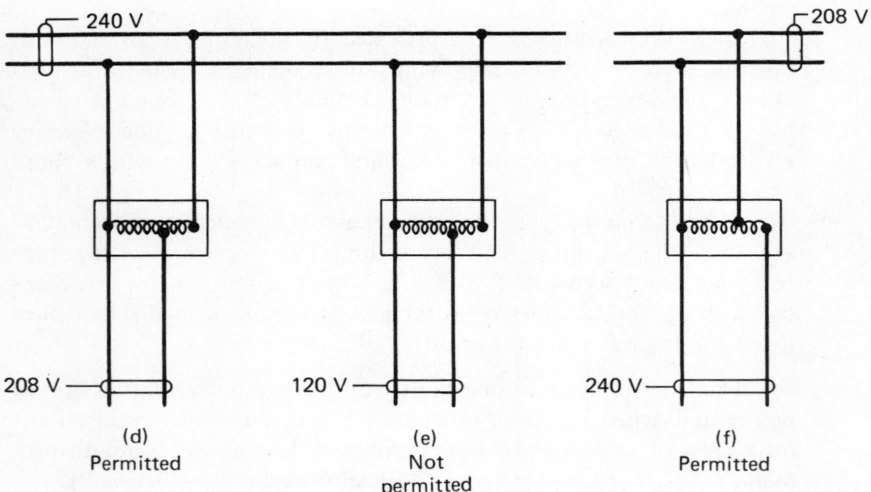

Fig. 212

Branch circuits derived from autotransformers (Sect. 210-9).

(c) Not permitted because the grounded secondary wire is not directly connected to the grounded wire of the supply circuit.

(e) Not permitted. For a 240-volt supply, omitting the grounded conductor is allowed only when the secondary is 208 V.

An autotransformer may be used to supply branch circuits, but only if one of the secondary conductors is grounded, and connected direct to the grounded conductor of the primary circuit. (An exception is made in the case of transforming from 240 to 208 volts, or from 208 to 240 volts. Here the grounding rule need not be followed.) (See Fig. 212.) The restrictions of this rule apply only for autotransformers serving branch circuits. The grounding restrictions do not apply for autotransformers serving feeders or services.

210-10. Ungrounded Conductors Tapped from Grounded Systems

This rule permits the use of ungrounded branch circuits that are tapped from a circuit that is grounded. Thus, a two-wire, 240-volt circuit may be tapped from the two hot wires of a 120/240-volt grounded circuit. The neutral need not be carried along with the tapped circuit. Switches for the tapped circuits must have a pole in each conductor. Fig. 214 illustrates an application of this rule.

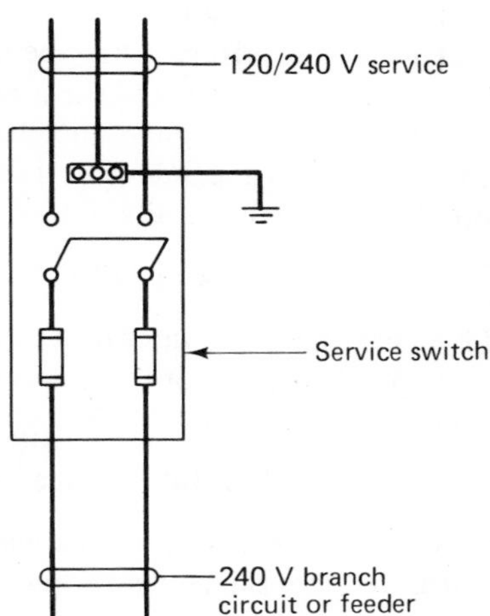

Fig. 214

Ungrounded conductors may be tapped from the ungrounded conductors of premises circuits having a grounded neutral conductor (Sect. 210-10). The above diagram illustrates an application of this rule.

Where only 240 volts is required in an occupancy, the neutral is run to the service switch along with the hot wires [this is required by Sect. 250-23 (b)]; 240 volts may be tapped from the ungrounded conductors; the neutral need not be carried along with the hot wires. See also Sect. 215-7.

B. Specific Requirements

210-19. Conductors—Minimum Ampacity and Size

(a) General

When the branch circuit has a "rating," the conductors are sized for the rating of the branch circuit. Thus, for a 15-amp. branch circuit, conductors must have a carrying capacity of at least 15 amps. (No. 14 minimum); for a 20-amp. branch circuit, conductors must have a carrying capacity of at least 20 amps. (No. 12 minimum); for a 30-amp. branch circuit, at least 30 amps. (No. 10 minimum); for a 50-amp. branch circuit, at least 50 amps. (No. 6 minimum).

For other than rated circuits the conductors shall have an ampacity not less than the maximum load to be served.

For efficiency of operation, the voltage drop in branch circuits should be held to 3% maximum.

Branch circuit conductors should be sized not only large enough to carry the load; they should be sized large enough to reduce voltage drop as well. For long runs, in order to reduce voltage drop, it may be advisable in some cases to size conductors above the size required for the amperage.

Voltage drop reduces the output of lights, appliances, and motors.

The amount of light produced by incandescent lights varies as the cube of the voltage. For a drop of 5% in voltage, the light output is reduced to

$$.95 \times .95 \times .95 = 85.7\% \text{ of full voltage output}$$

The heat generated by a heating unit (water heater, range element, immersion heater) is proportional to the square of the voltage. For a 5% reduction in voltage, the heat output is reduced to

$$.95 \times .95 = 90.2\% \text{ of full voltage output}$$

For motors, the power output is also proportional to the square of the voltage. A 5% voltage drop reduces the power output of the motor to 90.2% of full voltage output.

In addition to reducing the power output of equipment, voltage drop in a wiring system results also in dollar loss to the utilities customer because electric energy is paid for that is not used. The dollar loss is proportional to the voltage drop; a 5% voltage drop results in a 5% loss.

As an example, consider a 1,200-watt appliance served by a 120-volt circuit. If there were no voltage drop in the circuit, the voltage at the appliance would be 120 V, the appliance would draw 10 amps., the power consumed by the appliance would be $10 \times 120 = 1{,}200$ watts, and this would be the power consumption registered at the meter. The energy paid for would be the energy actually used.

With, say, a 5% voltage drop between meter and appliance, the voltage at the appliance would be 120 V minus 5% of 120, or 114 volts. With a 5% reduction in voltage, the current would be reduced by 5%, to 9.5 amps., and the power consumed by the appliance would be $9.5 \times 114 = 1{,}083$ watts. The voltage at the meter is 120 volts, and the power consumption would be registered on a basis of this voltage. Power consumption registered would be $9.5 \times 120 = 1{,}140$ watts. The difference between wattage registered and wattage used is $1{,}140 - 1{,}083 = 57$ watts. This represents a power loss of $57/1{,}140 = 5\%$. Five per cent of the watt hours registered at the meter are lost.

With a voltage drop throughout a wiring system of 5% from meter to load, $1 of each $20 of the electric bill goes for wasted energy.

Voltage drop also reduces the efficiency of operation of appliances, motors, and lights. Incandescent lighting is especially sensitive to voltage changes, the light produced being proportional to the cube of the voltage. A reduction of 5% in voltage results in a 14% reduction in light production.

Of course it is not possible to eliminate voltage drop entirely, but it is possible, and necessary, to keep voltage drop within reasonable limits that will assure efficient operation of electrical equipment and reduce loss of energy.

The voltage drop in a branch circuit should not exceed 3%. The voltage drop in a branch circuit plus the voltage drop in its feeder should not exceed 5%. This is not a Code rule. It is simply a recommendation intended to provide efficiency of operation of electrical equipment, and to reduce loss of energy in an electrical installation.

Example: Figuring Voltage Drop.

A 120-volt No. 14, two-wire branch circuit 75 ft long carries 12 amps. What is the voltage drop in the circuit?

Each wire is 75 ft long. Total length of both wires is 150 ft. From Table 8, p. 70-587 of the Code, the resistance of No. 14 is 2.68 ohms per 1,000 ft. The resistance of 150 ft would be

$$\frac{150}{1{,}000} \times 2.68 = .402 \text{ ohm}$$

$$E = I \times R = 12 \times .402 = 4.8 \text{ volts, voltage drop}$$

The percent drop would be $4.8/120 = 4\%$.

(b) Household Ranges and Cooking Appliances

This rule sets the minimum wire size for household range circuits at No. 8, for ranges of $8\frac{3}{4}$ kW or more rating. This is a minimum requirement. Larger conductors must be provided if required by the load.

Loads for household ranges need not be figured at the full kW rating of the range. It is assumed that all elements of a household range will rarely be "on" at the same time, rather only a percentage of them. Therefore, in figuring conductor sizes for household ranges, the Code allows a lower kW to be used than the full kW rating of the range. The actual kW allowed for household ranges is listed on p. 70-46 of the Code. Taking, for example, the case of a 10-kW range, Column A (this is the column usually used) shows the "demand" load to be 8 kW. This is the allowable load that may be used for figuring conductor size. The table also applies for wall-mounted ovens and counter-mounted cooking units. For these, see Note 4 following the table.

The neutral conductor of a household range circuit may be smaller than the hot wires. The ampacity may be 70% of that of the hot wires, but in no case smaller than No. 10. For a No. 6 circuit, the neutral may be No. 8. For a No. 8 circuit, the neutral may be No. 10.

Taps as small as No. 12 may be made to a 50-amp. or smaller circuit to supply ranges and cooking units, provided that No. 12 is adequate for the load. If not, larger conductors must be used.

Note that the rules of this Section apply only to *household* ranges and other *household* cooking appliances. They do not apply for commercial ranges or cooking appliances.

(c) Other Loads

For loads other than household ranges and cooking appliances, branch circuit conductors must have an ampacity at least equal to the load.

Conductors for "rated" branch circuits must have an ampacity equal to the branch circuit protection. Thus, for a 15-amp. circuit, conductors must have an ampacity of at least 15 A; for a 20-amp. circuit, conductors must have an ampacity of at least 20 A; etc. There are two exceptions:

1. *Tap Conductors*

   A No. 14 tap may be made to a circuit fused at 20 or 30 amps., or a No. 12 tap may be made to a 40- or 50-amp circuit, provided that:

   The tap supplies individual fixtures or lampholders, and is not over 18 in. long, or

   The tap supplies a high-temperature fixture set off from a box as per Section 410-67, or

   The tap supplies an individual receptacle or outlet, and is not over 18 in. long, or

   The tap supplies infrared heating appliances, or

   The tap supplies nonheating leads of de-icing cables or mats.

2. *Fixture Wires and Cords*

This is another exception to the rule of paragraph (a), which requires that conductors of a branch circuit have a carrying capacity equal to the branch circuit rating.

Fixture Wire

No. 18 fixture wire may be used on 15- or 20-amp. circuits.
No. 14 fixture wire may be used on 30-amp. circuits.
No. 12 fixture wire may be used on 40- and 50-amp. circuits.

Cord

No. 18 or larger cord of any type may be plugged into a 20-amp. circuit.

Cord with a 10-amp. or more carrying capacity may be plugged into a 30-amp. circuit. See Table 400-5, p. 70-239 of the Code. As is shown by the table, the cord may be as small as No. 18 for certain types of cord. Other types require larger sizes to meet the 10-amp. requirement.

Cord with a 20-amp. or more carrying capacity may be plugged into a 50-amp. circuit. As shown by the table, the cord could be as small as No. 14 for certain types of cord. Other types require larger sizes.

In the above cases the taps, fixture wire, and cord are "overfused," but these are exceptions to the general rule which are allowed by the Code.

210-20. Overcurrent Protection

(a) General

Branch circuit conductors must be protected by a fuse or circuit breaker (or other "overcurrent device"), the rating of which may not be more than the current-carrying capacity of the conductors. Thus, for No. 14 Type T conductors, a 15-amp. fuse is the largest size permitted for protection of the circuit; for No. 12 Type T, the largest size fuse permitted would be 20 amp.; etc.

Exceptions.

Protection for tap conductors may be higher than the ampacity of the tap [Section 210-19(c)].

Protection for fixture wires and cords may be higher than the ampacity of the fixture wire or cord [Section 210-19(c)].

210-21. Outlet Devices

(a) Lampholders

Circuits for medium-base lamps may not be fused at more than 20 amps. Mogul-base lamps may be used on circuits fused at up to 50 amps.

(b) Receptacles

Twenty, 30 and 50 amp. receptacles may not be connected to a circuit rated higher than the rating of the receptacle. Maximum circuit protection permitted for a 20-amp. receptacle is 20 amps.; for a 30-amp. receptacle, 30 amps.; for a 50-amp. receptacle, 50 amps.

A 15-amp. duplex receptacle may be connected to a 20-amp. circuit.

A 15-amp. *single* receptacle may be connected to a 20-amp. circuit only if there is at least one other outlet on the circuit. A single receptacle is defined by the Code as "a single contact device with no other contact device on the same yoke" (p. 70-12).

210-22. Maximum Loads

The Code recognizes five branch-circuit ratings: 15, 20, 30, 40, and 50 amp. The total load connected to a branch circuit may not exceed the branch-circuit rating. A 15-amp. branch circuit may be loaded to 15 amps.; a 20-amp. circuit to 20 amps.; etc.

A circuit supplying an individual load (a range circuit for example) is an individual branch circuit and does not take a branch-circuit "rating." For such circuits the conductors are sized according to the current requirement of the individual load.

The following subsections set forth the rules for figuring the load on branch circuits.

(a) Motor-Operated and Combination Loads

When a circuit supplies only motor-operated appliances, the rules of Article 430 must be followed. Article 430 says that when one motor is served by a circuit the load shall be figured at 125% of the full-load motor current. When several motors are served by a circuit, the load is figured at 125% of the full-load current rating of the largest motor, plus the sum of the full-load current ratings of the other motors in the group.

Example.

A circuit serves three appliances, one with a $\frac{1}{4}$-hp and two with $\frac{1}{6}$-hp, 115-volt single-phase motors. From Table 430-148, p. 70-316, full-load current of a $\frac{1}{4}$-hp motor is 5.8 amps., and of a $\frac{1}{6}$-hp motor, 4.4 amps. The load on the circuit is 125% of 5.8 + 4.4 + 4.4 amps., or

$$7.25 + 4.4 + 4.4 = 16.05 \text{ amps.}$$

For fixed equipment having a motor load combined with other loads, the circuit load is calculated on the basis of 125% of motor load (where the motor is over $\frac{1}{8}$-hp), plus the sum of the other loads. A dishwasher would come under this rule. The load for a 115-volt dishwasher having, say, a 1,000-watt heating element plus a $\frac{1}{6}$-hp motor would be figured on the basis of 125% of the full-load current rating of the motor, plus the current required for the heating element. From Table 430-148, full-load current rating of a $\frac{1}{6}$-hp, 115-volt motor is 4.4 amps. 125% of 4.4 = 5.5 amps. The current taken by the heating element is 1,000/115 = 8.7 amps. Total load for the dishwasher would be

$$9 + 5.5 = 14.5 \text{ amps.}$$

(b) Inductive Lighting Loads

Fluorescent lighting fixtures are an inductive lighting load. A fluorescent lamp draws more current than the lamp wattage would indicate, because the ballast consumes some wattage, in addition to the wattage of the lamp. A rule of thumb for figuring fluorescent lighting fixtures is to add 25% to the wattage of the lamp. This will produce about the same result as using the ampere rating of the fixture. For example, a 40-watt fluorescent would be figured at 50 watts, a 100-watt fluorescent at 125 watts, etc.

(c) Other Loads

Where in normal operation the load will continue for long periods (continuous load), the total connected load permitted is 80% of the branch-circuit rating. The Code defines "continuous load" as a load where the full circuit current is expected to continue for 3 hours or more. Store lighting is an example of a continuous load. Here, presumably, the lights would be in operation for 8 or 10 hours or more continuously. The same condition might exist in other occupancies, such as offices, banks, schools, drafting rooms, to name a few. Where there is "long continuing" operation of the load, a 15-amp. branch circuit may be loaded only to 12 amps. (80% of 15), a 20-amp. circuit only to 16 amps., etc.

Exceptions.

Exception No. 1. Continuous motor loads need not be reduced below the circuit rating.

Exception No. 2. Note 8 of Tables 310-16 through 310-19 requires derating of a conductor (i.e., a reduction in carrying capacity) when there are more than three conductors in a conduit or cable. When derating is made for this reason, no further derating is necessary because of "continuous load."

Exception No. 3. No derating of a "continuous-load" circuit is necessary where the protective assembly for the branch circuit is approved for continuous operation at 100% capacity.

210-23. Permissible Loads

The Code recognizes five branch-circuit "ratings": 15, 20, 30, 40, and 50 amp. One thing should be remembered: a circuit is not "classified" unless it has *two* or *more* outlets. A circuit supplying only one outlet is an individual circuit and is not given a classification.

There are rules governing the "permissible loads" (i.e. the type of equipment) that may be connected to circuits of different ratings. The rules are set down in paragraphs (a), (b) and (c), following.

(a) 15- and 20-Ampere Branch Circuits

Branch circuits coming under the 15 and 20-amp. classification may serve either medium- or heavy-duty lighting units and/or appliances. Appliances may be served direct or through receptacles.

A portable appliance or stationary appliance drawing more than 12 amps. may not be connected to a 15-amp. branch circuit. A portable or stationary appliance drawing more than 16 amps. may not be connected to a 20-amp. branch circuit. Other loads may also be on the circuit as long as the total load does not exceed 15 amps. for a 15-amp. circuit, or 20 amps. for a 20-amp. circuit.

When lighting, or portable appliances, or stationary appliances are on a circuit together with fixed appliances, the total rating of the fixed appliances is limited to $7\frac{1}{2}$ amps. for 15-amp. circuits and 10 amps. for 20-amp. circuits. If fixed appliances alone are on the circuit, the total rating of the fixed appliances may be 15 amps. for 15-amp. circuits; 20 amps. for 20-amp. circuits.

(b) 30-Ampere Branch Circuits

Medium-base lampholders may not be connected to a 30-amp. branch circuit. Lampholders on a 30-amp. branch circuit must be the heavy-duty type. Thirty-amp. lighting circuits may not be installed in residences, but may be installed elsewhere. Mogul-base lamps may be installed in residences, but if so they must be on 15- or 20-amp. branch circuits.

Thirty-amp. branch circuits may serve appliances or heavy-duty fixed lighting in other than dwellings, or appliances in dwellings. Note that a 30-amp. branch circuit may not serve *both* lights and appliances. In dwellings, a 30-amp. branch circuit may be used only for appliances. In other than dwellings one or the other may be served, but not both on the same circuit. Portable or stationary appliances used on 30-amp. branch circuits are limited to a 24-amp. rating for any one appliance. If the branch circuit protection is to be 25 amps. the rating is limited to 20 amps. maximum.

(c) 40- and 50-Ampere Branch Circuits

Medium-base lampholders may not be connected to a 40- or 50-amp. branch circuit. Forty- or 50-amp. branch circuits in other than dwellings may serve heavy-duty lampholders *or* infrared heating units *or* fixed cooking appliances. In dwellings, only fixed cooking appliances may be served.

The different classes of branch circuits, as applied to dwelling occupancies, are illustrated in the examples of Fig. 215.

210-24. Branch-Circuit Requirements—Summary

Table 210-24 of the Code sets down the rules of Section 210-23 in the form of a table. It should be mentioned here that, although it is not permissible to overfuse a circuit, it is permissible to *underfuse.* For example, if a circuit fulfilling all the requirements of the 30-amp. classification is fused at 15 amps. this does not make the circuit a "15-amp." circuit. It would still be a 30-amp. circuit, because 30-amp. fusing is permissible for the circuit.

It is the maximum *permissible* fusing that determines the circuit classification.

The size of the circuit conductors *and* the type of equipment on the circuit determine the maximum permissible fusing, which in turn determines the circuit classification.

To determine the circuit classification, set down the maximum-size fusing allowed for the circuit *conductors,* and also the maximum-size fusing allowed for the different types of *equipment* connected to the circuit. The *smallest* fuse size in the list determines the circuit classification. Here, and in the following examples, fusing is assumed to be the "branch-circuit overcurrent protection."

Examples.

1. A circuit supplies medium-base lamps and 15-amp. receptacles. Circuit conductors are No. 10. What is the circuit classification?

   Maximum fusing (overcurrent protection) allowed for No. 10 circuit wires 30 amps.

   Maximum fusing allowed for medium-base lamps (Table 210-24 lists "any type") 20 amps.

   Maximum fusing allowed for 15-amp. receptacles 20 amps.

   Smallest fuse size here is 20 amp. This is a "20-amp." circuit, which may be fused at 20 amps. maximum.

2. A circuit supplying mogul-base (heavy-duty) lamps in a residence. Circuit conductors are No. 14.

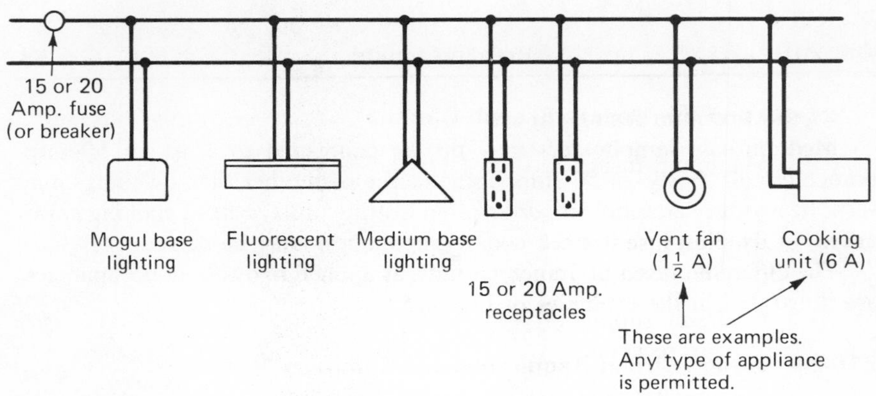

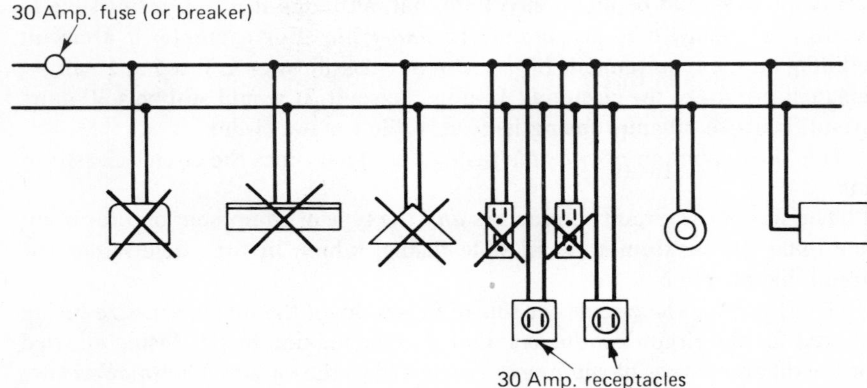

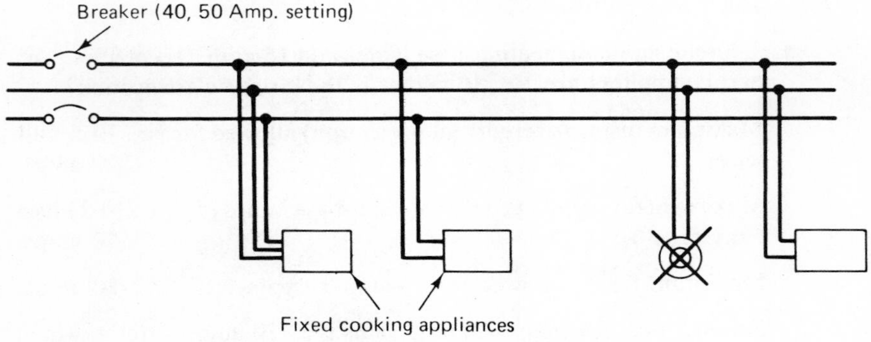

Fig. 215

Classified branch circuits in *dwellings;* examples showing type of equipment permitted (Sects. 210-23, 210-24).

Appliances of any type are permitted on 15-, 20-, and 30-amp. circuits.

No lighting is permitted on 30-amp. circuits; receptables for appliances must have 30-A rating. Only *fixed cooking* appliances are permitted on 40- and 50-amp. circuits.

Maximum fusing allowed for No. 14 circuit wires 15 amps.

Maximum fusing allowed for heavy-duty lamps in a residence 20 amps.

Smallest fuse size here is 15 amps. This is a "15-amp." circuit, which may be fused at 15 amps., maximum.

3. A circuit supplying mogul-base lamps, medium-base lamps, and 15-amp receptacles in a residence. Circuit conductors are No. 10.

   Maximum fusing allowed for No. 10 30 amps.

   Maximum fusing allowed for heavy-duty lamps in a residence 20 amps.

   Maximum fusing allowed for medium-base lamps 20 amps.

   Maximum fusing allowed for 15-amp. receptacles 20 amps.

   Smallest fuse size is 20 amps. This is a "20-amp." circuit, which may be fused at 20 amps. maximum.

4. A circuit supplying heavy-duty lamps in a factory. Circuit conductors are No. 8.

   Maximum fusing allowed for No. 8 40 amps.

   Maximum fusing allowed for heavy-duty lamps in other than residences 50 amps.

   Smallest fuse size is 40 amps. Therefore, this is a "40-amp." circuit, which may be fused at 40 amps., maximum.

5. A circuit supplying a range only. Circuit conductors are No. 6. This circuit supplies only *one* outlet. Therefore, it is an *individual* circuit and does not take a "classification" rating.

Some points to remember about branch circuits:

1. A circuit for two or more appliances, other than fixed cooking appliances, may not be fused at more than 30 amps.
2. A circuit for two or more fixed cooking appliances may be fused as high as 50 amps.
3. Lighting circuits for standard-type lamps may not be fused at more than 20 amps.
4. Lighting circuits for mogul-type lamps may be fused as high as 50 amps. in other than dwellings. In dwellings, maximum fusing is 20 amps.

5. A circuit for infrared heating lamps may be fused as high as 50 amps. Lamp sockets may be standard or mogul type.

6. A circuit serving *one* "non-motor" appliance rated 16.7 amps. or more may be fused at 150% of the appliance current rating [Section 422-27(e)]. No limit on appliance current rating.

If a group of appliances requires fusing above 30 amps., they must be either individually fused, or divided into groups drawing 30 amps. or less, with fusing for each group and a feeder (or service) serving the several branch circuits. (For fixed cooking appliances only, the limit is 50 amps.) There is no limit on feeder fusing as long as conductors are adequate for the load.

(It is understood that in the foregoing discussion "fusing" means overcurrent protection, and could be a circuit breaker or other overcurrent device.)

210-25. Receptacle Outlets Required

(a) General

In general, receptacles must be installed in all locations where portable cords are used.

There are some cases in which the Code allows cord to be used as fixed wiring, as for data-processing equipment [Section 645-2(b)]. Such locations would be exempted from the general rule.

(b) Dwelling Unit

This rule specifies the number of receptacles required in living areas of a home or apartment. The rule requires that "no point along the floor line in any wall space" be more than 6 ft from an outlet. This means that receptacles along a continuous wall may be spaced no more than 12 ft apart. Further, a receptacle is required in "any wall space two feet wide or greater." There may be, for example, two doors with 2 ft of wall space between them. A receptacle must be placed in this space (see Fig. 216).

Receptacles in sufficient number to meet the above rules must be installed in these or similar rooms:

Kitchen	Library
Family room	Den
Dining room	Sun room
Breakfast room	Bedroom
Living room	Recreation room
Parlor	

In the kitchen, family room, dining room, and breakfast room, all of these receptacles will be connected to the small appliance circuits required by Sec-

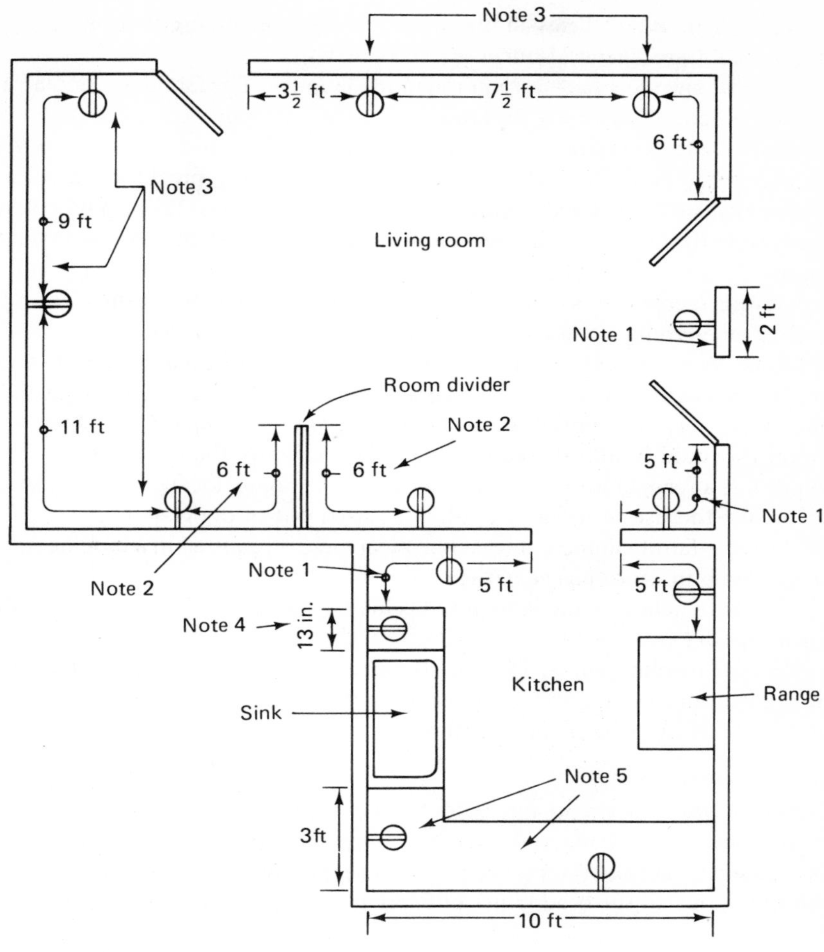

Note 1. Wall space 2 feet or more in width. Receptacle required.
Note 2. All parts of room divider are within 6 feet of a receptacle.
Note 3. All parts of wall are within 6 feet of a receptacle.
Note 4. Counter space wider than 12 inches. Receptacle required.
Note 5. 13 feet of counter space. Two receptacles recommended (One required by Code rules).

Fig. 216
Receptacle outlets required in dwellings (Sect. 210-25).

tion 220-3(b). Receptacles in the other rooms are required to be on other circuits, and are "general-purpose" receptacles.

At least one receptacle is required in the laundry. The laundry receptacle(s) would be connected to the 20-amp. circuit required by Section 220-3(c).

Receptacles are required at counters in the kitchen and dining areas. Any counter space more than 12 in. wide requires a wall receptacle. Each counter space must be considered separately. Thus, if there is a 12-in.-plus counter space on both sides of a sink, two receptacles are required, one for each counter space.

A wall receptacle is required adjacent to the bathroom basin.

For one-family homes, at least one receptacle is required to be installed outdoors. A receptacle installed in an enclosed or "screened-in" porch would not be considered an "outdoor" receptacle. Technically, a receptacle installed on a post, tree, open porch or on the outside wall of a separate garage on the premises would fulfill this requirement. But evidently the intent of the rule is to provide a receptacle on the outside wall of the home, located to provide easy access for the use of tools or appliances used out-of-doors.

For one-family homes, at least one receptacle is required in a basement, and at least one in an *attached* garage.

The basement receptacle required is in addition to any receptacles installed for a laundry.

For *all* dwelling units, 15- and 20-amp., single-phase receptacles installed in a bathroom, in a garage (attached or separate), or outdoors must have ground-fault protection (Sect. 210-8).

(c) Guest Rooms

The rules above also apply to hotels, motels, and similar occupancies, except that hotel and motel rooms are exempt from the "six foot" rule. In these occupancies, receptacles may be placed where convenient to suit the layout of the room, but all the other rules of Section 210-25(b) must be complied with.

(d) Show Windows

Receptacles are required in show windows, at least one receptacle for each 12 linear ft or major fraction thereof.

210-26. Lighting Outlets Required

(a) Dwelling Unit

At least one lighting outlet, *controlled by a wall switch,* must be installed in each "habitable" room, and in stairways, attached garages, outdoor entrances, attics, utility rooms, basements, hallways.

In living rooms, dens, bedrooms, lighting may be by floor lamps, and in these and similar rooms, one or more receptacles may serve as the lighting outlets, but the receptacle(s) must be controlled by a wall switch.

For hallways, stairways, and outside entrances, central control or automatic control is permitted in place of a wall switch.

(b) Guest Rooms

For guest rooms in hotels and motels, at least one lighting outlet (or receptacle) with wall-switch control shall be installed in each room.

ARTICLE 215 — FEEDERS

215-1. Scope

Article 100, Definitions, defines a feeder as follows: "All conductors between the service equipment (or generator switchboard of an isolated plant), and the final branch circuit overcurrent device." An example of a feeder would be a circuit from the service entrance to a distribution panel serving branch circuits.

215-2. Minimum Rating and Size

A feeder must be sized to have carrying capacity sufficient for the load that it will serve.

If a two-wire feeder supplies two or more branch circuits, it may not be smaller than No. 10, regardless of how small the load.

If a three-wire feeder supplies three or more two-wire, or two or more three-wire, branch circuits, it may not be smaller than No. 10, regardless of how small the load.

If a feeder carries the total load of the service entrance, the feeder must be the same size as the service entrance conductors, where the service is No. 6 or smaller. If the service conductors are larger than No. 6, the feeder may be sized to carry only the feeder load, which in this case could result in a feeder size smaller than that of the service.

215-3. Overcurrent Protection

Section 240-3 requires that conductors be protected according to their ampacities. Thus the fuse or circuit-breaker setting for a feeder is sized no greater than the ampacity of the feeder conductors, with these exceptions:

1. If the ampacity of a conductor does not correspond to the rating of a standard-size fuse or circuit-breaker setting, then the next-larger-size

fuse or circuit-breaker setting may be used. For example, the ampacity of No. 6 Type T is 55 amps. There is no 55-amp. fuse or circuit-breaker setting; therefore, the next higher standard size may be used—a 60 amp.

2. Feeders for motor circuits are allowed to have protection in excess of the current-carrying capacity of the feeder. Feeders for motors are protected according to the rules of Section 430–62 of the Code.

215-4. Feeders with Common Neutral

One neutral may serve for two or three sets of single-phase "hot" wires.

One neutral may serve for two sets of "hot" wires of a four-wire, three-phase system. Here there would be seven wires instead of eight, as would be the case if each circuit had its own neutral.

One neutral may serve two sets of "hot" wires of a five-wire, two-phase system. Here there would be nine wires instead of ten, as would be the case if each circuit had its own neutral.

When one neutral serves for two or three sets of feeders, and the feeders are run in metal raceway such as conduit, the Code requires that all conductors, including the neutral, be run in the same conduit.

If two conduits were used, induced currents could be set up in both conduits in the event of an unbalanced load condition.

If all conductors are grouped in the same conduit, the total current within the single conduit in one direction will at all times be equal to the total current in the other direction, and there will be no induced currents set up in the conduit wall.

215-5. Diagrams of Feeders

In cases where the electrical inspector requests a diagram of feeders, the following information must be included with the diagram:

1. Area of premises in square feet.

2. Total connected load.

3. Demand factors.

4. Computed load (demand factor × total connected load).

5. Size of conductors contemplated.

215-6. Feeder Conductor Grounding Means

This Section requires a grounding conductor in the feeder circuit, if a branch circuit connected to the feeder requires a grounding conductor. Note that this rule is for a *grounding* conductor, not a grounded neutral. The grounding conductor may be the metal sheath of cable, conduit, or raceway.

215-7. Ungrounded Conductors Tapped from Grounded Systems

Ungrounded circuits may be tapped from grounded circuits. Thus, a two-wire, 240-volt circuit may be tapped from the hot wires of a 120/240-volt circuit. The neutral need not be carried along with the hot wires.

215-8. Means of Identifying Conductor with the Higher Voltage to Ground

An example of an application of this rule would be three single-phase transformers connected delta-delta to a three phase line to produce a 240-volt three phase secondary. If, from one of the three transformers, a secondary neutral is brought out, this provides a four-wire secondary circuit, which may be used for 120/240-volt single-phase, or 240-volt three phase service.

Say that on a 240-volt three-phase delta-connected secondary, a neutral is brought out from the transformer connected between phase wires A and B. Then the voltage to neutral (ground) of the three-phase wires will be:

A to neutral: 120 volts

B to neutral: 120 volts

C to neutral: 208 volts

This Section requires that wire "C" (the phase conductor having the higher voltage to ground) shall either be orange in color or identified by tagging at connection points, if the neutral is present. (If the neutral is not present, identification is not necessary.) In this way the "high voltage to neutral" wire can be readily recognized (see Fig. 217).

215-9. Ground-Fault Personnel Protection

Section 210-8 requires that, for residences, when 15-amp. receptacles are installed outdoors, or in bathrooms, there must be ground-fault protection in the branch circuit supplying the receptacles. Ground-fault protection is also required for receptacles at construction sites.

This Section permits such ground-fault protection to be inserted in a feeder supplying the branch circuit as an alternative to having the ground-fault device in the branch circuit.

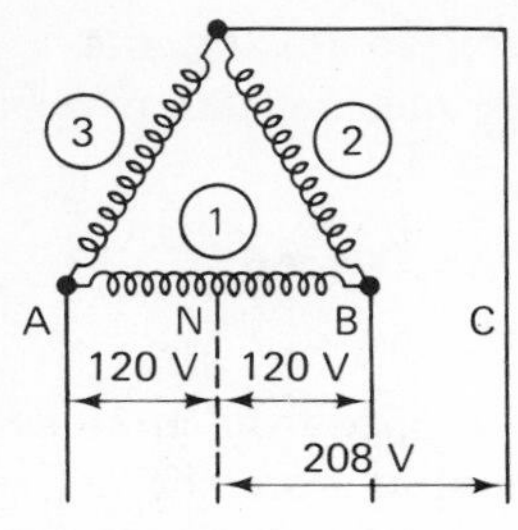

Schematic showing transformer secondary windings

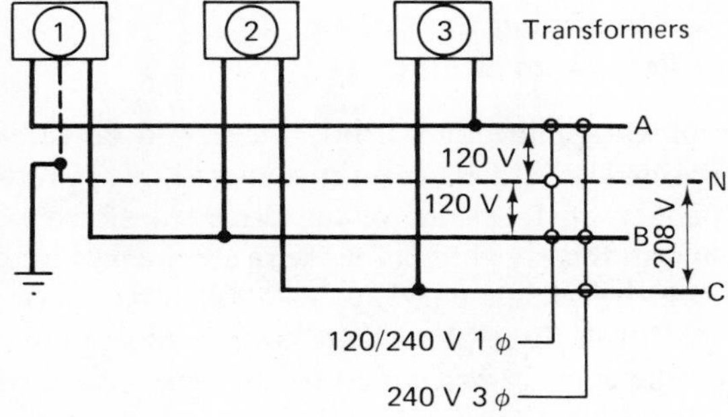

Fig. 217
Four-wire delta-connected secondary with midpoint of one phase supplying a grounded neutral. Conductor C shall either be orange in color or identified by tagging at connection points, if the neutral is present (Sect. 215-8). In this way the "high voltage to neutral" conductor can be readily recognized.

ARTICLE 220 — BRANCH-CIRCUIT AND FEEDER CALCULATIONS

A. General

220-1. Scope

To determine the number of branch circuits required for an "occupancy," it is first necessary to determine the total load for the occupancy. This part of the Code sets the rules for figuring the load.

There are three different types of "occupancy" to be considered:

1. Dwellings [listed in Table 220-2(b), p. 70-41].

2. Other occupancies listed in Table 220-2(b).

3. Occupancies *not* listed in Table 220-2(b).

1. DWELLINGS

For dwellings, the load would be divided into three parts:

(1) General lighting (3 watts per sq. ft of floor space).

(2) Small-appliance load.

(3) Special-appliance load.

The "small-appliance" load consists of the small-appliance receptacles installed in the kitchen, laundry, etc., for plugging in irons, toasters, and other small appliances.

The Code requires at least two such circuits in a residence (three if there is a laundry). Each small-appliance circuit is figured at 1,500 watts.

A "special appliance" would be any appliance not connected to a small-appliance circuit.

A water heater, clothes dryer, sump pump, dishwasher, or oil burner would be a "special-appliance load," and the load would be figured on the basis of the nameplate rating of the appliance.

Note that, in dwellings, no load need be figured for "general-purpose" receptacles. The fine print at the bottom of Table 220-2(b) exempts these receptacles as a load.

The number of branch circuits required for an occupancy will depend on the size of the lighting load, the number of small-appliance circuits, and the number of special appliances to be served.

2. OTHER OCCUPANCIES OF TABLE 220-2(b)

For all other occupancies listed in Table 220-2(b), the load would be comprised of the following three parts:

(1) General lighting.

(2) General-purpose receptacles.

(3) Special appliances.

General lighting is figured on a basis of watts per sq. ft of floor space, according to the unit load given in Table 220-2(b). For banks, it would be 5 watts per sq. ft; for stores, 3 watts per sq. ft; etc.

General-purpose receptacles in other than dwellings are figured at 180 VA per outlet. (A duplex receptacle is considered to be one outlet.)

A "special appliance" would be any appliance or load that is not portable. A freezer, dishwasher, air-conditioner, or an electric sign would be an example of special-appliance loads, and the load for each would be figured at nameplate rating.

3. OCCUPANCIES NOT LISTED IN TABLE 220-2(b)

For occupancies *not* listed in Table 220-2(b), the load would be comprised of the following three parts:

(1) General lighting.

(2) General-purpose receptacles.

(3) Special appliances.

General lighting in an unlisted occupancy is figured on a basis of number of outlets: 180 VA for each medium-base lamp, 600 VA per mogul-base lamp.

General-purpose receptacles are figured at 180 VA per outlet. (A duplex receptacle is considered to be one outlet.)

A special appliance would be any appliance or load that is not portable, and would be figured at nameplate rating.

Examples showing how to figure the load for different types of occupancies are given following Section 220-33.

220-2. Computation of Branch Circuits

(a) Continuous Loads

Generally, a branch circuit may be loaded to its rated capacity. However, where the load is a "continuous" load, the circuit may be loaded only to 80% of its rated capacity. A 20-amp. circuit, for example, could be loaded only to 80% × 20, or 16 amps. The Code defines "continuous load" as a load where the full circuit current is expected to continue for three hours or more. A store-lighting circuit is an example of a continuous load. Here, presumably, all the lights on the circuit would be in operation for 8 or 10 hours or more continuously. The same "continuous-load" condition might exist in other occupancies, such as offices, banks, schools, drafting rooms, etc.

Exception No. 1.

Note 8 of Tables 310-16 through 310-19 requires derating of a conductor (i.e., a reduction in carrying capacity) when there are more than three conductors in a conduit or cable (see p. 70-136 of the Code). When derating is made for this reason, no further derating is necessary because of "continuous load."

Exception No. 2.

No derating of a circuit is necessary where the protective assembly for the circuit is approved for continuous operation at 100% capacity.

(b) Lighting Load for Listed Occupancies

A "listed" occupancy is one that is listed in the table of p. 70-41. While this table includes quite a number of different types of occupancies, there are some types that are not listed. If a type of occupancy is not included in the table, it is not a "listed" occupancy.

Example: Lighting Load in a Listed Occupancy.

What is the minimum general lighting load that must be allowed for a two-story private home (called a "dwelling" in the Code), with first-floor outside dimensions of 30 by 50 ft, and upper floor 30 by 30 ft?

First, the square feet of floor area is figured from the outside dimensions of the building.

Only *finished* spaces need be included in figuring the floor area. An unfinished basement or unfinished attic need not be included. If the basement, or part of the basement, is used as "rumpus room" or play-room, the rumpus-room or play-room part of the basement must be included in the calculation. Similarly, if the attic space is used as a bedroom or a play-room it must be included.

Floor area would be:

First floor	30 × 50 =	1,500 sq. ft
Second floor	30 × 30 =	900
Total floor area		2,400 sq. ft

Next, turn to the Table on p. 70-41. For Dwelling Units the minimum to be allowed for lighting is 3 watts per sq. ft.

$$2{,}400 \times 3 = 7{,}200 \text{ watts minimum must be allowed for lighting for this home}$$

Figuring on a basis of 15-amp. branch circuits at 115 volts, each circuit would serve 115 × 15 = 1,725 watts.

$$\frac{7{,}200}{1{,}725} = 4.18 \text{ or five 15 amp. circuits minimum are required for lighting}$$

Each circuit should be arranged to carry, as nearly as practicable, one-fifth of the lighting load.

(c) Other Loads—All Occupancies

In unlisted occupancies, lighting is not figured on a watts per square foot basis, but according to the number of outlets on the lighting circuits. For example, for a barn with 10 lighting fixtures, the lighting load would be figured at 180 volt-amperes ($1\frac{1}{2}$ amps.) per fixture. If the fixtures were mogul base fixtures, the load would be figured at 600 volt-amperes (5 amps.) per fixture. Total load would be 15 A for 10 medium-base, 50 A for 10 mogul-base fixtures.

The rules of paragraph (c) apply for specific appliance loads, *and:*

1. In "listed" occupancies, other than dwellings, for figuring the general-purpose receptacle load. This would be 180 volt-amperes ($1\frac{1}{2}$ amps.) per receptacle. (In dwellings and hotel guest rooms, no additional load is figured for general-purpose receptacles; they are considered to be part of the lighting load.)

2. In "unlisted" occupancies, for figuring the load on both lighting outlets and other outlets, including general-purpose receptacles.

In listed occupancies the lighting load is always figured on a watts per square foot basis, not according to the number of outlets.

In "unlisted" occupancies, the lighting load is always figured on the basis of the number of outlets. For other than heavy-duty (mogul) lamps, the load for each fixture is figured at 180 volt-amperes ($1\frac{1}{2}$ amps). If mogul lamps are used, the load for each fixture is figured at 600 volt-amperes (5 amps.).

There are four exceptions to the rules of paragraph (c) above.

Exception No. 1: Multioutlet Assemblies.

This rule applies for such devices as "plug-in-strip," which is a sort of metal raceway with receptacle slots at intervals of perhaps 6 to 18 in. of length. In this case, each receptacle need not be figured at $1\frac{1}{2}$ amps. Regardless of the number of receptacle slots in the plug-in-strip, a load of only $1\frac{1}{2}$ amps. for each 5 ft is allowed. In places where the plug-in-strip is likely to be heavily loaded, with several appliances plugged in at one time, then the allowance must be $1\frac{1}{2}$ amps. *per foot.*

(The rule does not apply to dwellings and guest rooms of hotels; in this case the plug-in-strip could be connected to a "small-appliance" circuit along with other outlets in the circuit.)

Exception No. 2: Ranges.

Paragraph (c) sets the load for "outlets supplying specific appliances" as the "amp. rating of appliance." A range would be a specific appliance. However, the Code permits household range loads to be figured at a lower kW than the full kW rating of the range. The permissible loads allowed for household ranges are listed in the table on p. 70-46 of the Code.

It should be remembered that this table is for *household* ranges only. It does not apply to commercial ranges, such as ranges in a restaurant or hotel kitchen.

For ranges of less than $3\frac{1}{2}$ kW, Column B is used. For ranges of $3\frac{1}{2}$ to $8\frac{3}{4}$ kW, Column C is used. For ranges of 9 to 12 kW, Column A is used. (For ranges over 12 kW, see Notes 1 and 2 under the table.)

The following examples will explain the use of Columns A, B, and C.

1. Range rated at 3 kW: This range is in the less than $3\frac{1}{2}$-kW group. Therefore, Column B may be used. For one range, the demand factor is listed as 80%.

   80% × 3 = 2.4 kW, the demand load permitted for this range

2. Range rated at 8 kW: This range is in the $3\frac{1}{2}$- to $8\frac{3}{4}$-kW group. Therefore, Column C may be used. For one range, the demand factor is listed as 80%.

   80% × 8 = 6.4 kW, the demand load that may be allowed for this range

3. Range rated at 9 kW: This range is in the 9-12 kW group. Therefore, Column A must be used, giving a permissible demand load of 8 kW.

4. Range rated at 27 kW (see note 1, under the Table): For a 12-kW range, the demand load is 8 kW (column 1). For a 27-kW load 5% is added for each kW above 12. This would be 15 × 5 = 75%.

   8 kW + 75% of 8 kW = 14kW, permissible demand load

5. Five ranges, each rated at 10 kW: these ranges are in the 9-12 kW group; therefore, Column A must be used. From Column A, the permissible demand load for all five ranges combined is 20 kW.

6. Five ranges, each rated at 3 kW: Column B may be used. For five ranges of this rating, the load is taken as 62% of total kW.

   5 × 3 = 15 kW, total

   62% × 15 = 9.3 kW, permissible demand load

Exception No. 3: Show-Window Lighting.

This is not considered as general lighting, and is figured separately from the store general lighting.

Show-window lighting may be figured in either of two ways:

1. On the basis of $1\frac{1}{2}$ amps. per outlet for medium-base lamps, 5 amps. if mogul lamps are used.

2. On the basis of 200 watts per linear foot of show window.

Example.

A store has 85 linear ft of show window. There will be 32 mogul lighting outlets installed. What minimum load must be allowed?

On a basis of 5 amps. per outlet:

$$32 \times 5 = 160 \text{ amps.}$$

$$160 \times 115 = 18{,}400 \text{ watts}$$

On a 200 watts per linear ft basis:

$$85 \times 200 = 17{,}000 \text{ watts}$$

Exception No. 4: Telephone Exchanges.

In the case of telephone switchboards and frames, the $1\frac{1}{2}$ amps. per outlet rule need not be followed. In this case the load would be determined by the telephone company, according to the switchboard design, and wired to carry this load.

(d) Loads for Additions to Existing Installations

(1) Dwelling Units.

When figuring the lighting load for additions to an existing dwelling, if the new addition covers 500 sq. ft or less, outlets may be figured on either (1) a watts per square foot basis, or (2) at 180 VA per outlet (600 VA per outlet for mogul base lamps). If the new area to be wired covers more than 500 sq. ft, the lighting must be figured as for a new home or apartment, on the watts per square foot basis.

(2) Other Than Dwelling Units.

Lighting for additions to existing buildings other than dwellings may be figured either on the basis of watts per square foot or amperes per outlet, regardless of size of the addition.

220-3. Branch Circuits Required

(a) Number of Branch Circuits

The minimum number of lighting branch circuits required for an occupancy will depend upon the total lighting wattage required for the occupancy. This total wattage is figured on a watts per square foot basis for listed occupancies, and on a basis of number of outlets for unlisted occupancies. The Code specifies the watts per square foot that must be allowed for different types of listed occupancies; this information is listed in the Table on p. 70-41 of the Code. A sufficient number of circuits shall be provided to supply lighting and all other loads to be served.

The computed lighting load should be evenly divided among the branch circuits. If six branch circuits are to serve, say, 7,800 watts, each of the six circuits should be laid out so as to carry, as nearly as practicable, 1,300 watts (7,800 divided by 6).

(b) Small-Appliance Branch Circuits—Dwelling Unit

In homes, apartments, or other "dwelling occupancies," at least two "small-appliance" receptacle circuits must be provided to take care of such appliances as the toaster, iron, coffee maker, etc.

Receptacles for this purpose must be installed in each of these rooms: kitchen, pantry, family room, dining room, breakfast room.

These are 20-amp. circuits wired with No. 12 minimum conductors. With one exception (receptacles for electric clocks), *all* 15- and 20-amp. receptacles in these rooms must be connected to a small-appliance circuit. A receptacle for an electric clock may be connected to a general-purpose branch circuit or lighting circuit.

No small-appliance circuit shall serve any outlet outside of these rooms.

At least two small-appliance receptacle circuits are required for the kitchen. It might seem inconsistent to specify at least two circuits for the kitchen and only two for all rooms combined. Actually, one or both of the kitchen circuits could also serve other rooms, thus satisfying the minimum requirement of the rule with a total of two circuits to serve all the rooms. See Fig. 218.

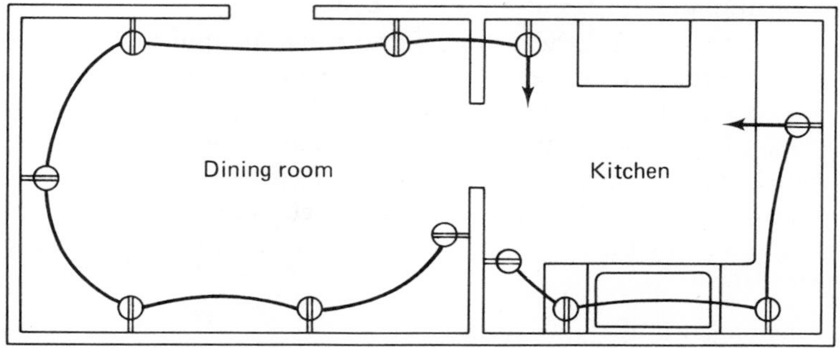

Fig. 218

Two small-appliance circuits serving kitchen and dining room. Both circuits must be represented in the kitchen.

(c) Laundry Branch Circuits—Dwelling Unit

At least one 20-amp. circuit must be provided for laundry receptacles.

(d) Load Evenly Proportioned Among Branch Circuits

For the occupancies listed in Table 220-2(b), lighting is figured on a watts per square foot basis. The lighting load should, as nearly as possible, be evenly divided among the required branch circuits. For example, a home with 1,500 sq. ft of area would require a minimum allowance of $3 \times 1{,}500 = 4{,}500$ watts for lighting.

$$\frac{4500}{115} = 39 \text{ amps.}$$

Three 15-amp. circuits would be required. Each circuit should be arranged to serve, as nearly as practicable, 1,500 watts (or 500 sq. ft).

B. Feeders

220-10. General

(a) Ampacity and Computed Loads

Feeder conductors shall have ampacity sufficient to carry the load. The feeder ampacity need not always be equal to the total of all loads on all branches connected to it. A study of the following sections will show that, in some cases, a "demand factor" may be applied to the total load. The demand factor permits a feeder ampacity to be less than 100% of the sum of all branch circuit loads connected to it.

(b) Continuous and Noncontinuous Loads

A "continuous" load is defined as a load where the full circuit current is expected to continue uninterrupted for three hours or more.

If all of the feeder load is a continuous load, the feeder must be sized to carry 125% of the load. Thus, a 40-amp. continuous load would require a feeder with a 50-amp. minimum carrying capacity.

In some cases, part of the feeder load may be continuous, part noncontinuous. In this case only the continuous part of the load would be subject to the 125% provisions.

Example.

A feeder serves three branch circuits. One branch circuit is a continuous load of 16 amps. The other two are noncontinuous loads of 20 amps. each. The calculated load on the feeder would be

$$125\% \times (16) + 20 + 20 = 20 + 20 + 20 = 60 \text{ amps.}$$

Exception.

Where the assembly including the overcurrent devices protecting the feeder is "listed" for operation at 100% of rating, the rule does not apply. Continuous loads need not be multiplied by 125%. (See definition of "listed," p. 70-10 of the Code.)

220-11. General Lighting

This Section gives the rules for figuring lighting load on feeders. The difference between figuring branch-circuit loads and feeder loads is that no demand factor is applied for a branch circuit, but may be applied in the case of a feeder. The load on a feeder is the sum of all the branch loads connected to the feeder, subject to demand factors allowed by the rules of this Section.

"Demand factor" is a percentage by which the total connected load on a feeder is multiplied to determine the greatest probable load that the feeder will have to carry. Take the case of lighting. In hospitals, hotels, apartment buildings, dwellings, it is not likely that all of the lights connected to every branch circuit served by a feeder would be "on" at the same time. Therefore, instead of sizing the feeder to carry all the load on all the branches, a percentage would be taken of this total load, and the feeder sized accordingly.

Referring to the table on p. 70-43, it can be seen that a demand factor for lighting may be applied only for dwellings, hospitals, hotels, motels, and warehouses. All other occupancies must be figured on a basis of total computed lighting wattage, and no demand factor is allowed.

220-12. Show-Window Lighting

This rule applies when figuring the feeder size for show windows, when the actual number of outlets is not known. In this case, show-window lighting must be figured at 200 watts per linear foot of show window, minimum.

If the number of outlets is known, then the show-window load may be figured according to Section 220-2(c) at $1\frac{1}{2}$ amps. per outlet (5 amps. per outlet if mogul lamps will be used).

220-13. Receptacle Loads—Nondwelling Units

In "dwellings," general-purpose receptacles are not counted as a load.

In other than dwellings, 180 watts ($1\frac{1}{2}$ amps) must be figured for each general purpose receptacle. For hospitals, hotels, motels, warehouses, this receptacle load may be lumped with the lighting load, and the demand factors of Table 220-11 may be applied to the total.

Or, for other occupancies not classed as "dwellings," a demand factor of 50% may be applied to receptacle loads in excess of 10 kW (Table 220-13 of the Code).

220-14. Motors

The load to be allowed for motors is:

1. For one motor: 125% of motor full-load current.
2. For more than one motor: 125% of full-load current of the motor with the highest current rating, plus the sum of full-load currents of remaining motors.

Examples.

(1) What load would be allowed for a $\frac{3}{4}$-hp, 115-volt, single-phase motor?

From Table 430-148, p. 70-316, full-load current for this motor is 13.8 amps.

125% of 13.8 = 17.25 or 18 amps., load allowance

(2) What feeder load would be allowed for two $\frac{3}{4}$-hp and two $\frac{1}{2}$-hp, 115-volt, single-phase motors?

From the table on p. 70-316 full-load current for a $\frac{3}{4}$-hp motor is 13.8 amps.; for a $\frac{1}{2}$-hp motor, 9.8 amps. Largest motor in the group is the $\frac{3}{4}$-hp motor, drawing 13.8 amps.

125% of 13.8 = 17.25 amps., allowance for largest motor in the group

13.8 amps., allowance for the other $\frac{3}{4}$-hp motor

19.6 amps., allowance for two $\frac{1}{2}$-hp motors

Total load 50.65 or 51 amps.

220-15. Fixed Electric Space Heating

The load for fixed space-heating equipment, such as unit heaters, radiant panels, etc., that are used for heating homes, factories, warehouses, etc., must be figured at the full rating of the heaters.

Exceptions.

1. When all heating units connected to a feeder are not expected to be in operation simultaneously, the feeder ampacity may be less than the total load, *but only by special permission.*

2. For dwellings only, the demand factor listed in Sections 220-30, 220-31, 220-32 may be applied when the "optional" method of figuring load is used.

220-16. Small Appliance and Laundry Loads—Dwelling Unit

This rule sets the load for the small-appliance and laundry circuits that the Code calls for in Section 220-3. The load is figured at 1,500 W for each such circuit; but when applying the demand factor for lighting, this load may be included with the lighting load (see examples following Section 220-33).

220-17. Fixed Appliance Load—Dwelling Unit(s)

It should be remembered that this rule applies only for "dwellings." When there are one, two, or three fixed appliances on a feeder, the load allowed would be the sum of the full nameplate ratings of the appliances. If there are four or more fixed appliances, the load allowed would be the sum of the full nameplate ratings multiplied by 75%. This applies for any fixed appliances except the range, clothes dryer, air-conditioning equipment, and space-heating equipment.

220-18. Electric Clothes Dryers—Dwelling Unit(s)

Electric clothes dryers in dwellings are figured at 5,000 W or nameplate rating, whichever is higher. A 4,000-watt dryer would be figured at 5,000 watts. A 5,000-watt dryer would be figured at 5,000 watts, a 6,000-watt dryer at 6,000 watts, etc.

If there are more than four dryers, a demand factor may be applied, as per Table 220-18, p. 70-45 of the Code.

Example.

What feeder load must be allowed for (5) clothes dryers, each rated at 3,000 watts?

According to the rule above, each individual dryer must be figured at 3,000 watts?

According to the rule above, each individual dryer must be figured at 5,000 watts:

$$5 \times 5{,}000 = 25{,}000 \text{ watts, total}$$

Table 220-18 allows an 80% demand factor to be applied for 5 dryers.

$$80\% \times 25{,}000 = 20{,}000 \text{ watts, feeder load}$$

220-19. Electric Ranges and Other Cooking Appliances—Dwelling Units

The feeder load for *household* ranges need not be figured on the basis of full nameplate rating. Hosuehold range loads may be figured according to Table 220-19, p. 70-46. Thus, a 12-kW range is figured at 8 kW rather than 12 kW (Column A). For five ranges, each rated at 12 kW, a load of 20 kW would be allowed rather than 60 (Column A).

For smaller ranges, a percentage of full nameplate rating may be taken as per Column B or C. For example, for one 4-kW range, a load of 80% × 4 = 3.2 kW would be allowed (Column C).

Table 220-19 may also be used for calculating *feeder* load for other household cooking units of over $1\frac{3}{4}$ kW rating.

220-20. Kitchen Equipment—Other Than Dwelling Units

For commercial cooking equipment, dishwasher booster heaters and other commercial kitchen equipment, the demand factors of Table 220-20, p. 70-47, may be used.

220-21. Noncoincident Loads

This is a special case of figuring the load to be allowed for feeders. An example of an application of this rule would be the case of two branch circuits, one for an air-cooling unit, the other for a heating unit for the same space, both connected to the same feeder. It is unlikely that both the cooling unit and the heating unit would be on at the same time. Therefore, the load on the feeder supplying the two branch circuits could, in this case, be figured as though it were feeding only the larger of the two branches. The smaller load may be omitted.

220-22. Feeder Neutral Load

If a three-wire, 120/240-volt feeder supplies a group of 120-volt branch circuits with half of the load connected to one side of the three-wire system, and half to the other side, then, if all the load were "on," there would be a perfect balance of load, and no current would flow in the neutral. If one of the feeder fuses blows, however, the neutral will be called upon to carry the same amperage as the remaining "hot" wire. The "maximum unbalance" in this case would be equal to the amps. carried by the "hot" wire.

This rule stipulates that "The feeder load shall be the maximum unbalance of the load. The maximum unbalanced load shall be the maximum connected load between the neutral and any one ungrounded conductor."

The maximum current would flow in the neutral when one of the hot wire fuses blows. The load on the neutral would then be the full load on the remaining leg, since the entire current in that leg must now flow through the neutral.

Loads connected across the "hot" wires do not count in figuring feeder neutral load. Since they are not connected to the neutral, they cannot contribute to neutral current.

Examples.

1. What neutral load would be figured for a three-wire, 115/230-volt circuit, feeding a 5-kW, 230-volt clothes dryer, and a 10-kW, 115-volt lighting and appliance load?

   Only the 10-kW load is considered. Assuming 5 kW to be connected across each 115-volt leg, the maximum current that could flow in the neutral would be

$$\frac{5{,}000}{115} = 43.5 \text{ amps.}$$

   This is the "maximum unbalance" for this feeder.

2. What neutral load in amperes would be figured for a three-wire, 115/230-volt circuit, with 2,300 watts connected across one leg and 3,450 watts connected across the other leg?

   Neutral load would be figured on the basis of the larger connected load, which is 3,450 watts.

$$\frac{3{,}450}{115} = 30 \text{ amps., neutral load}$$

3. What neutral load would be figured for a three-wire, 115/230-volt circuit, with a computed load of 300 amps. on each 115-V leg?

   The neutral would be figured to carry 100% of 200 amps. plus 70% of the current in excess of 200 amps., or

$$200 + 70\% \text{ (of 100)} = 270 \text{ amps.}$$

4. What neutral load would be figured for a five-wire, two-phase system, with 100-amps. line to neutral on each phase?

   For a five-wire, two-phase system, the neutral load is figured at 140% of the greatest line to neutral current.

$$140\%\text{(of 100)} = 140 \text{ amps., computed neutral load}$$

C. Optional Calculations for Computing Feeder and Service Loads

220-30. Optional Calculation—Single-Family Dwelling or Individual Apartment in Multifamily Dwellings

For single-family dwellings (or an individual apartment) an optional method of figuring the feeder load may be used in place of the method outlined in Part B, preceding.

This method may be used only where there would be a 100-A (or higher) service entrance.

To arrive at total kW or kVA load by this method:

1. List the air-conditioning load, if any.
2. Multiply central-heating load, if any, by 65%.
3. Multiply total load for space heating, if any, by 65%.
4. Add 100% of other loads, up to 10 kW.
5. Multiply remainder of "other" load by 40%.

The total load kW or kVA allowance is the sum of the above loads. The amperage load on a 115/230-volt service would be

$$\frac{\text{total kw (or kVA)}}{230}$$

220-31. Optional Calculation for Additional Loads in Existing Dwelling Unit

This optional calculation may be used only for additions to an existing occupancy with an existing 60-amp. service.

220-32. Optional Calculation—Three or More Multifamily Dwelling Units

This method for multifamily dwellings may be used only if all of the apartments have electric cooking *and* electric heating (or air conditioning). After figuring the load for each apartment, a demand factor can be applied to the total load for all apartments, according to Table 220-32. This would give the load on the feeder or service.

220-33. Optional Calculation—Two Dwelling Units

This Section would apply in figuring the feeder load, when a feeder serves two apartments. The feeder load would be figured in accordance with Part B, Feeders. After figuring the feeder load, the result would be checked against the feeder load for *three* apartments, figured on the optional calculation basis, according to Section 220-32.

In some cases the optional calculation may yield a smaller feeder load for three apartments than the Part B method yields for two apartments. In such cases, the Code permits the smaller load to be used for sizing the feeder to the two apartments.

220-34. Optional Method—Schools

For schools equipped with electric space heating, or electric air conditioning, the load may be figured according to Table 220-33.

It should be pointed out that the rules of Article 220 for calculating the load on feeders also apply for figuring the load on a service. A service, by official definition, is not a feeder (see definition of "feeder," p. 70-8 of the Code). However, the service carries the load of all branch circuits and, for the purpose of calculating load, the same rules apply as for calculating feeder load.

Examples: Figuring Service Load.

Single-family home, one story 40 by 50 ft with three small-appliance receptacle circuits (includes laundry), 12-kW range, 2-kW water heater, and 5-kW dryer.

1. *General Lighting Load*
   Area of the home is $40 \times 50 = 2{,}000$ sq. ft. Table 220-2(b), p. 70-41, requires a load of 3 watts per sq. ft to be allowed for "dwellings."

   $$2{,}000 \times 3 = 6{,}000 \text{ watts, lighting load}$$

2. *Small-Appliance Load*
   3 small-appliance circuits at 1,500 W each = 4,500 watts

3. *Special-Appliance Load*

Range (from Table, p. 70–46)	8,000 watts
Water heater	2,000 watts
Dryer	5,000 watts
Total special-appliance load	15,000 watts

4. *Lighting and Small-Appliance Demand Load*

Lighting	6,000 watts
Small appliances	4,500 watts
Total lighting and small-appliance load	10,500 watts
First 3,000 watts at 100%	3,000 watts
Remaining 7,500 watts at 35% (Table 220–11, p. 70–43)	2,625 watts
Lighting and small-appliance demand load	5,625 watts

5. *Total Load for Home*

Lighting and small-appliance load	5,625 watts
Special-appliance load	15,000 watts
Total	20,625 watts

For a 115/230-volt, 3-wire service, the amperage load on the service would be

$$\frac{20{,}625}{230} = 89.7 \text{ amps.}$$

Optional load calculation for same home:

2,000 sq. ft at 3 watts/sq. ft (lighting)	6,000 watts
Small-appliance circuits	4,500 watts
Range (at nameplate rating)	12,000 watts
Water heater	2,000 watts
Dryer	5,000 watts
Total	29,500 watts
First 10 kW at 100%	10 kW
Remainder (19.5 kW) at 40%	7.8 kW
Total allowable load	17.8 kW

For a 115/230-volt, 3-wire service, the amperage load on the service would be

$$\frac{17{,}800}{230} = 77.4 \text{ amps.}$$

Example: Load Calculation for a Small Restaurant.

Restaurant, 30 by 50 ft, with the following equipment:

Electric range	20 kW
Coffee maker	1,500 watts
Fry kettle	3 kW
Dishwasher	2 kW
Vegetable peeler	¼ hp (115 V)
Water heater	4.5 kW
Toaster	2.4 kW

There will be 10 general-purpose duplex receptacles.

1. *Lighting Load*

$$30 \times 50 \text{ ft} = 1{,}500 \text{ sq. ft area}$$

Table 220-2(b), p. 70-41, shows 2 watts per sq. ft as minimum allowance for lighting.

$$1{,}500 \times 2 = 3{,}000 \text{ watts}$$

Since the lighting will be a "continuous" load, it must be figured at

$$125\% \ (\times\ 3{,}000) = 3{,}750 \text{ watts.}$$

2. *Receptacle Load*
For the general-purpose receptacles, the load is figured at 180 volt-amperes (or watts) per receptacle.

$$10 \times 180 = 1{,}800 \text{ watts, receptacle load}$$

3. *Appliance Load*

Range	20,000	watts
Coffee maker	1,500	watts
Fry kettle	3,000	watts
Dishwasher	2,000	watts
Vegetable peeler (see note)	690	watts
Water heater	4,500	watts
Toaster	2,400	watts
	34,090	watts appliance load

Note: A $\frac{1}{4}$-hp, 115-volt, single-phase motor draws 5.8 (6) amps. (see Table 430-148, p. 70-316). $6 \times 115 = 690$.

4. *Total Load*

Lighting	3,750 watts
Receptacles	1,800 watts
Appliances	34,090 watts
Total	39,640 watts

$$\frac{39{,}640}{230} = 172.3 \text{ amps., total load on a 115/230-volt service}$$

D. Method for Computing Farm Loads

220-40. Farm Loads—Buildings and Other Loads

The load for a farm home is figured in the same way as the load for any other residence.

For other buildings on the farm, the load for each building is figured separately. If the ampere load for an individual building is over 60 A, the demand factors of Table 220-40 may be used.

The table specifies that "loads expected to operate without diversity" are to be figured at 100%. "Without diversity" means that the entire load is expected to operate at the same time, rather than with part of the load operating at one time and part of the load operating at another time. As an example, if all the lights in a building are operated by one switch, then, when the lights are on, all will be in operation at the same time. This is one example of a load operating without diversity.

Table 220-40 also specifies that not less than 125% of full-load current of the largest motor shall be figured at 100%, and further that not less than the first 60 amps. shall be figured at 100%. The motor rule would apply for large motors with full-load current ratings of more than 48 amps. at 230 volts. For example, if a building has a motor drawing 56 amps. at 230 volts, then the first 70 amps. (125% of 56) of load would have to be figured at 100%.

In most cases, the 60-amp. stipulation would prevail, computed loads of 60 amps. or less being figured at 100%.

The first 60 amps. of computed load on any one building is figured at 100%. The next 60 amps. is figured at 50%, and amperage over 120 amps., at 25%.

220-41. Farm Loads—Total

To figure the total load for a farm, first compute the amperage for the total connected load for one of the outbuildings. If the amperage for the building is 60 or less, set down the full amperage. If over 60, apply demand factors according to the amperage.

Do the same for each of the other outbuildings. Figure the load for the residence. Size the service (for the entire farm) at:

100% of the amperage for the outbuilding with the largest amperage.

Plus 75% of the amperage for the outbuilding having the second largest amperage.

Plus 65% of the amperage for the outbuilding having the third largest amperage.

Plus 50% of the amperage for all other outbuildings.

Plus 100% of the amperage for the residence.

ARTICLE 225 — OUTSIDE BRANCH CIRCUITS AND FEEDERS

225-1. Scope

Article 225 covers outside wiring and equipment. This Article would apply for installations in used-car lots, parking lots, overhead wiring between buildings, and other private outdoor installations. It does not apply for utility or power company lines.

225-2. Other Articles

In addition to the rules of Article 225, the rules of other articles of the Code, as listed in the table on p. 70-52, must also be complied with if applicable.

225-3. Calculation of Load

Branch circuit and feeder loads are figured in the same way as loads for interior wiring, according to the rules of Article 220.

225-4. Conductor Covering

Open wiring on insulators shall be insulated or covered if on a building or within 10 ft of a building.

Conductors in raceway or cables (except MI cable conductors) shall be either thermoplastic or rubber covered.

In wet locations, conductors shall be

1. Lead-covered, or
2. Type RHW, RUW, TW, THW, THWN, or XHHW, or
3. A type approved for the purpose.

Conductors for festoon lighting [see Section 225-6(b)] shall be either thermoplastic or rubber covered.

225-5. Size of Conductors

The amperage load on conductors shall not exceed the allowable ampacity of the conductor. Allowable ampacities for open wiring are listed in Tables 310-17, 310-19, pp. 70-133, 70-135; for conductors in raceway or cable, refer to Tables 310-16, 310-18, pp. 70-132, 70-134.

225-6. Minimum Size of Conductor

(a) Overhead Spans (Except Festoon Lighting)

Minimum size of conductor permitted is:

For 600 volts or under:
No. 10 for spans up to 50 ft.
No. 8 for spans over 50 ft.

For over 600 volts:
No. 6 for open wiring.
No. 8 for conductors in cable.

(b) Festoon Lighting

Festoon lighting is frequently used for lighting such locations as used-car lots. It consists of open conductors strung overhead, with light sockets attached to the conductors. The overhead conductors for festoon lighting may not be smaller than No. 12, except that, when supported by messenger wires, No. 14 may be used.

For spans exceeding 40 ft in length, a messenger wire must be provided for support of the conductors (Section 225-13).

225-7. Lighting Equipment on Poles or Other Structures

(a) General

Wiring of lights or lighting equipment installed on a single pole or structure shall comply with Article 210. Voltage shall not exceed the voltage specified in (c) below.

(b) Common Neutral

One neutral may serve for up to eight hot wires. Ampacity of the neutral shall be equal to the sum of the currents for all circuits served by the neutral.

(c) Voltage to Ground

Maximum voltage permitted for outdoor lighting on buildings or poles is 150 to ground, except that, when all of the following conditions are met, voltage may be as high as 300 to ground:

1. Fixtures are at least 8 ft above grade that is accessible to "unqualified" persons.

2. Fixtures are at least 3 ft from windows, platforms, fire escapes, and the like.

150 volts to ground would permit the use of a 240-volt circuit taken from the outside legs of a 120/240-volt circuit, or 208 volts taken from a 120/208-volt four-wire, three-phase circuit.

300 volts to ground would permit the use of a 480-volt circuit taken from a 277/480-volt, four-wire, three-phase circuit.

(d) Voltage Between Conductors

Where only the ballast(s) for permanently installed electric-discharge fixture(s) for area illumination are served, the circuit voltage may be as high as 500 *between conductors,* provided that the fixtures are at a height of at least 22 ft on poles, or 18 ft on other structures. (Electric-discharge fixtures would include fluorescent and mercury-arc fixtures.)

225-8. Disconnection

Disconnects for fuses shall be as required by Section 240-40.

225-9. Overcurrent Protection

The rating of fuses or setting of the circuit breaker protecting a branch circuit or feeder shall be in accordance with Section 240-3.

225-10. Wiring on Buildings

For wiring attached to the outside of a building, the following wiring methods are permitted:

For 600 volts and under:

1. Open wiring on insulators.
2. Approved multiconductor cable.
3. Type MI cable.
4. Rigid metal conduit.
5. Intermediate metal conduit.
6. EMT.
7. Busway.
8. Type MC Cable.

For over 600 volts:

1. Rigid metal conduit.
2. Rigid nonmetallic conduit, if encased in not less than 2 in. of concrete.
3. Approved multiconductor cable.
4. Cablebus.

5. If accessible only to qualified persons or effectively guarded, open wiring on insulators may be used.

225-11. Circuit Exits and Entrances

Where branch circuits or feeder circuits enter or leave a building, the rules of Sections 230-43, 230-52, and 230-54, as applying to services, shall apply.

225-12. Open-Conductor Supports

Glass or porcelain knobs, racks, brackets, and strain insulators are approved as supports for open conductors.

225-13. Festoon Supports

For festoon spans over 40 ft in length, a messenger wire must be provided for support of the conductors. The messenger must be fitted with strain insulators.

225-14. Open-Conductor Spacings

Distance Between Supports	Between Conductors	Clearance from Surface
For 600 volts or less:		
15 ft	12 in. minimum	2 in. minimum
9 ft	6 in. minimum	2 in. minimum
For 300 volts or less:		
4½ ft	3 in. minimum	2 in. minimum

For voltages above 600, see p. 70-542 of the Code.

Open conductors shall be separated from conductors of other systems by at least 4 in.

For conductors not on racks or brackets, minimum spacing for conductors on poles is 12 in. A minimum 30-in. climbing space must be provided between conductors, except that for voltages of 300 or less a 24-in. climbing space is permitted.

225-15. Supports Over Buildings

When wires pass over a building, they should, where practicable, be supported on poles on either side of the building, so that the wires passing over the building are suspended above the building without attachment to the building itself.

If necessary to attach the wires to the roof, some kind of support, such as a crossarm on a cradle, must be used to support the wires. The cradle or other support must be high enough so that the wires will have the clearance required by Section 225-19. Conductors passing over a building may not be fastened directly to the roof.

225-16. Point of Attachment to Buildings

See Section 230-26.

225-17. Means of Attachment to Buildings

See Section 230-27.

225-18. Clearance from Ground

For 600 volts or less, minimum height above ground for open conductors is as follows:

Above sidewalks or finished grade	10 ft
Above residential driveways	12 ft
Above parking lots, drive-ins not subject to truck traffic	12 ft
Above public streets, alleys, roads	18 ft

For clearance of conductors over 600 V, see *National Electrical Safety Code* (ANSI C2-1977).

225-19. Clearances From Buildings for Conductors of Not Over 600 Volts

(a) Over Roofs

Clearance of conductors over roofs must, in general, be at least 8 ft. There are two exceptions:

1. When the roof has sufficient slope, the clearance may be reduced to 3 ft for voltages of 300 or less between conductors. A roof with a steep slope is not likely to be walked on and would not therefore present a danger. This exception applies if the slope of the roof is no less than 4 in. in 12.

   For voltages above 300, an 8-ft clearance must be maintained, regardless of roof slope.

2. When conductors are attached to an entrance conduit extending through the roof, clearance may be reduced to 18 in. minimum if conductors do not pass over more than 4 ft of roof (i.e., if the entrance conduit is set back no more than 4 ft from the edge of the roof).

(b) Horizontal Clearances

Minimum horizontal clearance (from the building) for conductors not attached to a building is 3 ft.

(c) Final Spans

Conductors are permitted to be run on the outside wall of a building. When this is done, a clearance of at least 3 ft is required from windows, doors, porches, fire escapes and other locations that would permit the wires to be touched by persons. (Conductors run *above* a window need not have a 3-ft clearance from the window.)

(d) Zone for Fire Ladders

For buildings of over three stories (or over 50 ft high), overhead conductors shall, where practicable, be arranged so as not to interfere with the raising of fire-fighting ladders. There should be a clear space of at least 6 ft out from the building wherever possible.

225-20. Mechanical Protection of Conductors

See Section 230-50.

225-21. Multiconductor Cables on Exterior Surfaces of Buildings

See Section 230-51.

225-22. Raceways on Exterior Surfaces of Buildings

Raceways shall be raintight, and provision shall be made for drainage of moisture that might accumulate inside the raceway due to condensation. A drain hole at a low point in the raceway would provide drainage.

225-23. Underground Circuits

See Section 300-5.

225-24. Outdoor Lampholders

This Section applies for festoon lighting, a type of overhead lighting frequently used for lighting such locations as used-car lots. It consists of open conductors strung overhead with lampholders attached to the conductors.

When pigtail socket leads are spliced to the overhead conductors, the splices must be staggered so that the two splices will not be alongside one another (Fig. 221).

Some lampholders have leads fitted with terminals that puncture the insulation to make contact with the conductor. Lampholders of this type may be used only with stranded conductors. Solid conductors do not provide a reliable contact for devices of the puncture type.

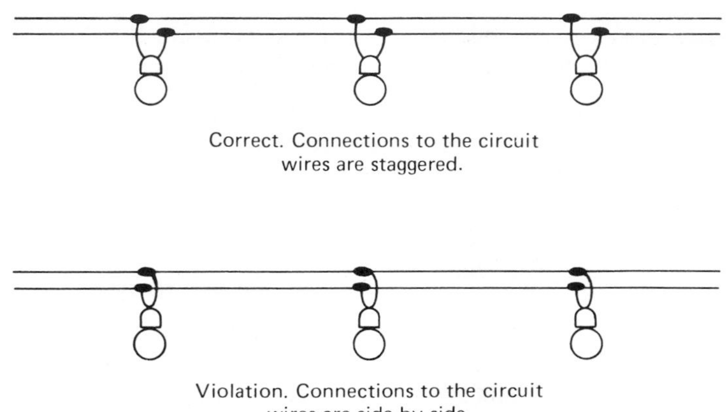

Correct. Connections to the circuit wires are staggered.
Violation. Connections to the circuit wires are side by side.

Fig. 221
Connection of outdoor lampholders to circuit wires (Sect. 225-24).

225-25. Location of Outdoor Lamps

Lamps for outdoor lighting shall be located *below* live conductors, transformers, and other electrical equipment. This is for safety of persons replacing lamps.

This requirement is waived when:

1. Clearances or other safeguards are provided to prevent contact with live parts by persons replacing lamps, or
2. The equipment concerned has a disconnect that can be locked in the open position.

ARTICLE 230 — SERVICES

A. General

230-1. Scope

To correctly interpret the rules relating to services, it is necessary to know precisely what is meant by the different terms used in the Code.

The following terms apply for overhead services:

The *service drop* is the overhead conductors between the last pole and the service entrance. The service drop ends at the point where the service-entrance conductors connect to the service drop.

The *service-entrance conductors* are the conductors between the service drop and the service disconnect, which is usually inside the building.

The *service conductors* are the conductors between the last pole and the service disconnect. The term "service conductors" is meant to include both the drop conductors and the service-entrance conductors.

The foregoing terms deal with conductors. The following terms include equipment as well as conductors:

The *service entrance* includes the service-entrance conductors *and* any equipment used. The term "service entrance" includes service-entrance conductors, conduit and fittings, meter, service switch and fuses, and any other equipment used in the run between the tap to the drop and the service disconnect.

The *service* includes the service-drop conductors, service-entrance conductors, *and* any equipment used between the last pole and the service disconnect.

When the service is underground, the conductors between the street main and the service entrance are a *lateral.* The lateral connects to the electric company's underground mains; or it could run underground to a pole, then up the pole to overhead mains.

For underground services, the lateral would take the place of the service drop in the above discussion.

230-2. Number of Services

The general rule is: only one service drop or lateral per building.

There are seven exceptions to the general rule. A building may have more than one service if needed for (1) fire pumps, (2) emergency lighting and/or power, (3) "multiple-occupancy" buildings (special permission required), (4) large capacity requirements (when a service larger than 3,000 amps. is required at 600 volts or less), (5) buildings covering a large area (special permission required), (6) different voltages, frequency, or phase, or where both AC and DC are used, or for different classes of use, (7) laterals.

(1) In the case of a fire pump in a building, safety precautions would dictate the use of a separate service to ensure against interruption of service to the fire pump.

(2) An emergency lighting or power system might be supplied to a building from a separate power source; in this case another service would be not only desirable but necessary.

(3) A "multiple-occupancy" building may be a duplex or an apartment house or any other building having more than one tenant. It may also be a commercial building with more than one tenant.

(a) of Exception No. 3 allows more than one service *drop* or *lateral* for such a building, only by special permission.

(b) of Exception No. 3 permits more than one set of service-*entrance* conductors for a multiple-occupancy building, all tapped to one service *drop* or *lateral.* Special permission is not required for this arrangement (Fig. 222).

More than one *drop* or *lateral* may be installed only by special permission.

(4) More than one service is permitted if capacity requirements are more than 3,000 amps. (at 600 volts or less); or if the electric company requires two or more services because of the load.

(5) For a building covering a very large area, it could be impractical to serve all parts of the building from one service center. For such buildings, more than one service may be installed by special permission. This exception is not concerned with height of a building—only with the extent of the area covered by the building.

(6) If a building requires, say, 480-volt service for power and 120/240-volt service for lighting, two services could be installed without special permission.

If certain equipment in a building operates on a special rate schedule, the Code permits an additional service for the special equipment because of the difference in class of use.

(7) More than one set of *laterals* is permitted if paralleled at the supply end. (Paralleling is permitted only for No. 1/0 and larger conductors.)

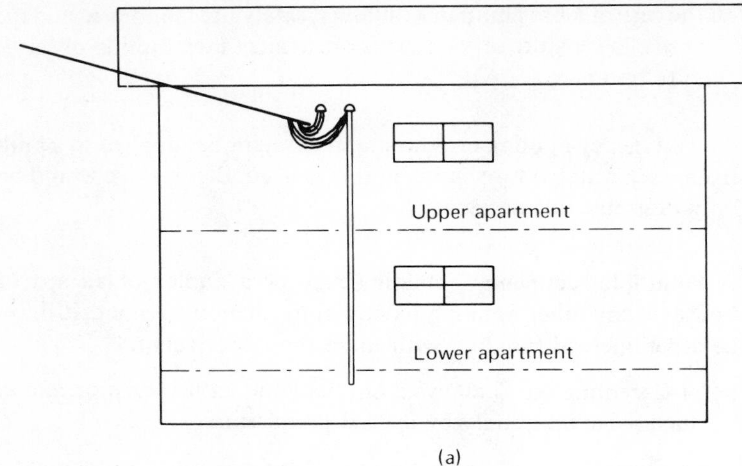

(a)

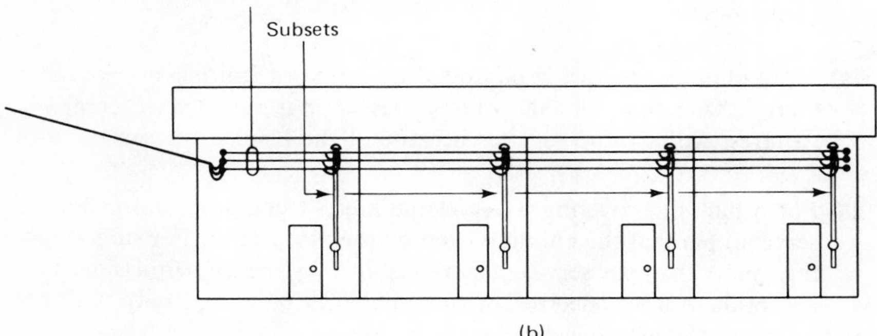

(b)

Fig. 222

Multiple-occupancy buildings with two or more separate sets of service-entrance conductors [Sect. 230-2, Exception No. 3(b)].

(a) Separate sets of service-entrance conductors tapped to one service drop.
(b) Several subsets of service entrance conductors tapped from a single set of main service-entrance conductors.

The arrangements shown are approved for multiple-occupancy buildings of one or two floors. For multiple-occupancy buildings of three or more floors, the different service disconnects must be grouped in a "common accessible location," and may not be located in each apartment as shown. [See Sect. 230-72(d).]

230-3. One Building or Other Structure Not to Be Supplied Through Another

No part of a service for a building may pass through the inside of another building, unless both buildings are occupied by, or under the management of, the same person or firm. [There is an exception to this rule. A service in conduit or duct may pass through another building if the conduit or duct is enclosed by concrete or brick at least 2 in. thick (see Section 230-44).]

A service may pass *under* another building, if covered by at least 2 in. of concrete. The service in this case need not be in conduit or duct, but must be a type suitable for burial in the earth.

A service may be run along the *outside* of one building to reach another.

B. Insulation and Size of Service Conductors

230-4. Insulation of Service Conductors

Service conductors must have an insulation suited for the conditions of use. This applies both to the service-drop and service-entrance conductors, as well as to underground services.

230-5. Size of Service Conductors

Service conductors shall have an ampacity at least equal to the amperage of the load. "Service conductors" includes conductors for drops, underground laterals, and service entrances. Each is treated separately in the following sections.

C. Overhead Services

230-21. Overhead Supply

A service drop is an "overhead supply."

The overhead conductors from the electric company pole to the point of connection of a service entrance is a service drop.

In farm wiring, a meter and/or disconnect are sometimes installed on a pole in the yard, with overhead spans to each of the buildings. The overhead spans are service drops, as well as the electric company's drop to the pole (Fig. 223).

All are required to be installed according to the rules of this part (C) of the Code.

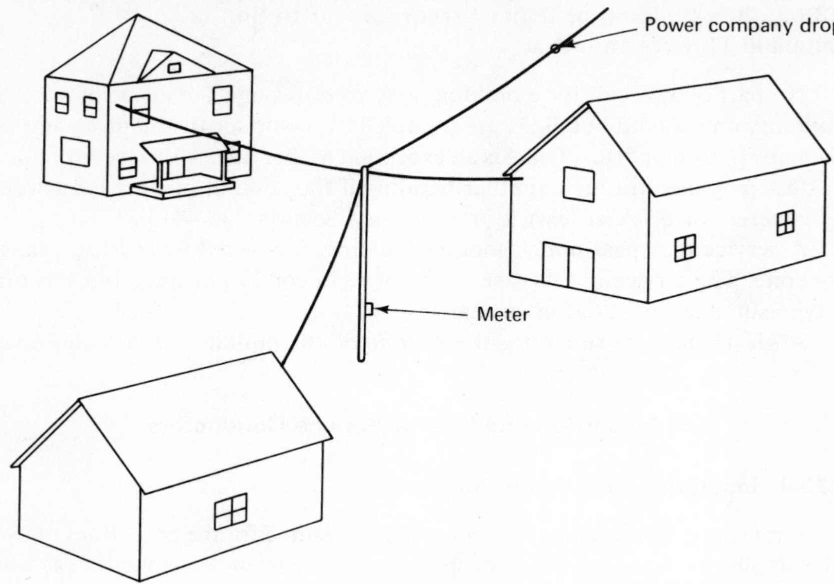

Fig. 223

Power company drop to a pole, with overhead spans from the pole to several buildings. The overhead spans are service drops, as well as the power company's drop, and subject to the Code rules of Article 230, Part C. Meter connects to power company drop, with a return run to the other drops (Sect. 230-21).

230-22. Insulation or Covering

(a) *Cable*

When the drop is in the form of cable, the conductor insulation must be thermoplastic (or other "vulcanizable" material). If the drop is individual wires run separately, the insulation may be any type suitable for the purpose.

When the drop is in the form of cable, a grounded neutral may be bare.

(b) When the drop is individual wires run separately, the neutral must be insulated in all cases.

230-23. Size and Rating

Minimum size permitted for overhead services is No. 8 copper or No. 6 aluminum, except for the special case where the drop serves a small load of only one branch circuit, in which case the conductors may be No. 12 hard-drawn copper.

In farm wiring, conductors may be run overhead to a building from a pole on which a meter or disconnect is installed. In this case, the overhead conductors are considered to be a service drop, and would have to be sized according to this rule.

230-24. Clearances

(a) Over Roofs

Clearance of a drop above roofs must in general be at least 8 ft. There are two exceptions:

1. When the roof has sufficient slope (at least 4 in. in 12), the clearance may be reduced to 3 ft for drops of 300 volts or less between conductors. A roof with a steep slope is not customarily walked on, and therefore the Code allows this exception. For voltages above 300, an 8-ft clearance must be maintained, regardless of roof slope.
2. Where a drop is attached to a service entrance conduit extending through the roof, clearance may be 18 in. minimum, if the drop does not pass over more than 4 ft of roof. This rule is for drops of 300 volts or less between conductors (Fig. 224).

(b) Clearance from Ground

For 600 volts or less, minimum height above ground for service drops is as follows:

Above sidewalks or finished grade	10 ft
Above residential driveways	12 ft
Above parking lots, drive-ins not subject to truck traffic	12 ft
Above areas subject to truck traffic	15 ft
Above public streets, alleys, roads	18 ft

(c) Clearance from Building Openings

A clearance of at least 3 ft is required from windows, porches, etc. At this distance the conductors could be touched only with difficulty. (Conductors passing *above* a window need not have a 3 ft clearance.)

230-26. Point of Attachment

This rule sets the minimum height for attachment of a drop to a building. In effect, the minimum height required is the height that will give the proper clearance of the drop above ground. For example, if the drop passes over a public street, it would have to be attached to the building at a height sufficient to give an 18-ft clearance over the street.

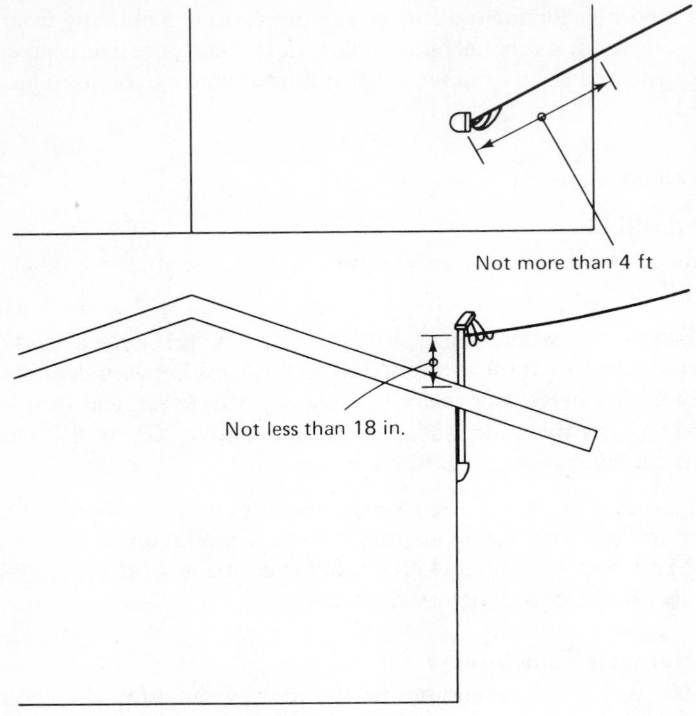

Fig. 224
Through-the-roof service of 300 V or less between conductors (higher-voltage services must have a clearance over roofs of at least 8 ft) [Sect. 230-24(a), Exception No. 2].

Since the minimum distance above ground for a drop is 10 ft, the point of attachment to the building can never be less than 10 ft above ground in any case.

230-27. Means of Attachment

For attaching service-drop *cable,* any standard form of fitting designed for outdoor use would be "approved for the purpose." A minimum clearance of 2 in. from the "surface wired over" is required for cables not approved for direct mounting [Section 230-51(b)].

Open wiring must be run on insulators or fittings approved for the purpose.

230-28. Service Masts as Supports

Service masts shall have adequate strength to withstand the strain imposed by the service drop. Service masts should be fitted with guys or braces.

230-29. Supports over Buildings

This Section recommends that when wires pass over a building they be supported on poles on either side of the building, so that the wires passing over the building are suspended in the air, without attachment to the building itself. If necessary to attach the wires to the roof, some sort of support, such as a crossarm on a cradle, must be used to support the wires. The cradle or other support must be high enough so that the wires will have the clearance above the roof required by Section 230-24.

D. Underground Services

230-30. Insulation

A lateral is an underground service. It may connect to an underground street main, or it may be run underground to a power company pole, thence up the pole to connect to the overhead lines. At the building, the lateral may enter a terminal box or meter, inside or outside the building wall. At that point the service-entrance conductors tap to the lateral and run to the service equipment in the building.

In some cases there may be no terminal box or meter inside or outside the building wall, and the underground run goes straight through to the service equipment, with no tap to a service entrance. In that case, the part of the run outside the building wall is considered to be the lateral. The part inside is considered to be the service entrance, and as such is subject to Code rules for service entrances. This would be a case of a single run having one designation for one part and another designation for the other part of the run. It is part lateral and part service entrance.

This rule requires that "service lateral conductors shall be insulated for the applied voltage." The rule would imply that the insulation may be any type of insulation rated high enough for the voltage and suitable for the conditions of use.

Grounded (neutral) lateral conductors in conduit may be bare. A fungus-resistant cable having an uninsulated neutral may be buried, regardless of soil conditions. A bare copper neutral may be buried directly, where soil conditions will not deteriorate the copper.

230-31. Size and Rating

Except where only a limited load of a single branch circuit is served, No. 8 copper (No. 6 aluminum or copper-clad aluminum) is the smallest size lateral permitted.

The neutral conductor may be sized to carry the "maximum unbalance of the load." For a 120/240-volt service, the maximum unbalance would be equal to the total amperage minus the amperage taken by equipment operating on 240 volts only. See Section 220-22 for examples of figuring neutral load.

If there were no 120-volt equipment (only 240-volt equipment) on the premises, the neutral would still have to be carried along with the service [this is required by Section 250-23(b)], but would carry no current. The neutral in this case may be sized the same as the grounding electrode conductor, according to Table 250-94, p. 70-101 of the Code.

E. Service-Entrance Conductors

230-40. Insulation of Service-Entrance Conductors

(a) The "hot" wires of a service-entrance must be insulated in all cases.

Grounded (neutral) service conductors in conduit or cable may be bare.

A bare copper grounded neutral may be buried directly, where soil conditions would not result in deterioration of the copper.

A fungus-resistant cable having an uninsulated copper or aluminum (or copper-clad aluminum) grounded neutral may be buried, regardless of soil conditions.

(b) If the service entrance is open wiring, the insulation must be thermoplastic or vulcanizable material.

230-41. Size and Rating

1. For a single-family home with six or more two-wire branch circuits, a 100-amp. minimum, three-wire service entrance is required. (This would require a No. 4 minimum conductor.*)
2. For a single-family home with a computed load of 10 kW or more, a 100-amp. minimum, three-wire service entrance is required.
3. For other occupancies, a 60-amp. minimum service entrance is required. (This would require a No. 6 in an RH or TH type, or a No. 4 TW.)

*See Note 3, p. 70-136 of the Code

Exceptions.

1. For loads of one or two two-wire branch circuits, conductors may be No. 8 copper.

2. For limited loads of a single branch circuit, conductors may be No. 12 copper.

3. By special permission, conductors may be No. 8 copper.

The neutral conductor of a service may be sized to carry the "maximum unbalance of the load." For a 120/240-volt service the maximum unbalance would be equal to the total amperage minus the amperage taken by equipment operating on 240 volts only. (See Section 220-22 for examples of figuring neutral load.)

If there were no 120-volt equipment—only 240 volt equipment—on the premises, the neutral would still have to be carried along with the service [this is required by Section 250-23(b)], but would carry no current. The neutral in this case may be sized the same as the grounding electrode conductor, according to Table 250-94, p. 70-101 of the Code.

F. Installation of Service Conductors

230-43. Wiring Methods for 600 Volts or Less

The following types of wiring are permitted for service entrances of 600 volts or less:

1. Open wiring on insulators.

2. Rigid metal conduit.

3. EMT.

4. Service-entrance cable.

5. Wireways.

6. Busways.

7. Auxiliary gutters.

8. Rigid nonmetallic conduit.

9. Cablebus.

10. Mineral-insulated, metal-sheathed cable.

11. Intermediate metal conduit.

12. Rigid nonmetallic conduit.

Types of approved service-entrance cable are:

Type SE.

Type SE (armored).

Type USE.

Type SD.

Type SE armored cable is type SE with a spirally wound steel tape armor for added protection. Type USE is for underground use.

Type SD cable is a service-drop cable, sometimes serving both as service drop and service entrance, being continuous from pole to service equipment.

Service-entrance cable must be approved for the voltage involved. Standard service-entrance cable is approved and marked for 600 V maximum. Approved cable carries the UL label.

230-44. Conductors Considered Outside of Building

Service conductors are considered to be outside a building if beneath the building and under at least 2 in. of concrete; or if within the building, and in conduit or duct covered by at least 2 in. of concrete or brick (see Section 230-3).

230-45. Separate Enclosures

The disconnect for a building may consist of up to six switches (or circuit breakers). As an example, an apartment building with six apartments could have six separate disconnects, one for each apartment, tapped to the service entrance, without a main switch for the building. For such an arrangement, all disconnects may be connected to one service entrance, or a separate service entrance may be run to each disconnect. Or two, three, four, five, or six separate service entrances may serve the group of disconnects. In short, one to six service entrances may be used to serve the six disconnects.

One, or more than one, service entrance may be used to serve two, three, four, five, or six disconnects. There may be more than one service entrance, but only one *drop* or *lateral* is permitted to serve the several entrances.

230-46. Unspliced Conductors

The general rule is that splices are not permitted in the service-entrance conductors; they must be continuous throughout their length between the service disconnect and the point of attachment to the drop (or lateral). There are, however, four exceptions to this rule.

Exception No. 1.

When a break in the conductors is necessary to connect a meter, such as a socket meter.

Exception No. 2.

In "multiple-occupancy" buildings, more than one service entrance is permitted. In this case one set of conductors could serve as a "main" entrance, with the individual entrances tapped to the main entrance [see Fig. 222(b)]. Each tap would constitute a "splice" but is permitted as an exception.

In multiple-occupancy buildings, as many as six entrance switches may be tapped to the same service entrance [Section 230-71(a)]. The necessary tap in the line, to connect each switch, is permitted as an exception.

Exception No. 3.

Underground service conductors may terminate in a connection box just inside the building. At this point the lead-covered underground service wires may be spliced to a nonwaterproof type of cable to continue to the service equipment. This exception makes it possible to change to a less expensive type of cable inside the building. A splice would not be permitted if the same type of cable as the underground service were used inside the building. (The cable inside must be a different type than the cable outside the building; otherwise, the splice is not permitted.)

Exception No. 4.

This rule would apply in a case where a service is already installed with the meter inside the building. Say that the inside meter is now removed and installed on the outside of the building. The taps are disconnected from the service drop. New service-entrance conductors are now tapped to the drop, and run in new conduit down to the outdoor meter, then up from the meter to a service head, where they are brought out and spliced to the old wires coming out of the old service head. The splice is permitted as an exception.

230-47. Other Conductors in Raceway or Cable

Other than for the exceptions listed, no conductors other than service conductors are allowed in the service raceway. Exceptions are (1) grounding conductors (2) control conductors from time switches.

230-48. Raceway Seal

It would not be desirable to allow moisture or gases to collect in a conduit or duct. The ends of the conduit or duct must be sealed with suitable sealing compound where an underground service enters a building.

Spare or unused raceway must likewise be sealed.

230-49. Protection Against Damage—Underground

See Section 300-5.

230-50. Protection of Open Conductors and Cable Against Damage—Above Ground

The rules of this Section can be summed up as follows:

Open Wiring:

Open wiring on insulators is *not* permitted within 8 ft of the ground.

Open wiring is *not* permitted where exposed to mechanical injury.

Service cable, when exposed to mechanical injury, must be protected by conduit, EMT, or other means.

Examples of locations "exposed to mechanical injury":

1. Near awnings, shutters, etc.

2. Alongside driveways.

3. Near coal chutes.

Conduit or EMT may be used as a service entrance in locations exposed to mechanical injury.

230-51. Mounting Supports

Service-entrance cables approved for direct-to-wall mounting must be strapped at not more than 4½ ft intervals, and within 12 in. of the service head.

Service cables that are not approved for direct-to-wall mounting must be mounted on insulators spaced not more than 15 ft apart. The cable must be held off the wall at least 2 in.

Individual open conductors shall be installed in accordance with Table 230-51(c), p. 70-62 of the Code.

Open wiring on insulators inside a building must be supported at intervals of not over 4½ ft. The conductors must be at least 2½ in. apart and 1 in. from the surface wired over.

230-52. Individual Conductors Entering Buildings or Other Structures

Nonabsorbent insulating tubes must be used for open wires passing into the building through the wall. Usually, porcelain tubes would be used, one for each wire. To prevent rain from entering the building through the tubes, the tubes must slant downward from inside to outside. As a further precaution against water entering the building, drip loops must be provided in the wire at the point outside where they enter the porcelain tubes. Individual conductors entering through the roof of a building shall enter through roof bushings.

230-53. Raceways to Drain

Service-entrance conduit (or other raceways), when exposed to the weather, shall be raintight. This means that raintight fittings must be used. Fittings for use with service entrances are made raintight by the manufacturer. Even though raintight fittings are used, it is possible for moisture from condensation to accumulate inside the conduit. Or, under extreme conditions, moisture could enter through the holes in the service head. For these reasons, the Code requires that provision be made for drainage. This could be a small drain hole in the bottom of the entrance ell, if this is the low point, or provision could be made for drainage inside the building, if the conduit enters the basement. Conduit entrances embedded in masonry must have provision for drainage.

230-54. Connections at Service Head

The sole purpose of this rule is to prevent moisture from entering into the service-entrance cable or conduit. Trouble has resulted from water following the exposed wires at the tap to the service drop, getting into the service-entrance cable or conduit, and passing into the meter. A service-entrance must be run up the building to a point above the service drop. This applies for both conduit and service cable.

The Code allows an exception to this rule in cases where it is impractical to have the service-entrance run up to a point above the service drop, provided the service head is not over 24 in. away *from* the point of attachment of the drop. Note that the word "from" not "below" is used in this rule. This would permit the service head to be 24 inches below the service drop attachment only when the service head is directly below the attachment. The 24-inch distance permitted refers to the straight line distance between head and point of attachment.

If cable is used for the service entrance, there are two approved ways of bringing out the wires from the cable for tapping to the service drop:

1. A service head with individual holes for each wire may be attached to the end of the cable and the wires brought out through the holes.
2. The service head may be omitted and the cable formed into a gooseneck above the drop, the cable being stripped back to allow splicing to the drop. The cable is taped and painted at the point where the wires leave the cable (Fig. 225).

If the gooseneck method is used, the Code allows reliance on the connections to the drop to preserve the gooseneck shape. The cable would come up through the top cable strap, and, because of the stiffness of the cable, loop out and down in the form of a gooseneck, the tap wires down to the drop being pulled up fairly tight to hold the gooseneck shape. Or a "fitting approved for the purpose" may be used. A metal fitting in the form of a gooseneck is on the market for this purpose. It clamps on to the cable and holds the gooseneck shape without relying on the taps to the drop for stiffness.

Conduit and EMT must be fitted with a service head.

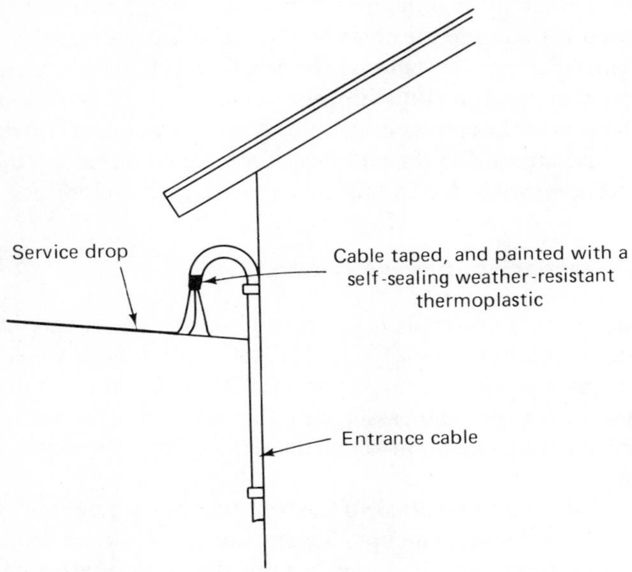

Fig. 225
Service cable formed in a gooseneck. No service head required [Sect. 230-54(b)].

230-55. Termination at Service Equipment

At the end of the service run inside the building, there must be a terminal box, cabinet, entrance switch, or similar type of enclosure. No live parts may be left exposed.

An exception is made to this rule when the service ends at an open-type switchboard. In this case no terminating box is required, but, for conduit, a bushing must be used where the wires are brought out of the conduit.

G. Service Equipment—Guarding and Grounding

230-62. Service Equipment—Enclosed or Guarded

All live parts of service equipment must be enclosed in a suitable cabinet, box, panel, or other enclosure so as to prevent accidental contact with live parts.

Exception.

For very large buildings, the service may terminate at a switchboard. Live parts on a switchboard need not be "enclosed" if suitably "guarded" in accordance with Sections 110-17 and 110-18.

230-63. Grounding and Bonding

Section 250-32 requires that metal enclosures for service conductors and equipment shall be grounded.

Service equipment to be grounded would include:

1. Service-entrance conduit.
2. Meter housing.
3. Service-disconnect enclosure.

Service equipment shall be grounded in accordance with Article 250. The following are rules taken from Article 250:

1. The grounded neutral may be used to ground service raceway, and meter housing.
2. The neutral must be bonded to the service-disconnect enclosure.
3. Service raceway or cable armor, meter fittings, and enclosures, boxes, and the service-disconnect enclosure must be bonded together.
4. The grounding electrode wire must be at least No. 8 wire.
5. If the grounding electrode wire size is only No. 8, it must be run in conduit, pipe, or tubing for protection from mechanical injury. The conduit, pipe, or tubing must be bonded to the service-switch enclosure.
6. A grounding electrode wire larger than No. 8 need not be so protected.
7. Soldered connections are not permitted; lugs, clamps, or pressure connectors must be used for making connections.

H. Service Equipment—Disconnecting Means

230-70. General

Every service must be provided with a disconnect that will disconnect the building served from the source of supply. Each disconnecting means shall be permanently marked to identify it as a service disconnect.

230-71. Maximum Number of Disconnects

Up to six switches or circuit breakers may serve as the disconnect for a premises, provided that the combined rating of the switches or breakers is not less than that required for a single switch or breaker. A 100-amp. entrance would require, for instance, at least four 30-amp. or two 50-amp. (rating) switches. The six or less switches or breakers may be the branch-circuit switches or breakers in a panelboard, or they may be separate units (Fig. 226). When single-pole switches are tied together so as to act as a two- or three-pole switch, the combination is counted as one switch.

230-72. Grouping of Disconnects

When two to six switches or circuit breakers serve as the disconnect for one home, apartment, or other premises (Section 230-71), they shall be marked to indicate the load served.

In "multiple-occupancy" buildings, such as apartment houses, up to six apartments may be served by the one service entrance, each apartment having a separate disconnect. No *main* disconnect is required in the service. If *more than six* disconnects are required, a single main disconnect must be installed ahead of the seven or more apartment disconnects.

For multiple-occupancy buildings having three or more floors, the individual switches for the apartments must be grouped together in a "common accessible location."

For multiple-occupancy buildings having three or more floors, not more than six service entrances may be tapped to one drop or lateral. Where there are three or more floors, the service entrances are not permitted to be run to each apartment, but must be run to a "common accessible location," where the different apartment disconnects would be grouped together.

For multiple-occupancy buildings of *one* or *two* floors, a variation in the general rules is permitted. Any number of service entrances may be tapped to one drop or lateral, with a separate service entrance run to each apartment. As can be seen, grouping of disconnects is not required, nor is a main disconnect required for this arrangement (Fig. 222).

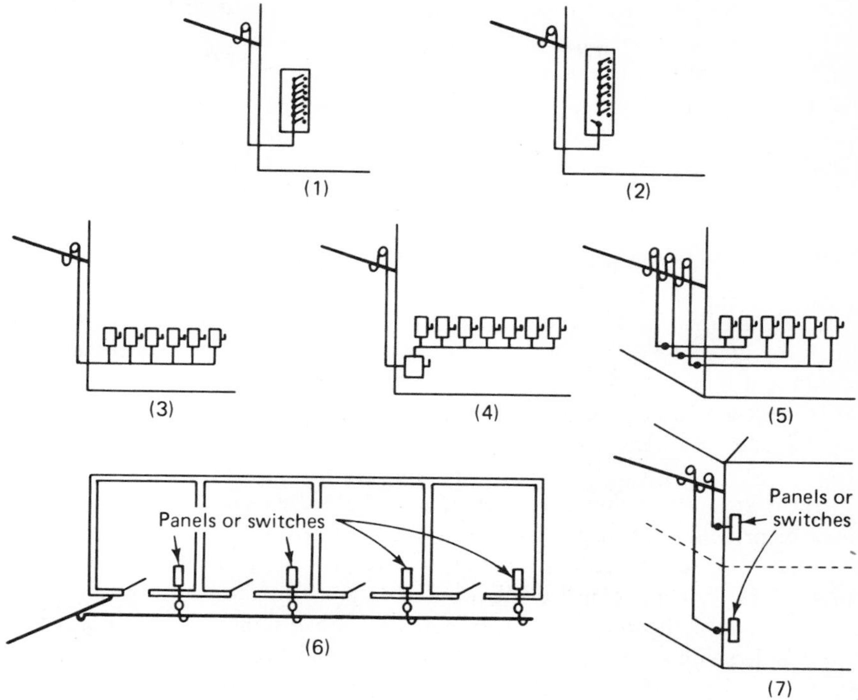

Fig. 226

Maximum number of disconnects permitted (Sect. 230-71).

(1) A panel with six or fewer switches or circuit breakers may serve as a disconnect.
(2) Panels with more than six switches or circuit breakers must have a main disconnect. [(1) and (2) frequently used for private homes.]
(3) Up to six separate switches or circuit breakers may serve as the disconnect for a building.
(4) More than six switches or breakers must have a main disconnect.
(5) The six or fewer disconnects of (3) may be served by one to six sets of service entrances. [The arrangements of (3), (4), and (5) are adapted to multiple-occupancy buildings of three or more floors, where all disconnects must be grouped as per Section 230-72(d).]
(6)(7) For multiple-occupancy buildings of one or two floors, the different disconnects need not be grouped. See also Fig. 222.

The service disconnect for any premises shall be installed in a readily accessible location, and as close as possible to the point where the service enters.

Disconnects for fire pumps or for emergency service shall be located at a remote point from the disconnect for the normal or regular service.

230-73. Working Space

Generally speaking, for service equipment of 150 volts or less to ground, clearance between the service disconnect and grounded walls or structures must be 3 ft minimum on each side of the service equipment. (See Section 110–16.)

230-74. Simultaneous Opening of Poles

230-75. Disconnection of Grounded Conductor

The disconnect must open all ungrounded conductors. Opening of the neutral is not required, but the disconnect may, if desired, also disconnect the grounded neutral. If the neutral is switched along with the hot wires, there must be simultaneous opening of all hot wires along with the neutral. For example, if it is desired to switch the neutral of a 120/240-volt entrance, the disconnect would have to be a three-pole switch or circuit breaker. You could not use one switch or circuit breaker for the neutral and another for the hot wires.

If the grounded neutral is not switched (this is the usual case), other means must be provided for disconnecting it. If the neutral is fastened to a terminal and may be disconnected by use of a screwdriver or wrench, this provides a satisfactory "other means" of disconnecting.

When only the hot wires are switched, the disconnect may consist of single-pole switches or breakers—one in each hot wire, provided the handles are tied together so as to be operable simultaneously [Section 230-71(b)].

If the neutral is to be switched along with the hot wires, ties are not permitted.

230-76. Manually or Power Operable

The following types of service disconnects are permitted:

1. Manual enclosed switch, such as an enclosed knife switch, or "pul-fuse" switch.

2. Manually operable circuit breaker.

A circuit breaker or switch may be operable by remote control, such as by a pushbutton, *provided it can also be opened manually.*

230-77. Indicating

The disconnect must be marked OFF and ON or with other marking that will clearly show whether the disconnect is in the open or closed position.

230-78. Externally Operable

The disconnect must be externally operable. Electrically operated circuit breakers need not be externally operable by hand to the closed position—only to the open position.

230-79. Rating of Disconnect

For installations having only limited loads of a single branch circuit, a 15-amp. (rating) disconnect may be used.

For installations of not more than two two-wire circuits, a single disconnect must have at least a 30-amp. rating.

For a single-family residence having six or more two-wire branch circuits, or having a load of 10-23 kW, a single disconnect must have at least a 100-amp. rating.

For installations other than the above, minimum single switch rating is 60 amps.

230-80. Combined Rating of Disconnects

Up to six switches or circuit breakers may serve as the disconnect for a premises, provided that the combined rating of the switches (or circuit breakers) is not less than that required for a single switch or circuit breaker. As an example, for a 100 amp. entrance with two switches, the rating of each switch would have to be at least 50 amp.; for four switches at least 25 amp., etc.

230-81. Connection to Terminals

The use of solder is prohibited for connection of service conductors to the service switch. A connector that applies pressure mechanically must be used, such as pressure connectors or bolted clamps.

230-82. Equipment Connected to the Supply Side of Service Disconnect

The following equipment may be connected in the line ahead of the service disconnect:

1. Fuses.
2. Meters, 600 volts and under (if grounded).
3. Surge protective capacitors.
4. Instrument transformers.

5. Lightning arresters.
6. Time switches.
7. Emergency circuits.
8. Fire and sprinkler alarms.
9. Fire-pump equipment.
10. Standby power systems.

When items 6 to 10 are connected on the supply side of the disconnect, they must be provided with a separate disconnect and "overcurrent device."

230-83. Emergency Transfer Equipment

Where there is an emergency source of supply as well as the regular source of supply, the service disconnect must be arranged so as to open the main supply before connection is made to the emergency supply. A double throw switch would fulfill the requirements of this rule. (Where the emergency and regular supply are intended to operate in parallel, the rule does not apply.)

230-84. More Than One Building or Other Structure

Where more than one building is on the same property and under the same management, each building must have a separate disconnect. The disconnect shall be located in or on each building in a "readily accessible" location, and as close as possible to the point where the conductors enter the building. The conductors to each building, even though served from another building, are a service drop (Section 230-21), the conductors entering the building are a service entrance, and the disconnect is required to be a type suitable for use as service equipment.

An exception is made for garages and outbuildings on *residential* property. A snap switch may be used as a disconnect for the garage or outbuildings. (The snap switch may be a three- or four-way switch, if desired.)

J. Service Equipment—Overcurrent Protection

230-90. Where Required

(a) Ungrounded Conductor

Either fuses or a circuit breaker may be used as the "overcurrent device" for a service entrance. When fuses are used, there must be a fuse in each "hot" wire, but a fuse is never permitted in a grounded neutral.

The general rule is that the fuse size or circuit breaker setting shall not be greater than the current-carrying capacity of the service-entrance conductors. If the service is No. 4 Type TW wire, the maximum fuse size would be 70 amps., since 70 amps. is the carrying capacity of the wire.

There are five exceptions to the general rule for sizing the "overcurrent devices" of a service:

Exception No. 1.

When motors comprise all or most of the load, fusing of the service can be according to the rules for motor fusing. For motors, the Code allows the conductors to be overfused (see Article 430).

Exception No. 2.

If there is no standard fuse size or circuit-breaker setting corresponding to the current-carrying capacity of the service wires, then the next higher fuse size or circuit breaker setting can be used.

As an example, say that No. 2 Type TW conductors are used for a service entrance. No. 2 Type TW has a current-carrying capacity of 95 amps. Since there is no 95-amp. standard fuse (or circuit-breaker setting), the Code allows the next higher size above 95 amps. to be used. A 100-amp. fuse or breaker may be used in this case.

Exception No. 3.

Up to six circuit breakers or six sets of fuses in an entrance panel may serve as the overcurrent protection for a service. As an example, for a 100-amp. entrance, there could be six circuit breakers, each set at 20 amps. The total of the six circuit breakers in parallel would be 120 amps., and the service would, in effect, be protected at 120 amps., which would be above the ampacity of the service, but permitted by Code rules.

Exception No. 4.

Up to six apartment disconnects can be tapped to the main service entrance, with no main disconnect required ahead of the six apartment disconnects.

Say that a single set of service-entrance conductors serves four apartments, each with its own service switch and fuses. The load on each of the four apartments is calculated at 52 amps. In calculating the load on the service-entrance conductors, a demand factor is applied in accordance with the rules for calculating the size of feeders. The calculated demand load on the service turns out to be, say, 163 amps. calling for No. 3/0 service-entrance conductors. Now, each apartment circuit might be fused at 60 amps. The total of the four sets of fuses in parallel is 240 amps., so the service-entrance conductors are, in effect, fused at 240 amps., which would be more than the ampacity of the No. 3/0 service entrance. This is allowable and is another exception to the general rule for fusing service conductors.

Exception No. 5.

Fire pumps. The service for a fire pump room may be fused high enough to carry the locked-rotor (stalled) current of the fire-pump motor(s). This would result in overfusing the service conductors, but is permitted as an exception.

(In the foregoing examples, where fuses or fusing are referred to, this should be taken to mean "overcurrent protection" and would include circuit breakers or other forms of circuit protection.)

(b) Not in Grounded Conductor

A fuse may not be placed in a grounded neutral. A circuit breaker may have an overcurrent coil in the neutral if, when the breaker opens, it simultaneously breaks all hot wires. In other words, it would be permissible in a three-wire grounded neutral service to use a three pole circuit breaker, because, on a neutral overload when the breaker opens, the hot wires will open along with the neutral. On the other hand, if the three wires were fused, the neutral fuse could blow independently, leaving the system throughout the building with two "live" hot wires and no neutral, which would constitute a hazard.

(c) More Than One Building

In a property comprising more than one building under single management, the overcurrent protection for all buildings may be grouped in one building, with a supply circuit from there to each of the other buildings (Fig. 228). This is permitted only if the overcurrent devices are "accessible" to tenants of the other buildings.

It should be noted that, with this arrangement, two disconnects would be required, one at the central building and one in each of the other buildings. Section 230-84(a) combined with the requirement of Section 230-72(c) requires a disconnect at each building, and Section 230-91 requires a disconnect to be either "integral with or adjacent to" the overcurrent device.

230-91. Location

Usually, the "service overcurrent device" is an integral part of the disconnecting means. A fused knife switch would be an example of this. Circuit breakers also combine the switch with the "overcurrent device." Switch and fuses must be either "integral" or "adjacent," except in the uncommon case where protection is required at the outer end of the service, in which case the overcurrent device may be outside, the disconnecting means inside.

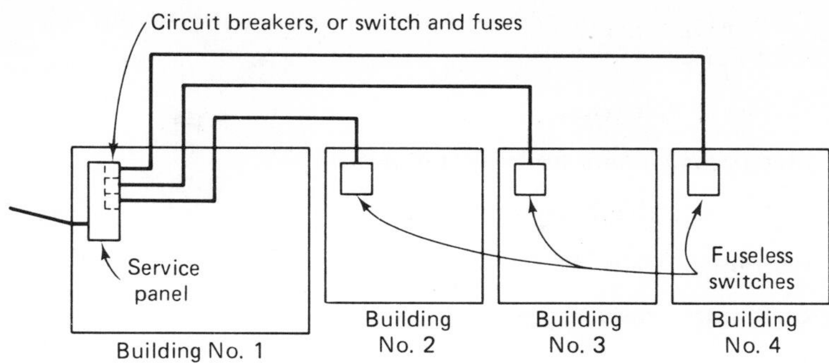

Fig. 228
Several buildings under single management. Buildings No. 2, 3, and 4 are served from building No. 1. Overcurrent protection for the services is located in building No. 1, rather than in each building [Sect. 230-90(c)]. The fuses or circuit breakers in building No. 1 must be accessible at all times to the occupants of buildings No. 2, 3, and 4. Panel also serves building No. 1. A disconnect is required at each building (Sect. 230-84). Disconnect may be a fuseless switch.

230-92. Location of Branch-Circuit Overcurrent Devices

An application of this Section would be the case of a service supplying only one branch circuit. If the service fuse is locked or sealed, another set of fuses must be installed, which will be accessible. These fuses must be of lower rating than the service fuses, so that, if a fuse blows, it will be one of the accessible fuses, rather than a locked or sealed fuse.

230-93. Protection of Specific Circuits

This Section allows an exception to the above. Where a water heater or other appliance is supplied on a flat rate or through a time switch on a special rate, the connection would be ahead of the meter, and to prevent unauthorized tapping to the circuit, sealing would be required. In this case no "accessible" fuses are required. A set of fuses that would permit tapping ahead of the meter would not be acceptable to the power company.

230-94. Relative Location of Overcurrent Device and Other Service Equipment

The effect of this Section, together with Section 230-82, would be to allow any sequence of service equipment. The equipment may be installed in a meter-switch-fuse sequence, or a switch-fuse-meter sequence, or any other arrangement.

The following equipment may be connected on the supply side of the overcurrent device:

1. Service switch.
2. Meters, 600 V and under (if grounded).
3. Surge protective capacitors.
4. Instrument transformers.
5. Lightning arresters.
6. Time switches.
7. Emergency circuits.
8. Fire and sprinkler alarms.
9. Fire-pump equipment.
10. Control circuit for power operable service equipment.

When items 6 to 10 are connected on the supply side of the service overcurrent device, they must be provided with separate overcurrent protection.

230-95. Ground-Fault Protection of Equipment

Ground-fault protection is required for grounded Wye connected services of more than 150 volts to ground and 1,000 amps. or more. This rule would apply principally for 480/277V Wye services. The maximum setting permitted for the ground-fault device is 1,200 amps. Note that this rule applies when the service *disconnect* is rated at 1,000 amps. or more.

230-96. Working Space

Generally, for service equipment of 150 volts or less to ground, clearance between the service equipment and grounded walls or structures must be 3 ft minimum on each side of the service equipment. See Section 110-16.

230-98. Available Short-Circuit Current

The available short-circuit current for an installation is the current that would momentarily flow in the line in case of a short circuit. The magnitude of a short-circuit current is dependent upon a number of factors, including the power company line, and has different values for different conditions. In some cases, the short-circuit current could be upwards of 25,000 amps. The power company probably could be helpful in estimating the approximate short-circuit current available for a premises wiring system.

In case of a short circuit, the service equipment would be momentarily subjected to a very high current, and must be built to withstand such a current without being damaged. If a circuit breaker is used as a service disconnect, it must be able to interrupt the high short-circuit current without damage to itself. Manufacturers specify the interrupting capacity of circuit breakers, and this interrupting capacity varies with the quality of the breaker. The interrupting capacity of the breaker must be equal to the short-circuit current that may be imposed upon it, and all other current-carrying parts of the service equipment must be built to withstand such currents without being damaged.

K. Services Exceeding 600 Volts Nominal

230-200. General

For services exceeding 600 volts, the rules of the preceding sections on services must be complied with, if applicable, as well as the provisions of Part K.

230-201. Classification of Service Conductors

For very large buildings, such as large hotels and office buildings, high-voltage primaries may be carried to step-down transformers located within the building. Here, the primaries are the service conductors, except in the case where they enter a vault, or where they enter metal-enclosed switchgear, or where they enter a locked room accessible only to qualified personnel, in which case the secondaries within the building are the service conductors, not the primaries entering the building. If the transformers are located outside the building, the secondaries entering the building are, of course, the service conductors (Fig. 230).

230-202. Service-Entrance Conductors

Types of wiring permitted for high-voltage service entrances are:

1. Rigid metal conduit.
2. Rigid nonmetallic conduit, if encased in not less than 2 in. of concrete.
3. Approved cable.
4. Open wiring on insulators.
5. Cablebus.
6. Intermediate metal conduit.

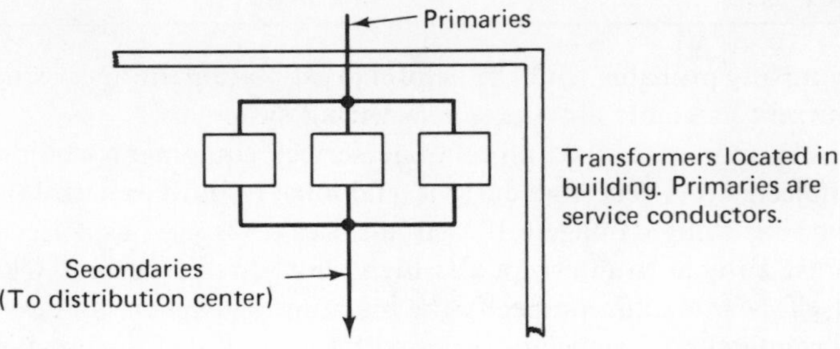
Primaries
Transformers located in building. Primaries are service conductors.
Secondaries (To distribution center)

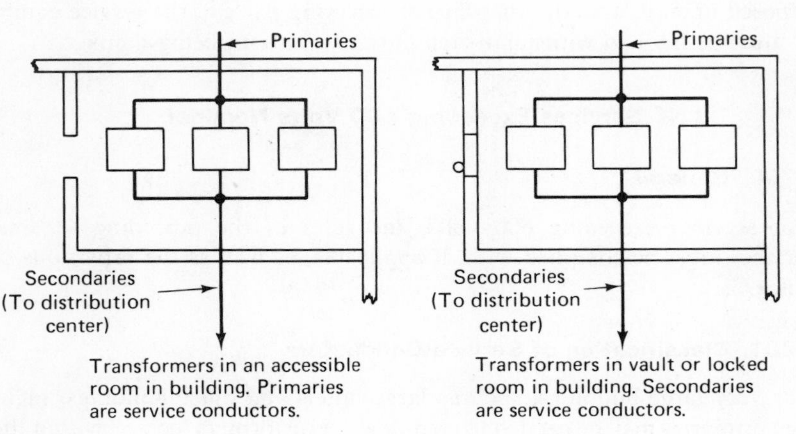
Primaries
Secondaries (To distribution center)
Transformers in an accessible room in building. Primaries are service conductors.
Primaries
Secondaries (To distribution center)
Transformers in vault or locked room in building. Secondaries are service conductors.

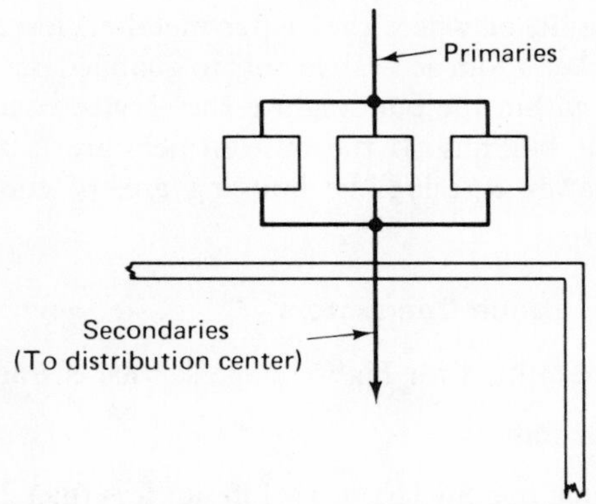
Primaries
Secondaries (To distribution center)

Transformers located outside of building, either outdoors or in another building. Secondaries are service conductors.

Fig. 230
Classification of service conductors (Sect. 230-201).

Cable tray systems may be used to support service cables.

Open wiring on insulators is permitted only if guarded against contact by persons, or if accessible to "qualified personnel" only.

Open wire services and service wires in conduit must be at least No. 6.

If cable is used, No. 8 is permitted.

When open wiring is used, the conductors must be solidly fastened to insulators having sufficient strength to withstand the stresses imposed on the wire and insulators in the event of a short circuit. This stress could in some cases amount to over 1,000 lbs. per ft of conductor.

When open wiring is used for a high-voltage service, it must be guarded by a fence or other suitable barrier, so that unauthorized persons cannot contact the wires.

(It would be preferable, in the case of high voltages, to keep the wires off the building altogether, and to enter the building through an underground conduit or duct from the pole to the building.)

For high-voltage services, a pothead is required, not only at the outer end but also at the inner end of a service-entrance conduit or cable.

Unless conductors suitable for wet locations are used, conduit exposed to the weather or embedded in masonry shall be arranged to drain.

Primaries exceeding 15,000 volts must be brought into a vault or to metal-enclosed switchgear.

230-203. Warning Signs

HIGH VOLTAGE signs must be posted where voltages above 600 are involved.

230-204. Isolating Switches

For certain types of disconnects, an isolating switch is required (Fig. 231). (Section 230-208 specifies the different types of disconnect approved for high-voltage services.)

(a) When oil switches or air or oil circuit breakers are used as the disconnecting means, an additional "isolating" switch must be installed ahead of the oil switch or the circuit breaker. "Isolating switch" is the term used for a switch that would be opened only when there is no load on the circuit. An isolating switch does not have to have a rating high enough to break the load current. A switch such as is called for in this Section would be opened *after* the oil switch or the circuit breaker is

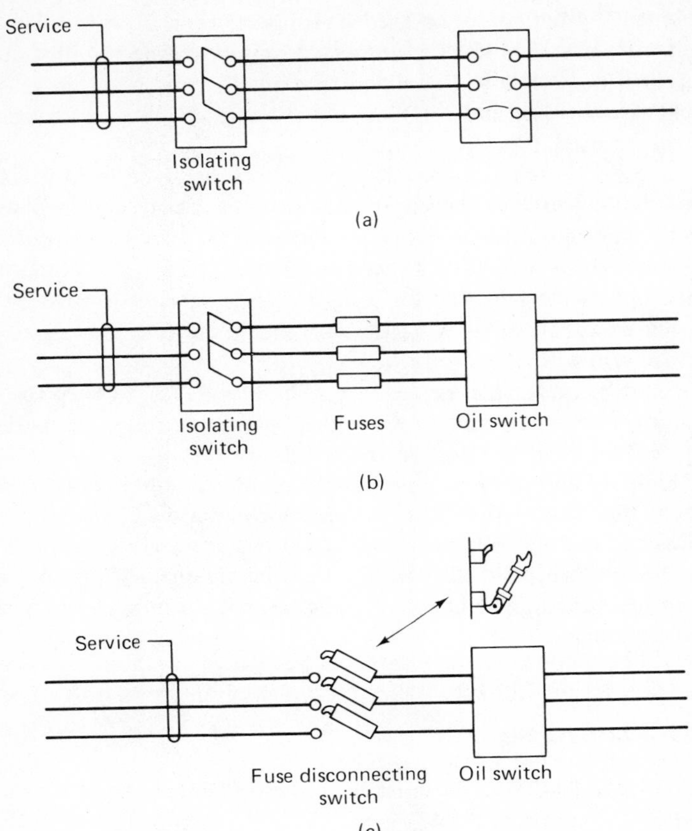

Fig. 231

Except where roll-out equipment is used, an isolating switch is required when an oil switch or a circuit breaker is used as a service disconnect:

(a) Circuit breaker acts as service disconnect and overcurrent protection combined.

(b)(c) Oil switch as disconnect; fuses provide the service overcurrent protection. When the fuses are the disconnecting type, as in (c), the fuses may act as the isolating switch.

opened. Opening the isolating switch would then kill the oil switch or circuit breaker so that it could be safely handled or worked on when servicing or repairs are required.

High-voltage service equipment of a type that can be rolled or pulled out from its switchgear or panel enclosure is available. An interlock allows the equipment to be removed only if the switch is open. When this type of equipment is used, an isolating switch is not required.

(b) If a nonautomatic oil switch and fuses are used as the disconnecting means, and the fuses are of a type that open and close like a switch, no isolating switch is required, but the disconnecting fuses have to be mounted in the line ahead of the oil switch.

(c) Isolating switches shall be accessible to qualified persons only.

(d) Isolating switches must provide means for "readily grounding" wiring on the premises. One way of doing this would be to use a double throw switch for the isolating switch, arranged so that in one position the load would connect to the line, and in the other position the load would connect to the ground connection.

230-205. Disconnecting Means

The service disconnecting means shall simultaneously disconnect all ungrounded conductors and shall be capable of being closed on a fault equal to at least the maximum available short-circuit current in the circuit. See Section 230-208 for types permitted.

230-206. Overcurrent Devices as Disconnecting Means

The different types of disconnect approved for high-voltage services are specified in Section 230-208, under Overcurrent Protection.

230-207. Equipment in Secondaries

This Section allows the disconnecting means (and overcurrent protection) in the secondaries to be omitted if there is a circuit breaker or load interrupter in the primary side of the line, and there is only *one* set of secondaries connected to a common bus. If there is a vault, this primary circuit breaker or load interrupter must be operable from outside the vault. Also, it must be of proper rating to protect the secondaries. If there are two or more sets of secondaries feeding the load, the rule does not apply and, even though there is a circuit breaker in the primary side, there must also be a disconnect and overcurrent protection on the secondary side.

230-208. Overcurrent Protection Requirements

The rules for both overcurrent protection and for disconnects are contained in this Section. There are two cases covered.

(a) When the service equipment is in a vault or consists of metal-enclosed switchgear.

(b) When the service equipment is *not* in a vault or does not consist of metal-enclosed switchgear.

A vault is a specially constructed room, with roof, walls, and floor of concrete or brick, and having fire-resistant doors. It must be constructed according to the specifications of Sections 450-41 to 450-48. Otherwise, it is not a vault.

Metal-enclosed switchgear is switchgear in an enclosure constructed of at least $\frac{1}{8}$-in.-thick metal.

(a) In Vault or Consisting of Metal-Enclosed Switchgear

When the service equipment is installed in a vault or consists of metal-enclosed switchgear, the overcurrent protection (and disconnecting means) may be any one of the following:

1. Oil switch and fuses.
2. Load interrupter and fuses.
3. Oil fuse cutout.
4. Automatic-trip circuit breaker.
5. Isolating switch and fuses.

If an oil fuse cutout is used, it could be a disconnect type, ie., a high-voltage fuse mounted with a hinge on one end so that it can be opened and closed, thus acting as a disconnect, as well as providing overcurrent protection.

A load interrupter is a switch or circuit breaker that does not provide overload protection; therefore, fuses are required when these are used. In this case the interrupter is the disconnect, and the fuses provide the overcurrent protection.

An "isolating" switch is not rated to interrupt load current and must not be opened under load. When an isolating switch is used as a primary disconnect, it must be interlocked with a disconnect in the secondary side in such a way that it would not be possible to open the primary isolating switch, unless the secondary switch is in the open position.

(b) Not in Vault or Not Consisting of Metal-Enclosed Switchgear

When the service equipment is *not* in a vault or does *not* consist of metal-enclosed switchgear, the overcurrent protection (and disconnecting means) may be:

1. Load interrupter and fuses located outside the building, or
2. Automatic-trip circuit breaker located outside the building.

(c) Fuses

Interrupting rating of fuses must be at least equal to the maximum possible short-circuit current for the circuit.

(d) Circuit Breakers

Circuit breakers must be the type that will trip independently of the circuit-breaker handle. With the handle closed, the breaker can trip internally without moving the handle. Thus, the breaker is "free to open in case it is closed on an overload." If a circuit breaker is used, it must be this type, or one having a separate handle for each pole. Circuit breakers must have an interrupting capacity at least equal to the maximum short-circuit current possible.

(e) Enclosed Overcurrent Devices

Section 220-10(b) requires derating of feeder conductors and overcurrent devices in cases of "long continuous" loads. For services over 600 volts, the derating requirement does not apply.

230-209. Surge Arresters (Lightning Arresters)

Lightning arresters are required only if requested by the inspector.

230-210. Service Equipment—General Provisions

Service equipment, including instrument transformers, shall conform to Article 710, Part B.

230-211. Metal-Enclosed Switchgear

Metal-enclosed switchgear shall consist of a substantial metal structure with a sheet-metal enclosure. Where installed over a wood floor, suitable protection shall be provided.

ARTICLE 240 — OVERCURRENT PROTECTION

240-1. Scope

The purpose of overcurrent protection is to keep the current in a circuit at a level that will prevent overheating of conductors and equipment. Current flowing in a wire generates heat, which raises the wire temperature. The wire temperature depends upon the amount of current flowing in the wire. If the current is excessive the high temperature of the wire could ignite the insulation and surrounding materials. Tests and experience have determined the safe carrying capacity for the different wire sizes and different types of insulation. These are listed in Tables 310-16 to 310-19 (pp. 70-132 to 70-135) of the Code. Table 310-16 is for copper conductors in raceway or cable, and is probably most frequently used.

Note that in the tables the allowable current-carrying capacity for a given wire varies according to the temperature rating of the type of insulation. Asbestos or varnished cambric covering, for example, allows higher amperages than rubber or thermoplastic insulation. This is in line with the principle of protecting the insulation (and surrounding materials) from excessive copper heat, which could damage the insulation. Rubber and thermoplastic insulation have less heat resistance, which necessitates lower permissible current for the conductors.

240-2. Protection of Equipment

For overcurrent protection of appliances, motors, generators, and the like, it is necessary to refer to the different Articles listed in this Section. In any installation, there are two parts that must be protected—the circuit conductors and the equipment. The fuse or circuit breaker protecting the installation should be of a rating small enough to protect both, according to the rules of the Code.

240-3. Protection of Conductors—Other Than Flexible Cords and Fixture Wires

The general rule is that conductors must be protected against overcurrent by a fuse or circuit breaker setting rated no higher than the ampacity of the conductor. For example, a No. 4 copper conductor with thermoplastic insulation has an ampacity of 70 amps. A 70-amp. fuse or circuit-breaker setting would be the largest size permitted for protection of this conductor.

However, there are exceptions to the general rule, and in some cases the Code allows the fuse or circuit-breaker setting to be above the ampacity of the conductor:

Exception No. 1: Next Higher Overcurrent Protective Device Rating.

If the ampacity of the conductor does not correspond with a standard size of fuse or circuit-breaker setting, the next higher size may be used. For example, the ampacity rating of a No. 2 copper conductor with thermoplastic insulation (Type T) is 95 amps. There is no standard 95-amp. fuse or circuit-breaker setting. Nearest standard size above 95 is 100 amp. The 100-amp. fuse or breaker setting may be used in this case for protection of the conductor.

The circuit breakers referred to here are meant to be the "nonadjustable type"; i.e., the overcurrent trip in the breaker is "set" at the factory and cannot be changed. The exception is also limited to fuses and circuit breakers rated at 800 amps. or less.

Exception No. 2: Tap Conductors.

Tap conductors are permitted to be overprotected under certain conditions. See Section 210-19(c); Section 240-21, Exceptions 2, 3, 5, 8; Sections 364-9 and 364-10; and Part D of Article 430.

Exception No. 3: Motor and Motor-Control Circuits.

Motor circuits are another exception to the general rule. Motor circuits are sized according to the rules of Article 430. A study of these rules will show that for motor circuits a fuse size or circuit-breaker setting in excess of the ampacity of the conductor is permitted by the Code. This exception is intended to provide fuse or circuit-breaker protection large enough to hold the high momentary current required for starting.

Exception No. 4: Remote-Control Circuits.

Remote-control circuits in general may have overcurrent protection of up to three times the ampacity of the conductor.

Motor-control circuits may be fused above their ampacity. An example of a motor-control circuit would be the circuit to a "start-stop" pushbutton from a magnetic motor controller. Here the protection for the control circuit could be the fuses or circuit breaker for the branch circuit.

For motor-control circuits the Code allows the protection for the control circuit to be up to 300% of the ampacity of the control circuit conductors. Or, to put it another way, the ampacity of the control circuit conductors need be only $\frac{1}{3}$ of the fuse or circuit-breaker rating. If the branch circuit is fused at 60 amps., the ampacity of the control circuit conductors need be only $\frac{1}{3} \times 60 = 20$ amps. A No. 12, which carries 20 amps., could be used for this control circuit. If the ampacity of the control circuit conductors is less than one-third of the fuse rating or circuit-breaker setting, the control circuit must be separately fused (see Section 430-72).

Exception No. 5. Transformer Secondary Conductors.

For a complete explanation, see Section 450-3.

Exception No. 6: Capacitor Circuits.

Capacitors draw a high inrush current on connection to the line. The Code permits circuit protection to be high enough to hold the inrush current, which would usually result in overfusing of the conductors, but permitted [see Section 460-8(b)].

Exception No. 7: Welder Circuits.

For welder circuits, conductor protection is permitted to be set at up to 200% of conductor ampacity [see Section 630-12(b) of the Code].

Exception No. 8:

Conductor overload protection is not required, if opening of a circuit would create an operational hazard, but short-circuit protection must be provided.

240-4. Protection of Fixture Wires and Cords

Fixture Wire

No. 18 fixture wire may be used on 15- or 20-amp. circuits.

No. 14 fixture wire may be used on 30-amp. circuits.

No. 12 fixture wire may be used on 40 and 50-amp. circuits.

Cord

No. 18 or larger cord of any type may be plugged into a 15- or 20-amp. circuit.

Cord with a 10-amp. or more carrying capacity may be plugged into a 30-amp. circuit. See Table 400-5, p. 70-239. As is shown by the table, the cord may be as small as No. 18 for certain types of cord. Other types require larger sizes to meet the 10-amp. requirement.

Cord with a 20-amp. or more carrying capacity may be plugged into a 40- or 50-amp. circuit. As shown by the table, the cord could be as small as No. 14 for certain types of cord. Other types require larger sizes.

240-6. Standard Ampere Ratings

Standard ratings for fuses and circuit breakers are: 15, 20, 25, 30, 35, 40, 45, 50, 60, 70, 80, 90, 100, 110, 125, 150, 175, 200, 225, 250, 300, 350, 400, 450, 500, 600, 700, 800, 1000, 1200, 1600, 2000, 2500, 3000, 4000, 5000, 6000 amps. For fuses only, 1, 3, 6, and 10 amps. are also standard sizes.

As applied to circuit breakers, the ratings listed are not circuit-breaker *sizes;* they are circuit-breaker *settings.* Circuit breakers are manufactured in a limited number of sizes, such as 50, 100, 225, 400, but each size can be adjusted at the factory for any one of a number of different settings. A 100-amp. breaker, for example, could have any standard setting from 15 up to 100 amps.; a 225-amp. breaker could have any standard setting from 110 up to 225 amps.; etc. The setting is the trip point. A circuit breaker with a 35-amp. setting, for instance, will trip (open) when the current goes above 35 amps.

240-8. Fuses or Circuit Breakers in Parallel

The Code prohibits paralleling of fuses or circuit breakers. (An exception is made for the special case of circuit breakers assembled in parallel and approved as a single unit.)

240-9. Thermal Devices

Thermal devices use a heater device inserted in the circuit, which, when it becomes sufficiently heated by overcurrent, operates to open the circuit. Such devices may not be used for short-circuit protection, because on short circuit they do not act immediately but require a time interval before operating. Such a time delay would be dangerous for short-circuit protection but may be used for overload protection. For short-circuit protection, fuses, fusetrons, or circuit breakers must be used. These devices have elements with no time delay and, on short circuit, open the circuit instantaneously.

240-10. Supplementary Overcurrent Protection

Certain electrical equipment might come with overcurrent protection within the equipment and provided by the manufacturer. The fact that there is overcurrent protection in the equipment does not mean that circuit overcurrent protection can be omitted. The Code considers overcurrent protection in equipment to be "supplementary," and Code rules for overcurrent protection of circuits supplying such equipment must be followed the same as though the equipment in question were without such protection.

240-11. Definition of Current-Limiting Overcurrent Protective Device

When a short-circuit occurs in a circuit a momentary high current flows in the line during the split second previous to the opening of the circuit by the fuse or circuit breaker protecting the circuit. Current-limiting overcurrent devices are so constructed as to substantially reduce the magnitude of the momentary current.

240-12. Electrical System Coordination

This Section permits installation, in industrial locations, of a special system of overload protection involving monitoring devices, and "selective fault-protective devices," where such a system is deemed necessary.

B. Location

240-20. Ungrounded Conductors

(a) Overcurrent Device Required

An overcurrent device "shall be connected in series in each ungrounded conductor." The "overcurrent device" may be a fuse or the trip element of a circuit breaker.

1. For two-wire DC systems without a grounded conductor, both conductors must have an overcurrent device.
2. For two-wire grounded DC systems, only one overcurrent device is required—in the ungrounded conductor.
3. For two-wire ungrounded AC systems, two overcurrent devices are required.
4. For two-wire AC systems with a grounded neutral, only one overcurrent device is required—in the hot wire.
5. For three-wire AC or DC circuits having a grounded neutral, two overcurrent devices are required—one in each hot wire.
6. For three-wire ungrounded systems, such as three-phase, three overcurrent devices are required.
7. For three-phase, four-wire systems, three overcurrent devices are required—one in each hot wire.

(b) Circuit Breaker as Overcurrent Device

The trip element(s) inside a circuit breaker are the "overcurrent device(s)." When any one of the trip elements operates, it trips the circuit breaker, opening all poles. A circuit breaker used for short-circuit protection is required to have a trip unit for each ungrounded conductor, and a pole for each ungrounded conductor.

For ungrounded two-wire circuits, two single-pole circuit breakers may be used in place of a two-pole circuit breaker.

Two single-pole circuit breakers—one in each hot wire—may be used for three-wire AC or DC single-phase circuits.

Circuit breakers for three-phase circuits must be three-pole breakers.

240-21. Location in Circuit

The general rule for location of fuses or circuit breakers in a circuit is that they must be at the source of the circuit. For example, if a branch circuit taps to a feeder, then the fuses or circuit breaker protecting the branch circuit must be at the point where the tap is made to the feeder.

There are exceptions to this general rule (where fuses are referred to, this is intended to mean a fuse, circuit breaker, or any other approved overcurrent device):

Exception No. 1: Smaller Conductor Protected.

A case that would apply for this rule would be one in which, say, a No. 14 circuit is tapped to a No. 6 feeder, and the feeder is fused at 15 amps. In this case the No. 14 circuit is properly protected by the 15-amp. feeder fuses, and no additional fuses are required at the point of tapping [Fig. 232(b)].

Exception No. 2: Feeder Taps Not Over 10 Feet Long.

An application of this rule would be a tap feeding a lighting panel. If the tap is not over 10 ft long, ends at the lighting panel, is mechanically protected by conduit, tubing, or metal gutters, and is sized to carry the total load on the lighting panel, no overcurrent protection is required for the tap [Fig. 232(c)].

Exception No. 3: Feeder Taps Not Over 25 Feet Long.

A tap to a larger sized conductor may be extended to a distance of up to 25 ft, provided the carrying capacity of the tap is at least $\frac{1}{3}$ that of the larger conductor. Overcurrent protection in this case is not required at the tap, but the tap must have overcurrent protection at the end of the run of proper size to protect the tap, and the tap must be protected from physical damage [Fig. 232(d)].

Exception No. 4: Service Conductors.

Fuses for services may be at the end of the run. This is of course the usual case for services.

Exception No. 5: Branch-Circuit Taps.

Section 210-19 allows taps of smaller conductors to be made to larger branch-circuit conductors for certain purposes, including taps for a small range. A No. 14 conductor may tap to a 20-, 25-, or 30-amp. circuit. A No. 12 may tap to a 40- or 50-amp. circuit. Fusing is not required at "the point of supply"; therefore, these are exceptions to the general rule for location of overcurrent devices in the circuit [see also Section 210-19(b) (c)].

Exception No. 6: Motor Circuit Taps.

See Sections 430-28 and 430-53(d).

Exception No. 7: Busway Taps.

Section 364-10 permits a reduction in size of a busway. In certain cases, no additional overcurrent protection is required for the smaller busway.

Exception No. 8: Transformer Feeder Taps with Primary Plus Secondary Not over 25 Feet Long.

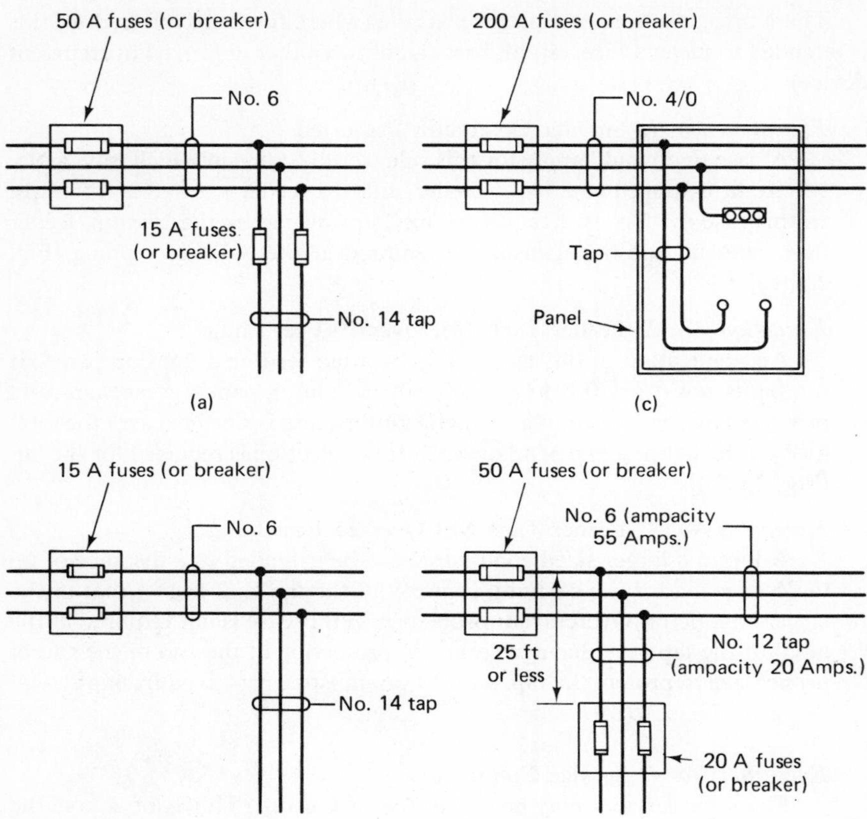

Fig. 232

Overcurrent protection for conductors. Location in circuit (Sect. 240-21).

(a) The general rule requires overcurrent protection at the point of tapping.

(b) *Example of Exception No. 1:* Fuses protecting larger conductor provide proper protection for smaller tap. No overcurrent protection required for tap.

(c) *Example of Exception No. 2:* No protection required for tap conductors as long as they are entirely within the enclosure, not over 10 ft long, and sized to carry the panel load.

(d) *Example of Exception No. 3:* If tap conductors have an ampacity at least $\frac{1}{3}$ that of the larger conductors, tap overcurrent protection may be at the end of the run, but tap conductors must be suitably protected from physical damage. Conductors in conduit, EMT, BX, or in an enclosed partition would be "suitably protected" from damage.

Overcurrent protection for a tap serving a transformer need not be at the point where the tap is made, provided:

1. Tap conductor ampacity is at least $\frac{1}{3}$ that of the feeder, and
2. Secondary conductor ampacity is at least $\frac{1}{3}$ that of the feeder, based on the primary-secondary transformer ratio, and
3. Total length of tap is not over 25 ft, primary plus secondary, and
4. All conductors are protected from physical damage, and
5. Secondary conductors terminate at a fuse or circuit breaker sized to protect the secondaries.

Example: Tap for a 480/240-Volt Dry-Type Transformer (Fig. 233).

Feeder is No. 1 Type T with an ampacity of 110 amps. Transformer primary current rating is 40 amps. Secondary of transformer feeds a panel with 100-amp. main fuses. Primary tap is 15 ft long. Secondary from transformer to panel is 10 ft long. Feeder fuse is 100 amps.

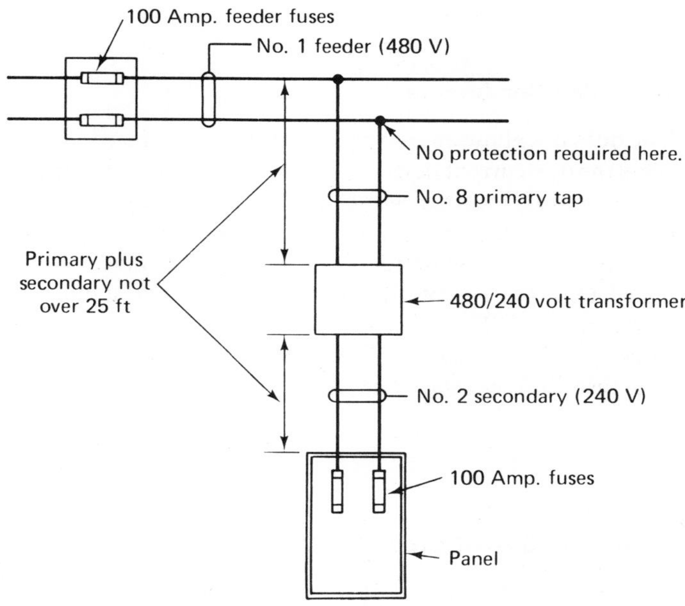

Fig. 233

Protection for a transformer tap may be at the end of the secondary run if the provisions of Sect. 240-21, Exception No. 8 are complied with. Fusing is not required at the point where the smaller conductors tap to the feeder.

The primary tap (from feeder to transformer) must have an ampacity $\frac{1}{3} \times 110 = 36\frac{2}{3}$ amp. A No. 8, which carries 40 amps., would be permitted.

Secondary ampacity must be at least $\frac{1}{3}$ that of the feeder based on primary-secondary transformer ratio, or

$$\frac{480}{240} \times \frac{1}{3} \times 110 = 73\tfrac{1}{3} \text{ amp.}$$

This would require a No. 2 secondary conductor.

Total length of tap is 15 + 10 = 25 ft, which is within requirements for total length.

Secondaries are No. 2. The 100-amp. fuse at the panel protects the secondaries (ampacity of No. 2 is 95 amps.).

Primary protection is the 100-amp. feeder fuse. Section 450-3(b) (2) requires primary protection not over 250% of the transformer primary rating, or 250% of 40, which is 100 amps. Transformer is properly protected by the 100-amp. feeder fuse. Fusing is not required at the point of tapping.

240-22. Grounded Conductors

The Code does not allow an overcurrent device to be placed in a grounded neutral, unless the overcurrent device operates to open the hot wires simultaneously with the neutral. In other words, a fuse is not allowed in the neutral, because the neutral fuse could blow without the hot wire fuses blowing. Then the neutral would be open while the hot wires are still alive, and this would create a hazard. Only one exception is made, which permits a fuse to be placed in a grounded conductor. This is for *running* protection of a three phase motor fed by a three-wire, three-phase circuit with one leg grounded. For *running* protection, a fuse may be placed in the grounded conductor (see Section 430-36).

240-23. Change in Size of Grounded Conductor

This Section states, in effect, that if a branch circuit is taken off a feeder it is not necessary to continue the neutral with the same size wire as the feeder neutral, but the neutral may also be reduced in size to suit the smaller "hot" wires of the branch circuit. The Code considers the smaller neutral to be protected by the fuses or circuit breaker in the hot wires of the branch circuit.

240-24. Location in or on Premises

A fuse or circuit breaker is an "overcurrent device."

Overcurrent devices shall be readily accessible. "Readily accessible" means capable of being reached easily. If the overcurrent device were located where it would be necessary to climb over or remove obstacles, or use a ladder to reach them, this would not be considered "readily accessible."

There are certain exceptions to the "accessibility" rule:

1. For services, the overcurrent protection is permitted to be at the beginning of the run, at the point where the service entrance taps to the drop. In this case the overcurrent device is not "readily accessible."
2. For busways, Section 364-12 permits overcurrent protection for a "plug-in" to be out of reach.
3. Some lighting fixtures and appliances are manufactured with built-in fuses. Here, the fuses are not required to be "readily accessible."

Overcurrent devices shall not be located where exposed to physical damage.

Overcurrent devices shall not be installed where ignitible materials are near enough to catch fire in case of accidental sparking or overheating of the overcurrent device.

Each occupant of a building or apartment must have "ready access" to the overcurrent devices for his occupancy. (An exception is made in the case of apartment buildings where a building employee is constantly in attendance.)

C. Enclosures

240-30. General

In general, fuses or circuit breakers must be enclosed. There are a few exceptions to this rule, as noted.

240-32. Damp or Wet Locations

In damp or wet locations, switch and fuse boxes must be "stooled off" the wall at least $\frac{1}{4}$ in.

240-33. Vertical Position

Boxes or cabinets containing fuses or other overcurrent devices should be mounted vertically on a wall, not horizontally. The Code allows horizontal mounting only if vertical mounting is not practicable.

D. Disconnecting and Guarding

240-40. Disconnecting Means for Fuses and Thermal Cutouts

Each set of cartridge fuses must have an individual disconnect on the supply side, so that any one set of fuses can be individually killed.

For other types of fuses and for thermal cutouts, the rule applies only for voltages of over 150 to ground.

If the fuses or cutouts are accessible only to qualified persons, such as building electricians, these requirements do not apply. (One disconnect may, for instance, serve a number of fused circuits; there need not be a disconnect for each circuit. Or, the disconnect may be omitted.)

The exception of Section 230-82 applies to services. In the case of services, any sequence of meter, fuse, and switch is permitted; for services the fuses can be ahead of the switch.

An exception is also made for the special case where there is only one disconnect for several motors on one machine, as with metal- or wood-working machines. Here each motor could have its own set of fuses, and the one disconnect may serve for the several sets. It is not necessary to have a disconnect for each circuit. The same exception applies where several space heaters are served by only one disconnect.

240-41. Arcing or Suddenly Moving Parts

In any installation of overcurrent devices, care should be taken to prevent possible physical injury caused by arcing or moving parts. A sudden opening of a large circuit breaker could be a source of danger. Such breakers should be the "trip free from handle" type. With this type of breaker, internal contacts open on overload without moving the circuit breaker handle, eliminating the danger of "suddenly moving parts."

E. Plug Fuses, Fuseholders, and Adapters

240-50. General

Plug fuses are rated at 125 volts (maximum); 125-volt plug fuses may be used in conductors of higher voltage, provided the voltage *to ground* of the conductor is 150 or less.

Thus, a 125-volt plug fuse may be used in a 240-volt conductor of a 120/240-volt grounded circuit, because the voltage to ground of the conductor is only 120.

Plug fuses are made in sizes up to 30 amps. Plug fuses of 15 amps. or less rating have a hexagonal window in the head. The 20-, 25-, and 30-amp. sizes have a round window.

Exposed live parts are not permitted on plug fuses, fuseholders, or adapters.

The screw-shell part of a fuseholder shall be connected to the load side of the circuit. This minimizes the danger of shock when the fuseholder is empty.

240-51. Edison-Base Fuses

Edison-base plug fuses have only one classification, 0 to 30 amps., which means that a fuseholder will take a plug of any rating up to 30 amps.

Plug fuses of the Edison-base type may be used only as replacements in existing installations, and then only if there is no evidence of overfusing or tampering. For new work, all fuses shall be Type S.

240-52. Edison-Base Fuseholders

Fuseholders installed in new work or to replace existing fuseholders shall be either Type S fuseholders or Edison-base fuseholders equipped with permanent adapters. An adapter is a device that is screwed into the Edison-base fuseholder. The adapter is equipped with a locking spring, and once the adapter is inserted it cannot be removed. Adapters will take only Type S fuses.

240-53. Type S Fuses

Construction of the Type S fuse is a radical departure from that of the Edison-base type. The screw part of the Type S fuse does not carry current, as with the Edison-base type. Instead there is a contact spring under the cap which, when the plug is seated, makes contact with a metal ring on the fuseholder. The spring connects to the fuse element within the plug. The fuse element connects to the line. The ring connects to the load. This arrangement makes tampering difficult. To bridge across the contacts, it is necessary to make a connection between the spring at the top and the button contact at the bottom of the plug. With the Edison-base plug fuse, a coin placed in the fuseholder could bridge across the contacts to bypass a blown fuse, leaving the circuit with no protection. Bridging the contacts in this way is not possible with a Type S fuse.

The threads of the Type S fuse have a different shape than the threads of the Edison-base type. It is not possible to use an Edison-base fuse in a Type S fuseholder, or vice versa.

Classification of Type S fuses is 0 to 15 and 16 to 30 amps. A 0- to 15-amp. fuseholder will not take a 16- to 30-amp. fuse, and vice versa.

The threads on 15-amp. fuses are different from the threads on 20-, 25-, and 30-amp. fuses. This prevents overfusing of 15-amp. circuits.

The rating must be marked or stamped on each Type S fuse by the manufacturer. As with the Edison-base-type fuse, 0- to 15-amp. fuses have a hexagonal-shaped window. Those of 16- to 30-amp. rating have a round window.

240-54. Type S Fuses, Adapters, and Fuseholders

This Section gives construction specifications for Type S equipment.

Type S adapters shall be built to fit Edison-base fuseholders.

Type S fuseholders and adapters shall be so constructed as to take only Type S plug fuses.

Adapters shall be so constructed that, once seated in a fuseholder, they cannot be removed.

Type S fuses, fuseholders, and adapters shall be so constructed as to make tampering "difficult."

Fuses, fuseholders, and adapters shall be standardized as to dimensions by the different manufacturers.

F. Cartridge Fuses and Fuseholders

240-60. General

There are two types of cartridge fuses, the "ferrule" type and the "knife-blade" type. The ferrule type makes contact through copper rings around the ends of the cartridge. The knife-blade type has copper blades in the form of flat bar $\frac{1}{8}$ in. thick or so projecting from each end. Contact is made to the blades. The fuseholder, i.e., the clips that the fuse fits into and makes contact with, is circular in shape for the ferrule-type fuse and straight in shape for the knife-blade type.

The ferrule type is made in sizes up to 60 amp. Larger sizes are the knife-blade type.

240-61. Classification

"Classification" simply means that all fuses within a certain range of rating are of the same physical size. For example, all cartridge fuses in the 0–30-amp. range are 2 in. long. In the 31–60-amp. range they are 3 in. long. Fuseholders are sized accordingly. You could not put a 35-amp. cartridge fuse in a 0–30-

amp. holder, nor could you use a 100-amp. cartridge fuse in a 31–60-amp. holder.

This size difference between the different classifications satisfies the requirement that fuses within a certain class range be "noninterchangeable" with fuses outside their class range.

Cartridge fuses come in voltage ratings of 250 and 600 volts. Fuses may not be used in a circuit of higher voltage than the fuse voltage rating, but may be used in circuits of lower voltage than their rating. Thus, a 600-volt fuse may be used in a 240-volt circuit, but a 250-volt fuse may not be used in a 600-volt circuit.

G. Circuit Breakers

240-80. Method of Operation

Circuit breakers of all ratings must be capable of opening or closing *by hand.*

Operation "by hand" means that the breaker must have a handle of some kind that can be grasped by the operator for opening or closing. With electrical or pneumatic operation only, of a breaker, the electrical or pneumatic control might at some time become inoperative, or the breaker might "stick" in the closed position and there would be no way of getting the circuit opened. If provision is made for "hand" operation, the circuit can still be opened should the electrical or pneumatic control fail to operate.

If a breaker is operated by remote control, then also *in addition* it must be operable by hand.

240-81. Indicating

Circuit breakers must be marked ON, OFF, or otherwise marked so that there will be no doubt about the circuit breaker "position."

240-82. Nontamperable

Circuit breakers shall be so constructed that the tip point or the time delay cannot be altered without dismantling of the breaker.

240-83. Marking

This Section requires circuit breakers to be marked by the manufacturer to show the circuit-breaker rating.

H. Overcurrent Protection over 600 Volts Nominal

240-100. Feeders

For short-circuit protection of high-voltage feeders, fuse rating may be up to three times the conductor ampacity. Circuit-breaker setting may be up to six times conductor ampacity. These values apply for short-circuit protection only, and are not meant to provide overcurrent protection. An overcurrent feature of a lower rating could be included in the same fuse or circuit breaker.

240-101. Branch Circuits

High voltage branch circuits shall have a short-circuit protective device in each ungrounded conductor. Or, as an alternative, if circuit breakers are used for protection, two overcurrent relays operated from two current transformers in each of two phases, is permitted.

The ampacities of high-voltage conductors are shown in Tables 310-39 through 310-50, pp. 70-141 through 70-148 of the Code. Table 310-40 is for copper conductors in *isolated* cable. Table 310-41 is for copper conductors in *isolated* conduit. The Code definition of "isolated" is "not readily accessible to persons unless special means for access are used." Note that No. 8 is the smallest conductor size listed in the tables.

ARTICLE 250 — GROUNDING

A. General

250-1. Scope

There are two kinds of grounding:

1. Circuit and system grounding.

2. Equipment grounding.

Circuit and system grounding consists of connecting one of the current-carrying conductors of a distribution system or premises wiring system to ground. Equipment grounding consists of connecting non-current-carrying metal parts of a wiring system to ground. "Metal parts" would include conduit, motor frames, the enclosing metal case of switches, appliances, and other equipment.

B. Circuit and System Grounding

If a primary wire should make accidental contact with one of the secondary conductors feeding a premises wiring system that is not grounded, the voltage to ground of the premises wiring conductors would become that of the primary conductor, say 2,400 volts. Anyone contacting one of the premises wiring conductors while in contact with ground would receive a shock that could be fatal.

If the premises wiring system is grounded, current will flow through the premises ground connection to ground, and back to the primary system through the primary ground connection. The voltage difference between the premises conductors and ground will now be the voltage drop in the grounding connection. The drop will be equal to the current times resistance of the grounding connection. With a ground to a water-piping system, this resistance might be 2 ohms. Assuming a current of 50 amps, the voltage difference would be $50 \times 2 = 100$ volts, rather than 2,400. Protection of premises wiring systems against accidental high voltages is one advantage of circuit and system grounding.

If a system is grounded, lightning surges will be drained off to ground through the ground wire. This is another advantage of circuit and system grounding.

250-3. Direct-Current Systems

(a) Two-wire DC systems of over 50 up to 300 volts supplying premises wiring shall be grounded, except:

1. A system equipped with a ground detector and supplying only industrial equipment in limited areas.
2. A rectifier-derived DC system supplied from an AC system which is grounded as required by Section 250-5.
3. DC fire-protective signaling circuits having a maximum current of .03 amps. as specified in Article 760, Part C of the Code.

(b) The neutral of all three-wire DC systems supplying premises wiring shall be grounded, regardless of voltage.

250-5. Alternating-Current Circuits and Systems to Be Grounded (See also Section 200-2)

(a) Alternating-Current Circuits of Less Than 50 Volts

Indoor AC circuits of less than 50 volts need be grounded only if the circuit is taken from a transformer having an ungrounded primary circuit or a primary circuit of over 150 volts to ground.

A low-voltage bell-ringing circuit in a residence with 120/240-volt service need not be grounded, since the circuit is taken from a transformer with a grounded primary circuit of only 120 volts to ground.

Low-voltage AC circuits run *outdoors* overhead must be grounded in all cases.

(b) Alternating-Current Systems of 50 to 1,000 volts (See Fig. 234)

1. All AC systems of 50 to 150 volts to ground must be grounded, except:
   - (a) Circuits for electric furnaces.
   - (b) Separately derived systems used exclusively for rectifiers supplying only adjustable-speed industrial drives.
   - (c) Separately derived systems with primaries under 1,000 volts, and used exclusively for control circuits.
   - (d) Circuits in anesthetizing locations [See Section 517-104(b)].
2. Wye connected 480Y/277-volt, three-phase, four-wire systems must be grounded (Fig. 234).
3. Three-phase, delta-connected, 240-volt systems must be grounded if one phase has a neutral. In this case the neutral of the one phase would be grounded (Fig. 234).
4. Any uninsulated service conductor must be grounded.

(c) Alternating-Current Systems of 1 kV and Over

AC systems of 1 kV and over shall be grounded if supplying portable equipment. Other AC systems of 1 kV and over need not be grounded, but *may* be grounded if desired.

(d) Separately Derived Systems

Separately derived systems used in premises wiring are subject to the rules of (a) and (b) above. A separately derived system is a system supplied by a private generator, or by a converter or by a private transformer on the premises.

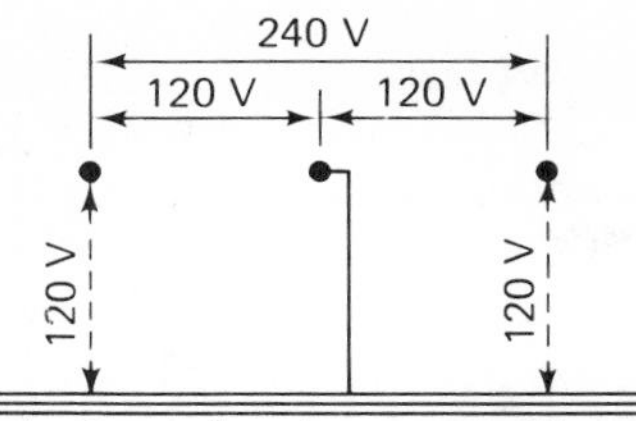

120/240 V circuit. Grounding the neutral will result in a maximum voltage to ground of less than 150. Shall be grounded.

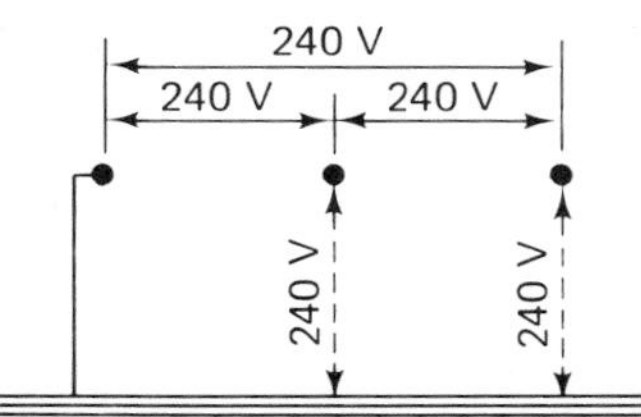

240 V, 3-phase circuit. Grounding any conductor results in a voltage to ground of more than 150 for each of the other two conductors. Need not be grounded.

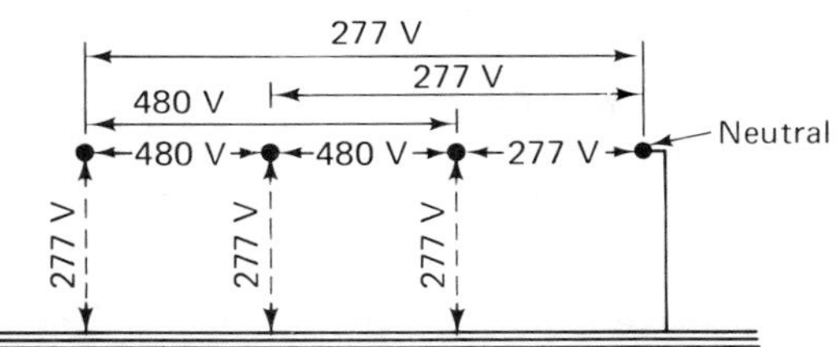

480/277 V, 3-phase, 4-wire circuit. Grounding the neutral results in a voltage to ground of 277 for the hot wires, but the neutral must be grounded.

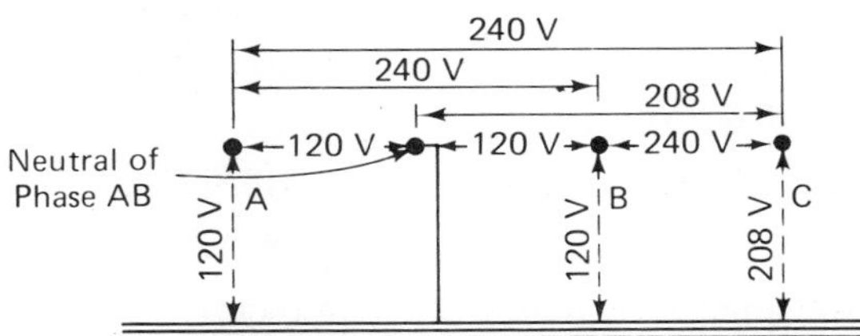

240/120 V, 3-phase, 4-wire circuit with midpoint of phase AB used as a neutral. Grounding the neutral results in a maximum voltage to ground of 208 V, but the neutral must be grounded.

Fig. 234

Grounding AC circuits (Sect. 250-5). The general rule permits circuits of over 150 V to ground to be ungrounded. The last two examples are exceptions to the rule.

Large buildings are sometimes supplied by a high-voltage primary terminating in a vault within the building. A 480Y/277-volt circuit is run from the vault to transformers located at different points or different floors in the building. The transformers reduce the voltage to a 120/240-volt single-phase system for general use. The 120/240-volt system is a *separately derived* system, and must be individually grounded.

250-6. Portable and Vehicle-Mounted Generators

(a) Portable Generators

The frame of a portable generator need not be grounded if the generator supplies only equipment mounted on the generator, or if the generator supplies cord and plug connected equipment through receptacles mounted on the generator, *provided:*

1. That the equipment grounding conductor for the receptacles is bonded to the generator frame, and
2. Exposed metal parts of the equipment served are bonded to the generator frame. This would require the use of grounding-type plugs for all equipment plugged to the receptacles. The exposed metal parts of equipment would then be bonded to the frame through the grounding conductor in the cord.

   If these conditions are not met, the generator frame would have to be grounded under any of the conditions set down in Section 250-42.

(b) Vehicle-Mounted Generators

The frame of the vehicle may serve to ground a circuit supplied by a generator on the vehicle *provided:*

1. The generator frame is bonded to the vehicle frame, and
2. The generator supplies only equipment mounted on the vehicle, or if the generator supplies cord and plug connected equipment through receptacles mounted on the vehicle, and
3. Exposed metal parts of the equipment served are bonded to the generator frame either direct or through the receptacles.

These rules would apply only for circuits that require grounding according to Section 250-5. Two-wire DC or two-wire AC circuits of less than 50 volts need not be grounded. All three-wire DC circuits must be grounded. DC circuits of 51 to 300 volts must be grounded. AC circuits of 50 to 150 volts must be grounded.

(c) Neutral Conductor Bonding

If the generator is a component of a separately derived system, a neutral must be bonded to the generator frame.

250-7. Circuits Not to Be Grounded

Regardless of voltage, the following circuits shall *not* be grounded:

1. Circuits for electric cranes operating over combustible fibers in Class III hazardous locations. See Section 503-13.
2. Circuits in anesthetizing locations. See Section 517-63(b).

C. Location of System-Grounding Connections

250-21. Objectionable Current over Grounding Conductors

Objectionable current in grounding conductors could result from (1) a highly unbalanced load, or (2) "multiple" grounds.

When there is a grounded neutral, as with a 120/240-volt system, the unbalanced current will have two parallel paths for the return to the power company transformer, one through the neutral, the other through the grounding conductor and ground. The amount of current flowing through ground will depend upon the resistance of the ground path compared to that of the neutral. In most cases the ground current would be small, but in some cases the ground current, on excessive unbalance, could be "objectionable." The obvious remedy in such a situation would be to balance the load.

"Multiple" grounds (more than one ground on the same system) can also result in objectionable current flow between ground connections.

If multiple grounds are the cause of objectionable ground currents, one or more of the following changes shall be made:

1. Discontinue one or more grounding connections.
2. Change locations of grounding connections.
3. Interrupt (break) the conductive path interconnecting grounding connections.
4. Take other action satisfactory to the authority having jurisdiction.

"Objectionable ground current" as described above does not include the large current that would necessarily flow through grounding conductors under accidental conditions. A hot wire making accidental contact with a grounded neutral would result in a large momentary current to ground, which could be considered "objectionable." It is not the intent to eliminate ground current resulting from accidental conditions. Such currents are a necessary function of the grounding system, and are not included as "objectionable" current.

250-22. Point of Connection for Direct-Current Systems

DC systems shall *not* have a system ground at the service entrance. The ground shall be at the supply stations only.

250-23. Grounding Connections for Alternating-Current Systems

(a) AC grounded systems must have a system ground at each service. A "grounding electrode" conductor is run from the neutral to a cold-water pipe or other "electrode," thus grounding the system. Connection to the neutral must be on the supply side of the service disconnect. In the usual case the neutral runs straight through, and in that case there would in fact be no supply side. But in cases where the neutral is switched along with the hot wires, the rule would require the grounding connection to be made on the supply side of the switch. This arrangement provides a ground for the service entrance when the service switch is in the open position.

Generally, no grounding connection is permitted on the load side of the service disconnect. However, there are four exceptions:

1. For separately derived systems (Section 250-26).
2. For separate buildings on the same premises (Section 250-24).
3. For ranges, counter-mounted cooking units, wall-mounted ovens, clothes dryers. (Enclosures for this equipment may be bonded to the neutral for grounding; Section 250-60-61.)
4. For services that are dual fed and employing a secondary tie, a grounding electrode connection to the tie point from each power source is permitted.

In addition to the ground at the building, the Code also requires a power-company ground at the transformer.

(b) This subsection requires that, where the power company secondary system is grounded, the grounded conductor must be run to each service. This rule would forbid running only the two outside legs of a 120/240-volt grounded secondary to a building. If only 240-volt service

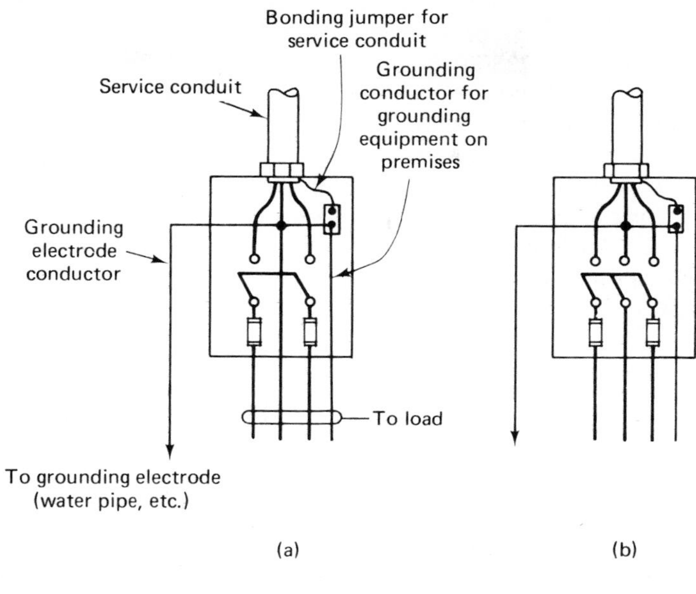

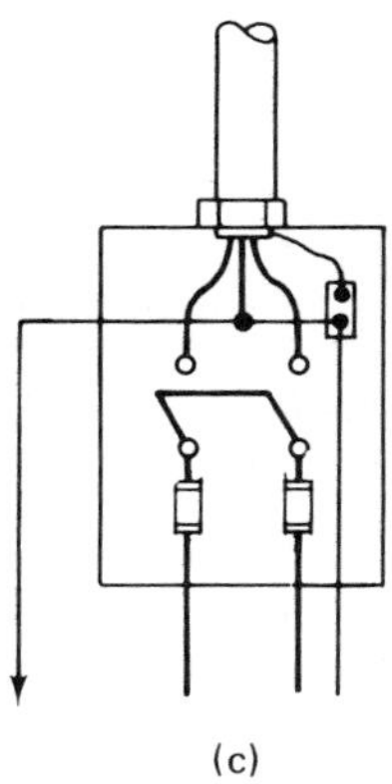

Fig. 236

Grounding connections for AC systems. (120/240-V service shown). The neutral, service conduit, grounding electrode conductor, service enclosure, and any grounding conductors for equipment on the premises must all be bonded together [Sects. 250-50(a), 250-53(b)].

(a) Service switch with straight through neutral.

(b) Service switch with switched neutral.

(c) When only 240 volts is required, neutral must still be brought to the service equipment and grounded [Sect. 250-23(b)].

is required, the grounded neutral still must be carried along with the hot wires [Fig. 236(c)]. The grounded neutral would not be a current-carrying conductor, but would function only as a path for fault currents, and may be sized as a grounding electrode conductor, according to Table 250-94, p. 70-101 of the Code.

In the usual case where the grounded neutral acts as a current-carrying conductor, it would be sized as a neutral feeder, according to Section 220-22, and except for larger-size services would be the same size as the hot wires.

250-24. Two or More Buildings Supplied from Single Service Equipment

When each of two or more buildings has a *service* fed from a main AC service, such as might be the case with farm buildings, then the service to each building must be separately grounded. (For ungrounded services, such as three-phase, three-wire, the grounding electrode conductor would connect only to the service disconnect enclosure, since there is no neutral that requires grounding.)

If the main service is run to one of the buildings, with a *feeder* or *branch circuit* serving another building from the main building, the feeder or branch circuit must be grounded to an electrode at the "other" building, *except:*

1. When there is only one branch circuit in the "other" building, and no equipment that requires grounding.
2. When an equipment-grounding conductor is run with the feeder or branch circuit, *and* no livestock are housed in the building.

The following examples might serve to clarify the rules of this Section as applying to different cases.

For buildings supplied by a feeder or branch circuit from the main building (assume a 120/240-volt, AC system):

1. A building with feeder from the main building, two branch circuits in the building, no equipment that requires grounding, building houses livestock.

   The building houses livestock, and in addition has more than one branch circuit. The neutral must be grounded to a water pipe or other electrode at the building.

2. A building fed by one branch circuit from the main building, no equipment that requires grounding, building houses livestock.
   The building houses livestock, *but* has only one branch circuit and no equipment to be grounded. No grounding is required.

3. A building fed by one branch circuit from the main building, has equipment that requires grounding, building houses livestock.
   The building houses livestock and has only one branch circuit, *but* has equipment that requires grounding. Both the neutral and equipment must be grounded to a water pipe or other electrode at the building. Grounding through a grounding conductor run with the circuit conductors is not permitted, because of the livestock.

4. A building fed by one branch circuit from the main building, building wired with BX, no livestock in the building.
   BX requires grounding. Since no livestock are present, a grounding conductor run with the branch circuit conductors can be used to ground the BX.

5. A building fed by one branch circuit from the main building, has equipment that requires grounding, no livestock in building.
   The building has only one branch circuit but has equipment to be grounded. Since no livestock are present, a grounding conductor, run with the circuit conductors from the main building, can be used to ground the equipment.

6. A building with feeder from the main building, two branch circuits, no equipment that needs grounding, no livestock in building.
   Where there is more than one circuit, there must be either an equipment grounding conductor, or a separate electrode.

7. A private garage fed by a branch circuit from the residence, no equipment that requires grounding, garage wired with Romex.
   There is only one branch circuit, and no equipment to be grounded. No ground wire or grounding is required.

The rules of this Section apply for buildings served by a feeder or branch circuit run from the main building, i.e., tapped to the *load* side of the service switch. If tapped to the supply side, the run to the "other" building would be a separate service, and subject to the grounding rules governing services.

Note that, when livestock are housed in a building, both the neutral and any equipment that requires grounding must be grounded to a water pipe or other electrode at the building, except in the one case of a single branch circuit with nothing in the building that requires grounding. Figure 237 illustrates applications of the rules of this Section.

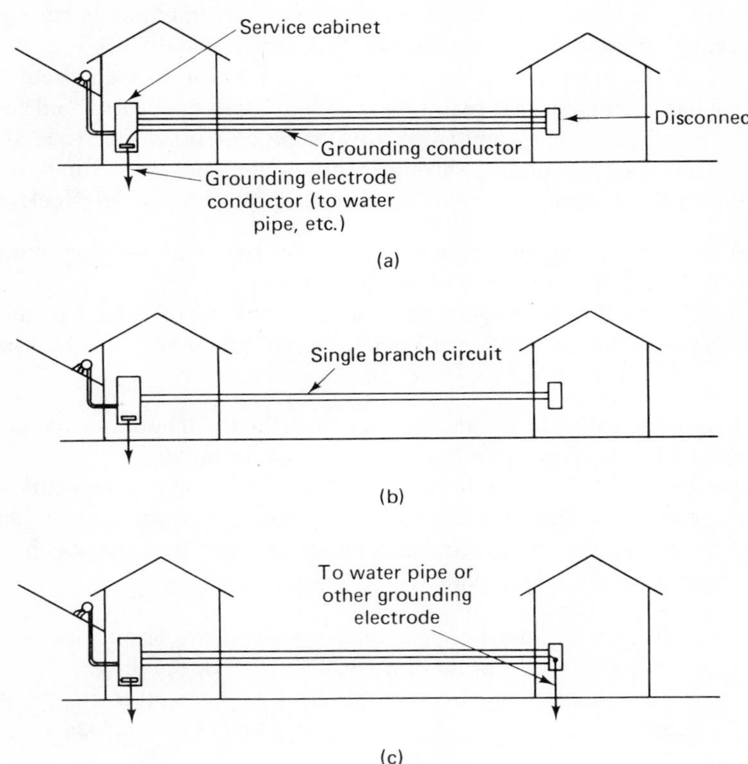

Fig. 237

Two or more buildings served from single service equipment (Sect. 250-24).

(a) The "other" building has no livestock, but has equipment that requires grounding. Separate electrode not required. A grounding conductor may be run with the circuit conductors for grounding the equipment.

(b) "Other" building has no livestock, and no equipment that requires grounding. No separate electrode or grounding conductor required.

(c) The "other" building houses livestock. Separate electrode always required, except for the one case where the "other" building has only *one* branch circuit *and* no equipment that requires grounding. Grounding conductor method is never permitted when livestock are present. Neutral must connect to electrode.

250-25. Conductor to Be Grounded—Alternating-Current Systems

The conductor to be grounded is as follows:

Single-phase, two-wire; the "white" wire.

Single-phase, three-wire; the neutral ("white" wire).

Three-phase, four-wire; the neutral ("white" wire).

Two-phase, three-wire; the neutral ("white" wire).

Three-phase, with one phase grounded; the neutral ("white" wire).

250-26. Grounding Separately Derived Alternating-Current Systems

Large buildings are sometimes supplied by a high-voltage primary terminating in a vault within the building. A 480Y/277-volt circuit is run from the vault to transformers located at different points or different floors in the building.

The transformers reduce the voltage to 120/240-volt single-phase systems for general use. Each 120/240-volt system is a *separately derived* system, since it is not in metallic contact with the primary system. The 120/240-volt system must be individually grounded, as though it were a service, with the neutral grounded and also bonded to the main switch for the system.

If the building is of metal construction, which is in turn grounded, the neutral may be grounded to a structural member of the building. Or a grounded water pipe may serve as the grounding electrode. Note that the rule does not specify a *cold*-water pipe.

If neither a structural member nor a water pipe is available, any of the electrodes specified in Sections 250-81 and 250-83 may be used as a third choice. The point of connection to the structural member, water pipe, or other electrode shall be as close as possible to the point of connection to the neutral. In other words, the grounding wire run must be kept as short as possible.

In summary, any interior wiring system that gets its power from a transformer within the building must be independently grounded, if the system is one that requires grounding according to Section 250-5(a) and (b).

This rule for grounding also applies where the wiring system is supplied by a converter, a private generator, or a motor generator.

D. Enclosure Grounding

Examples of "conductor enclosures" would be conduit, EMT, and BX sheath. These are grounded to prevent shock to persons coming in contact with the conduit, EMT, or BX sheath when the metal might happen to be "charged" through accidental contact with a hot wire.

If, as an example, metal conduit is used for the wiring in a 120/240-volt wiring system of a building and the conduit is *not* grounded, a hot wire accidentally coming in contact with the conduit will put the conduit at hot-wire potential, and present the same danger of shock as an exposed hot wire.

Grounding serves to maintain the conduit and metal enclosures of equipment at or near ground potential. If a conductor makes accidental contact with the metal, current will flow to ground through the grounding conductor, and the voltage between metal and earth will be limited to the comparatively small voltage drop in the grounding connection.

When there is a grounded neutral, as with 120/240-volt AC, the neutral is grounded at the service cabinet to the same ground wire that grounds conduit and metal enclosures. If a hot wire makes contact with the conduit or metal enclosure, this would be the same as a short circuit to neutral. The short circuit will instantly open the circuit fuse or circuit breaker, removing the danger.

250-32. Service Raceways and Enclosures

Metal service raceways and metal service equipment must be grounded. Metal raceways would include conduit, EMT, and the metal sheath or armor of service cables. Grounding can be accomplished by bonding the conduit, EMT, metal sheath, or armor to the grounded service-entrance cabinet. Bonding shall be in accordance with Section 250-72.

250-33. Other Conductor Enclosures

Conduit, EMT, and BX sheath, wherever used, must be grounded.

Exception No. 1.

An exception to this rule is allowed if a short piece of conduit, EMT, or BX is added to a nonmetallic wiring system, such as Romex. If the conduit, EMT, or BX is less than 25 ft in length and free from probable contact with ground, metal lath, piping, or conductive material, it need not be grounded. If 25 ft or more in length, it must always be grounded. If within reach of ground or a grounded object, it must be grounded regardless of length.

Exception No. 2.

Where a metal enclosure, such as conduit, is used merely as protection for cable, the metal enclosure need not be grounded.

E. Equipment Grounding

250-42. Fixed Equipment, General

"Equipment" means service switches, motor cases, outlet boxes, switch boxes, motor controllers, or any other exposed metal parts of electrical equipment.

The metal enclosures of equipment must be grounded:

(a) If equipment is within reach of a person who while touching the equipment could at the same time be in contact with ground or a "grounded object." The "grounded object" could be a water faucet in a bathroom or kitchen, or a radiator. If the electrical equipment is close enough to a pipe, faucet, etc., so that a person could touch both the electrical equipment and the pipe, faucet, etc., at the same time, the equipment must be grounded regardless of type of wiring. An exposed metal part that is within 8 ft vertically or 5 ft horizontally of ground or a grounded object is considered to be "within reach."

(b) If equipment is located in a wet or damp location and "not isolated"; i.e., if it is readily accessible to persons, then regardless of type of wiring used, such equipment must be grounded.

(c) In all cases where metal equipment is mounted on metal or metal lath.

(d) If the equipment is in a "hazardous location."

(e) In *all cases* where the wiring system is metal conduit, tubing, BX, or any other "metal-clad" type of wiring.

(f) If the voltage is over 150 to ground, the equipment must be grounded in all cases. This would include equipment on three-phase, three-wire, 220-volt circuits.

There are three exceptions to this last rule, which are self-explanatory.

250-43. Fixed Equipment—Specific

This Section lists specific equipment that must be grounded. Subparagraph (c) of the Code lists "motor frames as provided in Section 430-142." This Section is quoted in the listing below.

The following equipment is to be grounded regardless of voltage:

(a) In general, metal switchboard frames.

(b) In general, motors and generators in electric organs.

(c) Motors, stationary (the following is taken from Section 430-142):

If supplied by metal-clad wiring (conduit, BX, etc.), *or*

If located in a wet place *or*

If in a hazardous location.

(d) Motor controllers. (Exception: snap switches for controlling small motors need not be grounded if lined with an insulating material.)

(e) Motors, switches, boxes, and any other electrical equipment used with elevators and cranes.

(f) All electrical equipment used in garages, theaters, and movie studios. (Exception: Pendant lampholders operating at not more than 150 volts to ground are exempt.)

(g) Electric signs, including boxes, switches, and any other metal equipment used in conjunction with a sign. (Exception: If insulated from ground and metal objects, *and* accessible only to authorized persons, need not be grounded.)

(h) Motion-picture projection equipment.

(i) Equipment supplied by Class I and Class 2 remote-control and signaling circuits, where the remote-control *circuit* requires grounding. This rule would apply to a motor-control pushbutton, where the circuit for the pushbutton is taken off a transformer in the controller, and the circuit must be grounded as required by Section 250-5(a). If the transformer circuit requires grounding, the pushbutton must be grounded.

250-44. Nonelectrical Equipment

(a) Tracks and operator's cab of electric cranes must be grounded in all cases.

(b) Metal frame of an elevator operated nonelectrically (hydraulically, for instance) if there is wiring to the elevator (for lights etc.) must be grounded.

(c) Shifting cables on electric elevators must be grounded. (This does not mean the cables that raise and lower the elevator.)

(d) Metal enclosures of all kinds around high-voltage (over 750) equipment must be grounded, except when in substations or vaults operated by the electric company.

(e) Sections 550-9 and 551-23 require the frames of mobile homes and recreational vehicles (trailer homes) to be grounded.

250-45. Equipment Connected by Cord and Plug

(a) As in the case for fixed equipment, portable equipment must be grounded when located in a hazardous location. Any and all metal electrical equipment in a hazardous location must be grounded.

(b) Cord-and-plug connected equipment operating on a voltage of over 150 to ground must be grounded. This includes stationary as well as portable equipment.

Exceptions to this rule are:

1. Motors, if guarded. This means that if the motor is covered, shielded, enclosed, or otherwise protected by suitable covers or casings in such a way as to remove the possibility of shock, then the motor need not be grounded.
2. Heating appliances: grounding may be omitted if special permission is granted by the "authority having jurisdiction." Otherwise must be grounded.

(c) In residences, the following equipment must, in all cases, be either grounded or double insulated:

1. Refrigerators, freezers.
2. Air conditioners.
3. Washing machines.
4. Clothes dryers.
5. Dishwashers.
6. Sump pumps.
7. Electrical aquarium equipment.
8. Portable tools, hedge clippers, lawn mowers, wet scrubbers, snowblowers, handlamps.

"Double-insulation" portable appliances are appliances specially insulated by the manufacturer according to Underwriters Laboratories specifications. A number of such appliances are on the market, and these are exempt from grounding.

(d) For other than residences, the list of equipment to be grounded is the same as that for residences. In addition, *any* appliance or tool likely to be used in damp locations, or inside tanks or metal boilers, must be grounded. As in residences, double insulation may substitute for grounding.

250-46. Spacing from Lightning Rods

Raceways, such as conduit, and all metal cases enclosing electrical equipment, should be separated at least 6 ft from lighting rod conductors. If impossible to obtain 6 ft of separation, the metal enclosure and the lightning rod conductor must be bonded together by a copper wire or other metallic connection.

F. Methods of Grounding

250-50. Equipment Grounding Connections

(a) For Grounded System

In a grounded system, the neutral is grounded at the service switch to the "grounding electrode conductor." The grounding electrode conductor runs from the service switch to the "grounding electrode" (water pipe, for example).

The equipment grounding conductor may be a grounding wire run along with the circuit conductors, or, if the wiring on the premises is conduit, the conduit (or any other form of metal-clad wiring) could be the equipment grounding conductor. The grounding wire (or conduit) and the neutral must be connected or bonded to the grounding electrode conductor. Section 250-53(b) requires that the connection shall be made within the service enclosure, and that the service enclosure shall also be bonded to the same connection (see Fig. 236).

(b) For Ungrounded System

In an ungrounded system there is no neutral to be grounded. In this case the equipment grounding conductor alone is connected to the grounding electrode conductor. As noted above, the equipment grounding conductor could be a grounding wire, or if the wiring on the premises is conduit, the conduit (or any other form of metal-clad wiring) could be the equipment grounding conductor.

An exception to (a) and (b) above is allowed when, in an old installation, a branch circuit is extended to install a grounding-type receptacle, and the old wiring has no equipment grounding path. In this case it is not necessary to run a grounding conductor back to the service enclosure. The receptacle may be grounded to any convenient *cold*-water pipe. Note that this exception applies only for *receptacles*

250-51. Effective Grounding Path

The "path to ground" mentioned here would include the equipment grounding conductor (a wire, or conduit or other metal-clad wiring) and the grounding electrode conductor (Fig. 240).

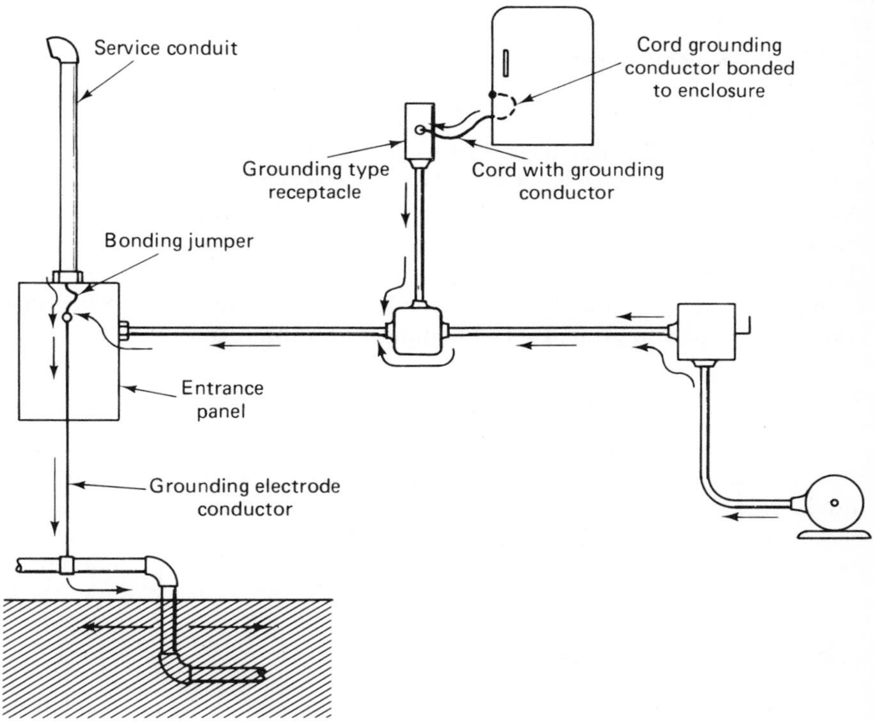

Fig. 240
The "path to ground" of Sect. 250-51. Here conduit is used as the grounding "conductor." All connections along the line must have good metal-to-metal contact to provide a continuous and effective path to ground.

This "path to ground" should be permanent, continuous, of low resistance, and have enough current-carrying capacity to safely conduct any fault current.

A high resistance in the "path to ground" would increase voltage to ground when current is flowing due to a fault in the wiring system.

Also, with a high resistance to ground, a fault current could be reduced to a point where the circuit fuse or circuit breaker would fail to open.

A low-resistance grounding path is necessary and desirable for safety.

250-53. Grounding Path to Grounding Electrode

The "grounding electrode conductor" is the conductor from the service disconnect enclosure to the "grounding electrode" (water pipe, etc.).

For a grounded wiring system, such as a 120/240-volt AC, single-phase system, the grounding electrode must be used to ground:

The neutral.

The service equipment.

The equipment grounding conductor.

All equipment grounding conductors must be bonded to the service enclosure. The neutral must be bonded to the service enclosure. The service enclosure is bonded to the grounding electrode conductor, thus grounding service enclosure, neutral, and equipment grounding conductor to the same electrode (Fig. 236). The equipment grounding conductor could be conduit, EMT, or a separate wire run with the circuit conductors. The equipment grounding conductor is used to ground metal equipment on the premises.

250-54. Common Grounding Electrode

If an AC wiring system has a grounded circuit conductor (neutral), the same electrode (water pipe, ground rod, etc.) that grounds the neutral must also be used to ground equipment. The 120/240-volt system has a neutral. The neutral is the grounded *circuit conductor* (which is grounded at the service enclosure). The same *electrode* that grounds the neutral also grounds equipment on the premises.

250-55. Underground Service Cable

A continuous underground system provides grounding for the conduit or metal sheath of the underground services (laterals) connected to the underground system. Therefore, in this case the conduit or metal sheath of the service (lateral) need not be grounded at the building. This exception applies for laterals connected to "continuous underground systems," and does *not* apply for a lateral run underground to a pole and overhead conductors.

The grounded neutral and service enclosure must be grounded, just as for overhead services.

250-56. Short Sections of Raceway

An example of an "isolated" section of metal raceway would be a short run of BX, or conduit, installed in a run of Romex. Grounding of the metal raceway or BX sheath is required if the run is over 25 ft long or within reach of ground, or if the run is in contact with grounded metal.

One of the methods of Section 250-57, following, must be used for grounding an isolated section of raceway [usually method (b)].

250-57. Fixed Equipment Grounding

Following are approved methods of grounding metal equipment enclosures:

(a) When "metal-clad" wiring is used, such as conduit, BX, or EMT, the conduit, BX, or EMT may serve as the grounding conductor for equipment.

(b) A grounding wire may be run along with the circuit wires and bonded to the equipment to be grounded. The grounding wire would make connection to the grounding electrode conductor in the service enclosure.

The grounding wire may be bare, but if insulated, the insulation must have a green color.

(When a grounding wire is larger than No. 6, it need not have a green color; but if not, it must be either (1) colored or painted green at each outlet, or (2) be stripped of insulation at each outlet.)

For DC circuits, the grounding wire may be run separate from the circuit wires.

(c) If special permission is obtained, other methods than the above may be permitted.

250-58. Equipment Considered Effectively Grounded

(a) If equipment is bolted or otherwise fastened to a metal rack or other metal support and the rack is grounded, the equipment is considered to be grounded.

(b) If an elevator machine is grounded, the elevator cab frame is considered to be grounded through the hoisting cables.

250-59. Cord- and Plug-Connected Equipment

There are three ways of grounding the metal cases of portable equipment and plug-connected stationary equipment:

(a) If the cord used is metal covered, such covering may serve as the ground wire. A plug with a grounding prong would be used. The equipment would be bonded to the cord's metal covering at one end, and the metal covering would be bonded to the grounding prong at the plug end. The receptacle would have a slot for the grounding prong.

(b) By using cord with a grounding conductor and a plug with a grounding prong. The grounding conductor in the cord may be bare or insulated. If insulated, the insulation must be green in color.

(c) A separate flexible wire or strap may be used, if part of the portable equipment.

250-60. Frames of Ranges and Clothes Dryers

Electric ranges, wall-mounted ovens, counter-mounted cooking units, and clothes dryers may be grounded by bonding to the neutral, when the circuit is 120/240-volt, single-phase, or 120/208 derived from a three- phase, four-wire wye-connected supply, but only under the following conditions:

The neutral must be at least No. 10, *and*

The neutral must be insulated (except that if the neutral is part of a Type SE cable and the branch circuit originates at the service equipment it may be bare), *and*

Grounding contacts of any receptacles furnished as part of the equipment must be bonded to the equipment.

250-61. Use of Grounded Circuit Conductor for Grounding Equipment

(a) Supply-Side Equipment

The neutral may be used to ground all metal parts of equipment on the supply side of the service disconnect. This would include meter housing and service conduit. Note that the neutral is *required* to be connected to the service equipment enclosure [Section 250-53(b)].

(b) Load-Side Equipment

On the load side of the service disconnect, the neutral may be used to ground the following equipment:

1. Frames of ranges, wall-mounted ovens, counter-mounted cooking units, and clothes dryers (see Section 250-60).
2. When the main service is in one building and other buildings are served from the main building, the "other" buildings are in some cases required to have a separate ground. In this case the neutral would be bonded to the disconnect enclosure for the other buildings, which are on the load side of the main service disconnect (see Section 250-24).
3. When a meter is on the load side of the service disconnect, the neutral may be used to ground the meter housing, provided:

   (a) There is no service ground-fault protection.

   (b) Meter is near the service disconnect.

Except in these three cases, the neutral may not be used for grounding purposes on the load side of the disconnect, unless special permission is obtained from the authority having jurisdiction.

250-62. Multiple Circuit Connections

In some cases a piece of equipment may be served by more than one circuit. If the equipment requires grounding, there must be a separate ground for each circuit.

G. Bonding

250-70. General

250-71. Bonding Service Equipment

"Bonding" means joining together the metal parts (boxes, cabinets, conduit, etc.) of the wiring system in such a way that good metallic contact is made between the different parts. This is done so as to join the exposed metal parts of the system together in a continuous metallic system, thus assuring a good electrical path to ground throughout the system for boxes, cabinets, and other items that require grounding.

Section 250-71 refers to service equipment *only.* The parts of the service equipment to be grounded are:

1. The service entrance raceway (such as conduit), or the service cable sheath or armor.
2. Meter bases and meter housings.
3. Service equipment enclosures.
4. Any other metal service equipment.

These must be bonded together in good metal-to-metal contact. Section 250-72, following, lists the accepted methods of doing this.

The exception of Section 250-55 refers to underground service entrances that connect to continuous underground cable systems. An underground service raceway or cable need not be grounded if it connects to a continuous underground system.

250-72. Method of Bonding Service Equipment

This Section lists the allowable methods of "bonding" service equipment (see Fig. 241).

(a) One or all of the parts listed above may be bonded to the neutral. For bonding to the neutral, pressure connectors, clamps must be used. Soldering is not permitted.

(b) Threaded connections. A threaded connection is considered an adequate bond. Therefore, if a piece of conduit can be threaded into a meter base, or into a service enclosure, this serves as a bond. Of course, a service enclosure would have to be fitted with threaded hubs or be made of cast metal to allow the use of threaded connections.

(c) Threadless couplings are considered adequate for bonding sections of tubing or metal conduit together if made up tight.

(d) Where a box has concentric knockouts, and only the smaller ones are punched out, leaving one or more rings of knockouts still in the box, a jumper must be used to bond conduit or tubing to the box. The knockout rings remaining in the box, being loosely connected, would impair the path to ground, and the Code requires that a jumper be used around them.

(e) An application of this rule permitting "other devices" to be used would be in the case where *no knockout rings* remain in the box where the conduit or cable enters. In this case, the box has solid metal around the conduit or cable and the Code allows other methods besides a jumper to be used.

Grounding bushings and grounding "wedges" are on the market that are approved as "other devices." Grounding wedges are equipped with set screws, which when tightened bond the conduit or cable to the box so as to satisfy the Code requirements for bonding.

250-73. Metal Armor or Tape of Service Cable

When the service entrance is a metal-armored cable with bare grounded neutral, and the metal armor is wound around the bare grounded neutral, the armor needs no further grounding. The armor need not be bonded to the service enclosure in this case. Since the bare neutral will be bonded to the service enclosure, and the cable armor is in metallic contact with the bare neutral, this effectively grounds the armor and serves as a bond to the service enclosure (Fig. 241).

250-74. Connecting Receptacle Grounding Terminal to Box

The grounding slot of grounding-type receptacles must have a connection to ground. If the wiring system is conduit, EMT, or BX, the outlet box will be grounded through the conduit, EMT, or BX.

The general rule is that a bonding *jumper* shall be used to connect the grounding terminal of a grounding-type receptacle to a grounded box.

There are four exceptions where the connection may be made by other means than a jumper:

1. When the box is surface-mounted, a device yoke having metal-to-metal contact with the box may be used.
2. When the box is flush-mounted, a yoke can be bonded to the box through the mounting screws of the box.
3. Floor boxes specially designed in such a way as to provide good contact between the box and receptacle need not have a bonding jumper.
4. Where required to reduce electromagnetic interference, the receptacle grounding slot need not be connected to a grounded box, but may be grounded to a separate insulated grounding conductor run with the circuit conductors.

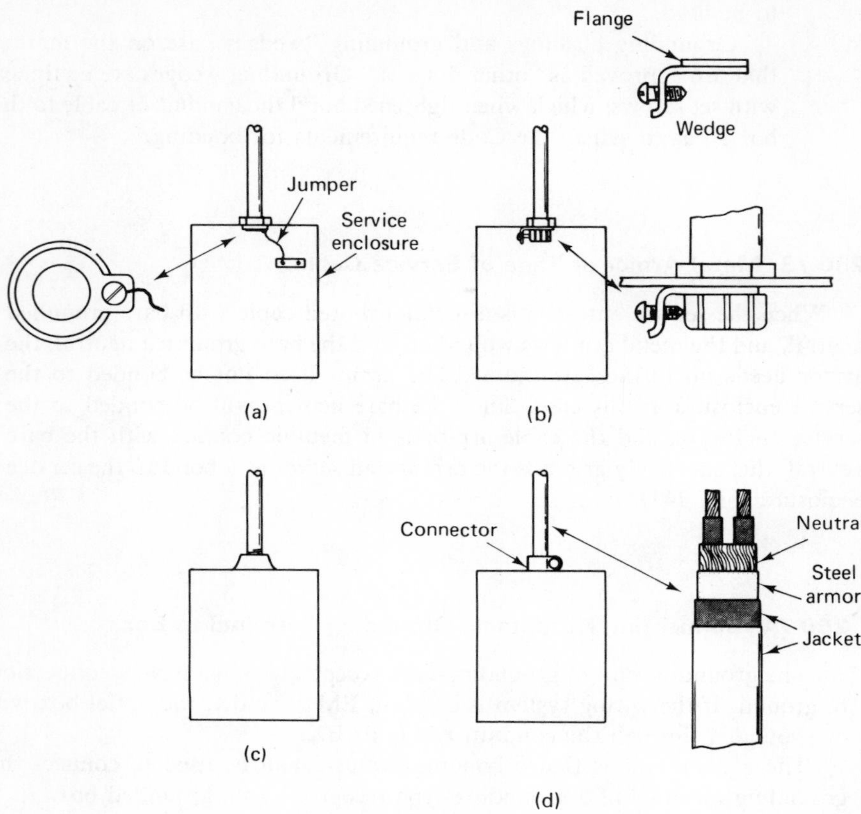

Fig. 241

Methods of bonding service equipment (Sects. 250-72, 250-73).

(a) Service conduit bonded to service enclosure through a jumper and grounding bushing.

(b) Service conduit bonded to service enclosure through a grounding wedge. Flange of wedge slips into wall of enclosure. When set screw is tightened, flange presses against metal of enclosure. Bottom part of wedge grips conduit. Wedges may be used only if no knockout rings are left in enclosure, around the conduit. Where knockout rings are present, a jumper must be used.

(c) Conduit threaded to service enclosure. No further bonding required.

(d) Service cable with steel armor in contact with bare neutral. Steel armor is grounded by contact with neutral. Bonding to service enclosure not required.

250-75. Bonding Other Enclosures

Where conduit, metal raceway, or cable armor serves as the grounding means for equipment, care must be taken to see that there are no breaks in the metallic continuity of the conduit (or other metal raceway) throughout the premises. Where conduit enters painted boxes, the paint should be removed where contact is made (the paint would usually be removed when a locknut or bushing is tightened up).

This rule does not specify the method of bonding between raceways and metal enclosures or between sections of raceway. The rule simply states that "the electrical continuity" shall be assured.

250-76. Bonding for over 250 Volts

For circuits, other than services, of more than 250 volts *to ground,* one of the following methods of bonding must be used:

(1) For bonding between sections of metal conduit or EMT:

1. Threaded couplings for conduit.

2. Threadless couplings made up tight for conduit or EMT.

The above should not be construed to mean that BX, Romex, or other types of wiring are forbidden for all circuits above 250 volts to ground. One of the two methods above must be used if conduit or EMT is the wiring method. If BX is used, there is no need for joining sections of the cable together. It is always continuous from outlet to outlet. (*Note:* BX may be used for voltages up to 600 only.)

(2) For bonding between metallic raceways and metallic boxes, cabinets, and the like, the following bonding methods are approved:

1. Jumpers, or

2. Two locknuts, one inside and one outside of the box or cabinet, or

3. Threaded bosses, or

4. Other "approved" devices.

Note that a locknut and bushing is not permitted for *bonding* at boxes or cabinets for circuits of more than 250 volts to ground. Two locknuts are permitted, but not a locknut and bushing. Locknuts and bushings may be used, but not *for bonding.* If used, they must have a bonding jumper around them (see Fig. 242).

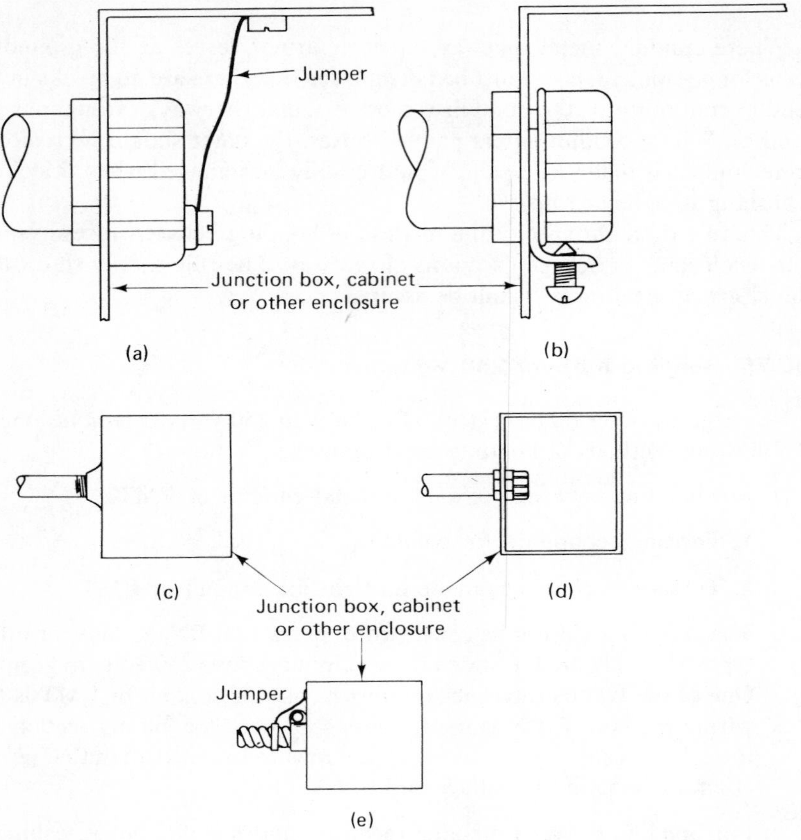

Fig. 242

Bonding for over 250 volts to ground (Sect. 250-76).

(a) Grounding bushing.
(b) Grounding wedge (may be used only if no knockout rings are left in enclosure wall, around the conduit).
(c) Threaded connection.
(d) Two locknuts—one inside, one outside of enclosure. Bushing used over inside locknut (this method may be used only if no knockout rings are left in enclosure wall, around the conduit).
(e) Jumper used around BX connector.

These bonding methods are required for 480/277 V, three-phase, four-wire; 440 or 480 volt, three-wire, three-phase. Not required for 120 or 240 volt circuits.

250-77. Bonding Loosely Jointed Metal Raceways

Expansion joints are placed in long straight runs of conduit or EMT to allow for expansion and contraction due to temperature changes. When expansion joints are used, they must be bridged across with jumpers (or other approved means), since an expansion joint is not considered a reliable bond.

250-78. Bonding in Hazardous Locations

In hazardous locations one of the following methods of bonding must be employed (this applies regardless of voltage).

(It should be noted that EMT is permitted only in Class II, Division 2 hazardous locations. Threaded rigid metal conduit may be used in any hazardous location. For wiring methods permitted in the different classes of hazardous locations, refer to Chapter 5.)

For bonding between sections of metal conduit or EMT:

1. Threaded couplings for conduit.

2. Threadless couplings made up tight for EMT or conduit.

For bonding between metallic raceway and metallic boxes, cabinets, and the like:

1. Threaded connection (for conduit), or

2. Bonding jumpers, or

3. Other devices approved for the purpose.

250-79. Main and Equipment Bonding Jumpers

(a) Material

(b) Attachment

Bonding jumpers must be of "corrosion-resistant" material such as copper. Steel jumpers are not permitted.

Jumpers must be attached to circuit, conduit, equipment by means of lugs, connectors, or clamps. Soldering is not permitted.

(c) Size—Equipment Bonding Jumper on Supply Side of Service and Main Bonding Jumper

A main bonding jumper would be a jumper used in the service cabinet to connect the equipment grounding conductor and the service equipment enclosure to the neutral [Section 250-53(b)].

Any bonding jumpers used in the service must be sized according to Table 250-94, p. 70-101. For example, a service entrance of No. 4 copper requires a No. 8 minimum jumper (if copper); a No. 2/0 copper entrance requires a No. 4 minimum; etc. Note that jumpers used at the service are required to be at least the minimum size required for the grounding electrode conductor.

(d) Size—Equipment Bonding Jumper on Load Side of Service

A bonding jumper used on *any other equipment than the service equipment* must be sized according to Table 250-95, p. 70-102. Generally, a No. 14 jumper is the smallest allowed. This size may be used for equipment on 15-amp. branch circuits. For branch circuits of higher rating, larger jumpers are required, as can be seen from the table.

(e) Installation—Equipment Bonding Jumper

If a wire is used to bond two equipments together, and the wire is exposed, wire length is limited to 6 ft maximum. If in a conduit or raceway, the length is not limited.

250-80. Bonding of Piping Systems

(a) Metal Water Piping

A metal water piping system in a building is required to be bonded to either the service equipment enclosure, or to any other electrode that may be used for grounding (metal frame of the building, driven pipe, etc.) An underground piping system, used for grounding, would be bonded to the service enclosure by the grounding electrode conductor, and this would satisfy the requirement of the rule. Or, as an alternative, a piping system could be bonded to another electrode, the other electrode being connected to the service enclosure through a grounding electrode conductor.

(b) Other Metal Piping

Nonmetallic pipe has come into use as water pipe. Sections of nonmetallic piping inserted in a metallic piping system would break the continuity of the metal-to-metal contact throughout the piping system. Nonmetallic unions or joints would have the same effect.

If an isolated section of metallic water (or gas) piping should become charged, this would create a hazard. Grounding all isolated sections would remove the hazard.

Where there is a possibility that any metallic water (or gas) piping on a premises might come in contact with a "hot" wire, all nonmetallic breaks must be bridged over with a bonding jumper, and the whole piping system grounded to the grounding electrode. The bonding jumper must be no smaller than the size permitted by Table 250-95 of the Code.

H. Grounding Electrode System

250-81. Grounding Electrode System

The Code lists four types of electrode that collectively constitute the first choice as the grounding electrode system. If two, three, or four are available on the premises, the two, three, or four must be bonded together and used collectively as the "grounding electrode." If one of these is available, that must be used as the grounding electrode. A conductor used for bonding must be at least as large as the grounding electrode conductor size required by Table 250-94, p. 70-101 of the Code.

The four "first choice" electrodes are:

1. Underground metal water piping (which is underground for at least 10 ft).
2. Metal frame of the building, if the frame is in good contact with the earth.
3. A bare copper conductor located within and near the bottom of a concrete footing in contact with the earth. Conductor must be at least No. 4 and at least 20 ft long.
4. A steel reinforcing bar at least 20 ft long, located within and near the bottom of a concrete footing.
5. A bare copper conductor encircling the building or structure. Conductor must be at least No. 2.

Metal water piping may not be used alone as the grounding electrode. Must be supplemented by an additional electrode, which may be a rod, pipe, plate, or No. 2, 3 or 4 above.

250-83. Made and Other Electrodes

If no first choice electrode is available, any of the following may be used as a second choice:

1. Metal plates.
2. Pipes.
3. Solid rods.
4. Gas pipe (may be used only if acceptable to the authority having jurisdiction).

Iron or steel plates shall be at least $\frac{1}{4}$ in. thick. Brass, bronze, or copper plates shall be at least $\frac{1}{16}$ in. thick. Metal plates shall present not less than 2 sq. ft. of surface to the soil. (A plate 1 sq. ft. in area would present 2 sq. ft. to the soil, for the two sides of the plate.) Plates shall, where practicable, be buried below the permanent moisture level.

The smallest size permitted for pipe electrodes is $\frac{3}{4}$ in. Iron pipe must be galvanized. "Black iron" pipe is not permitted.

Steel or iron rods shall be at least $\frac{5}{8}$ in. in diameter. Copper, bronze, or brass rods shall be at least $\frac{1}{2}$ in. in diameter.

Pipe or rod electrodes shall be at least 8 ft long.

Except where solid rock is struck, pipes or rods shall be driven to a depth of 8 ft. When solid rock is struck, a depth of only 4 ft is required.

When solid rock is struck at a depth of less than 4 ft, the pipe or rod shall be buried horizontally.

Made electrodes may be used only if no first- or second-choice electrode is available.

250-84. Resistance of Made Electrodes

The maximum resistance of a made electrode should not exceed 25 ohms. "Made" electrodes may, in some cases, where buried only the minimum 4 ft, or where driven in dry or sandy soil, have a resistance higher than this.

There are ground testers on the market for measuring the resistance of an electrode to ground. If the resistance of a "made" electrode is found to be over 25 ohms, two or more electrodes must be connected in parallel.

The electrodes of Section 250-81 usually have a resistance to ground of below 25 ohms.

250-86. Use of Lightning Rods

The use of a lightning-rod system as the electrode for wiring systems is prohibited.

In addition to the electrodes required by the Code for the wiring system, there may be electrodes for other systems, such as communications, on the premises. This Section recommends that where there are two or more electrodes on the premises they be bonded together. If bonded together, the two or more electrodes will necessarily be at the same potential, and consequently there can be no flow of current from one electrode to the other. Current flow between electrodes would be undesirable.

J. Grounding Conductors

250-91. Material

(a) Grounding Electrode Conductor

This rule requires that the wire used as the "grounding electrode conductor" be copper, aluminum, or copper-clad aluminum. The grounding electrode conductor is the wire from the service enclosure to the water pipe, ground rod, etc. Splices are not permitted in a grounding electrode wire (a splice is permitted in bus-bar).

(b) Types of Equipment Grounding Conductors (See Fig. 243)

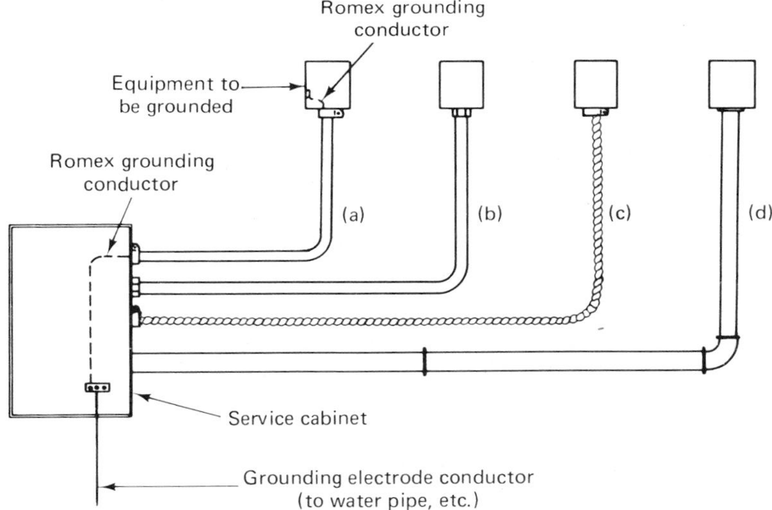

Fig. 243

Types of equipment grounding conductors [Sect. 250-91(b)].

(a) Grounding conductor run with circuit conductors. (Romex shown.)

(b) Rigid metal conduit or EMT used as a grounding "conductor."

(c) Sheath of BX used as a grounding "conductor." Sheath of Type MI, aluminum-sheathed or copper-sheathed cable may also be used as a grounding conductor.

(d) Wireway enclosure used as a grounding "conductor." The enclosure of other approved raceways may also be used as a grounding conductor.

The conduit, BX sheath, wireway enclosure are in metallic contact with equipment to be grounded and with the service cabinet. Service cabinet is bonded to the grounding electrode conductor, which connects to ground.

An equipment grounding "conductor" may be any one of the following:

1. A copper (or other "corrosion-resistant") wire.
2. Rigid metal conduit.
3. Intermediate metal conduit.
4. EMT.
5. BX armor.
6. Sheath of Type MI cable.
7. Sheath of Type MC cable.
8. Cable trays.
9. Other raceways approved for grounding purposes.

Other raceways approved for the purpose include:

Wireways.

Underfloor raceways.

Cellular metal floor raceways.

Busways.

Cablebus.

Flexible metal conduit (Greenfield) may be used for grounding if (1) length is not over 6 ft, (2) the enclosed circuit is protected at 20 amps. or less, and (3) fittings used are approved for the purpose.

Liquidtight flexible metal conduit in $1\frac{1}{2}$ in. and larger sizes may be used for grounding. In the $1\frac{1}{4}$ in. and smaller sizes it is permitted only in lengths of 6 ft or less.

(c) Supplementary Grounding

Supplementary grounding electrodes may be used in conjunction with the conductors listed in (b) above.

250-92. Installation

(a) Grounding Electrode Conductor

Following are the rules for installing the grounding conductor from service disconnect enclosure to water pipe or other "electrode." There are three cases:

1. *Wire No. 4 or larger*

When the grounding wire is No. 4 or larger it may be stapled direct to the surface wired over. No protection is needed except where exposed to severe damage.

2. *No. 6 wire*

A No. 6 grounding conductor may be unprotected, if run over a flat surface and securely stapled. Otherwise it must be in conduit, EMT, or cable armor.

3. *No. 8 wire*

A No. 8 grounding conductor must in all cases be run in conduit, EMT, or cable armor.

(b) Equipment Grounding Conductor

The "equipment grounding conductor" is the grounding path for boxes, cabinets, and the like. Conduit, tubing, or BX armor could be used for this purpose. But in cases where a separate wire is needed, it must be sized according to Table 250-95, p. 70-102 of the Code. Thus, for equipment on a circuit fused at, say, 60 amps. a No. 10 wire (if copper) would be required for grounding equipment.

250-93. Size of Direct-Current System Grounding Conductor

For grounding three-wire DC circuits, the size of the grounding conductor must be at least equal to the largest circuit conductor, but in no case smaller than No. 8.

"Balancer sets" or "balancer windings" are sometimes used to obtain a neutral from a two-wire DC generator.

A "balancer set" is a set of two smaller DC generators connected in series across the two lines of the main DC generator. A lead is brought out from the midpoint between the smaller generators, and this constitutes the neutral, or third wire. The main generator may be, say, 230 volt. The two balancer generators would then be 115 volts each.

Another way of obtaining a neutral from a two-wire DC generator is by "balancer windings." The two hot wires are brought out as usual from the generator. Two additional sets of leads (properly tapped within the generator armature) are brought out through collector rings. Each pair of leads feeds a "balancer winding." The midpoints of the two balancer windings are joined together by a jumper. Connection to this jumper supplies the third wire, or neutral, for the system.

When balancer sets or balancer windings are used, and are protected against excessive current [as per Section 445-4(d)], the size of the grounding conductor need not be equal to the largest circuit conductor, but only equal to the size of the neutral. For other DC systems, the grounding conductor shall be no smaller than the largest circuit conductor, but in no case smaller than No. 8.

As noted in Section 250-22, DC systems are not grounded at the service, as with AC systems. DC systems are grounded only at the supply station. However, a grounding conductor is required for DC systems—to ground the service enclosure and any other equipment on the premises that requires grounding.

250-94. Size of Alternating-Current Grounding Electrode Conductor

The "grounding electrode conductor" is the conductor that runs from the service switch enclosure to the "grounding electrode" (e.g., water pipe, etc.). A grounding electrode conductor may be no smaller than the size listed in Table 250-94 of the Code. The size of the grounding electrode conductor is based on the size of the service-entrance conductors. For example, if the service-entrance conductors are No. 2/0 copper, the grounding electrode conductor must be at least a No. 4.

Where the grounding electrode is a "made" electrode, such as a rod driven into the ground, then the grounding electrode conductor need never be larger than No. 6, regardless of size of the service entrance. This is because "made" electrodes have more resistance than electrodes such as water pipes, and the grounding electrode conductor would not at any time be called upon to carry currents requiring a larger conductor.

250-95. Size of Equipment Grounding Conductors

Table 250-95 lists minimum size of grounding conductor for grounding equipment (except service equipment) when the grounding conductor is a wire. Here the size of grounding conductor depends upon the size of the fuse, or setting of the circuit breaker used for protecting the circuit. Generally, No. 14 wire is the smallest permissible (except that, when part of a cord assembly, No. 18 is permitted).

Conduit, EMT, BX sheath, and other metal-clad cable sheath may also be used as the grounding "conductor" [see Section 250-91(b)].

When circuit conductors are run in parallel in separate raceways, and the grounding conductor is a wire, a separate ground wire must be run with each set of circuit conductors and sized according to Table 250-95.

An equipment grounding wire need never be larger than the circuit conductors to the equipment.

250-97. Outline Lighting

For bonding together different *sections* or *parts* of a complete assembly for outline lighting, the bonding wire need not be larger than No. 14. However, the grounding conductor for the whole group of parts must be sized in accordance with Table 250-95.

250-98. Grounding Conductor in Common Raceway

When the grounding conductor is a wire, it may be included in the same conduit or other raceway with the circuit conductors.

250-99. Grounding Conductor Continuity

(a) Separable Connections

Grounding-type plugs shall be so constructed that the grounding prong of the plug will make contact before the circuit conductors make and break contact after the circuit conductors break. A grounding prong longer than the circuit prongs would satisfy these requirements.

Interlocked equipment so constructed as to accomplish the same result is also acceptable.

(b) Switches

This rule would cover the unusual case of an automatic disconnect being placed in the grounding conductor. (The *grounding* conductor should not be confused with the *grounded circuit conductor,* the neutral.) If such a disconnect is placed in the grounding conductor, the disconnect must open all circuit conductors at the same time that it opens the grounding conductor.

K. Grounding Conductor Connections

250-111. To Raceway or Cable Armor

The raceway (conduit, EMT, etc.) is usually grounded at the service switch, where the conduit, EMT is metallically connected to the grounding electrode conductor. This satisfies the rule requiring the point of connection of the grounding conductor "to interior metal raceways, cable armor and the like" to be "as near as practicable to the source of supply."

250-112. To Grounding Electrode

The grounding conductor, if connected to a water pipe, should, if possible, be connected on the "street" side of the meter. If it cannot be connected on the street side of the meter, the meter must be bridged across with a jumper, since the meter is a piece of equipment that is likely to be disconnected at times for repair or replacement.

250-113. To Conductors and Equipment

The use of solder is not permitted for connecting a grounding wire to any piece of equipment, or to the neutral. Solder is not permitted for attaching a bonding jumper. Lugs, pressure connectors, clamps, or "other approved means" must be used for this purpose.

250-114. Continuity and Attachment of Branch-Circuit Equipment Grounding Conductors to Boxes

One application of this rule would be the case of a circuit feeding a number of grounding-type receptacles, and having a grounding wire run along with the circuit conductors. Here, a box for a receptacle could have "more than one grounding conductor," one entering and one leaving the box. The Code requires that the two grounding conductors be connected together in such a way that removing the receptacle would not break the grounding circuit. Both grounding conductors could not be connected to the grounding terminal on the *receptacle,* because if this were done, removing the receptacle could result in opening the grounding circuit at that point.

In metal boxes the two conductors must both be connected to a grounding screw in the box, with a connection to the receptacle made from the screw. In nonmetallic boxes, the two conductors could be joined together and a pigtail connection to the receptacle made from the joint. Connecting the grounding conductors in one of these ways would eliminate the possibility of breaking the grounding circuit, if a receptacle were removed.

The same precaution should be taken in all cases where grounding conductors enter and leave *any* box or enclosure.

250-115. Connection to Electrodes

The grounding electrode conductor may be attached to the electrode (water pipe, rod, plate, etc.) in the following ways:

1. By a bolted clamp. Clamp must be either cast bronze or brass, or iron or malleable iron.

2. By a sheet-metal strap-type clamp. Strap must have a rigid metal base that seats on the electrode. Strap must be heavy enough so as not to stretch after installation.

3. By a pipe fitting, pipe plug screwed into a fitting of a pipe electrode.

Clamps used on copper, brass, or lead pipe should be of copper. Clamps used on galvanized iron or plain iron pipe should be galvanized iron.

Methods 2 and 3 would be suitable for underground piping or a driven rod or pipe. For connection to a plate electrode or metal frame of a building, method 1 would be suitable.

For connecting the grounding electrode wire to a clamp or pipe fitting, lugs or pressure connectors must be used. Soldered connections are not permitted.

In addition to the methods of 1, 2, 3 above, "equally substantial approved means" may be used for attachment.

250-117. Protection of Attachment

If the ground connection must be made in a location that would expose the connection to damage, a protective covering shall be provided. The object of the rule is to protect the ground connection from present or future mechanical injury, which might break the connection.

250-118. Clean Surfaces

The Code of course requires good metal-to-metal contact in the ground connections. Paint or other foreign substances that might impair conduction should be scraped off at connection points.

L. Instrument Transformers, Relays, Etc.

250-121. Instrument Transformer Circuits

Current and potential instrument transformers are small transformers used to take a reduced current or voltage from a circuit, the lower current or voltage being wired to an ammeter or voltmeter, which is scaled to read correct current or voltage for the circuit.

The secondary circuit of such transformers would be the circuit leading to the ammeter, voltmeter, or other instrument. The rules for grounding the secondary circuits can be summed up as follows:

On switchboards:

1. Primary over 750 volts: always grounded.
2. Primary 0 to 750 volts: must be grounded if any live parts or wiring are exposed or accessible to "unauthorized" persons. Otherwise need not be grounded.

Not on switchboards:

1. Primary over 750 volts: always grounded.
2. Primary 300 to 750 volts: must be grounded if any live parts are exposed or accessible to "unauthorized" persons. Otherwise, need not be grounded.
3. Primary less than 300 volts to ground: need not be grounded.

250-122. Instrument Transformer Cases

Potential transformer cases, if accessible to other than qualified persons, must be grounded regardless of voltage. If not accessible, grounding is never required.

Current transformer cases require grounding only if the primaries are over 150 volts, and then only if "accessible." If not accessible, grounding is never required.

250-123. Cases of Instruments, Meters, and Relays—Operating Voltage 750 or Less

250-124. Cases of Instruments, Meters, and Relays—Operating Voltage over 750

These Sections refer to enclosing cases of ammeters, voltmeters, wattmeters, relays, etc.

The rules can be summed up as follows:

1. Not on switchboards: if voltage at instrument is between 300 and 750 volts to ground and instrument is accessible to other than qualified persons, cases shall be grounded. Under 300 V need not be grounded.
2. On switchboards, 0 to 750 volts: On dead front switchboards, cases shall be grounded. On live front switchboards, cases shall *not* be grounded.

3. Over 750 volts to ground (any location): Cases shall not be grounded, but shall be isolated or suitably protected [except for cases of electrostatic ground detectors having internal segments connected to the case, with the detector isolated by elevation (out of reach); these may be grounded].

250-125. Instrument Grounding Conductor

This Section sets the size of grounding conductor for the foregoing Sections.

The grounding conductor must be at least No. 12 copper (or equal). If the instruments are mounted on a grounded metal surface, they are considered properly grounded, and no additional grounding is required.

M. Connecting Lightning Arresters

250-131. Services of Less Than 1,000 Volts

Lightning arresters are not required by the Code except in certain industrial stations (Section 280-10). However, lightning arresters *may* be installed, if deemed advisable, on either secondary or primary circuits. A lightning arrester in elementary form is simply a device having a small air gap. One side of the air gap is connected to the circuit wire; the other side of the gap is connected to ground. The normal voltage of the circuit will not jump the gap. However, the large voltage surges caused by lightning will arc across the gap and be drained off to ground.

The Code permits four methods of connecting the ground side of secondary circuit arresters to ground:

1. They may be grounded to the "grounded service conductor" (the neutral).
2. They may be grounded to the "grounding electrode conductor."
3. They may be grounded to the grounding electrode for the service.
4. They may be connected to the equipment grounding terminal in the service equipment.

Connections for lightning arresters are illustrated in Fig. 244.

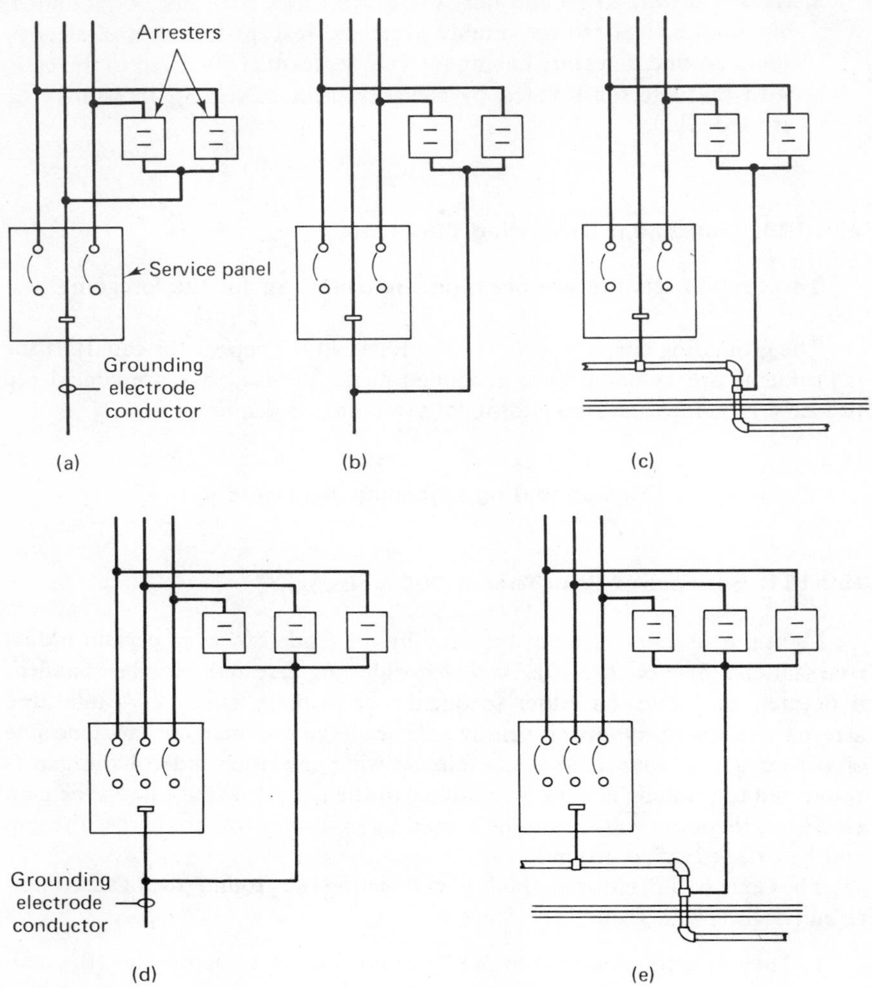

Fig. 244

Connecting lightning arresters on services of less than 1,000 volts (Sect. 250-131).

(a)(b)(c)	120/240-V grounded service.
(d)(e)	Three phase, three-wire service.
(a)	Connection to grounded neutral.
(b)(d)	Connection to grounding electrode conductor.
(c)(e)	Connection to grounding electrode.

250-132. On Circuits of 1 kV and Over

The ground side of a lightning arrester for a transformer primary may be connected to the transformer secondary grounded neutral. Connection may be made:

1. Direct to the secondary neutral only.
2. Direct to the secondary neutral *and* to an arrester ground.
3. To the secondary neutral through a spark gap, *and* to an arrester ground.

Method 1 may be used only if the transformer secondaries serve four or more premises within a distance of one mile, and each service is grounded to a city water system.

Method 2 may be used when one or more premises are served by the transformer secondaries, and each service is grounded to a continuous water piping system.

Method 3: when the transformer serves a premises having a "made" electrode for a ground (driven rod, pipe, plate), the primary arrester ground may be made to the secondary neutral, but only through a "spark gap."

Of course, a primary lightning arrester may also be independently grounded without connection to a secondary neutral.

The question might be asked, why should primary arresters having their own ground connection have, also, a ground connection to the secondary neutral? The answer is that a lightning discharge will at times set up an arcing between the primary and secondary bushings of a transformer. Such arcing can be prevented or at least reduced by the ground connection to the secondary neutral.

Other methods of grounding primary arresters to the secondary neutral may be used, if special permission is granted by the authority enforcing the Code.

N. Grounding of Systems and Circuits of 1 kV and Over (High Voltage)

250-150. General

Except when supplying portable equipment, the neutral of AC systems of 1 kV and over is not required to be grounded, but may be grounded [Section 250-5(c)].

For three-wire DC systems serving premises wiring of 1 kV and over, the neutral shall be grounded [Section 250-3(b)].

The following Sections set down the rules for grounding these high-voltage systems. In addition to the rules of this Part (N), the general rules for grounding must also be followed, where applicable.

250-151. Derived Neutral Systems

A neutral derived from a grounding transformer may be used for grounding, rather than grounding direct to the neutral.

250-152. Solidly Grounded Neutral Systems

(a) Neutral Conductor

600-volt insulation is permitted on the neutral of high-voltage circuits. The neutral may be bare *copper* when used as a neutral of a service entrance, or where used as the neutral of buried feeders.

A bare neutral (copper or other metals) may be run overhead outdoors.

(b) Multiple Grounding

A high-voltage neutral may be grounded at more than one point for:

1. Services.
2. Buried feeders having a bare *copper* neutral.
3. Conductors outside overhead.

Otherwise, only one ground is permitted.

250-153. Impedance-Grounded Neutral Systems

The neutral of a high-voltage system may be grounded through an impedance coil placed in the grounding wire. When an impedance coil is used, no direct ground is permitted.

The impedance neutral shall be identified and insulated. Insulation shall be equal to that of the phase wires.

Equipment grounding conductors may be bare.

250-154. Grounding of Systems Supplying Portable Equipment

(a) Portable equipment shall be supplied from a system having an impedance ground.

(b) Exposed metal parts of portable equipment shall be grounded to the point at which the neutral impedance is grounded.

(c) Maximum ground-fault current shall not develop a voltage between equipment frame and ground of over 100 volts.

(d) A ground-fault detection system must be provided that will disconnect a high-voltage system which has developed a ground fault. A detection system must be provided that will disconnect the high-voltage circuit to the portable equipment in case of a break in the grounding conductor.

(e) The grounding electrode for the high-voltage circuit feeding the portable equipment shall be separated at least 20 ft from any other electrode.

(f) High-voltage trailing cables and couplers for interconnection of portable equipment shall be of a type approved for the purpose.

250-155. Grounding of Equipment

All non-current-carrying metal parts of fixed and portable equipment, including associated fences, housings, etc., shall be grounded.

Exceptions.

1. Where isolated from ground and located so as to prevent any person who can make contact with ground from making contact with metal parts of equipment, when equipment is energized.
2. Pole-mounted distribution apparatus, as provided in Section 250-42, Exception No. 3.

   Grounding conductors not an integral part of a cable assembly shall be not smaller than No. 6.

ARTICLE 280 — LIGHTNING ARRESTERS

B. Industrial Stations

280-10 Where Required

280-11 Number Required

280-12. Where Connected

Lightning arresters are required in indoor or outdoor industrial stations (i.e., individual substations or generating stations not owned by the utility company) located where thunderstorms are frequent.

A lightning arrester is required for each ungrounded *overhead* conductor. An exception to this rule is allowed for the case of a single main bus feeding two (or more) outgoing circuits. If the single main bus is protected by arresters, this one set of arresters may serve for all the outgoing circuits.

With this arrangement, when an outgoing line is disconnected from the main bus, it would also be disconnected from the lightning arrester. For protection of the line when disconnected, the disconnect switch would be a double throw switch with a ground connection on one side. Then when the outgoing line is disconnected it will be connected to ground.

Arresters must be connected on the "line" side of all apparatus.

C. Other Occupancies

280-20. Utilization Equipment

Lightning arresters installed for the protection of utilization equipment (i.e., meters, motors, etc.) may be installed either indoors or outdoors.

Arresters on circuits of 750 volts or less may be either:

1. Enclosed, or if not enclosed
2. Made inaccessible to "unqualified" persons.

Arresters on circuits above 750 volts must always be made inaccessible to unauthorized persons, whether enclosed or not.

D. Installation

280-30. Location

Arresters installed indoors must be well separated from:

1. Other equipment.
2. Passageways.
3. Combustible materials, such as wood.

280-32. Arrester Conductors—Size and Material

Connections to lightning arresters must be:

1. Of copper wire or cable, minimum size No. 6 (except as provided for services in Section 250-131 for services of 1000 volts or less).
2. As short and straight as practicable.

280-33. Insulation

Arrester accessories must have insulation at least equal to insulation required elsewhere in the circuit.

280-34. Switch for Isolating Arrester

It may be desirable to install a switch for disconnecting the lightning arresters from the line. The Code requires that the switch be able to withstand a voltage test between live parts of at least 10 percent more than the voltage test that the live parts will withstand to ground. "Between live parts" would be the gap across the switch when open, also the gap between poles, where a two or three pole switch is used.

280-35. Grounding

The general rules of Article 250 of the Code must be complied with when grounding lightning arresters. Grounding conductors shall not be run in metal enclosures unless bonded to both ends of the metal enclosure.

Chapter 3. Wiring Methods and Materials

ARTICLE 300 — WIRING METHODS

A. General Requirements

300-1. Scope

The provisions of Article 300 apply to all wiring installations, except that for wiring systems such as remote-control systems, certain sections of Article 300 are not applicable. For wiring of these systems, refer to the following articles:

1. For remote-control circuits (circuits between thermostats and heating system controls, for example), Article 725.
2. For "low-energy" circuits that operate devices (electric door openers, circuits from a juke box to remote coin slots, etc.), Article 725.
3. For low-energy signal circuits (door-bell circuits, etc.), Article 725.
4. For fire-protection signaling circuits (alarms, etc.), Article 760.
5. For communication circuits (telephone, telegraph circuits), Article 800.

300-2. Voltage Limitations

The rules of Chapter 3 apply for voltages up to 600 (which is also the voltage limit for conductors for general wiring). For circuits of over 600 volts, there are additional requirements, which are set down in Article 710 of the Code.

300-3. Conductors of Different Systems

(a) Conductors of 600 volts or less may occupy the same conduit, raceway, or other enclosure with conductors of 600 volts or less, provided that all conductors are insulated for the highest voltage present. A 600-volt circuit may be run with a 6-volt circuit, if all of the conductors are insulated for 600 volts.

(b) Conductors of over 600 volts may *not* occupy the same conduit, raceway, or other enclosure with conductors of 600 volts or less, except as in (c), (d) and (e) following.

(c) Secondary wiring to electric-discharge (such as fluorescent) lamps of 1,000 volts or less may occupy a fixture enclosure with the branch-circuit conductors. The branch-circuit conductors are not required to have insulation suited for the high voltage of the secondary wiring (Fig. 310).

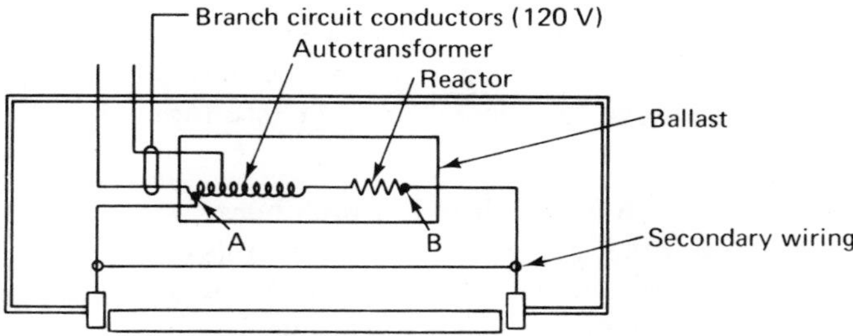

Fig. 310

The general rule does not permit conductors of over 600 volts to occupy the same enclosure with conductors of 600 volts or less. Instant-start (cold cathode) fluorescent lighting fixtures are one of the exceptions to the rule. The autotransformer above produces a voltage of over 600 at points A and B. Normally, the high voltage is present only during the instant of starting. But, if a tube burns out, or if the branch circuit is energized when there is no tube in the fixture, the high voltage will be continuous. The high-voltage secondaries are permitted to be in the same fixture enclosure with the 120-volt conductors [Sect. 300-3(c)].

(d) Primary leads of electric-discharge lamp ballasts, if contained within the individual wiring enclosure, may occupy a fixture enclosure with the branch-circuit conductors.

(e) Excitation, control, relay, and ammeter conductors used in connection with an *individual* motor or starter may occupy the same conduit, raceway, or other enclosure with the motor circuit, regardless of difference in voltage.

300-4. Protection Against Physical Damage

(a) Through Wood Framing Members

When holes must be bored in wooden joists, beams, rafters, or studs for conduit or cable, the Code requires that the holes be bored at the approximate center. Holes drilled at the centerline of a structural member result in the least weakening of the member.

Cables passing through holes in studs must be kept at least $1\frac{1}{4}$ in. from the edge of the stud, or if the stud is not wide enough to allow a $1\frac{1}{4}$ in. distance from the edge, the cable must be protected from nails that might later be driven into the stud. A steel plate placed on the face of each stud over the cable, or a steel bushing can be used at each stud. The plate or bushing is required to have at least a $\frac{1}{16}$-in. thickness. This precaution is required only for cables. Conduit or EMT provide their own protection against driven nails.

Where drilling is not possible and the strength of the member permits, notches may be cut in the edge of a joist, beam, rafter, or stud, and cable laid in the notches. A steel plate at least $\frac{1}{16}$ in. in thickness is required over the cable at each notch. Note that notching is permitted only when cable is used. Notching is not permitted for conduit or EMT (see Fig. 311).

(b) Cables Through Metal Framing Members

When Romex or other nonmetallic sheathed cable passes through holes in metal, either a bushing shall be provided, or the holes shall be so formed that there will be no cutting or abrasion of the cable.

300-5. Underground Installations

(a) Minimum Cover Requirements

Minimum depth for buried cable is 24 in.; for rigid metal conduit, 6 in.; for rigid nonmetallic conduit or other raceway approved for direct burial, 18 in.

There are several exceptions:

1. If a 2-in.-thick pad of concrete is placed over cable or nonmetallic conduit, depth may be reduced to 18 and 12 in., respectively.
2. Where there is heavy vehicular traffic, the minimum depth for any conduit or raceway shall be increased to 24 in.

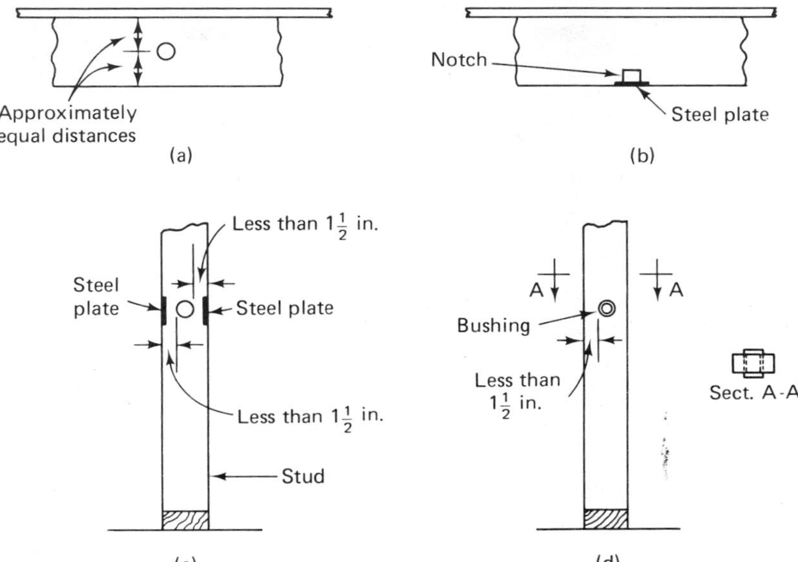

Fig. 311

Cables through wood framing members (Sect. 300-4).

(a) Holes shall be drilled at the approximate center of joists, studs, and rafters.

(b) Where the member has sufficient strength, a notch may be cut in the face of the member. A steel plate must be provided at each notch.

(c)(d) When a hole is less than $1\frac{1}{4}$ in. from the edge of a stud, a steel plate or a bushing must be provided.

3. For residential branch circuits of 300 volts or less, and 30 amps. or less, such as a circuit from house to garage, required depth for cable or nonmetallic conduit may be reduced to 12 in.
4. Lesser depths may be permitted where access to splices or boxes is required.
5. In airport runways and adjacent areas where trespassing is prohibited, depth for cables may be reduced to 18 in.
6. Ducts and raceways in solid rock may be buried at a lesser depth, if covered by at least 2 in. of concrete.
7. Control circuits for irrigation and landscape systems, 30 volts and under, may be buried at a 6 in. depth.

(For conduit or raceway under 4 in. or more of concrete the above minimums do not apply).

(b) Grounding

Underground conduit and the metal sheath of underground cable shall be grounded.

(c) Underground Cables under Buildings

Cables under a building shall be installed in conduit or raceway. The conduit or raceway shall extend under the building and to a suitable distance beyond the building wall.

(d) Protection from Damage

Conductors and cable emerging from the ground shall be protected by conduit or other metal raceway.

Underground conductors or cable that are run up a pole must be protected by rigid metal conduit or PVC Schedule 80, up to a height of at least 8 ft.

Conductors or cable entering a building must be protected by rigid metal conduit or metal raceway. Protection must extend into the ground below the surface.

(e) Splices and Taps

Underground splices or taps may be made without use of a splice box.

(f) Backfill

When backfilling, care should be taken to avoid damage to conduit or cable.

(g) Raceway Seals

If conditions are such that moisture may enter a conduit or raceway, the conduit or raceway shall be sealed.

(h) Bushing

A bushing or seal shall be used where a cable leaves a protecting conduit underground.

(i) Single Conductors

All conductors of a circuit shall either be in the same conduit or raceway or, if single conductor cables are used, they shall be grouped together.

300-6. Protection Against Corrosion

Certain materials, like brass and aluminum, are corrosion-resistant in themselves. Equipment made of such materials does not require a corrosion-resistant coating.

Steel or iron conduit and boxes must be galvanized or cadmium-coated.

Boxes or cabinets marked "Raintight" or "Outdoor Type" may be used outdoors.

Enameled conduit and fittings may not be used outdoors, nor indoors in wet or corrosive locations.

In wet indoor locations, conduit, cable, and fittings must be stooled off the surface at least $\frac{1}{4}$ in.

300-7. Raceways Exposed to Different Temperatures

(a) Sealing

If conduit enters into a cold storage room, there will be a considerable difference in temperature between that section of the conduit inside and that section of the conduit outside the refrigerated space. If the warm air in the section of conduit outside the refrigerated space circulates to the cold section of conduit inside the refrigerated space, moisture in the warm air will condense when it strikes the cold section, resulting in an objectionable accumulation of water inside the conduit. To prevent this, a seal is required in the conduit at the point where it enters the cold space.

(b) Expansion Joints

A run of conduit will expand with high temperatures and contract with cold temperatures. For long runs that are exposed to wide temperature changes, expansion and contraction could result in a damaging strain on connections at the ends of the run. Expansion joints must be placed in such conduit runs. An expansion joint allows movement of the conduit in the joint, relieving the strain on connections.

Application of this rule would be principally for outdoor installations. Indoor installations would not normally be subjected to wide temperature changes. For outdoor installations in some regions of the country, the summer temperature of a conduit run may differ from the winter temperature by as much as 150°F. With such variations in temperature, there could be enough contraction and expansion in a long straight conduit run to require the use of an expansion joint.

Where and when expansion joints are required would be a matter of judgment, and would be subject to the opinion of the "authority having jurisdiction."

300-9. Grounding Metal Enclosures

Conduit, BX sheath, metal raceway, boxes, cabinets, fittings shall be grounded where required by Sections 250-32, 250-33, and 250-42.

300-10. Electrical Continuity of Metal Raceways and Enclosures

If the wiring is metal raceway, such as conduit or metal-covered cable, such as BX, then the conduit or BX sheath must have good metallic contact with boxes, cabinets, etc., and with other sections of conduit, BX sheath so that there is no break in the metallic continuity of the grounding path. Where a metal-sheathed cable or metal conduit enters a metal box or enclosure, the tightened connector or locknut and bushing provides the metallic continuity between the cable sheath or conduit and the box or enclosure.

According to this rule, it would not be permissible to use nonmetallic boxes with metal conduit or BX, because a nonmetallic box would break the "electrical continuity" of the metal raceway.

300-11. Secured in Place

All boxes, cabinets, raceway, cable, fittings shall be "securely fastened in place." Except as provided in Section 370–13, boxes used with conduit must be independently fastened. (If installed in accordance with Section 370-13, *threaded* boxes not over 100 cubic inches in size may be supported by the conduit only.)

Wooden plugs driven into masonry are not permitted as a method of securing equipment in place. Wooden plugs are not considered a reliable footing for the screws. When equipment is to be mounted on masonry, expansion plugs (anchors) should be used.

300-12. Mechanical Continuity—Raceways and Cables

Splices in cables are not permitted.

300-13. Mechanical and Electrical Continuity—Conductors

(a) The Code does not permit splices to be contained within conduit or tubing.

Auxiliary gutters and wireways (which are sheet-metal troughs) may contain splices if the splices are accessible.

(b) When multiwire (three-wire, four-wire) circuits are used to supply a divided load, device terminals may not be used as a connection for a neutral entering and leaving the enclosure. The following example will illustrate the reason for this rule:

Consider a three-wire, 120/240-volt circuit serving receptacles, with the receptacle load divided between the two legs of the circuit. Suppose that the neutral wire entering and the neutral wire leaving one of the receptacle boxes are both attached to the screw terminal on the "device" (receptacle). If the receptacle is later removed, the neutral could be left open. Now, beyond the break, receptacles on one leg would be in series with the receptacles on the other leg, across the 240-volt circuit. If there is an unbalance of load, a higher-than-normal voltage will be impressed on the receptacles with the lesser load in operation. The unbalance in voltage will be proportional to the size of the respective loads connected to the receptacles.

If, say, a load of 500 watts is operating in series with a 1,500-watt load, the voltage across the loads will be in the ratio of 3 to 1. Voltage across the 1,500-watt load would be $\frac{1}{4} \times 240 = 60$ volts, and across the 500 watt load the voltage would be $\frac{3}{4} \times 240 = 180$ volts. 180 volts impressed across 120-volt equipment could damage the equipment, or in the case of incandescent lamps, the lamps could be burned out.

The importance of maintaining an unbroken neutral in a three-wire circuit serving a divided load is apparent from this example. A device terminal may not be used as a means of continuation of the neutral. The ends of the neutral should be joined together in a permanent splice, with a pigtail from the splice to the device terminal. In this way, removal of the device could not break the continuity of the neutral.

Note that the rule applies only for "multiwire" circuits. It does not apply for two-wire circuits. With two-wire circuits, a broken neutral would result only in a dead circuit beyond the break. (See Fig. 313).

300-14. Length of Free Conductors at Outlets and Switch Points

The Code requires at least 6 in. of free conductor at outlets, for making up joints or for connections.

300-15. Boxes or Fittings—Where Required

(a) Box or Fitting

This rule permits splices to be made in condulets, but it should be noted that Section 370-6 stipulates that splices may be made only in condulets with provisions for *three or more* conduit entries (Fig. 314). The general rule is that

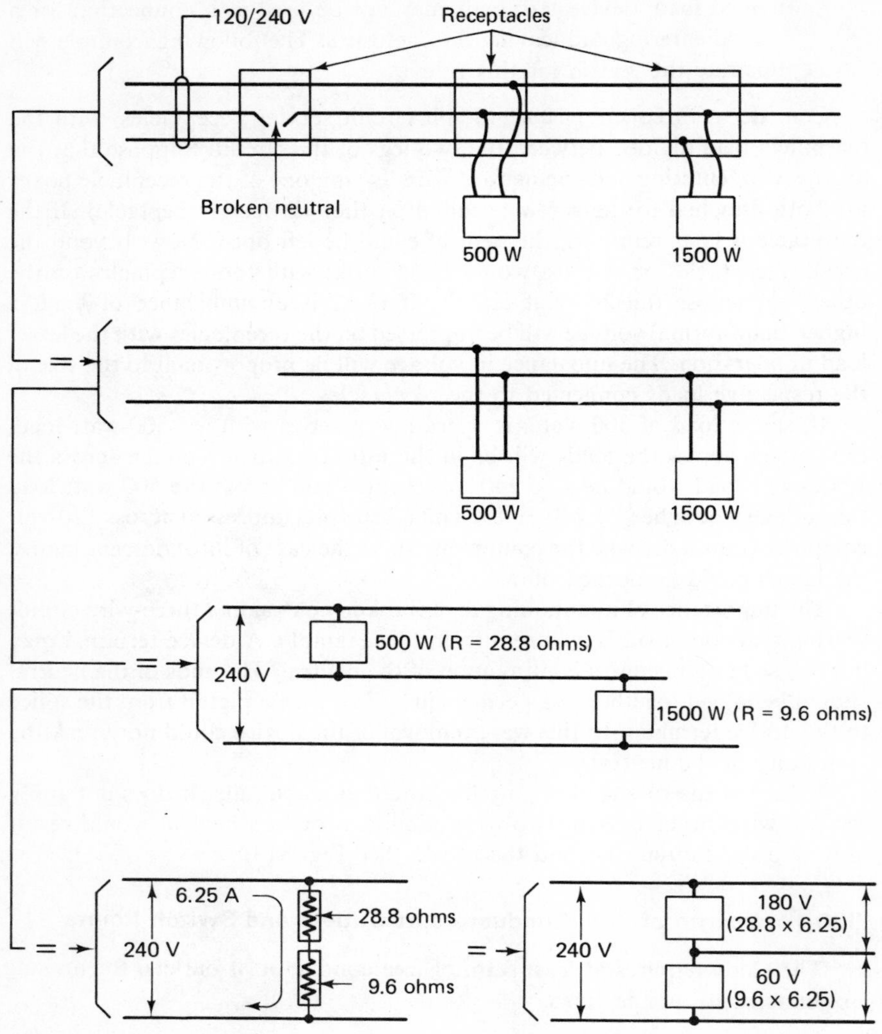

Fig. 313
Illustrating the effect of a broken neutral in a three-wire, 120/240-volt circuit. If the neutral is broken when unequal loads are connected across the two legs of the circuit, a high voltage will be impressed across one load, a low voltage across the other.

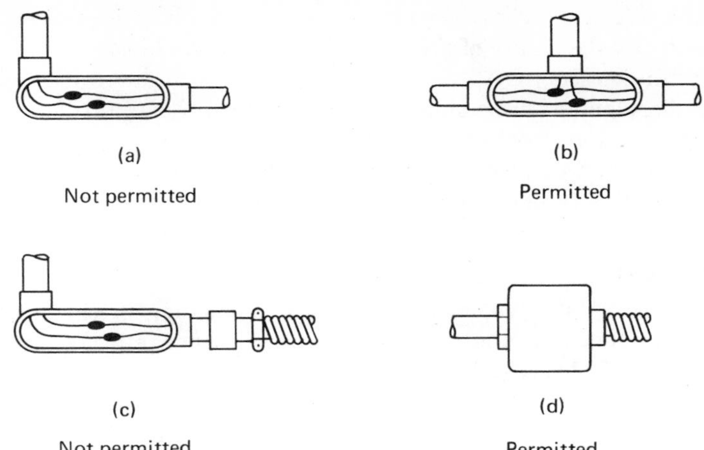

Fig. 314

Boxes or fittings—where required (Sect. 300-15):

(a) Splices may not be made in conduit fittings with two or less entries.
(b) Splices may be made in conduit or EMT fittings with *more than two* conduit entries.
(c) A fitting may *not* be used for changing from conduit or EMT to cable. A box must be used for this purpose (d).

a box *or fitting* must be provided at each junction, splice, outlet, switch point, pull point, and connection point in a run of conduit, tubing, raceway [for *cables,* see (b), following]. There are exceptions that apply for:

1. Surface raceways with removable covers.
2. Wireways with removable covers.
3. Header ducts with removable covers.
4. Multioutlet assemblies.
5. Auxiliary gutters with removable covers.
6. Fixtures approved for end-to-end mounting [see Section 410-31, Exception 2(a)].

Surface raceways, such as Wiremold, are not made for use with boxes. Outlets such as receptacles are mounted directly on the wall, without a box.

Wireways are sheet metal troughs with removable covers. Splices may be made in the trough without the use of a box.

Header ducts are underfloor ducts laid in cement flooring. The header duct carries the feeders to cellular raceway systems in the floor. No box is required if the header has a *removable* cover.

Multioutlet assemblies are metal raceways assembled with built-in receptacle outlets. By the nature of this type of wiring, it would be impossible to use boxes at the outlets.

Auxiliary gutters are similar to wireways. One use of auxiliary gutters is to carry the feeders from the service equipment to individual metered services for the different apartments in an apartment building. Splices may be made in auxiliary gutters without the use of a box, if the gutter has a removable cover.

(b) Box Only

For cables, a box must be provided at each junction, splice, outlet, switch point, pull point. A box is also required where a change is made from cable to conduit or EMT.

Exceptions to these rules are:

1. When bakelite or composition receptacles, switches, and other outlets are used in surface work, they may be mounted directly on the wall with the cable entering through an opening built into the device. No box is needed at the outlet.
2. Rosettes made for mounting directly on the ceiling require no box. The cable enters the rosette through an opening built into the rosette.
3. For Type MI cable, an "approved fitting" rather than a box may be used at a splice point, providing the splice is a "straight through" splice, not a junction point.
4. When conduit or tubing is used only for protection of a cable, no box is required where the cable leaves the conduit or tubing.
5. When Romex is used, a "wiring device" is permitted to be used without a box.

300-16. Raceway or Cable to Open or Concealed Wiring

(a) If a change is made from conduit or cable to open wiring on insulators, the conduit or cable must be brought into a box, and the open wiring must leave the box through a separate hole for each wire. Or, when conduit is used, a fitting similar in construction to a service entrance head may be used. Such fittings allow the wires to come straight out from bushed holes in the end of the fitting. Splices are not permitted in a fitting of this kind. Conductors must pass straight through (see Fig. 315).

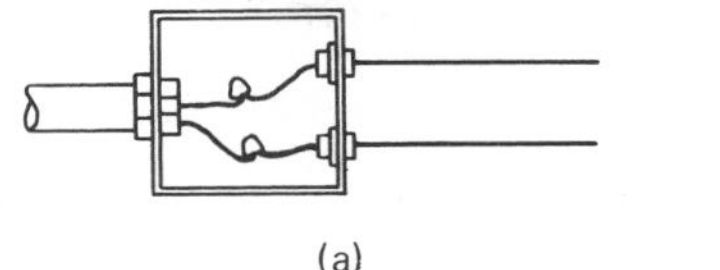

(a)

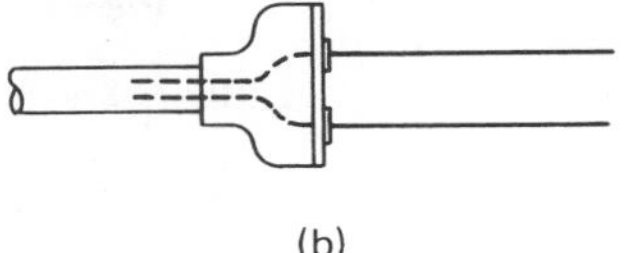

(b)

Fig. 315

Change from conduit to open wiring [Sect. 300-16(a)].

(a) Box with bushed holes.

(b) Fitting with bushed holes. When a fitting is used, the wires must pass straight through. Splicing is not permitted within the fitting.

(b) Where conduit or EMT terminates behind an *open* switchboard or *unenclosed* control equipment, a box is not required, but a bushing must be provided where the conductors leave the conduit or EMT. The bushing must be an insulating type, except that for leaded conductors a noninsulating-type bushing is permitted.

300-17. Number and Size of Conductors in Raceway

The number of conductors in conduit, tubing, or other raceway should be limited to a number that will permit pulling in or removing the wires without damage to the insulation.

The number of conductors should also be limited to a number that will allow proper dissipation of heat. Too many conductors in a raceway will result in the inside conductors reaching an excessive temperature that could damage the insulation.

The maximum number of conductors permitted in conduit or tubing of different sizes has been compiled in table form, and can be read from Tables 3A, 3B, and 3C, pp. 70-579 to 70-581 of the Code. These tables are used when the conductors are all the same size.

If the conductors are of different sizes, the number permitted must be calculated. Table 4, p. 70-582 would be used, together with Table 5, p. 70-583.

Example.

What minimum-size rigid metal conduit is required for (3) No. 4 and (3) No. 1/0 Type T conductors?

First, figure total cross-sectional area of all conductors. From Table 5, p. 70-583, the cross-sectional area of a No. 4Type T is .1087 sq. in. (Column 5).

$$3 \times .1087 = .3261 \text{ sq. in., area of 3 conductors}$$

Cross-sectional area of a No. 1/0 is .2367 sq. in. (Column 5).

$$3 \times .2367 = .7101 \text{ sq. in., area of 3 conductors}$$

$$.3261 + .7101 = 1.0362 \text{ sq. in., total area of all conductors}$$

Turn to Table 4, p. 70-582. Under the column headed "Over 2 Cond. 40%," run down this column to 1.0362, or the nearest figure above 1.0362. This would be 1.34. Moving to the left under "Trade Size," a 2-in. conduit would be required.

300-18. Inserting Conductors in Raceways

The rules of this Section can be summed up as follows:

1. No conductors shall be installed until raceway installation is complete. (Exception: raceways with removable cover or capping, such as surface metal raceways, or busways.)
2. Where possible, conductors shall not be placed in raceways until all mechanical work on the building that may damage conductors is completed.
3. Where possible, conductors shall not be placed in raceway while exposed to the weather.
4. Pull wires are not to be put in the raceway before the raceway installation is complete.
5. Grease or cleaning agents shall not be used as a lubricant for pulling in wires. Graphite or talc should be used for this purpose.

300-19. Supporting Conductors in Vertical Raceways

If a long wire is suspended in the air from a support above, the weight of the wire will impose a strain on the support and on the wire itself at the upper end.

The purpose of this Section is to specify supports that are capable of carrying the weight of wire in vertical installations and also to limit the length of wire hanging free, thereby limiting the strain on the wire itself. Three methods of support are recommended:

1. When conduit is used, insulating wedges can be inserted in the top end of the conduit. The weight below squeezes the wire between the insulating wedges, thus securing the conductors.

2. The wires may be secured to insulators in a box.

3. A right-angle bend of the wires in a vertical run, with the wires tied to insulators with tie wires, is approved as a support.

Figure 316 illustrates the three approved methods of support.

Vertical supports may be spaced no further apart than the distances listed in Table 300-19(a) of the Code, when method 1 or 2 is used. For method 3, spacing is limited to 20% of the spacings listed in the table.

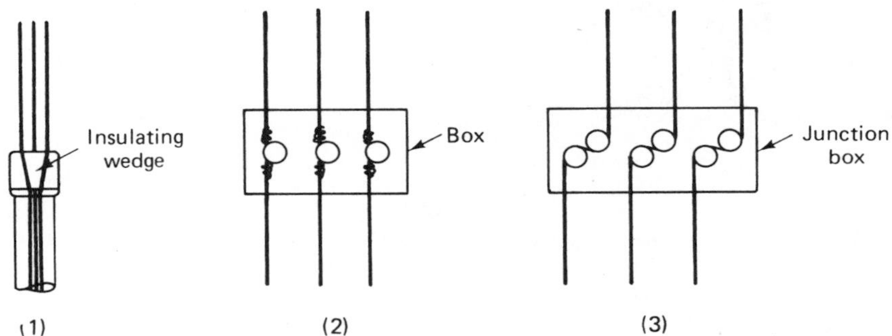

Fig. 316

Approved methods of supporting long vertical runs (Sect. 300-19).

(1) Clamping devices. The conductors are held by the tapered wedges owing to the squeezing action resulting from the conductor weight.

(2) Box with insulating supports. The conductors are fastened to the insulators by tie wire or other means. A cover must be provided for the box.

(3) Conductors deflected at least 90 degrees in a junction box. This method is also suitable for support of cables. When this method is used, the length of run that can be supported is limited to 20 percent of that permitted for methods (1) and (2).

Method (1) is particularly adapted to conduit. Methods (2) and (3) are better adapted to other forms of raceway, but may also be used for conduit runs.

300-20. Induced Currents in Metal Enclosures or Metal Raceways

Alternating current flowing in a conductor sets up a varying magnetic field around the conductor. The magnetic field sets up induced currents in surrounding metal, like conduit. If all conductors of a circuit are grouped together in the same conduit, the field set up by one conductor will neutralize that of the other(s) since the currents are at all times in opposite directions. There will be no magnetic field and, consequently, no induced currents in the conduit.

If only one leg of an AC circuit is contained in a conduit, there will be no opposite field to neutralize its field, and the resulting current set up in the metal conduit could be of sufficient magnitude to raise the temperature of the conduit to an objectionable point. The Code requires that, when AC conductors are run in metal conduit or raceway, all conductors of a circuit shall be grouped together in the same raceway (Fig. 317). (For nonmetallic conduit the rule does not apply, since induced currents cannot be set up in nonconducting material; conductors may be grouped or run single.)

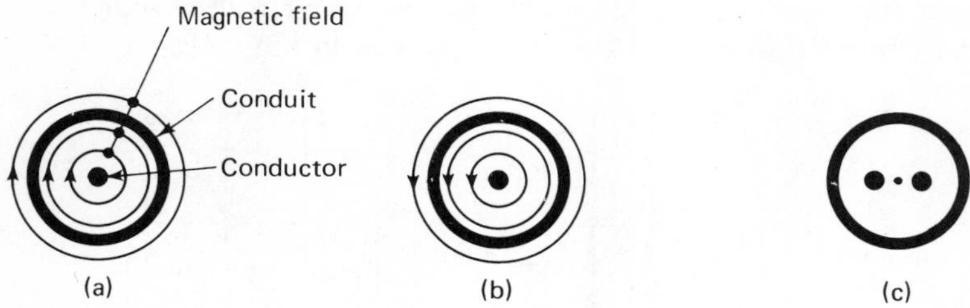

Fig. 317

Induced currents in metal conduit (Sect. 300-20). If the conductors of an AC circuit are run in separate metal conduits, as in (a) and (b), there will be a magnetic field surrounding each conductor. The magnetic field will cause a current to flow in the wall of the conduits. When both legs of the circuit are brought together, as in (c), the magnetic field set up by one conductor neutralizes that of the other. No magnetic field is present to set up a current in the conduit.

Where a single AC conductor passes through a separate hole in the steel wall of a box or enclosure, heating of the steel will result due to *hysteresis.* To avoid heating, all conductors of a circuit should if possible be grouped together, and enter through one bushing. Or, if it is necessary for each conductor to enter through an individual hole, heating can be avoided by cutting slots in the metal between the individual holes. The slots will break the magnetic path in the steel (Fig. 318). It should be noted that enclosures made of nonferrous metals (aluminum, brass, bronze) require no slots when individual conductors pass through individual holes. Nonferrous metals are subject to induced currents but are *not* subject to *hysteresis.*

DC does not cause induced currents or hysteresis, and the precautions necessary when dealing with AC do not apply to DC circuits.

300-21. Prevention of Fire Spread

When holes are made in fire-resistant walls, partitions, ceilings, the fire resistance is destroyed. When a hole must be made for a cable to pass through, space around the cable must be plugged with a fire-resistant material, such as asbestos powder paste.

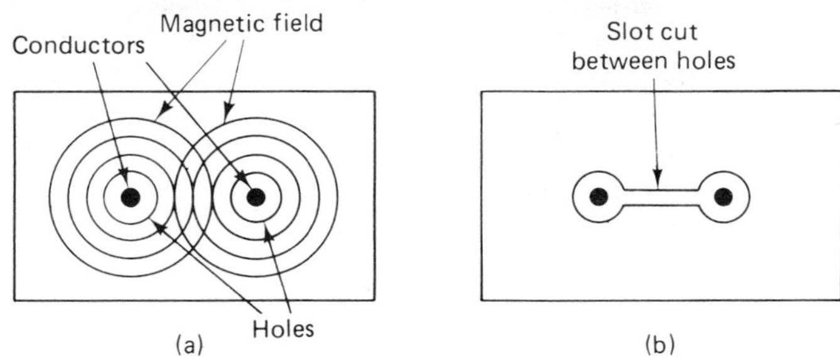

Fig. 318

(a) When a single conductor carrying alternating current passes through an individual hole in a steel enclosure, a magnetic field is set up in the enclosure wall. The varying field causes heating of the steel, due to hysteresis.

(b) Cutting a slot in the metal will break the magnetic path, eliminating the heating effect (Sect. 300-20).

300-22. Wiring in Ducts, Plenums, and Other Air-Handling Spaces

(a) Wiring may not be installed in ducts handling dust, loose stock, flammable vapors. Wiring may not be installed in ducts used with commercial cooking units.

(b) Ducts or Plenums Used for Environmental Air

Wiring of the following types may be present in air-conditioning or heating ducts:

1. Type MI (mineral-insulated) cable.
2. Rigid metal conduit.
3. Intermediate metal conduit.
4. EMT.
5. Type MC cable.

Greenfield and liquidtight flexible metal conduit may be installed in lengths not over 4 ft, where flexibility is required.

The only electrical equipment permitted in ducts or plenums are thermostats and other control equipment necessary to operation of the vent system, and lighting fixtures necessary for servicing of the control equipment. Such fixtures, if installed, shall be enclosed, gasketed-type fixtures.

(c) Hollow Spaces Used as Ducts or Plenums for Environmental Air

An example of the hollow spaces referred to would be the space above a ceiling or false ceiling that is used as an air duct. The following types of wiring are permitted:

1. Type MI cable.
2. Rigid metal conduit.
3. Intermediate metal conduit.
4. Metal surface raceway.
5. Liquidtight flexible metal conduit.
6. Greenfield.
7. BX.
8. EMT.

Liquidtight flexible metal conduit is permitted in lengths of 6 ft or less.

Lighting fixtures and other electrical equipment are permitted in these spaces.

(d) Wiring used for data-processing systems, and located within air-handling areas created by raised floors, shall conform to Article 645.

B. Requirements for Over 600 Volts, Nominal

300-31. Covers Required

Suitable covers shall be installed on all boxes, fittings, and enclosures.

300-32. Conductors of Different Systems

Over-600-volt conductors may not be in the same raceway or enclosure with conductors of 600 volts or less, except:

1. For motor, switchgear, and control assemblies.
2. In manholes.

300-33. Inserting Conductors in Raceways

Same requirements apply as for conductors of 600 volts or less. See Section 300-18.

300-34. Conductor Bending Radius

Conductors may not be bent to a radius of less than 8 times overall diameter.

Shielded or lead-covered conductors may not be bent to a radius of less than 12 times overall diameter.

300-35. Protection Against Induction Heating

AC circuits in metal ducts could cause circulating currents in the wall of the duct. Induced heating of the ducts can be avoided by grouping all conductors of a circuit together in the same conduit or cable, or binding single conductor cables together in circuit groups.

300-36. Grounding

All wiring and equipment shall be grounded in accordance with Article 250.

ARTICLE 305 — TEMPORARY WIRING

A. 600 Volts Nominal or Less

305-1. Scope

This Article of the Code is intended to apply to temporary wiring necessary on construction sites, for example, or wiring for a carnival. The rules do not apply for any wiring that is intended to remain for a period of over 90 days.

305-2. General

1. The regular rules for services, as given in Article 230, must be followed for temporary wiring.
2. Feeders for temporary wiring may be in the form of cord or cable, or if not subject to mechanical injury may be open wiring on insulators.
3. Branch circuits may be cable or cord or open wiring. Branch circuits shall originate in a power outlet or panelboard.

   When run as open wiring for receptacles or "fixed" equipment, a separate grounding wire must be run with the circuit wires.

4. All receptacles must be grounding-type receptacles, grounded back to the service equipment and service grounding electrode.
5. Bare conductors are not permitted. Earth returns are not permitted.
6. When cable is used for feeders or branch circuits, the plug may serve as a disconnect.
7. Lamps less than 7 ft above ground must be fitted with suitable guards.
8. A box is not required for splices in multiconductor cord or cable. [For splicing requirements see Sections 110–14(b) and 400–9.]

305-3. Grounding

The rules of Article 250 must be complied with.

B. Over 600 Volts, Nominal

Temporary wiring over 600 volts is permitted during periods of construction, tests, experiments, emergency. Suitable fences or barriers must be provided to prevent access of unauthorized persons. Wiring shall be removed immediately after serving its purpose. Equipment shall be grounded as required by Section 250-42.

ARTICLE 310 — CONDUCTORS FOR GENERAL WIRING

A. General

310-1. Scope

The insulation of conductors should be suitable for the conditions of use. Conditions such as temperature, exposure to moisture, or exposure to oil, gasoline, or corrosive fumes would be factors affecting choice of insulation.

310-2. Conductors to Be Insulated

Generally, conductors must be insulated.

Exceptions allowing uninsulated conductors to be used are:

1. For services, the neutral may be a bare wire [Section 230-40(a)].
2. A grounding electrode conductor may be bare [Section 250-91(a)]. The grounding electrode conductor is the conductor from the service cabinet to the water pipe or other electrode.
3. For grounding the metal enclosures of equipment, a bare wire may be used [Section 250-91(b)].

310-3. Stranded Conductors

Conductors No. 8 and larger, if installed in raceways, must be the stranded type. Smaller sizes may be the solid type. Sizes No. 8 and larger, if solid, would be too stiff for pulling in, and damage might result to the conductor insulation. Solid conductors of any size may be used in knob and tube work.

310-4. Conductors in Parallel

Conductors smaller than No. 1/0 may not be run in parallel, except for elevator lighting (Section 620-12 of the Code). No. 1/0 and larger sizes, if run in parallel, must conform to the following rules:

1. All conductors must be the same size. That is, a No. 1/0 could not be run in parallel with a No. 2/0. Two or more No. 1/0 could be run in parallel, or two or more No. 2/0, but not a 1/0 and 2/0 together.
2. All conductors must be the same length. This rule, as well as (1) above, is to ensure that the resistance in each path for the current is the same.
3. Insulation must be the same type. A Type RH insulated wire may not be run in parallel with a Type T insulated wire, for example.
4. All conductors must be of the same material. Copper conductors may not be run in parallel with aluminum conductors.
5. Paralleled conductors must be attached to the same solid connection at the terminals.

310-5. Minimum Size of Conductors

Minimum size for conductors is No. 14 copper, No. 12 aluminum, except:

1. Flexible cords may be No. 18 (Section 400-12).
2. Fixture wire may be No. 18 (Section 410-23).

3. For wiring to a fractional horsepower motor, if the junction box for the motor is 6 ft or less removed from the motor, conductors as small as No. 18 may be run from the box to the motor in Greenfield (see Sections 430-22 and 430-145).

4. Crane and hoist control circuit conductors may be No. 16 (Section 610-14 of the Code).

5. Conductors for elevator control and signal circuits may be No. 20 minimum (Section 620-12 of the Code).

6. Conductors for remote-control and signal circuits may be No. 18 minimum (Section 725-16 of the Code).

7. Conductors for fire-protective signaling circuits may be smaller than No. 14 (Sections 760-16 and 760-30 of the Code).

310-6. Underground Conductors

Cables that are to be run underground must be a type made for that purpose. Type USE (underground service entrance) cable and Type UF (underground feeder) cable are approved for direct burial in earth. These types may be laid directly in a trench and covered with earth; no protection is needed if the cables are buried at a depth of 18 in. or more.

310-7. Wet Locations

There are other locations, besides those exposed to the weather, that must be considered "wet locations." Conductors installed underground in concrete slabs or other masonry are considered to be in a wet location. Some inside locations, such as car-wash areas, are wet locations. Where condensation is expected within a raceway, this must be considered a "wet" location.

In such locations, conductor insulation must be either suitable for "wet locations" or lead-covered. If lead-covered, the insulation need not be suitable for wet locations.

310-8. Corrosive Conditions

Conductor insulation directly exposed to oil, grease, or gasoline must be a special type. Suitable insulation types are listed by Underwriters Laboratories, including a nylon-jacketed Type TW suitable for locations exposed to gasoline. Lead-covered conductors are approved for locations exposed to oil, grease, gasoline, or fumes. When the conductors are lead-covered, no special insulation is required.

310-9. Temperature Limitation of Conductors

"No conductor shall be used under such conditions that its *operating* temperature will exceed that specified for the type of insulation involved."

Table 310-13 of the Code lists maximum operating temperatures for different conductor types. A Type T, for example, has a maximum operating temperature of 140°F. Operating temperature is the temperature of the conductor *when carrying current.* A Type T used in a 140°F temperature would exceed the 140°F limit when carrying current owing to the heating effect of the current. The maximum *room* temperatures would have to be lower than 140°F in order to keep the *operating* temperature within the 140° limit.

310-10. Conductor Identification

(a) Grounded Conductors

Insulated conductors used as a grounded neutral are required to have a white or natural gray color, for sizes No. 6 and smaller.

Exceptions:

The neutral of varnished cloth cables, fixture wires, Type MI (mineral insulated) cables need not have a white or natural gray color.

Insulated neutral conductors No. 4 and larger need not be white or natural gray, but if not they must be painted or colored white at all boxes, terminals and outlets. (See also Section 200-6.)

(b) Grounding Conductors

A *grounding* conductor is a conductor used to ground metal equipment. This should not be confused with the *grounded* conductor, which is the neutral. Insulated conductors used as grounding conductors are required to have either a solid green color or green with yellow stripes for sizes No. 6 and smaller. For No. 4 and larger, grounding conductors need not be green in color, but if not, either (1) the insulation must be colored green at every box or outlet, or (2) all the insulation must be removed at every box or outlet.

(c) Ungrounded Conductor

Ungrounded conductors (the hot wires) may be any color other than green, white, or natural gray.

310-11. Marking

Conductors and cable must be marked by the manufacturer to show:

Maximum voltage and AWG size.

Type letter of the insulation: T, RH, etc.

Manufacturer's name or trademark.

The marking may be on the wire or cable, with marking every 24 in. or less, or the marking may be on a tag attached to the coil or reel.

For certain types of metal-covered cable (including BX, Type MC) the marking may be on a marker tape within the cable.

For cords and cables, a type letter showing whether the conductors of the cord or cable are laid parallel or twisted together must be included. D indicates two conductors laid parallel. M indicates two or more conductors twisted together.

310-12. Conductor Application

310-13. Conductor Construction

Table 310-13 of the Code lists the different types of insulated conductors used for general wiring. The conductors listed may be used for any voltage up to and including 600 volts, but not above.

Some conductor types are suitable for both wet and dry locations. Others are suitable only for dry locations. Conductors listed as suitable for "Dry Locations" may not be used in damp or wet places.

The "Max. Operating Temp." (maximum operating temperature) is listed for each conductor type. The maximum operating temperature is the temperature of the conductor *when carrying current. Room temperature* would have to be lower than the listed Max. Operating Temp., in order to offset the heating effect of the current.

It should be noted that when a conductor is used in a location having a temperature above 86°F, the allowable carrying capacity is reduced. Refer to Table 310-16, p. 70-132 of the Code. Take as an example a No. 12 Type T conductor used in a 103°F location. For Type T conductors the maximum operating temperature is 140°F (first column, top of page). The "correction factors" table below shows that, for 140°F conductors used in temperatures between 86° and 104°F, the correction factor is .82. (First listing below the 140°F column above.)

A No. 12 Type T has a normal ampacity of 20 amps., but in a temperature of 103°F, the ampacity is reduced to $.82 \times 20$, or 16.4 amps. This is the maximum load that may be put on a No. 12 Type T in a 103°F temperature.

For temperatures between 105° and 122°F, the correction factor is .58, which would limit the ampacity of a No. 12 Type T to $.58 \times 20 = 11.6$ amps. Although Code rules permit a Type T to be used, it would be advisable in such high temperatures to use instead a higher-temperature conductor, like a Type RHH. For a Type RHH (a 194°F type) the ampacity would be reduced only to 82% of normal ampacity, as is shown by the table.

"Type Letters" of Table 310-13 would be interpreted as follows:

R: rubber.

L: lead-covered.

H: heat-resistant.

T: thermoplastic.

C: cotton.

A: asbestos.

S: silicone rubber.

RU: latex rubber.

W: moisture-resistant.

MI: mineral insulated.

V: varnished cambric.

Thus, a Type TW wire would be one with a thermoplastic and moisture-resistant insulation; a Type RUH would be a wire with a latex-rubber, heat-resistant insulation; etc.

ARTICLE 318 — CABLE TRAYS

318-1. Scope

318-2. Uses Permitted

Cable trays are used where there are a number of cables in one run. A tray is a runway consisting of steel or aluminum members used to support the cable run (Fig. 319). The cables are carried on racks, troughs, or hangers incorporated in the tray. There may be several tiers of cable, one above the other.

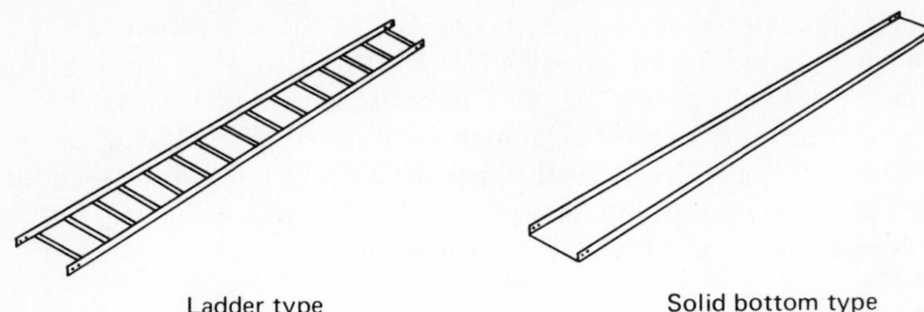

Fig. 319
Cable trays. Sections are end-bolted together to form a run of the desired length. Curved sections are available for making turns.

Such cable trays may be used for the following types of cables:

1. Mineral insulated, metal sheathed (Type MI).
2. Metal clad (Type MC).
3. Armored cable (BX).
4. Nonmetallic-sheathed (Romex).
5. Service-entrance cable (Type SE and USE).
6. Underground feeder cable (Type UF).
7. Shielded nonmetallic (Type SNM).
8. Power and control tray cable (Type TC).
9. Power-limited tray cable.

Conduit or other raceway may also be run in cable trays.

In industrial establishments, 250 MCM or larger single conductors, and Type MV cable may be installed in ladder type or ventilated through cable trays, but only where it is assured that qualified people will service the installation.

318-3. Uses Not Permitted

Cable trays may not be used in hoistways.

318-4. Construction Specifications

Cable trays must be sturdily constructed, and have no sharp edges that might damage cable covering.

318-5. Installation

The entire cable support must be complete before pulling in the cables.

In locations subject to possible damage to the cables, suitable protection must be provided. If separation of the cables is necessary, because of differences in voltage or for other reasons, a partition must be provided.

Cable trays must be exposed and accessible.

Sufficient space must be provided alongside the structure and between tiers to permit access to the cables for installation and maintenance. A spacing of at least 12 in. is desirable between tiers.

318-6. Grounding

The cable support must have good metallic connection between parts, and the entire structure must be grounded.

The minimum-sized steel or aluminum cable permitted for use in the different cable trays is listed in Table 318-6(b)(2) of the Code (p.70–156).

318-7. Cable Installation

(a) Splices may be made in cable trays.

(b) In horizontal runs, the cables need not be fastened. In vertical or sloping runs, the cables must be strapped or otherwise fastened.

(c) A box is not required where cables are installed in bushed conduit used for protection or support.

(d) When conductors are installed in parallel, they shall be run in two or more groups, each group consisting of a complete circuit. To illustrate, if a three-wire, three-phase circuit is run in parallel with two single conductor cables per leg, the six single-conductor cables must be grouped ABC, ABC, each group including all three phase-conductors of the circuit.

Single-conductor cables must be bound together in circuit groups.

318-8. Number of Multiple-Conductor Cables in Cable Trays (Cables Rated 2,000 Volts or Less)

For ladder or ventilated trough trays:

1. Where all cables are No. 4/0 or larger, total diameter of cables shall not exceed the cable tray width.

2. Where all cables are smaller than No. 4/0 use Table 318-8 of the Code, Column 1.

3. Where there is a mixture of No. 4/0, or larger, and smaller than No. 4/0 cables, use Table 318-8, Column 2.

4. For a tray having a usable inside depth of 6 in. or less, and containing only control and/or signal cables, the sum of the cross-sectional areas of cables shall not exceed 50% of the cross-sectional area of the tray.

For solid-bottom trays:

1. Where all cables are No. 4/0 or larger, total diameter of all cables shall not exceed 90% of cable tray width. Cables shall be installed in a single layer.

2. Where all cables are smaller than No. 4/0, use Table 318-8, Column 3.

3. Where there is a mixture of No. 4/0, or larger, and smaller than 4/0 cables, use Table 318-8, Column 4.

4. For a tray having a usable inside depth of 6 in. or less, and containing only control and/or signal cables, the sum of the cross-sectional areas of cables shall not exceed 40% of the cross-sectional area of the tray.

For ventilated channel-type trays:

The sum of the cross-sectional areas of all cables shall not exceed 1.3 square inches for 3-in. wide trays, or 2.5 square inches for 4-in. wide trays.

318-9. Number of Single Conductor Cables in Cable Trays (Cables Rated 2,000 Volts or Less)

For ladder or ventilated trough trays:

1. Where all cables are 1,000 MCM or larger, total diameter of all cables shall not exceed the cable tray width.

2. Where all cables are smaller than 1,000 MCM, refer to Table 318-9 of the Code, Column 1.

3. Where 4-in.-wide, ventilated, channel-type trays contain single-conductor cables, total diameter of cables shall not exceed the channel width.

318-10. Ampacity of Cables in Cable Trays

(a) Multiconductor Cables

The ampacity of cables with two or more conductors is given in Table 310-16 and 310-18 of the Code.

The tables apply when cables in the tray are without a cover. If the tray is covered (for more than 6 ft), ampacities must be reduced to 95% of that given in the tables.

(b) Single-Conductor Cables

1. **600 MCM and Larger**
   Use Tables 310-17 and 310-19. Ampacities are limited to 75% of ampacities given in the tables. If cables are covered (for 6 ft or more), reduce ampacities to 70% of that given in the tables.
2. **250 MCM Through 500 MCM**
   Ampacity for uncovered cables is limited to 65% of that given in Tables 310-17 and 310-19. If cables are covered (for 6 ft or more), ampacities are limited to 60% of that given in the tables.

When single conductors are separated by at least one cable diameter, Tables 310-17 and 310-19 may be used without restriction for both covered and uncovered cables. (This applies for 250 MCM and larger cables.)

318-11. Number of Type MV and Type MC Cables in Cable Trays (Cables rated over 2000 volts)

The sum of the diameters shall not exceed the cable tray width. They may not be stacked. They must be installed in single layers.

Type MV cable is permitted to be installed in cable trays only if the cable is approved for cable tray installation (See Article 326).

318-12. Ampacity of Type MV and Type MC Cables in Cable Trays (Cables rated over 2000 volts)

(a) Multiconductor Cables

For copper conductors refer to Tables 310-45, p. 70-144 of the Code; Table 310-46 for aluminum conductors. The tables are for uncovered cables. If cables are covered (for more than 6 ft) ampacities must be reduced to 95% of ampacities shown in the tables.

(b) Single Conductor Cables

For copper conductors refer to Table 310-39 of the Code; Table 310-40 for aluminum conductors. The tables apply for cables installed in a single layer, with spacing of at least one cable diameter between cables.

If there is no spacing, ampacities for uncovered cables 250 MCM and larger must be reduced to 75% of the ampacities shown in the tables.

If there is no spacing, and cables are covered (for more than 6 ft), the ampacities, for cables 250 MCM and larger, must be reduced to 70% of the ampacities shown in the table.

ARTICLE 320 — OPEN WIRING ON INSULATORS

320-1. Definition

Open wiring on insulators is a method of wiring that consists of single insulated wire attached to insulators, such as glass insulators or porcelain knobs or cleats. Split porcelain knobs, having a nail assembled with the two pieces of the knob, are available for No. 14 or No. 12 wire. Split cleats are also available. Split knobs and split cleats require no tie wire for fastening the wire, the conductor being gripped between the two pieces of the knob or cleat when the nail or screw is driven into place.

For solid knobs, it is necessary to fasten the conductor to the knob with a "tie wire." This would be a short piece of insulated wire wrapped around the conductor and knob, then "served up" around the conductor on each side of the knob.

320-2. Other Articles

Open wiring on insulators must conform to Articles 225 and 300. Not all the rules of Article 300 would be applicable to open wiring on insulators. Rules that would apply are:

Section 300-2 Voltage Limitations.

Section 300-4 Protection Against Physical Damage.

Section 300-6 Protection Against Corrosion.

Section 300-9 Grounding Metal Enclosures.

Section 300-14 Length of Free Conductors at Outlets and Switch Points.

320-3. Uses Permitted

Use of open wiring on insulators is limited to agricultural or industrial establishments for circuits of 600 volts or less.

Open wiring on insulators may be used:

1. Inside and exposed.
2. Outside and exposed.
3. In wet as well as dry locations.
4. In spaces having corrosive vapors.
5. For services.

Open wiring on insulators is *not* permitted in:

1. Commercial garages.
2. Theaters.
3. Motion-picture studios.
4. Hoistways.
5. Hazardous locations (except as follows).

There is one type of "hazardous location" in which open wiring on insulators may be used. This is a Class III, Division 2 hazardous location. Such a location is a location in which "easily ignitible fibers" are stored. "Easily ignitible fibers" would include rayon, cotton, jute, hemp, cocoa fiber, oakum, excelsior, and similar materials. This is the only type of "hazardous" location in which open wiring on insulators is permitted [see Section 503-3(b)].

320-5. Conductors

The type of conductor used must be suitable for the location and conditions of use. Table 310-13 of Article 310 lists the different types of conductors and specifies whether for use in dry or wet locations, also maximum operating temperature. Certain types may not be used for general wiring, and therefore are not permitted under any circumstances for use in open wiring on insulators. Those not permitted would include types TA, A, AA, AI, and AIA.

Current-carrying capacities for the different types and sizes of copper conductors are listed in Table 310-17, p. 70-133. This table is for conductors in free air, which applies for open wiring on insulators.

320-6. Conductor Supports

"Conductors shall be rigidly supported on noncombustible, nonabsorbent insulating materials." A "noncombustible, nonabsorptive" insulating material is one that will not burn, that will not absorb moisture, and is a nonconductor. Glass is an example of such a material.

Where a tap or splice is made, a knob or cleat must be placed in each conductor meeting at the tap or splice at a distance of not more than 6 in. from the junction.

A knob or cleat must be placed within 12 in. of a lampholder, receptacle, or rosette.

Supports (knobs or cleats) must be spaced not more than $4\frac{1}{2}$ ft apart.

Exception.

Conductors No. 8 and larger may be installed in spans of up to 15 ft, provided that spacers are placed in the span at $4\frac{1}{2}$-ft maximum intervals to maintain a separation of at least $2\frac{1}{2}$ in. between conductors.

An exception to the general rule of $4\frac{1}{2}$ ft between supports is also made for wiring in buildings of "mill construction." The mill-type of construction is used for buildings such as warehouses and mills. It differs from ordinary construction in that, instead of floor joists being spaced 16 in. apart, heavy timbers are used, spaced usually 8 to 12 ft apart.

In buildings of this type spacers are not required. Knobs or other insulators are required only at each timber, providing the wire size is at least No. 8, and the wires are "out of the way" of possible disturbance and separated at least 6 in.

320-7. Mounting of Conductor Supports

Nails for nailing knobs must be not smaller than 10-penny. (A 10-penny nail is 3 in. long.)

Nails for nailing cleats must be long enough to penetrate the wood to a depth equal to at least the thickness of the cleat. Thus, for a cleat of standard $1\frac{1}{8}$-in. height, a nail long enough to penetrate the wood at least $1\frac{1}{8}$ in. is required. An 8-penny nail ($2\frac{1}{2}$ in. long) would meet this requirement.

When screws are used for fastening cleats, they also must be long enough to penetrate the wood to a depth equal to at least the thickness of the cleat. For fastening knobs, the screw must be long enough to penetrate the wood to a depth equal to at least one-half the height of the knob (see Figure 320).

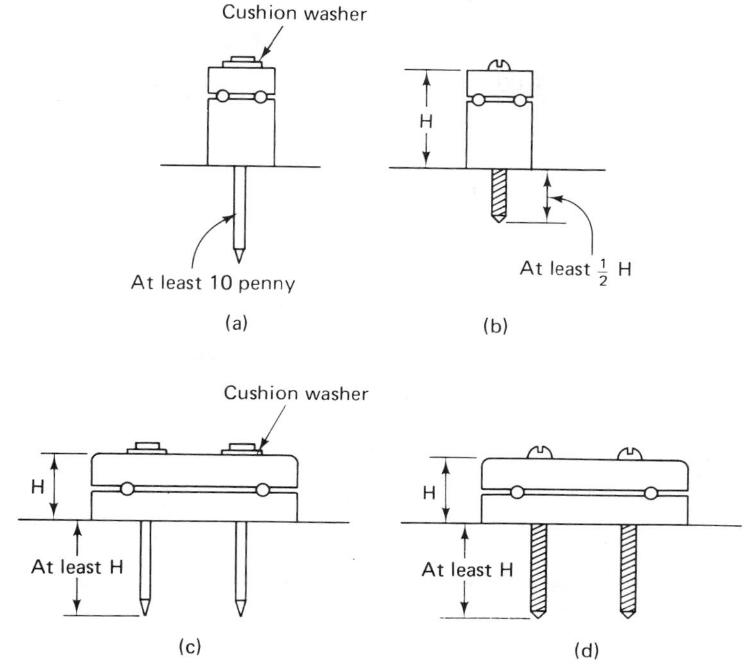

Fig. 320

Mounting of conductor supports (Sect. 320-7).

(a) Nails for fastening knobs shall be not smaller than 10-penny.

(b) Screws for fastening knobs must be long enough to penetrate the wood to a depth of at least $\frac{1}{2}$ height of the knob.

(c)(d) Nails or screws for mounting cleats must be long enough to penetrate the wood to a depth of at least the height of the cleat.

Cushion washers are required with nails.

320-8. Tie Wires

Knobs for conductors smaller than No. 10 would usually be split-type knobs.

For conductors No. 10 and larger, it may be preferable to use a solid knob instead of a split knob. The conductors are secured to solid knobs by means of tie wire. This rule requires that the tie wire have insulation "equivalent to the conductor." The tie wire could be a short length of the same wire that is used for the circuit conductor.

320-10. Flexible Nonmetallic Tubing

This is an exception to the rule of Section 320-6, which requires insulators to be used for supporting the conductors.

In some locations it may be difficult to install knobs or cleats. In such cases, and in dry locations only, the conductors may be encased in flexible tubing, such as loom, and strapped directly to the surface without the use of knobs, cleats, or other insulators.

This kind of installation is limited to 15 ft of continuous length. There may be more than one 15-ft length in a wiring system, but no one continuous length may be more than 15 ft long.

320-11. Through Walls, Floors, Wood Cross Members, Etc.

Porcelain tubes are the most common example of tubes of "noncombustible, nonabsorptive" insulating material. These are used for passing through timbers, walls, floors, partitions, etc. Each conductor must have an individual tube.

There are cases where a tube is not long enough to reach completely through a timber or wall. In this case a waterproof sleeve may be inserted into the hole, and two porcelain tubes used, one inserted into the hole from each side. The sleeve must be of noninductive material.

"Noninductive" material is material that will not carry induced currents. Sleeves made of hard rubber or fiber would be acceptable. Steel sleeves would not be permitted.

See Fig. 321.

320-12. Clearance From Piping, Exposed Conductors, Etc.

Minimum clearance from other conductors or from any kind of metal, including pipes, is 2 in. unless the conductors are protected by an insulating sleeve. If a 2-in. separation cannot be obtained, a sleeve in the form of a porcelain tube could be slipped over the conductor where it passes a pipe or another conductor. The tube should be taped to the conductor to hold it in place (see Fig. 322).

320-13. Entering Spaces Subject to Dampness, Wetness, or Corrosive Vapors

A drip loop is required in wires that enter a building from the outside or where wires enter a damp or wet location, such as a refrigerated space. The drip loop would be made on the outside of the building or inside the refrigerated space.

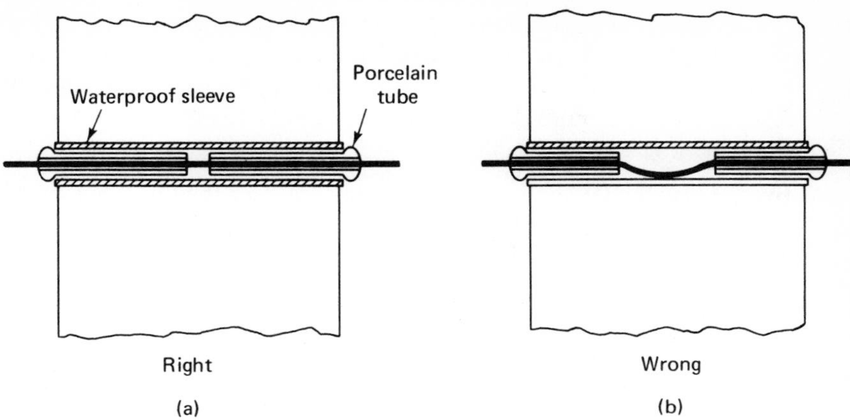

Fig. 321
Passing through members or partitions where two tubes are required (Sect. 320-11). (b) is a violation. The tubes are too short and permit the conductor to contact the sleeve. Conductor must be **kept** out of contact with the sleeve, as in (a).

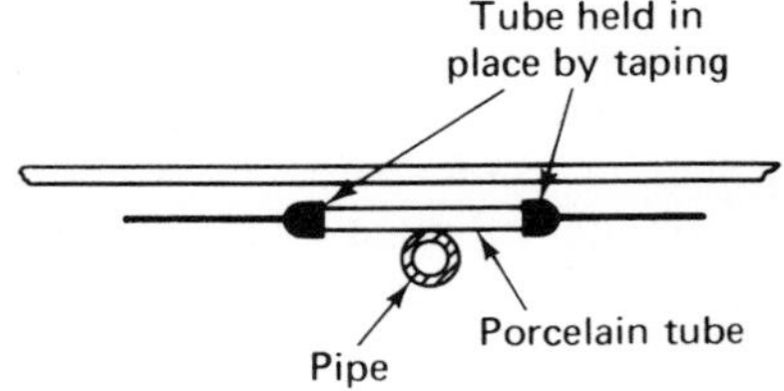

Fig. 322
Where it is necessary for wiring to be installed within 2 in. of pipes or other metal, an insulating tube is required. The tube must be secured at the ends (Sect. 320-12).

320-14. Protection from Physical Damage

Any conductor exposed to mechanical injury or any conductor that is less than 7 ft above the floor shall be protected by one of the following four methods:

1. Guard strips in the form of boards may be nailed in place on both sides of the run—narrow boards placed on end. This method would be used where there is danger of mechanical injury from the side of the run.
2. By using guard strips the same as above and, in addition, placing a "running" board in back of the run. This protects the run from the sides and the back. This method is often used for protecting a run across the face of joists or beams. It might be used, for instance, for a run across

the ceiling joists in a basement, where there is danger of mechanical injury from the side and where, in addition, objects such as implements or tools might be rested on the wires. A running board must extend not less than 1 in. or more than 2 in. outside conductors. The guard strips must be at least 2 in. high.

3. By using method 2 above and adding a board over the top. This would completely box in the run. This method would be used where there is danger of mechanical injury from all sides of the run.

4. The conductors may be placed in pipe, or in conduit. When this is done, all conductors of a circuit must be grouped in the same pipe or conduit. A separate pipe or conduit for each conductor is not permitted. EMT may also be used for protection.

   If *pipe* is used, loom or tubing must be placed on the wires before putting them into the pipe. If conduit or EMT is used, no loom or tubing is required.

320-15. Unfinished Attics and Roof Spaces

An unfinished attic is one having exposed studding, rafters, or floor joists. Spaces with 3 ft or more of headroom are treated as attics.

In unfinished attics, conductors may not be run across the face of studding, rafters, or floor joists. Conductors must be run either through holes in the members or on the side of the members.

If the attic has a stairway or ladder leading to it, a "through" run must be protected by a running board nailed across the face of the beams over the run. This is for runs *through* floor joists, and for runs *through* studding or rafters in the wall or ceiling that are within 7 ft from the floor. Runs on the *side* of studding, rafters, or floor joints require no protection.

If there is no stairway or ladder leading to the attic, no protection is required for any run, whether through or with the beams.

For roof spaces with less than 3 ft of headroom and wired *after* the building is completed, the above rules do not apply. Wiring may be run on the face of beams and without protection. If the wiring is installed during construction of the building, the rules do apply, the same as though the roof space were an attic.

320-16. Switches

Snap switches of the surface type used with open wiring on insulators do not require a box, but they must be mounted on some kind of insulating base at least $\frac{1}{2}$ in. thick (Fig. 323).

Other switches require metal enclosures.

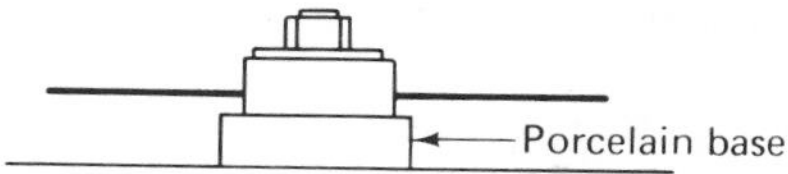

Fig. 323
Surface-type snap switch with insulating base, used with open wiring on insulators [Sects. 320-16, 380-10(a)]. The insulating base is part of the switch.

ARTICLE 324 — CONCEALED KNOB-AND-TUBE WIRING

324-1. Definition

Concealed Knob-and-Tube wiring is similar to open wiring on insulators, except that for concealed knob-and-tube work, knobs or cleats are used as supports. In Open Wiring on Insulators, other types of supports, such as glass insulators, would also be used in some cases.

Concealed knob-and-tube work, as the name indicates, is always concealed. Open wiring on insulators is exposed.

324-2. Other Articles

The general rules of Article 300, as well as the rules of this Article (324), apply for concealed knob-and-tube work.

324-3. Uses Permitted

Concealed knob-and-tube work may be used only for *extensions* to *existing* installations, and then only in the following spaces:

1. In hollow spaces of walls and ceilings.
2. In unfinished attic and roof spaces.

324-4. Uses Not Permitted

Concealed knob-and-tube work may *not* be used in:

1. Commercial garages.
2. Theaters.
3. Motion-picture studios.

4. Hazardous locations.
5. Assembly halls.

324-5. Conductors

Conductors must be suitable for the location and conditions of use (wet or dry, temperature, etc.) as specified for the different types of conductors listed in Table 310-13, Article 310 of the Code. For example, in a wet location, Type T could not be used; this type is approved only for dry locations. Type TW could be used, since this type of conductor is approved for both dry and wet locations.

Only single, insulated conductors may be used in concealed knob-and-tube work.

324-6. Conductor Supports

Supports (knobs or cleats) must be spaced not more than $4\frac{1}{2}$ ft apart; also, a knob or cleat must be placed not over 6 in. from a tap or splice.

When conductors are installed in the hollow space of a dry partition, the wires may be installed without supports, provided that each wire is in loom or flexible tubing. This method may be used in other dry locations where it is impossible or impractical to install knobs or cleats.

324-7. Tie Wires

Tie wires shall have insulation equivalent to that of the conductor.

324-8. Conductor Clearances

Minimum separation between conductors is 3 in. Miminum clearance *from surface wired over is* 1 in. (Knobs and cleats are manufactured so as to provide 1-in. clearance from the surface wired over.)

In places where the 3-in. separation between conductors cannot be maintained, loom or flexible tubing must be used. At boxes, switches, etc., the conductors would usually have to be brought within 3 in. of one another; if so, loom would be required on each conductor where it enters the box or switch.

When a run is parallel to the studding or joist, each conductor should be run on a separate studding or joist, where practicable.

324-9. Through Walls, Floors, Wood Cross Members, Etc.

(a) The provisions of Section 320-11 apply.

(b) Where a vertical run within a partition passes out through the floor at the bottom, a tube is required where the run penetrates the timber or 2 by 4. This rule requires that, for *plastered* partitions, in addition to the tube in the timber or 2 by 4, another tube be placed above it, so that the wire is protected to a height of at least 3 in. The purpose of this rule is to protect the wire from falling plaster that may accumulate around the tube. The same rule also applies for conductors passing through a header or other horizontal cross piece within a plaster partition.

324-10. Clearance from Piping, Exposed Conductors, Etc.

See Section 320-12.

324-11. Unfinished Attics and Roof Spaces

An unfinished attic is one having exposed studding, rafters, or floor joists. Spaces with 3 ft or more of headroom are treated as attics.

In unfinished attics, conductors may *not* be run across the face of studding, rafters, or floor joists. Conductors must be run either through holes in the members or on the side of the members.

If the attic has a stairway or ladder leading to it, a "through" run must be protected by a running board nailed across the face of the beams over the run. This is for runs *through* floor joists, and for runs *through* studding in the wall or rafters in the ceiling that are within 7 ft from the floor. Runs on the *side* of studding, rafters, or floor joists require no protection.

If there is no stairway or ladder leading to the attic, no protection is required for any run, whether through or with the beams.

For roof spaces with less than 3 ft of headroom and wired *after* the building is completed, the above rules do not apply. Wiring may be run on the face of beams and without protection. If the wiring is installed during construction of the building, the rules *do* apply, the same as though the roof space were an attic.

324-12. Splices

Splices must be soldered or, as an alternative, approved splicing devices may be used.

324-13. Boxes

Both metallic and nonmetallic boxes may be used in knob-and-tube work.

324-14. Switches

Flush-mounted snap switches used with concealed knob-and-tube work shall be enclosed in switch boxes. In wet locations, switch enclosures shall be weatherproof.

ARTICLE 326 — MEDIUM VOLTAGE CABLE

Type MV

Type MV cable is rated for voltages over 2,000.

It may be used in raceways, or buried directly in the earth, for power systems up to 35,000 volts.

Unless approved for the purpose, it may not be used where exposed to direct sunlight, or in cable trays, or supported by messenger.

Conductors may be copper, aluminum, or copper-clad aluminum.

ARTICLE 330 — MINERAL-INSULATED METAL-SHEATHED CABLE

Type MI

330-1. Definition

Type MI cable is a high grade metal-covered cable. The conductors are embedded in a mineral-type insulation (magnesium oxide), which will last almost indefinitely without deterioration, and will withstand very high temperatures. The covering or sheath is usually copper, which does not corrode, is waterproof, and gastight. The cable can be coiled or bent the same as any other type of cable. It has the advantage of being suitable for use in practically any location, including embedding in masonry. Special fittings are needed for use with this type of cable.

330-2. Other Articles

In addition to the rules of this Article (330), the rules for general wiring, as set down in Article 300, must be complied with.

330-3. Uses Permitted

330-4. Uses Not Permitted

Type MI cable may be used:

1. For feeders and for services.
2. For branch circuits.
3. In dry locations.
4. In wet locations.
5. Embedded in plaster.
6. Embedded in concrete or masonry.
7. Underground, where suitably protected against damage.
8. Where exposed to oil or gasoline.
9. In hazardous locations.
10. In any corrosive location not harmful to copper sheath.

Mineral-insulated metal-sheathed cable may not be used where corrosive conditions would be harmful to the copper sheath.

B. Installation

330-10. Wet Locations

In wet locations, boxes, fittings, and all other parts of the wiring system must be weatherproof and rustproof.

In locations such as dairies, laundries, canneries, and other wet locations, boxes, fittings, and cables must be "stooled off" the surface at least $\frac{1}{4}$ in.

330-11. Through Joists, Studs, or Rafters

When passing through wooden studs, joists, or rafters, the hole should always be drilled, where possible, at the center section of the member. A hole drilled at the center of a beam weakens the beam the least.

When no other way is possible, and a beam has enough strength to permit it, a notch for the cable may be cut in the edge of the beam. The cable must be covered at each beam by a steel plate of at least No. 16 gauge. This method should be used only where it is not possible to drill through a center section of the beam.

330-12. Supports

Straps or hangers for Type MI cable must be spaced not more than 6 ft apart, except where the cable is fished.

330-13. Bends

Type MI cable may not be bent to a radius of less than five times the diameter of the cable. Thus, a cable 1 in. in diameter may be bent to a radius of not less than 5 in. Larger bends are of course preferred, where possible; the Code specifies the minimum. The purpose of this rule is to prevent "kinking" or otherwise damaging the cable with sharp bends.

330-14. Fittings

Type MI cable requires special fittings for connection to boxes and other equipment. A typical fitting would consist of a gland, gland nut, and compression ring. When the gland nut is turned up, it grips the cable, holding it tight. The cable end is sealed as required by Section 330-15 (see Fig. 324).

330-15. Terminating Seals

Because of the nature of the insulation, it is important that no moisture be allowed to enter Type MI cable. For this reason, the cable end must be sealed with an approved sealing compound as soon as it is cut. Also, the bare conductors extending from the cable must be covered with insulating material. An insulating sleeve could be used for this purpose.

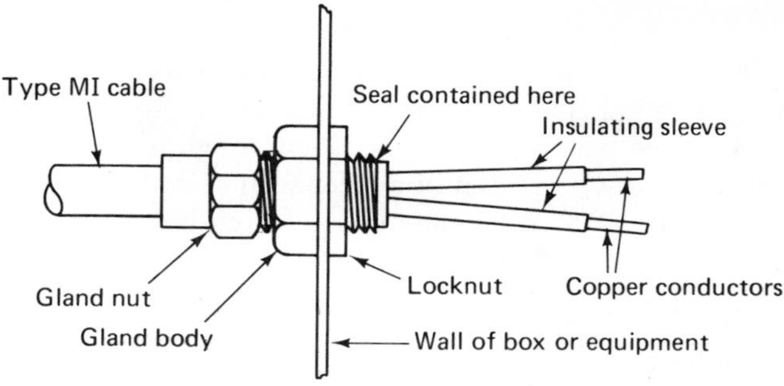

Fig. 324

Fitting for Type MI cable (Sects. 330-14, 330-15).

C. Construction Specifications

Conductors are solid copper, without individual insulation.

Insulation is a highly compressed refractory mineral.

Outer sheath is of sheet copper.

ARTICLE 333 — ARMORED CABLE

331-1. Definition

For details of cable construction, see Section 333-4 below.

333-2. Other Articles

In addition to the rules of this Article (333), the rules for general wiring, as set down in Article 300, must be complied with.

333-3. Marking

The manufacturer is required to mark the cable as per Section 310-11. For Type AC cable there is an additional requirement that external markers identifying the maker be provided on the cable throughout its length.

333-4. Construction

The individual copper conductors are covered with a standard-type insulation, then a cotton braid. The two, three, or four conductors are laid together, the assembly wrapped with a moisture-resistant, tough paper, and encased in an armored jacket, which consists of a steel strip spirally wound. Type AC cable is also known as BX. It is made in sizes from No. 14 to No. 2, and is intended to be used primarily as branch circuit and feeder cable.

333-5. Conductors

Conductor insulation may be any of the types used for general wiring. Type ACT has thermoplastic conductor insulation.

333-6. Use

Type AC and ACT may be used only in dry places. Type ACL has lead-covered conductors and may be used in wet locations, but may not be used for direct burial in the earth.

Types AC, ACT, ACL cable may *not* be used:

1. In theaters.
2. In motion-picture studios.
3. In hazardous locations.
4. In locations having corrosive fumes or vapors.
5. On cranes or hoists (except for flexible connections).
6. In storage battery rooms.
7. In hoistways or on elevators (except as per Section 620-21).
8. In commercial garages.

333-7. Supports

Maximum spacing between straps is $4\frac{1}{2}$ ft, with a strap not over 12 in. from each box or fitting, except where the cable must be fished.

An exception to the rule requiring a strap within 12 in. of each box or fitting in exposed work would be the case of an unsupported short lead to a motor or other piece of equipment where flexibility is required. In this case a 24 in. length of cable is permitted without supports.

333-8. Bends

Minimum radius for bends is six times cable diameter.

333-9. Boxes and Fittings

A fitting must be provided where the armor terminates. The armor would terminate only in a box, cabinet, or other piece of equipment, and the "fitting" would be a connector in most cases. A connector will protect the wires from abrasion as required by this rule. An "insulating bushing" must be used with the connector. This would consist of a short sleeve of insulating material that slips over the wires and under the cable armor. The insulating bushing must be partly exposed inside the box so as to be visible for inspection.

For lead-covered cable (Type ACL) no insulating bushing is required, but the lead covering must be visible for inspection inside the box.

333-10. Through Studs, Joists, and Rafters

When passing through wooden studs, joists, or rafters the hole should always be drilled, where possible, at the center section of the member. A hole drilled at the center of a beam weakens the beam the least.

When no other way is possible, and a beam has enough strength to permit it, a notch may be cut in the top or bottom of the beam for the cable. The cable must be covered at each notch by a steel plate of at least No. 16 gauge for protection of the cable against driven nails.

333-11. Exposed Work

In general, armored cable must "hug" the surface wired over. Unlike conduit, armored cable is not made to withstand a great deal of mechanical abuse. Therefore (with certain exceptions), the Code prohibits bridging across open spaces. (An exception is made for installations in attics, where the cable may be without backing between joists, studs, and rafters, if installed in accordance with Section 333-13, following.)

There are other exceptions to this rule; in the following cases the cable may be without backing:

(a) When flexibility is required, a box may be installed near a motor or appliance, using a short piece of free cable between the box and motor or appliance. The cable may be up to 24 in. long. This would allow flexibility in the connection when a motor or appliance is subject to vibration.

(b) When the cable is fished, as in a partition or when the cable is run on a rack, as per Article 318, backing is not required.

(c) In basements only, where the run is *not subject to physical damage,* the cable may be run across the underside of the floor joists above, and strapped at each joist. No guard strips are required.

333-12. In Accessible Attics

In unfinished attics, the cable may be run across the face of floor joists or across the face of rafters and studding. In "accessible" attics, *substantial* guard strips must be installed for runs across floor joists, and for runs across studs or rafters that are within 7 ft of the floor. Guard strips are simply wooden strips or boards nailed in place close to the cable on both sides. They protect the cable from injury from the side and from the front. (An accessible attic is one having a stairway or *permanent* ladder leading to it.)

If the attic is "inaccessible" (without a stairway or permanent ladder leading to it), such guard strips need be installed only within 6 ft of the scuttle hole or trapdoor.

When the cable is run along the *sides* of floor joists, rafters, and studding, guard strips are not required, either in accessible or inaccessible attics.

Figure 325 illustrates the requirements for BX installed in attics.

ARTICLE 334 — METAL-CLAD CABLE

Type MC

334-1. Definition

For details of cable construction, see Section 334-4, below.

334-2. Other Articles

In addition to the rules of this Article (334), the rules for general wiring, as set down in Article 300, must be complied with.

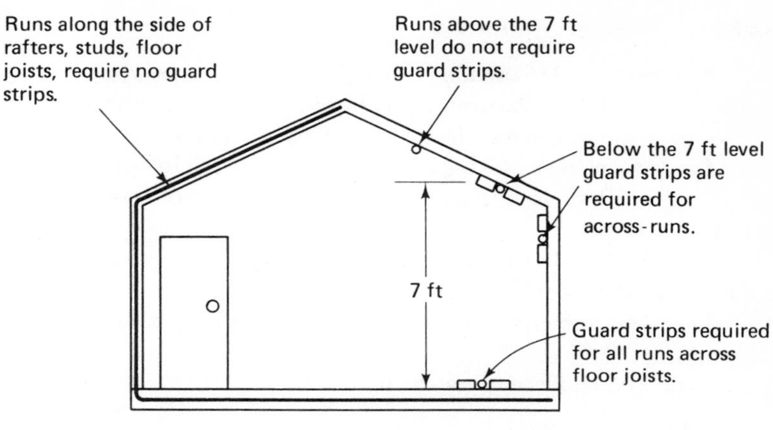
Runs along the side of rafters, studs, floor joists, require no guard strips.
Runs above the 7 ft level do not require guard strips.
Below the 7 ft level guard strips are required for across-runs.
7 ft
Guard strips required for all runs across floor joists.

Accessible attic

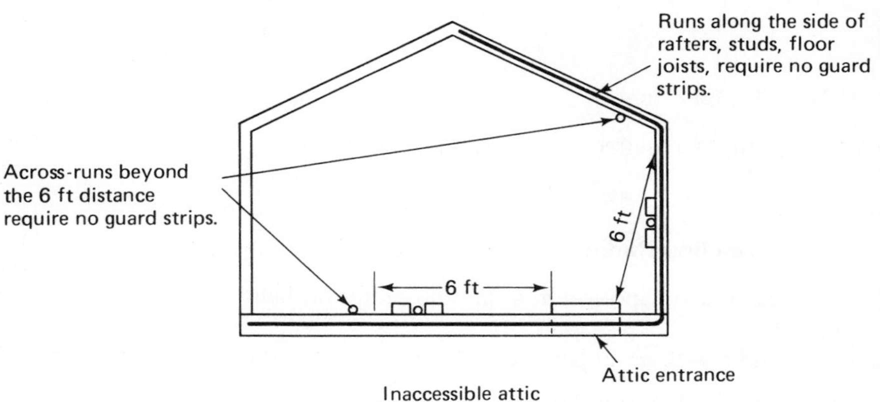
Runs along the side of rafters, studs, floor joists, require no guard strips.
Across-runs beyond the 6 ft distance require no guard strips.
6 ft
6 ft
Attic entrance

Inaccessible attic

Runs within 6 ft of attic entrance require guard strips, if on the face of members. For runs along the side of members, no guard strips are required.

Fig. 325

BX installed in attics (Sect. 333-12).
Nonmetallic-sheathed cable installed in attics (Sect. 336-9).
Flexible metal conduit installed in attics (Sect. 350-1)

334-3. Uses Permitted

334-4. Uses Not Permitted

Type MC cable is made with either a metal tape armor wound spirally around the cable, or the armor may be in the form of an impervious corrugated tube, or a smooth metal sheath. It comes in sizes up to 1,000 MCM.

Type MC cable with tape armor may not be used in wet places, unless there is a lead sheath under the armor or the conductors are a waterproof type, such as TW, RHW.

Type MC cable with an impervious tube or with a smooth metal sheath may be used in wet as well as dry places.

Type MC cable (if suitable for wet places) may be used as a service entrance.

Type MC cable may *not* be used:

1. Buried in concrete.

2. Directly buried in the earth.

3. Where exposed to corrosive acids or caustic alkalis.

334-10. Installation

Strapping is required at intervals of not over 6 ft.

334-11. Bending Radius

For cable with tape armor, minimum radius for bends is seven times cable diameter.

For cable with an impervious tube armor, minimum radius for bends is:

1. 10 times diameter for $\frac{3}{4}$ in. and smaller.

2. 12 times diameter for $\frac{3}{4}$–$1\frac{1}{2}$ in. cable.

3. 15 times diameter for cable over $1\frac{1}{2}$ in.

For shielded conductors, minimum radius of bends is 12 times cable diameter.

334-12. Fittings

Approved fittings shall be used with Type MC cable.

Construction Specifications

Conductors may be copper, aluminum, or copper-clad aluminum, solid or stranded. Minimum conductor size is No. 18 copper, No. 12 aluminum or copper-clad aluminum.

Insulation may be any standard type, except that, for No. 16 and No. 18, insulation must be one of the types listed for fixture wire, Table 402-3 of the Code.

ARTICLE 336 — NONMETALLIC-SHEATHED CABLE

Types NM and NMC

336-1. Definition

336-2. Construction

Nonmetallic-sheathed cable consists of two or three conductors covered individually with rubber or thermoplastic insulation, then a cotton braid, then a wrapping of tough paper, which is saturated with a moisture-resistant compound. The two or three conductors are then covered with a nonmetallic jacket, which is moisture- and fire-resistant. The two-conductor cable is elliptical in shape, the three-conductor, circular.

Type NM has a flame-retardant and moisture-resistant outer covering.

The outer covering of Type NMC is flame-retardant and moisture-resistant; in addition, it is fungus-resistant and corrosion-resistant.

Nonmetallic-sheathed cable is also known as Romex.

336-3. Uses Permitted or Not Permitted

Use of types NM and NMC is limited to *structures of three floors or less.*

(a) Type NM

Type NM cable may be used in dry locations except for the following: Type NM may *not* be used:

1. In corrosive locations (such as a battery room).

2. In *commercial* garages.

3. In theaters.

4. In motion-picture studios.

5. In hoistways.

6. In hazardous locations.

7. Embedded in plaster.

(b) Type NMC

Type NMC cable may be used in dry, wet, and corrosive locations, except as follows.

Type NMC may *not* be used in:

1. *Commercial* garages.

2. Theaters.

3. Motion-picture studios.

4. Hoistways.

5. Hazardous locations.

6. Storage-battery rooms.

Neither type NM or NMC may be buried in concrete.

336-4. Other Articles

In addition to the rules of this Article (336), the rules for general wiring, as set down in Article 300, must be complied with.

336-5. Supports

Maximum spacing between straps is $4\frac{1}{2}$ ft, with a strap not over 12 in. from each box or fitting, except that where cable must be fished no strapping is required.

336-6. Exposed Work—General

(a) Types NM and NMC cable must, in general, "hug" the surface wired over. There are, however, two exceptions to the rule (see Sections 336-8 and 336-9).

(b) This rule specifies that the cable "shall be protected from mechanical injury *where necessary.*" "Where necessary" would be a matter of judgment. It should be remembered, however, that types NM and NMC cable are rather easily damaged, and protection should be provided wherever there is any possibility of damage to the cable.

Where passing through a floor, the cable must be run in rigid or intermediate metal conduit or pipe up to a height of at least 6 in. above the floor. This rule is, of course, for exposed work. Cable passing through a floor inside a partition would not require protection.

336-7. Through Studs, Joists, and Rafters

When passing through wooden studs, joists, or rafters, the hole should always be drilled, where possible, at the center section of the member. A hole drilled at the center of a beam weakens the beam the least.

When no other way is possible, and a beam has enough strength to permit it, a notch for the cable may be cut in the edge of the beam. The cable and notch must be covered at each beam by a steel plate of at least No. 16 gauge for protection against driven nails.

336-8. In Unfinished Basements

In unfinished basements, types NM and NMC cable may be run across the face of the beams without protection, but *only in sizes* of *No. 8, three-wire* or *No. 6, two-wire,* or larger.

For smaller sizes, the cable, if run across the face of the beams, must be mounted on a running board. Cable of any size may be run through bored holes in the joist without backing.

If the run of cable is "with" the floor joists rather than across them, the Code permits cable of any size to be run on the face of, as well as the side of, joists in unfinished basements (see Fig. 326).

336-9. In Accessible Attics

In accessible unfinished attics, the cable may be run across the face of the floor joists or across the face of rafters and studding, but guard strips (*substantial* guard strips) must be installed for runs across floor joists and for runs across studs or rafters that are within 7 ft of the floor. Guard strips are simply wooden strips or boards nailed in place, close to the cable, on both sides. They protect the cable from injury from the side and front. (An "accessible" attic is one having a stairway or *permanent* ladder leading to it.)

If the attic is "inaccessible" (without a stairway or permanent ladder leading to it), such guard strips need be installed only within 6 ft of the scuttle hole or trap door.

When the cable is run along the sides of floor joists, rafters, or studding, guard strips are not required (see Fig. 325).

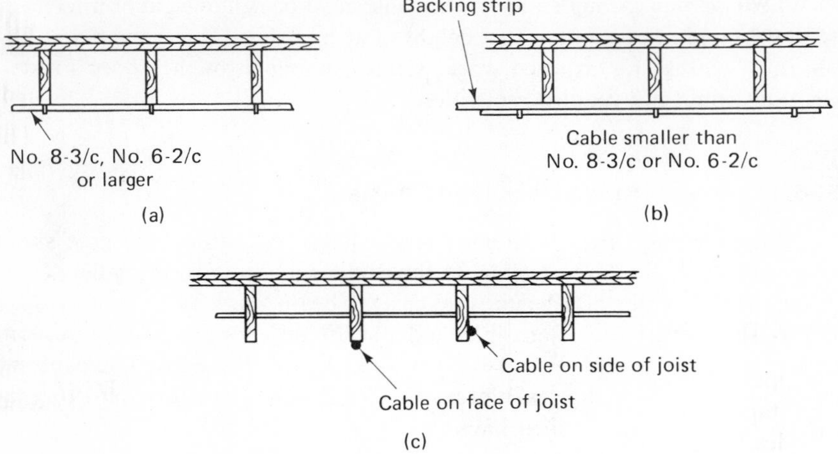

Fig. 326

Romex in unfinished basements (Sect. 336-8).

(a) Romex in size No. 8-3/c, No. 6-2/c, or larger may be run across the face of the joist, without backing.
(b) For smaller sizes, a backing strip must be provided.
(c) Any size Romex may be run through the joists, on the side of the joists, or lengthwise on the face of the joists.

336-10. Bends

Minimum radius of bends is five times the cable diameter. Since type NM and NMC two-conductor cable is not circular but elliptical in shape, this could be taken to mean five times the larger dimension of the cable.

336-11. Devices of Insulating Material

The "devices" referred to in this Section are the switches, receptacles, and lampholders made of bakelite or similar material that are on the market for use in surface wiring. The general rule of Section 300-15 requires that a box be installed at each outlet or switch point. The wiring devices referred to are an exception to this rule, no junction boxes being required at the switches or outlets.

336-12. Boxes of Insulating Material

Nonmetallic boxes may be used with types NM and NMC cable. This does not mean that metal boxes may not be used. Metal boxes are approved for use with all types of wiring. Nonmetallic boxes are approved for only nonmetallic sheath wiring. For types NM and NMC cable either metal boxes or nonmetallic boxes may be used.

ARTICLE 337 — SHIELDED NONMETALLIC-SHEATHED CABLE

Type SNM

337-1. Definitions

Type SNM cable is similar to Type NMC, except that Type SNM has a metal tape covering and a wire shield under the outer jacket. The wire shield provides protection from induced currents.

337-2. Other Articles

In addition to the rules of this Article (337), the rules for general wiring, as set forth in Article 300, must be complied with. Article 318 (Cable Trays) must also be complied with, when Type SNM is installed in cable trays. Type SNM is approved for use in Class I and Class II hazardous locations. When Type SNM is used in a hazardous area, the rules of Article 501 or 502 must also be complied with.

337-3. Uses Permitted

Type SNM may be used *only* as follows:

1. Where operating temperature does not exceed temperature marked on the cable.
2. In cable trays as per Article 318, or in raceway.
3. In Class I, Division 2, and Class II, Division 2, hazardous locations.

337-4. Bends

Minimum radius for bends is five times cable diameter.

337-5. Handling

Care should be taken in handling so as not to damage the cable. In cold temperatures (below 14°F), the insulation of Type SNM cable is subject to cracking, and this should be remembered in the handling of this cable.

337-6. Fittings

Fittings must be approved for use with this type of cable.

337-7. Bonding

The wire shield shall be bonded to all metal enclosures of electrical equipment and, at the supply end of the circuit, to the grounding bus.

337-8. Construction

Insulation is Type TFN, TFFN, THHN, or THWN.

Type SNM is made in sizes No. 18 through No. 2 in copper, and No. 12 through No. 2 in aluminum or copper-clad aluminum.

337-9. Marking

The manufacturer must mark the cable on the outside, showing type and operating temperature, voltage, manufacturer's name or trademark.

ARTICLE 338 — SERVICE-ENTRANCE CABLE

Types SE and USE

338-1. Definition

(a) Type SE has a flame-retardant, moisture-resistant outer covering. Type SE is unarmored, and not built to withstand mechanical abuse. (There is also an armored-type designated as Type ASE.)

(b) Type USE is for use underground. It has a moisture-resistant unarmored covering.

The neutral of Type SE or USE cable may be insulated or uninsulated.

338-2. Compliance with Article 230

This type of cable is used primarily for service entrances; when so used, the rules of Article 230 (Services) apply.

338-3. Uses Permitted as Branch Circuits or Feeders

In addition to its use for service entrances, Type SE cable is also approved for general interior wiring.

When used for general interior wiring, the neutral must be insulated. The insulation must be a rubber or thermoplastic type of insulation.

There are five exceptions, where, for general wiring, the neutral may be an uninsulated conductor:

1. Range circuit.
2. Wall-mounted oven circuit.
3. Counter-mounted cooking unit circuit.
4. Clothes dryer circuit.
5. Feeder from one building to another *on the same premises.*

For these circuits, the bare conductor of a Type SE cable may serve as the neutral, but the cable must be nonmetallic-sheathed, and the circuit voltage may not be over 150 volts (AC) to ground. (A 120/240-volt circuit is 120 volts to ground. A 120/208-volt three-phase circuit is 120 volts to ground.)

It should be understood that Type SE cable with an uninsulated conductor may be used for all interior wiring *as long as the uninsulated conductor is not used as a neutral or circuit conductor.* For instance, for a two-wire, 120-volt circuit, you could use a cable with two insulated and one uninsulated conductors, leaving the uninsulated conductor unused, or for use as a grounding conductor.

Type USE is not approved for interior wiring.

338-4. Installation Methods

(a) In addition to the rules of this Article (338), the rules for general wiring, as set forth in Article 300, must be complied with when service-entrance cable is used for interior wiring.

(b) Type SE cable used in interior wiring is also subject to the same rules that apply to nonmetallic-sheathed cable, as set forth in Article 336.

(c) When passing through wooden studs, joists, or rafters, the hole should always be drilled, where possible, at the center section of the member. A hole drilled at the center of a beam weakens the beam the least.

When no other way is possible, and a beam has enough strength to permit it, a notch for the cable may be cut in the edge of the beam. In this case the cable and notch must be covered at each beam by a steel plate of at least No. 16 gauge for protection against driven nails.

338-5. Marking

Service-entrance cable must be marked by the manufacturer to show voltage, type, and manufacturer's name or trademark. If the neutral is smaller than the phase wires, this also must be shown.

ARTICLE 339 — UNDERGROUND FEEDER AND BRANCH-CIRCUIT CABLE

Type UF

339-1. Description and Marking

(a) Description: Type UF cable is made for direct burial in the earth. The outer covering is flame-retardant, moisture-proof, fungus-resistant and corrosion-resistant. It comes in sizes No. 14 through 4/0, and may contain a bare grounding wire for grounding equipment. This wire may not be used as a neutral.

(b) The manufacturer is required to mark the cable, showing voltage, type, and manufacturer's name or trademark.

339-2. Other Articles

In addition to the rules of this Article (339), the rules for general wiring, as set forth in Article 300, must be complied with.

339-3. Use

Type UF cable may be used:

1. Directly buried in the earth.
2. Indoors in wet or dry locations.
3. Indoors in corrosive locations.

Type UF cable may *not* be used:

1. As service-entrance cable.

2. In commercial garages.

3. In theaters.

4. In motion-picture studios.

5. In storage-battery rooms.

6. In hoistways.

7. In hazardous locations.

8. Embedded in cement.

9. Where exposed to direct rays of the sun (unless approved for the purpose).

It may be used as single conductor cable, one cable for each leg of the circuit. When single conductors are buried, all conductors of the circuit must be grouped together in the same trench or raceway.

Unprotected cables underground must be buried to a depth of at least 24 in. Where this depth cannot be obtained, a protective covering must be provided, such as pipe, or a concrete protective covering. When so protected, a depth of at least 18 in. must be maintained (see Section 300-5).

339-4. Overcurrent Protection

339-5. Rated Ampacity

Overcurrent protection shall be provided, which shall be in accordance with the ampacity of the conductors in the cable. Refer to Table 310-16, p. 70-132.

ARTICLE 340 — POWER AND CONTROL TRAY CABLE

Type TC

340-1. Definition

Type TC cable is a factory assembly of two or more insulated conductors with a nonmetallic outer sheath. It may or may not contain grounding conductors.

340-2. Other Articles

In addition to the requirements of this Article (340), the rules for general wiring, as set forth in Article 300, must be complied with. When used in a cable tray, the rules of Article 318 (Cable Trays) also apply.

340-3. Construction

Conductor sizes are No. 18 through 1,000 MCM for copper, and No. 12 through 1,000 MCM for aluminum or copper-clad aluminum conductors. Insulation types for No. 16 and No. 18 conductors are listed in Section 725-16(b) of the Code. For larger sizes, insulation may be any of the standard types listed in Table 310-13 of the Code.

340-4. Uses Permitted

Type TC cable may be used *only in industrial establishments,* and then only if conditions of maintenance and supervision assure that the installation will be serviced by competent personnel.

It may be used as above for power, lighting, control, and signal circuits.

It may be used as above (1) in cable trays, (2) in raceways, (3) supported by messenger wire in outdoor locations, or (4) for Class I signal and control circuits.

It may be used as above in cable trays in Class I, Division 2, hazardous locations. (It is not approved for use in any other hazardous location.)

340-5. Uses Not Permitted

Type TC cable may *not* be used:

1. Where exposed to physical damage.

2. As open cable on brackets or cleats.

3. Exposed to direct rays of the sun unless approved for that purpose.

4. Directly buried, unless approved for the purpose.

340-6. Marking

Type TC cable must be marked by the manufacturer to show voltage, insulation type, AWG size, manufacturer's name or trademark.

340-7. Ampacity

For sizes up to and including No. 2, ampacities are listed in Table 400-5, p. 70-239 of the Code. The table applies for copper conductors, and for aluminum or copper-clad aluminum conductors.

For larger sizes, ampacities shall be taken from Section 318-10 of the Code.

ARTICLE 342 — NONMETALLIC EXTENSIONS

342-1. Description

One type of nonmetallic surface assembly consists of two No. 14 insulated conductors sewed into a narrow strip of specially treated cloth. In the space between the conductors is a flap, which covers the tacks or nails used to install the assembly.

Another type of assembly consists of simply a narrow flat strip of rubber. Molded into the rubber are two No. 12 conductors. Upholstery nails are used to install the assembly.

Nonmetallic surface extensions may be used only for extensions from *existing* outlets. A fitting in the form of a plug is obtainable for use on the end of the wiring strip, and this may be plugged into an existing receptacle. The wiring strip is then carried along the wall. Special receptacle outlets are available that may be inserted in the run of wiring strip (see Fig. 327).

342-2. Other Articles

In addition to the rules of this Article (342), the rules for general wiring, as set forth in Article 300, must be complied with.

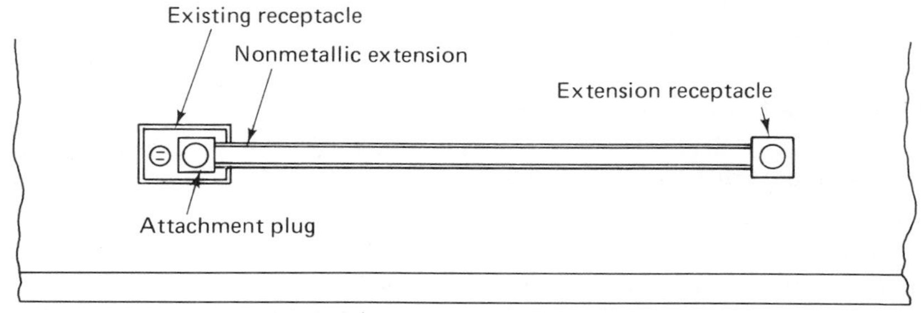

Fig. 327
Nonmetallic extension wiring.

342-3. Uses Permitted

Nonmetallic extensions may be used:

1. As a surface extension from an existing outlet on a 15- or 20-amp. branch circuit.
2. Only in dry locations, and exposed.
3. Only in *buildings occupied by* residences or offices.

(In industrial locations, it may be installed as aerial cable.)

342-4. Uses Not Permitted

Nonmetallic extensions may *not* be used:

1. As aerial cable in other than industrial locations.
2. In *unfinished* basements or attics.
3. On voltages over 150 volts (between conductors).*
4. In corrosive locations.

Nonmetallic extensions may not be run outside the room in which the run originates.

342-5. Splices and Taps

Splicing of the wiring strip is prohibited. Runs between outlets must be continuous and unbroken.

342-6. Fittings

The wiring strip may not be left with an exposed end. It must terminate in a receptacle, switch, or other device.

342-7. Installation

(a) Nonmetallic Surface Extensions

Surface extensions may not be installed within 2 in. of the floor.

Surface extensions may be installed only on woodwork or on plaster walls. They may not be installed on any kind of metal.

They must be fastened at least every 8 in., except that a distance of 12 in.

*When installed as aerial cable, voltages up to 300 maximum are permitted.

is allowed between the first fastener and the plug that plugs into an existing receptacle.

When making a right angle bend in the wiring strip, a special fitting in the form of a "cap" is required.

(b) Aerial Cable

When used as aerial cable in an industrial occupancy, the wiring strip must be strung on a messenger cable with turnbuckles at each end of the messenger. The messenger must be supported at intervals of not more than 20 ft. The messenger must be kept at least 2 in. away from steel structural members.

Minimum height above the floor is 10 ft (14 ft if there is vehicular traffic).

Minimum height above work benches is 8 ft from the floor.

The messenger cable may be used as a grounding wire for equipment.

342-8. Marking

Nonmetallic extensions must be marked by the manufacturer in accordance with Section 110-21.

ARTICLE 344 — UNDERPLASTER EXTENSIONS

344-1. Use

344-2. Materials

This type of wiring is permitted by the Code in order to provide a means of extending a branch circuit in a building where there are no open spaces in the walls for fishing from one outlet to the other, or where fishing would be expensive and difficult. An underplaster extension is illustrated in Fig. 328.

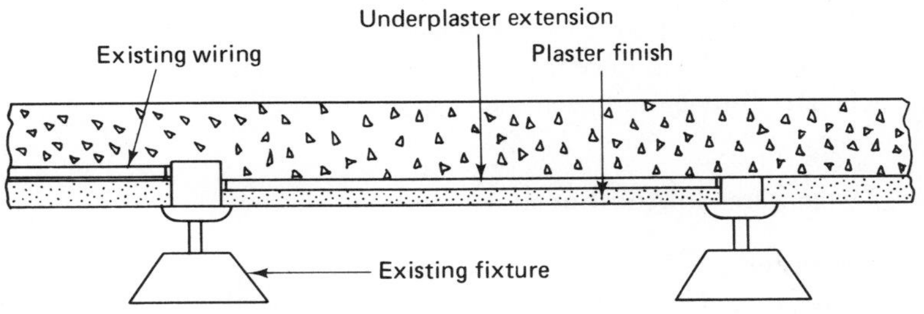

Fig. 328
Underplaster extension wiring.

In this type of installation, a channel is grooved in the plaster; the conduit or cable is placed in the groove, then plastered over.

Underplaster extensions are permitted only in buildings of "fire-resistive" construction.

Metal conduit, EMT, Type MI cable, Greenfield, BX, or approved metal raceway must be used for this type of wiring. Nonmetallic cable is not permitted.

Single conductors are permitted. This is an exception to the general rule of Section 300-20 for AC circuits in metal raceways. The general rule requires that all conductors of a circuit be enclosed in the same metal raceway. A single conductor in a metal cable or raceway sets up induced currents in the metal enclosure through induction. If the two or three legs of the circuit are all grouped in the same cable or raceway, the inductive effect is eliminated.

In the case of underplaster extensions, it is assumed that the currents will be very small and the inductive effect negligible; hence this exception to the general rule.

Standard sizes of raceway and cable must be used. The smallest standard size of conduit or tubing is $\frac{1}{2}$ in. This means that conduit or tubing smaller than $\frac{1}{2}$ in. may not be used. (An exception is made for single conductors. For a single conductor, conduit or tubing may be as small as $\frac{5}{16}$ in. inside diameter.)

344-3. Boxes and Fittings

The rules of Article 370 apply for boxes and fittings used with underplaster extensions.

344-4. Installation

For underplaster extensions, rigid conduit, Type MI cable, BX, flexible conduit, EMT, or approved metal raceway may be used.

This rule simply states that the general rules for the particular type of wiring used should be followed. If rigid conduit is used, then the general rules of Article 346 must be followed, and so on.

344-5. Extension to Another Floor

Underplaster extensions may be extended to include more than one floor of a building, if standard sizes of conduit, EMT, or cable are used for passing from one floor to the other.

ARTICLE 345 — INTERMEDIATE METAL CONDUIT

A. General

345-1. Definition

This is a lightweight rigid metal conduit with integral or associated couplings, connectors, and fittings. The average weight of intermediate conduit is about 75% that of standard rigid conduit. It is less expensive than standard conduit, and although of lighter construction, it will withstand severe mechanical abuse.

345-2. Other Articles

In addition to the rules of this Article (345), the rules for general wiring, as set forth in Article 300, must be complied with.

345-3. Uses Permitted

Uses Not Permitted

Intermediate metal conduit may be used in all hazardous locations.

Corrosion-proof intermediate conduit may be buried in earth or concrete. Galvanized conduit would be considered corrosion-proof.

It may not be buried in cinder fill subject to moisture unless made of material suitable for the corrosive action of cinder fill. Galvanized conduit would not be approved for this purpose. "Everdur" is a trade name for conduit made of a copper-silicon alloy. Intermediate metal conduit made of this material would be suitable for burial in cinder fill.

Galvanized intermediate metal conduit may be buried *under* cinder fill if kept at least 18 in. below the fill. Or if encased in at least 2 in. of concrete, it may be buried directly in the cinder fill.

Except for the above restrictions, regular intermediate metal conduit is approved for use in all locations.

B. Installation

345-5. Wet Locations

Straps, bolts, screws, and all other accessories used in the installation must be corrosion-proof. Galvanizing would meet this requirement.

345-6. Size

Smallest size permitted for use is $\frac{1}{2}$ in.; largest size, 4 in.

345-7. Number of Conductors in Conduit

When the conductors are all the same size, the size of conduit required can be read directly from Tables 3A, 3B, and 3C, Chapter 9 of the Code.

If conductors of different sizes are contained in a conduit, the required conduit size must be figured using Tables 4 and 5, Chapter 9. For an example, see Section 346-6 under Rigid Metal Conduit. The same method of figuring applies also for intermediate metal conduit.

345-8. Reaming and Threading

After cutting, the conduit must be reamed. When threading is done in the field, a conduit thread-cutting die with a taper must be used.

345-9. Couplings and Connectors

Threadless couplings and connectors may be used with intermediate metal conduit.

Occasionally it is necessary to cut a line of conduit and reinstall the cut lengths. Or a line may be installed from two directions and meet at a common point. When there are threaded connections at the far ends of the two meeting conduit lengths, and a threaded connection is also required at the junction, a special kind of connecting device is required at the junction. One type of connection device approved for use is the "Erickson" coupling. In principle, it serves the same purpose as a pipe union in a pipe line, permitting a tight threaded connection to be made at the junction.

It would be possible to use a coupling at the junction with one conduit having a long thread, as shown in Fig. 329(a). This method (the "running-thread" method) is *not* permitted.

(Where it is not required that the connections be threaded, there would be no need for a special connection device. A threadless coupling could be used at the junction.)

345-10. Bends—How Made

Minimum radius of bends is listed in Table 346-10, p. 70-183, of the Code. This is for field bends made with other than a one-shot bending machine. For one-shot machines, the radius of bends may be as shown in Table 346-10, Exception, p. 70-183. Smaller bends are permitted for one-shot machines. This table may be used only when conductors *without* lead sheath are to be used.

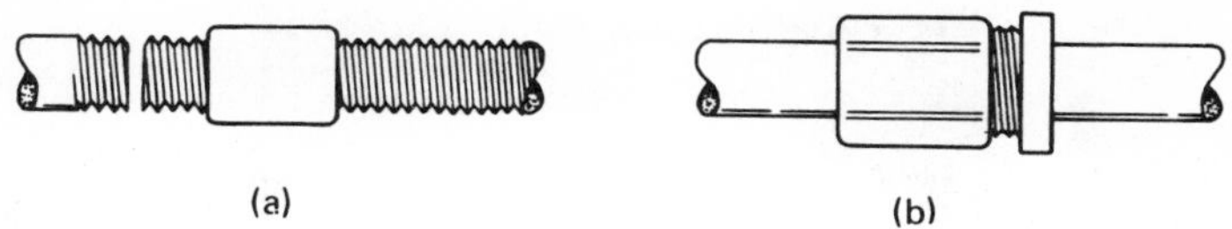

Fig. 329
(a) Running thread. The two conduits can be joined by turning the coupling counter-clockwise. Running threads are *not* permitted [Sect. 346-9(b)].
(b) Erickson coupling, approved for joining two sections of conduit.

When lead-sheathed conductors are to be used, Column 3 of Table 346-10 must be used in all cases.

Radius of bends is measured to the inner edge of the conduit.

345-11. Bends—Number in One Run

The total of all bends in a run of conduit (i.e., between outlets) may not total over 360 degrees. Four right-angle bends would equal 360 degrees. Or three right-angle bends plus two 45-degree offsets would equal 360 degrees.

345-12. Supports

Intermediate metal conduit must be strapped at least every 10 ft, and within 3 ft of outlets.

345-13. Boxes and Fittings

Boxes and fittings shall meet the requirements of Article 370.

345-14. Splices and Taps

Splices may not be contained in intermediate metal conduit. Splices shall be made only in boxes or "conduit bodies." (See definition of Conduit Body, p. 70-6 of the Code.)

345-15. Bushings

Bushings must be used over the end of conduit to protect conductor insulation from abrasion. This applies for conduit entering sheet-metal boxes, cabinets, enclosures.

C. Construction Specifications

345-16. General

(a) Intermediate metal conduit shall be shipped in 10-ft lengths, each length to include one coupling. (By special permission, other lengths may be shipped for special applications.)

(b) Conduit made of material other than steel (copper alloy, aluminum) shall be so marked.

(c) The letters IMC marked on each length at $2\frac{1}{2}$-ft intervals identifies the conduit as the intermediate metal type. The maker's name or trademark is required on each length (Section 110-21).

ARTICLE 346 — RIGID METAL CONDUIT

346-1. Use

Rigid metal conduit may be arbitrarily divided into three types:

1. Enameled steel conduit (now almost obsolete).
   May be used only indoors in noncorrosive atmospheres.

2. Standard conduit (galvanized steel conduit).
   May be used anywhere *except:*

   (a) In occupancies subject to severe corrosive influences.

   (b) Directly buried in cinder fill (see Section 346-3).

3. Special conduit.
   Everdur is a trade name for a conduit made of a copper-silicon alloy. It is made especially for use in severe corrosive atmospheres, and may be used in any location without restriction.
   Occupancies subject to "severe corrosive influences" would include tanneries, sugar mills, fertilizer plants, glue plants, chemical plants, paper mills, roundhouses, and stables. The corrosive atmosphere present in such locations will, in time, destroy the protective coating of standard conduit. Special conduit such as Everdur would be required in such locations.

Galvanized conduit may be installed in concrete, or directly buried in the earth.

Where practicable, boxes and fittings shall be of the same material as the conduit. Two "dissimilar" metals in contact will result in a destructive galvanic action being set up between the metals when moisture is present. Steel boxes and fittings used with Everdur conduit, which is a copper alloy, would result in such action. To avoid galvanic action, Everdur boxes and fittings shall be used with Everdur conduit, steel boxes and fittings with steel conduit. (There is an exception to this rule requiring similar metals. Aluminum fittings are approved, in all cases, for use with steel conduit.)

346-2. Other Articles

In addition to the rules of this Article (346), the rules for general wiring, as set forth in Article 300, must be complied with.

A. Installation

346-3. Cinder Fill

Cinders contain sulphur, and when moisture is present to any extent, sulphuric acid is formed, which will attack galvanized conduit. Galvanized conduit may not be buried directly in cinder fill that is outdoors or otherwise subject to moisture.

If galvanized conduit is used, it must be buried at least 18 in. *below* the cinder fill.

Everdur metal conduit may be buried directly in cinder fill. Rigid nonmetallic conduit is also approved for direct burial in cinder fill (Section 347-2).

If galvanized conduit is encased in at least 2 in. of concrete, it is considered protected by the concrete and may be buried in the cinder fill.

346-4. Wet Locations

In wet locations, supports, bolts, straps, screws, as well as the conduit and fittings, must be corrosion-resistant. Screws, straps, bolts, and nails must be galvanized or cadmium plated.

346-5. Minimum Size

$\frac{1}{2}$-inch conduit is the smallest size permitted.

Exceptions.

1. For underplaster extensions, $\frac{5}{16}$-in. inside diameter conduit may be used for single conductors (Section 344-2).

2. In the special case where a motor connection box is separated from the motor, $\frac{3}{8}$-in. conduit may be used (Section 430-145).

346-6. Number of Conductors in Conduit

The conduit size required for a given number of conductors of the same size can be read from Tables 3A, 3B, and 3C, Chapter 9, of the Code.

When conductors of different sizes are contained in the same conduit, the size of conduit required must be figured from the cross-sectional area of the conduit and the total cross-sectional area of all conductors, using Tables 4, 5, and 6, Chapter 9. Following are examples illustrating use of the tables.

What size conduit is required for (3) No. 6 Type T conductors?

Refer to Table 3A, p. 70-579. Under "Conductor Size," run down the column to 6. Following this line to the right, "3" is not listed. The nearest number above this is "4," which is listed in the column headed 1. A 1-in. conduit would be the smallest size permitted.

What is the minimum-size conduit required for three No. 2 and three No. 10 Type RH conductors?

First figure the total area of the conductors. From Table 5, p. 70-583, a No. 2 Type RH conductor has an area of .2067 sq. in. (Column 3, sixth listing from the bottom).

There are three No. 2 conductors.

$$3 \times .2067 = .6201 \text{ sq. in., area of the three conductors}$$

No. 10 Type RH has an area of .0460 sq. in. (Column 3, seventh listing from the top). The area of the three conductors is

$$3 \times .0460 = .1380 \text{ sq. in.}$$

Total area of all conductors is .6201 + .1380 = .7581 sq. in.

Now turn to Table 4, p. 70-582. Six conductors are going into the conduit. Under the column headed "Over 2 Cond.," run down this column to find a figure of at least .7581; .82 would be closest. Following this line to the first column (headed "Trade Size"), a $1\frac{1}{2}$-in. conduit is listed as the minimum size permitted.

346-7. Reaming and Threading

All conduit ends must be reamed after cutting. When conduit is threaded in the field, a standard cutting die with $\frac{3}{4}$ in. taper per foot must be used.

346-8. Bushings

Bushings must be used over the end of conduit to protect wire insulation from abrasion. This applies for conduit entering sheet-metal boxes or fittings. Bushings obviously could not be used on cast-metal equipment having threaded bosses.

346-9. Couplings and Connectors

(a) Threadless couplings may be used with rigid-metal conduit (but not in hazardous locations). In wet locations the threadless couplings must be the raintight type; when buried in concrete, the concrete-tight type.

(b) Occasionally it is necessary to cut a line of conduit and reinstall the cut lengths. Or a line may be installed from two directions and meet at a common point. When there are threaded connections at the far ends of the two meeting conduit lengths, and a threaded connection is also required at the junction, a special kind of connecting device is required at the junction. One type of connection device approved for use is the "Erickson" coupling. In principle, it serves the same purpose as a pipe union in a pipe line, permitting a tight threaded connection to be made at the junction.

It would be possible to use a coupling at the junction with a long thread (running thread) length of conduit on one side, as shown in Fig. 329(a). This method, the "running-thread" method, is *not* permitted.

(Where it is not required that the connections be threaded, there would be no need for a special connection device. A threadless coupling could be used at the junction.)

346-10. Bends—How Made

Tables 346-10 and 346-10, Exception (p. 70-183 of the Code), list the *minimum* radius of bend permissible for the different sizes of conduit. Note that the radius is measured to the *inside* edge of the conduit, not to the center or outside edge.

When a one-shot bending machine is used, generally a smaller radius of bend is permitted, compared with bends made by other methods. This is shown in Table 346-10, Exception. This table applies only when nonleaded conductors are to be used in the conduit. Where leaded conductors are to be used, Table 346-10, Column 3, applies in all cases.

346-11. Bends—Number in One Run

The total of all bends in a run of conduit (i.e., between outlets) may not total over 360 degrees. Four right-angle (90-degree) bends would equal 360 degrees. Or three right-angle bends plus two 45-degree offsets would equal 360 degrees.

346-12. Supports

Generally, rigid metal conduit must be strapped every 10 ft, and within 3 ft of each outlet or fitting.

For straight runs using *threaded* couplings, the 10-ft spacing may be increased for the larger sizes, as per Table 346-12 of the Code.

An exception is also made for vertical risers from machine tools and the like, where distance between supports may be increased to 20 ft.

346-13. Boxes and Fittings

Boxes and fittings shall meet the requirements of Article 370.

346-14. Splices and Taps

Splices may not be contained in rigid metal conduit. Splices shall be made only in boxes or "conduit bodies." (See definition of Conduit Body, p. 70-6 of the Code.)

B. Construction Specifications

346-15. General

(a) The Code requires that conduit be shipped in 10-ft lengths, with one coupling furnished with each length. In special cases, shorter or longer lengths may be shipped.

(b) Nonferrous, corrosion-resistant conduit shall be so marked.

(c) Manufacturer's name (or trademark) must appear on each length of conduit.

ARTICLE 347 — RIGID NONMETALLIC CONDUIT

347-1. Description

Nonmetallic conduit is made from nonmetallic materials, such as fiber, soapstone, polyvinyl chloride, polyethylene. The conduit is waterproof, rotproof, and rustproof, but does not have the strength of rigid metal conduit. Rigid nonmetallic conduit is also known and merchandised as "plastic conduit."

347-2. Uses Permitted

Rigid nonmetallic conduit may be used:

1. Directly buried in the earth (depth at least 18 in.).
2. In walls, floors, ceilings (concealed work).
3. For exposed work, if not subject to damage.
4. In severe corrosive atmospheres.
5. In cinder fill.
6. In wet as well as dry locations.

347-3. Uses Not Permitted

Rigid nonmetallic conduit may *not* be used:

1. In hazardous locations (except as per Sections 514-8 and 515-5). (May be used for underground runs in gas stations and bulk-storage plants.)
2. For fixture or equipment support.
3. Where subject to physical damage.
4. In temperatures above the maximum temperature permitted for the conduit.
5. For conductors with insulation suited for higher temperatures than that permitted for the conduit.
6. For voltages above 600 (unless encased in concrete).

347-4. Other Articles

In addition to the rules of this Article (347), the rules for general wiring, as set forth in Article 300, must be complied with.

A. Installations

347-5. Trimming

When a cut is made, the conduit ends must be reamed to remove sharp edges.

347-6. Joints

Joints are made up with the use of cement and sockets made for the purpose.

347-8. Supports

Conduit must be strapped at intervals not greater than those shown in Table 347-8, p. 70-186 of the Code. In addition, a strap is required within 4 ft of each outlet.

347-9. Expansion Joints

For long runs that are exposed to wide temperature changes, expansion joints must be inserted in the run to take up expansion and contraction. See Section 300-7(b).

347-10. Minimum Size

Minimum size for rigid nonmetallic conduit is $\frac{1}{2}$ in.

347-11. Number of Conductors

Requirements are the same as for metal conduit (see Section 346-6).

347-12. Bushings

Bushings must be used where conduit enters a box, cabinet, or fitting.

347-13. Bends—How Made

Field bends may be made only with approved bending equipment suitable for this type of conduit. Minimum radii for bends are the same as those listed in Table 346-10, 70-183 of the Code for rigid metal conduit.

347-14. Bends—Number in One Run

The total of all bends in a run of conduit (i.e., between outlets) may not total over 360 degrees. Four right-angle 90-degree bends would equal 360 degrees. Three right-angle bends plus two 45-degree offsets would equal 360 degrees.

347-15. Boxes and Fittings

Boxes and fittings must conform to the requirements of Article 370.

347-16. Splices and Taps

Splices may not be contained in rigid nonmetallic conduit. Splices shall be made only in boxes or "conduit bodies." (For definition of Conduit Body, see p. 70-6 of the Code.)

B. Construction Specifications

347-17. General

Conduit must be shipped in 10-ft lengths, except that other lengths may be shipped in special cases. Each length must be fitted with a coupling and marked with the manufacturer's name or trademark.

ARTICLE 348 — ELECTRICAL METALLIC TUBING

348-1. Use

Electrical metallic tubing, commonly called EMT, may be divided into two types:

1. Standard EMT (galvanized or sherardized).
2. "Everdur" EMT.

Everdur is a trade name for a type of EMT made of a copper-silicon alloy. This type of EMT is highly resistant to corrosive influences, and may be used in locations where corrosive fumes or vapors are present.

Standard EMT may be used in any location *except:*

1. Where subject to severe mechanical injury.

2. Directly buried in damp cinder fill.

3. In *cinder* concrete.

4. In severe corrosive atmospheres.

5. In most hazardous locations (may be used only in Class II, Division 2 locations).

Everdur EMT may be used in any location *except:*

1. Where subject to severe mechanical injury.

2. Directly buried in damp cinder fill.

3. In most hazardous locations (may be used only in Class II, Division 2 locations).

Note that EMT, regardless of type, may never be buried directly in damp cinder fill nor less than 18 in. underneath the fill.

If placed directly in cinder fill, EMT must be encased in a 2-in. jacket of concrete.

EMT having corrosion protection "suitable for the condition" may be installed in concrete, or directly buried in the earth. Galvanized or sherardized EMT would be suitable for direct burial in the earth (but not in damp cinder fill). It may also be installed in concrete (but not cinder concrete).

"Dissimilar" metals in contact with one another set up a galvanic action, which deteriorates the metal. As with conduit, the use of "dissimilar metals" should be avoided. (The Code makes an exception that permits aluminum fittings to be used with steel EMT, in any location.)

348-2. Other Articles

In addition to the rules of this Article (348), the rules for general wiring, as set forth in Article 300, must be complied with.

A. Installation

348-4. Wet Locations

In wet locations, supports, bolts, straps, screws, as well as the EMT and fittings, must be corrosion-resistant. Screws, straps, bolts, and nails must be galvanized or cadmium-plated.

348-5. Size

As with conduit, the smallest-size EMT permitted is $\frac{1}{2}$ in. except:

1. For underplaster extensions, $\frac{5}{16}$ in. inside diameter EMT may be used (Section 344-2).
2. In the special case where a motor junction box is separated from the motor, $\frac{3}{8}$ in. may be used (Section 430-145).

Unlike rigid conduit, there is a restriction on maximum size; 4-in. EMT is the largest size permitted. (There is no upper limit on rigid conduit size.)

348-6. Number of Conductors in Tubing

Number of conductors allowed in EMT follows the same rules that govern conduit (see Section 346-6 for examples).

348-7. Threads

EMT may not be threaded, except that integral couplings used with EMT may be factory threaded.

348-8. Couplings and Connectors

In *wet* locations, couplings and connectors shall be the "raintight" type. For difference between "wet" and "damp" locations, see p. 70-10 of the Code. EMT buried in masonry or concrete must have "concrete-type" couplings and connectors.

348-9. Bends—How Made

Tables 346-10 and 346-10, Exception (p. 70-183 of the Code) list minimum radius of bend permissible for rigid conduit. The same tables apply to EMT. Table 346-10 is used for all bends except field bends. When field bends are made with a "machine designed for the purpose," Table 346-10 Exception may be used, except for leaded conductors. For leaded conductors, Table 346-10 must be used in all cases.

348-10. Bends—Number in One Run

Maximum number of bends is the same as for conduit; not over four 90-degree bends, or equivalent, are permitted between outlets.

348-11. Reaming

When EMT is cut, the cut ends must be reamed to remove sharp edges that might damage the conductor insulation.

348-12. Supports

EMT must be strapped at least every 10 ft, and within 3 ft of outlets or fittings.

348-13. Boxes and Fittings

Boxes and fittings shall comply with the applicable requirements of Article 370.

348-14. Splices and Taps

Splices may not be contained in electrical metallic tubing. Splices shall be made only in boxes or "conduit bodies." (For definition of Conduit Body, see p. 70-6 of the Code.)

B. Construction Specifications

348-15. General

(a) EMT must be manufactured with a circular cross section (not oval).

(b) The outer finish must be such that, after installation, it can be readily distinguished from rigid metal conduit.

(c) Threaded couplings (these are rarely used) must be designed to prevent bending of the tubing at the threads.

ARTICLE 349 — FLEXIBLE METALLIC TUBING

349-1. Scope

Flexible metallic tubing is a liquidtight tubing. It does not have a nonmetallic jacket, like liquidtight flexible metal conduit (Article 351), but is entirely metallic. It is approved for use only in lengths of 6 ft or less.

349-2. Other Articles

In addition to the rules of this Article (349), the rules for general wiring, as set forth in Article 300, must be complied with.

349-3. Uses Permitted

349-4. Uses Not Permitted

Flexible metallic tubing *in lengths of 6 ft or less* may be used either concealed, or, if not subject to damage, for exposed work.

Flexible metallic tubing may *not* be used:

1. In storage battery rooms.
2. In hoistways.
3. In hazardous locations.
4. Embedded in concrete, or directly buried in the earth.

349-10. Size

Smallest size permitted is ½ in. except that ⅜ in. is permitted:

1. For use in air plenums and ducts.
2. For the run from a recessed fixture to a box set off from the fixture (see Section 410-67).

Largest size permitted is ¾ in.

349-12. Number of Conductors

For the ½ and ¾ in. size, percentage of fill shall be no greater than that listed in Table 1, p. 70-577 of the Code.

For the ⅜ in. size, refer to Table 350-3, p. 70-191 of the Code.

349-16. Grounding

349-18. Fittings

May be used for grounding in lengths up to 6 ft, provided the circuit in the tubing is rated at not over 20 amps.

May be used only with approved fittings.

349-20. Bends

See Table 349-20(b), p. 70-190 of the Code.

ARTICLE 350 — FLEXIBLE METAL CONDUIT

Flexible metal conduit is commonly known as Greenfield. It consists of a steel strip spirally wound, and has the appearance of BX cable.

350-1. Other Articles

In addition to the rules of this Article (350), the rules for general wiring, as set forth in Article 300, must be complied with.

Installation of Greenfield would also follow certain rules of Article 333, as applied to BX.

As with BX, Greenfield, in general, must "hug" the surface wired over. That is, it must lay flat against the surface; in this way it will have "backing" at all points. There are three exceptions to this rule:

1. A 3-ft unsupported lead to a motor or appliance where flexibility is required.
2. In unfinished attics, Greenfield may be run across the face of floor joists, or across the face of rafters and studding. If installed on or within 7 ft of the floor joists or floor, guard strips are required but no backing. Above 7 ft, no guard strips are required.

   If the attic is "inaccessible," guard strips are required only within 6 ft of a trap door or scuttle hole. See Fig. 325.
3. In basements, where *not subject to physical damage,* Greenfield may be run across the underside of the floor joists above and strapped at each joist. No backing or guard strips required.

350-2. Use

Greenfield may *not* be used:

1. In wet locations (unless conductors are lead-covered or moisture-resisting types, such as RW, TW, etc.).
2. In hoistways, except for certain control circuits and except for short extensions on elevator cars (see Section 620-21 of the Code).
3. In storage-battery rooms.
4. In hazardous locations, except Class I, Div. 2 [Section 501-4(b)].

5. Exposed to oil, gasoline, etc., unless the conductor insulation is of a type that will not be damaged by the oil, gasoline, etc., or is lead-covered.
6. Underground or embedded in poured concrete.

350-3. Minimum Size

Minimum size permitted is $\frac{1}{2}$ in. except:

1. For underplaster extensions, Greenfield with $\frac{5}{16}$-in. inside diameter may be used (Section 344-2).
2. Where a motor junction box is separated from the motor, $\frac{3}{8}$ in. may be used, as per Section 430-145.
3. When used as part of an approved assembly or on lighting fixtures, $\frac{3}{8}$-in. Greenfield is permitted (6 ft maximum).

350-4. Supports

Straps must be spaced not over $4\frac{1}{2}$ ft apart and not over 12 in. from boxes and fittings, except that where Greenfield must be fished no strapping is required. When flexibility is required, as at a vibrating connection, the 12-in. distance may be increased to 36 in.

Another exception is the run of Greenfield from a box to a recessed fixture, installed as per Section 410-67. The run of Greenfield need not be strapped.

350-5. Grounding

The metal sheath of Greenfield may be used for grounding of equipment *only in lengths of 6 ft or less,* and then only if the circuit conductors in the Greenfield are protected at 20 amps. or less [see Section 250-91(b)].

350-6. Bends in Concealed Work

Concealed runs may not contain more than the equivalent of four quarter-bends between outlets.

ARTICLE 351 — LIQUIDTIGHT FLEXIBLE METAL CONDUIT

351-1. Scope

351-2. Definition

Liquidtight flexible metal conduit is, in construction, similar to Greenfield, except that it has a watertight outer jacket of synthetic material. This jacket is impervious to oil, grease, chemicals, and corrosive fumes. One company manufactures this flexible conduit under the trade name of Sealtite.

351-3. Other Articles

In addition to the rules of this Article (351), the rules for general wiring, as set forth in Article 300, must also be complied with.

351-4. Use

Liquidtight flexible metal conduit may be used where protection from liquids, solids, or vapors is required, or where flexibility is required. A typical use would be connection of a motor or portable piece of equipment in a wet location or a location where the connection would be subjected to oil, grease, gasoline, or corrosive fumes, and where in addition a flexible connection is required.

It may be used in hazardous (except Class I, Div. 1) locations where flexibility is required.

Liquidtight flexible metal conduit may *not* be used:

1. Where subject to mechanical injury.
2. In temperatures above that approved for the material of the conduit.
3. In Class I, Division 1, hazardous locations.

351-5. Size

Maximum size is 4 in. Minimum size permitted is $\frac{1}{2}$ in., except that $\frac{3}{8}$ in. may be used:

1. For flexible connections to motors (see Section 430-145).
2. As part of an approved assembly, or for use with lighting fixtures (length not over 72 in.).

351-6. Number of Conductors

Rules are the same as for conduit (see Section 346-6).

351-7. Fittings

Special fittings are required for use with this type of conduit.

351-8. Supports

Liquidtight flexible metal conduit must be strapped at least every $4\frac{1}{2}$ ft, and within 12 in. of outlets, except where fished.

351-9. Grounding

The metal sheath of liquidtight flexible conduit in the $1\frac{1}{2}$-in. and larger sizes may be used for grounding equipment if the conduit and fittings are "approved for the purpose." In the $1\frac{1}{4}$-in. and smaller sizes it may be used for grounding, but only in lengths of 6 ft or less.

351-10. Bends in Concealed Work

For concealed work, the total of bends (between boxes, outlets, etc.) may not total over 360 degrees. Four right-angle bends would equal 360 degrees.

ARTICLE 352 — SURFACE RACEWAYS

A. Metal Surface Raceways

352-1. Description and Uses Permitted

There are various shapes and sizes of metal surface raceway. A few models are illustrated in Fig. 331. "Wiremold," a trade name for surface raceway, comes in several sizes, the smallest measuring about $\frac{1}{2}$ in. wide by $\frac{3}{8}$ in. deep, the largest $4\frac{3}{4}$ in. wide by $3\frac{9}{16}$ in. deep. The small size Wiremold will take three No. 14 conductors. The largest size will accommodate up to eleven No. 2/0.

The raceway consists of two pieces, the base and the cover. The base is fastened to the surface; the conductors are laid into the base, then the cover is snapped on. (Some models require pulling in of conductors after the cover is in place.)

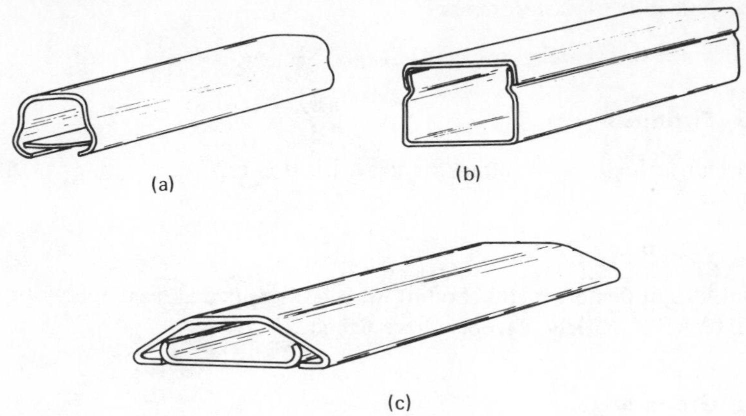

Fig. 331
Metal surface raceway.
(a)(b) Wall-mounting types.
(c) Floor-mounting type.

There is also a Wiremold that may be used for wiring across a floor [Fig. 331(c)]. This type of Wiremold is very shallow, and made strong enough so that it is not damaged by hand trucks or traffic which a raceway might be subjected to, when laid on a floor. The sides are sloped so that it offers little obstruction to foot traffic. It is approved for use "where subject to severe mechanical injury."

Specially made receptacles and switches are used with wall-mounted surface metal raceway.

Surface metal raceway comes in different lengths (usually 5 or 10 ft), which are joined together on the job.

Surface metal raceway may *not* be used:

1. In damp locations.
2. Where subject to severe mechanical injury (unless approved for the purpose).
3. Where subjected to corrosive vapors.
4. In hoistways.
5. In hazardous locations.
6. Concealed, except for underplaster extensions (Article 344), or data-processing systems (Article 645).

If voltage between conductors is 300 or over, a raceway with .040-in.-thick metal must be used. Most models of Wiremold raceway are made for voltages exceeding 300.

Locations that are considered to have "corrosive vapors" would include meat-packing plants, tanneries, paper mills, and battery rooms.

352-2. Other Articles

In addition to the rules of this Article (352), the rules for general wiring, as set down in Article 300, must be complied with.

352-3. Size of Conductors

Different raceways are designed to take different size conductors, and the recommended conductor size must not be exceeded.

352-4. Number of Conductors in Raceways

The number of conductors approved for use in a raceway is specified by the manufacturer for each size of raceway, and the recommended number must not be exceeded.

352-5. Extension Through Walls and Floors

Metal surface raceway may pass from room to room through *dry* floors or partitions, but a joint is not allowed within a partition.

352-6. Combination Raceways

"Combination" metal surface raceway is made with two separate compartments within the raceway, one for signaling circuits, such as bell-ringing circuits, etc., the other for lighting and power circuits.

Lighting and power circuits may not be run in the same compartment with signaling circuits.

The interior of the two compartments of a combination raceway must be of different colors so as to be easily identified, thereby preventing the reversing of compartments for the two systems anywhere along the line.

352-7. Splices and Taps

Surface metal raceway having a removable cover may contain splices or taps, if the removable cover allows access to the wiring after installation.

352-8. Construction

Metal surface raceway shall be so constructed that connections between sections will provide a good electrical and mechanical joint. Holes for screws must be made so as to allow screw heads to be flush with the metal surface.

B. Nonmetallic Surface Raceways

352-21. Description

This type of raceway is similar to the metallic type, the principal difference being in the material used in the manufacture. Nonmetallic raceways are resistant to chemical atmospheres, and may be used in locations subjected to chemical vapors. The metallic type of surface raceway may not be used in such locations.

352-22. Use

Surface nonmetallic raceway may *not* be used:

1. In damp locations.

2. Concealed.

3. Where subject to severe physical damage.

4. For voltages of 300 or more.

5. In hoistways.

6. In any hazardous location.

7. In temperatures above 122°F.

8. With conductors having insulation rated above 75°C.

Conductors rated above 75°C include types RHH, THHN, XHHW, TA, MI, SA, FEP, V, AVA, AVL, AVB. These types not permitted.

352-23. Other Articles

In addition to the rules of this Article (352), the rules for general wiring, as set forth in Article 300, must be complied with.

352-24. Size of Conductors

Different raceways are designed to take different size conductors, and the recommended conductor size must not be exceeded.

352-25. Number of Conductors in Raceways

The number of conductors approved for use in a raceway is specified by the manufacturer, and the recommended number must not be exceeded.

352-26. Combination Raceways

Lighting and power circuits may not be run in the same compartment with signaling circuits.

"Combination" raceways provide two separate compartments within the raceway, one for signaling circuits, such as bell-ringing circuits, the other for lighting and power circuits.

The interior of the two compartments of a combination raceway must be of different colors so as to be easily identified, thereby preventing the reversing of compartments for the two systems anywhere along the line.

352-27. Construction

Surface nonmetallic raceways shall be so constructed that connections between sections will provide a good mechanical joint. Holes for screws must be made so as to allow screw heads to be flush with the surface.

ARTICLE 353 — MULTIOUTLET ASSEMBLY

The Wiremold company manufactures a multioutlet assembly with the trade name Plugmold. Plugmold comes in lengths of 1, 3, 5, 6 ft. Receptacles are spaced 6, 9, 12, or 18 in. apart. Connection to the branch circuit is made through a connection hole in the base of the assembly. Multioutlet assembly is a convenient form of supplying a number of receptacle outlets within a small area. A typical use would be over a counter or workbench (Fig. 332).

353-1. Other Articles

In addition to the rules of this Article (353), the rules for general wiring, as set down in Article 300, must be complied with.

353-2. Use

Multioutlet assemblies may *not* be used:

1. In damp locations.
2. Concealed.
3. Where subject to severe mechanical injury.
4. Where subject to corrosive vapors.

5. In hoistways.

6. In hazardous locations.

If voltage between conductors is 300 or more, the metal thickness must be at least .040 in.

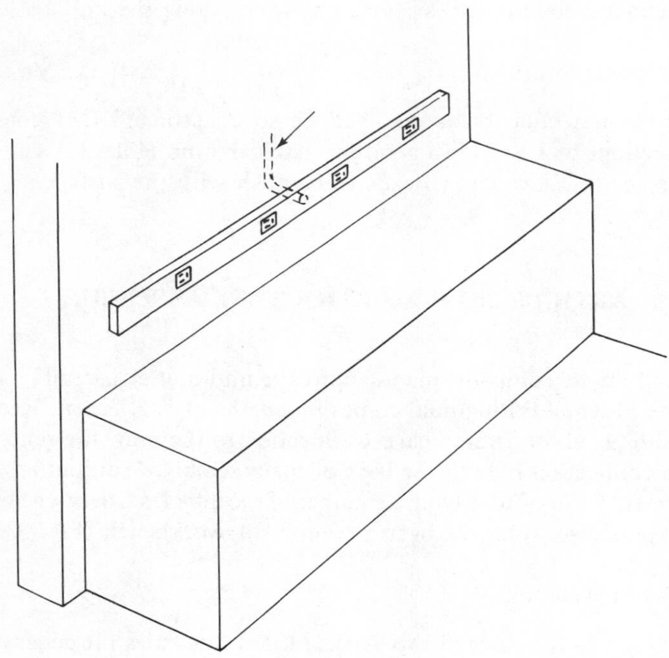

Fig. 332
Multioutlet assembly.

353-3. Metal Multioutlet Assembly Through Dry Partitions

Metal multioutlet assemblies may be extended from one room to another through a *dry* partition, provided this is done in such a way that it will not prevent the cover from being removed. A receptacle outlet may not fall within a partition.

ARTICLE 354 — UNDERFLOOR RACEWAYS

Underfloor raceway is a system of ducts laid in the floor of office or commercial buildings during construction of the building. Floors of these buildings are usually concrete, and the underfloor raceway system is laid in before the concrete is poured. Underfloor raceway may be either the metallic or nonmetallic type. Underfloor raceways may be rectangular or in the shape of a half-circle. They come in various sizes, ranging from about $1\frac{1}{8}$ by $1\frac{3}{4}$ in. to $1\frac{1}{2}$ by $6\frac{1}{2}$ in. or larger. This type of wiring provides a convenient raceway system throughout the building from which taps can be brought out through the floor to serve desks and equipment. Junction boxes are placed at different points in the network for pulling in wires and splicing. The junction boxes have screwed caps that are flush with the floor for access to the junction box after the building is completed. Usually, conduit is run from a wall cabinet to a junction box to feed the raceway system.

354-1. Other Articles

In addition to the rules of this Article (354), the rules for general wiring, as set forth in Article 300, must be complied with.

354-2. Use

This type of wiring may be used in any type of occupancy, *except:*

1. If subject to corrosive vapors.
2. In hazardous locations.

354-3. Covering

1. Half-round and flat-top raceways 4 in. or less in width must have at least $\frac{3}{4}$ in. of concrete *or wood* covering.
2. *Flat-top* raceways over 4 and up to 8 in. in width, and spaced 1 in. or more apart, must have at least 1 in. of *concrete* covering. Raceways over 4 and up to 8 in. in width, and spaced less than 1 in. apart, must have at least $1\frac{1}{2}$ in. of *concrete* covering.
3. In *office occupancies only,* flat-top raceway not over 4 in. wide may be laid flush with a concrete floor, provided:
    1. The raceway is approved for flush mounting.
    2. The raceway is covered with linoleum or equivalent floor covering

of at least $\frac{1}{16}$ in. thickness. (Carpeting would not be considered "equivalent" to linoleum.)

Trench-type raceways with removable covers may be laid flush with the floor surface in any occupancy (see Fig. 333).

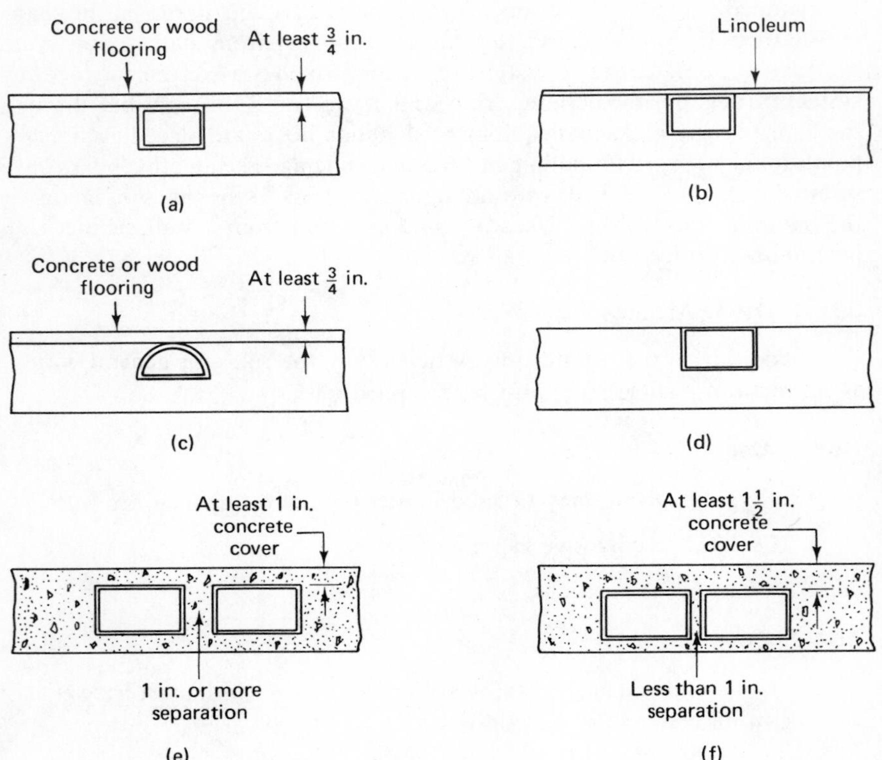

Fig. 333

Underfloor raceway covering (Sect. 354-3):

(a) Flat-top raceway 4 in. or less in width may have wood or concrete cover.

(b) *In offices only,* flat-top raceway 4 in. or less in width may be flush with floor surface provided it is covered with linoleum at least $\frac{1}{16}$ in. thick, or equivalent covering.

(c) Half-round raceway 4 in. or less in width may have wood or concrete cover.

(d) Trench-type raceway with removable cover may be installed flush with floor surface.

(e)(f) Requirements for raceway over 4 in. and up to 8 in. in width.

354-4. Size of Conductors

Different raceways are designed by the manufacturer for different size conductors, and the maximum size must not be exceeded.

354-5. Number of Conductors in Raceway

The cross-sectional area of all conductors or cables in a raceway may not exceed 40% of the cross-sectional area of the raceway.

Example.

How many No. 12 Type RH conductors would be permitted in a raceway with interior dimensions of $1\frac{1}{8}$ by $1\frac{3}{4}$ in.?

Cross-sectional area of the raceway is

$$1.125 \times 1.75 = 1.96 \text{ sq. in.}$$

$$40\% \text{ of } 1.96 = .784 \text{ sq. in.}$$

.784 sq. inches of the raceway may be occupied by conductors.

Area of No. 12 Type RH is .0278 sq. inches (Table 5, p. 70-583 of the Code).

$$\frac{.784}{.0278} = 28 \text{ plus}$$

A maximum of 28 No. 12 conductors would be permitted in this raceway.

354-6. Splices and Taps

Splices or taps may be made only in header access units (junction boxes). When a circuit serves several inserts, the circuit is run to a header access unit. A separate set of conductors is required from the access unit to each outlet, except when the outlets are "loop-wired." In loop wiring the conductor insulation is stripped for each outlet connection, but the wire is not cut. In this way an unbroken circuit may serve several inserts (outlets). It is not necessary to run a separate set of conductors for each insert (Fig. 334).

354-7. Discontinued Outlets

Unused conductors are not permitted to remain in the raceway. A taped (reinsulated) conductor is not permitted in the raceway. Where an outlet has a separate set of conductors run from a header access unit and the outlet is discontinued, the conductors between access unit and outlet must be removed.

Where an outlet is loop-wired and the outlet is discontinued, you cannot tape the bare spots in the insulation and leave the conductors in the raceway. The bared conductors must be removed.

354-8. Laid in Straight Lines

354-9. Markers at Ends

The purpose of these two rules is to facilitate "finding" the raceway after the building is completed. If the raceway is installed in straight lines and marked at the ends by an adjustable marker screw or some such device extending through the floor (but flush with the floor), the electrician will know where to drill the floor to strike the raceway, for installation of taps.

354-10. Dead Ends

The ends of raceway must be "capped" with a suitable fitting.

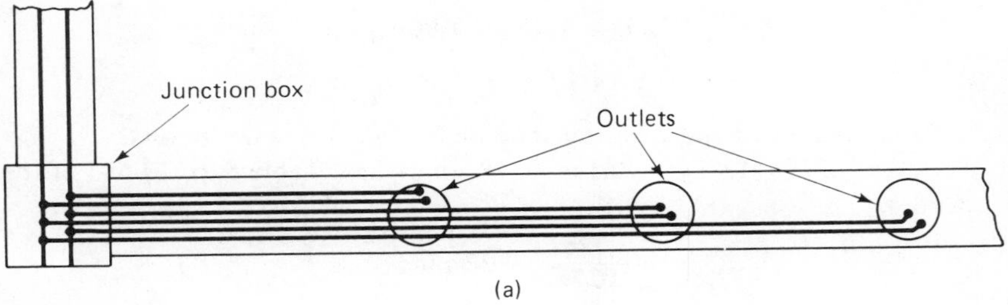

(a)

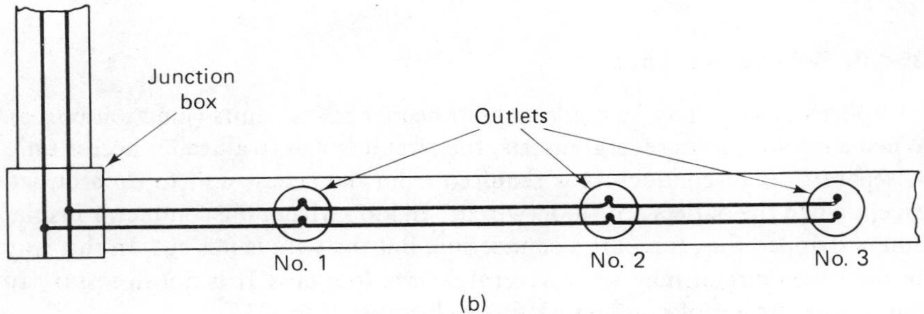

(b)

Fig. 334

Wiring to outlets in underfloor raceways

(a) Conventional wiring. A separate set of conductors is run from the junction box to each outlet. If an outlet is discontinued, its set of conductors must be removed.

(b) Loop wiring, with one set of conductors serving several outlets. In loop wiring the conductors *must not be cut,* and must be attached direct to the outlet device (receptacle, etc.). Taps are not permitted from the conductors to the device. If outlet No. 1 or No. 2 is discontinued, the entire length of conductors must be removed and a new set inserted. If only outlet No. 3 is discontinued, only the conductors between outlets No. 2 and No. 3 need be removed.

354-13. Junction Boxes

Junction boxes are installed with the access cap level with the floor. This is a Code rule. They must be moistureproof, and, if the raceway is metal, junction boxes must be metal.

354-14. Inserts

Inserts must be leveled to the floor (Fig. 335). "Inserts" are taps made into the raceway for a future outlet to a desk, etc. They may be installed before or after the floor is laid. Care must be taken, when drilling into a raceway after the floor is laid, to avoid damaging wires already in the raceway.

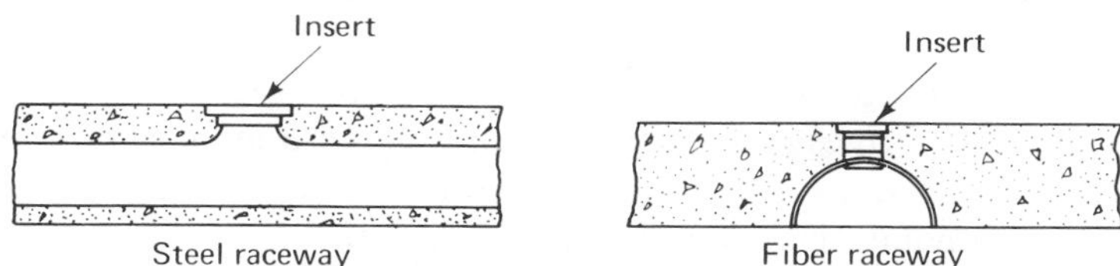

Fig. 335
Inserts must be leveled to floor grade (Sect. 354-14).

354-15. Connections to Cabinets and Wall Outlets

Wiring methods permitted for the run between the wall cabinet and the raceway system are:

1. Rigid metal conduit.
2. Flexible metal conduit (may not be buried in concrete).
3. Intermediate metal conduit.
4. EMT.
5. Approved fittings.

ARTICLE 356 — CELLULAR METAL FLOOR RACEWAYS

356-1. Definitions

This type of raceway is a part of the building structure and is installed by the structural crew. The entire floor of the building consists of sheet-metal cells, or tubes, laid side by side to form the floor structure, and afterwards covered with a layer of concrete. The cells come in sections of several cells to the section and of various lengths. The cells all run "one way." They come in different sizes, the cell size depending upon the floor loading (weight that the floor will have to carry). Generally, they are in the neighborhood of 4 in. in width and 3 or 4 in. in height. It can be seen that, with this type of construction, a ready-made raceway system is available under the entire floor (Fig. 336).

In order to feed the different cells, "headers" are installed in a direction at right angles to the cells. The header is a metal raceway of rectangular cross section, which connects with the cells. The header is installed by the electricians. Where the cells connect to the header, there are "access fittings" (junction boxes), which have screwed-on brass covers, which, after the concrete is poured, are flush with the floor and serve as access to the header and cells. Another type of header, recently developed, is the "trench-type" header. This type of header is fitted with removable covers so arranged as to be a part of the floor. The brass covers are eliminated, making for a more attractive floor appearance. The headers are connected to wall cabinets by conduit, tubing, flexible metal conduit, or fittings made for the purpose.

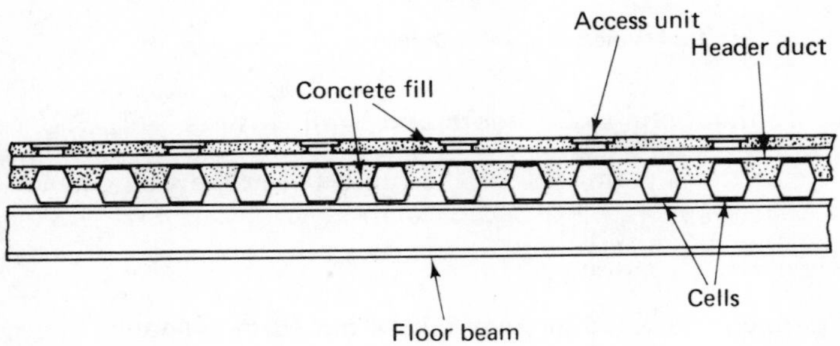

Fig. 336
Section of cellular metal floor raceway.

356-2. Use

This type of wiring is *not* permitted:

1. Where subject to corrosive vapors, such as in tanneries, sugar mills, etc.
2. In hazardous locations, such as coal-pulverizing plants, grain-processing plants, etc.

Cellular metal floor raceways in the floor of a commercial garage may not be used for wiring to any part of the garage, but may be used for wiring the rooms below the garage.

Raceways in the floor above the garage may be used for wiring ceiling outlets in the garage.

The cells of cellular metal floors are also used for piping. Wiring may not be run in the same cell with a pipe.

356-3. Other Articles

In addition to the rules of this Article (356), the rules for general wiring, as set forth in Article 300, must be complied with.

A. Installation

356-4. Size of Conductors

Maximum size conductor permitted with this type of wiring is No. 1/0. Larger sizes may be installed only if special permission is obtained from the authority enforcing the Code.

356-5. Maximum Number of Conductors in Raceway

The cross-sectional area of all conductors or cables in a cell or header may not exceed 40% of the cross-sectional area of the cell or header.

356-6. Splices and Taps

Splices or taps may be made only in the header access units or junction boxes. When a circuit serves several inserts, the circuit is run to a header access unit, with a separate set of conductors from the access unit to each outlet.

An exception is made for "loop" wiring. In loop wiring the conductor insulation is stripped for each outlet connection, but the wire is not cut. In this way an unbroken circuit may serve several inserts (outlets). For loop wiring it is not necessary to run a separate set of conductors for each outlet.

356-7. Discontinued Outlets

Unused conductors are not permitted to remain in the raceway. A taped (reinsulated) conductor is not permitted in the raceway.

Where an outlet has a separate set of conductors run from a header access unit and the outlet is discontinued, the conductors between access unit and outlet must be removed.

Where an outlet is loop-wired and the outlet is discontinued, you cannot tape the bare spots in the insulation and leave the conductors in the raceway. The bared conductors must be removed.

356-8. Markers

The purpose of this rule is to facilitate "finding" the cells after the concrete is laid over the cells. The cells would be marked by adjustable marker screws extending up from a cell through the concrete (but having the head flush with the finished floor). To identify different systems, markers with different-shaped heads could be used; a round-head marker could be used for power lines, a square-head marker for telephone lines, etc.

356-9. Junction Boxes

As with underfloor raceways, junction boxes (header access units) must be installed with the access cap level with the floor. Since all cellular metal floor raceways are made of metal, junction boxes must also be metal. All boxes must be moisture-proof.

356-10. Inserts

Inserts are nipple-like devices, which are tapped into the cells through the concrete. The upper part of the insert is threaded to receive an outlet, such as a receptacle. Inserts may be installed for future outlets, in which case they are closed with a threaded cap installed in the floor until such time as the outlet is installed. The caps must be installed flush with the finished floor. When drilling into the cell through the concrete, care must be taken not to allow chips from the drilling to fall into the cell. Also, care must be taken to avoid damaging wires that may be in the raceway.

356-11. Connection to Cabinets and Extensions from Cells

The headers may be connected to wall cabinets by rigid metal conduit, intermediate metal conduit, EMT, flexible metal conduit, or fittings made for the purpose. (Flexible metal conduit may *not* be installed in concrete.)

B. Construction Specifications

356-12. General

The raceways must be constructed so as to have good mechanical and electrical contact between sections. They shall be completely enclosed and free from burrs or sharp edges that might damage conductor insulation.

ARTICLE 358 — CELLULAR CONCRETE FLOOR RACEWAYS

358-1. Scope

Cellular concrete floor raceways are used for the same purpose as cellular metal floor raceways. They come in sections in the form of concrete slabs, with hollow spaces (cells) running lengthwise of the slab. Headers for concrete raceways are metal, the same as for cellular metal raceways. Headers are laid on top of and at right angles to the cells. Suitable fittings connect the header to cells that are to be used for wiring. The provisions of Article 300, as well as the provisions of this Article, apply for their installation.

358-2. Use

Cellular concrete raceways may *not* be used:

1. Where subject to corrosive vapors, such as in tanneries, sugar mills, etc.

2. In hazardous locations.

Cellular concrete floor raceways in the floor of a commercial garage may not be used for wiring to any part of the garage, but may be used for wiring the rooms below the garage.

Raceways in the floor above the garage may be used for wiring ceiling outlets in the garage.

358-3. Header

The header for cellular concrete floor raceways is installed by the electricians. The header is a metal duct, which is installed on top of and at right angles to the cells before the cement floor is poured. The header connects to the wall cabinet from which the different circuits originate. "Access units" are placed in the header over selected cells. The wiring passes from header to cell through a hole or knockout in the bottom of the header and a hole drilled in the top of the cell. The access units are fitted with screwed covers, which are leveled so as to be flush with the finished floor.

The following rules apply to installation of the header:

1. Must be installed in a straight line.

2. Must be at right angles to the cells.

3. Must be fastened to the cellular concrete floor.

4. Must be moisture-proof; end joints must be closed.

5. Must be metallically continuous.

6. Must be bonded to the distribution center enclosure.

358-4. Connection to Cabinets and Other Enclosures

The method permitted for connecting the header to the cabinet is through "metal raceway and fittings approved for the purpose."

358-5. Junction Boxes

Junction boxes must be installed with the access cap level with the floor. Boxes must be metal, and moisture-proof.

358-6. Markers

Markers must be installed to locate cells; markers must also be installed where the header crosses a cell that is intended for future use. In this case there would be no access fitting at the cross-over point, and a marker would locate the cross-over for the electrician, if, later, a fitting is to be installed.

358-7. Inserts

Inserts must be installed so as to be flush with the finished floor.

Receptacles used with inserts must be grounding-type receptacles. The cell into which the insert and receptacle is fitted is of concrete and provides no metallic connection, as in the case of cellular metal raceway. The receptacle (and insert) must be grounded back to the metal header by means of a copper wire. The metal header is required to be grounded by Section 250-33; thus the receptacle and insert would also be grounded.

If, when drilling through a cell wall, chips fall into the cell, they shall be removed. It is a Code rule that "chips and other dirt shall not be allowed to remain in the raceway." It is also required that the tool used for the drilling shall be of such design as to prevent injury to conductors in the cell.

358-8. Size of Conductors

358-9. Maximum Number of Conductors

358-10. Splices and Taps

358-11. Discontinued Outlets

All four rules are identical to those for cellular metal raceway. See Sections 356-4 through 356-7.

ARTICLE 362 — WIREWAYS

362-1. Definition

Wireways (also called duct) are sheet-metal enclosures. They come in sections, three sides having closely spaced knockouts, the fourth side being fitted with a hinged or screwed-on cover for access in installing or removing wires. Both ends of the section are open and the ends are either flanged, or if not flanged joined with connector pieces. Flanged ends of the sections are butted together and bolted to form a continuous raceway (Fig. 338). At each joint a hanger is inserted. The open ends of a completed raceway are closed with closing plates. Tees and junction boxes are also made for use with this duct. The wires are laid in after the raceway is completely assembled. The duct comes in different sizes: $2\frac{1}{2}$, 4, 6 in., etc. Short pieces, 1 and 2 ft long, are available, so that a continuous raceway of any length within 1 ft can be made up without cutting the duct.

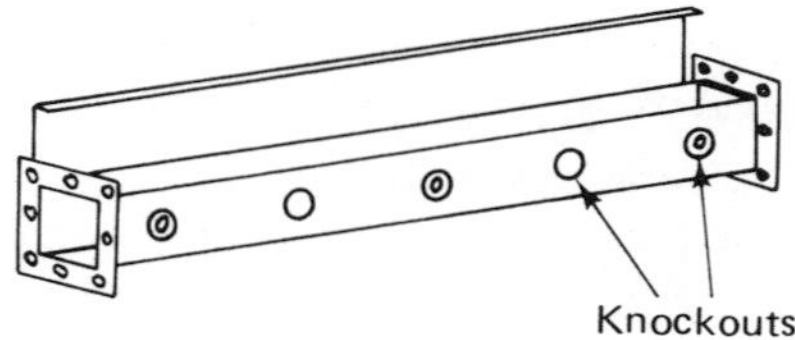

Fig. 338
Section of wireway.

This type of wiring is used principally in industrial plants, theaters, and garages in dry locations and usually carries feeders or mains. Taps are taken off for motors, etc. wherever needed, usually through conduit, BX, or flexible conduit, the knockouts in the duct being used for this purpose. One advantage of wireways is that circuits can be easily added, removed, or replaced with larger conductors if needed to meet changing conditions.

362-2. Use

The standard-type wireway is intended for use indoors in dry locations. Wireways installed outdoors must be of approved raintight construction. Wireways may be used only for exposed work.

Wireways may *not* be used:

1. Where subject to severe mechanical injury.

2. In corrosive atmospheres.

3. In most hazardous locations. (Wireways may be used in Class II, Division 2 locations, provided they are dust tight.) See Section 502-4(b).

362-3. Other Articles

In addition to the rules of this Article (362), the rules for general wiring, as set forth in Article 300, must be complied with.

362-4. Size of Conductors

Conductors installed in wireways shall not be larger than the maximum size for which the wireway was designed.

362-5. Number of Conductors

Maximum number of current-carrying conductors permitted, of any size, is 30.

Sum of the cross-sectional areas of *all* conductors must not exceed 20% of the interior cross-sectional area of the duct.

Grounding conductors are not current-carrying conductors and need not be counted as one of the 30, as long as the total fill of all conductors does not exceed 20% of the wireway cross-sectional area.

Signaling-circuit conductors, motor-control circuits (for starting duty) are not considered as current-carrying conductors, and need not be counted, as long as the total fill of all conductors does not exceed 20% of the wireway cross-sectional area.

Example.

How many 500 MCM Type RH conductors may be placed in a 4-in. square duct?

$$4 \times 4 = 16 \text{ sq. in., area of duct}$$

$$20\% \text{ of } 16 = 3.2 \text{ sq. in., available for conductors}$$

From Table 5, p. 70-584 of the Code, the area of 500 MCM Type RH is .9834 sq. in.

$$\frac{3.2}{.9834} = 3.25$$

A maximum of three 500 MCM conductors would be permitted in this duct.

There are exceptions permitting more than 30 current-carrying conductors:

1. For wireways used in connection with elevators, dumbwaiters, es-

calators, or moving walks, any number of conductors is permitted as long as the fill does not exceed 50%.

2. For theaters, the 30 conductor limit does not apply. (The 20% fill limit does apply.) See Section 520-5.
3. For wireways, the correction factors of Note 8, p. 70–136 of the Code are not required to be used, but if applied, any number of conductors is permitted as long as the fill does not exceed 20%.

362-6. Splices and Taps

Splices may be made in wireways without the use of a junction box, "provided they are accessible." A hinged cover or a removable cover would provide accessibility.

Where splices are made, the wireway duct may be filled to 75% of the cross-sectional area of the duct. Unspliced wire may fill only 20% of the duct area, but more space is naturally required for a splice than for a single wire. Hence, the Code raises the allowable "fill" to 75% in places within the duct where splices or taps are made. It would be difficult to calculate exactly how many splices or taps could be made in a given duct. Different methods of splicing or tapping would result in different sizes of splices and taps. The percentage of "fill" existing where splices and taps are made would have to be judged by appearance.

362-7. Supports

In general, distance between horizontal supports must not be over 5 ft. This would apply for all standard ducts. Spacing over 5 ft is permitted only in cases where special duct is used, and then the spacing of supports shall be not over 10 ft.

For vertical runs, spacing between supports may be 15 ft provided there is not more than one joint between supports.

362-8. Extension Through Walls

Wireways may not be concealed, but may pass through a wall, provided a joint does not fall within the wall.

362-9. Dead Ends

The open ends of a completed wireway installation (dead ends) are capped with closing plates provided for the purpose. Open ends are not permitted in the completed wireway.

362-10. Extensions from Wireways

Other types of wiring may connect to wireways to serve outlets beyond the wireway. Types of wiring permitted for this purpose are:

1. Rigid metal conduit.
2. Intermediate metal conduit.
3. Greenfield.
4. EMT.
5. Surface metal raceway.
6. BX.

362-11. Marking

Wireways must be marked with the manufacturer's name or trademark.

ARTICLE 363 — FLAT CABLE ASSEMBLIES

Type FC

363-1. Definition

This is a method of surface wiring, that uses metal surface raceway (see Article 352) with a flat cable assembly taking the place of conductors within the raceway.

Note that nonmetallic surface raceway may not be used for this type of wiring.

363-2. Other Articles

In addition to the rules of this Article (363), the rules for branch circuits, grounding, and general wiring, as set forth in other articles of the Code, must be complied with.

Since metal surface raceway is used with this type of wiring, the rules of Article 352 also apply.

363-3. Uses Permitted

1. This type of wiring is approved only for *branch circuits* of not over 30 amps. It cannot be used as a feeder.
2. It may be used only for exposed work.

363-4. Uses Not Permitted

Flat cable assemblies may *not* be used:

1. Where subject to corrosive vapors (unless specially approved for such locations).
2. In hoistways.
3. In hazardous locations.
4. In wet or damp locations (unless specifically approved for wet or damp locations).
5. Where subject to severe damage.

363-5. Installation

The surface metal raceway must be completely installed before inserting the Type FC cable.

363-6. Number of Conductors

363-7. Size of Conductors

363-8. Conductor Insulation

1. Number of conductors in Type FC cable is limited to four.
2. Type FC cable conductors must be No. 10, stranded copper—no larger, no smaller.
3. Insulation may be a rubber, thermoplastic, or asbestos type, or any other type approved for general wiring.

363-9. Splices

Splices may be made only in junction boxes, using terminal blocks.

363-10. Taps

Taps may be made only to a phase wire and the neutral. Taps may not be brought out from the hot wires only.

Tap devices, such as receptacles, must be rated not less than 15 amps., and not more than 300 volts.

363-11. Dead Ends

All dead ends of the metal raceway must be closed with an end-cap.

363-12. Fixture Hangers

363-13. Fittings

Fixture hangers must be a type approved for the purpose.

Fittings must be approved for the purpose, and installed with care so as to avoid damage to the cable.

363-14. Extensions

Flat cable assemblies may be joined to other types of wiring, as an extension, to reach outlets beyond the flat cable wiring. The extensions may be joined to the flat cable wiring only at the junction boxes at the ends of the flat cable run. An extension may not be taken off at any other point.

363-15. Supports

Type FC cable must be properly supported within the surface metal raceway.

The metal raceway is fastened to the surface by wood screws using the holes provided by the manufacturer.

363-16. Rating of Circuits

This type of wiring may be used only for *branch circuits* of 30 amps. or less.

363-17. Marking

Type FC cable must be marked by the manufacturer to show the temperature rating of the cable.

363-18. Protective Covers

A run installed less than 8 ft above the floor must be suitably protected by a metal cover approved for the purpose.

363-19. Identification

The neutral of Type FC cable must show a white or natural gray color.

363-20. Terminal Block Identification

The terminal blocks required by Section 363-9 must be color-coded, showing white for the neutral and black, red, and blue for phase wires.

ARTICLE 364 — BUSWAYS

Busways are sheet-metal enclosures of square or rectangular cross section, having conductors built in at the factory. The conductors are copper bus bar supported on insulators. Busways come usually in 10-ft sections, which can be bolted together on the job, the bus bar within the sections being also bolted together, to form a continuous busway. This type of wiring is used principally in industrial buildings for power distribution. Busways are particularly adapted to plants in which changes in machine layout are continually being made.

Busways come in three main types:

1. Without plug-ins.
2. With plug-ins.
3. With trolley.

Busways without plug-ins are used for a main supply run, such as from the switchboard to the distribution area. On a run such as this there would be no need for "take-offs" along the run.

The plug-in type is made with suitable outlets spaced at intervals along the busway. Specially designed plug-ins are used for connecting the loads to the busway (see Fig. 339).

Busways with trolley have an open bottom. The trolley runs on four wheels along the overhead housing. Contact is made through the open bottom of the

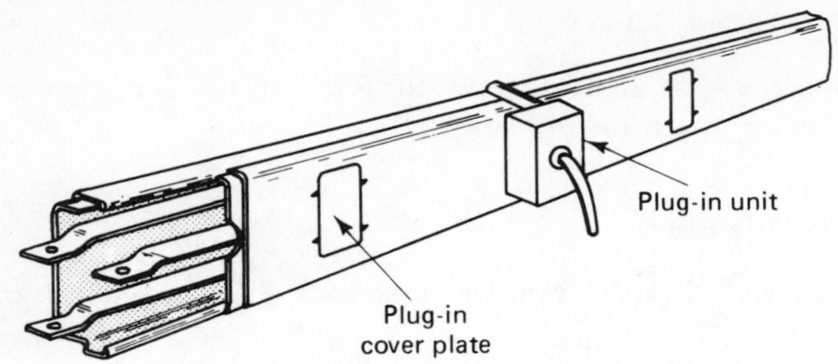

Fig. 339
Section of plug-in-type busway, showing plug-in unit and arrangement of busbars.

busway by brushes or rollers bearing on the bus bars within. Busways with trolley are used for feeding portable tools, as in industrial establishments.

364-3. Other Articles

In addition to the rules of this Article (364), the rules for general wiring, as set forth in Article 300, must be complied with.

364-4. Use

Busways may be used only for exposed work. (There is an exception permitting a busway to be installed behind panels.)

Busways are approved as a service entrance for voltages up to 600 (Section 230-43).

Busways may *not* be used:

1. Where subject to severe mechanical injury or corrosive vapors.
2. In hoistways.
3. In hazardous locations, except that in Class I, Division 2 locations only, enclosed gasketed busways are permitted [Section 501-4(b)].
4. In damp or wet locations (unless specifically approved for such locations).

364-5. Support

For horizontal runs, maximum distance between supports is 5 ft (except for busway approved and marked for 10-ft spacing).

For vertical runs, the maximum distance between supports is 16 ft.

364-6. Through Walls and Floors

Busways may pass through dry walls or floors provided a joint does not fall in the partition or between the floors.

Where passing through floors, the busway must be totally enclosed up to a height of at least 6 ft above the floor.

364-7. Dead Ends

The open ends (dead ends) of a busway must be closed off. Closing plates are available for this purpose.

364-8. Branches from Busways

Where taps or branches are taken off busways, seven types of wiring are permitted:

1. Rigid *metal* conduit.
2. Flexible metal conduit (Greenfield).
3. EMT.
4. Surface metal raceway (see Article 352).
5. Armored cable (BX).
6. Hard-usage cord assemblies.
7. Intermediate metal conduit.

The following cords fall into the "hard-usage" classification:

1. Junior hard-service cord: Types SJ, SJO, SJT, SJTO.
2. Hard-service cord: Types S, SO, ST, STO.

364-9. Overcurrent Protection

364-10. Rating of Overcurrent Protection—Feeders and Subfeeders

The allowable current-carrying capacity of a busway is stamped on the busway by the manufacturer. The overcurrent protection for the busway shall not exceed this value; a 90-amp. busway would be protected by a 90-amp. maximum fuse or circuit breaker setting; a 225-amp. busway by a 225-amp. maximum fuse or breaker setting; etc.

Where the current rating of the busway does not correspond to a standard fuse or circuit breaker setting, the next higher size may be used.

364-11. Reduction in Size of Busway

Where a busway is reduced to a smaller size, it is not necessary to provide additional overcurrent protection for the smaller busway, provided that the smaller busway:

1. Has a carrying capacity of at least $\frac{1}{3}$ the overcurrent setting, *and*
2. Is not over 50 ft long, *and*
3. Is not in contact with combustible material.

Thus, a 400-amp. busway, fused at 400 amps., could be reduced to a 150- or 200-amp. size, 50 ft long, with no separate overcurrent protection.

If reduced to a 100-amp. size, the smaller bus would have to be fused at the take-off point, since 100 is less than $\frac{1}{3}$ of 400.

364-12. Subfeeder or Branch Circuits

In general, taps taken off a busway must have overcurrent protection at the point of connection of the tap.

When a busway is used as a feeder, and a branch circuit is taken off the feeder through a plug-in connection, the overcurrent protection for the branch circuit must be included in the plug-in. The overcurrent protection is required to be a circuit breaker or fusible switch. Plug-in units of this type may be obtained from the busway manufacturers.

The following are exceptions to this rule:

1. No overcurrent protection is required if the tap conductors are of such size as to be properly protected by the busway fuse or circuit breaker.
2. Overcurrent protection may be at the termination of the tap, rather than at the plug-in, if the tap is not over 25 ft long, has an ampacity of at least $\frac{1}{3}$ that of the feeder, and the conductors are protected from damage.
3. For fixtures with cords, the overcurrent device may be part of the fixture cord plug.
4. For fixtures that are plugged directly into the busway, the overcurrent device may be mounted on the fixture.

364-13. Rating of Overcurrent Protection—Branch Circuits

This rule states, in effect, that the overcurrent protection for busways used as branch circuits follows the same rules as if any other type of wiring were used for the branch circuit.

In other words, if the circuit is a 20-amp. branch circuit, a maximum 20-amp. fuse or circuit-breaker setting may be used. If the circuit is a 30-amp. branch circuit, the maximum protection would be 30 amps.; etc.

364-14. Length of Busways Used as Branch Circuits

Branch-circuit busways with plug-ins shall be limited in length. The purpose of this rule is to prevent overloading of the busway. A long busway invites more take-offs or plug-in loads. If the busway is limited in length, there will be fewer take-offs and consequently less loading. A rule of thumb would be to limit the busway length to three times the ampere rating of the busway. Thus, a 30-amp. busway would be limited to a length of 90 ft.

364-15. Marking

Busways must be properly marked by the manufacturer to show voltage, current rating, and manufacturer's name or trademark.

B. Requirements for Over 600 Volts Nominal

364-21. Identification

High voltage busways must be marked by the manufacturer to show voltage, rated current, frequency, rated impulse withstand voltage, rated 60-Hertz withstand voltage, rated momentary current, manufacturer's name or trademark.

364-22. Grounding

Metal busways shall be grounded.

364-23. Adjacent and Supporting Structures

Alternating current may induce circulating currents in nearby metal. Metal busways should be so installed that any circulating currents set up in the metal enclosure will not result in an objectionable temperature.

364-24. Neutral

A neutral bus shall be sized to carry the maximum possible current that it will be required to carry.

364-25. Barriers and Seals

Unless the busway is forced-cooled, a vapor seal must be provided where a busway passes from inside to outside the building. The purpose of the seal is to minimize condensation of moisture within the busway.

364-26. Drain Facilities

Drains must be provided at low points to remove any possible accumulation of moisture.

364-27. Ventilated Bus Enclosures

Ventilated bus enclosures must be installed in accordance with Article 710, Part D of the Code.

364-28. Terminations and Connections

Where flammable gas is present, seal-off bushings shall be provided at terminations.

In long straight runs, means shall be provided to take up expansion and contraction due to temperature changes.

364-29. Switches

Switches and disconnecting links shall have a momentary current rating equal to that of the bus. Isolating switches shall be interlocked to prevent opening under load.

364-30. Low-Voltage Wiring

Secondary wiring and control devices shall be insulated from primary wiring and equipment by fire-retardant barriers.

ARTICLE 365 — CABLEBUS

365-1. Definition

Cablebus consists of insulated conductors mounted on insulating supports within a square or rectangular ventilated metal enclosure (Fig. 340). Cablebus is used principally as a feeder for heavy loads, but may be used for *individual* branch circuits.

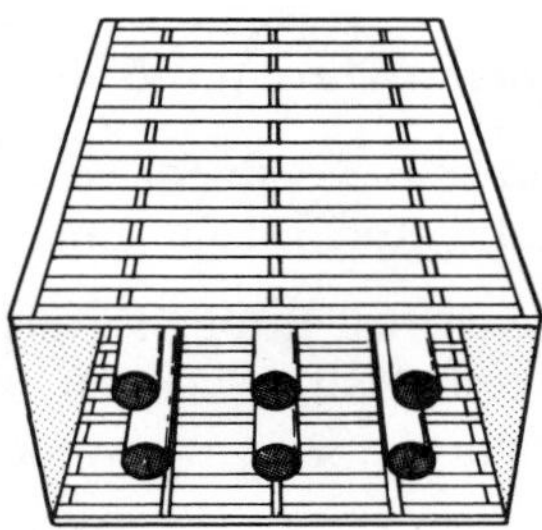

Fig. 340
Section of cablebus.

365-2. Use

Cablebus may be used only for exposed work. Cablebus used in damp or corrosive locations must be specifically approved for such locations. Standard cablebus may not be used in hoistways. Cablebus used in hoistways must be a type specifically approved for such use.

Cablebus is approved as a service entrance for voltages of 600 and below (Section 230-43).

The metal enclosure of cablebus may be used as a grounding conductor for grounding equipment, but may not be used as a neutral.

365-3. Conductors

Conductors must have insulation rated 75°C or above. This would include the following types of conductor insulation: RH, RHH, RHW, RUH, THHN, THW, THWN, MI, SA, FEP, V, AVA, AVL, AVB.

No. 1/0 is the *smallest* conductor permitted.

Different cablebus is designed for different sized conductors, and the recommended conductor size must not be exceeded. Number of conductors must not exceed the number recommended by the manufacturer.

Supports for the conductors within the enclosure must be spaced not more than 3 ft apart for horizontal runs, $1\frac{1}{2}$ ft for vertical runs. Spacing *between* conductors must be not less than one conductor diameter at points of support.

365-5. Overcurrent Protection

If there is no standard-size fuse or circuit breaker setting corresponding to the current rating of the cablebus, the next higher size fuse or breaker setting may be used.

365-6. Support and Extension Through Walls and Floors

(a) The cablebus assembly must be supported at intervals of not more than 12 ft, unless specifically designed for longer spans.

(b) The cablebus may be carried through walls (other than fire walls) as long as a joint does not fall within the wall, and provided the cablebus, where it passes through the wall, is unventilated at that point.

(c) Except where fire stops are required, cablebus may extend through a *dry* floor provided that the cablebus is totally enclosed to a height of at least 6 ft above the floor.

(d) Except where fire stops are required, cablebus may extend through a floor in a wet location if:

1. Curbs are provided around the floor opening, and
2. The cablebus is totally enclosed to a height of at least 6 ft above the floor.

365-7. Fittings

Approved fittings must be provided for turns, dead ends, and terminations at equipment or apparatus.

In places where the assembly could be subjected to damage, it shall be suitably guarded by such additional protection as may be required.

365-8. Conductor Terminations

Approved fittings must be used for connections to cablebus conductors.

365-9. Grounding

This Section requires good, reliable metal-to-metal contact throughout the metal enclosure. At joints or other places where good metal-to-metal contact is not obtained, a bonding jumper must be used.

Metal raceways must be grounded (Section 250-33), and the purpose of this rule is to provide a good grounding path throughout the metal enclosure.

365-10. Marking

Each section of cablebus must be marked by the manufacturer showing the maximum number and diameter of cables, voltage rating, ampacity, and manufacturer's name or trademark.

ARTICLE 366 — ELECTRICAL FLOOR ASSEMBLIES

A. General

366-1. Description

Electrical floor assemblies consist of conductive panels and units for housing receptacles. They are used in indoor locations to serve branch circuits, signaling circuits, and communication circuits.

366-2. Other Articles

In addition to the requirements of this Article (366), the requirements of Articles 210, 220, 250, and 310 must also be complied with. When signaling or communication circuits are served, the requirements of Articles 725 and 800 shall also apply.

366-3. Definitions

(a) Panels

Laminated panels containing sheets of electrical conducting material separated by insulating material(s).

(b) Receptacle Housing Unit

A special housing designed for insertion into the panels and containing power and/or signaling/communication outlets and filtering as required.

(c) Signaling/Communications Receptacle Outlet

An outlet whose use is specifically limited to signaling and/or communications circuits.

(d) Termination Unit

A special unit that presents the proper impedance to the high-frequency signaling and communication circuits within the electrical floor assemblies without affecting the 60-Hertz power.

(e) Base Unit

That portion of the receptacle housing unit which contains terminal probes and means for terminating the various receptacle outlets.

(f) Terminal Probe

A special probe that makes contact only with the conductive sheet(s) with which it is designed to do so.

(g) Interpanel Connector

Connectors specifically designed with three conductors, one each for phase, neutral, and grounding connections to interconnect the panels, and/or panel input units to panels, and/or termination units to panels.

(h) Panel Input Unit

A unit specifically designed to permit connections between panels and the power branch circuit and the signaling/communication circuits, or for only power branch circuits whenever signaling/communications circuits are not used.

(i) Holddown Bar

A bar designed specifically to secure the floor panels in place on the floor.

366-4. Uses Permitted

366-5. Uses Not Permitted

366-6. Branch Circuit

This type of wiring may be used for:

1. Lighting branch circuits.
2. Appliance branch circuits.
3. Signaling circuits.
4. Communication circuits.

The rating (and circuit protection) for any branch circuit is limited to 20 amps, 120 volts, *two-wire,* single phase.

This type of wiring may *not* be used:

1. Where subject to corrosive vapors.
2. Outdoors or in damp or wet locations.
3. In hazardous locations.

B. Installation

366-10. Panels

Panels may be installed only on flat, smooth surfaces.

366-11. All Circuits

15- and 20-amp. branch circuits shall be extended from their branch circuit panelboards.

Signaling and communication circuits shall be extended from Class 2 sources [see Table 725-31(a), p. 70-550 of the Code].

Wiring method must be *metal* conduit or *metal* raceway.

Combination 15- and 20-amp. branch circuits and signaling and/or communication circuits shall terminate in a panel input unit.

366-12. Circuits

For lighting or appliance branch circuits, maximum length of panels permitted to be connected in series is 200 ft. Total area of all panels forming a single lighting or appliance branch circuit is 1,024 ft.

Signaling and communication circuits may serve any number of panels.

366-13. Receptacle Units

Suitable tools shall be used for installing or removing receptacle units.

366-14. Grounding

A copper grounding conductor, No. 12 minimum, must be carried along with the branch circuit between the branch circuit panelboard and the panel input unit. The grounding conductor shall be connected to a grounding terminal screw in the panelboard and in the panel input unit.

ARTICLE 370 — OUTLET, SWITCH, AND JUNCTION BOXES, AND FITTINGS

A. Scope and General

370-1. Scope

This part of the Code applies to switch boxes, junction boxes, and fittings, including conduit fittings with covers.

In hazardous locations, the special rules of Articles 500 through 517 also apply.

370-2. Round Boxes

When a locknut or bushing is used on a box, the locknut or bushing requires a flat bearing surface.

Round boxes do not provide such a flat bearing surface; locknuts and bushings are not permitted to be used with these boxes.

Octagonal or square boxes must be used when locknuts and bushings are required.

370-3. Nonmetallic Boxes

If nonmetallic boxes were used with metal-sheathed cable such as BX, or with metal conduit or EMT, the metallic continuity of the wiring system would be broken at each box. This would be in violation of Section 300-10.

Nonmetallic boxes, such as bakelite or porcelain boxes, may be used only with nonmetallic-sheathed cable, such as Romex, or with open-type wiring, such as knob-and-tube work, or with nonmetallic conduit.

Nonmetallic boxes may *not* be used with "metallic-sheathed" types of wiring, such as BX, metal conduit, EMT.

(There is an exception permitted for nonmetallic boxes of over 100 cubic inches. If furnished *by the manufacturer* with a bonding means to bond together the entering conduit or cable sheath, these larger nonmetallic boxes are permitted to be used with metal conduit or metal-sheathed cable.)

Metal boxes may be used with *all types* of wiring.

370-4. Metal Boxes

All metal boxes mounted on metal or metal lath must be grounded (see also Section 250-42). If a metal-sheathed type of wiring is used, such as metal conduit, EMT, or BX, the conduit, EMT or metal sheath of the BX would provide the grounding path. If the wiring is a nonmetallic type such as Romex or nonmetallic conduit, the boxes would have to be grounded through a grounding conductor run with the circuit conductors.

B. Installation

370-5. Damp or Wet Locations

A "damp" location is a location subject to a moderate degree of moisture, such as some barns, or basements.

A "wet" location is one subject to *saturation* with water. An *unprotected* outside location would be a wet location. But an outside location partly protected, like an open porch with a roof, is not considered a wet location. Because of the protecting roof, it would be classified as a "damp" location.

In "wet" locations, boxes and fittings must be weatherproof.

In "damp" locations, standard boxes and fittings may be used, but if used must be "so placed as to prevent moisture or water from entering and accumulating within the box."

370-6. Number of Conductors in Switch, Outlet, Receptacle, Device, and Junction Boxes

When the conductors in a box are *all the same size,* the size of box required can be read from the Table, p. 70-211 of the Code.

The upper part of the table is for junction boxes. The "device" listings are for device boxes. A box of the type used for switches and receptacles is an example of a "device" box.

Each circuit conductor terminating in a box counts as one conductor. "Straight through" conductors count as one.

One or several *grounding* conductors count as only one conductor.

Fixture wires need not be counted.

A conductor that is entirely within a box need not be counted. A pigtail from a splice within a box to a receptacle in the box would be an example of such a conductor.

Each "device" strap counts as one conductor. A switch or receptacle is a "device." One *or more* cable *clamps* count as one conductor (connectors do not count). One *or more* fixture studs or hickeys count as one conductor.

Examples.

1. Three No. 14, two-conductor cables with grounding wire terminate in a junction box with clamps. What size junction box is required?

   There are six circuit conductors. The three grounding wires count as one conductor. The clamps count as one conductor. The box will be sized to accommodate eight No. 14 conductors (Fig. 343). From Table 370-6(a), a 4 × $2\frac{1}{8}$ in. round or octagonal box or a 4 × $1\frac{1}{4}$ in. square box would be the smallest permitted.

2. A junction box without clamps contains a fixture stud, six No. 12 conductors, three grounding conductors, and two fixture wires. What size box is required?

Box contains:
6 No. 14 conductors
3 grounding wires (1 conductor)
Clamps (1 conductor)
Box is sized for (8) No. 14 conductors

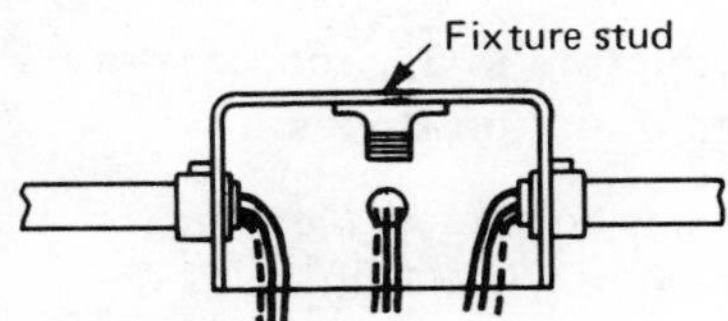

Box contains:
6 No. 12 conductors
3 grounding wires (1 conductor)
Fixture stud (1 conductor)
Box is sized for (8) No. 12 conductors

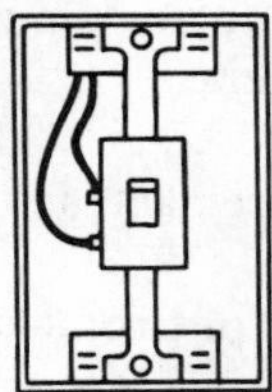

Box contains:
2 No. 14 conductors
Clamps (1 conductor)
Switch (1 conductor)
Switch box is sized for (4) No. 14 conductors

Fig. 343
Number of conductors in boxes (Sect. 370-6).

The fixture wires need not be counted. The three grounding conductors count as one conductor. The fixture stud counts as one conductor. The box will be sized to accommodate eight No. 12 conductors (Fig. 343). From Table 370-6(a), a 4 × $2\frac{1}{8}$ in. round or octagonal box or a 4 × $1\frac{1}{4}$ in. square box would be the smallest size permitted.

3. A switch box with clamps, containing a toggle switch and two No. 14 conductors.

   The switch strap counts as one conductor, the clamps as one conductor.This would be a "device" box sized to accommodate four No. 14 conductors (Fig. 343). From Table 370-6(a), a 3 × 2 × 2 in. box would be the smallest size permitted.

When conductors of different sizes are contained in a box, the minimum-sized box required must be calculated.

Example.

What is the smallest-size square box required for two No. 14–3 conductor and two No. 12–3 conductor cables meeting in a junction?

There will be six No. 14 conductor ends in the box, and six No. 12 conductor ends. From Table 370-6(b), p. 70–212 of the Code, 2 cu. in. is required for each No. 14 conductor and 2.25 cu. in. for each No. 12 conductor.

$$\begin{aligned} \text{The No. 14 wires require } 6 \times 2 &= 12 \text{ cu. in.} \\ \text{The No. 12 wires require } 6 \times 2.25 &= \underline{13.5} \text{ cu. in.} \\ & 25.5 \text{ cu. in.} \end{aligned}$$

From Table 370-6(a), a $4\frac{11}{16}$ × $1\frac{1}{4}$ in. square box would be the minimum size permitted.

Splices may be made in condulets having provisions for *three or more* entries. For condulets with less than three entries, splices may be made only if the condulet is specially marked, by the manufacturer, with cubic inch capacity.

370-7. Conductors Entering Boxes or Fittings

(a) All openings in a box must be suitably closed.

(b) Metal Boxes and Fittings

When *metal* boxes are used with knob-and-tube wiring, two methods of entering the box are permitted:

1. In damp places, insulating bushings (such as porcelain) must be used.
2. In dry places, each conductor may be encased in loom, and the encased conductor clamped where it enters the box. The loom must extend to the last knob or cleat [Fig. 344(b)].

In dry places, insulating bushings are not required, but of course may be used if desired. In damp places, insulating bushings *must* be used.

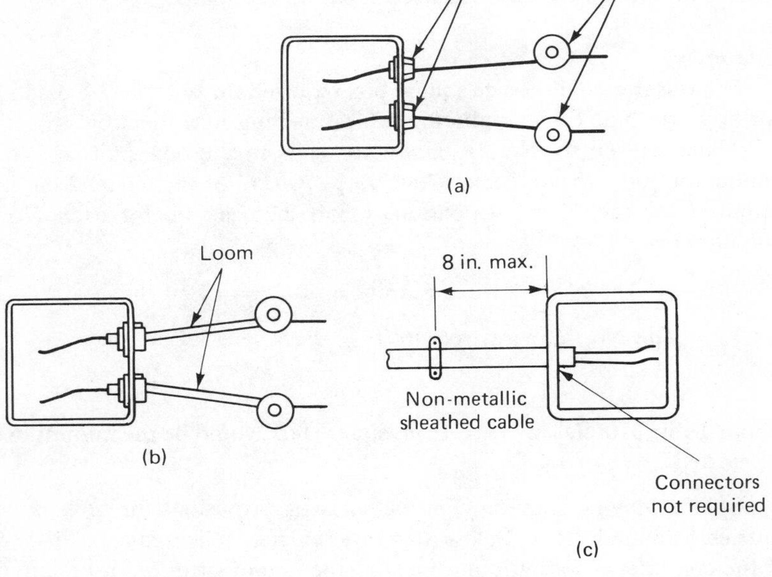

Fig. 344

Conductors entering boxes (Sect. 370-7):

(a) Open wiring entering metal boxes in damp places. An insulating bushing must be provided for each conductor.

(b) Open wiring entering metal boxes in dry places. Conductors may be encased in loom and enter through connectors. Loom must extend to nearest insulator.

(c) Where nonmetallic-sheathed cable enters a *single gang* nonmetallic box, connectors are not required. Last support must be no further than 8 in. from box.

(c) Nonmetallic Boxes

Where nonmetallic boxes (bakelite etc.) are used with nonmetallic-sheathed cable, connectors are not required if the box is a *single gang* box.The only requirement is that the last support be no more than 8 in. from the box. For knob-and-tube or Romex work, nonmetallic boxes have the advantage that an accidental ground within the box would create no hazard. When nonmetallic boxes are used with knob-and-tube work, each conductor must enter the box through an individual hole (Fig. 344). Connectors must be used for nonmetallic conduit.

370-8. Unused Openings

Unused openings in boxes (or fittings) must be closed with a plug or plate. Metal knockout closures are available for this purpose. Metal plugs used in nonmetallic boxes must be recessed at least $\frac{1}{4}$ in. into the box. Recessing reduces the possibility of contact by persons with metal that could become energized.

370-9. Boxes Enclosing Flush Devices

This rule would apply for wall switches or plug receptacles, which are usually installed in switch boxes. The boxes have ears for attaching the box to the wall, and another set of ears for attaching the switch or plug receptacle. The screw used for attaching the box may not be used to attach the switch or receptacle. A separate attachment screw must be used for this purpose.

370-10. In Wall or Ceiling

A box set in a wall or ceiling of wood or other material that will burn must be flush with the surface. The purpose of this practice is to keep material that will burn away from possible contact with the wires. If the box is flush with the surface, there will be no combustible material exposed to possible sparking or arcing within the box.

Boxes set in a wall or ceiling of material that will not burn, such as concrete, may be recessed up to $\frac{1}{4}$ in.

370-11. Repairing Plaster

The purpose of this rule is to eliminate exposed wooden lath, which might be a fire hazard. Plaster must come up flush with the box, so as to seal out wooden lath that might ignite in case of a fault within the box. Broken plaster around a box must be repaired to eliminate open gaps or spaces around the box.

370-12. Exposed Surface Extensions

Where it is desired to install an exposed surface run of wiring from a recessed box, the Code requires an extension ring to be mounted on the recessed box to accommodate the surface wiring. Or as an alternative, another box may be mounted over the recessed box. The box or extension ring must be fastened to and in good metallic contact with the box; separate fastening is not permitted (see Fig. 345).

370-13. Supports

Threaded boxes of not over 100 cubic inches that do not support a fixture or contain a device (such as a receptacle) need not be fastened, if conduit on at least two sides is *threaded* to the box, and the conduit is strapped within 3 ft of the box. If the box supports a fixture or contains a device, and conduit straps are within 18 in., the box need not be fastened (Fig. 346).

Boxes larger than 100 cubic inches must be independently fastened to the surface, regardless of connection to the conduit. A 6 × 6 × 3 in. box, for instance, would exceed the 100 cubic inches specified and must be independently fastened, even if threaded to conduit.

Where wiring is concealed in partitions and in ceiling spaces of frame

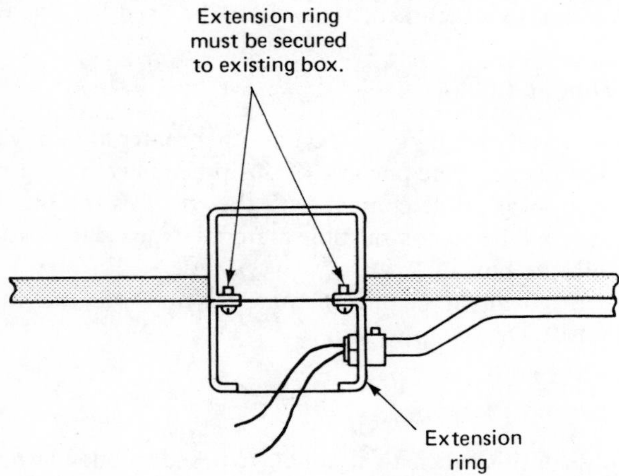

Fig. 345
Exposed surface extension (Sect. 370-12).

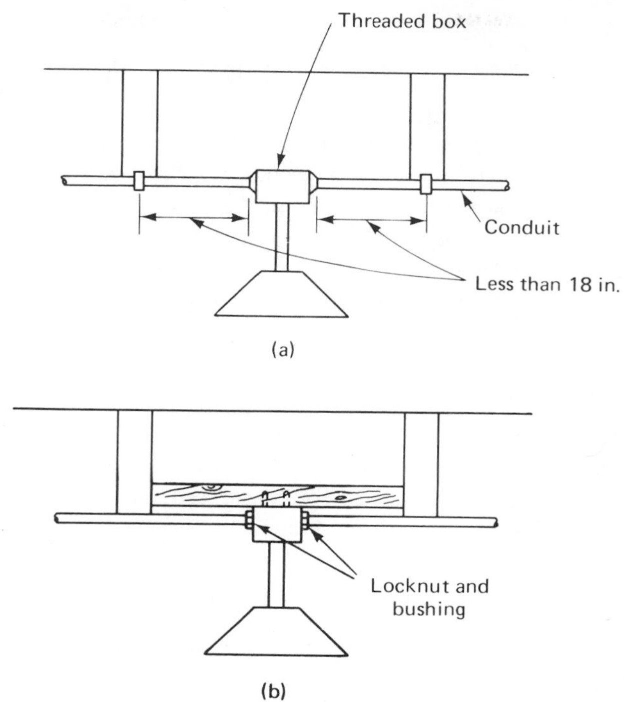

Fig. 346

Box supports (Sect. 370-13):

(a) A threaded box of 100 cubic inches or less supporting a fixture may be supported by the conduit straps if straps are within 18 in. of box.

(b) Boxes with locknut and bushing must be separately fastened regardless of size.

buildings, boxes and other fittings must be fastened to the studs, or a metal or wooden support may be used to bridge across between studs or joists and the box or fitting fastened to the metal or wooden support. Bar hangers are an example of a metal support.

Boxes or fittings may not be fastened to lath of any kind, except that in a finished building, with walls closed up, it is permissible to attach a switch or receptacle box to the wall using approved anchors or clamps.

370-14. Depth of Outlet Boxes

Minimum depth permitted for boxes enclosing "devices" such as switches and receptacles is $\frac{15}{16}$ in. For boxes used only for making splices, minimum depth permitted is $\frac{1}{2}$ in.

370-15. Covers and Canopies

(a) Metal covers may be used with bakelite or porcelain boxes.

(b) Each box must be covered.

If the box is exposed, a box cover plate must be used.

If a lighting fixture is hung beneath a box, the fixture canopy is considered to be a cover, and the box cover plate can be omitted.

If a fixture is hung on a combustible wall or ceiling, the space under the fixture canopy and around the box must be covered with noncombustible material such as asbestos. (See Fig. 413).

If the fixture is hung on a wall or ceiling of material that will not burn, this is not required. The idea of the rule is to have no combustible material around the box under the fixture canopy.

(c) Where a box cover has a hole for a cord, the hole is required to have a bushing or, if no bushing, smooth, well-rounded edges. Hard rubber and composition bushings are not considered adequate for this service, and are not permitted as a bushing.

370-16. Fastened to Gas Pipes

If a box is to be fastened to the threaded end of a gas pipe, it would be necessary to use a hickey or other suitable screwed fitting with a flange for fastening the box to the fitting.

370-17. Outlet Boxes

(a) Boxes at Lighting Fixture Outlets

This rule would be interpreted to mean that the box for a wall or ceiling fixture must be provided with a fixture stud (hickey) for supporting the fixture.

If boxes without fixture studs were installed at lighting outlets, there would be a strong incentive to attach the lighting fixture to the ceiling or the lath with screws. To remove this incentive, fixture studs, which are a more secure support, are required in all boxes used for lighting.

(b) Floor Boxes

Standard boxes may not be used for floor receptacles. Special boxes—floor boxes—must be used for floor receptacles.

An exception to this rule is made in the case of an *elevated* floor in a show window. In this case, standard boxes may be used, but *only by special permission.*

370-18. Pull and Junction Boxes

(a) Minimum Size

Note that the rules of this Section apply for $\frac{3}{4}$-in. or larger conduit (or raceway) that contains No. 4 or larger conductors, and for No. 4 or larger cables. Where conductors in raceway or cable are smaller than No. 4, it is not necessary that a pull or junction box have the full dimensions required by the following rules.

The purpose of the rule is to provide enough room in a pull or junction box so that conductors of the larger sizes (No. 4 or larger) can be properly installed without kinking or undue bending.

There are two cases:

1. Straight pulls.
2. Angle pulls.

Case 1 is that of a pull or junction box installed in a straight run of conduit.

Example.

A pull box is to be installed in a straight run of conduit, consisting of two 3-in., two 2-in., and one 1-in. conduit. What is the minimum length of box required?

The rule says that the length of the box shall be not less than eight times the trade diameter of the largest raceway. Here the largest raceway is a 3-in. conduit.

$$8 \times 3 = 24 \text{ in., minimum length of pull box}$$

The box need be only *wide* enough to accommodate the entering conduits, allowing for proper clearance between conduits for use of a wrench (Fig. 347).

Case 2 applies where a group of conduits enters a pull or junction box at one side and leaves at the top or bottom. This is a right-angle pull.

The rule as stated for Angle or U pulls would set the minimum *width,* as well as the minimum *length* of the box. In other words, the minimum length as figured from the rules would also be the minimum width.

Example.

A pull box is to be installed for a right-angle turn in a group of conduits consisting of four 3-in., two 2-in., and three $1\frac{1}{2}$-in. conduits. What size box is required?

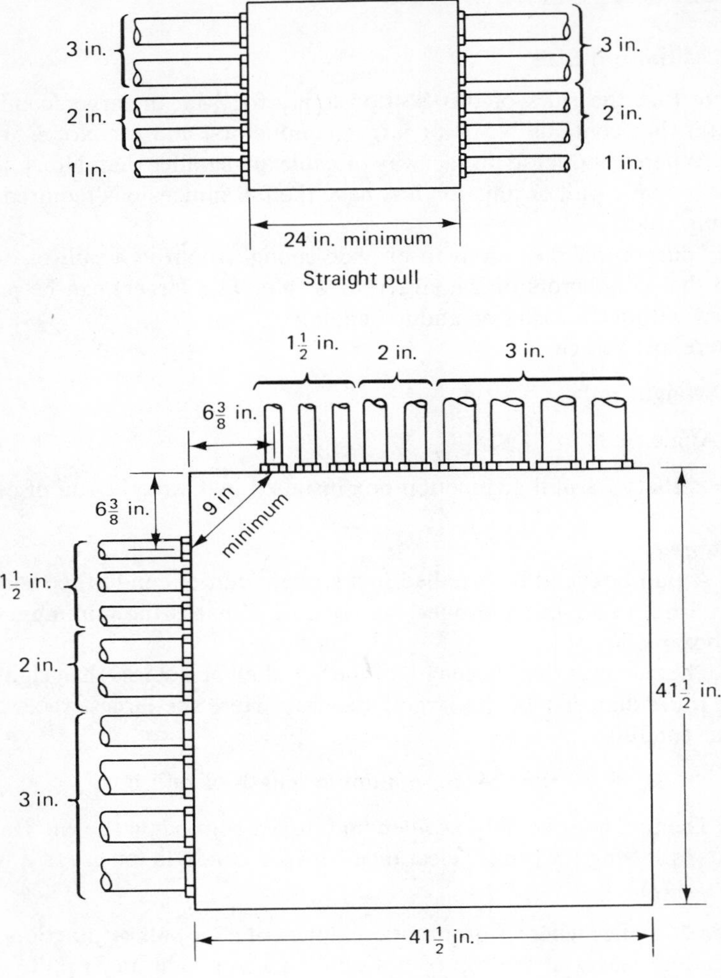

Fig. 347
Pull boxes (Sect. 370-18).

The inside length of the box shall be not less than 6 times the largest raceway diameter, plus the sum of the diameters of all additional raceways.

First, take six times the diameter of one of the largest conduits (3 in.); then add the diameters of all other conduits in the run.

$6 \times 3 \quad = 18$, this accounts for one 3-in. conduit

$3 \times 3 \quad = 9$, this accounts for the other three 3-in. conduits

$2 \times 2 \quad = 4$, this accounts for the two 2-in. conduits

$3 \times 1\frac{1}{2} = 4\frac{1}{2}$, this accounts for the three $1\frac{1}{2}$-in. conduits

$35\frac{1}{2}$ in.

The minimum length of the box would be $35\frac{1}{2}$ in. The minimum width of the box would be $35\frac{1}{2}$ in.

The rule also says that "the distance between raceway entries enclosing the same conductor shall not be less than six times the diameter of the larger raceway." Suppose in the example that the conduit run enters the box at the top and leaves at the left side. If the first conduit on the left at the top is $1\frac{1}{2}$ in. and the top conduit at the side is a $1\frac{1}{2}$ in., then the diagonal distance between the centers of these conduits where they enter the box must be at least $6 \times 1\frac{1}{2} = 9$ in. This means that the two conduits must be set far enough away from the corner to obtain the 9-in. diagonal distance between the two. The distance from the corner for each conduit would be equal to $.707 \times 9 = 6\frac{3}{8}$ in. There would be $35\frac{1}{2} - 6\frac{3}{8}$, or $29\frac{1}{8}$ in. left for the conduits.

This method gives minimum size for the box. The dimensions arrived at by this method should always be checked to determine whether the minimum size provides enough clearance between conduits to accommodate locknuts and for use of a wrench.

Corner-to-corner diameters of the locknuts used in the above example are:

For 3-in. conduit: $4\frac{1}{4}$ in.

For 2-in. conduit: $3\frac{1}{8}$ in.

For $1\frac{1}{2}$-in. conduit: $2\frac{5}{8}$ in.

The space occupied by the locknuts would be

$$(4 \times 4\tfrac{1}{4}) + (2 \times 3\tfrac{1}{8}) + (3 \times 2\tfrac{5}{8}) = 31\tfrac{1}{8} \text{ in.}$$

Allowing $\frac{1}{2}$ in. between locknuts

$$8 \text{ (spaces)} \times \tfrac{1}{2} = 4 \text{ in.}$$

Total space required for locknuts would be

$$31\tfrac{1}{8} + 4 = 35\tfrac{1}{8} \text{ in.}$$

Adding to this the $6\frac{3}{8}$ in. clear space required at the corner gives a total of $41\frac{1}{2}$ in. for width and length of the box (Fig. 347).

The larger dimension should always be used where the two sets of dimensions differ. (In some cases, the first method may yield the larger dimension.)

(b) Conductors in Pull or Junction Boxes

This rule applies particularly for large boxes above distribution switchboards, etc. If a pull or junction box has a dimension, any dimension, over 6 ft, the conductors must be either "served up" with twine or supported on insulated racks.

(c) Covers

All junction and pull boxes must be provided with suitable covers.

(d) When permanent barriers are installed in a box, each section shall be considered as a separate box.

370-19. Junction, Pull, and Outlet Boxes to Be Accessible

A box is considered "accessible" if the wiring in the box can be inspected without damaging the building structure. A box covered by a fixture canopy would be accessible. A box located at such a height that a ladder would be required to reach it would still be accessible. A box housing a receptacle or wall switch would be accessible. A box concealed within a closed partition would be "inaccessible."

Underground boxes are considered accessible if they can be reached simply by removing earth. If it is necessary to remove part of a sidewalk or part of a paved street or highway, they are considered inaccessible.

C. Construction Specifications

370-20. Metal Outlet, Switch and Junction Boxes, and Fittings

Must be corrosion-proof. Galvanized, cadmium-plated, or painted equipment would meet this requirement.

Smaller sheet-metal boxes must be at least 16 gauge. Larger boxes must conform to requirements for cabinets and cutout boxes (except for hinging).

Cast-metal boxes must have a wall thickness of at least $\frac{1}{8}$ in. ($\frac{3}{32}$ in. for malleable iron, aluminum, brass or bronze boxes).

370-21. Covers

Metal covers must be of the same thickness as the box, except that lined covers may be of smaller gauge.

370-22. Bushings

Where a box cover has a hole for a cord, the hole is required to have a bushing or, if no bushing, smooth well-rounded edges. Holes for individual wires must have insulating bushings such as porcelain—one bushed hole for each conductor.

370-23. Nonmetallic Boxes

370-24. Marking

Mounting ears or flanges must be on the outside of nonmetallic boxes. This is to prevent possible contact between mounting screws and conductors in the box, which would permanently energize the metal mounting screws. All boxes, conduit bodies, covers, etc., must be marked with the manufacturer's name or trademark.

D. Pull and Junction Boxes for Use on Systems over 600 Volts Nominal

Note that, for straight pulls, the length of a box must be 48 times the outside diameter of the largest cable or *conductor* entering the box. For angle or U pulls, minimum width and length are at least 36 times outside diameter of the largest cable or conductor. These requirements differ from those of Section 370-18 for 600 volts and under.

ARTICLE 373 — CABINETS AND CUTOUT BOXES

373-1. Scope

A "cabinet" or "cutout box" is by definition a box or enclosure fitted with *swinging doors.* (See Definitions, pp. 70-5 and 70-7 of the Code.) This distinguishes cabinets and cutout boxes from pull boxes or junction boxes, which have covers rather than swinging doors.

In a cutout box, the hinged door has a flange that "telescopes" with the side of the box. Cutout boxes are made for surface mounting. In a cabinet, the hinged door is usually flat, having no flange. Cabinets are made for either flush or surface mounting.

An example of a cabinet would be a lighting or power panel. An example of a cutout box would be the enclosure for a knife switch.

Fig. 348 shows a typical cabinet and cutout box.

A. Installation

373-2. Damp or Wet Locations

In a damp or wet location, cutout boxes and surface-mounted cabinets must be "stooled off" the wall at least $\frac{1}{4}$ in.

In wet locations, cabinets and cutout boxes must be the weatherproof type. In damp locations they need not be weatherproof, but if not weatherproof must be so placed or equipped as to prevent water from "entering and accumulating" within. "Accumulating" of water could be prevented by drilling drain holes in the bottom of the box.

(For definition of "damp" and "wet" locations, see p. 70-10 of the Code.)

373-3. Position in Wall

Recessed cabinets mounted in walls of wood, wood lath, or other combustible material must be mounted with the front edge flush or projecting from the surface. If mounted in walls of concrete or other noncombustible material, the front may be set back from the surface, but not more than $\frac{1}{4}$ in.

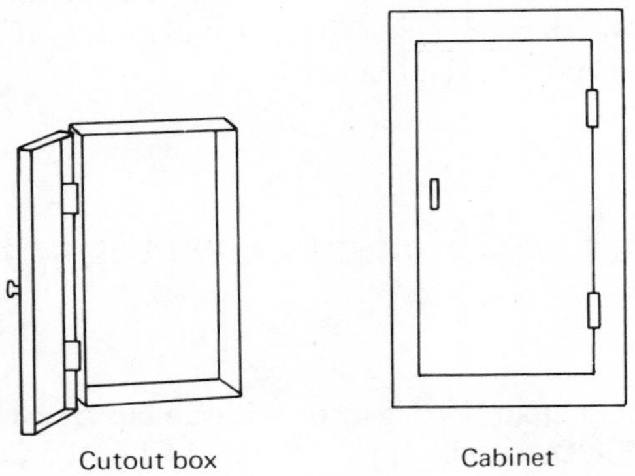

Fig. 348
Typical cabinet and cutout box.

373-4. Unused Openings

This rule is the same as the rule of Section 370-8 for boxes.

The provisions of the rule forbid an unused knockout hole that has been opened to be left open. The rule calls for protection "substantially equivalent to the wall of the cabinet or cutout box." The intent is to require that the material used for closing an opening should have a strength equal to that of the material of the cabinet or cutout box. A wooden plug or a piece of light-gauge metal would not be approved for this purpose.

If metal is used for closing an opening in a *nonmetallic* box or cabinet, the plug or plate must be recessed at least $\frac{1}{4}$ in.

373-5. Conductors Entering Cabinets or Cutout Boxes

(a) Openings to Be Closed

"Adequate closing" in this case would be afforded by a connector and locknut around a cable or conduit.

(b) Metal Cabinets and Cutout Boxes

When metal cabinets and cutout boxes are used with knob-and-tube wiring, two methods of entering the box are permitted:

1. In damp places, insulating bushings (such as porcelain) must be used.
2. In *dry* places, each conductor may be encased in loom, and the encased conductor clamped where it enters the box. The loom must extend to the last knob or cleat.

   In dry places, insulating bushings are not required, but of course may be used if desired. In *damp* places, insulating bushings *must* be used rather than loom.

373-6. Deflection of Conductors

A "gutter" or raceway in a cabinet is the space provided by the manufacturer between the panel in the box and the sheet-metal wall of the box ("tub"). This space is intended for the wiring. It varies in width according to the size of the cabinet.

The purpose of this rule is to avoid sharp bends in the entering conductors. A sharp bend in a narrow gutter would jam the conductors against the box with considerable force, and might eventually result in a ground.

Conductors may not be deflected within a cabinet or cutout box unless the width of the gutter is at least equal to the width specified in Table 373-6(a) of the Code. Larger conductors of course require a wider gutter than the smaller sizes.

If the width of the gutter is less than that specified in the table, the conductor would have to enter the cabinet or cutout box in such a way that bending would not be required. See Fig. 349.

"Hot" wires No. 4 or larger must enter a cabinet or cutout box through *insulating* bushings, rather than steel bushings. Bushings are on the market made of bakelite and other insulating materials. Wrought-iron bushings with built-in insulating rings are also available. Either of these types may be used.

Wires smaller than No. 4 are not likely to press against the bushing with force. Steel bushings may be used with No. 6 and smaller wire.

Two locknuts are required when the bushing is made entirely of bakelite or other insulating material. The locknut under the bushing relieves strain on the insulating bushing and provides a reliable connection. Wrought iron bushings with built-in insulating rings do not require an inside locknut.

373-7. Space in Enclosures

A cabinet or cutout box shall provide sufficient space for conductors without overcrowding.

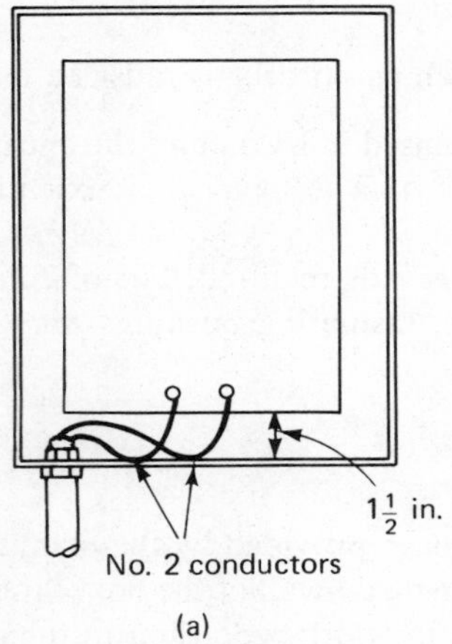

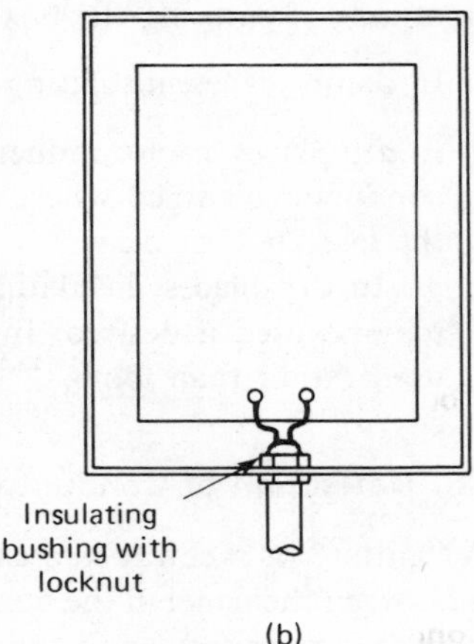

Fig. 349

Deflection of conductors in cabinets (Sect. 373-6):

(a) No. 2 conductors deflected in a 1½-in. gutter. This is a violation. There is not sufficient gutter width to make a deflection without forcing the conductors against the wall of the box. To make such a deflection, a 2½-in. gutter is required [Table 373-6(a)].

(b) The conductors may enter the 1½-in. gutter if without a deflection. Since the conductors are larger than No. 6, an insulating bushing is required.

373-8. Enclosures for Switches or Overcurrent Devices

Splices may be made in switch boxes and "overcurrent-device" enclosures, or conductors may be fed through, provided that there is enough free space in the box to accommodate the wires and splices. The allowable "fill" is specified as 40% for wires, 75% for splices. The percentage of fill applies to the free space—the wiring space—within the box, excluding the switch or overcurrent device.

373-9. Side or Back Wiring Spaces or Gutters

Cabinets and cutout boxes must be provided with wiring space in accordance with the construction specifications of Sections 373-11(c) and (d).

B. Construction Specifications

373-10. Material

Metal cabinets and cutout boxes must be corrosion-proof. Galvanizing, cadmium plating, or painting would meet this requirement.

Sheet metal used for construction of boxes and cabinets must be at least 16 gauge.

Nonmetallic cabinets may be used only by special permission.

373-11. Spacing

(a) General

1. *Base*
   A panel or other device must be stooled off the back wall of the enclosure at least $\frac{1}{16}$ in.
2. Door must be separated at least 1 in. from live parts, but if the door is lined with insulating material or is of at least 12-gauge metal, a $\frac{1}{2}$-in. separation is permitted.
3. At least a $\frac{1}{2}$-in. spacing must be maintained between live parts and the walls of the cabinet or cutout box. Spacing shall be increased for voltages above 250.

(b) Switch Clearance

Sufficient clearance must be maintained between switches and the door of the cabinet or cutout box.

(c) Wiring Space

Cabinets or cutout boxes accommodating more than eight conductors in addition to the supply conductors must be provided with wiring gutters inside the case.

(d) Wiring Space—Enclosure

Wiring spaces within a cabinet or cutout box must be provided with covers, barriers, or partitions.

ARTICLE 374 — AUXILIARY GUTTERS

374-1. Use

Auxiliary gutters are troughs made of sheet metal. They are similar to wireways or busways but have a different use. Wireways and busways are used for general wiring and between widely separated points. Auxiliary gutters are used for short runs between apparatus.

They are used, for example, in the service part of apartment-house wiring. An auxiliary gutter would be installed from the master service switch, with individual taps from the gutter to the metered services for the apartments.

Another use of auxiliary gutters is in connection with a distribution center for a group of motors, the gutter carrying the main or feeder, with taps to motor switches, which are mounted on a suitable frame.

Gutters may enclose only conductors, either bare, as in the form of a bus bar, or insulated wire. Switches, fuses, circuit breakers, etc., are not permitted inside auxiliary gutters.

374-2. Extension Beyond Equipment

Auxiliary gutters may not extend more than 30 ft beyond the equipment served (except that for elevators, length is not limited).

374-3. Supports

374-4. Covers

Supports must be installed at intervals of not more than 5 ft. Covers must be securely fastened to the gutter.

374-5. Number of Conductors

The sum of the cross-sectional areas of all conductors may not exceed 20 percent of the interior cross-sectional area of the gutter; but regardless of size of the gutter, not more than 30 conductors are permitted in any case. Grounding wires are not counted as conductors.

To determine the size of gutter required for any given number of wires, refer to Table 5, pp. 70-583 and 70-584 of the Code. This table gives the area in square inches for the different-sized conductors. After determining the total area of all wires going into the gutter, multiply by 5; this will give you the minimum cross-sectional area of the gutter required.

For example, consider a gutter that is to carry six 250 MCM Type RH wires. From the table the cross-sectional area of this wire is .5917 sq. in.

$$.5917 \times 6 = 3.5502 \text{ sq. in., total area of wires}$$

$$3.5502 \times 5 = 17.75 \text{ sq. in., required area of the gutter}$$

This would require a gutter about $4\frac{1}{4}$ by $4\frac{1}{4}$ in. minimum size. (The gutter need not be square in shape; it could be rectangular, but in either case it must have at least 17.75 sq. in. of area.)

There are exceptions to the rule limiting the number of conductors to 30. In the following cases more than 30 conductors are permitted:

1. Conductors for signaling circuits or motor-control circuits are not counted as conductors; 30 conductors in addition to these may be contained in an auxiliary gutter, as long as the total area of *all* conductors does not exceed 20% of the cross-sectional area of the gutter.

2. For auxiliary gutters used in connection with elevators, dumbwaiters, escalators, or moving walks, any number of conductors is permitted as long as the fill does not exceed 20%.

3. Any number of current-carrying conductors are permitted in an auxiliary gutter if the correction factors of Note 8, p. 70-136 of the Code, are applied.

374-6. Ampacity of Conductors

The correction factors of Note 8, p. 70-136 of the Code, ordinarily apply when there are more than three conductors in a raceway.

However, in the case of auxiliary gutters, the correction factors do not have to be applied unless there are more than 30 current-carrying conductors in the gutter.

Current-carrying capacity of copper bus bar in an auxiliary gutter is limited to 1,000 amps./in.^{2} of the bus bar cross-sectional area, 700 amps. for aluminum bus bar.

For example, a copper bus bar $\frac{1}{4}$ by 1 in. would have a cross-sectional area of $\frac{1}{4} \times 1 = \frac{1}{4}$ sq. in. The carrying capacity would be $\frac{1}{4} \times 1{,}000 = 250$ amps. maximum.

374-7. Clearance of Bare Live Parts

This Section refers to bare bus bars.

Minimum spacing of bare bus bars is as follows:

1. 2 inches between bus bars at points of support. Between supports, the bars may approach one another to a distance of 1 in. minimum between bars.

2. 1 inch between bus bar and walls of enclosure.

Example.

Three $\frac{1}{8}$ by 1 in. bus bars are to be installed in an auxiliary gutter. What is the minimum-sized gutter required? Assume the bus bars to be placed in a vertical position side by side.

A 2-in. spacing between bus bars would give:

$$\tfrac{1}{8} + 2 + \tfrac{1}{8} + 2 + \tfrac{1}{8} = 4\tfrac{3}{8} \text{ in., total space taken by bus bars at points of support}$$

One inch is required between the outside bars and walls of the enclosure. Total inside width of gutter would be

$$4\tfrac{3}{8} + 1 + 1 = 6\tfrac{3}{8} \text{ in., minimum}$$

The bus bars are 1 in. in height, and there must be 1 in. of clearance, both top and bottom, between the edge of the bus bars and the sheet metal of the gutter. Height of gutter would therefore be $1 + 1 + 1 = 3$ in. (inside height) minimum.

A gutter at least $6\frac{3}{8}$ by 3 in. would be required. This size would also fully satisfy the requirements of Section 374-5 as to the total cross-sectional area of conductors (bus bars in this case) not exceeding 20% of cross-sectional area of the gutter (Fig. 350).

374-8. Splices and Taps

(a) Splices and taps are allowed in auxiliary gutters. Splices or taps may not fill the gutter completely, only to 75% of the area of the gutter.

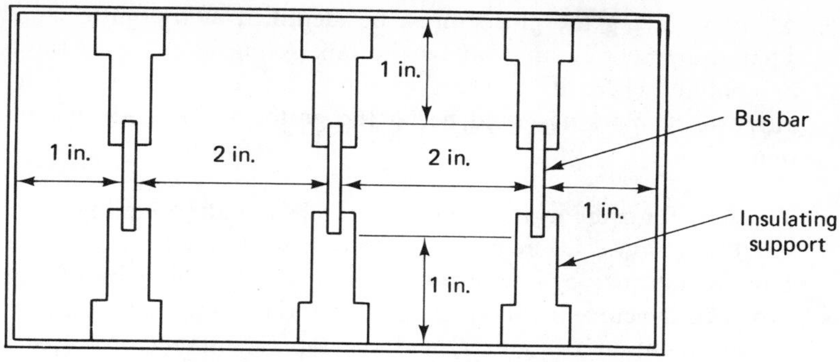

Fig. 350
Minimum clearance of bare live parts (Sect. 374-7). The clearances are for bus bar set in insulating supports having no live parts. Supports having live metal parts are subject to the same clearance requirements: 2 in. minimum between the live parts, and 1 in. minimum between the live parts and metal wall of enclosure.

(b) Insulated taps shall not be allowed to rest on, or come in contact with, bus bar of opposite polarity. Such practice might result in injury to the insulation by cutting or from excessive heating, and result in a short circuit. Taps to bare bus bars in a gutter shall leave the gutter opposite their connection to the bus bar. Taps shall be placed in such a way that the insulation will not come in contact with bus bar of opposite polarity (Fig. 351). All taps must be accessible. A cover attached by screws or bolts would fulfill the requirement for accessibility.

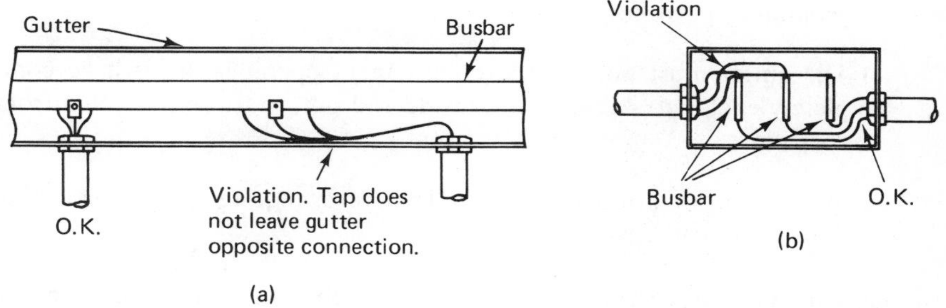

Fig. 351
Splices to bare conductors [Sect. 374-8(b)]:

(a) Taps must leave gutter opposite their terminal connections.
(b) Taps shall not be brought in contact with bare conductors of opposite polarity.

(c) All taps leaving the gutter must be identified at the gutter to show what equipment is supplied by the tap. A tag attached to the cable or conduit where it connects to the gutter could be used for this purpose, or marking could be on the gutter at the point of connection.

(d) The rules for overcurrent protection of taps in gutters could be summarized as follows: Overcurrent protection need not be at the point of tapping, but may be any distance within 25 ft of the point of tapping, provided the current-carrying capacity of the tap wires is at least $\frac{1}{3}$ that of the mains in the gutter, and the tap is suitably protected from damage.

For example, suppose that the mains in the gutter were No. 2/0 Type T wire. From Table 310-16, p. 70-132, the carrying capacity of No. 2/0 is 145 amps.

$$\tfrac{1}{3} \times 145 = 48\tfrac{1}{3} \text{ amps.}$$

If the tap were No. 6 or larger, the fuse or other overcurrent protection in the tap could be located up to 25 ft from the point of tapping.

If the tap were smaller than No. 6, the protection would have to be located at the point of tapping to the No. 2/0.

374-9. Construction and Installation

(a) Adequate electrical continuity must be provided. The parts should be joined together so that the enclosure forms a continuous conductor for grounding purposes.

(b) The gutter must not have any permanent openings; it must be completely enclosed. All surfaces, inside and out, must be protected from corrosion.

(c) Suitable bushings must be provided wherever required to protect insulation of the wires from abrasion.

(d) This subsection provides for adequate width, where the conductors are deflected or the gutter makes a turn. For turns and conductor deflection, the rules of Section 373-6 must be followed.

(e) Auxiliary gutters for use outdoors must be of raintight construction. See definition of "raintight," p. 70-12 of the Code.

ARTICLE 380 — SWITCHES

A. Installation

380-1. Scope

Article 380 applies to all switches and to circuit breakers used as switches.

380-2. Switch Connections

(a) Three-Way and Four-Way Switches

Three-way (and four-way) switches may switch only the "hot" wire.

If "metal-clad" wiring such as conduit, EMT, or BX is used for a switch circuit, a single conductor may *not* be run from the switch to the fixture. The other side of the circuit must be carried along with the switched wire. This is to prevent induced currents from being set up in the conduit, EMT, or BX sheath. If both sides of the circuit are in the same enclosure, there will be no induced current, because the inductive effect of the current in one conductor cancels the inductive effect of the other, the currents being always equal and opposite in direction (Fig. 352).

A switch wire may be run in conduit from a fixture box to a switch, if the return wire is carried along with it. In this case the current in the return wire would always be opposite in direction to the current in the supply wire, thus neutralizing the inductive effect.

For three-way or four-way switches, two "travelers" alone may not be run in conduit or other "metal-clad" wiring. The return wire must be run along with them, or if the return wire is not included, the neutral must be carried along with the switched travelers.

If non-metal-clad wiring such as Romex is used, switch wires may be run separately, since with non-metal-clad wiring there is no danger of induced currents being set up in the cable sheath.

(b) Grounded Conductors

This Section prohibits the use of a single-pole switch in the neutral or grounded conductor.

Switching the neutral only would create the danger of shock to persons, even though the switch were open. Also, an accidental ground beyond the switch could turn a circuit "on" even though the switch were "off." For example, if the metal case of a motor is grounded, and the neutral at the motor should accidentally come in contact with the case, then the circuit would be

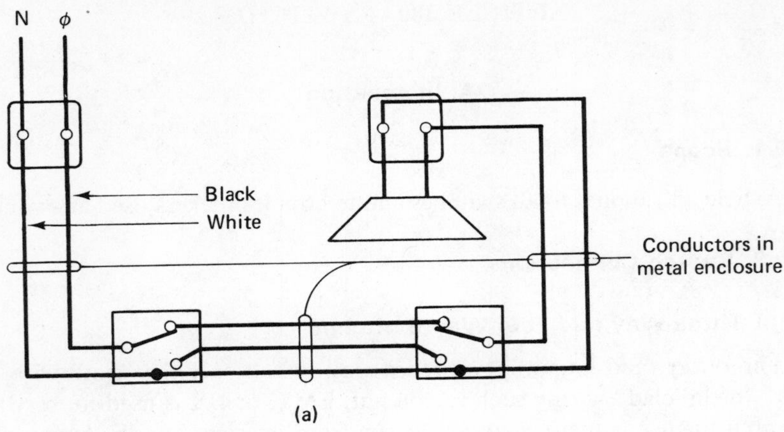

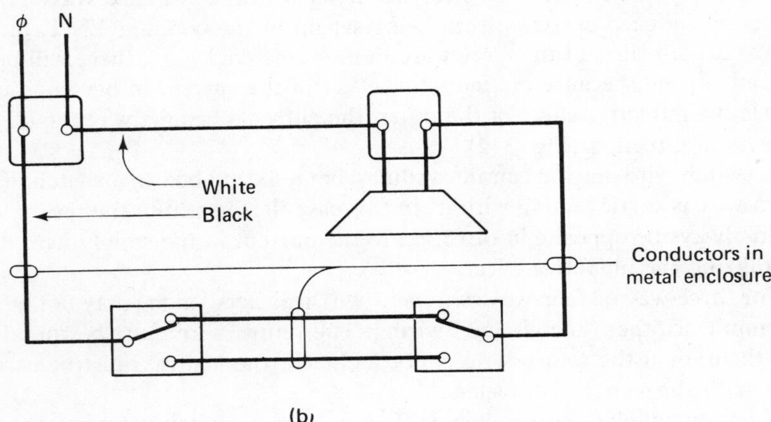

Fig. 352

Three-way switch circuits in metal enclosures (conduit, EMT, BX, etc.).

(a) Both polarities are in the same enclosure as required by Sect. 380-2(a).

(b) Violation. This arrangement would permit induced currents to be set up in the metal enclosures. If a nonmetallic wiring method is used (Romex, nonmetallic conduit, etc.), method (b) is permitted, since induced currents cannot be set up in nonmetallic enclosures.

completed through the case to ground, and the motor would operate even though the switch were "off."

The neutral of a two-wire grounded circuit may be switched, if a two-pole switch is used, thereby opening the hot wire along with the neutral. The neutral of a three-wire system may be switched if a three-pole switch is used.

380-3. Enclosure

In most cases, switches must be enclosed. This minimizes fire hazard, protects the switch from mechanical injury, and protects persons from contact with the bare parts of the switch. Switches and circuit breakers shall be externally operable.

Exception.
Pendant switches, surface-type snap switches, and knife switches mounted on an open-face switchboard or on a panelboard need not be enclosed.

380-4. Wet Locations

In wet locations, switches and circuit breakers must have weatherproof enclosures, and must be "stooled off" the wall at least $\frac{1}{4}$ in. (see definition of "wet location," p. 70-10 of the Code).

380-5. Time Switches, Flashers, and Similar Devices

This rule is intended to apply to any automatic switching device, which would of course include flashers used for control of sign lighting. All such devices must be enclosed in metal enclosures, except where mounted in switchboards or control panels or enclosed in "approved" individual housings.

380-6. Position of Knife Switches

380-7. Connection of Knife Switches

Single-throw knife switches *should* be mounted vertically, but, as indicated by the wording of this rule, *may* be mounted horizontally, as long as "gravity will not tend to close them." When mounted vertically, the hinge must be at the bottom. For both horizontal and vertical mounting, the incoming line is required to be connected to the side of the switch opposite the blades, so that the blades will be dead when the switch is in the open position [Fig. 353(a)].

Double-throw switches should be mounted *horizontally.* They may be mounted vertically, but if mounted vertically must be provided with a locking device that will ensure the blades remaining open when so set [Fig. 353(b) (c)]. The incoming line may be connected to the blade part of a double-throw switch.

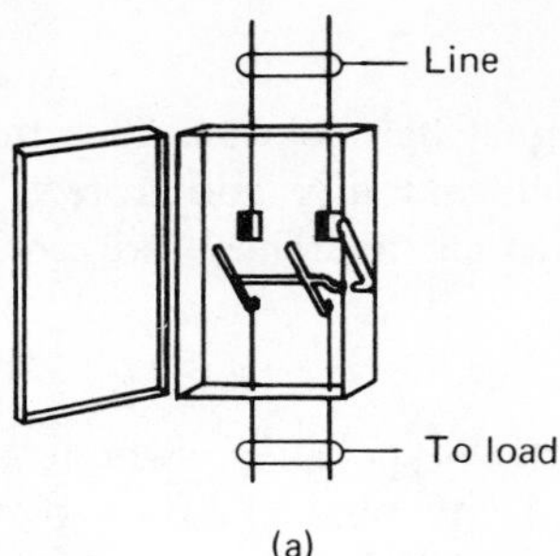

(a)

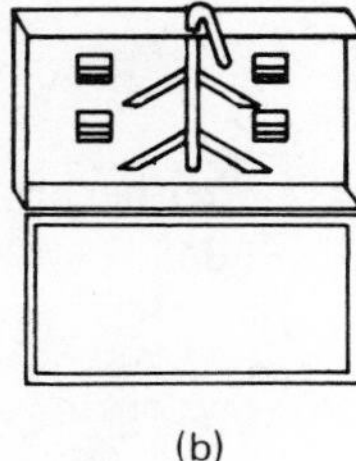

(b)

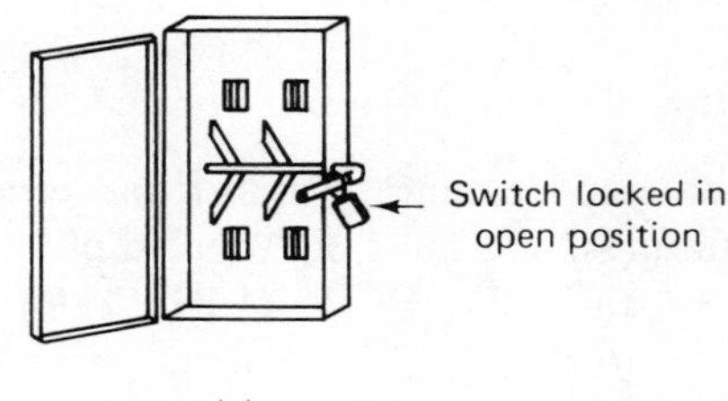

(c)

Fig. 353

Position of knife switches (Sect. 380-6):

(a) Single-throw knife switches must be mounted hinge end down, so that gravity will not tend to close them. The incoming line may not be connected to the hinge end. The load is connected to the hinge.

(b)(c) Double-throw switches may be mounted either horizontally or vertically. If mounted vertically, a locking device must be provided.

380-8. Accessibility and Grouping

(a) Switches and circuit breakers must be readily accessible. "Readily accessible," according to Code definition, means "capable of being reached quickly for operation . . . without removing or climbing over obstacles, or requiring the use of a ladder, chair, etc." In short, switches and circuit breakers must be so located that they may be reached and operated without delay.

The operating handle of any switch or circuit breaker may be not more than $6\frac{1}{2}$ ft above the floor level.

Exceptions.

1. On busways, fused switches and circuit breakers may be at the same level as the busway, as long as means are provided to operate the switch or circuit breaker from the floor.

2. Switches for motors, appliances, or other equipment, and mounted adjacent thereto, may be located at a greater height.
3. For hookstick-operated isolating switches, the handle height mav be more than $6\frac{1}{2}$ ft.

(b) Snap switches of different voltages may be ganged in boxes if the difference in voltage is not over 300 V. If over 300 V, barriers must be provided between switches.

380-9. Faceplates for Flush-Mounted Snap Switches

The box for a flush-mounted snap switch would be recessed in the wall and not liable to contact by persons. However, the *faceplate* would be exposed to contact. The faceplate has metallic contact with the box through the mounting screws and yoke, and if the faceplate is of metal, an accidental ground in an ungrounded box would permanently energize the plate. If the faceplate is within reach of ground or a grounded object, this would present a shock hazard; and under these conditions the Code requires that nonmetallic faceplates be used. If the faceplate is *not* within reach of ground or a grounded object, it may be of metal.

This rule is for *ungrounded* metal boxes. If the box is grounded, a metal faceplate may be used in any location, since an accidental ground in the box would immediately open the circuit fuse or circuit breaker and deenergize the plate.

380-10. Mounting of Snap Switches

(a) Surface Type

Surface-type snap switches used with open wiring on insulators must be mounted on a pad of insulating material not less than $\frac{1}{2}$ in. thick.

(b) Box Mounted

Section 370-10 permits a switch box installed in a "noncombustible" wall (such as concrete, masonry, etc.) to be recessed $\frac{1}{4}$ in. back from the surface. When the box is so recessed, the plaster ears of the switch must be seated against the surface of the wall, not recessed so as to seat against the box.

When the box is mounted flush with the surface of the wall, the switch must be attached to the box, not the wall.

380-11. Circuit Breakers as Switches

Circuit breakers are approved for use as switches.

380-12. Grounding of Enclosures

Metal enclosures for switches or circuit breakers operating at more than 150 volts to ground must be grounded regardless of location.

Metal enclosures for switches or circuit breakers operating at 150 volts or less to ground must be grounded only if:

1. Located within reach of ground or a grounded object (8 ft vertically or 5 ft horizontally is "within reach").
2. Located in a damp or wet location and subject to contact by persons.
3. Mounted in contact with metal.
4. Located in a hazardous location.

380-13. Knife Switches

General-use knife switches rated over 1,200 amps. at 250 volts or less and knife switches rated over 600 amps. at 251 to 600 volts, may be used only as isolating switches. They may not be used for interrupting current. To interrupt currents above these values, a circuit breaker or a specially designed switch must be used.

380-14. Rating and Use of Snap Switches

"Snap switch" as used here includes the tumbler and toggle switch. The Code divides snap switches into two classes, the AC general-use snap switch and the AC-DC general-use snap switch.

(a) AC General-Use Snap Switches

These may be used for:

1. Resistive loads, such as heaters and incandescent lights, and inductive loads, such as fluorescent lights.

   For such loads, the switch rating must be at least equal to the load amperes.
2. Motor loads. For motor loads the switch rating must be at least 125% of the motor full-load current rating.

(b) AC-DC General-Use Snap Switches

1. AC-DC snap switches used for controlling incandescent lights must be "T" rated. For other resistive loads, they need not be "T" rated, but in either case the switch rating must be equal to the load amperes.

2. When used to control inductive loads, such as fluorescent lights, the rating of the switch must be twice the load amperes. AC-DC general-use snap switches may *not* be used for motor control (Section 430-83).

B. Construction Specifications

380-15. Marking

Switches must be marked by the manufacturer showing volts, amps., and, if horsepower rated, with hp.

380-16. 600-Volt Knife Switches

600-volt knife switches of over 200 amps. must be fitted with auxiliary contacts.

380-17. Fused Switches

Paralleling of fuses is prohibited by the Code (Section 240-8).

ARTICLE 384 — SWITCHBOARDS AND PANELBOARDS

384-1. Scope

A "panelboard" according to definition is intended to be mounted in a cabinet or cutout box placed "in or against a wall or partition." A panelboard is for control of small-capacity circuits. The familiar lighting distribution panelboard consisting of a group of fuses or circuit breakers mounted inside a sheet metal cabinet is one example of a panelboard that fits the definition.

Switchboards, on the other hand, are larger, usually control circuits of higher capacity, and by definition are not intended to be installed in cabinets or mounted on the wall, but usually stand on the floor.

The Code rules governing switchboards do not apply to switchboards in power plants, or to switchboards for signal circuits operated by batteries. The rules governing panelboards include battery-charging panels.

384-2. Other Articles

The rules of Article 240 (Overcurrent Protection), 250 (Grounding), 370 (Boxes and Fittings), and 380 (Switches) must be complied with as well as the rules of this Article (384).

384-3. Support and Arrangement of Busbars and Conductors

(a) Conductors and busbars shall be firmly fastened and located so as to be free from damage.

(b) An alternating current flowing in a busbar or conductor will cause a current to flow in nearby metal enclosures because of induction. Proper arrangement of busbars or conductors will minimize or eliminate this effect. If all conductors of a circuit are grouped together, for example, the current in one direction will always be equal and opposite to the current in the other direction, and the inductive effect of the group will be neutralized.

(c) When panelboards or switchboards are used as service equipment, a grounding bar is required. The grounding bar must be bonded to the panel case or switchboard frame.

(d) Load terminals must be so arranged that connections may be made without reaching across a bus.

(e) In a three-phase delta-connected system, if a neutral is brought out from one of the phase transformers, the voltage to neutral of one phase will be higher than the voltage to neutral of the other two phase wires. As an example, consider a three-phase, 240-volt circuit. If a neutral is brought out from the transformer connected between phase wires A and B, the voltage between neutral and phase wire A will be 120 volts; between neutral and phase wire B, 120 volts. The voltage between neutral and phase wire C, however, will be 208 volts. When a circuit such as this is used in a switchboard or panelboard, the conductor with the higher voltage to ground (in this case C) must be marked or identified. (See Fig. 217)

(f) Phase arrangement of three-phase buses shall be A, B, C, from front to back, top to bottom, and from left to right as viewed from the front. (For additions to existing installations, other busbar arrangements may be permitted.)

(g) Gutter space and wire bending space provided in panelboards and switchboards shall be at least equal to that required by Table 373-6(a), p. 70-218 of the Code.

A. Switchboards

384-4. Location of Switchboards

A switchboard of the "live front" type of construction may not be placed in a damp or wet location. Live-front switchboards may be placed only in locations that are dry at all times, and then only if under competent supervision and accessible only to qualified persons.

384-5. Wet Locations

In a damp or wet location a switchboard must be of the "dead-front" type with no exposed current-carrying parts, and enclosed in a weatherproof enclosure.

384-6. Location Relative to Easily Ignitible Material

384-7. Clearance from Ceiling

These two Sections recognize the possibility of fire resulting from a switchboard being located too close to any material that might ignite in case of overheating of a part of the switchboard, or in the case of arcing due to an accidental short circuit or other causes. For a ceiling of wood, fiber, or any other material that will burn, the Code requires a minimum clearance of 3 ft between the ceiling and the top of the board unless (1) a fireproof shield is provided, or (2) the switchboard is totally enclosed.

384-8. Clearances Around Switchboards

Referring to Section 110-16, minimum clearances around a switchboard would be as follows:

When live parts are exposed, minimum clearance from an ungrounded wall would be 3 ft (if the wall is grounded, the minimum distance is $3\frac{1}{2}$ ft for voltages of 151 to 600 to ground). See Fig. 354.

For a dead-front switchboard (having no exposed live parts), minimum clearance required in front of the board is $2\frac{1}{2}$ ft. No clearance is specified for sides and rear, but it must be remembered that, when the board is being worked

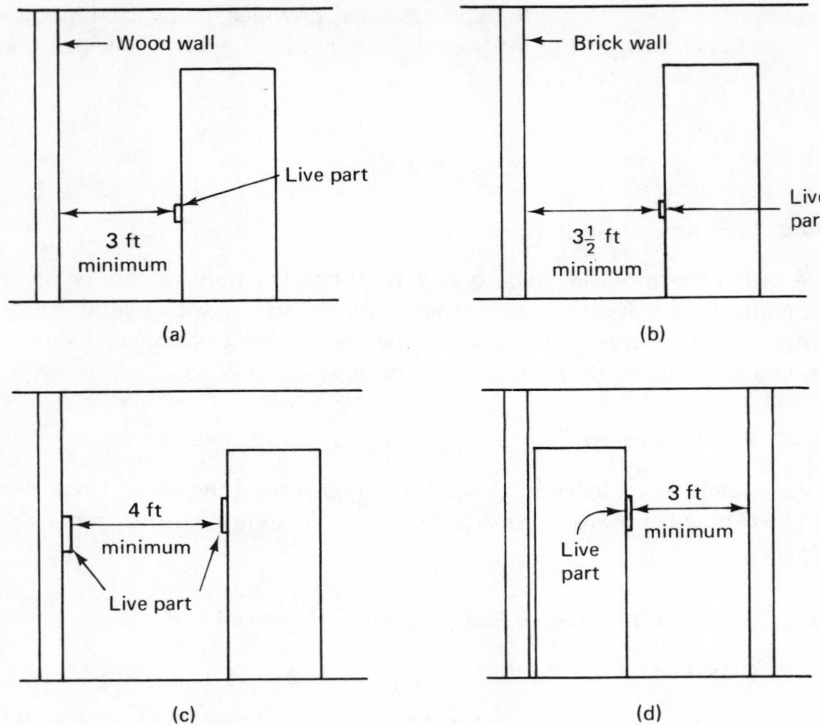

Fig. 354

Clearances around switchboards for voltages of 151 to 600 to ground (Sects. 384-8, 110-16):

(a)(b)(c) Minimum clearances required in back of switchboards.
(a) Minimum clearance between live parts and a nongrounded wall.
(b) Minimum clearance between live parts and a grounded wall (brick, concrete, tile walls are considered to be grounded).
(c) Clearance required when there are live parts on both sides.
(d) Minimum clearance required in front of switchboards.

on from the rear, with cover plates removed, there would be live parts exposed, and a minimum 3 ft clearance would be required. These are minimums. It is desirable to have at least 3 ft of working space in front of a switchboard.

384-9. Conductor Covering

Insulated conductors, where closely grouped, are required to have flame-retardant insulation. Instrument and control wiring, such as wiring to ammeters, voltmeters, wattmeters, and pilot lights, may be any one of the following types: RH, RHH, RHW, V, ALS, AVA, AVB, SIS, T, TA, TBS, TW, THHN, THWN, THW, MI, XHHW.

384-10. Clearance for Conductors Entering Bus Enclosures

Switchboards (and some large panelboards) are mounted on the floor.

Circuits may enter the switchboard or panelboard through the floor. When conduit or other raceway enters a switchboard (or floormounted panelboard) through the bottom, sufficient space must be provided for entry and installation of the conductors. Minimum space required between the bottom of the switchboard enclosure and bus bars or other obstructions is 8 in. for insulated bus bars, their supports, or other obstructions, and 10 in. for uninsulated bus bars. No part of an entering conduit or raceway, including fittings, may rise to a height of more than 3 in. above the bottom of the enclosure.

384-11. Grounding Switchboard Frames

384-12. Grounding of Instruments, etc.

All *AC* switchboard frames must be grounded.

Single-polarity DC switchboard frames should be grounded, but grounding is not required by the Code *if* the switchboard is "effectively insulated." (A single-polarity DC circuit is a two-wire DC circuit.)

For three-wire DC circuits, it is evidently the intent of the Code that the switchboard frames be grounded.

Sections 250-121 through 250-125 give the rules for grounding of instruments.

B. Panelboards

384-13. General

This rule requires that "panelboards shall have a rating not less than the minimum feeder capacity required for the load."

To illustrate, suppose that the computed load on a panel is 120 amps., divided among ten 120-volt branches. For a three-wire solid neutral panel, the load will be split between the two legs, with each of the panel mains carrying approximately 60 amps.

Panelboards are built with 50, 100, 200-amp. mains. A panel with 100-amp. mains would be required for the above load.

The intent of this rule is that the mains of a panel shall have sufficient capacity to carry the intended load. In practice, it is desirable to have one or more spare branches, and to size the mains large enough to allow for future additional loads.

384-14. Lighting and Appliance Branch-Circuit Panelboard

384-15. Number of Overcurrent Devices on One Panelboard

If more than 10 percent of the branch-circuit breakers (or fuses) on a panelboard are small breakers (or fuses), 30 amp. or less, and the panel has a solid neutral, it is called a "lighting and appliance branch-circuit panelboard."

Not more than 42 overcurrent devices are permitted in lighting and appliance branch-circuit panelboards. If all circuit breakers are single pole, this permits 42 circuits; if two pole, 21 circuits; if three pole, 14 circuits.

If 90 percent or more of the branch-circuit breakers or fuses are rated at over 30 amps. the panelboard is a power panelboard, not a "lighting and appliance branch-circuit panelboard." A power panelboard may have any number of overcurrent devices.

Note that certain requirements following apply only to lighting and appliance branch-circuit panelboards. Other requirements apply to panelboards in general.

384-16. Overcurrent Protection

(a) A lighting and appliance branch-circuit panelboard must have overcurrent protection. The overcurrent protection may be the fuses or circuit breaker protecting the feeder, as long as the feeder fuse or circuit-breaker rating is not greater than the panel rating. If the rating of the feeder fuse or breaker is too high for the panel rating, individual protection must be provided at the panel.

For panelboards used as service equipment for individual residential occupancies, individual protection is not required.

(b) Regardless of panelboard rating, when a panelboard has any *snap switches* rated 30 amps. or less, the rating of the fuse or circuit breaker protecting the panel may not exceed 200 amps.

(c) For "continuous loads," the load on a branch must be reduced to 80% of the branch rating. For a 15-amp. branch the load must not exceed

80% of 15 or 12 amps., etc.

(d) Where a panelboard is supplied through a transformer, overcurrent protection for the panelboard must be provided on the secondary side of the transformer.

Exception.

For two-wire secondaries, the protection may be on the primary side only.

(e) "Delta breakers" are not permitted in panelboards.

384-17. Panelboards in Damp or Wet Locations

Panelboards installed in damp locations must be "stooled off" the wall at least $\frac{1}{4}$ in. but need not be weatherproof.

Panelboards installed in wet locations must be *weatherproof,* and stooled off the wall at least $\frac{1}{4}$ in. (see definition of "damp" and "wet" locations, p. 70-10 of the Code).

384-18. Enclosure

Panelboards must be enclosed by a cabinet, usually of sheet metal. Open panelboards are not permitted.

Exception.

Panelboards other than the enclosed type are permitted if accessible only to qualified persons.

384-19. Relative Arrangement of Switches and Fuses

Fuses must be on the load side of switches. This eliminates danger of shock when fuses are being changed or replaced.

Exception.

For service equipment, fuses may be on the supply side of the switches (see Section 230-82).

C. Construction Specifications

384-20. Panels

Switchboard panels must be of moisture-resistant noncombustible material, such as steel or slate.

384-21. Busbars

Bare busbars are permitted if rigidly mounted.

384-22. Protection of Instrument Circuits

Instruments on a switchboard must be protected in the same way as other electrical equipment. The Code allows fuses up to 15 amps. for instrument protection. Fuses must be standard fuses, except that for 2-amp. or less rating, midget fuses may be used.

384-23. Component Parts

Switches, fuses, and fuseholders must conform to applicable rules of Articles 240 (Overcurrent Protection) and 380 (Switches).

384-24. Knife Switches

For exposed knife switches, the hinged part must be connected to the load, not the supply side of the circuit.

384-26. Minimum Spacings

Table 384-26 of the Code lists minimum spacing for busbars of different voltages.

384-27. Grounding of Panelboards

Panelboard cases must be grounded. If supplied by a "metal-clad" feeder, such as conduit, EMT, or BX, the conduit, EMT, or BX sheath may be used for grounding. If the feeder is a nonmetallic type of wiring, such as Romex, a grounding wire, run with the feeder, must be used.

The panel must be equipped with a grounding bar, which would be used in the latter case, the grounding wire being connected to the grounding bar in the panel. This grounding bar is an equipment grounding bar, and must be kept separate from the neutral (except that when a panel is used as service equipment, the neutral may be connected to the grounding bar).

Chapter 4. Equipment for General Use

ARTICLE 400 — FLEXIBLE CORDS AND CABLES

A. General

400-3. Suitability

400-4. Types

Cords shall be "suitable for the condition of use and location."

Table 400-4 of the Code lists the different types of approved cords and shows the kind of service for which each cord is suited. Certain cords are approved only for pendant use. These may not be used for portable appliances. Others are approved for use with portable appliances. Some may be used for both purposes. There are three designations indicating "toughness" of a cord: Extra Hard Usage, Hard Usage, Not Hard Usage. Cords suitable for use with heaters are so indicated. These are approved for use with irons, toasters, soldering irons, and other appliances that would subject the cord to high temperatures. The foregoing would be conditions of use.

Certain cords are suitable for use in dry places only. Others may be used also in damp places. These would be "conditions of location."

400-5. Ampacity of Flexible Cords and Cables

Table 400-5 of the Code lists the ampacities of the different types of cord. For certain types the ampacity depends upon the number of conductors used as "current carrying" conductors. If two, use column B; if three, use column A; if four or more, multiply the column A listing by 80%. Note that the ampacity does not depend upon the number of conductors in a cord, but on the number of conductors used for carrying the current. (The neutral of three-wire or four-wire circuits is not considered a "current carrying" conductor.)

400-6. Marking

The manufacturer is required to attach a printed tag to a reel or carton of cord. The cord must list the allowable voltage, type of cord, size, and the manufacturer's name or trademark.

For type SJ, SJO, SJT, SJTO, S, SO, ST, and STO cords, the cord itself must be marked at 24-in. intervals with type, size, and number of conductors.

400-7. Uses Permitted

Cords may be used only:

1. For pendants.
2. For wiring of fixtures.
3. To connect portable lamps and appliances.
4. As elevator cables.
5. For wiring cranes and hoists.
6. For connection of stationary equipment when frequent moving is necessary.
7. For prevention of noise and vibration.
8. To facilitate removal of fixed or stationary appliances.
9. For data processing wiring.

Cords for appliances and portable lamps must be equipped with plugs and plugged to a receptacle. They may not be plugged into a light socket nor wired direct to the supply circuit.

An example of (1) above would be the cord supporting a pendant lighting fixture.

An application of (7) would be where a machine has so much vibration that it would be impractical to connect the machine to a permanent-type wiring, such as conduit, Romex. In this case the Code allows the permanent wiring to be brought to a box near the machine, and a short piece of cord used between the box and the machine to take up the vibration.

An application of (8) would be the cord connection for a household range or refrigerator.

Data processing equipment may be wired with flexible cord [Section 645-2(b)]. This is the only exception to the rule of Section 400-8, which prohibits using cord for permanent wiring in buildings. (Cords may be used to wire cranes and hoists.)

400-8. Uses Not Permitted

Article 645 permits cords to be used for interconnection of separate units in a data processing room. In effect, this amounts to permanent wiring and is an exception to the general rules of this Section.

Except for data processing wiring, the following rules apply:

1. Cord may not be used to wire a building or part of a building.
2. May not pass through a hole in walls, ceilings, or floors.
3. May not pass through doorways or windows.
4. May not be permanently strapped or fastened to building surfaces.
5. May not be run concealed, as in a partition.

400-9. Splices

Splices may be made in No. 12 and larger hard service cords. Table 400-4 shows that the only hard service cord made in sizes No. 12 and larger are types S, SO, ST, STO, HS, HSO, SJ, SJO, SJT, SJTO, HSJ, and HSJO. No splices are permitted in any other type of cord of any size.

400-10. Pull at Joints and Terminals

Cords shall be connected to plug terminals and other terminals in such a way as to relieve the strain on the connection when the cord is pulled on. A knot in the two conductors, known as the Underwriters knot, is commonly used for this purpose on plug terminals (Fig. 410).

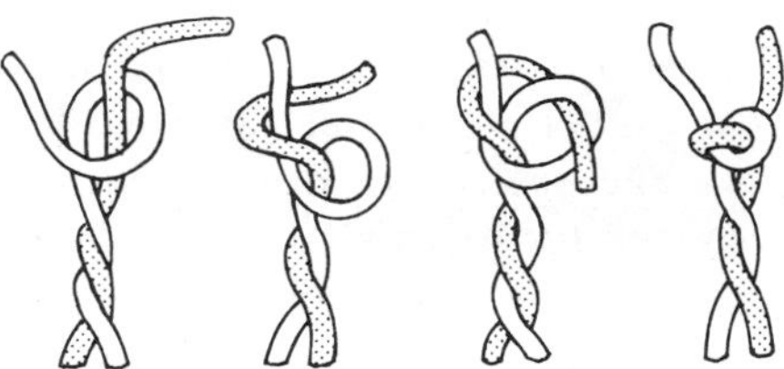

Fig. 410
Underwriters knot.

400-11. In Show Windows and Showcases

Cords used in show windows or showcases must be one of the following types: S, SO, SJ, SJO, ST, STO, SJT, SJTO, AFS.

All except the last named are cords suitable for hard usage, and are the toughest cords made. Type AFS is a heat-resistant cord.

Exceptions.

(1) Cord attached to display merchandise (merchandise for sale) and

(2) Cord used for ceiling fixtures hung from a chain. These may be other types than those listed.

400-12. Minimum Size

Cords for general use are made in conductor sizes down to No. 18 minimum. Tinsel cord has No. 27 conductors, but is approved only for cord attached to an appliance by the manufacturer.

400-13. Overcurrent Protection

Cords do not require separate overcurrent protection. The branch circuit fuse or circuit breaker serves as protection. No. 18 cord and tinsel cord may be used on a 20-amp. circuit; 10-amp. capacity cord may be used on a 30-amp. circuit; 20-amp. capacity cord may be used on a 40- or 50-amp. circuit. Table 400-5 lists the ampacities of the different types of cord.

Only the cords listed in Table 400-4 are permitted for use, unless special permission for the use of other types is obtained from the Underwriters Laboratories.

Following is a description of the different types of cord covered by the preceding sections.

Referring to Table 400-4, the first four general types listed are tinsel cord —parallel (types TP and TPT), and jacketed (types TS and TST). In the parallel cord, the conductors are laid parallel. In the jacketed type the two or three conductors are twisted together. These cords are made only in size 27 and have a carrying capacity of $\frac{1}{2}$ amp. (see Table 400-5 for ampacities of the different types of cord). The tinsel cords may be used in lengths of not over 8 ft, in damp or dry locations, for attachment to portable appliances of not over 50 watts. Insulation on the individual conductors is either rubber or thermoplastic with an outer covering of either rubber or thermoplastic. Maximum voltage is 300 volts.

Asbestos-Covered (types AFC and AFPD) and Cotton-Covered (type CFPD) are heat-resistant cords. They are made in sizes 18 to 10, two- and three-conductor. Insulation on the individual wires of the asbestos-covered type is impregnated asbestos, and on the cotton-covered type, impregnated cotton. The conductors are twisted together, and have an outer jacket of cotton, rayon, or saturated asbestos. These cords may be used only for pendants in dry places. The principal use of these cords is for fixtures where they are exposed to high temperatures. Ampacities are 6, 8, 17, 23, 28 amps. for Nos. 18, 16, 14, 12, 10, respectively.

All Rubber Parallel Cord comes in three types: types SP-1, SP-2, and SP-3. Type SP-1 comes in size No. 18, two- or three-conductor (one conductor of the three is a grounding wire). Conductors are rubber insulated, laid parallel, then covered with a rubber outer covering. It may be used for pendants or portables in damp or dry places and where not subject to hard usage. Maximum voltage is 300 between conductors, ampacity 10 amps.

Type SP-2 is the same as type SP-1, except that type SP-2 comes in sizes 18 and 16 two- or three-conductor (one conductor of the three is a grounding wire). Ampacity is 10 amps. for the No. 18, 13 amps. for the No. 16. Maximum operating voltage is 600 between conductors. SP-3 comes in sizes 18 to 12, two- or three-conductor (one conductor of the three is a grounding wire). Individual conductors are rubber insulated, laid parallel, then covered with a rubber outer jacket. It may be used in damp places and is recommended for refrigerators or room air conditioners. Ampacities are 10, 13, 18, and 25, for Nos. 18, 16, 14, 12, respectively. Maximum voltage is 600.

All Plastic Parallel Cord comes in three types: types SPT-1, SPT-2, and SPT-3.

Type SPT-1 comes in size No. 18, two- or three-conductor (one conductor of the three is a grounding conductor). Individual conductors are thermoplastic insulated, laid parallel, and then covered with a thermoplastic outer jacket. It may be used for pendants and portables in damp or dry places where not subjected to hard usage. Ampacity is 10 amps., maximum voltage 300.

Type SPT-2 is constructed the same as type SPT-1, except that SPT-2 comes in sizes 18 and 16, two- or three-conductor (one conductor of the three is a grounding wire). Ampacities are 10 amps. for the No. 18, 13 amps. for No. 16. Maximum voltage between conductors is 600.

Type SPT-3 is made in sizes 18 to 10, two- or three-conductor (one conductor of the three is a grounding wire). Construction is the same as for SPT-1 and SPT-2. This type is recommended for refrigerators or room air conditioners where not subjected to hard usage. Ampacities are 10, 13, 18, 25, 30 for Nos. 18, 16, 14, 12, 10, respectively. Maximum voltage is 600.

Lamp Cord, type C, is made in sizes from 18 to 10, two or more conductors. This is a twisted cord, each conductor having rubber insulation covered by a cotton braid. There is no outer covering. Type C may be used for pendants or portables in dry places only, and where not subjected to hard usage. It is seldom used for portables. Ampacities are 10, 13, 18, 25, 30 amps. for Nos. 18, 16, 14, 12, 10, two-conductor; 7, 10, 15, 20, 25 amps. for the three-conductor. Maximum voltage is 300.

Twisted Portable Cord, type PD, is type C cord with an outer covering of cotton or rayon applied over the twisted conductors. Same carrying capacities and uses as type C. Maximum voltage is 600.

Vacuum Cleaner Cord types SV, SVO, SVT, SVTO. Type SV has rubber insulation with a rubber jacket. Types SVO, SVT, SVTO have thermoplastic insulation with a thermoplastic jacket. Types SVO and SVTO are oil resistant. Sizes are No. 18 and 17. All are two-conductor or two-conductor with grounding wire, for use with pendants or portables, in dry or damp places, where not subjected to hard usage. Ampacity is 10 amps. for the No. 18, and 12 amps. for the No. 17; maximum voltage between conductors is 300.

Junior Hard Service Cord is made in four types: SJ, SJO, SJT, and SJTO. Sizes are Nos. 18 to 10, with two, three or four conductors. Individual conductors of types SJ and SJO are rubber insulated. Type SJ has a rubber outer jacket; type SJO has an outer jacket of an oil-resistant compound. Types SJT and SJTO have thermoplastic or rubber-insulated individual conductors covered by a thermoplastic outer jacket. These cables are suitable for hard usage and may be used with portables or pendants in dry or damp places. Ampacity is 10 amps. for the No. 18, two-conductor, 7 amps. for the three-conductor No. 18, 18 amps. for the No. 14, two-conductor, 15 amps. for the No. 14 three-conductor. Maximum voltage is 300.

Hard Service Cord, types S, SO, ST, and STO is made in sizes 18 to 2, with two or more conductors. Individual conductors of types S and SO are rubber insulated. Type S has a rubber outer jacket; type SO has an outer jacket of an oil-resistant compound. Types ST and STO have thermoplastic or rubber-insulated individual conductors. The outer jacket of type ST is thermoplastic; that of type STO is oil-resistant thermoplastic. The outer covering of these cords is a very tough material that will withstand severe mechanical abuse. It may be used on theatre stages, in garages, on construction sites, and at other locations where subjected to extrahard usage. Ampacities are 10, 13, 18, 25, 30, 40, 55, 70, 95 for No. 18, 16, 14, 12, 10, 8, 6, 4, 2, two-conductor, and 7, 10, 15, 20, 25, 35, 45, 60, 80 amps. for the three-conductor. Maximum voltage is 600.

Rubber-Jacketed Heat-Resistant Cord, types AFS and AFSJ, has two or three conductors, sizes No. 18 to No. 12. Individual insulation is impregnated asbestos, with an outer jacket of rubber. Suitable for portable heaters in dry or damp places. Ampacities are 10, 15, 20 amps. for No. 18, 16, 14, respectively. Maximum voltage is 300.

Heater Cord, type HPD, is made in sizes 18 to 12, with two, three, or four conductors. Individual insulation is rubber or thermoplastic with asbestos or all neoprene. Type HPD has an outer jacket of cotton or rayon. These cords are suitable for portable heaters in dry places. Ampacities are 10, 15, 20, 30 amps. for Nos. 18, 16, 14, 12, respectively. Maximum voltage is 300.

Rubber-Jacketed Heater Cord, type HSJ: conductor sizes are 18 to 12, with two, three, or four conductors. Individual conductors are insulated with rubber, thermoplastic-asbestos, or neoprene, then given an outer jacket of cotton and rubber. It is suitable for portable heaters in dry or damp places. Ampacity is 10 amps. for the No. 18, 15 amps. for the No. 16; 300 volts maximum.

Jacketed Heater Cord, types HSJO, HS, HSO, is similar to type HSJ, except that types HSJO and HSO have an oil-resistant outer jacket. Type HSJO comes in sizes 18 to 12. Types HS and HSO in sizes 12 and 14; all have two, three, or four conductors. They are suitable for portable heaters in damp places. Ampacities are 10, 15, 20, and 30 amps. for Nos. 18, 16, 14, and 12, respectively.

Parallel Heater Cord, type HPN, is made in sizes 18 to 12, two or three conductors. Has thermosetting insulation and outer jacket. Suitable for portables in dry or damp places. Ampacities are 10, 15, 20, and 30 amps. for Nos. 18, 16, 14, and 12, respectively. Maximum voltage is 600.

Range, Dryer Cable, types SRD and SRDT, is made in sizes 10 to 4, three- or four-conductor. Individual insulation on the SRD is rubber with a rubber or neoprene outer jacket; on the SRDT it is thermoplastic with a thermoplastic outer jacket. Recommended for ranges and dryers. May be used in damp places. Ampacities are 25, 35, 45, and 60 amps. for Nos. 10, 8, 6, and 4, respectively, for three-conductor, and 20, 28, 36, and 48 amps. for the four-conductor. Maximum voltage is 600.

Data Processing Cable is made in size 32 (minimum), has thermoplastic, rubber, or cross-linked synthetic polymer insulation and covering. It is used in data processing systems, in dry places.

Elevator Cable, types E, EO, EN, ET, ETLB, ETP, ETT: conductor size 18 to 14, two or more conductors. Individual insulation is rubber or thermoplastic. Outer jacket is cotton, neoprene, or thermoplastic. Types EN and ET have flame- and moisture-resistant outer jackets. Types EO, ETP, and ETT may be used in hazardous locations. There may be steel supporting fillers incorporated in the cable (these are required for cables exceeding 100 ft between supports). These cables are used for elevator lighting and control circuits. Ampacities are 10, 13, and 18 amps. for Nos. 18, 16, and 14, two-conductor, and 7, 10, and 15 amps. for the three-conductor.

B. Construction Specifications

400-20. Labels

Underwriter-approved cords have a label showing underwriter approval.

400-21. Nominal Insulation Thickness

Table 400-4 lists the insulation thickness, in mils, specified for the different types of cord. A mil is 1/1,000 in. 15 mils is approximately 1/64 in., 30 mils 1/32 in., 60 mils 1/16 in.

400-22. Grounded-Conductor Identification

This rule is for the neutral conductor, not the grounding conductor. The neutral conductor may have white or natural gray braid, or insulation. Or the cord may have a white or natural gray separator. Or the neutral may be distinguished by a tracer in the braid or by marking on the outside of the cord. Finally, the neutral may be a tinned conductor, while the hot wire is untinned. The tinning identifies the neutral.

The "identified" conductor should be connected to the "identified" terminal of appliances (see Section 200-9), or when connected direct to a circuit, it should be connected to the neutral of the circuit.

400-23. Grounding-Conductor Identification

When a cord has a grounding wire intended for the purpose of grounding the metal enclosures of equipment, this wire always shows a green color in the braid or insulation.

400-24. Attachment Plugs

This Section says, in effect, that when a cord has a green grounding conductor the plug shall be equipped with a grounding prong.

C. Portable Cables Over 600 Volts Nominal

400-30. Scope

The rules of Sections 400-31 to 400-36 apply to high-voltage cables connecting mobile equipment and machinery, such as a crane or hoist.

400-31. Construction

(a) Conductors shall be no smaller than No. 8. Only stranded conductors are permitted.

(b) Cables operating at more than 2,000 volts shall be shielded. Shielding here refers to electrical shielding, not mechanical shielding.

(c) All cables shall have a grounding conductor sized according to Table 250-95, p. 70-102 of the Code.

400-32. Shielding

All shields shall be grounded.

400-33. Grounding

Grounding conductors shall be grounded in accordance with Part K of Article 250.

400-34. Minimum Bending Radii

Bends shall have sufficient radius to prevent damaging cables.

400-35. Fittings

Lengths of cable may be connected together with connectors. Connectors shall be the locking type, and arranged to prevent opening or closing while energized.

400-36. Splices and Terminations

Splices are not permitted, unless permanent, vulcanized, or other approved type.

Terminations shall be accessible only to authorized personnel.

ARTICLE 402 — FIXTURE WIRES

402-3. Approved Types

Only the fixture wires listed in Table 402-3 of the Code are permitted to be used.

402-5. Ampacity of Fixture Wires

Maximum allowable ampacities are No. 18, 6 amps.; No. 16, 8 amps.; No. 14, 17 amps.

402-6. Minimum Size

No. 18 is the smallest size permitted.

402-7. Number of Conductors in Conduit

Section 725-16 permits certain types of fixture wire to be used for signaling and communication circuits. When so used, the fixture wire may be in conduit. Table 2, p. 70-578 of the Code specifies the maximum number of wires permitted in the different sizes of conduit or tubing.

Except for signaling and communication circuits, fixture wires are to be used only for wiring or connecting lighting fixtures.

402-8. Grounded-Conductor Identification

If one conductor of fixture wires is intended to be connected to the neutral, it must be marked or identified by means of stripes in the insulation, or by one of the means listed in Section 400-22(a) through (e).

402-9. Marking

Fixture wire shall be marked by the manufacturer to show maximum voltage, type letter, size, and manufacturer's name or trademark. Thermoplastic fixture wire must be marked on the insulation at intervals of 24 in. Other fixture wire may be marked by means of a printed tag attached to the reel or carton.

402-10. Uses Permitted

Fixture wires may be used for wiring of lighting fixtures or for connecting lighting fixtures to the branch circuit conductors.

402-11. Uses Not Permitted

Except for signaling and communication circuits, fixture wires may not be used for general wiring.

402-12. Overcurrent Protection

No. 16 and No. 18 fixture wire are considered as protected by a branch circuit fuse or circuit breaker rated at 20 amps. or less.

No. 14 fixture wire is considered protected by a branch circuit fuse or circuit breaker of 30 amps. or less.

ARTICLE 410 — LIGHTING FIXTURES, LAMPHOLDERS, LAMPS, RECEPTACLES, AND ROSETTES

A. General

410-1. Scope

410-2. Application to Other Articles

410-3. Live Parts

Article 410 sets down the rules governing the construction of lighting fixtures, lamps, receptacles, and the rules for their installation. The construction would be the responsibility of the manufacturer. Approved fixtures carry a UL label.

Generally, no exposed live parts are permitted on fixtures or receptacles.

B. Fixture Locations

410-4. Fixtures in Specific Locations

(a) Fixtures installed outdoors or in wet locations indoors must be weatherproof or watertight.

(b) Fixtures installed in corrosive locations, such as battery rooms, must be of material that will not deteriorate by the action of corrosive fumes.

(c) Lighting fixtures may not be installed in hoods over *nonresidential* ranges unless the fixture is a vaporproof type. The recessed fixture must be corrosion-proof. Wiring must be outside of hood.

410-5. Fixtures near Combustible Material

Combustible material would include lamp shades. Combustible material on or near a fixture may not be subjected to temperatures above 194°F.

410-6. Fixtures over Combustible Material

Fixtures installed over highly combustible material, such as paper, must be fixtures *without* switches. Switching of the fixtures would have to be by a wall switch. Unless each fixture has an *individual* wall switch, fixtures must be at least 8 ft above the floor or so located as to be protected from damage.

410-7. Fixtures in Show Windows

No externally wired fixture is permitted in a show window except a chain-supported fixture (which is classed as "externally wired" because it would require open wiring between the fixture and the outlet box on the ceiling above). Fixtures attached direct to the ceiling or wall are not externally wired types, and may be used in show windows.

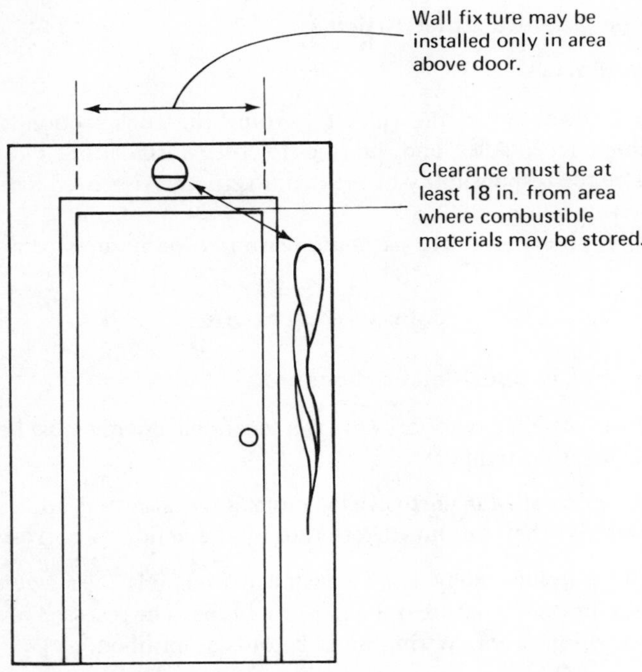
Wall fixture may be installed only in area above door.
Clearance must be at least 18 in. from area where combustible materials may be stored.

Fig. 411
Wall fixtures in clothes closets [Sect. 410-8(a)(1)].

410-8. Fixtures in Clothes Closets

Wall fixtures may not be installed in clothes closets anywhere except over the door (Fig. 411). The reason for this rule is to avoid the possibility of clothes being hung over the wall fixture. If the wall fixture is anywhere except over the door, this is likely to happen and would constitute a fire hazard.

Ceiling fixtures in closets must have at least an 18-in. clearance from areas where combustible items, such as clothing, might be stored. This means that a ceiling fixture would have to be kept at least 18 in. horizontally from an elevated shelf in the closet.

Flush recessed fixtures equipped with a solid lens are considered to be outside of the closet, and may be installed anywhere in the closet (Fig. 412).

Fixtures hanging from a cord are not permitted in clothes closets.

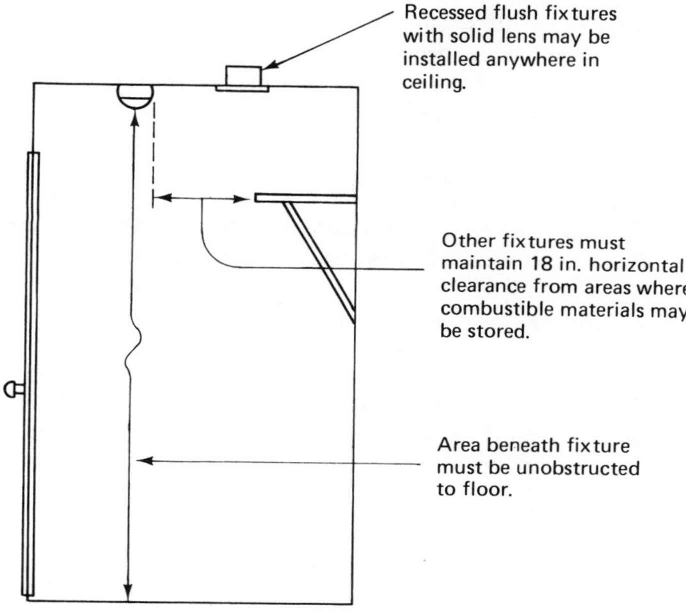
Recessed flush fixtures with solid lens may be installed anywhere in ceiling.
Other fixtures must maintain 18 in. horizontal clearance from areas where combustible materials may be stored.
Area beneath fixture must be unobstructed to floor.

Fig. 412
Ceiling fixtures in clothes closets [Sect. 410-8(a)(2)].

410-9. Space for Cove Lighting

There shall be adequate space in coves for changing of lamps, ballasts, etc.

C. Provisions at Fixture Outlet Boxes, Canopies, and Pans

410-10. Space for Conductors

The box in the ceiling above a ceiling fixture must have sufficient space to accommodate the wires and connections. Table 370-6(a), p. 70-211 of the Code, shows the number of conductors permitted in boxes of different sizes. Information on use of the table is given in Section 370-6.

410-11. Temperature Limit of Conductors in Outlet Boxes

Certain types of fixtures, such as recessed fixtures, would subject the conductors in the outlet box to abnormally high temperatures. Care should be taken to provide circuit conductors that have a type of insulation suited for the temperature. If the box temperature is expected to be over 140°F, Type T conductors are not permitted, since 140°F is the temperature limit for Type T.

A circuit may not pass through an outlet box that is *integral* with an *incandescent* fixture, unless the fixture is specifically approved for "through" wiring (see also Section 410-31).

410-12. Outlet Boxes to Be Covered

If an outlet box is covered by a fixture or fixture canopy, it is considered "covered." If not so covered, it must be fitted with a box cover.

410-13. Covering of Combustible Material at Outlet Boxes

Wallboard or other combustible ceiling or wall material inside a fixture canopy must be covered with a noncombustible material, such as plaster, asbestos, or sheet metal (Fig. 413).

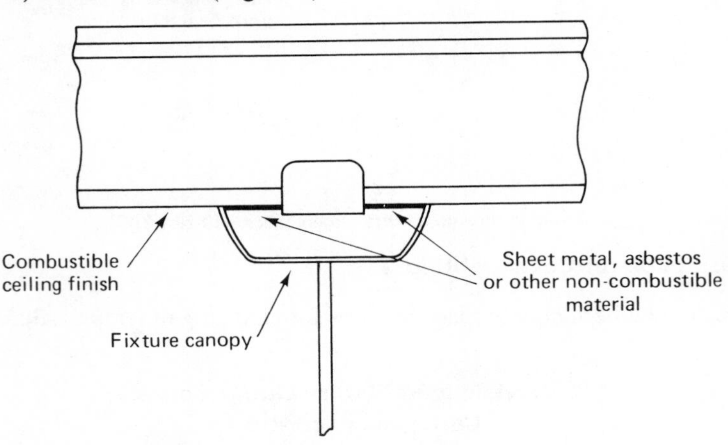

Fig. 413

Covering of combustible material at outlet boxes (Sect. 410-13).

410-14. Connection of Electric-Discharge Lighting Fixtures

When electric-discharge (fluorescent) fixtures are hung from the ceiling, the wiring to the fixture must be metal raceway, metal-clad cable, or nonmetallic sheathed cable.

Exception.

If the fixture is equipped (by the manufacturer) with a cord, the cord may be used for this purpose and plugged into a box receptacle. The plug and receptacle must be the grounding type, and the cord must be visible for its entire length.

Electric-discharge fixtures with *mogul-base screw-shell* lampholders may be connected by cord to circuits rated up to 50 amps. Other fluorescents may be connected to circuits rated only up to 20 amps. "Rating" refers to circuit protection—fuse size or circuit-breaker setting for the circuit.

D. Fixture Supports

410-15. Supports—General

A fixture may not be hung from the screw shell of a light socket if the fixture weighs over 6 pounds or measures over 16 in. in any dimension.

410-16. Means of Support

Fixtures weighing 50 pounds or less can be attached to the outlet box for support.

Fixtures weighing over 50 pounds must be independently supported by ceiling joists or other substantial ceiling members (Fig. 414).

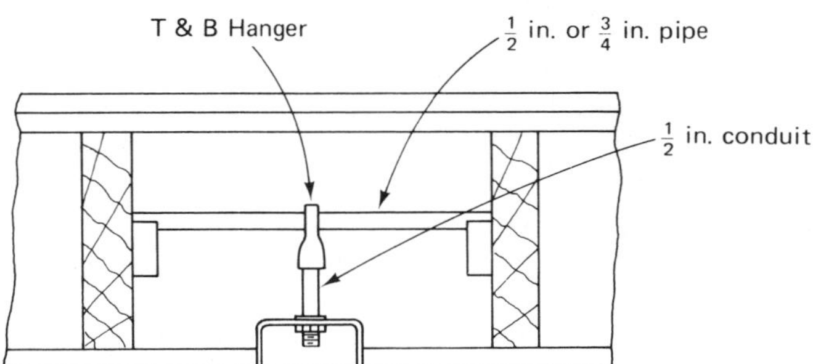

Fig. 414
Hanger for fixture weighing more than 50 lb. This arrangement provides a support for the fixture which is "independent of the outlet box," as required by Section 410-16.

E. Grounding

410-18. Fixture Grounding

This Section refers to fixed lighting fixtures.

Subsection (a) of the Section requires that, if the wiring system to a fixed lighting fixture provides a means for grounding, any "exposed conductive parts" (exposed metal parts) shall be grounded.

Subsection (b) requires that, if the wiring system to the fixture does not provide a means for grounding, the fixture must be nonmetallic.

If there is a means for grounding, the fixture must be grounded.

If there is no means for grounding, the fixture must be nonmetallic.

The effect of the two rules is that *all fixed metal lighting fixtures,* regardless of voltage or location, *must be grounded.*

It should be noted that this rule does not apply to movable cord-connected lighting fixtures—desk lamps, floor lamps, etc. It applies only to lighting fixtures fastened in place.

It should be noted also that Section 410-19, following, requires that *all* lighting fixtures—fixed or any other type—if operating at more than 150 volts to ground shall be grounded regardless of location.

For voltages of 150 volts or less to ground, cord-connected lighting fixtures that are not fixed in place require grounding only if located in a hazardous location [Section 250-45(a)]. Portable handlamps require grounding in all cases—regardless of location [Section 250-45(c) and (d)].

410-19. Equipment over 150 Volts to Ground

Metal fixtures operating at more than 150 volts to ground must be grounded regardless of location. This applies for both fixed and portable fixtures.

(240-volt fixtures connected to a 120/240-volt AC circuit would be operating at a voltage of 120 to ground.)

Note: Lamp tie wires, mounting screws, clips, etc., need not be grounded if spaced at least $1\frac{1}{2}$ in. from lamp terminals.

410-21. Methods of Grounding

For methods of grounding, refer to Section 250-91(b).

F. Wiring of Fixtures

410-22. Fixture Wiring—General

410-23. Conductor Size

410-24. Conductor Insulation

410-25. Conductors for Certain Conditions

410-26. Conductors for Movable Parts

These sections set down Code requirements for the construction of fixtures. Compliance with these rules would be the responsibility of the manufacturer.

410-27. Pendant Conductors for Incandescent Filament Lamps

"Pigtail" sockets are made with short leads permanently attached to the socket. They are often used for overhead lighting with the sockets connected to overhead wires. This Section requires that when used in this way the pigtail leads be *soldered* to the overhead wires.

The overhead wires may not be used to hold up the sockets. A third wire, or a steel messenger cable, could be used for support, with each socket independently hung from the wire or cable. The rules of this Section apply where pigtail sockets are used "in other than festoon wiring" (see Sections 225-6 and 225-13).

Subsections (b) and (c) are manufacturer's requirements.

410-28. Protection of Conductors and Insulation

(a) Fixture conductors shall be secured in a manner that will not tend to cut or abrade the insulation.

(b) Where conductors pass through a canopy or into a metal light socket, a bushing shall be provided to protect the conductor insulation.

(c) When a light socket is hung from a cord, the light socket shall have an insulating bushing to protect the cord from abrasion.

410-29. Cord-Connected Showcases

Showcases (other than fixed showcases) may be connected together by cord. Cord must be a type suitable for hard service. Types permitted would be SJ, SJO, SJTO, S, SO, ST, and STO. Cords must have a grounding conductor.

The showcase cords may be coupled together by locking-type connectors. One of the group would be connected by cord and plug to a permanent receptacle, which would supply the current for the group. The receptacle would usually be a floor receptacle, which may be on a standpipe.

Receptacles, connectors, and plugs shall be grounding type, 15- or 20-amp. rating.

Not more than six showcases may be connected together in this way.

Cords must be secured to the underside of the showcases.

Showcases may be separated by not more than 2 in.

The free lead at the *end* of the group of showcases must have a female fitting in or on the showcase.

Equipment other than showcases shall not be connected to any showcase.

Standpipes of floor receptacles shall allow floor cleaning equipment to be operated without damage to receptacles.

410-30. Connections, Splices, and Taps

(a) Fixtures shall be so installed that the connection between the fixture wires and the circuit wires may be readily inspected. If the connections can be inspected by removing a canopy, this requirement would be fulfilled.

(b) Splices are not permitted in fixture arms or stems.

(c) Unnecessary splices are not permitted on a fixture.

(d) When a fluorescent is mounted over a concealed box, there shall be suitable openings in back of the fixture to provide access to the box.

410-31. Fixtures as Raceways

When a number of fixtures (such as a string of ceiling fixtures) is served by the same circuit, the circuit may not be "run through" the fixtures. Each fixture must have an individual take-off from a separate box.

An exception is made when the fixtures are a type specially approved for end-to-end installation. In this case the circuit may be run "straight through," using the fixtures as a raceway. Such an arrangement is frequently used in the installation of fluorescent ceiling fixtures.

Two circuits serving the fixtures may be carried through the fixtures. One may be a three-wire circuit, the other a two-wire circuit. Three two-wire circuits are not permitted. Two three-wire circuits are not permitted.

When a branch circuit is run through fixtures, and conductors come within 3 in. of a ballast in a fixture, the branch circuit conductors must be a type suitable for a temperature of 194°F. Suitable types are RHH, THW, THHN, FEP, FEPB, SA, XHHW, and AVA.

410-32. Polarization of Fixtures

All screw shells of a fixture shall be connected to the same wire, and this wire shall be connected to the neutral when the fixture is installed.

G. Construction of Fixtures

This part of the Code sets forth the construction rules that must be followed in the manufacture of lighting fixtures.

H. Installation of Lampholders

410-47. Screw-Shell Type

Screw-shell lampholders may be used only for light bulbs. They may not be used to serve appliances, or for any other purpose than as lampholders.

410-48. Double-Pole Switched Lampholders

In the unusual case of a 240-volt switched lampholder served from the two outside legs of a 120/240-volt circuit, the lampholder switch must be two-pole.

Note: A study of Section 210-6(a) together with Sections 210-6(c) and (d) will show that *mogul-base* lampholders of the switched type would be permitted, in *other than* residences, on the 240 volt legs. Medium-base lampholders, switched or unswitched, would not be permitted.

410-49. Lampholders in Damp or Wet Locations

Damp or wet locations would include not only the outdoors, but certain inside locations as well. Dairies, breweries, and damp basements are examples. In such locations lampholders must be the weatherproof type.

J. Construction of Lampholders

This part of the Code provides construction specifications for the manufacture of lampholders (light sockets).

K. Lamps and Auxiliary Equipment

410-53. Bases, Incandescent Lamps

The base of a lamp (light bulb) is the threaded part that screws into the light socket. Medium-base lamps have 1-in.-diameter bases, and come in sizes up to 300 watts. Mogul-base lamps have $1\frac{1}{2}$-in.-diameter bases, and come in sizes of from 300 to 1,500 watts.

410-54. Enclosures for Electric-Discharge Lamp Auxiliary Equipment

Resistors and regulators for this type of equipment reach temperatures high enough to be treated as heat sources. Wiring to the resistors and regulators must have insulation suited to the high temperature.

410-55. Arc Lamps

This Section requires that arc lamps used in theaters, projection machines, and on constant-current systems be approved types.

L. Receptacles, Cord Connectors, and Attachment Plugs (Caps)

410-56. Rating and Type

Receptacles and plugs shall have a rating not less than 15 amps., 125 volts; 15 amps., 250 volts (10-amp, 250-volt receptacles may be used for limited service, in nonresidential occupancies).

The receptacle face must project from *metal* plates at least .015 in. For insulating-type plates, the receptacle face need not project from the plate, but must be at least flush with the plate (Fig. 415). All metal receptacle faceplates must be grounded.

410-57. Receptacles in Damp or Wet Locations

Receptacles exposed to the weather must be weatherproof, not only when the cover is closed; they must also be weatherproof when in use, i.e., with the cover open and a plug inserted in the receptacle. This rule is not intended to apply to outdoor receptacles that would be used only intermittently for portable tools or other portable equipment. Such outdoor receptacles need not be

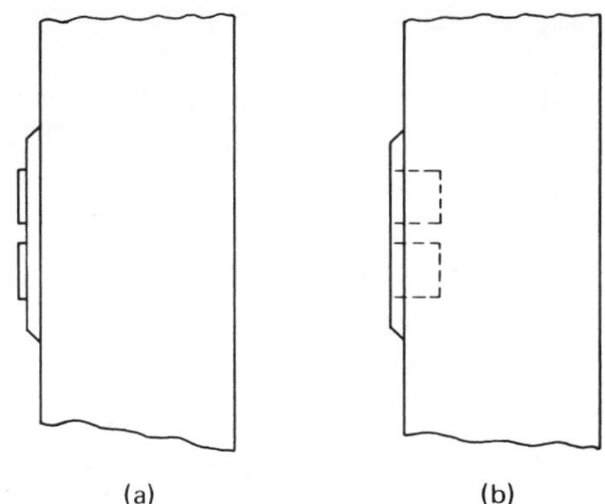

Fig. 415
Installation of receptacles (Sect. 410-56):

(a) Metal plate. Receptacle face must project from plate at least .015 in. May not be flush with plate.
(b) Composition plate. Receptacle face may be flush with plate (or project from plate).

weatherproof with the receptacle in use. The only requirement is that they have a *self-closing* gasketed cover—one that automatically snaps shut when the plug is removed. A closing spring on the cover would satisfy this rule. Outdoor receptacles in a residence could be this type in most cases, but an open-and-closed-weatherproof type would be required for equipment left plugged to a receptacle indefinitely.

Receptacles installed outdoors but protected from the weather must be of a type that is weatherproof only when the cover is closed. They need not be of a type that is weatherproof when in use. An example of a location protected from the weather would be an open porch with a roof over the porch.

Receptacles installed outdoors must be high enough above the ground to be above the level of snow or water accumulation.

410-58. Grounding-Type Receptacles, Adapters, Cord Connectors, and Attachment Plugs

Grounding-type plugs must have a grounding prong. For portable *hand-held* tools or appliances only, the grounding prong may be a movable self-restoring type for voltages up to 150 (between conductors).

For voltages above 150, the grounding prong must be a fixed type for hand-held and all other equipment.

Grounding-type plugs must be so constructed that the grounding prong makes contact before the circuit wires make contact.

Grounding-type receptacles must have a slot to receive the grounding prong of the plug.

The receptacles and plugs must have a grounding terminal for connection to the grounding wire. The grounding terminal must show a green color.

A grounding terminal may not be used for any other purpose than as a grounding connection.

M. Rosettes

Rosettes are used to support a drop cord. They are attached to the ceiling or to a box in the ceiling, and the cord projects through a hole in the rosette. They are small in size, usually not more than 3 in. in diameter, and constructed of porcelain or other insulating material.

A type of rosette formerly in use contained a small fuse wire. This rosette had two parts that could be separated by a twist of the hand for fuse replacement. Fused rosettes are no longer permitted.

N. Special Provisions for Flush and Recessed Fixtures

Flush and recessed fixtures reach higher temperatures than other types. This is due to the fact that the heat from the fixture is not radiated fast enough to keep it at a normal temperature. There are special rules for the wiring of such fixtures.

410-64. Approved Type

Such fixtures must be approved for recessed mounting. A fixture carrying a UL label is an approved fixture.

410-65. Temperature

(a) Flush and recessed fixtures "shall be so constructed or installed that adjacent combustible material will not be subjected to temperatures in excess of 194°F." "Combustible material" includes wood, wood lath, and anything else that will burn.

The Underwriters Laboratories have established a temperature of 194°F as the highest safe temperature for any object adjacent to or in contact with combustible material. Construction of the fixture would be the responsibility of the manufacturer. UL-approved flush and recessed fixtures are manufactured according to the rules of Part P, following, and will maintain a temperature within the specified 194°F, but only if properly installed. The fixture should not be installed in such a way that all radiation of heat is cut off. A fixture embedded in insulation, for example, would result in an excessive fixture temperature, even in a UL-approved fixture.

(b) In a fire-resistant building the Code allows a higher temperature than 194°F. In such buildings the fixture temperature may go as high as 302°F. Recessed fixtures built for this service must be so marked by the manufacturer.

410-66. Clearance

This rule requires at least a ½-in. clearance all around the fixture, except at attachment points. Thermal insulation shall not be installed within 3 in. of the side of recessed fixtures (Fig. 418).

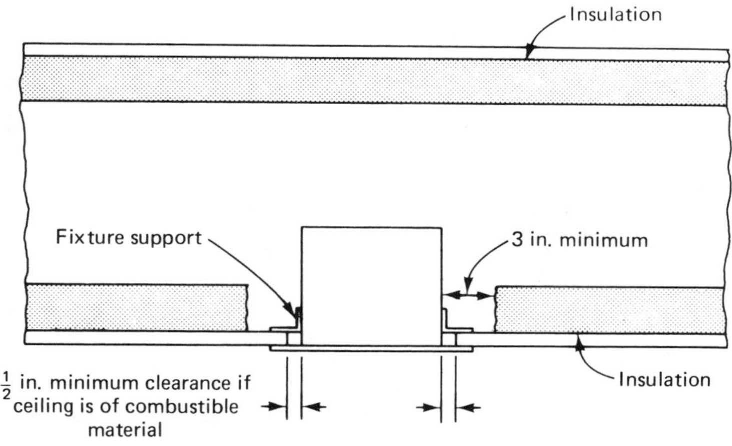

Fig. 418
Clearance required for recessed fixtures (Sect. 410-66). (Clearance above shall permit free air circulation.)

410-67. Wiring

The temperature of recessed fixtures generally will exceed 75°C (167°F), and they must be wired with conductors having insulation suitable for the high temperature. None of the thermoplastic or rubber-covered types would be suitable, except Types RHH, THHN. If the branch-circuit conductors are high-temperature conductors, the fixtures can be wired direct, like any other fixture. If the branch-circuit conductors are a type not suitable for temperatures above 167°F, they may not be run directly to the fixture, but may be run to a junction box set off from the fixture, with Type AF conductors run from the box to the fixture in Greenfield (Fig. 419). When this is done, the box must be at least 1 ft removed from the fixture, and the run of Greenfield not less than 4 nor more than 6 ft in length. The run is limited to 6 ft because Type AF conductors are approved only for fixture wiring; if held to 6 ft, the run is considered to be part of the fixture. The 4-ft minimum length is specified to prevent too much heat from being conducted along the Greenfield from the fixture to the box. The box must be "accessible."

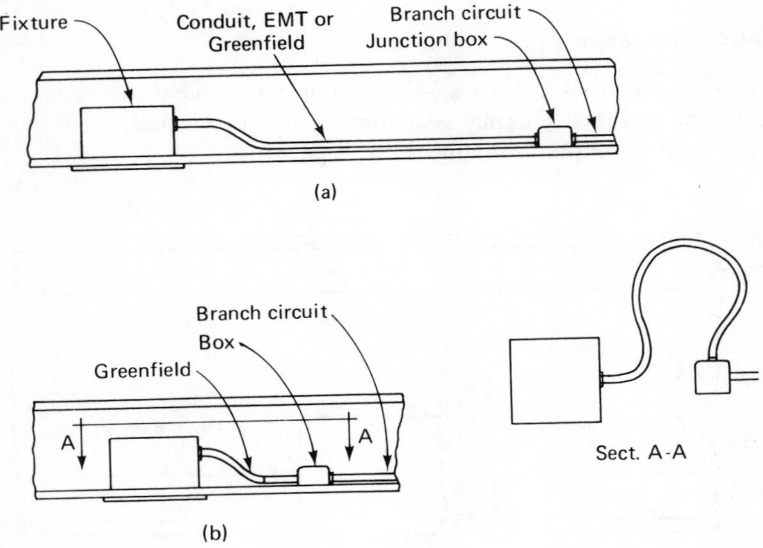

Fig. 419

Wiring flush or recessed fixtures, when branch circuit conductor insulation has a temperature rating less than required, and tap conductors are used as per Sect. 410-67(b)(2).

(a) Junction box 4 to 6 ft from fixture. Type AF conductors in run of conduit, EMT, or Greenfield, from box to fixture.

(b) Junction box less than 4 ft from fixture. Type AF conductors in Greenfield. Run from box to fixture is looped to obtain minimum 4-ft length required by the rule. Junction box must be accessible.

It might seem inconsistent to specify a minimum 4-ft run to a box that could be only 1 ft from the fixture. Where the box is less than 4 ft from the fixture, there must be a loop in the Greenfield between the fixture and the box in order to get the minimum 4-ft run required by the rule.

If the box is 4 ft or more from the fixture, a run of conduit or EMT could be used between box and fixture. It should be noted that other recessed fixtures may be served direct from the first fixture, using Type RHH, THHN conductors between fixtures. No additional boxes would be required.

"Branch-circuit conductors," such as Types RHH, THHN, can be used in place of Type AF fixture wires (which are "tap conductors"). In this case the conductors may be run from a box located anywhere in the branch circuit. Length of the run is not limited to 6 ft, but must be at least 4 ft long.

P. Construction of Flush and Recessed Fixtures

This part of the Code gives manufacturers' construction specifications for flush and recessed fixtures.

Q. Special Provisions for Electric-Discharge Lighting Systems of 1,000 Volts or Less

410-73. General

Fluorescent fixtures are one form of electric-discharge lighting. The rules of this part of the Code apply for fluorescent fixtures of 1,000 volts or less. The 1,000 volts refers to the starting voltage of the fixture, not the operating voltage. Fluorescent fixtures require a high momentary starting voltage to start the arc in the tube. As soon as the arc is started, the voltage drops back to a value near or below circuit voltage. In a 120-volt fluorescent, this "operating" voltage may be in the neighborhood of from 50 to 100 volts. The high starting voltage is supplied momentarily by the ballast during the instant that the starter contacts break, or for "instant-start" fluorescents, the starting voltage is supplied by an autotransformer. This part of the Code is for fluorescents with starting voltage of 1,000 volts or less.

410-74. Direct-Current Equipment

Most fluorescent fixtures operate on alternating current. There are some DC fluorescents, and the Code requires that these must be marked by the manufacturer to show that they are intended for DC operation.

410-75. Voltages—Dwelling Occupancies

(a) Fixtures with starting voltages of more than 1,000 volts are not permitted in residences.

(b) Fixtures with starting voltages of 300 to 1,000 volts are permitted in residences only if no live parts are exposed while lamps are being inserted, removed, or while the lamps are in place.

410-76. Fixture Mounting

(a) When ballasts are exposed (i.e., on the outside of the fixture), the fixture must be so mounted that the ballast will not be in contact with combustible material.

(b) When the ballast is inside the fixture, and the fixture is mounted on "combustible low-density cellulose fiberboard," the fixture shall be approved for such mounting, or if not approved, there must be a $1\frac{1}{2}$-in. air space between fixture and fiberboard.

410-77. Equipment Not Integral with Fixture

(a) "Auxiliary equipment" would include the ballast. When installed separate from the fixture, the auxiliaries must be in a metal cabinet.

(b) A circuit from a ballast to a display case may not extend beyond that display case, unless the display case is a permanent type.

410-78. Autotransformers

In instant-start fluorescents, the ballast consists of an autotransformer. Fluorescent fixtures having autotransformers producing more than 300 volts are permitted only on grounded circuits.

410-79. Switches

Snap switches must have an ampere rating high enough to carry the load. Fluorescent fixtures are an inductive load, and some snap switches are not rated to switch inductive loads equal to the full ampere rating of the switch (see Section 380-14).

R. Special Provisions for Electric-Discharge Lighting Systems of More Than 1,000 Volts

This part of the Code applies to neon tube lighting, and to fluorescent tube lighting requiring more than 1,000 volts, also to "cold-cathode" fluorescent tube lighting requiring more than 1,000 volts.

Neon tube lighting requires voltages up to 15,000 volts for starting, the voltage depending on the length of the tube. High voltages are also required for operation of the tubes after starting.

Note that this part of the Code applies to neon *lighting.* Article 600 applies to neon *signs.*

The transformers used have a high reactance and the secondary voltage drops off abruptly when a load is applied. A 15,000-volt transformer, for example, has 15,000 volts at the secondary end only on open circuit. As soon as a load is applied, the voltage drops. The greater the current, the less the secondary voltage. Secondary current is measured in milliamps. A 15,000-volt transformer, for example, might be built to deliver a maximum of 100 milliamps ($\frac{1}{10}$ amp.) of secondary current.

410-80. General

(a) Equipment for use with electric-discharge lighting systems of more than 1,000 volts shall be approved for the service. Among other things, special wire or cable approved for the high voltage would have to be used on the secondary side of transformers. (Standard conductors, used for general wiring, are approved for voltages only to 600 volts.)

(b) When one end of a fluorescent tube is inserted into the socket of a fixture, and the voltage at the socket is over 300 volts, the other end of the tube is considered as alive.

(c) High-voltage lighting systems must conform with the general rules for lighting, as well as the rules of this part of the Code.

410-81. Control

(a) A switch must be provided in the primary (low-voltage) transformer leads. The switch must break all hot wires.

(b) The switch must be within sight of the fixtures or tubes, or if it is not possible to have the switch within sight of all the lighting controlled by the switch, the switch must be provided with a lock for locking in the open position. Such an arrangement is necessary to the safety of persons engaged in servicing the equipment or replacing lamps.

410-82. Lamp Terminals and Lampholders

The fixture and tube sockets must be so designed that no live parts are exposed while a tube is being inserted or removed from the lamp sockets.

410-83. Transformer Ratings

This Section limits transformer secondary voltage to 15,000 volts (1,000 volts additional is allowed on test).

Secondary current rating is limited to 120 milliamps for 7,501- to 15,000-volt transformers, and 240 milliamps for transformers of 7,500 volts and under.

410-84. Transformer Types Permitted

Only dry-type or askarel-filled transformers are approved for service on electric-discharge lighting systems of more than 1,000 volts.

410-85. Transformer Secondary Connections

The high-voltage (secondary) windings of transformers may not be connected in parallel.

The high-voltage windings of two transformers may be connected in series, provided one end of each of the two secondaries is connected to its transformer case, and grounded by an insulated conductor not smaller than No. 14 (Fig. 420).

410-86. Transformer Locations

(a) Transformers shall be located so as to be accessible. A transformer would be considered "accessible" if it could be reached and worked on without difficulty. See definition of "accessible," p. 70-4 of the Code.

(b) Transformers shall be installed as close to the load as possible.

(c) Transformers shall be kept clear of combustible material.

410-87. Transformer Loading

The length of tubing connected to a transformer shall be no more than the length of tubing for which the transformer was intended. If too much tubing is connected to a transformer, the milliamps. in the secondary will go down, and the transformer secondary voltage will go up. Electric-discharge transformers are built to operate at a certain secondary voltage, specified by the manufacturer, and this voltage should not be exceeded.

The secondary voltage can be kept within limits by keeping the tubing length within the limits recommended by the manufacturer. The permissible length of tubing will depend on the tubing size. For larger sizes, a greater length of tubing is permitted. For smaller-size tubing, the permissible length of tubing would be less.

410-88. Wiring Method—Secondary Conductors

Conductors must be suited to the high secondary voltage. (Standard-type conductors are approved only for voltages up to 600.)

The high-voltage secondary circuit must be wired with approved gas-tube sign cable, with voltage rating suitable for the secondary voltage. This type of

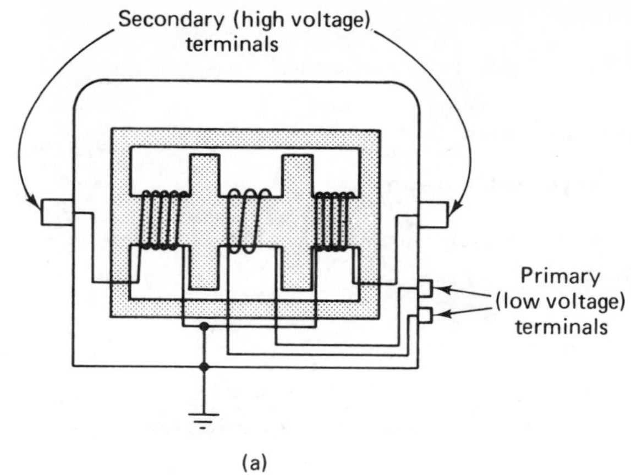

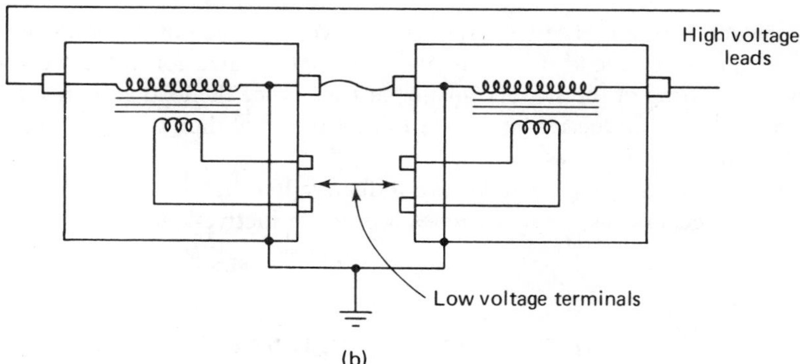

Fig. 420
Transformers for electric-discharge lighting:

(a) Conventional transformer with midpoint grounded. Midpoint-grounded transformers may not be connected in series.

(b) Transformers with one end of high-voltage winding grounded, connected in series as per Sect. 410-85.

cable is made in voltage ratings of 5,000, 10,000, and 15,000 volts.

The cable may be installed in one of the following ways:

1. As concealed wiring on insulators.

2. In rigid or intermediate *metal* conduit.

3. In flexible metal conduit.

4. In liquidtight flexible metal conduit.

5. In EMT.

(See also Section 600-31 of the code.)

410-89. Lamp Supports

410-90. Exposure to Damage

Lamps must be securely supported. They shall not be located where exposed to damage.

410-91. Marking

High-voltage warning signs must be provided for lamps, tubing, and for secondary wiring if the open circuit voltage is above 1,000.

410-92. Switches

A switch is required in the primary (low-voltage) side of the transformer. This is an inductive load. For switches that are not rated for inductive loads, the ampere rating of the switch must be at least twice the load amperes. If the switch is rated for inductive loads, the ampere rating of the switch need be only equal to the load amperes.

AC general-use snap switches are inductive-load rated.

AC-DC general-use snap switches are not inductive-load rated.

ARTICLE 422 — APPLIANCES

A. General

422-1. Scope

422-2. Live Parts

422-3. Other Articles

The rules of Article 422 are for all appliances, including motor appliances.

Appliances shall have no exposed live parts except where necessary to the operation of the appliance, as for toasters, cooking units, etc.

Appliances having motors (such as garbage grinders, peelers, dishwashers) are subject to the rules of Article 430 as well as to the rules of this Article. Sizing of conductors, circuit overcurrent protection, etc., for motors shall be according to the rules of Article 430.

B. Branch-Circuit Requirements

422-5. Branch-Circuit Sizing

(a) The general rule for "individual" circuits is that the conductors shall have an ampacity at least equal to the current rating marked on the appliance. There are a few exceptions to this rule:

1. In the case of motors, Article 430 requires a conductor with an ampacity of 125% of the current rating of the motor. If there is no current rating marked on the appliance, conductors must be sized at 125% of motor rated current.

2. For appliances without motors that are expected to operate continuously at full load, conductor ampacity must be 125% of current rating of the appliance. (Three hours or more of operation at a time is considered a "continuous" load.)

3. *Household* cooking appliances. Here the conductor ampacity need not be equal to the full nameplate current rating of the appliance. The kW load is figured according to Table 220-19, p. 70-46 of the Code. This will be less than the nameplate rating. (It should be emphasized that this exception applies only to *household* cooking appliances. It does not apply to commercial cooking appliances or any cooking appliances used in other than a household.)

   As an example, consider a 12-kW range. At 12 kW and 230 volts, the amperage would be 12,000/230 = 52.5 amps. This would require a No. 6 (Type T) conductor. According to Table 220-19 the range kW may be figured at 8 rather than 12 kW. At 8 kW the amperage would be 8,000/230 = 34.8 amps., which requires only a No. 8 conductor.

   The Code permits the No. 8 conductor to be used. In other words, a conductor with ampacity less than the appliance nameplate rating is permissible.

(b) When there are other loads on the circuit besides appliances, the conductors must be sized to carry both loads.

422-6. Branch-Circuit Overcurrent Protection

The fuse size or circuit-breaker setting for protection of other than motor appliances must be kept within the ampacity of the circuit conductors. If a protection rating is marked on the appliances, the fuse or breaker rating may be no higher than the marked rating.

For motor appliances the protection may be sized according to Table 430-152, p. 70-320 of the Code. (The branch-circuit protection for motor-operated appliances may be rated higher than the ampacity of the circuit conductors.)

Examples: Appliances Not Marked with a Current Rating.

1. A 2,000-watt, 115-volt hotplate:

Current rating is 2,000/115 = 17.4 amps. From Table 310-16, p. 70-132, minimum conductor size is No. 12 (Type T). Ampacity of No. 12 is 20 amps. A 20-amp. fuse or circuit breaker may be used for circuit protection.

2. A $\frac{1}{3}$ hp, 115-volt AC garbage grinder (disposer):

From Table 430-148, p. 70-316 of the Code, full-load current of the motor is 7.2 amps. Conductor ampacity must be 125% of 7.2, or 9 amps. A No. 14 branch-circuit conductor may be used.

Referring to Table 430-152, p. 70-320 of the Code, for a single-phase motor a branch-circuit fuse may be sized up to 300% of motor full-load current rating (under Nontime Delay Fuse, first listing at the top); 300% of 7.2 is 21.6 amps. There is no fuse this size; therefore, the Code allows the next higher standard size to be used. A 25-amp. fuse may be used for circuit protection. If a circuit breaker is used, it may be sized up to 250% of motor full-load current (fourth column of the table). This would be 250% of 7.2, or 18 amps. A circuit breaker set at 20 amps. may be used for circuit protection.

3. A 115-volt dishwasher with a 1,000-watt heater and $\frac{1}{6}$ hp motor:

Full-load current rating of the motor is 4.4 amps. Conductor ampacity for the motor would be 125% of 4.4, or 5.5 amps. Heater current is 1,000/115 = 8.6 amps. Conductors must be sized to carry 5.5 + 8.6, or 14.1 amps. A No. 14 (Type T) conductor would be required.

Maximum-size branch-circuit fuse permitted would be 300% of the motor current, plus the heater current.

$$(300\% \text{ of } 7.2) + 8.6 = 21.6 + 8.6 = 30.2 \text{ amps.}$$

A 30-amp. fuse could be used. If a circuit breaker is used, its rating would be

$$(250\% \text{ of } 7.2) + 8.6 = 18 + 8.6 = 26.6 \text{ amps.}$$

A 30-amp. circuit-breaker setting would be permitted.

If a current rating is marked on an appliance, it is not necessary to calculate the current rating. The branch-circuit conductors and overcurrent sizing would be according to the nameplate current rating.

C. Installation of Appliances

422-7. General

422-8. Flexible Cords

If a cord is to be subjected to hard usage, a hard-usage cord is required. If the cord is to be used in a damp or wet location, a cord approved for damp places is required.

Cord for hotplates, irons, toasters, heaters, ranges, and other appliances that produce high temperatures must be heater cords. Table 400-4 lists the different types of heater cord approved for use with appliances. Approved types are AFSJ, AFS, HPD, HSJ, HSJO, HS, HSO, HPN, SRD, SRDT.

Cord-and-plug connected waste disposers, trash compactors and dishwashers for use in dwellings must be either double-insulated, or if not double-insulated, grounded through the cord.

Cord shall be three-conductor, not less than 18 nor more than 36 inches long. Cord must be one of these types: S, SO, ST, STO, SJO, SJT, SJTO, SPT3.

Receptacle shall be accessible. (Need not be "readily accessible.")

422-9. Cord- and Plug-Connected Immersion Heaters

These should be so constructed that current-carrying parts are safe from contact with the liquid in which the heater is immersed. Compliance with this requirement would be the responsibility of the manufacturer.

422-10. Protection of Combustible Material

Fixed appliances producing heat, such as ranges, ovens, and hotplates, shall be located away from combustible material.

422-11. Stands for Portable Appliances

Appliances such as flatirons, soldering irons, and curling irons must be equipped with stands. If there were no stand, there would be danger of a hot appliance being set down on combustible material.

422-12. Signals for Heated Appliances

For appliances such as smoothing irons installed or used elsewhere than in residences, a signal (such as a light) must be provided to show when the appliance is "on." (If the appliance is provided with a temperature switch, a signal is not required.)

422-13. Flatirons

Flatirons used in residences must be equipped with temperature-limiting means. This would be a temperature switch inside the iron that will open the circuit when the iron reaches a certain temperature.

422-14. Water Heaters

Water heaters must be equipped with a temperature safety switch that will prevent the water from reaching a dangerously high temperature. The safety switch must be either a "manual reset" type, or equipped with a replacement element.

All fixed storage water heaters of 120 gallons or less are considered a "continuous" load, and circuit conductors must be sized for at least 125% of the full-load current of the water heater.

422-15. Infrared Lamp Industrial Heating Appliances

Medium-base screw-shell lampholders may be used for infrared lamps up to 300 watts. Lampholders must be the *unswitched,* porcelain type (or other types approved for the purpose).

Screw-shell lampholders may not be used for infrared lamps above 300 watts unless especially approved for the purpose.

In industrial occupancies only, infrared lamps may be connected in series across circuits of 230 volts or higher. Note that, when infrared lamps are connected in series across the line, the lampholder (not the lamp) must have a voltage rating at least equal to the circuit voltage. Lampholders come in 250 and 600-volt types. Lamps are usually 120-volt. Thus for two lamps in series across a 240-volt line, 250-volt lampholders could be used. For four lamps across a 480-volt line, the lampholders would have to be the 600-volt type.

422-16. Grounding

Metal enclosures for appliances operating at above 150 volts *to ground* must be grounded in all cases. Other appliances are to be grounded if required by Sections 250-42 or 250-45.

422-17. Wall-Mounted Ovens and Counter-Mounted Cooking Units

For stationary appliances, a cord and plug is acceptable as the disconnecting means. The Code does not classify wall-mounted ovens and counter-mounted cooking units as stationary appliances. They are considered to be fixed appliances. A cord and plug is not acceptable as a disconnect. A disconnect switch is required for these units.

D. Control and Protection of Appliances

422-20. Disconnecting Means

Appliances generally must be provided with some kind of disconnecting means. This may be a switch near the appliance, or for cord-connected appliances it may be the cord and plug. The intent of the Code is that the disconnect shall completely disconnect all hot wires from all parts of the appliance, and that the disconnect shall be hand-operated. A switch on an appliance is not considered a disconnect.

When more than one circuit serves an appliance, the two or more disconnect switches shall be grouped, and each switch must be marked to show which part of the appliance is served by the switch.

422-21. Disconnection of Fixed Appliances

422-22. Disconnection of Portable Appliances

Disconnection of Stationary Appliances

See definitions of Fixed, Portable, and Stationary Appliance, p. 70-4 of the Code.

Water heaters, wall-mounted ovens, garbage grinders, and dishwashers would be examples of fixed appliances. These are fixed appliances even if connected by cord and plug because they are "secured in place." *Any* appliance that is wired direct, rather than by cord and plug, is a fixed appliance. Direct wiring "secures" an appliance in place.

Any appliance that is customarily and easily moved from place to place in normal use is a portable appliance. These would have to be cord and plug connected; otherwise, they could not be easily moved.

Household refrigerators and freestanding household ranges connected by cord and plug are examples of appliances that do not fall into either the fixed or portable classification. Since they are not secured in place, they could not be classified as fixed appliances. They are not customarily or easily moved from place to place; therefore, they could not be classified as portable appliances. Such appliances are designated as stationary appliances.

The rules of these Sections may be summed up as follows:

1. *Fixed Appliances*

   300 watts and under, or $\frac{1}{8}$ hp and under: no disconnect required.

   Over 300 watts or $\frac{1}{8}$ hp: disconnect required. May be branch-circuit switch if "readily accessible."

2. *Portable Appliances and Stationary Appliances with Cord and Plug*

   Cord and plug qualifies as the disconnect.

422-24. Unit Switches as Disconnecting Means

A switch (or switches) on an appliance is not considered a disconnecting means. When a fixed appliance rated at over 300 volt-amps. or $\frac{1}{8}$-hp has a switch (or switches), a separate disconnect must be provided, in addition to the switch on the appliance.

The following are permitted as the disconnect for an appliance *with a switch:*

1. *Multifamily Dwellings (Such As Apartment Buildings)*

   Disconnect may be outside the apartment, but must be on the same floor. This would permit the disconnect to be a branch-circuit switch or circuit breaker in a distribution panel for the apartment.

2. *Two-Family Dwellings*

   Disconnect may be outside the apartment and on another floor. This would permit the disconnect to be a branch-circuit switch or circuit breaker in a panel in the basement.

3. *Single-Family Dwellings*

   May be the service disconnect. Need not be on the same floor as the appliance.

4. In other occupancies, the branch-circuit switch or circuit breaker, *if readily accessible,* may serve as the disconnect.

The above rules would not apply for portable appliances or for stationary appliances connected by cord and plug (a cord-connected range, for example). In this case the cord and plug would act as the disconnect, and no additional disconnect would be required. The rules *do* apply for all appliances wired direct.

For wall-mounted ovens and counter-mounted cooking units connected by cord and plug, the cord and plug may *not* serve as the disconnect (Section

422-17). These units require a separate disconnect, which may be one of the four listed.

422-25. Switch and Circuit Breaker to Be Indicating

The disconnecting switch or circuit breaker must be marked OFF, ON, or otherwise marked to show switch position.

422-26. Disconnecting Means for Motor-Driven Appliances

For fixed motor-driven appliances of more than $\frac{1}{8}$ hp, without a switch on the appliance, the disconnect must be within sight of the motor controller.

If there is a switch on the appliance, the disconnect may be located as per Section 422-24.

For cord- and plug-connected motor-driven appliances of any rating the cord and plug may serve as the disconnect (Section 422-22).

422-27. Overcurrent Protection

(a) Appliances generally are considered protected by the branch-circuit protection provided by Section 240-3.

Motor-operated appliances must have running overload protection, in addition to the branch-circuit protection (see Part C of Article 430).

(b) If a *household* range or *household* appliance with surface heating elements has a current rating (according to Table 220-19, p. 70-46) of over 60 amps., the appliance must be served by more than one circuit—a circuit for each 50 amps. or fraction. For 230-volt appliances, this rule technically would apply only for an appliance rated at 27 kW. To illustrate, turn to Table 220-19. Note 1 under the Table specifies that, for ranges over 12 kW, the demand of Column A shall be increased 5% for each additional kW over 12. For a 26-kW range, the demand would be

$$8 \text{ kW} + 70\% \text{ of } 8 \text{ kW} = 13.6 \text{ kW}$$

$$\frac{13{,}600}{230} = 59.2 \text{ amps, current rating}$$

A 26 kW, 230-volt appliance would not come under the rule. Since the Table is for ranges only up to 27 kW, the rule would apply only for a 27-kW, 230-volt range or appliance. The rule *would* apply for *115*-volt surface heating appliances rated $8\frac{3}{4}$ to 27 kW.

(c)(d) Overcurrent protection for infrared heating appliances and open-coil or sheathed-coil heating elements of the commercial type are limited to 50 amps.

(e) When an individual circuit supplies only one appliance, and the appliance is rated at 16.7 amps. or more, the circuit fuse size or circuit-breaker setting is limited to 150% of the current rating of the appliance. An appliance drawing 16.7 amps. might be wired with No. 10 circuit conductors. Ordinarily, a 30-amp. fuse would be permitted, since No. 10 has a 30-amp. current-carrying capacity. In this case, however, the fuse size would have to be limited to 25 amps, which is 150% of the appliance current rating. (The rule does not apply to motor-driven appliances. These may be fused higher than 150%. See Section 422-6, Example No. 2.)

(f) This Subsection specifies rules for factory-installed overcurrent devices.

E. Marking of Appliances

This part of the Code specifies the information that the manufacturer must provide on the appliance nameplate.

ARTICLE 424 — FIXED ELECTRIC SPACE HEATING EQUIPMENT

A. General

424-1. Scope

Article 424 applies for all types of electric heating systems for rooms and buildings. This would include baseboard heaters, cables laid in wall or ceiling plaster or in floors, central electric heating systems where water or air is heated in a boiler or furnace, and any other electric heating systems for rooms or buildings.

424-2. Other Articles

Code rules for wiring and overcurrent protection, as set down in other sections of the Code, must be followed, as well as the rules of this Article (424).

424-3. Branch Circuits

(a) Branch-Circuit Requirements

Branch circuits may be any amperage as long as only one heating unit is on the circuit.

If more than one unit is on the circuit, the branch-circuit size is limited to 30 amps. maximum (50 amps. for industrial infrared heaters).

(b) Branch-Circuit Sizing

This refers to sizing of conductors feeding a heating cable or other heating equipment. The conductors, generally, must have an ampacity equal to 125% of the load. For example, if the load is 40 amps., the conductors must have an ampacity of 125% of 40, or 50 amps minimum.

B. Installation

424-9. General

424-10. Special Permission

424-11. Supply Conductors

Conductors used for general wiring, such as latex rubber and thermoplastic-covered wire, are approved for temperatures only up to 60°C.

If the heating unit requires conductors with over 60°C insulation, the manufacturer is required to mark the equipment with this information. Conductors suitable for over 60°C include types RH, RHH, RHW, RUH.

If the equipment is not marked, latex rubber or thermoplastic conductors (types RUW, T, TW) may be used for the wiring.

424-12. Locations

Heating equipment shall not be installed where exposed to damage.

If installed in a damp or wet location, the equipment must be approved for such locations.

424-13. Spacing from Combustible Materials

This rule would not apply for heating cables embedded in plaster. It would apply for other types of electric heating units that are heated to a high temperature, such as space heaters. The latter type must be kept clear of combustible material.

424-14. Grounding

Exposed metal parts of space heating equipment must be grounded.

C. Control and Protection of Fixed Electric Space Heating Equipment

424-19. Disconnecting Means

For motor-driven heaters of more than $\frac{1}{8}$ hp, the disconnect must be within sight from the motor controller, except that if the heater is equipped with supplementary overcurrent protection, a disconnect with provision for locking in the open position may be out of sight.

For heaters without a motor, the branch-circuit switch or circuit breaker can serve as the disconnect, if "readily accessible."

For heaters having a motor of 1/8 hp or less, the branch circuit switch or circuit breaker can serve as the disconnect, if "readily accessible." (See definition of "readily accessible," p. 70-12 of the Code.)

Unit Switches as Disconnecting Means

A switch on a heating unit is not considered a disconnecting means. When the heating unit has a switch, a separate disconnect is required, but it may be in another room and may be the branch-circuit switch.

The following are permitted as the disconnect for a heater *with a switch:*

1. *Multifamily Dwellings (Such As Apartment Buildings)*
   Disconnect may be outside the apartment, but must be on the same floor. This would permit the disconnect to be a branch-circuit switch or circuit breaker in a distribution panel for the apartment.

2. *Two-Family Dwellings*
   Disconnect may be outside the apartment and on another floor. This would permit the disconnect to be a branch-circuit switch or circuit breaker in a panel in the basement.

3. *Single-Family Dwellings*
   May be the service disconnect. Need not be on the same floor as the appliance.

4. In other occupancies, the branch-circuit switch or circuit breaker, *if readily accessible,* may serve as the disconnect.

424-20. Thermostatically Controlled Switching Devices

(a) Thermostats that control line current (not current for a relay) must operate to open all hot wires, and must have an "off" position.

(b) Thermostats with no "off" position need not open all hot wires.

(c) The above rules (a and b) do not apply to remote-control thermostats.

(d) The thermostat described in (a) above may serve as a disconnect. When used as a disconnect, the thermostat must have a manual "off" position, and the "off" position shall open all hot wires. It shall be so constructed that, when manually put in the "off" position, it cannot reconnect automatically.

424-21. Switch and Circuit Breaker to Be Indicating

Switches and circuit breakers must have an ON, OFF marking.

424-22. Overcurrent Protection

Heating units are considered as protected by the branch-circuit fuse or circuit breaker. Motors require running overcurrent protection in addition to the branch-circuit protection.

Resistance-type space heating units rated over 48 amps. must be subdivided by the manufacturer into loads of not over 48 amps. Manufacturer shall furnish overcurrent protection for each load, either in the unit, or separate.

When overcurrent protection is separate, conductors from the overcurrent devices to the unit may be sized at 100% of load, for heaters rated under 50 kW.

For heaters rated 50 kW or more, conductors may be sized at 100% only if the heater has temperature control, *and* is marked for 100% conductors. Otherwise they must be sized at 125% of load.

D. Marking of Heating Equipment

424-28. Nameplate

424-29. Marking of Heating Elements

Heating equipment must be provided with a nameplate, giving volts and amperes (or watts).

E. Electric Space Heating Cables and Panels

424-34. Heating Cable Construction

Leads for connecting heating cables or panels to the circuit shall be furnished, and attached to the heating cable or panel by the manufacturer. The leads must be at least 7 ft long.

424-35. Marking of Heating Cables and Panels

(a) Heating Cables

The connecting leads of a heating cable must be marked by the manufacturer to show the voltage to be used with the cable.

Different colors on the conductor insulation denote different voltages: 120 volts, yellow; 208 volts, blue; 240 volts, red; 277 volts, brown. Marking on the conductors must be within 3 in. of the terminal end of the conductor.

(b) Heating Panels

Heating panels must be permanently marked by the manufacturer.

424-36. Clearances of Wiring in Ceilings

Ceiling wiring must have at least a 2-in. clearance above the ceiling.

All wiring in the space above a ceiling containing cable or panel heating is considered to be operating at a temperature of 50°C (122°F). Conductors operating at this temperature will have a reduced carrying capacity, in accordance with the correction factors of Table 310-16. (If there is 2 in. or more of insulation between the wiring and heated ceiling, a correction factor need not be applied.)

Example.

What size Type RH conductor is required for a circuit run above the ceiling, for ceiling heating cables with a full-load current rating of 16 amps.?

The conductor must be sized to carry 125% of the full load [Section 424-3(b)].

$$125\% \text{ of } 16 = 20 \text{ amps.}$$

Referring to Table 310-13, p. 70-124, Type RH is rated at 75°C.

Refer now to the correction factors on p. 70-132. In the first column go down to 50°, which is our operating temperature. Opposite, in the third column, a demand factor of .75 is listed. This is the correction factor for a 75°C conductor operating in a temperature of 50°C. To carry 20 amps.

in a 50°C temperature the conductor ampacity must be 20/.75 = 26.7 amps. A No. 10 conductor would be required.

424-37. Clearances of Branch-Circuit Wiring in Walls

(a) Wiring in outside walls must be run outside the wall insulation. No correction factor is necessary for cables run in outside walls (see Fig. 424).

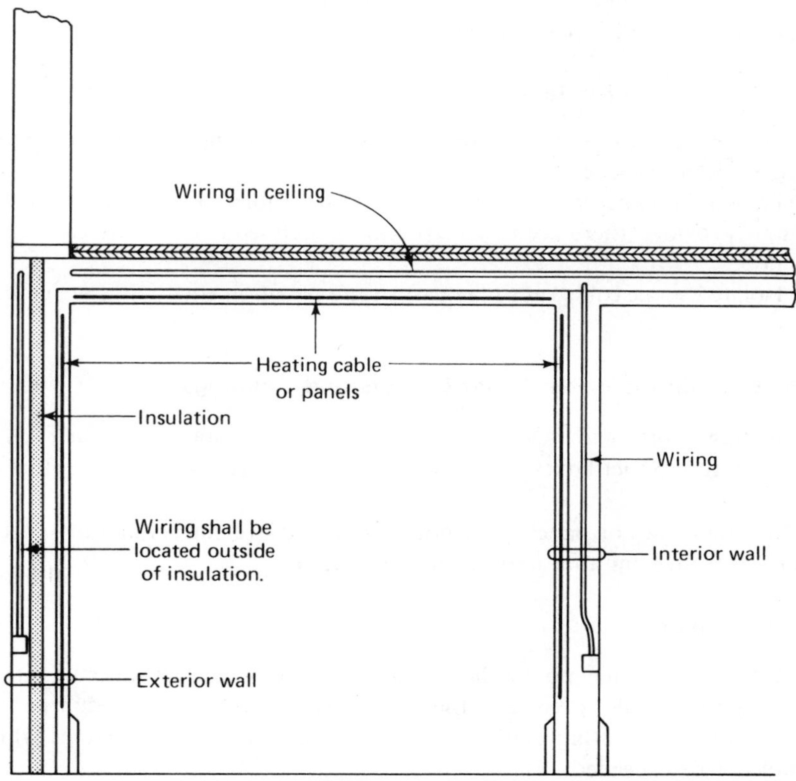

Fig. 424

Wiring in heated walls and ceilings (Sects. 424-36, 424-37).

No correction factor required for wiring in exterior wall.

Wiring in interior wall subject to 40°C correction factors.

Wiring in ceiling subject to 50°C correction factors (unless separated from heating cables by at least 2 in. of insulation).

(b) The correction factor for heating circuits and all other circuits in inside walls is based on a 40°C temperature.

Example.

What size Type T conductor is required for the circuit to inside wall heating panels drawing 16 amps.?

The conductor ampacity would be 125% of 16, or 20 amps. Type T is a 60°C conductor. Referring to the Correction Factor Table, p. 70-132, the correction factor for a 60°C cable in a temperature of 40°C is .82. To carry 20 amps. the conductor must have an ampacity of $20/.82 = 24.4$ amps. A No. 10 conductor would be required.

424-38. Area Restrictions

The general rule is that heating cables or panels may not extend beyond a single room or be installed over a partition or closet.

(For humidity control only, low-temperature cables are permitted in closet ceilings, provided there are no obstructions, such as a shelf, between ceiling and floor.)

(Isolated single cable runs may pass over a partition where they are embedded.)

424-39. Clearance from Other Objects and Openings

Heating cables and heating panels may not be installed within 8 in. of surface fixture outlet boxes, or within 2 in. of recessed fixtures or ventilation openings.

Heating cables or panels may not be installed over or behind any part of surface-mounted lighting fixtures (see Fig. 425).

424-40. Splices

Heating cables may not be shortened. One good reason for this rule is that, if the length of cable is reduced, the total resistance is reduced, resulting in a greater current. Heating cables are made to take a certain current, which should not be exceeded.

Splices in heating cables may be made only if absolutely necessary.

424-41. Installation of Heating Cables on Dry Board, in Plaster, and on Concrete Ceilings

(a) Heating cables are permitted in ceilings but may not be installed in walls.

(b) Cables rated $2\frac{3}{4}$ watts per foot and under must be separated at least $1\frac{1}{2}$ in. on centers.

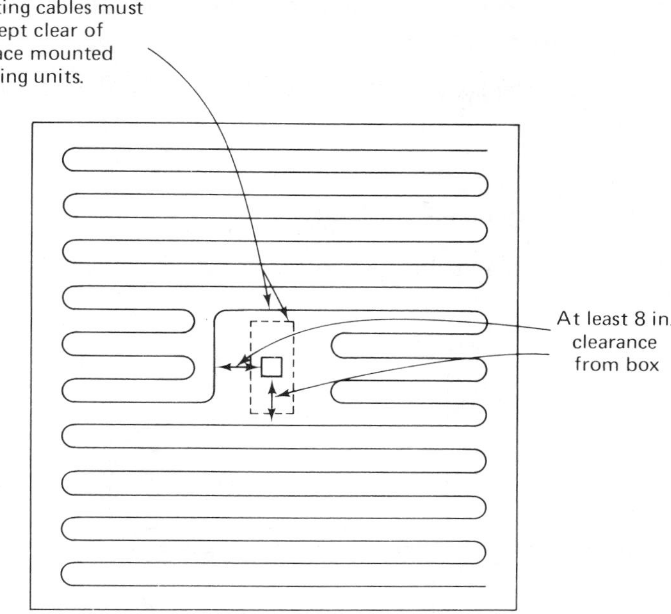
Heating cables must be kept clear of surface mounted lighting units.
At least 8 in. clearance from box

Fig. 425
Clearance of heating cables from boxes and lighting fixtures (Sect. 424-39).

(c) Heating cables may be installed only on fire-resistant surfaces, but not directly on metal or metal lath. Metal or metal lath must have a coat of plaster before the heating cables are installed.

(d) Both the heating cables and at least 3 in. of the heating cable connecting leads must be embedded in the plaster or dry board.

(e) Ceilings must have a $\frac{1}{2}$-in.-thick coating of noninsulating plaster as a finish coat, after the installation is complete.

(f) Cables must be strapped or otherwise secured in place at least every 16 in. (Cables specifically approved for the purpose may be strapped at 6-ft intervals.)

(g) In dry board ceiling installations, a coating of thermally conducting plaster is applied after the cables are in. The ceiling is then covered with gypsum board, not over $\frac{1}{2}$ in. thick.

(h) Cables may not be laid on or be in contact with metal or metal lath.

(i) In dry board installations, heating cables may not be run directly under a joist. The cables may not cross the joist unless absolutely necessary.

This rule would require cables to be run parallel to the joists and under the space between joists.

(Fig. 426 shows a plaster finish installation; Fig. 427 illustrates a dry board installation.)

424-42. Finished Ceilings

Ceilings may be painted or papered after the job is finished.

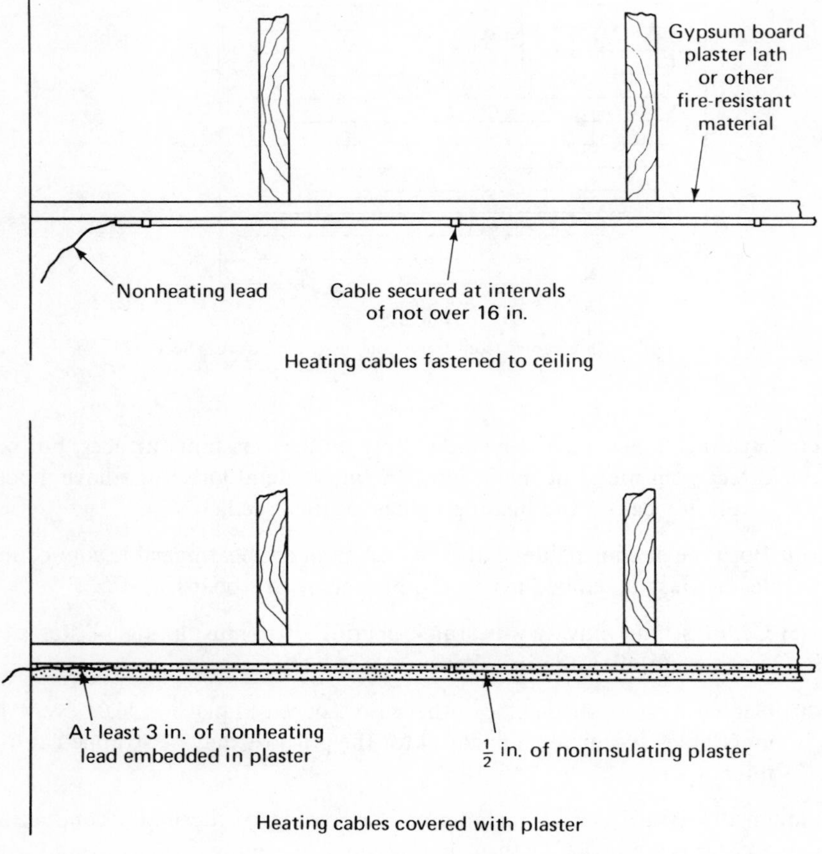

Fig. 426
Installation of ceiling heating cables in plaster finish (Sect. 424-41).

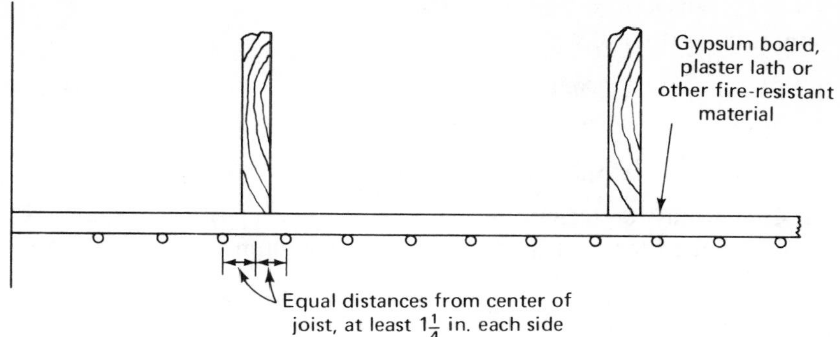

Heating cables fastened to ceiling

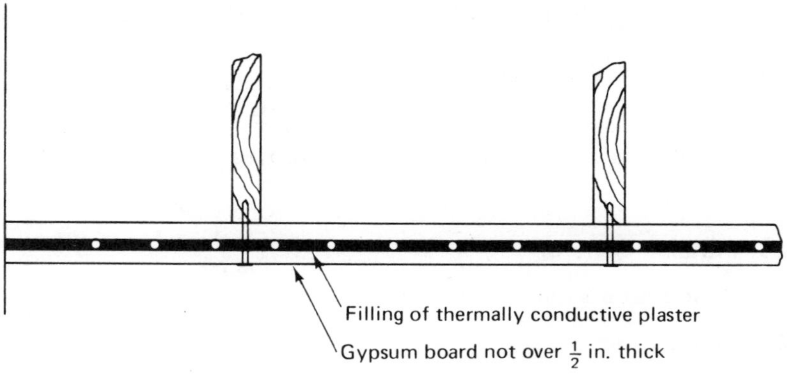

Heating cables covered with gypsum board

Fig. 427
Installation of ceiling heating cables, dry board installations. Cables shall be installed parallel to joists. Cross over only at ends of cable run.

424-43. Installation of Nonheating Leads of Cables and Panels

This Section refers to the 7-ft nonheating leads that the manufacturer is required to furnish attached to the heating cable. When these leads are run to a junction box, at least 6 in. of lead must show in the box. A nonheating lead must not be cut. If the leads are too long for the box location, the excess must be attached to the ceiling and embedded in the plaster. Nonheating leads of *panels* may be cut as required.

424-44. Installation of Panels or Cables in Concrete or Poured Masonry Floors

(a) Panels or cables shall be rated at not more than 33 watts per square foot of panel, or $16\frac{1}{2}$ watts per linear foot of cable.

(b) Cables shall be spaced not less than 1 in. apart on centers.

(c) Cables must be secured in place before pouring of the concrete. The device used for securing in place must be nonmetallic.

(d) Cable must be kept clear of metal, such as reinforcing bars in the concrete.

(e) Connecting leads, where they are brought through the floor, must be in metal conduit or tubing, or other approved enclosure.

(f) The conduit or tubing must be fitted with a bushing at the lower end.

424-45. Inspection and Tests

Care must be taken to prevent damage to cables.

Cable installations shall be inspected and approved before pouring of the concrete.

424-46. Panels—General

424-47. Panels to Be Complete Units

424-48. Installation

These Sections apply for panels of less than 25 watts per square foot, that are assembled in the field to form a heating installation for one room or area.

The panels must be installed as complete units and connected together by approved wiring methods.

Nails or staples may not be used where they penetrate current-carrying parts. Metal fasteners may be used if they are insulated.

F. Duct Heaters

424-57. General

424-58. Approved

This part (F) of the Code is for heaters mounted inside air ducts. Such heaters must be approved for duct mounting and installed in an approved manner.

424-59. Air Flow

There must be a uniform flow of air over or through a heater. This is necessary to avoid overheating.

424-60. Elevated Inlet Temperature

Duct heaters used with high inlet temperatures must be approved for the purpose and marked for such use by the manufacturer.

424-61. Installation of Duct Heaters with Heat Pumps and Air Conditioners

Duct heaters installed less than 4 ft from a heat pump or air conditioner must be a special type approved for the purpose.

424-62. Condensation

Air conditioners or air coolers could cause condensation to form within the duct. For this reason the Code requires that, when duct heaters are used with such equipment, the duct heaters be "approved for use with air conditioners."

424-63. Fan Circuit Interlock

If a duct heater were in operation without air flowing within the duct, this could result in damage. The Code requires that duct heater circuits be interlocked with the fan circuit in such a way that the heater will not operate with the fan "off."

An interlock arrangement is illustrated in Fig. 430.

424-64. Limit Controls

Duct heaters must be provided with a built-in safety device that will limit the temperature of the heater to a safe value.

424-65. Location of Disconnecting Means

The heater disconnect must be within sight of the heater controller.

424-66. Installation

Duct heaters shall be installed according to manufacturer's instructions. Duct heaters shall be located so as to permit access to the heater.

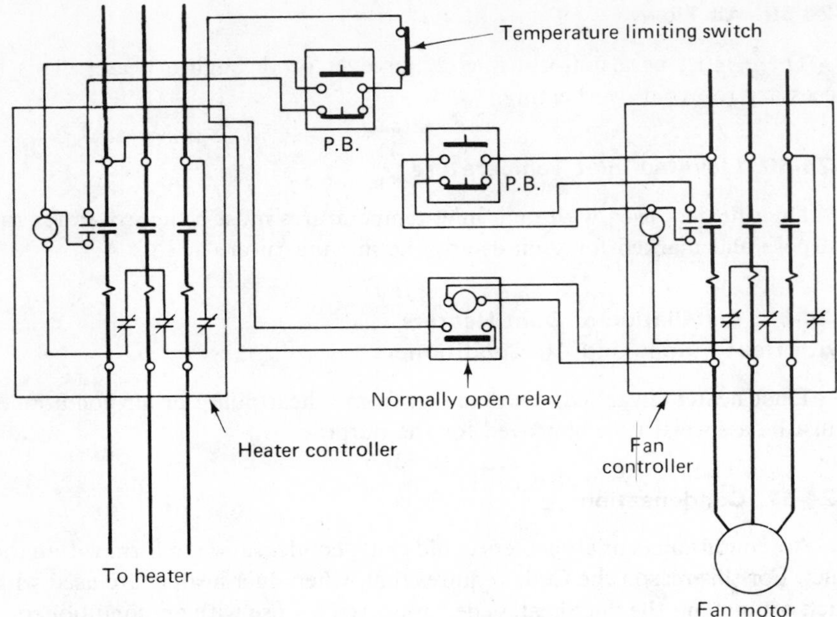

Fig. 430
Fan circuit interlock (Sect. 424-63). One method of interlocking fan circuit with heater circuit. The normally open relay prevents energizing of the heater circuit unless fan motor is energized.

G. Resistance-Type Boilers

424-70. Scope

424-71. Approved

This part of the Code applies to boilers using resistance-type electric heating elements. Immersion heaters are one form of resistance-type heater. Resistance-type boilers must be "approved for the purpose" and installed in an approved manner.

424-72. Overcurrent Protection

(a) For immersion heaters contained in an ASME rated and stamped vessel, the load on any one circuit is limited to 120 amps. If the load is greater than 120 amps, there must be more than one circuit—one for each 120 amps. or fraction. Circuit protection for each circuit may be not more than 150 amps. rating.

(b) For immersion heaters *not* contained in an ASME rated and stamped vessel, the load on any one circuit is limited to 48 amps. If the load is greater than 48 amps, there must be more than one circuit—one for each 48 amps. or fraction. Circuit protection for each circuit may be not more than 60 amps. rating.

(c) Overcurrent protection for the above shall be factory-installed.

(d) Branch-circuit protection must be provided in addition to the factory-installed protection.

For heaters rated 50 kW or more and having factory-installed overcurrent protection, the branch circuit conductors may be sized at the nameplate rating on the heater, *provided* the heater has temperature control. (For other heaters, conductors must be sized at 125% of the load amperes.)

424-73. Over-Temperature-Limit Control

This rule is for boilers "designed so that . . . there is no change in state of the heat transfer medium." The heat-transfer medium would be water. In a steam boiler, the water changes to steam; there is a "change in state" of the heat-transfer medium. The rule does not apply to steam boilers.

For boilers having no "change in state" of the heat-transfer medium, a temperature-limiting switch (a "limit" switch) must be provided to open the circuit on excessive temperature.

424-74. Over-Pressure-Limit Control

This rule would apply to steam boilers. For steam boilers a pressure-limiting switch must be provided to open the circuit on excessive pressure.

424-75. Grounding

All non-current-carrying metal parts shall be grounded.

H. Electrode-Type Boilers

424-80. Scope

424-81. Approved

This part of the Code applies to boilers that heat the liquid by passage of a current through the liquid.

Electrode-type boilers shall be "approved for the purpose" and installed in an approved manner.

424-82. Branch-Circuit Requirements

Conductors must be sized on a basis of 125% of the load. An 80-amp. load would require a conductor with an ampacity of 125% of 80, or 100 amps.

(For electrode boilers rated 50 kW or more, the circuit conductors may be sized at the nameplate rating of the boiler, *provided* the boiler has temperature or pressure control, and is marked by the manufacturer for 100% conductors.)

424-83. Over-Temperature-Limit Control

This rule is for boilers "designed so that . . . there is no change in state of the heat-transfer medium." The heat-transfer medium would be water. In a steam boiler, the water changes to steam; there is a "change in state" of the heat-transfer medium. The rule does not apply to steam boilers.

For boilers having no "change in state" of the heat-transfer medium, a temperature-limiting switch (a "limit switch") must be provided to open the circuit on excessive temperature.

424-84. Over-Pressure-Limit Control

This rule would apply to steam boilers. For steam boilers a pressure-limiting switch must be provided to open the circuit on excessive pressure.

424-85. Grounding

All exposed non-current-carrying metal parts shall be grounded. This includes supply and return piping. The pressure vessel containing the electrodes must be *isolated* and *insulated* from ground.

424-86. Markings

Electrode-type boilers must be marked to show manufacturer's name, volts, amps., kW, type of current, and labeled "Electrode-Type Boiler." A warning sign must be provided reading ALL POWER SUPPLIES SHALL BE DISCONNECTED BEFORE SERVICING, INCLUDING SERVICING THE PRESSURE VESSEL.

ARTICLE 426 — FIXED OUTDOOR ELECTRIC DE-ICING AND SNOW-MELTING EQUIPMENT

A. General

426-1. Scope

426-2. Other Articles

426-3. Branch-Circuit Requirements

Article 426 applies to de-icing and snow-melting cables, units, and panels of the *embedded* type.

Such an installation is considered a "continuous load." This means that the circuit conductors must be sized to carry 125% of the load. For instance, if the load is 40 amps., the conductors must have a 50-amp. carrying capacity.

B. Installation

426-9. General

426-10. Use

Equipment and cables must be UL-approved for the purpose. Cables may be installed only in the material for which they are approved. If approved only for cement, they may not be embedded in any material other than cement.

426-11. Complete Units

Heating cables may not be shortened.

426-12. Special Permission

Equipment not conforming to the requirements of this Article (426) may not be installed, unless special permission is granted to do so.

C. Control and Protection

426-20. Disconnecting Means

A disconnect switch or circuit breaker must be provided. The disconnect must break all hot wires.

Where "readily accessible," the branch-circuit switch or circuit breaker may serve as the disconnecting means. The disconnect must have an ON, OFF marking [see also Section 426-21(a)].

426-21. Controllers

(a) Thermostats that interrupt line current (not a relay circuit) and which have an "off" position may be used as the disconnect, provided the "off" position opens all hot wires.

(b) Thermostats must be so designed that, when manually put in the "off" position, they will remain "off" until put in the "on" position.

(c) Thermostats without an "off" position need not open all hot wires. Thermostats without an "off" position may not be used as a disconnect.

426-22. Overcurrent Protection

The equipment is considered as protected by the branch-circuit fuse or circuit breaker.

426-23. Nonheating Leads

The heating cable manufacturer is required to furnish leads attached to the cable for connection to the circuit conductors.

426-24. Installation of Heating Cables, Units, or Panels

(a) These must be designed for use in the material (cement, asphalt, etc.) in which they are to be embedded.

(b) Maximum wattage permitted is 120 watts per sq. ft of area.

(c) Spacing between cables must be at least 1 in. between centers.

(d) Cables and panels must be installed on an asphalt or masonry base at least 2 in. thick, then covered with a coating of asphalt or masonry at least $1\frac{1}{2}$ in. thick.

Or they may be installed on other approved bases and embedded in $3\frac{1}{2}$ in. of masonry or asphalt, but not less than $1\frac{1}{2}$ in. from the top.

(e) Cables must be secured in place before pouring of the asphalt or masonry.

(f) Cables may not bridge expansion joints unless adequately protected.

426-25. Installation of Nonheating Leads

(a) Leads with a grounding sheath (metal sheath) may be embedded the same as the heating cables.

(b) Leads without a grounding sheath must be in conduit or tubing. The conduit or tubing must be run to within 6 in. of the factory splice, but may not be closer than 1 in.

(c) The conduit or tubing must have an insulating bushing at the embedded end.

(d) Leads must be protected by conduit or tubing where they emerge from asphalt or masonry.

(e) At least 6 in. of lead must be left in the junction box.

Fig. 435 shows a nonheating lead installation.

426-26. Marking

The manufacturer must mark cables and panels with voltage, amperage (or watts), and catalog number.

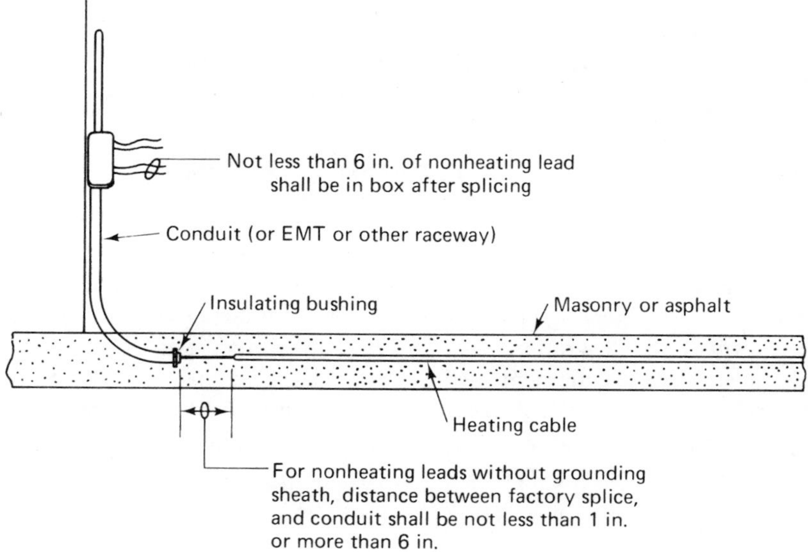

Fig. 435
Installation of nonheating lead (Sect. 426-25).

426-27. Junction Boxes

All splices made in the field must be in junction boxes.

426-28. Grounding

(a) Grounding is required for all metal parts, such as boxes, cable sheath, etc.

(b) Grounding means (such as copper braid, copper or lead sheath) shall be provided on the cable by the manufacturer.

(c) A No. 14 minimum, insulated copper grounding conductor must be run to the distribution panel for the purpose of grounding the installation. Grounding conductor to be without splices.

426-29. Inspection

Cables, panels, and other equipment must be inspected and approved before pouring of the masonry or asphalt.

ARTICLE 427 — FIXED ELECTRIC HEATING EQUIPMENT FOR PIPELINES AND VESSELS

A. General

427-1. Scope

Article 427 specifies rules for the installation of electrical equipment used for the purpose of heating pipe, usually to prevent freezing. A heating element in the form of a cable wrapped around water pipe would be an example of such "equipment." Any equipment used to heat "vessels" associated with the pipeline also comes under the rules of this article. Heating cable in various lengths, connected by cord and plug and equipped with a plug-in thermostat, is available for pipe-heating purposes.

427-2. Definitions

This Section explains what is meant by the terms "pipeline," "vessel," and "integrated heating system," as used in the sections following.

A "pipeline" is any length of pipe, including also pumps, valves, flanges, control devices, strainers, and similar equipment along the pipeline.

A "vessel" is a container such as a barrel, drum, or tank.

An "integrated heating system" would include all pipe, appurtenances, vessels—the complete system including the heating equipment.

427-3. Application of Other Articles

In addition to the rules of this Article, the general rules of the Code must also be complied with.

427-4. Branch-Circuit Requirements

Branch-circuit conductor size is figured on a basis of 125% of the load amperes. A 20-amp. load would require a conductor with an ampacity of 125% of 20, or 25 amps.

B. Installation

427-10. General

427-11. Use

Equipment shall be approved for the purpose and installed in such a manner that the equipment will be protected from damage.

427-12. Integrated Electrical Heating System

(a) If the piping and/or vessels are to be heated to a temperature of more than 140°F, any piping and/or vessels that may be touched or contacted by persons shall be covered or insulated. Piping and/or vessels out of reach need not be covered or insulated.

(b) Signs must be posted so that persons having occasion to contact the piping and/or vessels will know that electrical heating equipment is present. This applies for all electrical heating equipment, regardless of temperature.

(c) Heating elements shall be fastened at intervals of not more than 12 in. (For wrap-around cable, the wrapping would secure the cable along its length; fastening would be required only at the cable ends.) Pipe insulation may not be used as a means of securing cable.

(d) Thermostatic control is required only if the heating cable is *not* in direct contact with the pipe or vessels.

(e) Where a heating cable bridges an expansion joint in a pipeline, provision shall be made to take up expansion and contraction. This could be done by providing a loop at the expansion joint.

(f) If installed on flexible piping, heating elements shall be a type able to withstand flexing.

C. Control and Protection

427-20. Disconnecting Means

(a) A disconnect switch shall be provided. The disconnect must have a "positive lockout" in the "off" position.

(b) For heating cable with a cord-and-plug connection, the cord and plug is approved as a disconnect, *provided:*

1. Amperage is not over 20.
2. Voltage is not over 150 to ground.

If amperage is over 20 or if voltage is over 150 to ground, a separate disconnect switch must be provided.

A branch-circuit switch or circuit breaker, if *readily accessible,* may serve as a disconnect. Thermostatic controls are not acceptable as a disconnect unless they can be locked out in the "off" position.

427-21. Controls

1. Thermostatic controls that interrupt line current (not relay current) and have an "off" position shall have a pole for each hot wire. Such controls may serve as a disconnect provided they have a positive lockout for the "off" position, which will prevent automatic restarting.
2. Thermostatic controls without an "off" position need not open all hot wires. Such thermostatic controls may *not* serve as a disconnect.
3. Remote-control thermostats may not serve as a disconnect.

427-22. Overcurrent Protection

Overcurrent protection shall be provided in accordance with Section 210-20.

427-23. Nonheating Leads

(a) At least 6 in. of nonheating leads must be left in the junction box.

(b) Where nonheating leads leave a pipeline or vessel, they shall be protected by metal conduit or EMT.

(c) Connections between lengths of heating cable may be covered with pipe insulation.

427-24. Markings

Heating cable must be marked by the manufacturer with identification symbol, catalog number, volts, watts (or amperes).

427-25. Electrical Connections

(a) Nonheating connections concealed by piping insulation must be made with insulated connectors.

(b) Other connections must be in a junction box or fitting.

427-26. Grounding

All exposed metal parts likely to become energized shall be grounded.

ARTICLE 430 — MOTORS, MOTOR CIRCUITS AND CONTROLLERS

A. General

430-1. Motor Feeder and Branch Circuits

Sections 430-1 through 430-17 are general requirements that apply to motors, controllers, and motor circuits. Diagram 430-1, p. 70-286, includes all of the possible circuits and equipment covered by Article 430. The diagram is for a wound-rotor motor with secondary control through separate resistors. All of the circuits and components shown in this diagram would not necessarily be included for the wiring and control of every motor.

430-2. Adjustable-Speed Drive Systems

The term "power-conversion equipment" as used in this Section would include motor generators. If power-conversion equipment is part of an adjustable-speed drive system, circuit conductors, overcurrent protection, etc., are sized on a basis of current input (motor current). If the motor has overload protection, no overload protection is required for the generator of an M.G. set. A disconnect in the incoming line (to the motor) may serve as the disconnect for the outgoing line (from the generator).

430-3. Part-Winding Motors

A part-winding-start induction motor is a special type having two separate windings, one for starting and the other brought into the circuit for running. The Code requires that, when each of the windings has individual overcurrent protection, the protection for each be sized at half of that permitted for the full motor horsepower.

430-4. In Sight From

The term "in sight from" is used frequently in the succeeding pages. A motor is considered "in sight from" its controller if the motor is visible and not more than fifty feet distant. A motor located 51 ft from its controller is not considered "in sight from" the controller, even though it may be seen from the controller location.

430-5. Other Articles

Attention is here drawn to the fact that motor installations for certain applications, such as air conditioning and cranes, must comply with Article 430, and also with articles listed for these special cases.

430-6. Ampacity and Motor-Rating Determination

(a) General Motor Applications

Tables 430-147 through 430-150 (pp. 70-315 through 70-318 of the Code) list full-load currents for all sizes and types of motors. These current values are used for figuring conductor size, size of branch-circuit fuses (or breaker), controller size, disconnect size.

The tables are not used for sizing the *running overload protection.* For running overload protection, the current rating on the motor nameplate is used. In many cases the nameplate current for a given motor will be lower than the current listed in the tables.

The above rules apply for all motors except:

1. Multispeed motors.
2. Shaded pole or permanent-split-capacitor fan and blower motors.
3. Torque motors.
4. AC adjustable voltage motors.

For multispeed motors, conductor size and branch-circuit protection are based on nameplate current rating [see Sections 430-22(a) and 430-52]. Other determinations are as above.

For shaded pole or permanent-split capacitor fan and blower motors, nameplate current rating is used for all determinations.

Torque motors: see (b) below.

AC adjustable-voltage motors: see (c) below.

(b) Torque Motors

A torque motor is one that is built to operate in the stalled position, in this way exerting a torque (turning force) without rotating. For torque motors, the locked-rotor (stalled) current marked on the motor nameplate is used for all determinations.

(c) AC Adjustable Voltage Motors

Nameplate current rating is used for sizing conductors, branch-circuit fuses (or breaker), controller, disconnect, and running overload protection—all determinations.

430-7. Marking on Motors and Multimotor Equipment

430-8. Marking on Controllers

430-9. Marking at Terminals

These Sections list the items of information that the Code requires on the motor nameplate, and on controllers. Marking of terminals is required where terminal marking is necessary to ensure proper connections.

430-10. Wiring Space in Enclosures

Unless the design of the enclosure is such as to provide adequate space for additional conductors, motor controllers and disconnects may contain only the wiring necessary for operation of the motor. Tapping to conductors in controllers or disconnects for the purpose of feeding other than the motor circuits is prohibited; conductors for other apparatus may not feed through a controller or disconnect unless "adequate space" is provided.

430-11. Protection Against Liquids

When a motor is installed where there is dripping or spraying of water or oil, the motor should be an enclosed-type motor built for use in such locations. If the motor is not a type suitable for such locations, it must be protected by a suitable cover.

430-12. Motor Terminal Housings

430-13. Bushing

These Sections list the rules governing the size and construction of motor terminal housings. Compliance would be the responsibility of the motor manufacturer.

430-14. Location of Motors

A motor shall not be so located that it would be difficult to lubricate or make any necessary replacements.

All motors require a certain amount of air circulation to carry away the motor heat. Motors shall be so located that the proper circulation of air will be provided.

Open motors with commutators or collector rings shall be located at a safe distance from combustible material.

430-16. Exposure to Dust Accumulations

In locations where dust is present and accumulates, such as in feed mills, motors must be the enclosed type and rated for high temperatures. In extreme cases, it may be necessary to pipe in clean air from outside the room to cool the motor. In this case an enclosed, separately ventilated motor would be used. These motors have openings in the motor case for admission and discharge of the air, the inlet and outlet pipes being connected to the openings.

430-17. Highest Rated (Largest) Motor

Certain sections following refer to the "highest rated" motor in a group. The "highest rated" motor is simply the motor with the greatest full-load current. The full-load current for motors of all types and sizes is given in Tables 430-147 through 430-150 (pp. 70-315 through 70-318 of the Code).

B. Motor Circuit Conductors

430-21. General

430-22. Single Motor

Section 430-22 specifies the rules for figuring the minimum size conductor permitted for a circuit supplying an *individual* motor. The rules of this Section do *not* apply for cases where other equipment, such as lighting or receptacles, are on the same circuit with the motor.

Section 430-22 applies for the case in which a *single motor only* is supplied by the circuit.

THE GENERAL RULE IS THAT CONDUCTORS SUPPLYING A SINGLE MOTOR MUST HAVE A CURRENT-CARRYING CAPACITY OF NOT LESS THAN 125 PERCENT OF THE MOTOR FULL-LOAD CURRENT RATING.

Tables 430-147 through 430-150 (pp. 70-315 through 70-318 of the Code) list the full-load current ratings of motors of different types and sizes. These tables are used for figuring the conductor size.

Example.

What minimum size Type T branch-circuit conductor is required for a 15-hp, 230-volt, three-phase motor?

From Table 430-150, p. 70-318, full-load current rating of the motor is 42 amps.

$$125\% \text{ of } 42 = 52.5 \text{ amps.}$$

The conductors must have a current-carrying capacity of at least 52.5 amps. From Table 310-16, No. 6, which carries 55 amps., would be the smallest size Type T conductor permitted for this motor.

There are special cases in which the ampacity of conductors may be less than 125% of motor full-load current. Where a motor operates on short time duty, with periods of rest in between, the conductors have a chance to cool, and the Code allows a smaller size conductor than that required for a continuous load.

Example.

What minimum size Type T conductor is required for a 15-hp, 230-volt, three-phase motor driving a pump, operating on 15-minute cycles?

From Table 430-150, p. 70-318, full-load current rating of the motor is 42 amps. Referring to Table 430-22(a), p. 70-295, the table lists the required carrying capacity of conductors in this case as 85% of full-load current rating.

$$85\% \text{ of } 42 = 35.7 \text{ amps.}$$

The conductors must have a current-carrying capacity of at least 35.7 amps. From Table 310-16, No. 8, which carries 40 amps., would be the smallest Type T conductor permitted.

Table 430-22(a) also lists some special cases where a current-carrying capacity of over 125% is required.

Any motor is considered a *continuous-duty* motor unless there is no possibility of its running continuously under any circumstances.

A stoker motor normally runs only periodically, but it could run continuously if, for example, the hopper is empty. Because there is a possibility of continuous operation, such a motor is considered a continuous-duty motor.

A motor operating a drawbridge could not operate continuously since "limit switches" shut the motor off at the end of the travel of the draw. This would be considered periodic duty, since there is *no possibility* of the motor operating continuously.

Multispeed three-phase induction motors are made in three types: constant horsepower, constant torque, and variable torque.

For the constant horsepower type, the horsepower output does not change with the speed. For a motor of this type the current rating would be the same for all speeds.

In the constant torque type, horsepower output varies directly with the speed. For a 900/1,800 rpm two-speed motor of this type, the horsepower output at 1,800 rpm would be twice the horsepower output at 900 rpm.

In the variable torque type, the horsepower output varies as the square of the speed. For a 900/1,800 rpm two-speed motor of this type, the horsepower output at 1,800 rpm would be four times the horsepower output at 900 rpm.

For a three-phase multispeed motor, there would be six or more conductors between controller and motor, the number depending upon number of speeds and type of motor—whether constant horsepower, constant torque, or variable torque.

For multispeed motors, full-load current rating is taken from the motor nameplate rather than the tables. Here there would be a current rating for each speed, and the highest rating given would be used to figure conductor size *to the controller.* The conductors between controller and motor are sized according to the current rating for the different speeds.

For a constant horsepower two-speed motor, the high-speed and low-speed conductors between the controller and the motor would be the same size.

For a constant torque two-speed motor or a variable torque two-speed motor, the required size of the high-speed conductors would be larger than that of the low-speed conductors.

Paragraph (b) of this Section deals with a special case in which the motor connection requires some flexibility, as in the case of a motor that must be movable on its base to adjust belt tensions. Here, a run of conduit could terminate at a point near the motor, and a short length of flexible cable provided between the end of the conduit run and the motor. This is permitted only for motors up to 1 hp.

In general, no conductor smaller than No. 14 is permitted by the Code (Section 310-5). However, an exception is allowed in the case of this flexible connection; conductors may be as small as No. 18. (See Section 430-145.)

430-23. Wound-Rotor Secondary

Wound-rotor motors are three-phase induction motors operating on the same principle as the squirrel-cage motor. The difference between the wound-rotor motor and the squirrel-cage type is that the wound-rotor type has two sets of leads, the main leads and a set of "secondary" leads. The secondary leads connect to the rotor through slip rings. The other end of the secondary leads connects, through a controller, to a set of resistors. The amount of resistance in the rotor circuit can be varied by the controller to vary the speed of the motor. The greater the resistance, the less is the speed of the motor. The resistances may be a part of the controller, or they may be separate, with a separate set of leads from the controller to the resistor bank for each of the several resistor segments (Fig. 436).

In general, the secondary leads between the motor and the controller must be sized for 125% of the secondary full-load current of the motor. Secondary full-load motor currents are not listed in the Code. They must be read from the motor nameplate or obtained from the manufacturer. They will always be less than the full-load motor current.

[For a "periodic-service" motor, the secondary conductor ampacity may in some cases be less than 125% of secondary full-load current, and Table 430-22(a), p. 70-295, may be followed.]

When there is a resistor bank separate from the controller, the leads

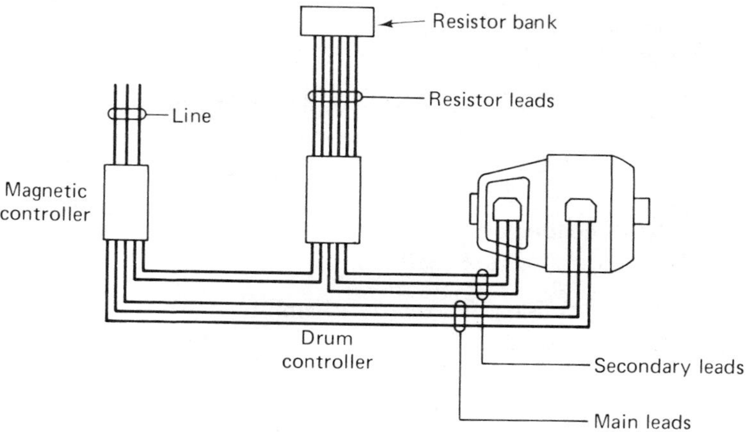

Fig. 436

Wound-rotor motor with drum controller; resistors separate from controller. Resistor leads are sized according to Table 430-23(c) of the Code.

between the *controller* and the *resistor bank* are sized according to Table 430-23(c) of this Section of the Code. The conductors referred to here are shown in the diagram on p. 70-286 of the Code, at the bottom of the page. (In some cases there would be several sets of such leads.)

Wound-rotor motors are used not only for speed control purposes. They are also used for applications that require a high starting torque. Inserting the proper resistance in the rotor circuit at starting will result in a starting torque two to three times that of a squirrel-cage motor of the same horsepower.

When used only for starting duty, the resistor leads (between controller and resistor bank) carry current only during the short starting period, and may be sized smaller than when used for speed control. According to Table 430-23(c), if the resistor leads are used *only for starting,* the ampacity of the leads between controller and resistor need not be over 55 percent of the *secondary* current of the motor.

If the resistor bank is used for *speed control,* then the carrying capacity required is 65 to 110% of *secondary* current. In the usual case, for speed control, the resistor leads would be sized on a basis of 110%.

Example.

A 20-hp, 230-volt, three-phase wound-rotor motor has a secondary full-load current rating of 40 amps. Resistor bank is separate from controller and used for speed control. What minimum size Type T conductors are required for

1. main leads
2. secondary leads
3. resistor leads (leads between controller and resistor bank)

1. From Table 430-150, p. 70-318 of the Code, full-load current rating of the motor is 54 amps.

$$125\% \text{ of } 54 = 67.5 \text{ amps.}$$

A No. 4 conductor, which carries 70 amps., would be required for the main leads (Table 310-16).

2. Secondary full-load current is 40 amps.

$$125\% \text{ of } 40 = 50 \text{ amps.}$$

From Table 310-16, No. 6, which carries 55 amps., would be the minimum size for the secondary leads.

3. Resistor leads would be sized for 110% of secondary full-load current rating.

$$110\% \text{ of } 40 = 44 \text{ amps.}$$

From Table 310-16, No. 6, which carries 55 amps., would be the minimum size for the resistor leads.

430-24. Conductors Supplying Several Motors

Section 430-22 applies for the case where there is *only one* motor on the circuit (i.e., the motor has an *individual* circuit).

Section 430-24 applies where there are two or more motors on the same circuit (Fig. 437). In this case the conductors must be sized to carry 125% of the full-load current rating of the highest-rated (most-current) motor plus the sum of full-load current ratings of all other motors on the circuit.

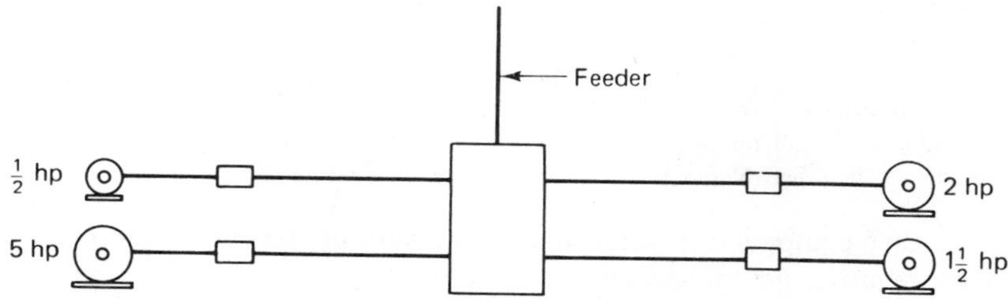

Fig. 437
Conductors supplying several motors (Sect. 430-24). Feeder ampacity must be at least equal to 125% of full-load current rating of the 5-hp motor plus the sum of the full-load current ratings of the other motors.

Example.

What minimum size Type T feeder conductors are required to feed two 10-hp and one 3-hp, 230-volt, three-phase motors?

From Table 430-150, p. 70-318 of the Code, full-load current rating of the 10-hp motor is 28 amps.; of the 3-hp motor, 9.6 amps. The conductors must be sized to carry

$$125\% \text{ of } 28 + 28 + 9.6 \text{ or } 35 + 28 + 9.6 = 72.6 \text{ amps.}$$

From Table 310-16, p. 70-132, No. 3 conductors would be required.

430-25. Conductors Supplying Motors and Other Loads

(a) Combination Load

When one or more motors are on the same circuit with other equipment, such as lights or appliances (Fig. 438), the minimum size conductor required for the whole load is figured as follows:

First, the carrying capacity required for the motor or motors is figured as though only motors were on the circuit. Then the carrying capacity required

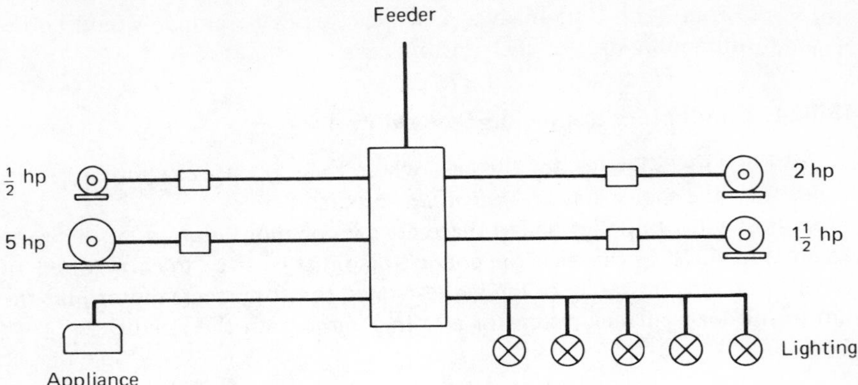

Fig. 438

Combination load [Sect. 430-25(a)]. Feeder ampacity must be at least equal to 125% of full-load current rating of the 5-hp motor, plus the sum of the full-load current ratings of the other motors, plus the amperage of the lighting and appliances.

for the other equipment is determined. The sum of the two is the carrying capacity required for the circuit.

Example.

What minimum size Type T conductors are required for a circuit for two $\frac{1}{4}$-hp single-phase motors, and also a heater drawing 10 amps.? Circuit is 115 volts AC, single phase.

From Table 430-148, p. 70-316 of the Code, full-load current of a $\frac{1}{4}$ hp, 115-volt, single-phase motor is 5.8 amps. Carrying capacity required for the two motors is

$$125\% \text{ of } 5.8 + 5.8 \text{ or } 7.25 + 5.8 = 13.05 \text{ amps.}$$

Carrying capacity required for the heater is 10 amps. Total carrying capacity required is

$$13.05 + 10 = 23.05 \text{ amps.}$$

From Table 310-16, p. 70-132, No. 10 conductors, which carry 30 amps., are required.

(b) Multimotor and Combination-Load Equipment

A single piece of equipment may contain more than one motor. Or it may contain a motor, or motors, and in addition an appliance load. A dishwasher is an example of such equipment, containing both a motor and a heater. If the circuit ampacity is marked on the equipment by the manufacturer, the conductor ampacity shall be at least equal to the marked ampacity. If not marked, conductor size would be calculated as above.

430-26. Feeder Demand Factor

For some motor installations, there might be a special situation in which a number of motors are connected to one feeder, and the nature of operations may be such that at no time would all the motors connected to the feeder be in operation simultaneously.

Such cases are special cases in which the authority having jurisdiction may grant permission to reduce the feeder size for a group of motors below that required by the above rules.

430-27. Capacitors with Motors

Capacitors are sometimes installed on circuits feeding AC induction motors. The purpose of the capacitors is to improve the power factor of the load. When capacitors are used in this way, less current is drawn from the line by the motor(s). This would require a lower setting for the overcurrent device protecting the motor(s). Conductors to the capacitor are sized in accordance with Section 460-8.

430-28. Feeder Taps

When more than one motor is on a feeder circuit, each motor is "tapped" to the feeder. The tap is protected by the motor branch-circuit protection. The motor branch-circuit protection will be at the end of the tap, and the following rules apply:

1. If the tap conductors are the same size as the feeder, there are no special requirements. The tap may be any length.
2. If the length of the tap is 25 ft or less, conductor ampacity need be only $\frac{1}{3}$ that of the feeder, provided that the conductors are protected from physical damage. Conduit, EMT, flexible metal conduit, or BX sheath would provide suitable protection for the conductors.
3. If the length of the tap is 10 ft or less, conductors with ampacity less than $\frac{1}{3}$ that of the feeder may be used, provided that the conductors are in raceway or entirely within a controller. Note that, in this case, cable is not permitted for the tap run.

The "length of tap" above is the length of conductor between the point of tapping to the feeder and the motor branch-circuit fuse or circuit breaker.

C. Motor and Branch-Circuit Running Overcurrent and Overload Protection

A motor branch circuit includes the following components, which are required by the Code:

1. Motor-running overload protection.
2. Branch-circuit short-circuit protection.
3. A motor controller.
4. A motor disconnect.

One or more of these may be included in the same enclosure or each may be separate. Or in some cases one device may serve a dual purpose, but all four functions must be provided for most motor circuits. (There are certain exceptions that permit motor-running overload protection to be omitted.) Figs. 439 to 446 illustrate different types of motor branch circuits, each of which includes the four essential components.

430-31. General

A motor circuit requires two kinds of protection:

1. Protection against overload.
2. Protection against short circuit.

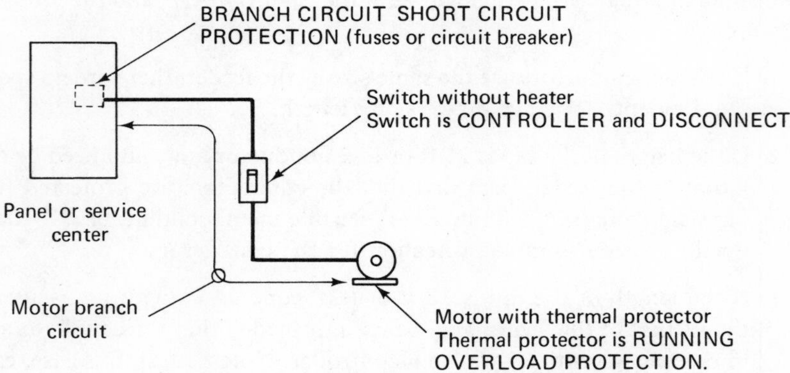

Fig. 439

Motor-running overload protection integral with motor. Switch may be single-pole for 120 V, single-phase; must be two-pole for 240 V, single-phase; three-pole for three-phase.

This part (C) of the Code deals with protection against overload.

An "overloaded" motor will draw more current than it was designed for. Excessive current due to overloading could result in damage to motor and controller and cause dangerous overheating of the circuit conductors. Failure

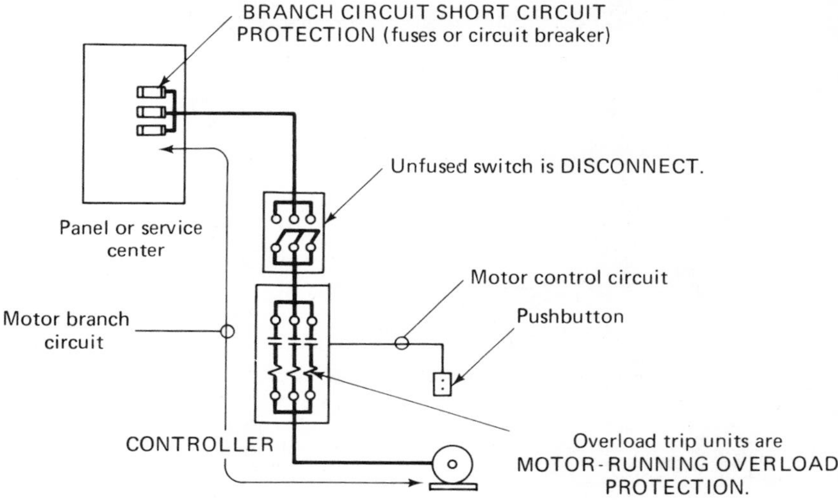

Fig. 440

Motor circuit with fusetrons. Switch may be single-pole for 120 V, single-phase; must be two-pole for 240 V, single-phase; must be three-pole for three-phase.

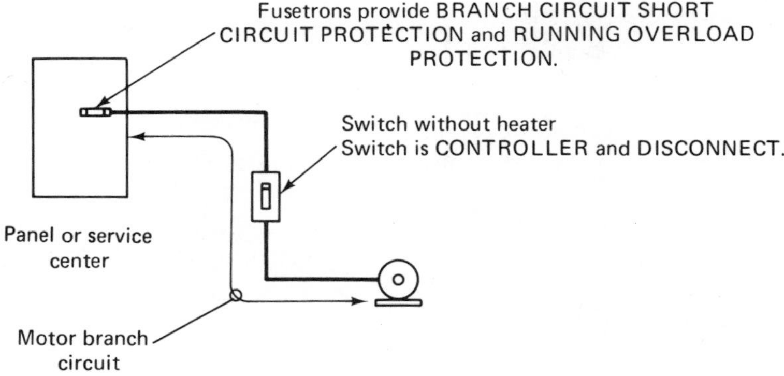

Fig. 441

Motor circuit with magnetic controller. Disconnect separate from controller. Three-phase circuit shown.

to start could also result in an excessive current continuing long enough to result in overheating. The running-"overload device" required by this part of the Code is intended to protect motor, controller, and branch-circuit conductors against overheating due to continuing excessive current.

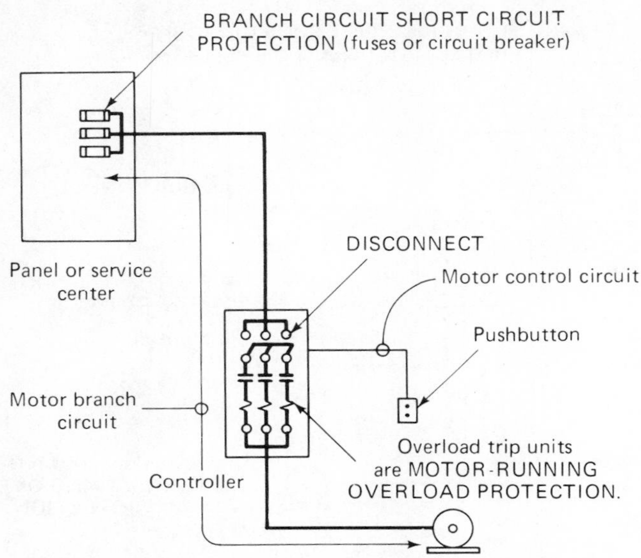

Fig. 442

Magnetic controller with disconnect in controller. Three-phase circuit shown.

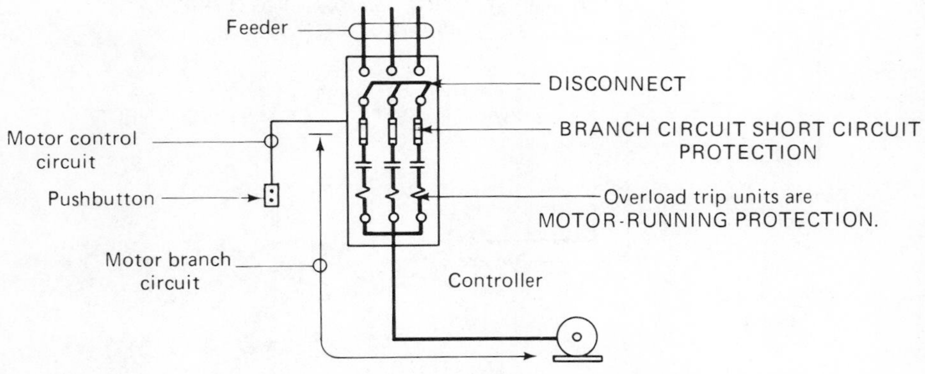

Fig. 443

Controller with disconnect, short-circuit protection, and running overload protection in one enclosure. Three-phase circuit shown.

Motors, on starting, draw a high current during the short time interval required to attain full speed. The starting current could be on the order of five times the full-load current of the motor. A momentary high starting current is not objectionable because of its short duration, but continuing overcurrent in a motor will result in damage or deterioration.

A good "overcurrent device" will have the "time-delay" feature that allows the momentary high current required for starting, but will open the circuit on prolonged overcurrent that could result in damage to the motor.

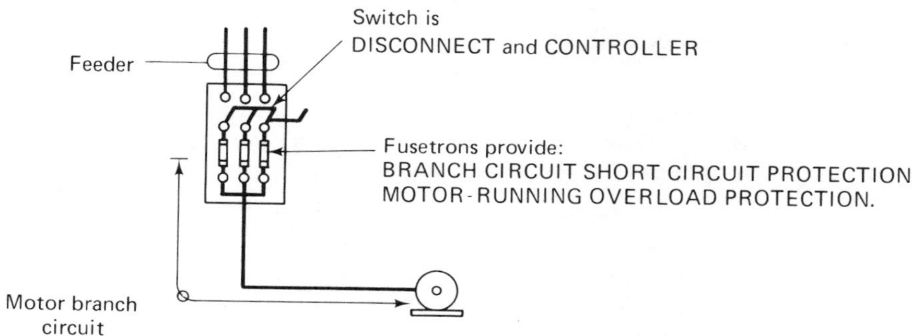

Fig. 444

Manual motor switch with fusetrons provides four functions: disconnect, controller, short-circuit protection, and motor-running overload protection. Three-phase circuit shown.

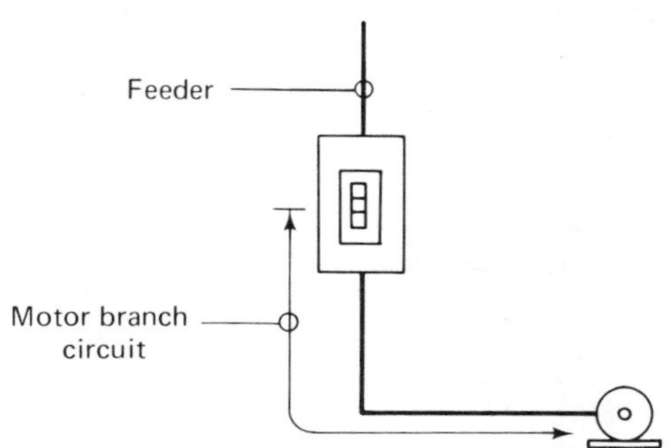

Fig. 445

Manual circuit breaker with thermal and magnetic trip for motor control and protection. Thermal trip element is MOTOR-RUNNING OVERLOAD PROTECTION. Magnetic trip element is BRANCH-CIRCUIT SHORT-CIRCUIT PROTECTION. Hand-operated contacts are CONTROLLER and DISCONNECT.

The following devices are commonly used for motor-running overload protection:

1. Fusetrons.
2. Thermal relays.
3. Motor switches with built-in "thermal devices."
4. Thermal cutouts.
5. Circuit breakers.
6. Thermal device built into the motor.

1. Fusetrons are so constructed as to provide the time-delay characteristic required for motor-running protection. In one type of cartridge fusetron, current flows through a heater element in the form of a piece of metal. A spring soldered to the heater element is arranged in such a way that when there is an overload the heat from the high current melts the solder, the spring is released, and the circuit opens. The time required for an overload to heat the solder to the melting point gives the fuse its time-delay characteristic.

   In series with the time-delay feature, fusetrons also contain a fuse link. The fuse link is sized for about 500% overcurrent, but on short circuit it opens instantaneously like an ordinary fuse. The fusetron thus provides both motor-running and short-circuit protection.

2. Thermal relays are made in several different forms, but all operate on the same principle. They consist of a "heater" in the form of a short strip

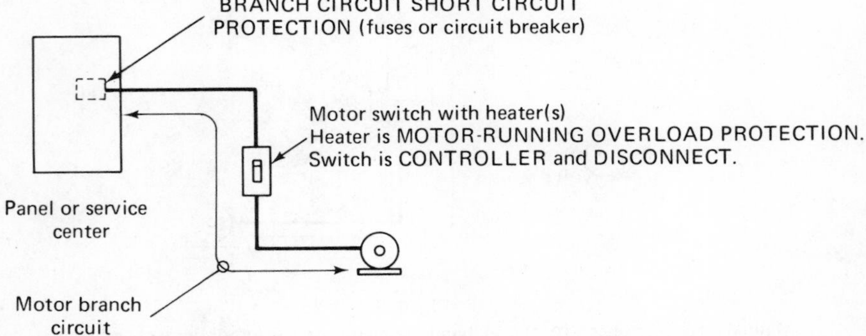

Fig. 446

Motor switch with heater. Switch may be single-pole for 120 V, single-phase; must be two-pole for 240 V, single-phase; three-pole for three-phase.

of high-resistance metal and a set of contacts arranged in such a way that, if the heater reaches a high temperature, the contacts open.

The heater is connected in the motor circuit and takes the motor current. The contacts are connected in an "auxiliary" circuit. The auxiliary circuit is wired to the holding coil of the main disconnect contacts for the motor. When the heater contacts open, the holding coil is deenergized, opening the main contacts for the motor circuit.

Thermal relays are customarily used in "magnetic" motor starters, and are a part of the starter. One form of relay unit consists of a heater, melting pot, and ratchet wheel. Continued overcurrent through the heater melts the alloy in the melting pot and allows the ratchet wheel to rotate and open the relay contacts. These units are interchangeable and may be obtained in a number of different ratings. By changing the relay unit, the controller overload protection can be adapted to different size motors.

3. Motor switches are usually used for smaller-size motors, but may be obtained for motors up to 5 hp, 230 volts. They come with "heaters" that, on continued overload, open the circuit. The "heaters" are the "overcurrent device" in this case. Heaters may come separate from the switch, and if so it is the responsibility of the installer to select the proper size heater for the motor horsepower, and install it in the switch.

4. Thermal cutouts are similar in appearance to plug fuses, except that thermal cutouts are larger. Inside the cutout is a contact arm made of spring steel, which makes contact through a fusible link. When an overload continues for a certain period, the heat generated by the high current melts the fusible link, and the spring steel contact opens, opening the circuit.

5. Circuit breakers used on motor circuits have a built-in "thermal device" that heats up and releases a trigger if an overload continues for a length of time. The breaker contacts then open. Breakers also provide short-circuit protection.

6. Motors are on the market that have an overload device mounted inside the motor frame. Usually, it is in the form of a contact made by a metal strip, which is enclosed in a small circular-shaped case. Heat affects the metal strip in such a way that it snaps the contacts open on prolonged overload. The contacts are connected in the motor circuit. When an overload occurs, the heat from the high current, and also the heat from the motor itself, causes the contacts to open, thus opening the circuit.

Ordinary fuses may also be used as the "running overcurrent device."

Ordinary fuses, however, are a poor form of overload protection for motors, because they do not have time-delay; they either blow quickly or not at all. Usually, a fuse sized small enough to properly protect the motor against overload will blow on the starting current; to hold the starting current, the fuse rating required would usually be too high to properly protect the motor.

For running protection of motors, the protective device should have "time-delay."

430-32. Continuous-Duty Motors

(a) More Than One Horsepower

(1) All continuous-duty motors of more than 1 hp are required to have running overload protection. For intermittent-duty motors, running overload protection may be omitted (Section 430-33).

The rating or trip setting of the overcurrent device shall be not more than either 125 or 115% of the full-load current rating of the motor.

The most common type of motor is the one built for a temperature rise of 40°C. Such motors are usually built to take a 125% overload for a long period, and the "overcurrent device" may be rated at 125% of the motor full-load current.

Certain motors, such as totally enclosed motors, are built for a temperature rise of 55 or 75°C. These motors are not built to take a 125% overload, and the overcurrent device may be rated at only 115% of the motor full-load current.

The overcurrent device would be a thermal relay or any one of the six types of overcurrent devices mentioned above.

For multispeed motors, overload protection is required for each speed.

The general rule is that motor-running overcurrent (overload) protection shall be sized at not more than 125% of the motor nameplate full-load current rating.

If a 125% rating will not hold the starting current of the motor, this may be increased to 140% of motor full-load current rating. This increase would be permitted only if it can be shown that the lower rating is insufficient for the starting current.

Example.

What is the maximum size fusetron that could be used for running overload protection of a 15-hp, 230-volt, three-phase motor with a nameplate current rating of 42 amps.?

$$125\% \text{ of } 42 = 52.5 \text{ amps.}$$

A 50-amp. fusetron would be the largest size permitted.

(2) This paragraph lists the maximum setting permissible for a thermal protector built into the motor. The proper setting would be the responsibility of the motor manufacturer. Note that the permissible setting for a thermal protector is higher than that permitted for other forms of protection—up to 170% of motor full-load rating.

(3) Motors that are part of an "approved assembly" need not have separate overload protection. The protection for the motor is built into the assembly by the manufacturer. The motor in a household refrigerator would be an example of a motor that is part of an approved assembly.

(4) For very large motors (above 1,500 hp) "temperature detectors" are required in place of the "overcurrent devices" called for in paragraphs 1 and 2. Temperature detectors are usually thermocouples. Thermocouples are sensitive to heat, and this principle is used for protection of very large motors.

(b) One Horsepower or Less, Manually Started

(1) Motor-running overload protection is not required for a motor that is

1. Not over 1-hp rating, and
2. Not permanently installed, and
3. Manually started, and
4. Within sight from the controller.

A $\frac{1}{2}$-hp floor sander would meet these requirements, the motor being not over 1 hp, portable (not permanently installed), and manually started with a switch mounted on the machine. Vacuum cleaners and hand tools would fall in this classification. Such motors do not require motor-running overload protection, and may be plugged to circuits protected at 20 amps. or less.

(2) Permanently installed (fixed) motors of 1 hp or less that are started manually are subject to the same rules as automatically started motors of 1 hp or less. See Subsection (c) following.

(c) One Horsepower or Less, Automatically Started

Some examples of "automatically started" motors would be:

Stoker motors.

Oil-burner motors.

Refrigerator motors.

Water-pump motors.

Compressor motors.

It should be noted that Subsection (c) applies not only for automatically started motors. It applies for *"any* motor of one horsepower or less which is permanently installed" [Section 430-32(b)(2)]. The rules then would apply also for manually started fixed motors of 1 hp or less.

The rules of Subsection (c) can be condensed as follows:

All automatically started AC motors of rating $\frac{1}{20}$ to 1 hp must have overload protection, unless part of an approved assembly.

Manually started *fixed* AC motors of rating $\frac{1}{20}$ to 1 hp must have overload protection, unless part of an approved assembly.

An "approved assembly" would be an assembly that has controls that will automatically shut the motor off in case of stalling or overload, such as in the case of an oil burner.

All *fixed* DC motors of rating 0 to 1 hp must have overload protection unless part of an approved assembly.

To sum up all the foregoing rules for running overload protection of AC motors:

A. FIXED-CONTINUOUS DUTY MOTORS (for intermittent duty, see Section 430-33).

1. *All fixed motors above 1 hp must have running overload protection.*
2. All fixed motors $\frac{1}{20}$ to 1 hp must have overload protection, unless "part of an approved assembly."

   [There is an exception that permits running overload protection for motors of fractional hp to be omitted. When motors of 6 amps. or less rating are connected to a general-purpose branch circuit, individual running overload protection is not required. See Section 430-42(a).]
3. Fixed motors less than $\frac{1}{20}$ hp do not require running overload protection.

B. PORTABLE MOTORS.

1. *All portable motors above 1 hp must have running overload protection.*
2. Portable motors $\frac{1}{20}$ to 1 hp need not have overload protection, if *manually started* within sight of the motor.

3. Portable motors $\frac{1}{20}$ to 1 hp must have overload protection if *automatically* started, unless "part of an approved assembly."

4. Portable motors less than $\frac{1}{20}$ hp do not require overload protection.

(d) Wound-Rotor Secondaries

Wound-rotor motors are three-phase motors. These motors have two sets of leads—the main leads, that connect to the field, and the secondary leads, that connect to the rotor. The secondary leads are used for speed control of the motor.

No separate overload protection is needed for the secondary circuit; it is considered to be protected by the overload protection in the main leads.

430-33. Intermittent and Similar Duty

The foregoing rules are intended to apply to "continuous-duty" motors.

Most motors are "continuous-duty" motors, but there are some motors that serve for "intermittent duty." Table 430-22(a), p. 70-295 of the Code, lists some of them.

In the case of "intermittent-duty" motors, it is permissible to omit the "overload" protection.

430-34. Selection of Overload Relay

The general rule is that running overload protection for a motor may be sized at not over 125% of motor full-load current rating. If a 125% rating will not hold the motor starting current, this may be increased to 140%. (For 115% motors the rating may be increased to 130%.)

430-35. Shunting During Starting Period

An advantage of the shunting method of starting a motor lies in the fact that ordinary fuses will function satisfactorily as motor-running overload protection. For conventional starting methods, the high current drawn by a motor on starting would blow a fuse having no time-delay. In the shunt method, this objection is overcome by shunting the fuses out of the circuit during the brief starting period.

By use of a double throw switch, the fuses are bypassed, or "shunted out" of the circuit, while the motor is coming up to speed. After the motor is up to speed, the double throw switch is thrown to the "running" position, and the fuses are brought back into the circuit. Shunt-start switches must be so constructed that the switch cannot be left in the starting position. The shunting method may be used only for manual or pushbutton starting. For automatic starting, it is not permitted.

It can be seen that, during the starting period, the motor is without overload protection because the fuses are out of the circuit. The Code permits this on condition that the branch-circuit fuses (or circuit breaker) be rated or set at not over 400% of the motor full-load current.

A 15-hp, three-phase, 230-volt motor has a current rating of 42 amps. If this motor is started by the "shunting" method, the branch-circuit protection may be no larger than 400% of 42, or 168 amps. A 150-amp. fuse or circuit-breaker setting would be the largest allowable in this particular example.

430-36. Fuses—In Which Conductor

Fusetrons are fuses. When fusetrons are used for motor-running overload protection, a fusetron is required in each "hot" wire.

Fuses or fusetrons are not permitted in a grounded conductor, except in the special case of a three-wire, three-phase circuit having one leg grounded. Here the Code *requires* a running overload fuse or fusetron in the grounded conductor when fuses are used in the hot wires.

430-37. Devices Other Than Fuses—In Which Conductor

"Devices other than fuses" would be:

Thermal relays.

Thermal devices in motor switches.

Thermal cutouts.

Circuit breaker trips.

Thermal devices built into the motor.

When any of these is used for overload protection, the number used shall be in accordance with the Table on p. 70-300 of the Code. See Fig. 453.

430-38. Number of Conductors Opened by Overload Device

"Motor-running protective devices" most generally used for motor-running protection are:

1. Fusetrons.

2. Thermal cutouts.

3. Thermal protectors (thermal device built into the motor).

4. Thermal relays.

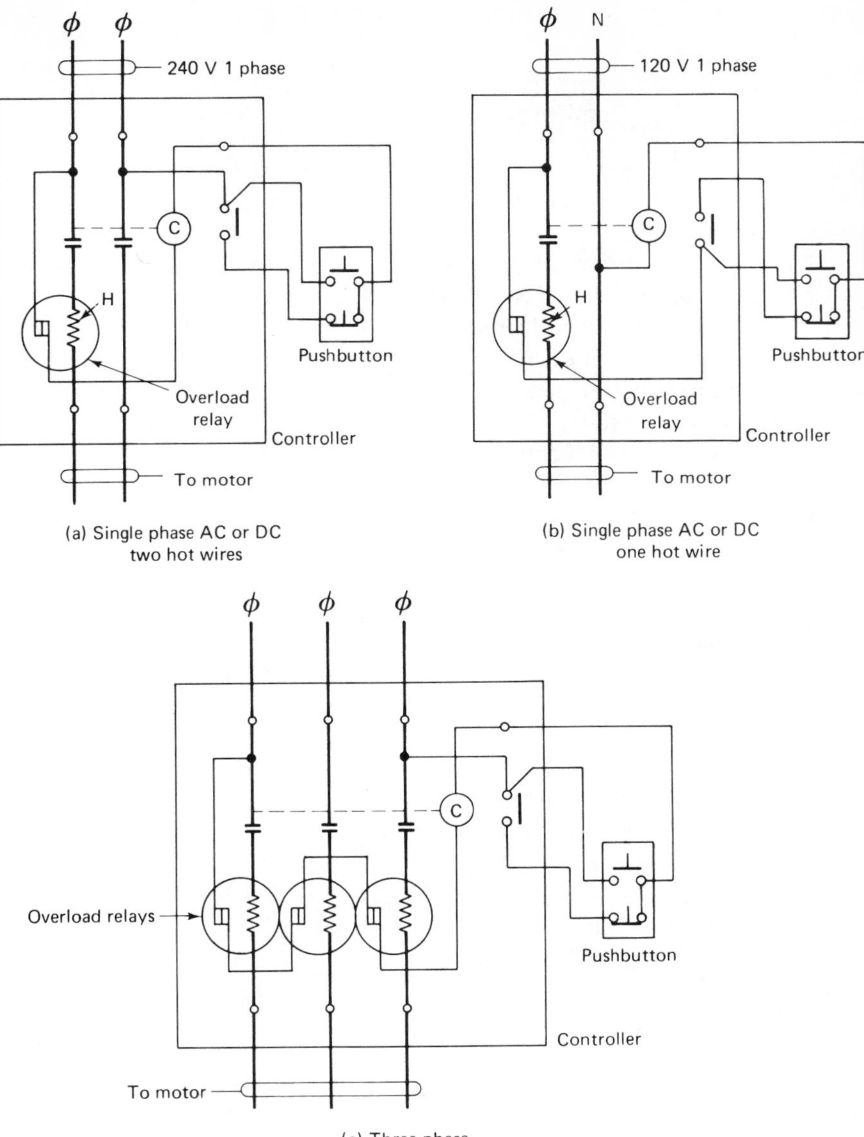

Fig. 453

Running overload units required (Sect. 430-37):

(a) For two-wire ungrounded motor circuits, one overload relay is required.

(b) For two-wire grounded motor circuits, one overload relay is required. Must be in the hot wire.

(c) For three-phase motor circuits, three overload relays are required.

Operation of the pushbutton starts the motor. On overload the heat generated by the heater(s) (H) is sufficient to open the relay contacts, deenergizing the operating coil (C). Main contacts open, stopping the motor.

5. Motor switches with "heaters."

6. Circuit breakers with heaters (thermal trip).

The rule of this Section applies for protective devices other than fuses (or fusetrons), thermal cutouts, or thermal protectors. It applies for items 4, 5, and 6, listed above.

These three types of overcurrent devices are different in operation from the other three listed. When a thermal relay operates, it does not break the line directly, but opens the control circuit, which in turn opens the line. In this way a single thermal relay could open two or three conductors of a circuit at once. The same is true of the heaters contained in motor switches and circuit breakers. The heater does not open the line directly, but springs the motor switch or circuit-breaker contacts, which in turn opens the line.

When a fusetron, thermal cutout, or thermal device built into the motor opens, it opens directly only the one conductor in which it is placed. As mentioned, the rule of this Section does not apply to these.

A thermal relay in a magnetic controller, a heater in a motor switch, or heater in a circuit breaker must, when it operates, open a "sufficient number of ungrounded conductors to interrupt current flow to the motor."

For any single-phase AC motor, or for any DC motor, breaking one conductor would comply with the rule. In other words, a single-pole magnetic controller, motor switch, or circuit breaker can be used as a controller.

For a three-phase motor, more than one conductor must be opened to satisfy the rule. If only one conductor of a three-phase motor circuit is opened, the motor will not stop; it will keep on running. This is called "single phasing." If two conductors are opened, the motor will stop, and the intent of the rule is satisfied. Table 430-37 of the Code requires three overcurrent devices, but any one of the three could operate to open all poles of the controller, which may be two pole. (While this rule permits a two pole controller to be used for a three-phase motor, good practice would dictate the use of a three pole controller, which will open all conductors.)

430-39. Motor Controller as Running Overload Protection

According to Code definition, any switch of any kind that is used to stop and start a motor is a motor controller. In the trade, usually only the larger-sized switches are called controllers. A snap switch used to stop and start a motor is not customarily called a "controller." It is referred to as a switch.

However, according to the Code, even a small motor switch is a motor controller, and this interpretation should be remembered when reading this Section.

In the usual case, the "running overcurrent device" is combined in the same enclosure with the controller. For instance, magnetic controllers have thermal relays contained in the controller. A small motor switch may have overload "heaters" in the switch. The thermal relays and the heaters are the "running overcurrent devices."

A fused knife switch may be used as the motor controller. It could contain fusetrons, which are the running overcurrent device.

Circuit breakers used for motor control contain heaters, which are the "running overcurrent device."

In all these cases, the motor controller serves also to provide "running overcurrent protection." This Section merely confirms such an arrangement as permissible.

430-40. Thermal Cutouts and Overload Relays

The rule of this Section applies when thermal cutouts, thermal relays, and other devices that are not capable of opening short circuits are used for running protection of a motor.

A thermal relay does not provide short-circuit protection. A motor switch with heater does not provide short-circuit protection.

A thermal cutout does not provide short-circuit protection.

A thermal device built into the motor does not provide short-circuit protection.

These devices provide only motor running (overload) protection.

A fuse or fusetron provides short-circuit protection.

Circuit breakers provide short-circuit protection.

The Code requires that short-circuit protection must always be provided for a motor and its overload device. Short-circuit protection may be in the form of a fuse or a circuit breaker placed in the line somewhere ahead of the controller. Or in some cases the fuses or circuit breaker that provide short-circuit protection might be incorporated in the controller itself, along with the motor-running overcurrent device.

There are also cases where the short-circuit protection is provided by the same device that provides the motor-running protection. One example is the fusetron. A fusetron provides *both* short-circuit protection *and* motor-running protection within the same fuse. Most circuit breakers also combine both short-circuit protection and motor-running protection in the same circuit breaker. (For "dual service," sizing must be as per Section 430-32.)

"Thermal devices" used alone do not provide short-circuit protection, only motor-running overload protection. Short-circuit protection must be separately provided when thermal devices alone are used for motor-running overload protection.

A fuse or circuit breaker used only for short-circuit protection must be rated according to Table 430-152, p. 70-320 of the Code. The table lists the maximum fuse size or circuit-breaker setting permitted for different types of motors.

Column 1 of the table is for ordinary fuses.

Column 2 is for fusetrons.

Column 3 is for circuit breakers having instantaneous trip only (no thermal trip element).

Column 4 is for circuit breakers having both instantaneous and thermal trip elements.

(When the ratings specified by the table are not high enough to hold the starting current of the motor, they may be increased.) See also Section 430-52.

430-42. Motors on General-Purpose Branch Circuits

(a) When motors of 1 hp or less, and 6 amps. or less rating are connected to a 15- or 20-amp., 120 volt, general-purpose branch circuit, or to a 15-amp., 240 volt general-purpose branch circuit, running overload protection is not required. For single-phase, the rule would limit the size of 120 volt motors to $\frac{1}{4}$ hp; for 240 volt motors, $\frac{1}{2}$ hp maximum. Larger sizes would require running overload protection.

Note that running overload for these motors may be omitted only if the circuit is a *general-purpose* branch circuit, protected at not more than 20 amps. A general-purpose branch circuit is, according to Code definition, "a branch circuit that supplies a *number of outlets* for lighting and appliances."

Small motors connected to other than general-purpose branch circuits must be provided with running overload protection, in accordance with Section 430-32(b)(2) and 430-32(c).

(b) Motors of more than 6 amps. full-load rating (or over 1 hp), if connected to a general-purpose branch circuit, must have running overcurrent (overload) protection, and, in addition, the controller (and overload device) must be "approved for group installation." Controllers approved for group installation are special controllers, and from a practical standpoint, it would be advisable in the case of larger motors to provide a separate circuit for each motor. Separate circuits would permit the use of standard controllers.

(c) When small motors (6 amps. or less rating) are plug-connected into a general-purpose circuit, and running overcurrent protection is omitted (as permitted for manually started portable motors), the receptacle rating may not exceed 15 amps. at 125 volts, or 10 amps. at 250 volts.

(d) The overcurrent device protecting a general-purpose branch circuit shall have sufficient time-delay so that it will not open on the high starting current of the motor or motors. The rating of the fuse or circuit breaker must be kept within the limits permitted for the circuit. Fusetrons are permitted. Standard fuses are not permitted.

430-43. Automatic Restarting

Some overcurrent devices are so constructed that, after tripping and opening the circuit, they will, after a short time, "reset," thus automatically restarting the motor. Thermal devices that are built into the motor frame can be made so that they automatically reset. Thermal relays could also be the "automatic" reset type. Or either of these may be so constructed that, after tripping, they must be reset by hand, usually by pushing a reset button.

Overcurrent devices that will automatically restart a motor, after tripping, are not permitted unless specially approved. The reason for this rule is to prevent injury to a person who might happen to be working on a motor, and have it unexpectedly start up, when the overcurrent device automatically resets after tripping. Thermal protectors in motors shall be a type that requires resetting by hand. Motors with automatic-reset protectors shall not be installed where automatic restarting would result in injury to persons.

D. Motor Branch-Circuit Short-Circuit and Ground-Fault Protection

430-51. General

430-52. Rating or Setting for Individual Motor Circuit

The branch-circuit protection for a motor would be a fuse or circuit breaker located in the line at the point where the branch circuit originates.

The fuse or circuit breaker could be at a service cabinet or distribution panel or in the motor controller.

When there is only one motor on a circuit, the fuse or circuit breaker is sized according to Table 430-152, p. 70-320 of the Code.

Use of the table will require some explanation. In the first place, there is the matter of "code letters." A code letter shows certain electrical characteristics of the motor. The code letter is based on the amount of inrush current that the motor takes on starting. Motors with code letter A take the least inrush current. The amount of inrush current increases up to code letter V, which shows the greatest inrush current.

To use the table it is necessary to know the different *types* of motors. Different types are as follows:

1. Single-phase, AC.
2. Squirrel cage.
3. Wound rotor.
4. DC.
5. Synchronous.

Squirrel-cage motors are three-phase motors. Wound-rotor motors are three-phase motors with speed control. Squirrel-cage motors are more extensively used than the wound-rotor type.

Synchronous motors are AC motors, which are used usually in large sizes only. They require a source of DC for field excitation. Synchronous motors are built in sizes from 20 to 5,000 hp and are found principally in steel mills, paper mills, cement mills, and similar locations.

Single-phase AC and three-phase squirrel-cage motors are the most widely used types.

As to method of starting a motor, there are four methods included in the table:

1. Full voltage.
2. With a resistor.
3. With a reactor.
4. With an autotransformer.

AC motors up to about 10 or 15 hp are usually started on full voltage. For larger motors, a resistance or reactance is inserted in the motor circuit at starting to reduce the starting current. Or the voltage at starting is reduced by use of an autotransformer.

There are four columns in Table 430-152.

Column 1 is for ordinary fuses.

Column 2 is for fusetrons.

Column 3 is for circuit breakers having instantaneous trip only (may be used only if specially approved).

Column 4 is for circuit breakers having both instantaneous trip and thermal trip elements (the most common type).

If there is no standard fuse or circuit-breaker setting of the size required, the next higher size may be used.

Examples.

1. What is the maximum size branch-circuit fuse (not fusetron) permitted for a 20-hp, 230-volt, 3-phase squirrel-cage motor, with no code letter, and resistor starting?

   From Table 430-150, p. 70-318 of the Code, full-load current rating of the motor is 54 amps.

   Table 430-152 lists a permissible fuse rating of 300% of full-load current (under Nontime Delay Fuse, second listing from the top). This would be 162 amps. There is no 162-amp. fuse; therefore, the next higher standard size, a 175 amp., may be used for branch-circuit protection.

2. What is the maximum size branch-circuit fuse permitted for a $\frac{1}{2}$ hp, 230-volt, single-phase motor with no code letter?

   From Table 430-148, p. 70-316, full-load current rating is 4.9 amps. Table 430-152 lists a permissible fuse rating of 300% of motor full-load current (under Nontime Delay Fuse, first listing at the top). This would be 14.7 amps. A 15-amp. fuse may be used for branch-circuit protection.

3. What is the maximum size circuit-breaker setting permitted for a 20-hp, 230-volt, 3-phase wound-rotor motor?

   From Table 430-150, full-load current is 54 amps. Table 430-152 lists a permissible circuit-breaker setting of 150% of full-load current (under Inverse Time Breaker, third listing from the bottom). This would be 81 amps. A 90-amp. circuit-breaker setting may be used.

   (If the ratings taken from the table will not hold the motor starting current, ratings may be increased to a maximum of 400% for fuses, 225% for fusetrons, 400% for circuit breakers.)

430-53. Several Motors or Loads on One Branch Circuit

This Section deals with the case where only one set of branch-circuit fuses (or a circuit breaker) is to serve for two or more motors.

(a) This rule is for motors drawing 6 amps. or less and 1 hp or less. This would limit the size of single-phase motors to $\frac{1}{4}$ hp on a 120-volt circuit or $\frac{1}{2}$ hp on a 240-volt circuit. Three-phase motors would be limited to $\frac{3}{4}$ hp at 115 volts and 1 hp at 230 and higher voltages.

Several motors of these sizes or smaller may all be served by a single set of branch-circuit fuses (or one circuit breaker), provided that the fuse (or breaker setting) is not larger than 20 amps. at 125 volts or less, or 15 amps. at 126 to 600 volts [Fig. 454(1)]. Other loads are also permitted on the circuit [Fig. 454(2)].

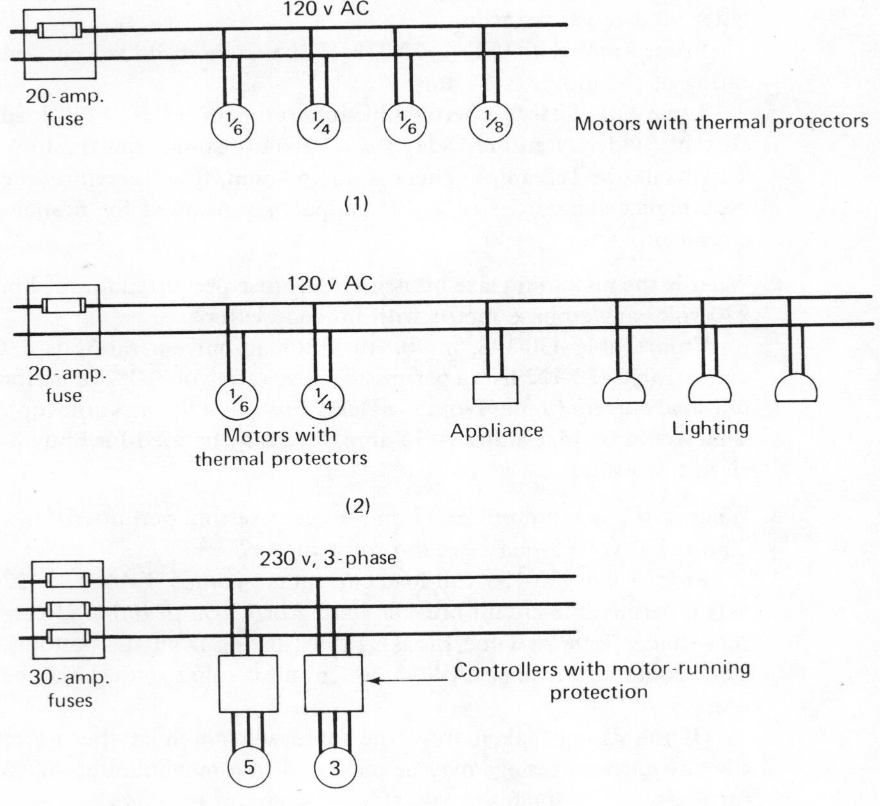

Fig. 454

Several motors or loads on one branch circuit (Sect. 430-53):

1. Several small motors on one branch circuit.
2. Small motors and other loads on one branch circuit. The total amperage of all loads must be held to 20 amps. maximum to conform with Sect. 210-22.
3. Two motors of more than 1 hp on one branch circuit.

The rule stipulates that individual running overcurrent protection shall conform to Section 430-32. Most motors above $\frac{1}{20}$ hp require running protection. Motors that do not require motor-running protection are the exception rather than the rule. Each motor would have its own individual motor-running protection, as required, but it is not necessary to provide branch-circuit protection for each motor. One set of fuses (or a circuit breaker) may serve as branch-circuit protection for all motors of the group.

(b) Two or more motors of any size may be connected to a single branch circuit, provided that the branch-circuit fuse or circuit breaker setting is no higher than that permitted by Table 430-152, p. 70-320, for the *smallest* motor in the group. Each motor must have individual running protection [Fig. 454(3)].

Example.

One 3-hp and one 5-hp, 230-volt three-phase squirrel-cage motor with full-voltage starting are connected to the same branch circuit. What is the largest-size fuse (not fusetron) permitted for branch-circuit protection?

From Table 430-150, p. 70-318 of the Code, full-load current of the 3-hp motor (the smallest) is 9.6 amps.

Table 430-152 lists a permissible fuse rating of 300% of 9.6, or 28.8 amps. A 30-amp. fuse would be the largest size permitted.

It should be noted that, in applying this rule, the branch-circuit protection is sized for the smallest motor. This could in some cases result in a situation where a larger motor of the group could not be started without opening the branch-circuit fuse or tripping the breaker.

(c) Two or more motors of any size may be connected to a single branch circuit protected by fuses, or a circuit breaker rated for the *largest* motor of the group, provided that each motor controller is approved for "group installation."

Each motor must have individual running overload protection, and each overload device must be approved for group installation. While the arrangement of this subsection is permissible, it would not be advisable except where no other arrangement is possible. Controllers approved for group installation are expensive and not readily obtainable. Rather than go to the expense of providing special controllers, it would be better to install fuses or a breaker at the point where each motor taps to the line. In this way the main line, which was a branch circuit, now becomes a feeder, and the individual lines to each motor would now be branch circuits. Each motor now has its individual branch-circuit protection, and there is no special problem. You can tap any number of branch circuits to one feeder (if the feeder conductors are adequate) as long as you provide branch-circuit protection for each motor at the point of tapping.

(d) Where a single branch circuit serves several motors, the tap conductors for the individual motors must be the same size as the branch-circuit conductors, except that, for taps 25 ft or less in length, a tap conductor with ampacity of $\frac{1}{3}$ that of the branch-circuit conductors is permitted, if the tap is suitably protected from physical damage.

430-54. Multimotor and Combination-Load Equipment

Multimotor equipment would be equipment containing two or more motors.

Combination-load equipment would be equipment containing one or more motor loads, plus another type of load. A dishwasher would be an example. Here there is a motor and a heater in the same piece of equipment.

The rule of Section 430-7(d) requires the manufacturer to provide a nameplate on such equipment, showing the size of branch-circuit fusing (or circuit-breaker setting) permitted for the equipment.

The branch-circuit fuse size or circuit-breaker setting may not exceed the size specified on the nameplate.

430-55. Combined Overcurrent Protection

Fusetrons can serve a dual purpose in motor circuits—as combined motor-running overload protection, and branch-circuit short-circuit protection. Circuit breakers also can combine the two functions. When used to serve as both motor-running and branch-circuit overcurrent protection, the fuses or the circuit breaker setting must be sized according to Section 430-32, which would be 125% or 115% of motor full-load current rating. The time-delay feature of the fusetrons, the thermal unit of the breaker, will serve to hold the starting current of the motor.

It should be pointed out that, although permissible as motor-running overload protection, circuit breakers are seldom used for this purpose. They are, however, used extensively for branch-circuit overcurrent protection.

430-56. Branch-Circuit Protective Devices—In Which Conductor

Section 240-20 specifies the number of fuses required for branch-circuit protection, or, if a circuit breaker is used, the number of trip units that must be provided within the breaker. The rule is that there must be a fuse, or a trip unit, in each ungrounded conductor. Thus, for a 120-volt, two-wire circuit with a neutral, one fuse or trip unit is required—in the hot wire.

For a three-phase circuit, three fuses or trip units are required.

430-57. Size of Fuseholder

The branch-circuit fuseholder shall be large enough to accommodate the required branch-circuit fuse. Branch-circuit fuses are sized according to Table 430-152, p. 70-320 of the Code, and the fuseholder is required to be *no smaller* than that required to accommodate the largest-size fuse permitted by the table.

The Code lists an exception to this rule: "Where fuses having time delay appropriate for the starting characteristics of the motor are used, fuseholders of smaller size . . . shall be permitted."

As an example of what is meant by this exception, say that a certain motor has a full-load current of 15 amps. Ordinary fuses (not fusetrons) are to be used for branch-circuit protection, and Table 430-152 allows a fuse sized at 300% of motor rating, as per Column 1. This would call for a 45-amp. fuse and would require a 60-amp. fuseholder. A 30-amp. fuseholder would not be permitted. However, fusetrons may be used instead of fuses, and serve as both branch-circuit protection and running overload protection combined (Section 430-55). The fuse (tron) would be rated at 125% $\times$ 15 = 18.75 (20) amps. This would permit a 30-amp. fuseholder to be used, rather than a 60 amp.

430-58. Rating of Circuit Breaker

Section 430-52 and Table 430-152 specify the maximum *setting* permissible in a circuit breaker for motor branch-circuit protection. Section 430-110 sets the minimum *size* at 115% of motor full-load current rating. See Section 430-110 for elaboration on these requirements.

E. Motor Feeder Short-Circuit and Ground-Fault Protection

430-61. General

430-62. Rating or Setting—Motor Load

Section 430-62 specifies the rule for figuring the maximum size of fuse or circuit breaker setting that may be used to protect a feeder that supplies two or more branch circuits for motors.

The feeder fuse or circuit breaker would probably be at a distribution panel or entrance cabinet. Branch-circuit protection for each of the motors could be in the motor controllers. Or the feeder could feed a distribution panel, with the individual motor circuits branching out from there, each branch circuit having individual protection at the panel.

The fuse or circuit breaker protecting the feeder can have a rating equal to:

> The highest *branch-circuit* rating for any motor of the group as per Table 430-152, p. 70-320, *plus* the sum of the full-load currents of the rest of the motors connected to the feeder.

Examples.

1. What is the maximum size fuse (not fusetron) permitted for protection of a feeder that supplies one 10-hp, one 5-hp, and one 3-hp, 230-volt, three-phase motor branch circuits? Motors are squirrel-cage motors with full-voltage starting.

   From Table 430-150, p. 70-318, the full-load current of the 10-hp motor is 28 amps., of the 5 hp, 15.2-amps., and of the 3 hp, 9.6 amps.

   Table 430-152 shows that the branch-circuit fuse for a squirrel-cage motor with full-voltage starting may be rated at 300% of motor full-load current (under Nontime Delay Fuse, second listing down).

   The maximum fusing for the feeder will be equal to the highest branch-circuit fusing permitted for any individual motor in the group *plus* the sum of the full-load currents of all the other motors.

   The motor that would take the highest branch-circuit fusing is the 10-hp motor. This motor has a full-load current of 28 amps.

$$300\% \text{ of } 28 = 3 \times 28 = 84 \text{ amps.}$$

Since there is no 84-amp. fuse, the next higher size, 90 amps, could be used for branch-circuit protection of the 10-hp motor alone.

Adding to this, the full-load currents of the other motors:

$$90 + 15.2 + 9.6 = 114.8 \text{ amps.}$$

A 110-amp. fuse would be the largest size permitted for protection of the feeder. (In figuring overcurrent protection for the *group,* you cannot go to the next higher size.)

2. What is the maximum size fuse (not fusetron) permitted for protection of a feeder that supplies one 25-hp wound-rotor motor, one 20-hp and one 15-hp squirrel-cage motor branch circuits? All motors are 230 volt, three-phase resistor starting.

   From Table 430-150, the full-load current of the 25-hp motor is 68 amps., of the 20 hp, 54 amps., and of the 15 hp, 42 amps.

   From Table 430-152, the maximum branch-circuit fusing permitted for a wound-rotor motor is 150% of motor full-load current (under Nontime Delay Fuse, third listing from the bottom). For squirrel-cage motors, the maximum is 300% of full-load current.

For the 25-hp wound-rotor motor, maximum branch-circuit fusing permitted would be

$$150\% \text{ of } 68 = 1\tfrac{1}{2} \times 68 = 102 \text{ amps.}$$

For the 20-hp squirrel-cage motor, maximum branch-circuit fusing would be

$$300\% \text{ of } 54 = 3 \times 54 = 162 \text{ amps.}$$

This motor takes the highest branch-circuit fusing.

There is no 162-amp. fuse. The next higher size, 175 amps., could be used for branch-circuit protection of this motor alone.

The feeder fuse rating would be

$$175 + 68 + 42 = 285 \text{ amps.}$$

A 250-amp. fuse would be the largest permitted for feeder protection. This example shows that, when there are different types of motors connected to the feeder, it is not always the largest motor that would take the highest branch-circuit fusing.

3. What is the maximum size fusetron permitted for protection of a feeder that supplies three 5-hp, 230-volt, three-phase motor branch circuits? All are squirrel-cage motors with full voltage starting.

From Table 430-150, full-load current of each motor is 15.2 amps. From Table 430-152, the maximum branch-circuit fusetron for a squirrel-cage motor is 175% of full-load current (under Dual Element Fuse, second listing from top). The largest motor in the group is a 5-hp motor.

$$175\% \text{ of } 15.2 = 1.75 \times 15.2 = 26.6 \text{ amps.}$$

Since there is no fusetron of this size, a 30-amp. fusetron could be used for branch-circuit protection of this motor alone. Adding to this the full-load currents of the other two motors:

$$30 + 15.2 + 15.2 = 60.4 \text{ amps.}$$

A 60-amp. fusetron would be the largest permitted for feeder protection.

There may be special cases where a feeder is "oversized" for one reason or another, so that the feeder conductors have a carrying capacity that is actually greater than the calculated feeder fuse size. For instance, in the last example, the calculated feeder fusing is 60 amps. Suppose that the feeder conductors which were installed are No. 0 Type T wire. No. 0 Type T carries 125 amps. In this special case, because of the large feeder size, a 125-amp. fusetron could be used for feeder protection.

430-63. Rating or Setting—Power and Light Loads

The following example will show how to figure the maximum feeder fuse size (or circuit breaker setting) permitted, when lighting or appliance circuits are connected to a feeder along with the motor circuits.

Example.

What is the maximum size fusing permitted for a feeder that supplies two $\frac{1}{2}$-hp and one $\frac{1}{3}$-hp motor circuits, also a lighting circuit of 3 kW? The circuit is single-phase, two-wire, 115 volt AC.

First, the feeder fusing is figured for the motors alone, as though only motor circuits were connected to the feeder. From Table 430-148, p. 70-316 of the Code, full-load current of the $\frac{1}{2}$-hp, single-phase motor is 9.8 amps., of the $\frac{1}{3}$-hp motor, 7.2 amps. From Table 430-152, maximum branch-circuit fusing permitted for single-phase motors is 300% of full-load current.

$$300\% \text{ of } 9.8 = 3 \times 9.8 = 29.4 \text{ amps.}$$

The next higher fuse size, 30 amps., could be used for branch-circuit protection of the $\frac{1}{2}$-hp motor alone. Adding to this the full-load currents of the other two motors:

$$30 + 9.8 + 7.2 = 47 \text{ amps., maximum feeder fusing permitted for motors alone}$$

Now figure the current taken by the lighting load.

$$\frac{3{,}000 \text{ (watts)}}{115 \text{ (volts)}} = 26 \text{ amps., lighting load}$$

Adding this to the maximum motor fusing:

$$47 + 26 = 73 \text{ amps.}$$

A 70-amp. fuse would be the largest permitted for feeder protection.

F. Motor Control Circuits

430-71. General

This part of the Code deals with control circuits that are connected to motor controllers.

Examples of such circuits would be:

1. The circuit from a magnetic controller to a pushbutton. The pushbutton may be located at some distance from the controller. The START and STOP buttons on the pushbutton operate the contacts in the magnetic controller to start and stop the motor.
2. The circuit from a magnetic controller to a pressure switch. Motors driving water pumps and air compressors usually are started and stopped automatically by a pressure switch connected into the water pipe or air pipe. When the water or air pressure drops to a certain value, the pressure switch closes, operating the contacts in the magnetic controller and starting the motor. When the pressure rises to a preset value, the pressure switch opens, stopping the motor.
3. The circuit from a magnetic controller to a thermostatic switch. A thermostatic switch is actuated by heat. Such a switch might be used in connection with a heating system, to operate a stoker motor, or in connection with a hot water circulating system.

430-72. Overcurrent Protection

Some controllers are equipped with control circuit transformers, which supply low voltage for the control circuit. Control circuits supplied by such a transformer shall have individual protection rated or set at not more than 200% of the control circuit ampacity, and not more than 200% of the transformer rated secondary current [Fig. 455(1)].

Motor control circuits without transformers are considered protected if the fuse or breaker size protecting them is not more than 3 times the ampacity of the control circuit conductors [Fig. 455(2)].

If the control circuit operates a "vital" machine, such as a fire pump, no control circuit fusing is ever required, regardless of how small the control circuit conductors, and regardless of the size of the motor branch-circuit overcurrent protection. The Code *requires* overcurrent protection to be omitted rather than risk the possibility of an open circuit at a time of emergency.

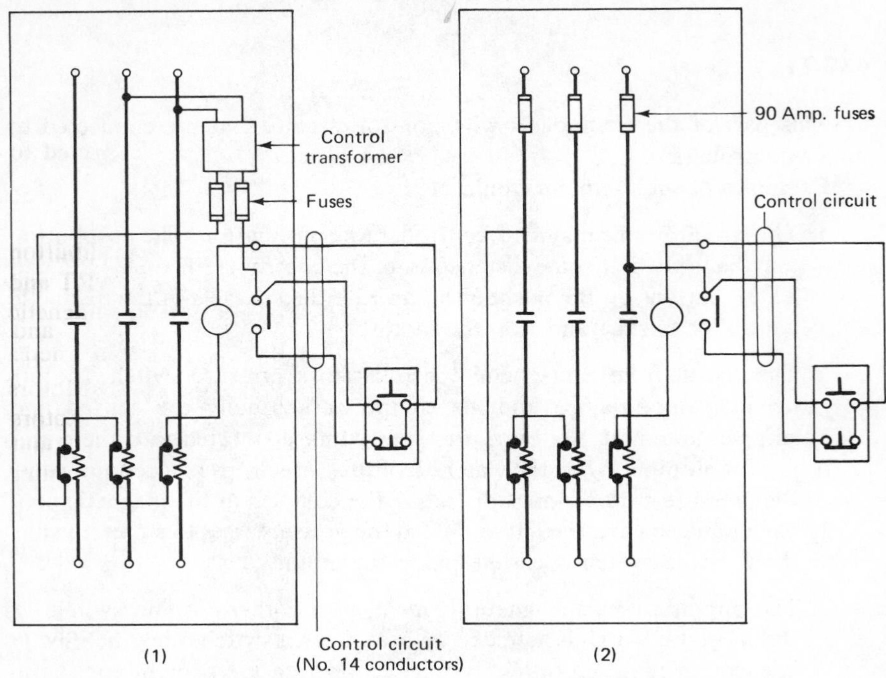

Fig. 455

Overcurrent protection for motor control circuits (Sect. 430-72).

1. Controller with control circuit transformer. Overcurrent protection must be provided in the transformer secondary when the control circuit extends beyond the controller. Control circuit fuse size may be no larger than 200% of ampacity of the control circuit conductors. In the example, fuse size would be limited to a maximum of $15 \times 2 = 30$ amps.
2. Controller without control circuit transformer. Control circuit conductors must have an ampacity equal to at least $\frac{1}{3}$ of the fuse size. In the example, this would be $\frac{1}{3} \times 90 = 30$ A.

Examples.

1. The branch-circuit fuses for a 15-hp, 230-volt, three-phase motor (not a "vital" motor) are 90-amp. fuses. What is the smallest size conductor that can be used to wire a remote pushbutton station for the controller without fusing the circuit to the pushbutton? (Controller does not have a control circuit transformer.)

The control circuit conductors must have a carrying capacity of

$\frac{1}{3}$ of 90 amps., or 30 amps. From Table 310-16, p. 70-132 of the Code, a No. 10 Type T conductor would be required for the control circuit [Fig. 455(2)]. Smaller conductors could be used for the control circuit, but if so, the control circuit would have to be *separately fused* at the ampacity of the control circuit conductors.

2. Branch-circuit fuses for a 25-hp fire-pump motor are 200-amp. fuses. What is the smallest size conductor that may be used for a pushbutton circuit for this motor, without fusing the pushbutton circuit?

   The conductors may be the minimum size for an unfused control circuit—No. 14. This is a "vital" machine, and control circuit fusing is not permitted.

430-73. Mechanical Protection of Conductor

If the motor drives a "vital" machine, such as a fire pump, an "open" in the control circuit would create an undesirable, even dangerous situation.

The control circuit for a vital machine shall be installed in conduit or EMT, or otherwise protected from damage.

For grounded control circuits in conduit, the hot wire shall be used for the control circuit to and from the pushbutton or switch.

When the control circuit for a motor is in conduit, EMT, BX, or any other type of metallic enclosure, an accidental ground in the conduit, EMT, or BX could start the motor, if the *neutral* is used for the control circuit. If there were a ground on the return wire from the pushbutton or switch, the circuit to the starting coil would be completed through the grounded conduit, EMT, or BX sheath, starting the motor. (Connecting to the grounded conduit, EMT, or BX sheath would be the same as connecting to the neutral.)

If a hot wire is used for the control circuit, an accidental ground could not start the motor (see Fig. 456).

430-74. Disconnection

The control circuit must have a disconnect. The main disconnect may disconnect both the motor and control circuit, or there may be a separate disconnect for the control circuit.

The control circuit is sometimes a low-voltage circuit obtained from a small transformer in the controller. The switch that disconnects the control circuit must also disconnect its transformer.

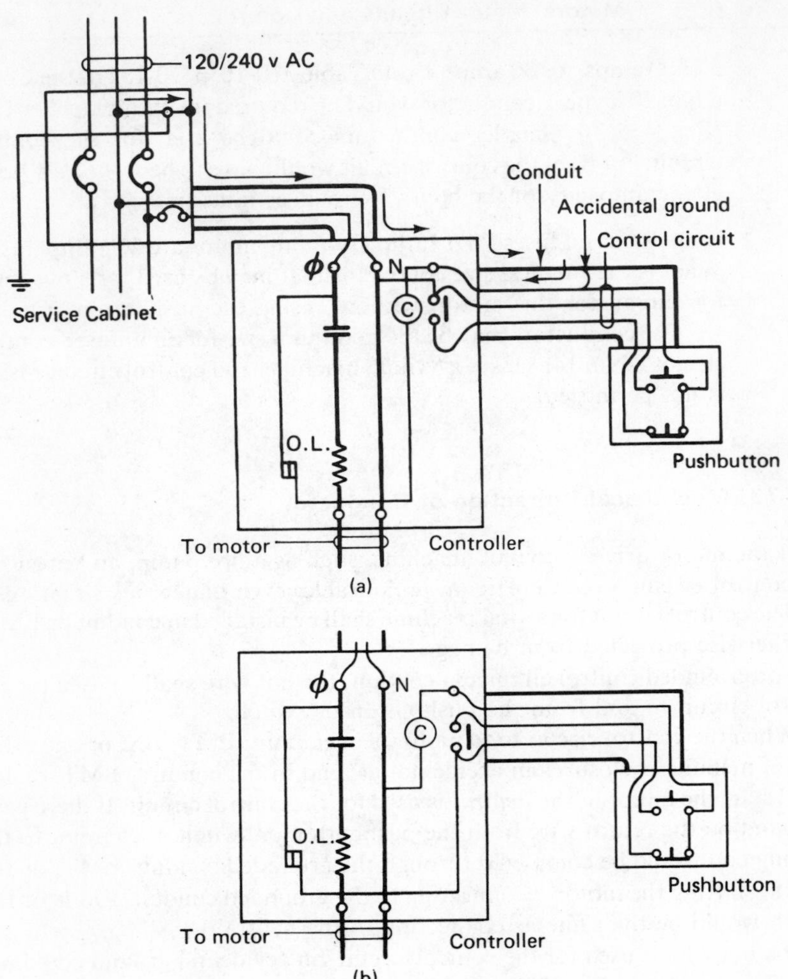

Fig. 456

Correct and incorrect wiring of control circuit for a 120-volt AC motor. (a) Incorrect wiring. The neutral is used for the pushbutton supply. An accidental ground, as shown, will start the motor even with the pushbutton in the stop position. The control circuit conduit is in metallic contact with the service switch, which is bonded to the neutral. The accidental ground completes the circuit to the operating coil (C), as shown by the arrows. The control circuit wiring of (a) would be in violation of Sect. 430-73 (second paragraph). The hot wire must be used for the control circuit, as shown in (b).

G. Motor Controllers

430-81. General

In studying this part of the Code, on motor controllers, it is first necessary to know the Code interpretation of the word "controller." By Code definition, any switch of any kind, large or small, that is used to start and stop a motor is a controller. A snap switch used to start and stop a small motor is a controller, as well as the largest motor-control device.

Motor controllers may be divided into two classes:

1. Full voltage starters.
2. Reduced voltage starters.

AC motors up to about 10 or 15 hp are usually started on full voltage, or to use a more common term, "across the line," which means that the motor is thrown directly across the line on starting without the use of a resistance, reactance, or autotransformer.

Reduced voltage starters use resistors, reactors, or autotransformers to reduce the voltage during starting. After the motor gets up to speed, the resistor or reactor is switched out of the circuit, allowing full line voltage to be applied for running. An autotransformer has low-voltage taps, which are used for starting. After the motor gets up to speed, it is switched to full line voltage.

A motor switch with heater combines two functions. The switching part is the controller, and the heater is the motor-running protection. A fused knife switch with fusetrons could also serve both as controller and motor-running protection. A fused knife switch with fusetrons can, in fact, serve four purposes: as controller, motor-running protection, branch-circuit protection, and disconnect. The switch is the controller and disconnect, and the fusetrons can serve double duty as motor-running protection and branch-circuit protection combined.

Stationary motors of $\frac{1}{8}$ hp or less that are normally left running, such as clock motors and the like, do not require a controller.

Portable motors of $\frac{1}{3}$ hp or less do not require a controller. The cord and plug may serve to start and stop the motor, although such an arrangement could be in practice an inconvenient method of motor control.

430-82. Controller Design

The design and construction of motor controllers shall conform with the requirements of this Section. For horsepower-rated controllers, compliance would be the responsibility of the manufacturer, and UL-approved controllers would be built according to these requirements.

The nameplate on motor controllers shows the horsepower, voltage, and type of circuit (single-phase, three-phase, DC) for which the controller is intended. The horsepower rating of a controller should be equal to the motor horsepower, and the voltage rating of the controller suited to the voltage of the motor.

430-83. Rating

The general rule is that motor controllers shall be rated in horsepower, and have a horsepower rating equal to the motor horsepower.

There are exceptions that permit other than horsepower-rated controllers to be used:

1. For stationary motors of 2 hp or less, and 300 volts or less, the controller need not be horsepower rated. It may be a general-use switch, such as a knife switch, rated in amperes rather than horsepower, provided the ampere rating of the switch is at least twice the full-load current rating of the motor. Or, for AC, the controller may be a general-use AC snap switch, provided the ampere rating of the snap switch is at least 125% of the full-load current rating of the motor. (AC-DC general-use snap switches are not permitted as motor controllers.)

2. A circuit breaker rated in amps. may be used as a motor controller for any size motor.

3. Torque motors are a special case. Such motors are intended to operate in the stalled position only. For torque motors, the controller may be ampere rated for any size motor.

Switches are marked by the manufacturer, either in horsepower rating or ampere rating. Those marked only with an ampere rating are general-use switches. Those marked in horsepower are motor switches. Circuit breakers are usually marked with an ampere rating only.

Examples.

1. Controller for a $1\frac{1}{2}$-hp, 230-volt, 3-phase motor. Full-load current 5.2 amps. (Table 430-150).

   Since the motor is not over 2 hp and not over 300 volts, the controller need not be horsepower rated. The controller may be any of the following:

   (a) 2-pole AC snap switch with ampere rating of at least $1\frac{1}{4} \times 5.2$ amps. (See note on p. 408.)

   (b) 3-pole general-use knife switch with ampere rating of at least 2×5.2 amps.

   (c) 3-pole horsepower-rated switch.

   (d) 3-pole magnetic motor controller.

   (e) 3-pole circuit breaker with ampere rating at least 5.2 amps.

2. Controller for a $\frac{1}{2}$-hp, 115-volt, single-phase motor with full load current of 9.8 amps. (Table 430-148).

   Since the motor is not over 2 hp and not over 300 volts, the controller need not be horsepower rated. The controller may be any one of the following:

   (a) Single-pole AC snap switch with ampere rating of at least $1\frac{1}{4} \times 9.8$ amps.

   (b) Single-pole general-use knife switch with ampere rating of at least 2×9.8 amps.

   (c) Single-pole horsepower-rated switch.

   (d) Single-pole magnetic motor controller.

   (e) Single-pole circuit breaker with ampere rating of at least 9.8 amps.

3. Controller for a 3-hp, 230-volt, 3-phase motor. Full-load current 9.6 amps. (Table 430-150).

   The motor is over 2 hp. The controller must be either horsepower rated or a circuit breaker. It may be any one of the following:

   (a) 3-pole horsepower-rated knife switch.

(b) 3-pole motor switch. Motor switches are always horsepower rated.

(c) 3-pole magnetic motor controller. Magnetic motor controllers are always horsepower rated.

(d) 3-pole circuit breaker with ampere rating of at least 9.6 amps.
Note: Technically, controllers for three-phase motors may be 2-pole (Section 430-84), but 3-pole controllers are recommended.

430-84. Need Not Open All Conductors

The intent of this rule is that the controller need open only a sufficient number of conductors to stop the motor. Thus, for a single-phase AC motor, a single-pole controller would be permitted; for a 3-phase motor, a 2-pole controller would be permitted; etc.

If the controller also acts as the "disconnect" (see Section 430-111), then the controller must open *all hot wires* in the circuit.

430-85. In Grounded Conductors

The grounded neutral of a motor circuit may not be opened by the controller unless the hot wire, or wires, are simultaneously opened along with the neutral. This simply means that, when the circuit has a grounded neutral, you cannot have one switch in the neutral and a separately operated switch in the hot wire or wires. If the neutral is to be opened, the switch must have enough poles to open all hot wires simultaneously with the neutral.

430-86. Motor Not in Sight from Controller

The general rule is that the motor must be within sight from the motor controller (see definition of "in sight from," Section 430-4). This is a reasonable safeguard against accidents.

There are exceptions to the general rule:

(1) The controller may be out of sight of the motor, if it has a locking device that will permit locking in the open position [Fig. 457(a)]. It can be seen that, with this arrangement, the danger inherent in a controller located out of sight is eliminated.

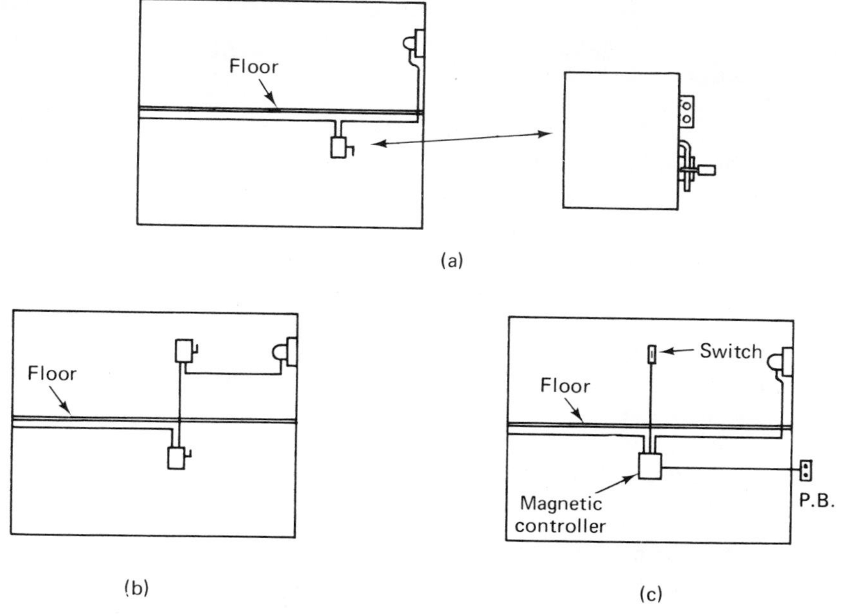

Fig. 457

Motor not in sight from controller (Sect. 430-86):

(a) Motor may be out of sight from controller if the disconnect can be locked in the open position.

(b)(c) Motor may be out of sight from the controller if a second switch, a manually operated switch, is placed within sight from the motor. In (b) the switch is in the main motor circuit. (c) shows a magnetic controller operated by a pushbutton. The switch in the room above is wired to kill the pushbutton circuit, and may be a toggle switch or other manually operated switch.

(2) The controller is allowed to be out of sight if there is an additional switch for disconnecting the motor, which is "within sight" from the motor [Fig. 457(b)(c)]. This switch may be in the main circuit, or it may be in a pushbutton circuit for the motor controller, connected in such a way that the controller cannot be operated when the switch is open.

430-87. Number of Motors Served by Each Controller

The general rule requires that each motor have an individual controller. There are exceptions to the general rule that apply for motors of 600 volts or less.

When a single machine is operated by several motors, one controller may control the entire machine, rather than only one motor. Such an arrangement would be almost a necessity for proper operation of certain large machines.

If all motors in a group are within the same room and all within sight of the controller, a single controller may serve several motors.

Where several motors are on the same branch circuit. Section 430-53(a) allows several fractional horsepower motors to be supplied by a single branch circuit. For clock motors and the like, the branch circuit switch could be the "controller" for several such motors.

It should be remembered that, where a single controller is to serve two or more motors, the controller must be sized large enough to handle the total horsepower or current of all the motors combined. For a horsepower-rated switch, the horsepower rating of the switch must be equal to the sum of the horsepower ratings of all the motors in the group.

430-88. Adjustable-Speed Motors

The speed of DC motors is commonly controlled by varying the field current of the motor. A weak field (low field current) on starting would allow a dangerously high current to rush through the armature. The Code requires that controllers for DC motors be so constructed that, unless the motor is specifically designed for such starting, the motor cannot be started on a weak field. Actually, any UL-approved controller for a DC motor will comply with this rule.

430-89. Speed Limitation

Separately excited DC motors are susceptible to the danger of excessive motor speeds being reached under certain conditions. The principal danger lies in the weakening or accidental opening of the field circuit. A weak field increases the speed of a DC motor; if the motor is lightly loaded at the time of an accidental opening of the field circuit, the motor could reach a dangerously high speed. For series motors, loss of load constitutes a danger.

(1) The field circuit of a separately excited motor has, as the name indicates, a separate source of DC. Under this condition, if the field circuit should accidentally open, or if a fault should develop in the source of supply for the field current, the weakened motor field would cause the motor to reach an excessive speed, if the motor happened to be lightly loaded at the time.

(2) Series motors have an inherent danger, which must be carefully considered when dealing with this type of motor. If a series motor accidentally

loses its load, the motor speed will become excessive. As a rule, series motors are always coupled or geared to their load, so that they are always loaded. If a series motor is not geared or coupled to its load, there is always danger of the motor reaching a damaging speed.

(3) If a motor-generator is used for battery charging, and the power to the AC motor is accidentally cut off, the DC generator will then take power from the batteries and run as a motor, with the possibility of an excessive speed.

The same thing would be true if two or more motor generators were operating in parallel and feeding the same DC line. If one motor generator stops, its DC generator will take power from the DC line and run as a motor, sometimes at excessive speed.

Converters operating in parallel are also subject to this danger.

In cases such as the foregoing (1), (2), and (3), the Code requires a speed-limiting device to be provided unless the motor is *always* under manual control of a qualified operator, or unless the motor is connected to the load in such a way that the speed would be safely limited (a gear connection would safely limit the speed). The speed-limiting device could be a centrifugal overspeed switch mounted on the motor shaft.

AC motors are not subject to the danger of overspeed. This danger is characteristic of series-wound DC motors and separately excited DC motors.

430-90. Combination Fuseholder and Switch as Controller

When a fused switch is used as motor controller and motor-running overload protection combined, the fuse rating may be up to 125% of motor full-load current (Section 430-32). The purpose of Section 430-90 is to assure that the fuseholder is *large enough* to hold the maximum size fuse permitted. The rule is intended to prevent possible bridging of the fuseholders in cases where the fuses prove to be too small to hold the motor starting current.

H. Disconnecting Means

430-101. General

The Code requires a reliable and easy-to-reach means of disconnecting a motor.

In some cases the controller can function as a disconnect; but for certain types of controllers, a separate disconnect is required. Magnetic controllers are subject to possible operational faults. A magnetic controller could lock in the closed position, or a fault could develop in the control circuit, making it impossible to stop the motor. Magnetic controllers must be provided with a hand-operated disconnect, which may be in the same case with the controller or separate therefrom.

A disconnect is required to disconnect both motor and controller from all ungrounded conductors of the circuit.

The basic idea of this part of the Code is to provide a *hand-operated* means of stopping or disconnecting a motor. This may be an enclosed knife switch, a hand-operated circuit breaker, toggle switch, or motor switch, or, for portable motors, a cord and plug.

It should be noted that a separate disconnect is not always required. Certain types of controllers may serve not only as the controller, but as the disconnect as well.

If the controller for a motor is any type of hand-operated controller (except a compensator) *and* has a *pole for each hot wire,* no additional disconnect is required; the controller itself may function as the disconnect.

A separate hand-operated disconnect is mandatory if the controller is either (1) a magnetic controller or (2) a compensator (autotransformer controller).

430-102. In Sight from Controller Location

See definition of "in sight from," Section 430-4.

The disconnect must be located within sight from the controller. If the controller serves also as the disconnect, then the disconnect is obviously in sight from the controller.

An exception is made for motor circuits of *over* 600 volts. The disconnect may be out of sight of the controller if (1) the disconnect may be locked in the open position, and (2) the controller carries a warning sign giving location of the disconnect.

430-103. To Disconnect Both Motor and Controller

The disconnect switch, if required, must be in the line ahead of the controller. It may, however, be in the same enclosure with the controller, as long as it is wired to "kill" the working parts of the controller, when open. Many magnetic controllers, especially the larger ones, come with a disconnect switch included in the controller case.

430-104. To Be Indicating

The disconnect switch must be marked ON, OFF, or with similar marking, to indicate whether the switch is in the open or closed position.

430-105. Grounded Conductors

The neutral does not have to be opened by the disconnect, but may be, if desired. If the neutral is to be opened by the disconnect switch, all hot wires must open simultaneously along the neutral.

430-106. Service Switch as Disconnecting Means

The service switch may serve as the disconnect when a service is installed for one motor only, provided that the service switch is within sight of the controller.

430-107. Readily Accessible

The disconnect must be "readily accessible." See definition of "readily accessible," p. 70-12 of the Code.

430-108. Every Switch

All disconnects in the motor branch circuit shall comply with the requirements of Section 430-109 and 430-110.

430-109. Type

The general rule is that the disconnect must be a horsepower-rated switch or a circuit breaker. There are exceptions to this rule, as follows:

Exception No. 1.

Stationary motors of $\frac{1}{8}$ hp or less. No disconnect required.

Exception No. 2.

For stationary motors of 2 hp or less, and 300 volts or less, the disconnect need not be horsepower-rated. It may be a general-use switch, such as a knife switch, rated in amperes rather than horsepower, provided the ampere rating of the switch is at least twice the full-load current rating of the motor. Or, for AC the disconnect may be a general-use AC snap switch, provided the ampere rating of the snap switch is at least 125% of the full-load current rating of the motor. (General-use, AC-DC snap switches may not be used as motor disconnects.)

Exception No. 3.

The disconnect for a motor having an autotransformer controller may be a general-use switch for motors from 2 to 100 hp, provided the motor drives a generator with overcurrent protection, and provided further that the controller has the no-voltage release feature, and is provided with proper motor-running overload protection, and the branch-circuit fuse size or circuit-breaker setting is not more than 150% of motor full-load current rating.

Exception No. 4.

The disconnect for any stationary motor of more than 40 hp DC or 100 hp AC may be a general-use switch or an isolating switch *if* the switch is marked DO NOT OPERATE UNDER LOAD.

Exception No. 5.

For portable motors, the cord and plug may serve as the disconnect.

Exception No. 6.

For torque motors of any size the disconnect may be a general-use switch.

The type of disconnect permitted for fixed motors of different size and voltage is tabulated below.

	Type Permitted
Motors of 300 volts or less	
0– ⅛ hp	No motor disconnect required
⅙– 2 hp	AC snap switch (for AC only)
	General-use switch
	Horsepower-rated switch
	Circuit breaker
2½– 100 hp	Horsepower-rated switch
	Circuit breaker
Over 100 hp	General-use switch*
	Horsepower-rated switch
	Circuit breaker
	Isolating switch*
Motors of over 300 volts	
0– ⅛ hp	No motor disconnect required
⅙– 2 hp	Horsepower-rated switch
	Circuit breaker
2½– 100 hp	Horsepower-rated switch
	Circuit breaker
Over 100 hp	General-use switch*
	Horsepower-rated switch
	Circuit breaker
	Isolating switch*

Note: There is one exception that permits a general-use switch as a disconnect for motors of 2½ to 100 hp. See Exception No. 3.

*For D.C. this applies for motors over 40 hp.

Horsepower-rated switches are marked by the manufacturer with a horsepower rating. Switches marked only with an ampere rating are general-use switches. Enclosed knife switches may be obtained in either the horsepower-rated or ampere-rated-only type.

430-110. Ampere Rating and Interrupting Capacity

(a) The disconnect for motors of 600 volts or less must have an ampacity of not less than 115% of the motor full-load current rating.

For horsepower-rated switches, the switch would be built by the manufacturer to provide at least the 115% ampacity required by this rule.

Where a general-use switch is permitted, as for motors of 2 hp and less, the switch must have an ampere rating of twice the motor full-load current rating.

If an AC snap switch is used as the disconnect (this would be for smaller motors), the snap switch must have a rating equal to at least 125% of the motor full-load current rating.

If a circuit breaker is used as the disconnect, the size (carrying capacity) of the breaker must be at least 115% of motor full-load current rating.

There is a difference between *size* and *setting* of a circuit breaker. Circuit breakers come in 50, 100, 225, 400, and 600 amp. (and larger) sizes. This is called the frame size. The frame size is the maximum current-carrying capacity of the breaker. Each frame size has several different possible *settings.* (The setting fixes the amperage above which the breaker will trip.)

A 50-amp. breaker may be set at any standard setting between 15 and 50 amps.

A 100-amp. breaker may be set at any standard setting between 15 and 100 amps.

A 225-amp. breaker may be set at any standard setting between 110 and 225 amps., and so on.

When a circuit breaker is used as a disconnect, the circuit breaker *frame size* must be at least 115% of the motor full-load current rating. The rule does not refer to the *setting.*

(b) The nameplate on torque motors is marked in amperes only. The disconnect for a torque motor need not be horsepower-rated. May be rated in amperes only. The ampere rating of the disconnect shall be at least 115% of the ampere rating of the motor.

(c) Under certain conditions, one disconnect may serve for several motors (Section 430-112). The disconnect horsepower would equal the sum of the horsepowers of all motors of the group, plus any resistance loads (converted to horsepower).

430-111. Switch or Circuit Breaker as Both Controller and Disconnecting Means

The controller, if a hand-operated type, may serve double duty as both controller and disconnect, provided it has enough poles to open all hot wires.

1. If the controller is a hand-operated air-break switch, no separate disconnect is required, provided the switch opens all hot wires. "Airbreak switch" would include knife switches, toggle switches, motor switches, or any hand-operated switch except a compensator (autotransformer starter).
2. If the controller is a hand-operated circuit breaker, no separate disconnect is required, provided the circuit breaker opens all hot wires.
3. If the controller is an oil switch (not over 600 volts, 100 amps.), no separate disconnect is required, provided the oil switch opens all hot wires. (Oil switches of higher voltage or amperage require a separate disconnect.)

An autotransformer-type starter must have a disconnect. A magnetic controller, one operated by pushbutton control, or by a pressure switch, or similar control devices, must have a disconnect.

Note that the disconnect, if required, may be in the same enclosure with the controller.

430-112. Motors Served by a Single Disconnecting Means

The general rule requires that each motor shall have an individual disconnect (which may in some cases be the controller).

There are exceptions to the general rule:

1. When a single machine is operated by several motors, one disconnect may serve for the several motors.
2. If all motors of a group are within the same room, and all within sight of the disconnect, a single disconnect may serve several motors.
3. Where several small motors are on the same branch circuit, Section

430-53(a) allows several fractional-horsepower motors to be supplied by a single branch circuit. In this case, a single disconnect may serve for all the motors. For motors of $\frac{1}{8}$ hp or less, the disconnect may be the branch-circuit fuse or circuit breaker.

430-113. Energy from More Than One Source

This rule would apply for example when a motor has both a regular and an emergency supply. Both sources must be provided with a motor disconnect, which may be one double throw switch, or two separate disconnects.

Examples. Disconnects:

1. Disconnect for a 10-hp, 230-volt, three-phase motor with magnetic controller. Full-load motor current 28 amps. (Table 430-150):

   The motor is in the $2\frac{1}{2}$-100-hp range.

   Disconnect may be:

   1. 3-pole horsepower-rated switch, with rating of at least 10 hp, 230 volt AC.

   2. 3-pole circuit breaker, with frame size of at least 115% × 28 amps.

2. Disconnect for a $\frac{1}{3}$-hp, 115-volt, single-phase AC motor with magnetic controller. Full-load motor current 7.2 amps. (Table 430-148):

   The motor is in the $\frac{1}{6}$- to 2-hp range, and under 300 volts.

   Disconnect may be:

   1. Single-pole AC snap switch with ampere rating of at least $1\frac{1}{4}$ × 7.2 amps.

   2. Single-pole general-use switch with ampere rating of at least 2 × 7.2 amps.

   3. Single-pole horsepower-rated switch.

   4. Single-pole circuit breaker with frame size of at least 115% × 7.2 amps.

3. Disconnect for a 10-hp, 230-volt, three-phase motor. Controller is a three-pole hand-operated motor switch, horsepower-rated.

   The controller is hand-operated and has a pole for each hot wire. No separate disconnect is required.

J. Over 600 Volts Nominal

430-121. General

In addition to the general rules for motors and controllers, which are covered by Sections 430-1 through 430-113, there are special rules that apply to motors operating at more than 600 volts.

Article 710 specifies, among other things, that the wiring method for high-voltage circuits must be conduit, metal raceways, or "suitable" metal-armored cable.

It should be remembered that the insulation on conductors for general wiring is made for voltages only up to 600. For voltages above 600, conductors with high-voltage insulation must be used, and the insulation must be approved for a voltage at least as high as the voltage of the circuit.

430-122. Marking on Controllers

Controllers shall be marked with maker's name or identification, voltage, current or horsepower rating, control voltage.

430-123. Conductor Enclosures Adjacent to Motors

Flexible metal conduit in lengths of not over 6 ft may be used for connection to motor terminal enclosures.

430-124. Size of Conductors

Conductor ampacity must be at least equal to the current setting of the overload device.

430-125. Motor Circuit Overcurrent Protection

(a) General

For high-voltage motors, protective devices must be provided that will operate on motor-running overload, and when fault currents (such as a ground) occur in the motor, motor circuit, or motor control apparatus.

(b) Overload Protection

Motor-running overload protection may be in the form of a thermal protector built into the motor, or by "current-sensing" devices. Current-sensing devices would be devices that are set to operate when the current reaches a preset value. Thermal overload relays, heaters, fuses are not considered to be "current-sensing devices."

Sensing devices shall be the hand-reset type.

Sensing devices shall operate to open all ungrounded conductors.

Secondary circuits of wound-rotor motors do not require separate protection. These are considered as protected by the devices protecting the main motor circuit.

(c) Fault Current Protection

The following methods are approved for branch-circuit protection:

1. Circuit breakers. It should be mentioned that most circuit breakers are made for voltages only up to 600 volts. If circuit breakers are used for branch-circuit protection, they must have a voltage rating high enough for the voltage of the circuit.
2. Special high-voltage fuses. High-voltage fuses may be the "oil-filled" type. This type of fuse is built in the form of an oil chamber, with a fuse link submerged in special oil.

High-voltage "air" fuses, which act also as disconnects, may be used for branch-circuit protection. Usually, a hook stick is used to disconnect the fuse.

Standard fuses are made for voltages only as high as 600 and may not be used in high-voltage circuits. Fuses for high-voltage circuits must be specially constructed because of the large arc that is generated when the fuse blows. The higher the voltage, the greater will be the arc. High-voltage fuses are built to quickly extinguish the arc, and also to confine the arc so as to minimize fire hazard.

430-126. Rating of Motor Control Apparatus

Controllers and disconnects must have an ampere rating not less than the current setting of the overload protective device.

430-127. Disconnecting Means

All disconnects, regardless of location, must be equipped with a locking device that will lock the disconnect in the "open" position.

K. Protection of Live Parts—All Voltages

430-131. General

430-132. Where Required

This part of the Code applies for both low- and high-voltage motors (all motors operating at 50 volts or more).

Motors or controllers with exposed live parts of 50 volts or more must be specially located.

(Commutators and brush rigging with voltage of 150 or less *to ground,* if inside the motor end bracket, are not considered to be exposed live parts.)

Completely enclosed motors would have no exposed live parts. "Open"-type motors may, however, have exposed live parts. The end bell of an open-type motor has rectangular openings, and it would be possible for a person to accidentally come in contact with a live part through an opening. With this type of motor, special locating is required unless the live parts in the end bell are a commutator or brush rigging of 150 volts or less to ground.

When special locating is required, the motor must be installed in one of the following ways:

1. In an enclosure, or in a room accessible only to "qualified" persons.
2. In an elevated platform accessible only to qualified persons.
3. Elevated, in some way, at least 8 ft above the floor.

430-133. Guards for Attendants

This rule is intended to protect the "qualified" persons who would have access to motors specially located in a room, balcony, etc., as per Section 430-132. To protect "qualified" persons who work on and around the motor, insulating mats, such as rubber mats, must be installed on the floor around the motor, the mats being wide enough so that live parts of the motor could not be reached unless the attendant were standing on the mat. Controllers with exposed live parts must also be provided with mats. (Wooden platforms are acceptable as a substitute for mats.)

L. Grounding

430-141. General

430-142. Stationary Motors

Section 430-142 could be restated as follows:

1. Frames of fixed motors operating on circuits of more than 150 volts *to ground* must *always be grounded.*
2. Frames of fixed motors operating on circuits of 150 volts or less to ground must be grounded if they are:
   (1) Wired with metal conduit, BX, or other "metal-clad" wiring, or
   (2) Located in a wet location and within reach, or

(3) Located in a hazardous location.

Example of circuits with voltages of less than 150 to ground:

120-volt, single-phase, AC or DC (120 to ground).

240-volt, taken from outside legs of a three-wire 120/240-volt circuit with grounded neutral (120 to ground).

120/208-volt, four-wire, three-phase (120 to ground).

Examples of circuits with voltages of more than 150 to ground:

220-volt, three-wire, three-phase (220 to ground).

440-volt, three-wire, three-phase (440 to ground).

Note—Section 250-42 (c) (a) would also require grounding of motors mounted on metal, or within reach of ground or a grounded object.

Examples.

1. A 115-volt, single-phase motor, wired with Romex, is located in an attic. Is grounding required?
   The motor operates on less than 150 volts to ground, is not in a wet or hazardous location, and is not wired with "metal-clad" wiring. Grounding is not required.

2. A 115-volt, single-phase motor, wired with metal conduit, is located in an attic. Is grounding required?
   The motor operates on less than 150 volts to ground, is not in a wet or hazardous location, but is wired with conduit ("metal-clad" wiring). Therefore, grounding is required regardless of location.

3. A 230-volt, three-phase motor, wired with Romex, is located in an attic. Is grounding required?
   Yes. All motors of more than 150 volts to ground must be grounded.

430-143. Portable Motors

The rules of this Section and Section 250-45, can be summed up as follows:

1. Portable drills, hedge clippers, lawn mowers, wet scrubbers, sanders, and saws operating at 150 volts or less to ground must be either grounded or double-insulated.

2. For voltages above 150 to ground, these tools must be *grounded.* Double

insulation is not considered to be adequate protection where higher voltages are involved.

3. The insulation on a grounding wire in a cord must be green in color [Section 250-59(b)].

Note that Section 250-45 requires that refrigerators, freezers, air conditioners, washing machines, clothes dryers, dishwashers, and sump pumps must be grounded. These are not "portable" equipment, but if connected by cord and plug they come under the rules of Section 250-45.

430-144. Controllers

The general rule is that motor controllers must always be grounded, regardless of voltage or location.

However, there are two exceptions to this rule:

1. Controllers attached to ungrounded portable equipment. Examples would be the switch on a vacuum cleaner, sander, etc. These need not be grounded, unless the appliance is grounded.

2. Snap switches with lined covers, i.e., with an insulating lining, such as asbestos, need not be grounded.

430-145. Method of Grounding

There are two ways in which fixed motors, or controllers, may be grounded:

1. If metal conduit, EMT, or BX is used, then the conduit, EMT, or metal sheath of the BX can serve as the grounding conductor. The conduit, EMT, or BX sheath would be in metallic contact with the motor or controller, and would constitute a metallic circuit back to the service entrance, where it would be grounded, thus grounding the motor or controller.

2. A separate grounding wire may be run along with the circuit conductors. This method would be used when Romex or other nonmetallic-sheathed type of wiring is used to wire a motor or controller that must be grounded. Cable with a grounding wire would be used. The grounding wire would be bonded to the motor or controller at one end and to the grounded service disconnect enclosure at the other end, thus grounding the motor or controller.

A motor wired with metal conduit, EMT, or BX must have either a terminal housing or, if the motor does not have a terminal housing, a junction box must be provided. This junction box need not be installed on the motor; it may be separated from the motor by a distance up to 6 ft. Some kind of metallic-clad wiring must be used for the short run between the junction box and the motor; nonmetallic wiring is not permitted. The conductors for this run may be as small as No. 18 (provided that No. 18 will carry the motor current). See also Section 430-22.

ARTICLE 440 — AIR-CONDITIONING AND REFRIGERATING EQUIPMENT

A. General

440-1. Scope

440-2. Other Articles

Article 440 deals with a special type of equipment—sealed (hermetic-type) motor compressor units. The rules that apply for hermetic-type motors are in addition to the general motor rules of Article 430.

The National Electrical Manufacturers Association gives this definition of a hermetic motor: "A hermetic motor consists of a stator and rotor without end shaft, end shields or bearings for installation in refrigeration condensing units of the hermetically sealed type."

As the name implies, motor and compressor are contained in a sealed enclosure. "Hermetic" means "made perfectly close or airtight, so that no gas can enter or escape."

The rules of Article 440 apply also for room air conditioners, household refrigerators, drinking water coolers, and freezers, when such equipment contains a hermetic motor. Actually, these units are furnished as a complete package with all necessary controls provided by the manufacturer. (Such units are considered appliances, and are subject also to the applicable rules of Article 422.)

440-3. Marking on Hermetic Refrigerant Motor Compressors and Equipment

440-4. Marking on Controllers

Motor compressor and equipment nameplates must show:

Manufacturer's name, trademark, or symbol.

Identifying designation.

Phase.

Voltage.

Frequency.

Rated load current.

Locked-rotor current (for motors over 9 amps. 115 volts, and 4.5 amps. 230 volts, and all polyphase motor compressors).

(Some equipment also lists a "branch circuit selection current.")

Controllers must be marked with:

Identifying designation.

Manufacturer's name, trademark, or symbol.

Phase.

Voltage.

Horsepower (or full-load and locked-rotor current).

440-5. Ampacity and Rating

To properly connect and protect the motor, it is necessary to determine:

Conductor size.

Disconnect size.

Controller size.

Rating of motor overload protection.

Rating of branch-circuit short-circuit protection.

These are based on the rated load current on the equipment nameplate, *or* if a "branch-circuit selection current" is marked on the nameplate, the branch-circuit selection current shall be used to determine all the above *except* overload protection. Rated-load current is always used to determine motor overload protection.

If the equipment nameplate does not show a rated-load current, the rated-load current on the compressor nameplate is used.

440-6. Highest-Rated (Largest) Motor

This Section applies when two or more motors are fed from one circuit.

Section 430-24 requires that, when two or more motors are fed by one circuit, the circuit conductors shall have an ampacity equal to 125% of the largest (highest-current) motor, plus the sum of the full-load current ratings of all the other motors in the group.

Section 430-62(a) limits the rating of the circuit overcurrent protection to the rating for the motor having the highest permissible branch-circuit protection, as per Table 430-152, p. 70-320, plus the sum of the full-load currents of the rest of the motors connected to the circuit. This applies also for hermetic motors.

For hermetic motors, the motor current ratings are the nameplate ratings. (For other types of motors, the motor current rating is taken from Tables 430-148 through 430-150 of the Code.)

Example.

Determine conductor size (Type T conductor) and circuit fuse size for a circuit feeding three hermetic motors with nameplate currents of 12, 10, and 8 amps. All motors are three-phase squirrel-cage motors; full-voltage starting.

Conductors must have an ampacity equal to 125% of the highest motor current, plus the sum of the other motor currents, or

$$(125\% \times 12) + 10 + 8 = 15 + 10 + 8 = 33 \text{ amps.}$$

From Table 310-16, p. 70-132, a No. 8 conductor would be required. From Table 430-152, p. 70-320, maximum branch-circuit fusing permitted for a squirrel-cage motor with full-voltage starting is 300% of motor full-load current (under Nontime Delay Fuse, second listing from top). The 12-amp. motor would have the highest permissible branch-circuit protection, which would be

$$300\% \text{ of } 12 = 36 \text{ amps.}$$

Since there is no standard 36-amp. fuse, the next higher size could be used, a 40-amp. fuse. This would be the branch-circuit protection permitted for the 12-amp. motor alone. Adding this to the full-load current of the other motors:

$$40 + 10 + 8 = 58 \text{ amps.}$$

A 50-amp. fuse would be the largest permitted for the feeder. (In figuring overcurrent protection for the feeder, you cannot go to the next higher fuse size.)

440-7. Single Machine

An air-conditioning or refrigeration system may be comprised of several motors. The general Code rule for motors is that each motor must have its own individual controller and an individual disconnect. Sections 430-87, Exception, and 430-112, Exception, are exceptions to this general rule, and permit one controller or disconnect to serve for several motors. The exceptions apply also in the case of air-conditioning and refrigeration systems, when one system is comprised of several motors.

B. Disconnecting Means

440-11. General

440-12. Rating and Interrupting Capacity

The type of disconnect permitted for hermetic motors is the same as for other types of motors. The disconnect may be a horsepower-rated switch or a circuit breaker, or for certain size motors it may be a general-use switch (see Section 430-109).

The disconnect is sized on a basis of motor horsepower. If the nameplate rating (or branch-circuit selection current) for the motor or piece of equipment is in amperes, rather than horsepower, the horsepower corresponding to the ampere rating must be taken from Tables 430-148, 430-149, or 430-150 of the Code.

Or, if the locked-rotor current is listed on the nameplate, the horsepower corresponding to that current must be obtained from Table 430-151, p. 70-319.

The higher of the two horsepowers would determine the size of the disconnect.

Examples.

1. Determine the disconnect size for a hermetic motor with nameplate full-load current rating of 15 amps.; locked-rotor current is 115 amps. Motor is 230-volt, three-phase.

   From Table 430-150, p. 70-318, nearest higher horsepower corresponding to the full-load current rating of 15 amps. is 5 hp. From Table 430-151, nearest higher horsepower corresponding to the locked-rotor current of 115 amps. for a 230-volt, three-phase motor is $7\frac{1}{2}$ hp. A $7\frac{1}{2}$-hp disconnect would be required for this motor.

   If a circuit breaker is to be used as a disconnect, it is sized as follows: From Table 430-150, the current rating of a $7\frac{1}{2}$ hp, 230-volt, three-phase motor is 22 amps. The circuit-breaker size must be at least 115% × 22 = 25.3 amps. A 50-amp. frame circuit breaker would be permitted as a disconnect.

2. A single disconnect is to be used to serve three hermetic motors, with nameplate ratings as follows:

   (1) Full-load current, 12 amps; locked-rotor current, 65 amps.

   (2) Full-load current, 9 amps; locked-rotor current, 60 amps.

   (3) Full-load current, 5 amps; locked-rotor current, 33 amps.

All motors are 230-volt, three-phase. What size disconnect is required?

Referring to Table 430-150, nearest higher horsepower corresponding to the full-load currents is:

(1)	12 amps.	5 hp
(2)	9 amps.	3 hp
(3)	5 amps.	1½ hp
	Total	9½ hp

Referring to Table 430-151, for 230-volt, three-phase motors, nearest higher horsepower corresponding to the locked-rotor currents is:

(1)	65 amps.	5 hp
(2)	60 amps.	5 hp
(3)	33 amps.	2 hp
	Total	12 hp

Minimum hp rating of the disconnect would be the higher of the two totals: 12 hp.

Subsection 440-12(b)(2) requires the disconnect to have an ampacity rating of at least 115 percent of the total current. A disconnect selected on a horsepower basis will have a current-carrying capacity at least equal to this figure.

440-13. Cord-Connected Equipment

For cord-connected equipment containing hermetic motors, no disconnect is required. The cord and plug serves as the disconnect (except for certain air conditioners).

Note: for room air conditioners a cord and plug may *not,* in some cases, serve as a disconnect (see Section 440-63).

440-14. Location

The disconnect for air-conditioning or refrigerating equipment shall be in sight from and readily accessible from the equipment.

C. Branch-Circuit Short-Circuit and Ground-Fault Protection

440-21. General

This part of the Code sets down the rules for sizing the branch-circuit fuse or circuit-breaker setting for circuits supplying hermetic motors only, or where hermetic motors and standard-type motors are both on the circuit.

440-22. Application and Selection

(a) Rating or Setting for Individual Motor Compressor

For a single hermetic-type motor, branch-circuit protection may be sized at 175% of nameplate current rating of the motor. This may be increased to 225%, if necessary to hold the motor starting current.

As an example, for a motor with a nameplate rating of 20 amps., a branch-circuit fuse of 175% $\times$ 20 = 35 amps. may be used. If the 35-amp. fuse will not hold the starting current, the fuse size may be increased to 225% $\times$ 20 = 45 amps.

(b) Rating or Setting for Equipment

(1) When there is more than one hermetic-type motor on the circuit, the branch-circuit protection is sized at a rating equal to 175% of the nameplate current of the largest motor (or branch-circuit selection current, whichever is greater), plus the sum of the other motor nameplate currents.

Example.

What maximum size branch-circuit fuse is permitted for a circuit serving three hermetic-type motors, with nameplate currents of 16, 14, and 10 amps.?

$$(175\% \times 16) + 14 + 10 = 28 + 14 + 10 = 52 \text{ amps.}$$

A 50-amp. fuse could be used.

If the 50-amp. fuse will not hold the starting current, the size may be increased to

$$(225\% \times 16) + 14 + 10 = 36 + 14 + 10 = 60 \text{ amps.}$$

When both hermetic- and standard-type motors are on the circuit, and one of the hermetic-type motors is the largest, then the branch-circuit fusing is figured as above.

Example.

What maximum size branch-circuit fuse is permitted for a circuit serving two hermetic motors with nameplate currents of 20 and 16 amps., also a 3-hp, 230-volt three-phase blower motor?

From Table 430-150, p. 70-318, full-load current rating of the 3-hp motor is 9.6 amps. Largest rated motor is the 20-amp. hermetic motor. Maximum size of fusing permitted would be

$$(175\% \times 20) + 16 + 9.6 = 35 + 16 + 9.6 = 60.6 \text{ amps.}$$

A 60-amp. fuse would be permitted.

(2) When both hermetic- and standard-type motors are on the circuit, and one of the standard motors is the largest, branch-circuit fusing is figured on a basis of maximum fusing for the one (largest) standard motor, and all the other motor current ratings are added to this.

Example.

What maximum size branch-circuit fuse is permitted for a circuit serving two hermetic motors with nameplate currents of 20 and 16 amps., also a 10-hp, 230-volt, three-phase squirrel-cage blower motor with full-voltage starting?

From Table 430-150, full-load current rating of the 10-hp motor is 28 amps. This is the largest motor of the group. Branch-circuit protection for standard motors is figured according to Table 430-152, p. 70-320. From Table 430-152, maximum branch-circuit fusing for a squirrel-cage motor is 300% of motor full-load current (under Nontime Delay Fuse, second listing from top).

$$300\% \times 28 = 84 \text{ amps.}$$

A 90-amp. fuse could be used for branch-circuit protection for this motor alone. To this is added the current of the other motors.

$$90 + 20 + 16 = 126 \text{ amps.}$$

A 125-amp. fuse may be used.

There are two exceptions to the above rule, which make it unnecessary to calculate the size of the branch-circuit protection:

1. Where unit equipment will start and operate on a 15- or 20-amp. 120-volt circuit or a 15-amp. 208- or 240-volt circuit.

   Here the 20-amp. or 15-amp. protection is acceptable provided the 20-amp. or 15-amp. protection does not exceed the ampere protection rating marked on the equipment.

2. For cord and plug connected equipment operating at 250 volts or less, single phase (examples are household refrigerators, drinking water coolers, freezers, beverage dispensers).

   In this case the nameplate marking on the equipment determines the branch-circuit protection.

(c) When the rating or setting of a protective device for a piece of equipment is specified by the manufacturer, *and is less than the calculated rating,* the manufacturer's rating or setting shall be used.

D. Branch-Circuit Conductors

440-31. General

This part of the Code is intended to specify conductor sizes for wiring hermetic-type motors. The rules do not apply to wiring within equipment.

440-32. Single Motor Compressor

For a single hermetic-type motor, conductors must have an ampacity equal to at least 125% of nameplate current rating (or branch-circuit selection current, whichever is greater).

Example.

What size Type T conductors are required to serve a hermetic-type motor with a nameplate rating of 20 amps.?

$$125\% \times 20 = 25 \text{ amps.}$$

Conductors must have an ampacity of 25 amps. From Table 310-16, p. 70-132 of the Code, a No. 10 conductor is required.

440-33. Motor Compressor(s) With or Without Additional Motor Loads

For several motors, the conductors must have an ampacity equal to 125% of the largest motor current rating, plus the sum of all the other motor current ratings.

Example.

What size Type T conductors are required for a circuit serving hermetic type motors, with nameplate ratings of 20, 15, and 10 amps.?

The conductors must have an ampacity of

$$(125\% \times 20) + 15 + 10 = 25 + 15 + 10 = 50 \text{ amps.}$$

From Table 310-16, a No. 6 conductor is required.

440-34. Combination Load

When other loads are on the circuit along with the motors, conductor size is figured as above for the motors; then the current rating of the other loads is added to this.

Example.

What size Type T conductors are required for a circuit serving hermetic-type motors, with nameplate ratings of 12, 8, and 5 amps., also a 2,000-watt, 115-volt heater?

Conductor ampacity required for the motors alone:

$$(125\% \times 12) + 8 + 5 = 15 + 8 + 5 = 28 \text{ amps.}$$

Conductor ampacity required for the heater is

$$\frac{2{,}000}{115} = 17.4 \text{ amps.}$$

Conductor ampacity required for the entire load is

$$28 + 17.4 = 45.4 \text{ amps.}$$

From Table 310-16, p. 70-132, a No. 6 conductor is required.

440-35. Multimotor and Combination-Load Equipment

Where more than one motor is contained in a single unit of equipment, or where motors and other loads are contained in a single unit, it is not necessary to figure conductor sizes on the basis of the individual motors or loads. The conductors in this case would be sized according to the required conductor ampacity marked on the piece of equipment [marking is required by Section 440-3(b)].

E. Controllers for Motor Compressors

440-41. Rating

The method of figuring controller size for hermetic motors is the same as the method for figuring the disconnect size. The size is based on (1) the nameplate rated-load current (or branch-circuit selection current); (2) the locked-rotor current of the motor.

Example.

What size controller is required for a hermetic-type motor, with nameplate rated-load current rating of 26 amps., and locked-rotor nameplate current of 130 amps? Motor is a 230-volt, three-phase motor.

First, the equivalent horsepower corresponding to the full-load current rating is determined. For a three-phase motor, Table 430-150, p. 70-318, is used. The nearest current listing above 26 amps. is 28 amps. This corresponds to 10 hp.

Next, the equivalent horsepower corresponding to the locked-rotor current is determined from Table 430-151, p. 70-319. For a three-phase, 230-volt motor, the nearest current listing above 130 is 132 amps., corresponding to a $7\frac{1}{2}$-hp motor. The controller is sized according to the higher horsepower; a 10-hp controller would be required.

When one controller serves two or more motor-compressors, the controller is required to have a continuous current rating equal to 115% of the sum of all motor full-load currents, and, in addition, a locked-rotor current rating equal to 115% of the sum of all motor *locked-rotor* currents. (Locked-rotor currents for motors of different types and sizes are given in Table 430-151, p. 70-319.)

If there are other loads, besides motors, on the circuit, the amperage of these is added to the motor amperages to obtain the required ampere rating for the controller.

F. Motor-Compressor and Branch-Circuit Overload Protection

440-51. General

Sections 440-51 through 440-55 provide for protection against overload, i.e., continued overcurrent that would overheat motors, conductors, and apparatus.

440-52. Application and Selection

(a) Protection of Motor-Compressor

Overload protection may be one of the following types:

1. Relay that will trip at not over 140% of motor full-load current.

2. Thermal protector integral with the motor compressor.

3. Fusetron.

4. Circuit breaker having thermal overload trip.

5. Protective system furnished with the unit.

Thermal protectors are mounted inside the motor frame. Usually, they are in the form of a contact made by a metal strip enclosed in a small case. Heat affects the metal strip in such a way that it snaps the contacts open on prolonged overload. The contacts can be connected directly in the motor circuit or in a relay circuit, which would operate the main contacts in the controller. Proper setting of the device to prevent overheating would be the responsibility of the motor manufacturer.

In some cases, a protective system is built into a unit by the manufacturer, and no additional motor protection is required. The household refrigerator would be an example of such a unit.

When fusetrons or circuit breakers are used for overload protection, the required size or setting is a maximum of 125% of the rated-load current of the motor. Thus, for a motor with a 12-amp. full-load current rating, the maximum size fuse (or circuit-breaker setting) would be 15 amps.

(b) Protection of Motor-Compressor Control Apparatus and Branch-Circuit Conductors

This subsection permits the same type of protective devices called for by subsection (a), above, for protecting the motor to be used also to protect the controller and branch-circuit conductors against overload.

440-53. Overload Relays

Devices such as overload relays and thermal protectors do not provide short-circuit protection. They are delayed-action devices, which require a time interval in which to heat up to the operating point. Even on short circuit they do not operate instantly. Devices for short-circuit protection must operate instantaneously on short circuit.

This Section requires that short-circuit protection be provided for devices which are used for overload protection. The branch-circuit short-circuit protection required by Part C would provide such protection, in the usual case.

440-54. Motor-Compressors and Equipment on 15- or 20-Ampere Branch Circuits—Not Cord-and-Attachment Plug-Connected

Motor compressors and equipment may be connected to general-purpose branch circuits rated 15 or 20 amps. at 120 volts, or 15 amps. at 208 or 240 volts. Motor-running overload protection is required, but may be the branch-circuit fusetrons or circuit breaker if sized according to Section 440-52(a). (Fusetrons rather than fuses should be used on a branch circuit serving motors.)

440-55. Cord-and-Attachment Plug-Connected Motor-Compressors and Equipment on 15- or 20-Ampere Branch Circuits

Requirements are the same as for Section 440-54, above, with the additional requirement that the attachment plug and receptacle shall be rated not more than 20 amps. at 125 volts, or 15 amps. at 250 volts.

G. Provisions for Room Air Conditioners

440-60. General

Part G applies for air-conditioning units that are installed, as a unit, in a room. It does not apply for central air-conditioning machines.

All room air conditioners above 250 volts must be wired direct. They may not be connected by cord and plug. *Single-phase* room air conditioners of 250 volts or less may be connected by cord and plug.

All three-phase room air conditioners must be wired direct, regardless of voltage. They may not be connected by cord and plug.

440-61. Grounding

All plug-connected air conditioners must be grounded.

Air conditioners that are wired direct must be grounded if:

1. Within reach of ground or a grounded object (a pipe, radiator).
2. In contact with metal.
3. Operating at over 150 volts to ground.
4. Wired by metal-clad wiring, such as conduit or BX.
5. In a hazardous location.
6. In a damp location and within reach.

440-62. Branch-Circuit Requirements

A branch circuit may be loaded only to 80% of the circuit capacity when only cord-and-plug-connected air conditioners are on the circuit.

If lighting or other appliances are also on the circuit, the rating of the cord-and-plug-connected air conditioners is limited to ½ the circuit capacity.

440-63. Disconnecting Means

A cord and plug may serve as the disconnect for an air-conditioning unit, if:

1. Voltage is 250 or less, single-phase, and
2. Manual controls on the air conditioner are within 6 ft of the floor and readily accessible.

Otherwise, a readily accessible disconnect is required within sight of the unit (see Fig. 458).

440-64. Supply Cords

Length of cords is limited to 10 ft for 120 volts, 6 ft for 208 or 240 volts.

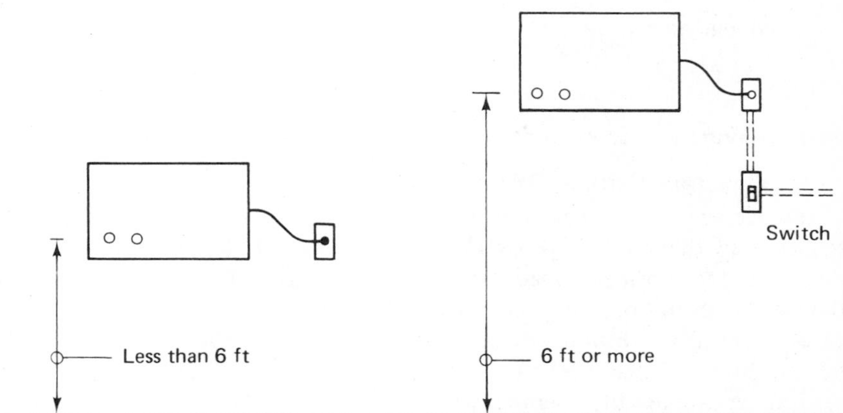

Fig. 458
Disconnect for cord-and-plug-connected single-phase room air conditioners of 120 or 240 volts. (Sect. 440-63). If the air conditioner controls are less than 6 ft above the floor, the cord and plug acts as the disconnect. If the controls are 6 ft or more above the floor, a disconnect switch must be provided for the receptacle. The switch may be an AC toggle switch or other manual switch within sight of the air conditioner (AC-DC toggle switches are not permitted). These rules do not apply for three-phase air conditioners, which must be wired direct, and require a disconnect switch in all cases.

ARTICLE 445 — GENERATORS

445-1. General

445-2. Location

Standard-type generators are designed to operate indoors in dry places. If a generator is to operate in a hazardous location, a specially designed generator, meeting Code requirements for hazardous locations, would have to be used.

445-3. Marking

A generator nameplate must show:

Maker's name.

kW, or kVA.

Volts.

Amps.

RPM.

Frequency.

Power factor.

445-4. Overcurrent Protection

(a) Constant-Voltage Generators

DC generators must have overcurrent protection. AC generators may be so designed that on a high overload the voltage of the generator falls off, thereby reducing the overload current to a safe value. It is for this reason that the Code does not require overload protection for all AC generators. In some cases, overload protection may be omitted. The generator manufacturer should be consulted on this question.

Exciters are usually operated without overload protection, rather than risk generator shutdown due to opening of a protective device in the exciter circuit.

(b) Two-Wire Generators

When two or more DC generators are operated in parallel, an "equalizer" conductor is connected to the positive terminal of each generator. The purpose of the equalizer is to maintain equal output voltage for each generator.

When equalizers are used, there could be a division of current at the positive terminal, part flowing to the equalizer, part to the positive generator lead. A fuse or circuit breaker placed in the positive generator lead would at times not have the full generator current. When DC generators are operated in parallel, only one overcurrent device is required—in the negative generator lead only (Fig. 459). The Code would not permit an overcurrent device in the generator positive lead only, because an overcurrent device in the positive lead would not always be actuated "by the entire current generated" (Fig. 459).

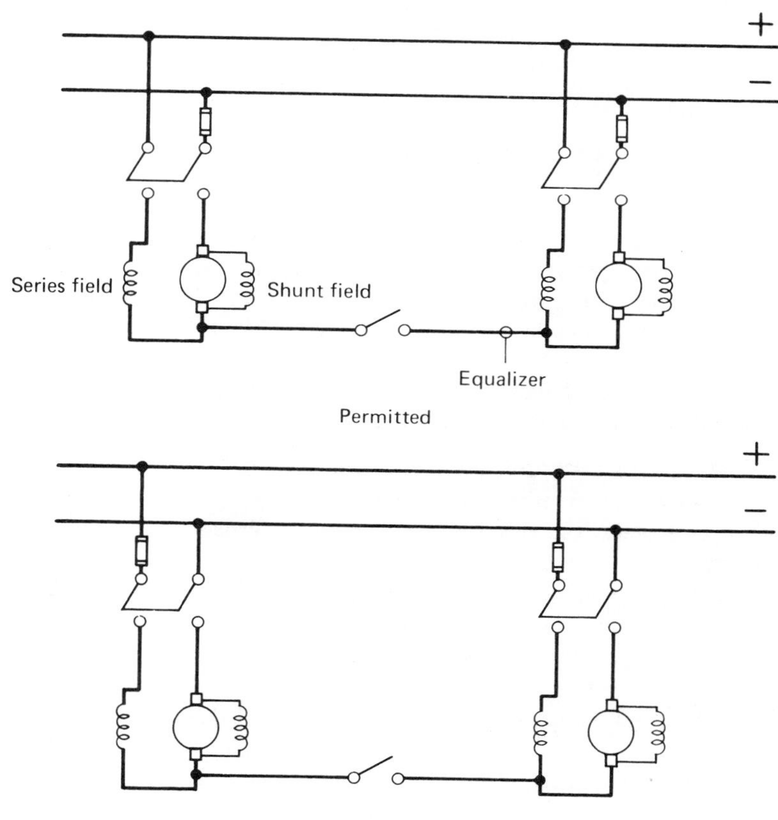

Fig. 459

Overcurrent protection for two-wire DC generators in parallel [Sect. 445-4(b)]. A single fuse may be used for protection of a two-wire DC generator, but the fuse must be so placed as to take the full current of the generator (except the shunt-field current). For generators operating in parallel, the one fuse must be in the negative lead. If placed in the positive lead, not all the generator current will pass through the fuse, since part of the current will at times be diverted to the equalizer. (For a generator not operating in parallel, the fuse may be in either lead.)

An overcurrent device is not permitted for the shunt field. If the shunt-field circuit were to open when the field is at full strength, a dangerously high voltage would be induced, which might damage the generator.

(c) 65 Volts or Less

This rule applies to motor generator sets with generators of 65 volts or less. If the fuse or circuit breaker protecting the motor is set to operate when the generator is not more than 50% overloaded, no protection is required in the generator leads. Where the generator voltage is above 65, it is evidently the intent of the Code to require separate overcurrent protection for the generator.

(d) Balancer Sets

Balancer sets consist of two smaller DC generators used with a larger two-wire generator. The two balancer generators are connected in series across the two-wire main generator line. A neutral is brought out from the midpoint connection between the two balancer generators. Each of the two balancer generators carries approximately one-half of any unbalanced load.

With such an arrangement, when there is a heavy unbalance in the load, the balancer generators may become overloaded, while there is no overload on the main generator. The balancer generators shall be equipped with an overload device that will actuate the main generator disconnect when they (the balancer generators) become overloaded.

(e) Three-Wire, Direct-Current Generators

As in two-wire generators, the overcurrent device protecting a three-wire generator must take the full generator current. When equalizer leads are present, the overcurrent device, if misplaced in the circuit, might take only part of the current. Three-wire DC generators operating in parallel have two equalizer leads. The overcurrent devices must be so placed in the circuit that they will take the full generator current.

A two-pole breaker placed ahead of the junction of the main and equalizer leads will accomplish this (Fig. 460). A four-pole breaker with two poles for the main leads and two poles for the equalizer leads can be used, provided that the operating coils of the circuit breaker are actuated by the full generator current.

445-5. Ampacity of Conductors

Generator leads must have an ampacity equal to at least 115% of the nameplate current rating of the generator.

Exception No. 1

If the design or operation of the generator is such as to prevent overloading, an ampacity of 100% is permitted.

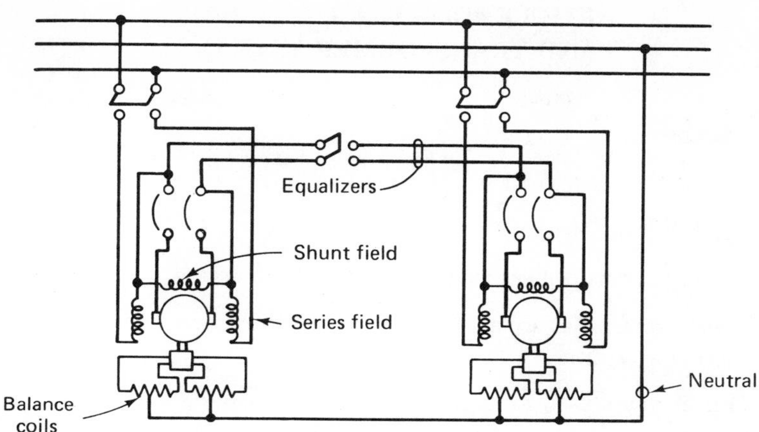

Fig. 460

Overcurrent protection for three-wire DC generators operating in parallel, using two-pole circuit breakers as the overcurrent device. With connections as shown, it can be seen that the circuit breakers take the entire current from the generator armature, as required by Sect. 445-4(e). Circuit breakers must have a trip coil in each lead. (Fuses are not permitted as overcurrent protection for three-wire DC generators.)

Exception No. 2

Where an integral overcurrent device is provided by the manufacturer, with leads connected to the device.

445-6. Protection of Live Parts

445-7. Guards for Attendants

When generators operate at more than 150 volts to ground, no live parts shall be exposed to contact by "unqualified" persons.

Section 430-133 requires insulating mats or platforms around motors. These are required for generators when the generator voltage is more than 150 to ground.

445-8. Bushings

Bushings shall be provided for the holes in the terminal housing.

ARTICLE 450 — TRANSFORMERS AND TRANSFORMER VAULTS

450-1. Scope

Article 450 applies to all transformers except:

1. Current transformers.
2. Dry-type transformers that are a part of apparatus.
3. Transformers that are a part of X-ray, high-frequency, or electrostatic-coating apparatus.
4. Transformers used for signal and control purposes.
5. Transformers used for sign and outline lighting.
6. Transformers for electric-discharge lighting.
7. Transformers used for power-limited fire-protective signaling.
8. Transformers used for research development, where effective safeguards are provided to prevent contact by persons with high-voltage terminals.

Some examples of the above transformers are:

1. Transformers used in connection with voltmeters, ammeters, on a switchboard.
2. Transformers used with welding machines.
3. Transformers for bell ringing.

Generally speaking, the rules of this Article are intended for power transformers, transformers that supply circuits feeding motors, lighting, appliances, etc.

A. General Provisions

450-2. Location

Transformers shall be located where "readily accessible" to qualified personnel for inspection and maintenance. If it were necessary to use a ladder to get to a transformer, it would not be considered readily accessible. See definition of "readily accessible," under Definitions, p. 70-12 of the Code.

There are two exceptions to the "accessibility" rule:

1. For dry-type transformers not over 600 volts, located on open walls. These need not be "readily accessible."

2. Dry-type transformers not over 600 volts and 50 kVA may be installed in fire-resistant hollow spaces of buildings. The transformers cannot be permanently closed in; there must be some access to the transformers although they need not be "readily" accessible.

Note that the two exceptions are for *dry*-type transformers. The exceptions do not apply for oil- or askarel-filled transformers.

450-3. Overcurrent Protection

There are two sets of rules for overcurrent protection of transformers: rules for transformers over 600 volts, and rules for transformers of 600 volts or less.

(a) Transformers over 600 Volts

1. The general rule is that the overcurrent device (fuse or circuit breaker) be in the primary side at the transformer. However, the feeder fuse or circuit breaker, if properly sized, may serve as transformer protection.

   Maximum permissible fuse size is 150% of rated primary current (or the next standard fuse size above 150%).

   Maximum permissible circuit-breaker setting is 300% of rated primary current.

2. Protection may be in the secondary side only, provided the rating of the fuse protecting the *primary feeder* is not over three times rated primary current, or, for a circuit breaker, six times rated primary current.

3. When protection is in the secondary side, the secondary fuse size or circuit-breaker setting may be 250% of current rating, for secondaries 600 volts or under. For secondaries of over 600 volts, maximum permissible fuse rating is 150%, maximum circuit-breaker setting 300%.

(b) Transformers 600 Volts or Less

1. The general rule is that the overcurrent device (fuse or circuit breaker) be in the primary side near the transformer. However, the feeder fuse or circuit breaker, if properly sized, may serve as the transformer overcurrent protection.

   Maximum permissible primary fuse size or circuit breaker setting is as follows:

For transformers having rated primary current of less than 2 amps.: 300% of rated primary current.

For transformers having rated primary current between 2 and 9 amps.: 167% of rated primary current.

For transformers having rated primary current of 9 amps. or more: 125% of rated primary current, or the next standard fuse size or circuit-breaker setting above 125% [Fig. 461(b)(c)].

2. Protection may be in the secondary side only, provided the fuse size or circuit breaker setting protecting the *primary* feeder is not over $2\frac{1}{2}$ times rated primary current.

3. When protection is in the secondary side, permissible fuse size or circuit-breaker setting is as follows:

   For transformers having rated secondary current less than 9 amps.: 167% of rated secondary current.

   For transformers having rated secondary current of 9 amps. or more: 125% of rated secondary current, or the next standard fuse size or circuit breaker setting above 125% [Fig. 461(a)].

4. Some transformers are equipped with overload protection by the manufacturer. In this case, primary protection can be omitted if the fuse size or circuit-breaker setting protecting the primary feeder is not more than six times rated primary current of the transformer.

Examples.

1. A 480/120-volt, 10-kVA transformer, tapped to a circuit fused at 45 amps.

   Rated primary current is

$$\frac{10{,}000}{480} = 20.8 \text{ amps.}$$

The circuit fusing of 45 amps, is less than $2\frac{1}{2}$ times the primary current rating; therefore, fusing at the transformer may be in the secondary side if desired.

Rated secondary current is

$$\frac{10{,}000}{120} = 83.2 \text{ amps.}$$

$$125\% \times 83.2 = 104 \text{ amps.}$$

A 110-amp. fuse or circuit breaker setting may be used in the secondary side.

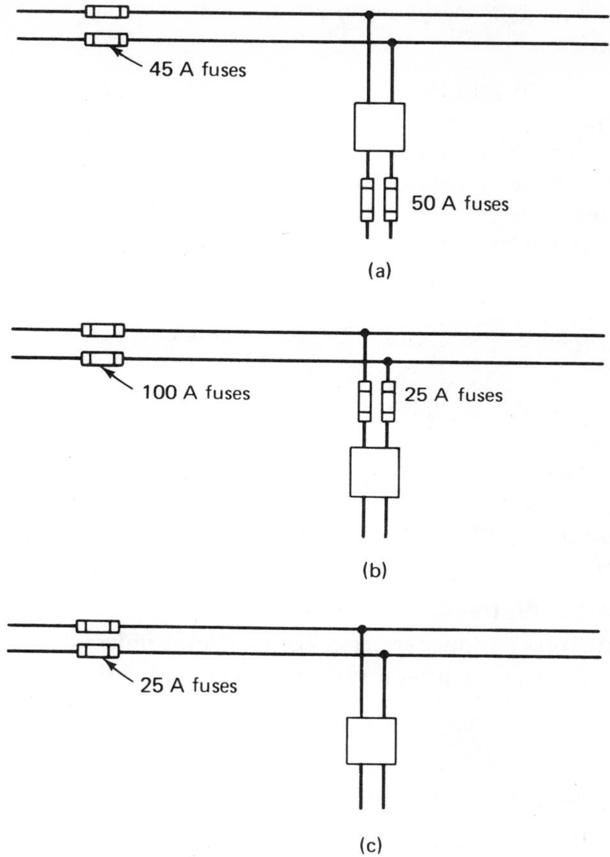

Fig. 461
Overcurrent protection for transformers (Sect. 450-3). In the examples above, the transformer is assumed to be a 480/240-V transformer, rated primary current 20 amps., rated secondary current 40 amps.

(a) Feeder fusing is less than $2\frac{1}{2}$ times primary current rating. Transformer protection may be in secondary side, and may be 125% of secondary current rating.
(b) Feeder fusing more than $2\frac{1}{2}$ times primary current rating. Transformer protection must be in primary side, and may be 125% of primary current rating.
(c) Feeder fusing of 25 amps. properly protects the transformer primary winding. No further protection required.

Or fusing may be at the transformer in the primary side only. Fuse size may be

$$125\% \times 20.8 = 26 \text{ amps.}$$

A 30-amp. primary fuse or circuit breaker setting would be permitted.

2. A 480/120-volt, 10-kVA transformer tapped to a circuit fused at 100 amps.

   Here the circuit fusing of 100 amps. is over $2\frac{1}{2}$ times the primary rated current; therefore, individual primary fusing is required for the transformer.

   Rated primary current is 20.8 amps.

$$125\% \times 20.8 = 26 \text{ amps.}$$

   A 30-amp. fuse or circuit breaker setting may be used in the primary side.

3. A 480/120-volt, 10-kVA transformer, tapped to a circuit fused at 25 amps.

   Here the primary is properly protected by the 25-amp. circuit fuse since the circuit fuse size is not over 125% of primary rated current of 20.8 amps. No further protection is required for this transformer.

(c) Potential (Voltage) Transformers

Potential (voltage) transformers, when installed indoors, must have fuses in the primary side. (Potential transformers are used with voltmeters, ammeters, etc.)

450-4. Grounding Autotransformers

(a) Three-Phase Four-Wire System

Autotransformers are single winding transformers, the single winding being common to both the primary and secondary circuits. To reduce the voltage, the primary is connected across the full winding, and the secondary across part of the winding. To boost the voltage, the primary circuit is connected across part of the winding, the secondary across the full winding.

Autotransformers are used when it is desired to derive a three-phase, four-wire grounded distribution system from a three-phase, three-wire ungrounded distribution system. This may be accomplished by star connecting three autotransformers (or one three-phase autotransformer) to the three-phase ungrounded circuit. A phase lead is brought out from each autotransformer, and the common junction of the three autotransformers provides the fourth wire, which may be grounded (Fig. 462). The voltage between phase conductors of the grounded system can be made either higher or lower than that of the ungrounded circuit, depending on the point of connection within the transformers. Autotransformers have been used in this way to transform

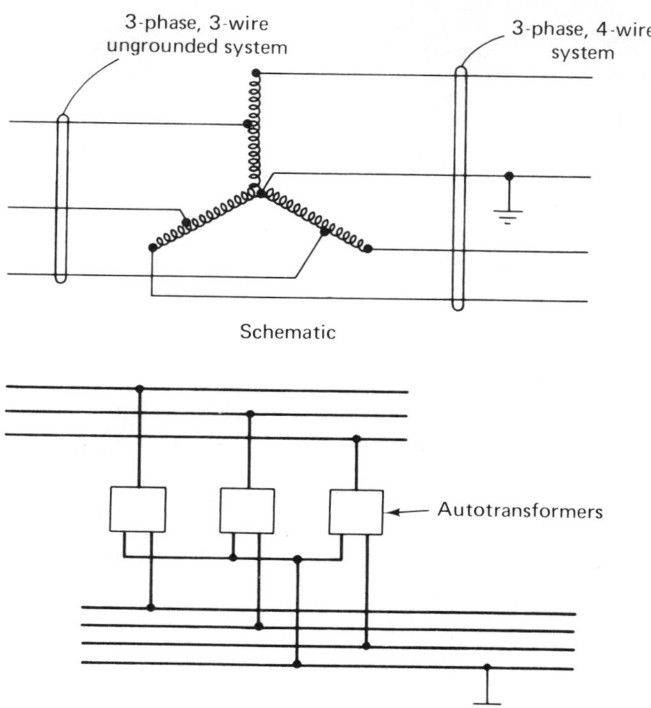

Fig. 462
Autotransformers connected to a three-phase, three-wire ungrounded system for the purpose of creating a three-phase, four-wire distribution system.

from a 2,300-volt, three-phase, three-wire circuit, to a 4,000Y/2,300-volt, three-phase, four-wire circuit.

The following rules apply for autotransformers so connected:

1. Transformers shall be directly connected to the ungrounded system. Switches or overcurrent protection between connection and autotransformer are not permitted.

2. Overcurrent protection in the form of a sensing device must be provided. The sensing device shall be set to trip at 125% of rated current in phase wire or in neutral.

3. A sensing system shall be provided to guard against single phasing or internal transformer faults.

4. Autotransformers shall have a continuous neutral current rating sufficient to handle the maximum possible unbalance on the four-wire system.

(b) Ground Reference for Fault Protection Devices

In addition to being used to provide distribution systems, autotransformers are used for the purpose of providing a means of detecting grounds on three-phase, three-wire systems. The transformers are star connected to the three-phase, three-wire system, and the common junction of the star connection is grounded. The transformers carry no appreciable current except when an accidental ground occurs on one of the phase wires. The current caused by the ground can be made to operate a protective device.

The following rules apply for autotransformers used for ground detection:

1. Autotransformers shall have a neutral continuous current rating sufficient to handle any ground-fault current that might be imposed on it.
2. An overcurrent protective device shall be provided. The protective device shall be set to trip at not over 125% of autotransformer phase current rating, or 42% of the rating of any protective device connected in the autotransformer ground connection.

(c) Ground Reference for Damping Transitory Overvoltages

Connections shall be as per (a)(1) above.

450-5. Secondary Ties

In large industrial plants a "network" distribution system is sometimes used for power loads. Three-phase banks of transformers are located at various points in the plant. There are usually two high-tension primary circuits feeding the transformers. A double throw switch at each transformer bank permits either primary circuit to feed any bank of transformers. The primary circuit conductors are sized large enough so that either circuit can carry the entire load if a fault develops in the other. Secondary voltage is usually 480 volts, three-phase. The transformer secondaries are joined together in a "network system," whereby all transformers share in feeding all loads.

The conductors connecting the transformer secondaries together are secondary ties.

Secondary ties must be protected at both ends. The protection may be by fuses, according to the current-carrying capacity of the conductors [Section 450-5(a)], or the ties may be protected by a "limiter" at each end [Section 450-5(a)(3)]. A limiter protects against short circuit, but does not protect against overload. Usually, limiters, rather than fuses, are used for protection of the ties.

When limiters only are used as protection, the following rules apply:

1. When all loads are connected to the tie at the point of a transformer connection to the tie, ampacity of the tie shall be at least 67% of rated secondary current of the largest transformer connected to the tie.
2. When any load is connected to the tie at a point *between* transformer connections to the tie, the ampacity of the tie shall be at least 100% of rated secondary current of the largest transformer connected to the tie.

There is usually a load center connected to the tie at the point where a transformer bank connects to the tie. The transformers would be protected by a circuit breaker in the secondary leads between the transformer and the load center. Circuit-breaker setting may be up to 250% of transformer secondary current rating [Section 450-5(b)]. In addition, a reverse power relay must be provided [Section 450-5(b)], which will open the circuit in case the transformer should go "dead." A reverse power relay is necessary to prevent current being fed to an incapacitated transformer from the other transformers of the network in such an emergency (see Fig. 463). When the secondary voltage is more than 150 to ground, ties must be provided with a switch at each end [Section 450-5(a)(5)].

Transformer, as used above, refers to a three-phase transformer. If a bank of three single-phase transformers is used, the secondary current rating would be the current rating of the bank of transformers, not the current rating of any one transformer of the bank.

450-6 Parallel Operation

Two or more transformers may be operated in parallel to serve the same load (this is the case above). All the transformers should have the same voltage regulation and impedance characteristics. One switch may serve all transformers, but each transformer must have proper overcurrent protection.

450-7. Guarding

Where transformers are so located as to be exposed to possible damage, they shall be suitably protected.

Where there is a possibility of injury to persons from contact with live transformer parts, suitable protective provisions should be made. Section 110-17 specifies the following, as suitable provisions:

1. Locating in a room accessible only to qualified persons.

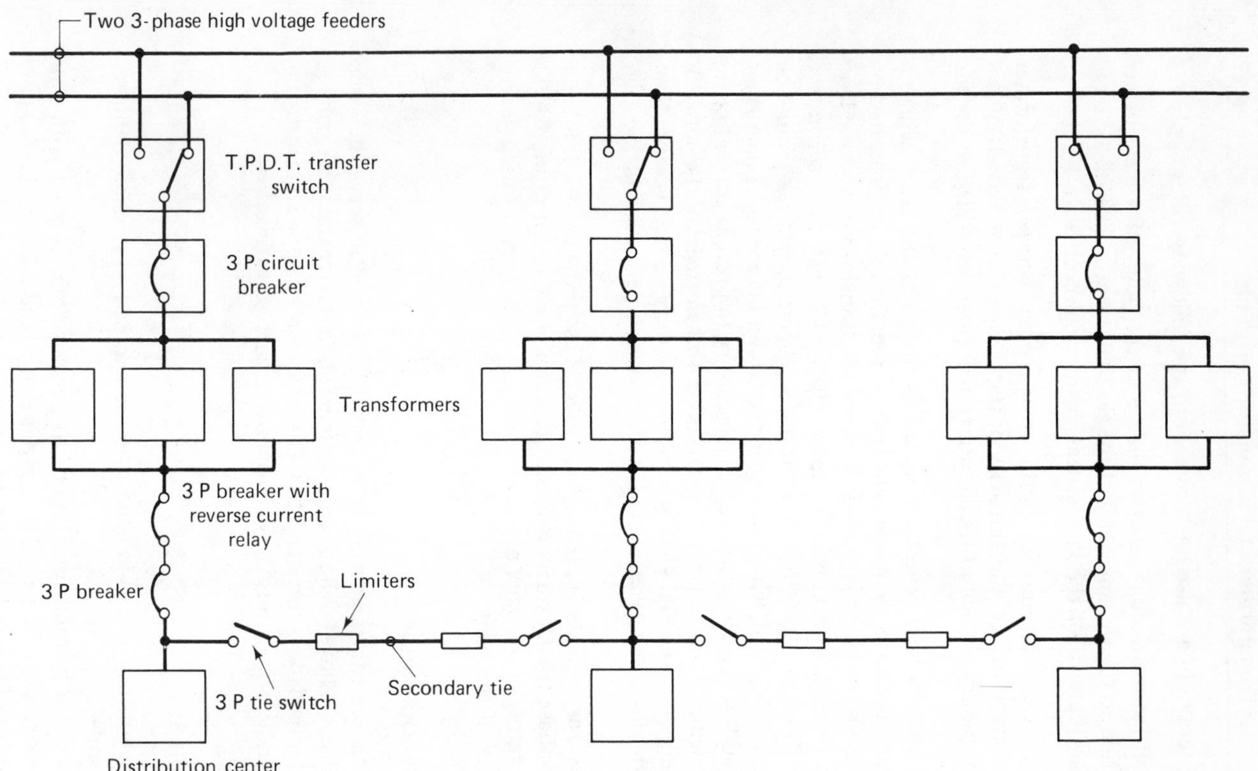

Fig. 463

Network distribution system for power loads. There are two circuit breakers in the secondary leads; one is a reverse power breaker, the other provides transformer overcurrent protection, both of which are required by Sect. 450-5(b). Limiters, at each end, provide tie circuit protection. Tie disconnect switches are also provided [Sect. 450-5(a)(5)].

Since there are no loads between the distribution centers, the secondary ties may be sized to carry 67% of the rated secondary current of the largest *bank* of transformers connected to the system [Sect. 450-5(a)(1)].

2. Providing permanent partitions or screens.

3. Elevating at least 8 ft above the floor.

450-8. Ventilation

Transformers shall be so located that there will be sufficient cool air to prevent overheating. They should not be installed in locations subject to abnormally high temperatures.

450-9. Grounding

Grounding of a transformer case would be required under any of the conditions set down in Section 250-42. Fences and guards around transformers are also required to be grounded.

450-10 Marking

Transformer nameplates must list the following:

1. Manufacturer's name.

2. kVA rating.

3. Frequency.

4. Primary and secondary voltage.

B. Specific Provisions Applicable to Different Types of Transformers

450-21. Dry-Type Transformers Installed Indoors

1. Dry-type transformers of more than $112\frac{1}{2}$ kVA, having Class B or Class H insulation, shall have a fire-resistant heat-insulating barrier between transformers and combustible material, or, if no barrier, shall be separated at least 6 ft horizontally and 12 ft vertically from the combustible material.

2. Dry-type transformers of more than $112\frac{1}{2}$ kVA, having other types of insulation, shall be installed in a fire-resistant transformer room.

3. Dry-type transformers rated $112\frac{1}{2}$ kVA or less shall have a fire-resistant heat-insulating barrier between transformers and combustible material, or, if no barrier, shall be separated at least 12 in. from the combustible material if voltage is over 600.

4. Dry-type transformers rated $112\frac{1}{2}$ kVA or less, and 600 volts or less, need not have a 12-in. separation or barrier if completely enclosed except for vent openings.
5. All indoor dry-type transformers of over 35,000 volts shall be installed in a vault.

450-22. Dry-Type Transformers Installed Outdoors

Dry-type transformers installed outdoors must have weatherproof enclosures.

(There is a difference between "weatherproof" and "watertight." See Definitions, p. 70-14 of the Code.)

450-23. High Fire Point Liquid-Insulated Transformers

Transformers using a high "fire-point" liquid may be installed indoors. The Code sets the minimum fire-point at 300°C (572 F). This would be the minimum temperature at which the transformer liquid would ignite. The Code requires that the liquid shall be "nonpropagating," that is, a type liquid that, should it ignite, will not induce the spread of fire beyond the liquid. Transformers meeting these requirements may be installed indoors, for voltages up to 35,000. Higher voltages require a vault.

450-24. Askarel-Insulated Transformers Installed Indoors

Askarel is a liquid that will not burn; therefore, it is safer than oil as a transformer liquid. However, arcing in askarel produces gases (nonexplosive gases).

Askarel-insulated transformers of over 25 kVA must be furnished with a relief vent to relieve the pressure built up by gases that may be generated within the transformer.

In well-ventilated rooms, the vent may discharge directly to the room.

In poorly ventilated rooms, the vent must be piped to a flue or chimney that will carry the gases out of the room. Or, as an alternative, the transformer can be fitted with a gas absorber placed inside the case. When there is a gas absorber, the vent may discharge to the room.

Askarel transformers of more than 35,000 volts must be installed in a vault.

450-25. Oil-Insulated Transformers Installed Indoors

1. Indoor oil-filled transformers of over 600 volts must be installed in a vault, with the following exceptions, where, regardless of voltage, a vault is not required:

Electric furnace transformers with a total rating of 75 kVA or less may be located in a fire-resistant room.

Oil-filled transformers may be installed in a building without a vault, provided the building is accessible to qualified persons only, and used solely for providing electric service to other buildings.

2. If suitable provisions are made to prevent a possible oil fire from igniting other materials, oil-filled transformers of 600 volts or less may be installed without a vault. When installed without a vault, the total kVA of all transformers permitted in a room (or section of a building) is limited to 10 kVA for non-fire-resistant buildings, 75 kVA for fire-resistant buildings.

450-26. Oil-Insulated Transformers Installed Outdoors

When oil-filled transformers are installed on or adjacent to combustible buildings or material, the building or material shall be safeguarded from possible fire originating in a transformer. Fire-resistant barriers, water-spray systems, and enclosures for the transformers are approved safeguards.

C. Transformer Vaults

450-41. Location

Wherever possible, transformer vaults shall be located at an outside wall of the building. This will permit ventilation direct to the outside without using ducts or flues.

450-42. Walls, Roof, and Floor

This Section sets the rules for construction of vaults. Floor, walls, and roof must be of fire-resistive material, such as concrete, and able to withstand heat from a fire within for at least three hours. A 6 in. thickness is specified for the walls and roof. The floor, when laid on earth, must be at least 4 in. thick.

450-43. Doorways

The door to a transformer vault must be built according to the standards of the National Fire Protection Association.

The door sill must be at least 4 in. high. This is to prevent any oil that may accumulate on the floor from running out of the transformer room.

Doors must be kept locked at all times to prevent access of unqualified persons to the vault.

450-45. Ventilation Openings

Where ventilation is direct to the outside, without the use of ducts or flues, the vent opening must have an area of at least 3 square inches for each kVA of transformer capacity, but never less than 1 square foot in area.

The vent opening must be fitted with a screen or grating, and also with an automatic closing damper made of at least No. 10 MSG steel.

If ducts are used in the vent system, the ducts must have sufficient capacity to maintain a suitable vault temperature.

450-46. Drainage

Drains should be provided to drain off oil that might accumulate on the floor due to an accidental leak in a transformer.

450-47. Water Pipes and Accessories

Piping for fire protection within the vault or piping to water-cooled transformers may be present in a vault. No other piping or duct system may enter or pass through a vault except by special permission. Valves or other fittings of a foreign piping or duct system are never permitted in a vault.

450-48. Storage in Vaults

Nothing of any kind may be kept in a vault other than the transformers and equipment necessary to their operation.

ARTICLE 460 — CAPACITORS

Three-phase induction motors draw a current that is out of phase with the line voltage; the current always lags behind the voltage. A lagging current in the line is undesirable to the power company, because with a lagging current less power can be delivered by the line. This means less revenue for the power company.

For this reason, the power company may impose penalty charges against a plant having a lagging current. It is therefore sometimes to the advantage of the plant to correct the condition of lagging current (which is also called low-power factor). By connecting capacitors to the line, the current can be brought more nearly "in phase" with the line voltage. Capacitors draw a leading current from the line, i.e., the current leads the voltage. This leading current counteracts the effect of the lagging current drawn by the motors, and raises the power factor of the plant. Capacitors draw current, but consume no power.

Capacitors are used in this way chiefly by larger industrial plants that have a great many induction motors in use. Small plants with relatively few motors might not realize enough saving on electric bills to warrant the expense of installing capacitors for power factor correction. Larger concerns, however, can often save enough money on reduced electric bills to make the investment in capacitors worthwhile.

Small capacitors can be connected to the line at each individual motor, or larger capacitors can be connected to the line near the service entrance and serve the whole group of motors. In any event, the power factor will be improved, and, for a given load, the current in the line will consequently be reduced up to the point where the capacitors are connected.

460-2. Enclosing and Guarding

Most capacitors may be installed in any convenient location, but capacitors containing over 3 gallons of *combustible* oil (not askarel) must be in a vault or outdoor fenced enclosure.

Capacitors shall be enclosed, located, or guarded so that persons cannot accidentally contact live parts.

A. Under 600 Volts Nominal

460-6. Drainage of Stored Charge

(a) Time of Discharge

(b) Means of Discharge

A capacitor will "hold" a charge after it is disconnected from the line. There will still be a voltage at the terminals of the capacitor after the capacitor is disconnected, and anyone coming in contact with live parts could be subjected to a dangerous shock.

For this reason, a means must be provided for drawing off the charge immediately after the capacitor is disconnected. This can be done by connecting a high resistance across the capacitor terminals. This will in no way affect the efficiency of the capacitor, except that the high resistance will draw a very small current from the line. When the capacitor is disconnected, its charge will drain off through the resistance. Note that a time limit of one minute is set for discharging a capacitor (down to 50 volts or less). The length of time required to drain the charge will depend upon the size of the resistance. The higher the resistance, the greater the length of time required for drainage.

460-7. Power Factor Correction—Motor Circuit

Capacitors are rated in kVAr, usually shortened to kVA. The maximum kVA ratings permitted for capacitors connected to motors of different sizes are not listed in the Code, but this information can be obtained from tables compiled by the motor manufacturers.

460-8. Conductors

(a) The conductors feeding a capacitor must have a current-carrying capacity of at least 135% of the current rating of the capacitor, and when the capacitor serves a motor, the capacitor leads must be at least $\frac{1}{3}$ the size of the motor leads.

Capacitors are usually used on three-phase lines, and the following examples will show how to figure conductor sizes for three-phase capacitors.

1. A 4-kVA capacitor is connected to the individual circuit of a 10-hp, 230-volt, three-phase squirrel-cage motor. What is the minimum size Type T conductor permitted for wiring the capacitor? The motor leads are No. 8 Type T.

$$4 \text{ kVA} = 4{,}000 \text{ volt amps.}$$

Rated current of the capacitor would be

$$\frac{4{,}000}{230 \times 1.73} = 10 \text{ amps.}$$

$$135\% \text{ of } 10 = 1.35 \times 10 = 13.5 \text{ amps.}$$

This amperage would require a No. 14 Type T conductor (Table 310-16, p. 70-132). The motor leads are No. 8, with a carrying capacity of 40 amps. No. 14 has a carrying capacity of 15 amps., which is more than $\frac{1}{3}$ of 40; therefore, No. 14 Type T conductors would satisfy both parts of this rule.

2. A 10-kVA capacitor is connected to the circuit of a 40-hp, 230-volt, three-phase motor. What is the minimum size Type T conductor permitted for wiring the capacitor? The motor leads are No. 2/0 Type T.

Rated current of the capacitor is

$$\frac{10{,}000}{230 \times 1.73} = 25.1 \text{ amps.}$$

$$1.35 \times 25.1 = 33.8 \text{ amps.}$$

This amperage would require a No. 8 conductor which carries 40 amps. The motor leads are No. 2/0 with a carrying capacity of 145 amps. $\frac{1}{3}$ of 145 is 49 amps., which would be the minimum carrying capacity of the capacitor leads to satisfy the "$\frac{1}{3}$" rule. No. 8 could not be used in this case. A No. 6 with a carrying capacity of 55 amps. would have to be used.

(b) Overcurrent Protection

A capacitor must have overcurrent protection, the same as any other piece of equipment. If the capacitor is connected to the line on the load side of the motor overcurrent protection, the motor overcurrent protection may serve as protection for the capacitor.

Otherwise, the capacitor must be individually protected by fuses or a circuit breaker in the capacitor circuit. The rule says that "the rating or setting of the overcurrent device shall be as low as practicable." The intent is to allow an overcurrent rating just high enough to prevent unnecessary opening of the circuit. It should be remembered that capacitors draw a momentary high inrush current when connected to the line.

Under average conditions, a rating or setting of 160 to 250% of the capacitor current rating should be satisfactory.

(c) Disconnecting Means

A capacitor must have a disconnect switch. If the capacitor is connected on the load side of the motor disconnect, then the motor disconnect can serve also as the capacitor disconnect.

Otherwise, an individual disconnect must be provided. The rating of the disconnect switch must be at least 135% of the current rating of the capacitor. For the capacitor of example No. 2, above, the switch rating must be at least $1.35 \times 25.1 = 33.8$ amps. If a knife switch is used, a 60-amp. knife switch would be required.

460-9. Rating or Setting of Motor-Running Overcurrent Device

This Section applies only when a capacitor is installed on the load side of the motor-running protection. Usually, the motor-running protection is in the controller, so that this rule would apply generally for capacitors connected on the load side of the controller.

When a capacitor is connected in a motor circuit, the current drawn from the line will be reduced up to the point of connection of the capacitor. If the capacitor is "behind" the controller, the current through the controller will be reduced. If the overload protection is in the controller, the current through the overload device will also be reduced.

Example.

If a 5-kVA capacitor is connected on the load side of a controller for a 15-hp, 230-volt, three-phase motor, the current through the controller will be reduced by 11%.

Assuming a motor full-load current rating of 40 amps., running overload protection for the motor may be rated at 125% of 40 = 50 amps.

A 50-amp. overcurrent device would be used, if there were no capacitor.

With a capacitor, the current through the controller will be reduced from 40 amps. to 35.6 amps., and for this current, the running overload protection would be rated at 125% of 35.6 = 44.5 amps. 45-amp. overload protection would be used, rather than the 50 amps. The reduction in size of the overload protection is required by the Code (see Fig. 464).

460-10. Grounding

All metal capacitor cases must be grounded in accordance with the rules of Article 250.

Exception.

Where the capacitor units are supported on a structure that is designed to operate at other than ground potential.

460-12. Marking

This Section requires the manufacturer to provide a nameplate on capacitors, and lists the information that must be given on the nameplate: voltage, frequency, kVAr, phase, type of liquid, etc.

B. Over 600 Volts Nominal

460-24. Switching

(a) One switch may serve for a group of capacitors. The switch must:

1. Have a continuous current rating not less than 135% of the sum of the rated currents of all capacitors of the group.
2. Have an interrupting capacity sufficient to interrupt the total rated current.
3. Be able to withstand the inrush current.
4. Be able to carry any fault currents.

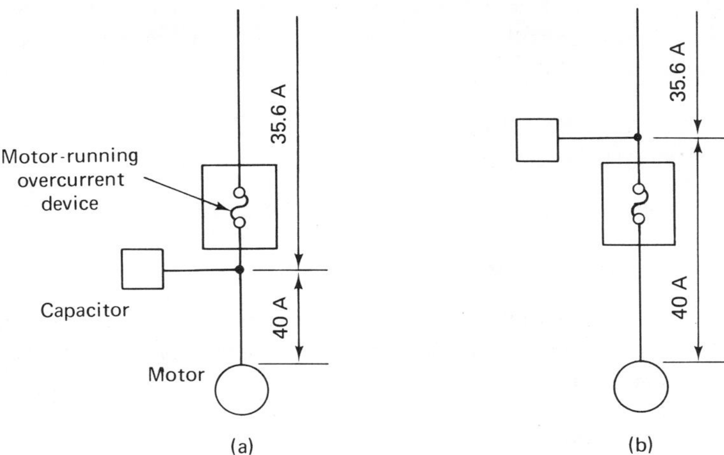

Fig. 464
A capacitor connected to a motor circuit reduces the current in the line up to the point of connection of the capacitor.

(a) Capacitor is connected on the load side of the motor-running overcurrent device, reducing the current through the overcurrent device to a value less than motor current. Rating of overcurrent device must be figured on a basis of the reduced current, in this case 35.6 amps. (Sect. 460-9).

(b) Capacitor is connected on the line side of the overcurrent device. Rating of the overcurrent device is figured on a basis of full motor current (40 amps).

Capacitors draw an excessive current at the instant of connection to the line. This is the "inrush" current, which is many times greater than the load current. The switch must be able to "make" the high inrush current without damage to itself.

(b) If a group of capacitors is intended to operate at times with one or more capacitors out of the circuit, such capacitors must be provided with "isolating" switches to remove them from service. Isolating switches are not intended to interrupt current, and as such would not have the interrupting capacity to permit opening under load. An isolating switch would be opened only after the circuit has been killed by the main switch.

Isolating switches must be interlocked with the main switch so that an isolating switch cannot be opened until the main switch is opened. Or, as an alternative, warning signs may be posted at the isolating switch locations warning against opening under load.

(c) Capacitors are sometimes connected in series. When this is done, a means must be provided to assure the proper switching sequence. This can be done:

1. Through mechanically sequenced bypass switches.
2. Through interlocks.
3. By using prominent signs showing the proper switching procedure.

460-25. Overcurrent Protection

High-voltage capacitors must be provided with fault current interrupting devices. One device may serve for a group of capacitors, or each may have individual protection.

460-26. Identification

The manufacturer is required to mark each capacitor with maker's name, rated voltage, frequency, kVAr or amperes, and amount of liquid required.

460-27. Grounding

Grounding shall be in accordance with Article 250.

460-28. Means for Discharge

A means must be provided for draining off the charge immediately after a capacitor is disconnected from the line. This can be done by connecting a high resistance across the capacitor terminals. When the capacitor is disconnected, its charge will drain off through the resistance. The time required to drain the charge will depend upon the size of the resistance. The greater the resistance, the longer the time required. The Code requires that the capacitor be drained down to a residual voltage of 50 volts or less within 5 minutes after disconnecting.

ARTICLE 470 — RESISTORS AND REACTORS

A. 600 Volts Nominal and Under

One use of resistors would be in connection with speed control for motors. It will be remembered that the speed of wound-rotor motors is controlled by cutting resistances into or out of the rotor circuit of the motor. The cutting in and out of the resistances is accomplished by means of the controller.

Resistors usually come in the form of individual sections of grids made of a high-resistance metal. The individual sections of grids are bolted to a framework, in the field, to build up a resistance bank of the desired size. The grids are then connected together, and leads from the controller are connected at different points in the resistor bank. Thus, different values of resistance may be cut into the motor circuit to obtain the different motor speeds.

Resistors may also be used in a motor circuit simply for starting the motor, rather than for speed control.

Reactors are used in connection with larger generators. They are connected in series with the main generator leads to limit the current on short circuit. Reactors are coils, which, while having a comparatively small resistance, have a very large *reactance;* they block high-frequency alternating currents. Reactors are also used with lightning arresters to block the passage of high-frequency lightning discharges, thus directing the charge to ground through the grounding circuit. Small reactors are used as dimmers in connection with stage lighting.

470-2. Location

Resistors and reactors shall not be placed where exposed to physical damage.

470-3. Space Separation

Resistors and reactors must be separated from all combustible material by at least 12 in. or, if a 12-in. separation is not possible, thermal barriers (asbestos, for example) must be provided.

470-4. Conductor Insulation

Resistors produce considerable heat when they are in use. Insulated conductors used to wire resistors must have insulation suited to high temperatures. The Table of conductors on pp. 70-124 through 70-131 of the Code lists the various types of insulation, and gives the highest temperature for which each type of insulation is suited. Conductors used to wire resistors must have insulation suitable for temperatures of at least 194 degrees F. From the table, the following types of conductors would be suitable: Types RHH, THHN, AVA, AVL, AVB, SA. As can be seen, thermoplastic (Type T) insulation would not be permitted, as this insulation is good for temperatures only up to 140°F.

(Other insulation types are permitted where resistors are used only for motor *starting.* In this case, the resistors will be in use only during the short starting period, and not much heat will be generated. However, when the resistors are used for *speed control* of the motor, they will be in use for longer periods, and high temperature conductors would be required.)

B. Over 600 Volts Nominal

470-18. General

1. Resistors and reactors shall be protected against physical damage.
2. Resistors and reactors shall be completely enclosed, or isolated by elevation to protect persons from accidental contact with live parts.
3. Resistors and reactors shall not be installed within 1 ft of combustible material.
4. Sufficient clearance shall be maintained between resistors or reactors and grounded objects.
5. Metallic enclosures and other metal parts shall be arranged so as not to create abnormally high temperatures that could constitute a fire hazard or a danger to personnel.

470-19. Grounding

Grounding shall be in accordance with Article 250.

470-20. Oil-Filled Reactors

The requirements of Article 450 for oil-filled transformers also apply to oil-filled reactors.

ARTICLE 480 — STORAGE BATTERIES

480-1. Scope

Article 480 applies for installations consisting of batteries of either the lead-acid or alkali type.

Lead-acid batteries use a dilute solution of sulphuric acid as the electrolyte. The positive plate is lead peroxide; the negative plate is composed of sponge lead. They are manufactured in 6-, 8-, and 12-volt sizes. Automobile batteries are lead-acid batteries.

The alkali-type battery uses a caustic soda solution as the electrolyte. In the nickel-iron alkali-type battery, the positive plate is made of nickel; the negative plate is of iron oxide. The open-circuit voltage of a nickel-iron cell is approximately 1.5 volts. These batteries are more rugged than the lead-acid type, but more expensive.

480-2. Definition of Nominal Battery Voltage

Batteries do not have a set voltage. The voltage of a battery at any particular time depends upon the state of charge, and the load on the battery. The voltage of a lead-acid battery may vary from 2.3 volts per cell down to 1.5 volts per cell, under different conditions. Since battery voltage is subject to fluctuations, a "nominal" voltage is used to designate battery voltage. Nominal voltage per cell is taken as 2 volts for the lead-acid type, 1.2 volts for the alkali type. Thus, a six-cell lead-acid battery is a 12-volt battery.

480-3. Wiring and Equipment Supplied from Batteries

Batteries are sometimes assembled in 120-volt banks to supply lighting and other loads. The wiring from battery banks is subject to Code rules for general wiring.

480-4. Grounding

Grounding shall be in accordance with Article 250.

480-5. Insulation of Batteries of Not Over 250 Volts

(a) Vented Lead–Acid Batteries

Lead-acid batteries with sealed, nonconductive heat-resistant containers do not require insulating supports. (The conventional automobile battery would be an example of such a battery.)

(b) Vented Alkaline-Type Batteries

Nickel-iron battery cells are sometimes contained in a steel container. Trays for these batteries are required to be of wood or other insulating material. If the sides and bottom of the container are glass or other nonconductive *and* heat-resistant material, the batteries may be installed on metal trays. The number of cells permitted in a tray is limited to 20 in series in any one tray, for batteries with steel containers.

(c) Rubber Jars

Cells in sealed rubber or composition containers need not have insulating supports if the voltage of the battery bank is 150 volts or less. If over 150 volts they must be supported on racks in groups of 150 volts or less.

(d) Sealed Cells or Batteries

Sealed batteries (or single cells) of "non-conductive, heat-resistant" material do not require insulating supports.

480-6. Insulation of Batteries of over 250 Volts

When the voltage of the battery bank is over 250 volts, it must be divided into banks of not over 250 volts and placed in racks.

480-7. Racks and Trays

Racks shall be of fiberglass, metal, or other suitable material. Metal racks must be provided with insulating material for supporting the cells.

Trays shall be resistant to deteriorating action by the electrolyte (sheet-lead resists the action of the electrolyte in lead-acid batteries).

480-8. Battery Locations

(a) Ventilation must be provided in battery rooms to carry off battery fumes.

(b) Guarding of live parts shall comply with Section 110-17.

480-9. Vents

Vented cells shall be equipped with a flame arrester. Nonvented cells shall be equipped with a pressure release vent.

Chapter 5. Special Occupancies

ARTICLE 500 — HAZARDOUS (CLASSIFIED) LOCATIONS

500-1. Scope—Articles 500 Through 503

Articles 500 through 503 deal with special locations—locations where (1) flammable gas or vapors, (2) combustible dust, or (3) ignitible fibers may be present in the air.

Such locations are divided by the Code into three classes:

Class I locations: flammable gas or vapor locations.

Class II locations: combustible dust locations.

Class III locations: ignitible fiber locations.

Class I locations include such locations as spray booths, gas generator rooms, and the area around the gasoline pumps in a service station.

Class II locations include such locations as feed mills, grain-processing plants, and coal-pulverizing plants.

Class III locations include such locations as rayon mills, cotton mills, and clothing manufacturing plants.

Unconfined arcing or sparking in hazardous atmospheres could result in an explosion or set off a damaging fire. Because of the hazards involved, the Code has special requirements applying to electrical installations in such locations. These requirements are set forth in Articles 501—503.

Garages and service stations are separately treated in Articles 511 and 514.

500-2. Special Precaution

Explosive gases/vapors are divided into four groups, A, B, C, and D. Group designations for the different gases/vapors are listed in Table 500-2, p. 70-350 of the Code. All of the listings in the table are (or produce) explosive gases or vapors, and fall in the Class I category.

Equipment used in a Class I hazardous location must be approved and marked for both the class and the group designation, according to the vapor or gas involved. For instance, gasoline is listed under Group D atmospheres. When the Code calls for equipment "approved for Class I locations," and gasoline vapors are involved, the equipment must be marked for use in Class I, Group D atmospheres.

Equipment for use in Class I hazardous locations must also be marked by the manufacturer with the operating temperature—the highest temperature that the piece of equipment will reach while operating. Operating temperature must of course be below the ignition temperature of the vapor involved. Groups A, B, and D vapors have ignition temperatures of 536°F. Group C vapors have an ignition temperature of 356°F.

Combustible dusts are divided into three groups: E, F, and G. Metal dusts (aluminum, magnesium) are Group E. Nonmetallic dusts (carbon black, charcoal, coke, coal dusts) are Group F. Grain, flour, and starch dusts are Group G. The three groups are in the Class II category. Equipment approved for Class II locations must be approved and marked for both the class and the group designation, according to the type of dust involved. Equipment for use in a location where coal dust is present, for example, must be marked for use in Class II, Group F atmospheres.

As with Class I locations, maximum operating temperature must also be marked on Class II approved equipment. Maximum operating temperatures for Class II equipment are given in Section 502-1 of the Code.

There are no group designations for Class III locations.

500-3. Specific Occupancies

Garages, aircraft hangars, service stations, bulk storage plants, finishing processes, and health-care facilities are separately treated in Articles 510 through 517.

500-4. Class I Locations

(a) Class I, Division 1

These are locations in which flammable gases or vapors are normally present, or may be present during repair operations, or because of leakage, or may be present because of breakdown or faulty operation of equipment.

(b) Class I, Division 2

These are locations in which flammable liquids or gases are in containers, and explosive vapors would not be present in the air except in case of an accident, such as breakage of a container.

500-5. Class II Locations

(a) Class II, Division 1

These are locations in which combustible *dusts* (including electrically conducting dusts such as magnesium or aluminum dusts) are normally present in the air, or *may* be present in the air because of machinery failure.

(b) Class II, Division 2

These are locations in which combustible dusts are not normally present in the air, but where such dusts may accumulate on electrical equipment to such an extent as to ignite or cause overheating of the equipment.

500-6. Class III Locations

(a) Class III, Division 1

These are locations in which ignitible *fibers* are handled, manufactured, or used.

(b) Class III, Division 2

These are locations in which ignitible fibers are stored or handled.

ARTICLE 501 — CLASS I LOCATIONS

501-1. General

In Class I locations, the rules of this Article (501) must be followed, as well as the general rules for wiring, as set forth in Chapters 2 and 3 of the Code.

501-2. Transformers and Capacitors

(a) Class I, Division 1

(1) *Containing a Liquid That Will Burn*

This rule is for oil-filled transformers and capacitors. The rule, in effect, forbids oil-filled transformers and capacitors to be installed in Class I, Division 1 locations. Oil-filled transformers and capacitors shall be installed only in approved vaults.

(2) *Not Containing a Liquid That Will Burn*

This rule applies for askarel-filled and dry-type transformers and capacitors. This type may be installed in Class I, Division 1 locations, but only if they are "approved for Class I locations."

(b) Class I, Division 2

Standard oil-filled, askarel-filled, and dry-type transformers may be installed in Class I, Division 2 locations, as long as the rules of Sections 450-21 through 450-26 are complied with.

501-3. Meters, Instruments, and Relays

(a) Class I, Division 1

Enclosures must be "approved for Class I, Division 1 locations."

(b) Class I, Division 2

(1) *Contacts*

This rule is for any make-and-break contact, such as a switch, circuit breaker, or pushbutton. In general, the contact enclosure must be "approved for Class I, Division 1 locations."

There are exceptions to this rule:

1. If the contacts are oil-immersed, or
2. Hermetically sealed, general-purpose enclosures are permitted.
3. For contacts interrupting very low currents, such as the voice contacts in a telephone, general-purpose enclosures are permitted.

(2) *Resistors and Similar Equipment*

Enclosures must be "approved for Class I, Division 1 locations."

Exception.

General-purpose enclosures may be used under the following circumstances:

1. If there are no sliding or make-and-break contacts, and
2. Maximum operating temperature of any exposed surface is not over 80% of the ignition temperature for the surrounding gas or vapor. (Maximum ignition temperature for Group C vapors is 356°F; for Groups A, B, and D vapors, it is 536°F.)

(3) *Without Make-or-Break Contacts*

Transformer windings, impedance coils, solenoids and similar windings installed in Class I, Division 2 locations may be the general-purpose type, if there are no sliding or make-and-break contacts incorporated in the equipment. If there are make-and-break contacts, the enclosures must be "approved for Class I, Division 1 locations."

(4) *General-Purpose Assemblies*

An assembly consisting of two or more of the different items listed in (1), (2), (3) above may have a general-purpose enclosure, provided that general-purpose enclosures are approved for each individual item, as per (1) (2) (3). For instance, if a fixed resistor and a transformer are together in one enclosure, the enclosure could be general purpose. If there were a switch or pushbutton also in the enclosure, the enclosure would have to be "approved for Class I, Division 1 locations," because of the switch.

(5) *Fuses*

This rule is for fuses that would be used for protection of instruments, such as voltmeters, and for the protection of the resistors, impedance coils, and solenoids mentioned above. Such equipment would usually be on a switchboard or panel. The fuses may be in general-purpose enclosures, provided:

1. That the instruments that the fuses are protecting are permitted to have general-purpose enclosures, and
2. Fuse rating is not over 3 amps. at 120 volts, and
3. A switch is placed in the circuit ahead of the fuse.

Otherwise, instrument fuses must have enclosures "approved for Class I, Division 1 locations."

(6) *Connections*

Process-control instruments may be connected by cord and plug, provided *all* the following requirements are fulfilled:

(a) A switch approved for Class I, Division 1 locations is provided.

(b) Current is not over 3 amps. at 120 volts.

(c) Cord is an extra-hard usage type (such as type S); or a hard-usage type (such as type SJ) with plug cap and receptacle of the locking-and-grounding-type, and protected.

(d) A sign is posted warning against unplugging under load.

(e) Cord is not over 3 ft long.

501-4. Wiring Methods

(a) Class I, Division 1

Three wiring methods are permitted in Class I, Division 1 locations:

1. Rigid *metal* conduit.

2. Type MI cable (mineral-insulated cable).

3. Threaded steel intermediate conduit.

Boxes and fittings must be explosion-proof. Explosion-proof boxes are always threaded; connectors are not permitted.

Short lengths of flexible cable are permitted where a flexible connection is required, but the flexible cable must be "approved for Class I locations."

(b) Class I, Division 2

In Class I, Division 2 locations, the following wiring methods are permitted:

1. Rigid *metal* conduit.

2. Enclosed gasketed busways.

3. Type MI cable (mineral-insulated cable).

4. Type MC cable (metal-clad power cable).

5. Threaded steel intermediate conduit.

6. Type SNM cable (shielded nonmetallic sheathed cable).

7. Type TC cable (power and control tray cable).

8. Type MV cable (Article 326).

9. Type PLTC cable (for remote control, signaling circuits).

Boxes, fittings, and joints need not be explosion-proof, but where a seal is required, the sealing fitting must be explosion-proof.

Cord or flexible conduit is permitted where a flexible connection is required. If cord is used, it must be an extra-hard usage type of cord, such as type S. Fittings must be an approved type.

501-5. Sealing and Drainage

Sealing is a very important part of electrical installations in hazardous locations. Where conduit enters a piece of equipment, such as a switch enclosure, a sealing fitting is inserted in the conduit run close to the switch. After the wires are pulled in, the fitting is filled with sealing compound. This closes off the opening in the conduit, isolating the switch from other parts of the wiring system. If the conduit were not sealed off, an explosion or ignition within the switch could travel along the conduit, causing damage at other outlets. Installations with improper sealing, or with a seal omitted, could present a potential danger to persons and property.

(a) Conduit Seals Class I, Division 1

(1) Seals must be placed in each conduit run entering the enclosure for

Switches

Circuit breakers

Fuses

Relays

Resistors

or any other device that could produce arcing, sparking, *or high temperature.* The seal must be no further than 18 in. from the enclosure.

(2) In each conduit run of *2-in.* or *larger* conduit, seals must be placed not only at the above enclosures, but also at junction boxes and fittings containing terminals, splices, or taps. The seal must be within 18 in. of the box or fitting.

(3) When a conduit run between two enclosures is 36 in. or less in length, one seal midway between the two would be 18 in. or less from either enclosure, and one seal may serve for both enclosures. See Fig. 510.

(4) A seal is required at the point in any conduit run where the conduit leaves a Class I, Division 1 area and passes to a nonhazardous area, or to a different class area, such as a Class I, Division 2 area. The seal does not have to be at the exact boundary of the hazardous area. It may be at a convenient point in the run on either side, but it is advisable to place

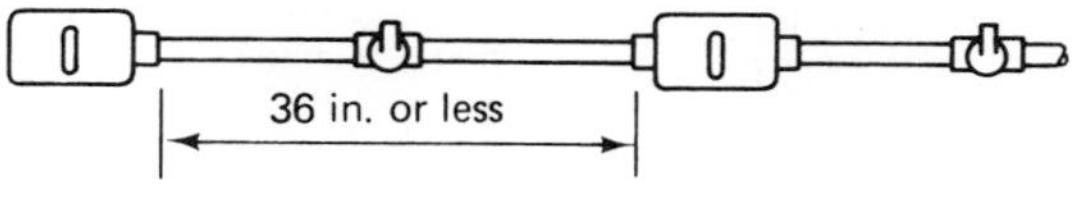

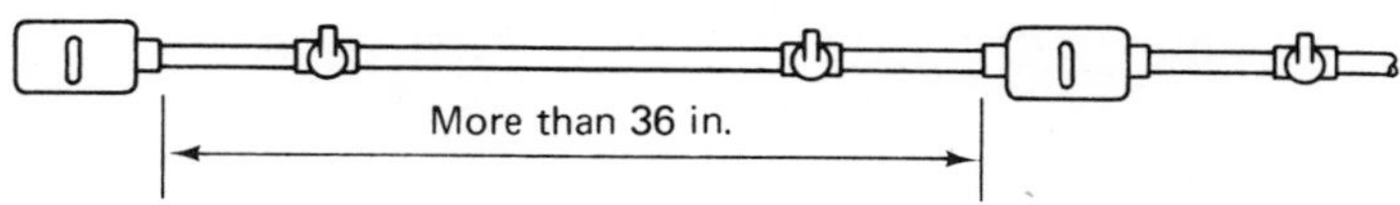

Fig. 510

Conduit seals [Sect. 501-5(a)]. One seal may serve two enclosures not more than 36 in. apart. For enclosures more than 36 in. apart separate seals are required for each enclosure. Seals in all cases shall be no farther than 18 in. from the enclosure.

the seal as near to the boundary as is practicable. Boxes, unions, couplings, or fittings are not permitted in the conduit run between the seal and the point where the conduit leaves the Class I, Division 1 area (Fig. 511).

An exception to the above is the case of a conduit run that simply "passes through" a Class I, Division 1 area from a *nonhazardous* area.

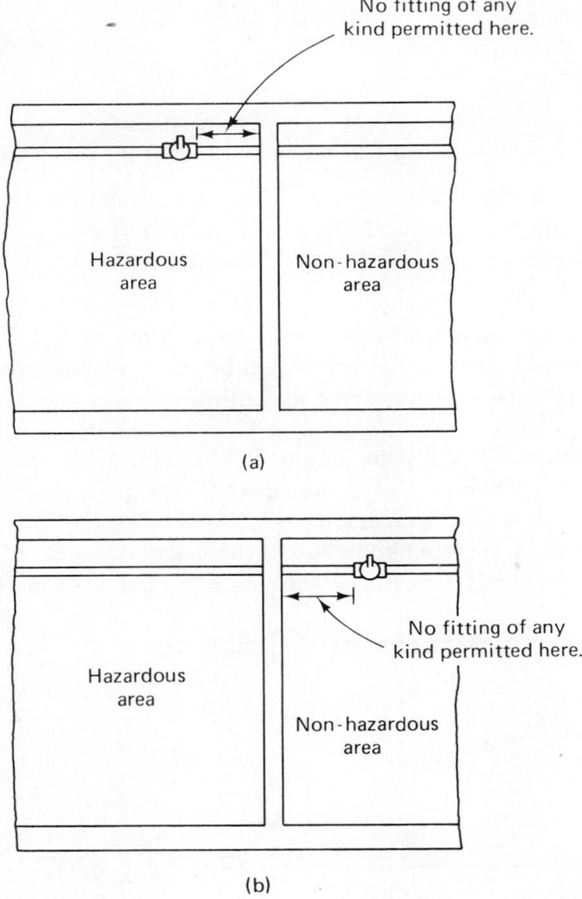

Fig. 511
Sealing for conduit runs leaving a Class I hazardous area (Sect. 501-5).

(a) Seal in hazardous area.
(b) Seal outside hazardous area.

Here no seal is required, provided the conduit run through (and 12 in. beyond) the hazardous area is without fittings (Fig. 512). Note that the area bounding the Class I, Division 1 area must be *nonhazardous.* If a conduit run "passes through" a Class I, Division 1 area from another kind of hazardous area, such as Class II or Class III, or Class I, Division 2, then a seal is always required.

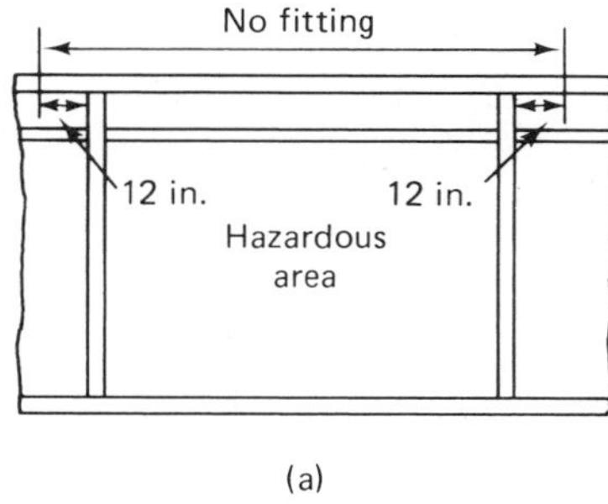

(a)

No fitting within, or 12 in. beyond the hazardous area.

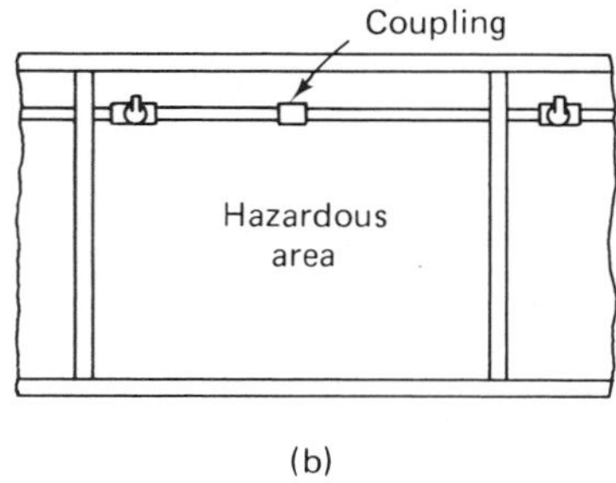

(b)

Fitting included in the run.

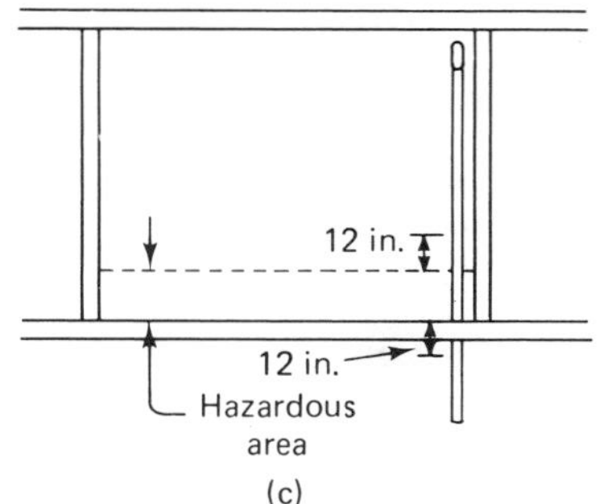

(c)

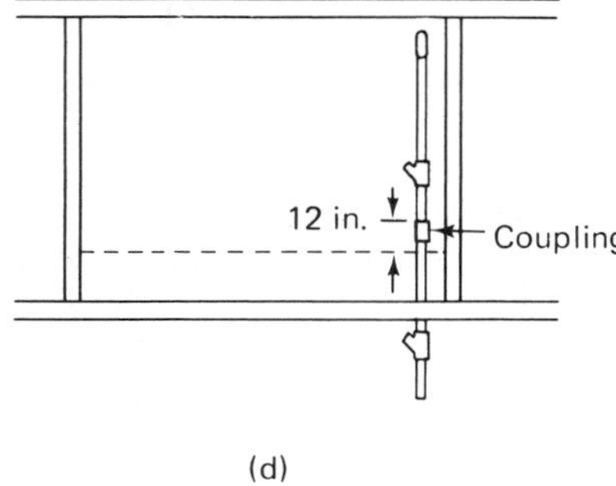

(d)

Fig. 512

Conduit passing through a Class I hazardous area.

(a) An unbroken run requires no seal.

(b) If there is a fitting in the run, seals must be provided. Seals may be inside or outside the hazardous area.

(c)(d) Conduit run through the Class I hazardous area of a commercial garage. In (c) the conduit is unbroken within and 12 in. beyond the hazardous boundary. No seal is required. In (d), the coupling within 12 in. of a boundary makes seals necessary.

(b) Conduit Seals, Class I, Division 2

(1) Sealing requirements are the same as for Class I, Division 1 locations, except that, for general-purpose type enclosures, sealing is not required. (In Division 2 locations, certain types of equipment may have general-purpose enclosures.)

(2) A seal is required at the point in a conduit run where the conduit leaves a Class I, Division 2 area and passes to a nonhazardous area. The seal does not have to be at the exact boundary of the hazardous area. It may be at a convenient point in the run, on either side, but it is advisable to place the seal as near to the boundary as practicable. Boxes, unions, couplings, or fittings are not permitted in the conduit run between the seal and the point where the conduit leaves the Class I, Division 2 area.

An exception to the above is the case of a conduit run that simply "passes through" a Class I, Division 2 area from a nonhazardous area. Here no seal is required, provided the conduit run through (and 12 in. beyond) the hazardous area is without fittings.

(c) Class I, Divisions 1 and 2

(1) Sealing fittings must be "approved for Class I locations."

(2) Sealing compound must be "approved for the purpose."

(3) Thickness of the seal must be not less than the trade size of the conduit, but never less than $\frac{5}{8}$ in.

(4) Splices or taps are not permitted in sealing fittings. Boxes having splices shall not be filled with compound.

(5) Assemblies shall be "approved for Class I locations."

(d) Cable Seals, Class I, Division 1

Impervious sheathed cable could confine a hazardous gas or vapor within the cable. If such gas or vapor is capable of traveling along the cable, the cable shall be sealed, as though it were a conduit.

When cables without an impervious sheath are run in conduit, the cable shall be sealed, and, for sealing purposes, treated as a single conductor.

(e) Cable Seals, Class I, Division 2

Seals for cables shall be at the point of entrance to the enclosure. Sealing compound shall surround each individual conductor of the cable.

Impervious sheathed cable could confine a hazardous gas or vapor within the cable. If such gas or vapor is capable of traveling along the cable, such cable shall be sealed where it leaves a Class I, Division 2 area and passes to a nonhazardous area.

(An exception is made where the cable simply "passes through" the Class I, Division 2 area. Here no seal is required.)

(f) Drainage

(1) Where a vertical run of conduit is brought down to a piece of apparatus and a seal inserted in the vertical run, moisture from condensation could be trapped in the conduit above the seal. Provision must be made either to prevent accumulation or to permit periodic drainage. Sealing fittings are available that are designed to provide for drainage of the vertical conduit run. The condensation accumulates in a small sump or drainage well, which may be periodically drained as required.

(2) Where there is a possibility of moisture accumulating in motors or generators, the entrance of moisture should be minimized by proper arrangement of joints and conduits.

(3) Certain operations depend on a single seal diaphragm or tube to prevent process fluids from entering into electrical conduit. Here the Code requires an additional seal to be provided, with a drain between the two seals.

501-6. Switches, Circuit Breakers, Motor Controllers, and Fuses

(a) Class I, Division 1

Must be approved for Class I locations.

(b) Class I, Division 2

(1) Must have enclosures approved for Class I, Division 1 locations, or be hermetically sealed or oil-immersed.

(2) Isolating switches in Class I, Division 2 locations may be the general-purpose type.

(3) Plug or cartridge fuses must have enclosures "approved for the purpose." Oil-immersed and hermetically sealed fuses may be in general-purpose enclosures.

(4) Distribution panels with *10 or less* circuits may be of the general-purpose type, provided that:

1. The panel serves only fixed lighting.

2. Fuses, if used, are enclosed.

3. The panel switches (or circuit breakers) are not used for switching lights on and off.

4. The fixed lighting is within one room or area.

501-7. Control Transformers and Resistors

This Section is for control transformers, resistors, and impedance coils. Examples would be the transformer in an autotransformer type of motor controller, or resistors used for motor control or as dimmers for lights.

(a) Class I, Division 1

Enclosures must be "approved for Class I, Division 1 locations."

(b) Class I, Division 2

(1) Switches used in conjunction with transformers, resistors, and impedance coils must be either (1) "approved for Class I, Division 1 locations" or (2) hermetically sealed, or (3) oil-immersed.

(2) Transformers and impedance coils may be the general-purpose type.

(3) Resistors must in general be "approved for Class I locations."

Fixed resistors may have general-purpose enclosures, provided operating temperature will stay below 80% of the ignition temperature of the surrounding vapor or gas. (Ignition temperature of most vapors is taken as 536°F.)

501-8. Motors and Generators

(a) Class I, Division 1

Must be either "approved for Class I, Division 1 locations," or totally enclosed, pipe ventilated, or a totally enclosed, inert-gas-filled type.

Pipe-ventilated motors are cooled by clean air forced through a pipe by a fan or blower. The clean air (from outside the hazardous area) is piped to the motor through an air intake in the motor housing and exhausted through an exhaust pipe, which conducts the warmed air to an area outside of the hazardous location. The blower system must be interlocked with the motor starter, so that the motor will not run unless the blower system is operating. Temperature detectors must be provided for the motor.

Pipe ventilation is used principally for very large motors.

(b) Class I, Division 2

In Class I, Division 2 locations, motors having brushes or switching mechanisms must be "approved for Class I, Division 1 locations." DC motors, "universal" motors, wound rotor motors, capacitor start motors belong in this category.

DC motors and "universal" motors have commutators. AC wound-rotor motors have slip rings. The brushes traveling over the commutator or slip ring could produce an arc or spark, and these motors must be "approved for Class I, Division 1 locations."

Capacitor start motors must be "approved for Class I, Division 1 locations" because of the centrifugal switching device in such motors, which could produce a spark.

Squirrel-cage motors, split-phase motors, and "single-value" capacitor motors may be the general-purpose type provided that there is no built-in thermal protector in the motor.

It should be noted that any motor having a built-in thermal protector must always be "approved for Class I locations," regardless of type. This is because the thermal protector has a make-and-break contact, which could produce a spark or arc.

Any generator having brushes or built-in make-and-break contacts or resistors must be "approved for Class I, Division 1 locations."

501-9. Lighting Fixtures

(a) Class I, Division 1

All lighting fixtures, including portable lamps, must be approved for Class I, Division 1 locations, and protected against physical damage.

Pendant fixtures must be suspended by *and wired by* metal conduit, which must be threaded to the box in the ceiling and to the fixture at the lower end.

For conduit stems that are more than 12 in. long, the conduit must be either braced at the lower end, or if the conduit is not braced, a fitting or a short piece of explosion-proof flexible tubing must be inserted at the upper end of the stem, not more than 12 in. below the ceiling box (Fig. 513).

Boxes shall be explosion-proof and a type approved for hanging fixtures.

(b) Class I, Division 2

Portable lamps must be "approved for Class I, Division 1 locations."

In Class I, Division 2 locations, fixed lighting fixtures need not be "approved for Class I, Division 1 locations," unless (1) the fixture is the switched type or (2) there is a possibility that the fixture will reach a temperature over 80% of the ignition temperature of the surrounding vapor or gas. (Ignition temperature of most vapors is taken as 536°F.)

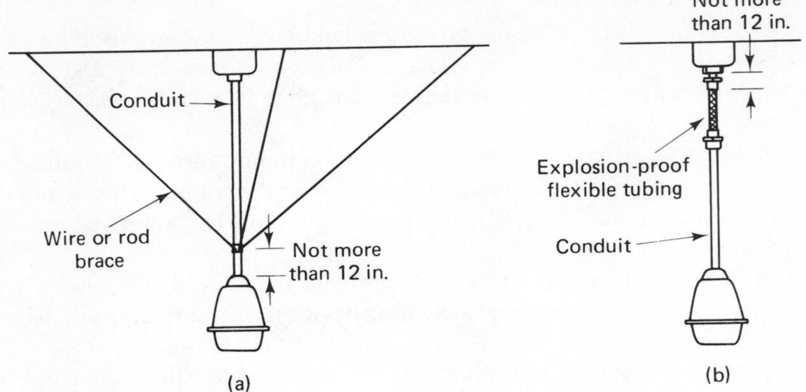

Fig. 513

Pendant fixtures in Class I locations (Sect. 501-9). Pendant fixtures with stems longer than 12 in. must be either braced at the lower end (a), or a flexible connection must be provided at the upper end (b).

If the fixture is a switched type, or if it might reach a temperature higher than 80% of the vapor ignition temperature, it must be "approved for Class I, Division 1 locations."

For fluorescent fixtures with starters, the starters must have enclosures "approved for Class I locations," or the entire fixture may be "approved for Class I locations." Boxes shall be a type approved for hanging fixtures, but need not be "approved for Class I locations."

Rules for installing pendant fixtures are the same as for Division 1 locations, except that, in addition to conduit, "other approved means" may be used for hanging the fixture.

501-10. Utilization Equipment

"Utilization equipment" would be appliances.

(a) Class I, Division 1

In Class I, Division 1 locations, appliances must be "approved for Class I, Division 1 locations."

(b) Class I, Division 2

(1) Heating appliances must be "approved for Class I, Division 1 locations." Heating appliances would include water heaters and room heaters. There are exceptions that allow heaters to be the general-purpose type:

(a) If the maximum operating temperature of any exposed surface will not exceed 80% of the ignition temperature of the gas or vapor surrounding the heater, when operating continuously at *120%* rated voltage, the heater may be the general-purpose type.

(b) If the maximum operating temperature of any exposed surface will not exceed 80% of the ignition temperature of the gas or vapor surrounding the heater, when operating continuously at *100%* rated voltage, the heater may be the general-purpose type, *provided* it is supplied with a temperature controller.

To meet the requirements of (b), the operating temperature marked on the heater would have to be no more than 80% of the ignition temperature of the gas or vapor.

To meet the requirements of (a), the marked operating temperature would have to be no more than 55% of the ignition temperature of the gas or vapor. (See Section 500-2 for ignition temperatures.) All heaters must be completely enclosed.

(2) Appliances with motors need not be "approved for the location" unless the motor has brushes, or a centrifugal switch, or a built-in thermal protector, in which case the appliances must be "approved for Class I, Division 1 locations" [see Section 501-8(b)].

(3) If an appliance has a switch, the switch must for all appliances be "approved for Class I locations." The rest of the appliance may in some cases have a general-purpose enclosure, but the switch must always be "approved for Class I locations."

Except as required by (1), (2), (3) above, appliances in Class I, Division 2 locations may be the general-purpose type.

501-11. Flexible Cords, Class I, Divisions 1 and 2

Cords may be used in all Class I locations, but only for *portable* lamps or appliances.

The cord must:

1. Be an extra-hard usage type. Extra-hard usage cords are types S, SO, HSO, ST, and STO.

2. Have a grounding conductor for grounding the lamp or appliance.

3. Be fitted with clamps at both ends to relieve pull on the connections.

4. Be sealed, if the lamp or appliance is an explosion-proof type.

501-12. Receptacles and Attachment Plugs, Class I, Divisions 1 and 2

In Class I locations, receptacles and plugs must be the grounding type and "approved for Class I locations."

[For process-control instruments, receptacles and plugs may be the general-purpose type, provided all the conditions of Section 501-3(b)(6) are complied with.]

501-13. Conductor Insulation, Class I, Divisions 1 and 2

In Class I locations where conductor insulation may be exposed to gasoline, oil, or corrosive vapors or liquids, the insulation must be a type suitable for the conditions. (If lead-covered, the insulation need not be of a type suitable for these conditions.) For some conditions, a nonleaded, thermoplastic nylon-covered type is approved for these conditions. The Underwriters Laboratories listing should be referred to for approved insulation types in locations such as the above.

501-14. Signaling, Alarm, Remote-Control, and Communication Systems

Signaling and alarm systems would include doorbells, alarm bells, buzzers. Remote control would include pushbutton circuits for starting and stopping motors. Communication systems would include telephones and telephone circuits.

(a) Class I, Division 1

In Class I, Division 1 locations, all equipment must be "approved for Class I, Division 1 locations." Wiring must be either metal conduit or Type MI cable. Seals must be provided where required by Section 501-5(a). Seals must comply with the requirements of Section 501-5(c).

(b) Class I, Division 2

For Class I, Division 2 locations, the Code does not require that all equipment be "approved for Class I locations." Different types of equipment have different requirements.

(1) Switches, circuit breakers, pushbuttons, or any other make-and-break device must be either (1) "approved for Class I, Division 1 locations," or (2) oil-immersed, or (3) hermetically sealed, or if the current and voltage involved are very small (such as the voice current in telephones), they may be the general-purpose type.

(2) "Fixed" resistors may be the general-purpose type, provided the temperature of the resistor will not exceed 80% of the ignition temperature of the surrounding gas or vapor.

Variable resistor enclosures must be "approved for Class I, Division 1 locations."

(3) Fuse enclosures may be the general-purpose type.

(4) Wiring methods permitted in Division 2 locations are listed in Section 501-4(b). Seals must be provided where required by Section 501-5(b) as applying to Class I, Division 2 locations. Seals must comply with the requirements of Section 501-5(c).

501-15. Live Parts, Class I, Divisions 1 and 2

No exposed live parts are permitted in any Class I location.

501-16. Grounding, Class I, Divisions 1 and 2

(a) All metal equipment must be grounded. This includes cabinets, switch boxes, appliances, fixtures, frames of motors, conduit, and all other exposed metal parts of electrical equipment.

(b) Bonding jumpers must be used for bonding conduit to boxes and equipment. Locknuts are not considered an adequate bond in hazardous locations.

Where flexible metal conduit is used, as per Section 501-4(b), bonding jumper must be provided to bridge the flexible conduit.

(c) In certain areas of the country, particularly in some southern states, lightning disturbances are at times quite severe. In such locations, the Code requires lightning arresters to be installed at the service entrance to Class I locations.

(d) Where there is a grounded neutral in the service, that neutral must be bonded to the raceway systems and to the grounding conductor. This applies for AC circuits only.

(e) If a grounded conductor is not required in an AC service, but there is a grounded conductor in the electric company line, the grounded conductor must be brought along with the service, and bonded to the raceway system.

(f) The grounding connections required by (d) and (e) above may not be abandoned.

The Code requirements for equipment in Class I locations are summed up in the two accompanying tables. Each equipment listing is followed by its Code reference Section.

In some cases equipment is required to have enclosures approved for Class I locations. This would permit general-purpose equipment to be used, if a box or enclosing case that is approved for Class I locations is provided for the equipment.

"Approved for Class I locations" means that the complete assembly, the enclosed apparatus as well as the enclosure, must be approved as a unit for use in Class I locations.

Summary of Equipment Requirements, Class I, Division 1 Locations

Equipment	Type Permitted
Appliances, Sect. 501-10(a)	"Approved for Class I locations"
Bells, buzzers, Sect. 501-14(a)	"Approved for Class I locations"
Boxes, fittings, Sect. 501-4(a)	Explosion-proof
Circuit breakers, Sect. 501-6(a)	"Approved for Class I locations"
Control transformers, Sect. 501-7(a)	Enclosures must be "approved for Class I locations"
Cords, Sect. 501-11	Type S, SO, ST, or STO; must have grounding conductor
Distribution panels, Sect. 501-6(a)	"Approved for Class I locations"
Fuses, Sect. 501-6(a)	"Approved for Class I locations"
Generators, Sect. 501-8(a)	"Approved for Class I locations," or totally enclosed, pipe-ventilated, or inert gas-filled
Lighting fixtures, Sect. 501-9(a)(1)	"Approved for Class I locations"
Loudspeakers, Sect. 501-14(a)	"Approved for Class I locations"
Motors, Sect. 501-8(a)	"Approved for Class I locations" or totally enclosed, pipe ventilated, or inert gas-filled
Motor controllers, Sect. 501-6(a)	"Approved for Class I locations"
Portable lamps, Sect. 501-9(a)(1)	"Approved for Class I locations"
Pushbuttons, Sect. 501-6(a)	"Approved for Class I locations"
Receptacles, Sect. 501-12	"Approved for Class I locations"
Resistors (control), Sect. 501-7(a)	Enclosures must be "approved for Class I locations"
Switchboard instruments, meters, resistors, etc., Sect. 501-3(a)	Enclosures must be "approved for Class I locations"
Switches, Sect. 501-6(a)	"Approved for Class I locations"
Transformers (oil-filled), Sect. 501-2(a)(1)	Not permitted
Transformers (askarel and dry-type), Sect. 501-2(a)(2)	"Approved for Class I locations"
Wiring methods permitted, Sect. 501-4(a)	Rigid or intermediate metal conduit, Type MI cable

Summary of Equipment Requirements, Class I, Division 2 Locations

Equipment	Type Permitted
Appliances, Sects. 501-10(b)(1), 501-10(b)(2)	Heating appliances must be "approved for Class I locations" [there is an exception allowing general-purpose heaters to be used; see Section 501-10(b)(1)]; appliances having a motor with brushes, or a capacitor start motor, or a motor with a thermal protector must be "approved for Class I locations"; other appliances without switches may be the general-purpose type
Bells, buzzers, Sect. 501-14(b)(1)	Enclosures must be "approved for Class I locations" *Note:* Enclosures may be general-purpose type if (1) contacts are oil-immersed or hermetically sealed, or if (2) contacts make and break very small currents, such as in telephones
Boxes, fittings, Sect. 501-4(b)	Need not be explosion-proof except where a seal is required
Circuit breakers, Sect. 501-6(b)(1)	Enclosures must be "approved for Class I locations," except where contacts are (1) hermetically sealed or (2) oil-immersed
Control transformers, Sect. 501-7(b)(2)	May be general-purpose type
Cords, Sect. 501-11	Type S, SO, ST, or STO; must have grounding conductor
Distribution panels, more than 10 circuit, Sects. 501-6(b)(1), 501-6(b)(3)	"Approved for Class I locations"
Distribution panels, 10 circuit or less, Sect. 501-6(b)(4)	May be general-purpose type if (1) feeding only fixed lighting fixtures, in one room or area, and (2) not regularly used for switching lights on and off; otherwise, must be "approved for Class I locations"
Fuses (other than distribution panel fuses), Sect. 501-6(b)(3)	Fuses must be in enclosures "approved for Class I locations" or oil-immersed or hermetically sealed
Generators, Sect. 501-8(b)	"Approved for Class I locations" if generator has brushes, or has devices with make-and-break contacts, or integral resistors; otherwise, may be general-purpose type
Isolating switches, Sect. 501-6(b)(2)	May be general-purpose type
Lighting fixtures, switched type, Sect. 501-9(b)(5)	"Approved for Class I locations"
Lighting fixtures, without switch, Sect. 501-9(b)(2)	May be general-purpose type
Loudspeakers, Sect. 501-14(b)	May be general-purpose type

Summary of Equipment Requirements, Class I, Division 2 Locations (*Cont.*)

Equipment	Type Permitted
Motors, squirrel-cage, single-value capacitor, or split-phase type, Sect. 501-8(b)	May be general-purpose enclosed, if there is no thermal protector in motor; if there is a thermal protector, must be "approved for Class I locations"
Motors, wound-rotor, capacitor-start, universal, or DC types, Sect. 501-8(b)	"Approved for Class I locations"
Motor controllers, Sect. 501-6(b)(1)	Enclosures must be either (1) "approved for Class I locations," or (2) may be general purpose if contacts are oil-immersed or hermetically sealed
Portable lamps, Sect. 501-9(b)(1)	"Approved for Class I locations"
Pushbuttons, Sect. 501-6(b)(1)	Enclosures must be "approved for Class I locations"
Receptacles, Sect. 501-12	"Approved for Class I locations"
Resistors (fixed), Sect. 501-7(b)(3)	May be general-purpose type if surface temperature will not exceed 80% of ignition temperature for gas or vapor involved; otherwise, must be "approved for Class I locations"
Resistors (with sliding contacts), Sect. 501-7(b)(3)	"Approved for Class I locations"
Switchboard instruments, meters, etc., having sliding or make-and-break contacts, Sect. 501-3(b)(1)	"Approved for Class I locations"
Switchboard instruments without sliding or make-and-break contacts, Sect. 501-3(b)(3)	May be general-purpose type
Switches, Sect. 501-6(b)(1)	Enclosures must be either "approved for Class I locations," or may be general-purpose if contacts are oil-immersed or hermetically sealed
Transformers, Sect. 501-2(b)	May be general-purpose type
Wiring methods permitted, Sect. 501-4(b)	Rigid metal conduit Type SNM cable Type MI cable Type MC cable Steel intermediate conduit Type PLTC cable Enclosed gasketed busways

ARTICLE 502 — CLASS II LOCATIONS*

502-1. General

In the following sections, equipment is in some cases required to be "dust-ignition-proof" or in other cases "approved for Class II locations." Dust-ignition-proof equipment is so constructed as to be able to withstand the effect of dust igniting within the equipment without transmitting a spark or arc to the outside. Equipment that is "approved for Class II locations" is dust-tight but is not required to be dust-ignition-proof. Equipment that is required to be dust-ignition-proof or "approved for Class II locations" must be suitable for the particular type of dust involved, whether Group E, F, or G. Group E dusts are metal dusts, Group F dusts include coal dust and coke dust. Group G dusts include flour, starch, grain, and hay dust.

It should be remembered that "explosion-proof" and "dust-ignition-proof" are two different things. Explosion-proof equipment might not, in some cases, be also dust-ignition-proof, and in Class II locations, explosion-proof equipment is not acceptable as a substitute for the dust-ignition-proof type.

This Section (502-1) sets down maximum operating temperatures permitted for equipment used in Class II hazardous locations. Equipment that is UL approved for Class II locations will meet these requirements.

In Class II locations, the rules of this Article (502) must be followed, as well as the general rules for wiring as set forth in Chapters 2 and 3 of the Code.

502-2. Transformers and Capacitors

(a) Class II, Division 1

(1) *Containing a Liquid That Will Burn*

This rule is for oil-filled transformers and capacitors. The rule, in effect, prohibits the use of oil-filled transformers and capacitors in Class II, Division 1 locations.

(2) *Not Containing a Liquid That Will Burn*

This rule applies for askarel-filled and dry-type transformers and capacitors. This type may be installed in Class II, Division 1 locations if "approved for Class II locations," but only if the dust involved is a nonmetallic dust.

*See Section 500-1 for definition of Class II locations.

(3) *Metal Dusts*

No transformer or capacitor of any type is permitted in a location where hazardous metallic dust is present.

(b) Class II, Division 2

(1) *Containing a Liquid That Will Burn*

This rule, in effect, prohibits the use of oil-filled transformers and capacitors in Class II, Division 2 locations.

(2) *Containing Askarel*

Askarel-filled transformers rated 25 kVA or less may be installed in Class II, Division 2 locations. The transformers may have general-purpose enclosures.

Askarel-filled transformers rated over 25 kVA may be installed in Class II, Division 2 locations but only if:

1. They have pressure-relief vents, to relieve the pressure which may be built up by gases generated within the transformer (askarel generates gases, when subjected to an arc).
   (If the pressure-relief vent exhausts directly to the room, the Code requires that, in addition, a gas absorber be provided inside the transformer.)
   (If the pressure-relief vent exhausts to the outside [this could be through a pipe flue], no gas absorber is required.)
2. The transformer is kept at least 6 in. clear of any combustible material.

(3) *Dry-Type Transformers*

Dry-type transformers operating at over 600 volts must be installed in vaults.

Dry-type transformers of 600 volts or less may be installed in Class II, Division 2 locations, provided the transformer case is without ventilating or other openings. Otherwise, they also must be installed in vaults.

502-3. Surge Protection, Class II, Divisions 1 and 2

In certain areas of the country severe lightning disturbances are likely. In such areas, lightning arresters and surge protectors must be installed. All grounds provided at the service must be metallically connected together. Capacitors used as surge protectors must be connected on the supply side of the service disconnect, and protected by 30-amp. fuses or a circuit breaker set at 30 amps.

502-4. Wiring Methods

(a) Class II, Division 1

In Class II, Division 1 locations, wiring method must be either metal conduit or Type MI cable (mineral-insulated cable).

(1) *Fittings and Boxes*

There are two parts to this rule:

1. For locations where the dusts are hazardous but not of a combustible electrically conductive nature. This would include grain, cocoa, dried egg and milk dust, starch dust, and hay dust locations.

   In such locations, boxes and fittings that contain splices or taps must be "approved for Class II locations."

   Boxes and fittings without splices or taps need not be "approved," but must have tight-fitting enclosures with no openings (such as screw holes).

2. For locations where dusts of a combustible electrically conductive nature are present. This would include coal dust, coke, carbon black, charcoal dust, magnesium, and aluminum dust locations.

   In such locations, *all* fittings and boxes, whether with or without splices or taps, must be "approved for Class II locations."

(2) *Flexible Connections*

In Class II, Division 1 locations, liquidtight flexible metal conduit, or Type S, SO, ST, or STO cord may be used. Unless other means are provided for grounding, cords shall have a grounding conductor. Where dusts of an electrically conducting nature are present, cords must have dust-tight seals at both ends.

(b) Class II, Division 2

In Class II, Division 2 locations the following wiring methods are permitted:

1. Rigid *metal* conduit.
2. Dust-tight wireways.
3. Type MI cable (mineral-insulated cable).
4. Type MC cable (metal-clad power cable).
5. Intermediate metal conduit.
6. Type SNM cable (shielded nonmetallic sheathed cable).
7. Electrical metallic tubing (EMT).

(1) *Wireways, Fittings, and Boxes*

Wireways, fittings, and boxes in Class II, Division 2 locations need not be "approved for Class II locations," but must have close-fitting enclosures, with no openings (such as screw holes) that might transmit sparks to the outside of the wireway, fitting, or box.

(2) *Flexible Connections*

Same requirements as for Class II, Division 1 locations.

502-5. Sealing, Class II, Divisions 1 and 2

A seal is required where a dust-ignition-proof and a non-dust-ignition-proof piece of equipment are both in the hazardous dust location, with a run of conduit or EMT between the two. As an example, suppose that a dust-ignition-proof switch and a fitting are in the same run of conduit, with the fitting 8 ft horizontally from the switch box. The fitting is not dust-ignition-proof; the switch is. Now, the hazardous dust can enter the fitting and travel inside the conduit to enter the switch enclosure. Hazardous dust inside the switch enclosure would be dangerous. To prevent passage of dust through the conduit, the Code requires a seal in the 8-ft conduit run between the switch and the fitting.

Dust inside a conduit will not travel over 10 ft horizontally. If the conduit run between the two equipments is horizontal and at least 10 ft long, a seal is not required between the two.

Dust inside a conduit run will not travel over 5 ft *upward,* but will travel a considerable distance *downward.* If the dust-ignition-proof equipment is vertically *above* the non-dust-ignition-proof equipment and 5 ft distant, no seal is required. If the dust-ignition-proof equipment is vertically *below* the other, a seal is always required, regardless of length of the run (Fig. 514).

502-6. Switches, Circuit Breakers, Motor Controllers, and Fuses

(a) Class II, Division 1

(1) Must be dust-ignition-proof, except as in (2) below.

(2) Where dusts of an electrically conductive nature are present, isolating switches must be dust-ignition-proof. If the dusts are not electrically conductive, isolating switches need not be dust-ignition-proof, but must have tight enclosures, with no openings of any kind. Electrically conductive dusts include coal, coke, carbon, magnesium, and aluminum dust.

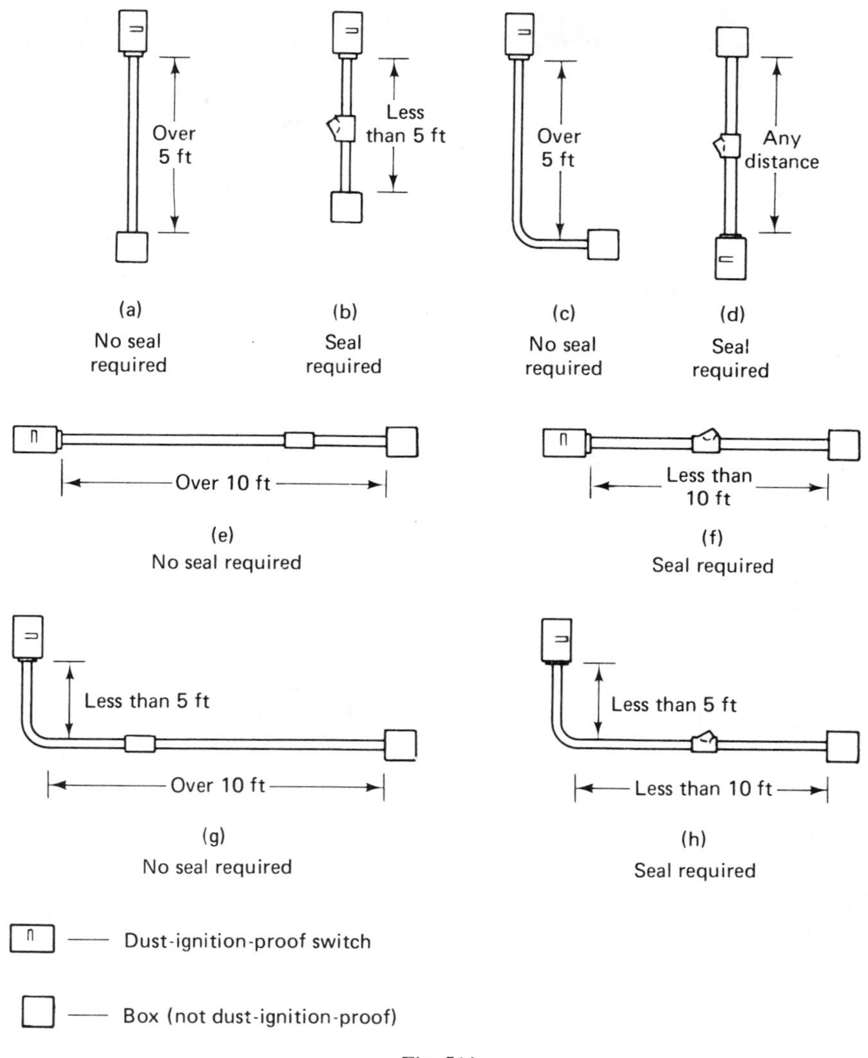

Fig. 514
Examples of application of the rule of Sect. 502-5 (sealing in Class II locations). When the switch is beneath the non-dust-ignition-proof box, a seal is always required (d).

When the switch is *above* or *horizontal with* the box, a seal is required only if both the vertical and horizontal distances are less than 5 and 10 ft, respectively (b)(f)(h). In (c) the horizontal distance is less than 10 ft, but the vertical distance is over 5 ft. In (g) the vertical distance is less than 5 ft, but the horizontal distance is over 10 ft. No seal required in either case.

(3) In locations where hazardous metal dusts are present, all switches (including isolating switches), circuit breakers, motor controllers, and fuses must have enclosures approved for metal dust locations.

These rules also apply to any other device for interrupting current, such as pushbuttons and relays.

(b) Class II, Division 2

In Class II, Division 2 locations, switches, circuit breakers, motor controllers, and fuse boxes need not be dust-ignition-proof, except where electrically conductive dust is present.

In Class II, Division 2 locations where electrically conductive dust is present, switches, circuit breakers, motor controllers, and fuses must be dust-ignition-proof.

502-7. Control Transformers and Resistors

This Section is for *control* transformers, solenoids, resistors, and impedance coils.

Examples would be the transformer for a pushbutton circuit in a motor controller, or resistors used for motor control or as light dimmers.

(a) Class II, Division 1

All such equipment must have dust-ignition-proof enclosures. In locations where hazardous *metal* dusts are present, such equipment must have special enclosures approved for metal dust locations.

(b) Class II, Division 2

Resistors must have dust-ignition-proof enclosures, except that, where the operating temperature of a *fixed* resistor will not exceed 248°F or is part of an automatically timed starting sequence, the enclosure may be a "tight metal housing."

Control transformers, solenoids, and impedance coils need not be dust-ignition-proof, but must have tight enclosures without any kind of opening (such as screw holes).

502-8. Motors and Generators

(a) Class II, Division 1

Shall be either "approved for Class II, Division I locations," or totally enclosed pipe-ventilated.

Pipe-ventilated motors are cooled by clean air forced through a pipe by a fan or blower. The clean air (from outside the hazardous area) is piped to the motor through an air intake in the motor housing, and exhausted through an exhaust pipe, which conducts the warm air to an area outside of the hazardous location. The vent pipes must be constructed according to the rules of Section 502-9, following.

(b) Class II, Division 2

Shall be either dust-ignition-proof, or totally enclosed, pipe-ventilated, except that standard motors and generators may be used in cases where the authority having jurisdiction judges that the conditions would not require dust-ignition-proof or pipe-ventilated equipment.

502-9. Ventilating Piping

When pipe-ventilated motors or generators are used in Class II locations, the piping must comply with the following requirements:

1. Vent pipes must be of metal not lighter than No. 24 MSG, or of equally substantial noncombustible material.
2. The air intake and exhaust must be outside.
3. The intake air must be clean and unpolluted.
4. Vents must be screened at the intake and exhaust end.
5. Must be rustproof (galvanized sheet metal would meet this requirement.)

The above requirements apply for both Divisions 1 and 2 locations.

(a) Class II, Division 1

Entire piping system must be dust tight. Seams must be:

1. Riveted and soldered, or
2. Bolted and soldered, or
3. Welded, or
4. Rendered dust tight by other equally effective means.

(b) Class II, Division 2

In Division 2 locations, the requirements are less stringent. The rule says that the vents shall be "sufficiently tight to prevent the entrance of *appreciable* quantities of dust." This would indicate that the vents need not be entirely dust tight.

In Division 2 locations it is not necessary to solder or weld the seams. Slip joints may be used in Division 2 locations.

502-10. Utilization Equipment

"Utilization equipment" would be appliances.

(a) Class II, Division 1

All appliances must be "approved for Class II locations." Where hazardous metal dusts are present, appliances must be specially approved for metal dust locations.

(b) Class II, Division 2

(1) Heating appliances must be "approved for Class II locations." Heating appliances would include water heaters and room heaters.

(2) For appliances having motors, the motor must be dust-ignition-proof. The rest of the appliance may have a general-purpose enclosure.

(3) If an appliance has a switch, the switch must have a tight enclosure. The switch enclosure must be without openings, such as screw holes, but need not be "approved for Class II locations."

(4) Transformers, impedance coils, and solenoids associated with appliances must have tight enclosures. Resistors must have dust-ignition-proof enclosures.

502-11. Lighting Fixtures

(a) Class II, Division 1

All fixtures, including portable lamps, must be "approved for Class II locations."

Pendant fixtures may be suspended by rigid conduit, chains, or "other approved means." When conduit is used, it must be threaded to the box in the ceiling and to the fixture at the lower end.

If the length of conduit is over 12 in. the conduit must be either braced at the lower end or, if the conduit is not braced, a flexible fitting must be provided at the upper end. (Requirements are the same as for Class I locations. See Fig. 513.)

Cord may be used for wiring a pendant fixture, but the fixture may not be hung from the cord. Other means must be used to support the fixture. The types of cord permitted are S, SO, ST, STO, SJ, SJO, SJT, and SJTO. When cord is used, seals must be provided at both ends.

(b) Class II, Division 2

(1) In Division 2 locations, portable lamps must be "approved for Class II locations."

(2) In Division 2 locations, *fixed* lighting need not be "approved for Class II locations," but must be a type that will not collect dust. The fixture housing must be tight enough to prevent escape of sparks or flame.

Starters in fluorescent lights must be in tight metal enclosures without opening of any kind (such as screw holes).

The rules for installing pendant fixtures are the same as for Division 1 locations, except that, when cord is used, seals are not required in Division 2 locations. In Division 1 locations, a seal is required at both ends of the cord.

502-12. Flexible Cords, Class II, Divisions 1 and 2

Cords must be type S, SO, ST, or STO, except that for wiring pendant fixtures types SJ, SJO, SJT, and SJTO are also approved (Section 502-11). All cords must have a grounding conductor. Clamps must be fitted at both ends, to relieve pull on the connections.

When a cord enters a box, fitting, or enclosure that is required to be dust-ignition-proof, a seal must be provided. A seal is not required for a box, fitting, or enclosure that is not required to be dust-ignition-proof.

502-13. Receptacles and Attachment Plugs

(a) Class II, Division 1

Must be grounding type and "approved for Class II locations."

(b) Class II, Division 2

In Class II, Division 2 locations, receptacles are not required to be "approved for Class II locations." However, the receptacle and plug must be the grounding type and must be a type that will not allow a make or break "while live parts are exposed." A "twist-lock" type of receptacle and plug would meet this requirement, since with this type the plug must be inserted in the receptacle, and then twisted before contact can be made, and the plug cannot be withdrawn until contact is broken inside the receptacle. The conventional type of receptacle, with the conventional type of straight blade plug, would not be permitted.

502-14. Signaling, Alarm, Remote Control and Communication Systems, Meters, Instruments, and Relays

(a) Class II, Division 1

(1) *Wiring Methods*

Wiring for signal, alarm, and intercommunication systems in Division 1 locations may be:

Rigid or intermediate metal conduit, or

Type MI cable, or

EMT.

Note that for wiring any other kind of equipment, only metal conduit or Type MI cable is permitted in Class II, Division 1 locations (see Section 502-4).

(2) *Contacts*

Any equipment having make-and-break contacts must have enclosures "approved for Class II locations." This would include buzzers, bells, pushbuttons, telephones.

Note: When make-and-break contacts are oil-immersed or sealed within a chamber, the enclosure may be the general-purpose type.

(3) *Resistors and Similar Equipment*

Resistors, transformers, and choke coils must have enclosures "approved for Class II locations."

(4) *Rotating Machinery*

Motors and generators must be "approved for Class II locations."

(5) *Combustible Electrically Conductive Dusts*

Where electrically conductive dusts are present, no general-purpose equipment is permitted. Electrically conductive dusts include coal, coke, carbon, charcoal, magnesium, and aluminum dust.

(6) *Metal Dusts*

Where metal dust is present, all equipment must be specifically approved for metal dust locations. Metal dusts include aluminum and magnesium dust.

(b) Class II, Division 2

(1) *Contacts*

Telephones may be the general-purpose type. Telephone equipment having make-and-break contacts for other than voice currents must have tight metal enclosures without openings of any kind.

(2) *Transformers and Similar Equipment*
Shall have tight metal enclosures without openings of any kind.

(3) *Resistors and Similar Equipment*
Resistors, thermomic tubes, and rectifiers must have enclosures "approved for Class II locations." (Exception: *Fixed* resistors operating at not over 248°F may have general-purpose enclosures.)

(4) Motors and generators generally must be either dust-ignition-proof, or totally enclosed pipe-ventilated, except that standard motors and generators may be used in locations where the authority having jurisdiction judges that the conditions would not require dust-ignition-proof or pipe-ventilated equipment.

502-15. Live Parts, Class II, Divisions 1 and 2

No exposed live parts of any kind are permitted in any Class II location.

502-16. Grounding, Class II, Divisions 1 and 2

(a) All metal equipment must be grounded. This includes cabinets, switch boxes, appliances, fixtures, frames of motors, conduit, and all other exposed metal equipment.

(b) *Bonding jumpers* must be used for bonding conduit or metal-clad wiring to boxes and equipment. This applies not only to equipment within the hazardous areas, but also to the entire run back to the service equipment. The idea is to provide a completely reliable grounding path extending from equipment back to the grounding electrode.

Where flexible metal conduit is used as per Section 502-4(a)(2), a bonding jumper must be provided to bridge the flexible conduit.

(c) In certain areas of the country, particularly in some southern states, lightning disturbances are at times quite severe. In such locations, the Code requires lightning arresters to be installed at the service entrance to Class II locations.

(d) Where there is a grounded conductor in an AC service, the grounded conductor must be bonded to the raceway system and to the grounding conductor.

(e) If a grounded conductor is not required in an AC service, but there is a grounded conductor in the electric company line, the grounded conductor must be brought along with the service and bonded to the raceway system.

(f) The grounding connections required by (d) and (e) above may not be abandoned.

The Code requirements for equipment in Class II locations are summed up in the accompanying tables. Equipment listings are followed by the Code reference section.

Summary of Equipment Requirements, Class II, Division 1 Locations

Equipment	Type Permitted
Appliances, Sect. 502-10(a)	"Approved for Class II locations"
Bells, buzzers, Sect. 502-14(a)(2)	Enclosures must be "approved for Class II locations"
Boxes, fittings, Sect. 502-4(a)(1)	Boxes and fittings in which taps, joints, and connections are made must be "Approved for Class II locations"; where electrically conducting dusts are present, must be "approved for Class II locations" whether with or without taps, joints, or connections
Circuit breakers, Sect. 502-6(a)(1)	"Approved for Class II locations"
Control transformers, Sect. 502-7(a)	Dust-ignition-proof enclosures
Cords, Sect. 502-4(a)(2), 502-11(a)(3)	Types S, SO, ST, and STO, except that, for wiring pendant fixtures, types SJ, SJT, SJO, and SJTO are also permitted; must have grounding conductor
Distribution panels, Sect. 502-6(a)(1)	Dust-ignition-proof
Fuses, Sect. 502-6(a)(1)	Dust-ignition-proof
Generators, Sect. 502-8(a)	"Approved for Class II locations," or totally enclosed, pipe-ventilated
Lighting fixtures, Sect. 502-11(a)(1)	"Approved for Class II locations"
Loudspeakers, Sect. 502-14(a)	May be general-purpose type
Motors, Sect. 502-8(a)	"Approved for Class II locations," or totally enclosed, pipe-ventilated
Motor controllers, Sect. 502-6(a)(1)	Dust-ignition-proof
Portable lamps, Sect. 502-11(a)(1)	"Approved for Class II locations"
Pushbuttons, Sect. 502-6(a)(1)	Dust-ignition-proof
Receptacles, Sect. 502-13(a)	"Approved for Class II locations"
Resistors (control), Sect. 502-7(a)	Dust-ignition-proof enclosures
Switches, Sect. 502-6(a)(1)	Dust-ignition-proof
Telephones, Sect. 502-14(a)(2)	"Approved for Class II locations"
Transformers (oil-filled), Sect. 502-2(a)(1)	Not permitted
Transformers (askarel), Sect. 502-2(a)(2)	"Approved for Class II locations"
Transformers (dry-type), Sect. 502-2(a)(2)	"Approved for Class II locations"
Wiring methods permitted, Sect. 502-4(a)	Rigid or intermediate metal conduit Type MI cable

Summary of Equipment Requirements, Class II, Division 2 Locations

Equipment	Type Permitted
Appliances: Sect. 502-10(b)(1)	Heating appliances must be "approved for Class II locations"
Sect. 502-10(b)(2)	For appliances with motors, the motor must be dust-ignition-proof
Sect. 502-10(b)(3)	If an appliance has a switch, the switch must have a tight enclosure
	Other appliances may be general-purpose type
Bells, buzzers, Sect. 502-14(b)(1)	Must have tight-fitting enclosures with no openings
Boxes, fittings, Sect. 502-4(b)(1)	Must have tight-fitting enclosures with no openings
Circuit breakers, Sect. 502-6(b)	Must have tight-fitting enclosures with no openings
Control transformers, Sect. 502-7(b)(2)	Must have tight-fitting enclosures with no openings
Cords, Sects. 502-4(b)(2), 502-4(a)(2), 502-11(b)(4)	Types S, SO, ST, and STO, except that, for wiring pendant fixtures, types SJ, SJT, SJO, and SJTO are also permitted; must have grounding conductor
Distribution panels, Sects. 502-6(b), 502-6(a)(2)	Fuses, switches, and circuit breakers must have tight-fitting enclosures with no openings
Fuses, Sects. 502-6(b), 502-6(a)(2)	Must have tight-fitting enclosures with no openings
Generators, Sect. 502-8(b)	Dust-ignition-proof, or totally enclosed, pipe-ventilated, except that by special permission other types may be used
Lighting fixtures, Sect. 502-11(b)(2)	Must have tight-fitting enclosures with no openings
Loudspeakers, Sect. 502-14(b)	May be general-purpose type
Motors, Sect. 502-8(b)	Dust-ignition-proof, or totally enclosed, pipe-ventilated, except that by special permission other types may be used
Motor controllers, Sect. 502-6(b), 502-6(a)(2)	Must have tight-fitting enclosures with no openings
Portable lamps, Sect. 502-11(b)(1)	"Approved for Class II locations"
Pushbuttons, Sect. 502-6(b)	Must have tight-fitting enclosures with no openings
Receptacles, Sect. 502-13(b)	Twist-lock, grounding type
Resistors (control), Sect. 502-7(b)(3)	Dust-ignition-proof enclosures except for *fixed* resistors operating at not over 248°F and resistors that are part of an automatically timed starting device

Summary of Equipment Requirements, Class II, Division 2 Locations (*Cont.*)

Equipment	Type Permitted
Switches, Sects. 502-6(b), 502-6(a)(2)	Must have tight-fitting enclosures with no openings
Telephones (without built-in bell), Sects. 502-14(b)(1)	May be general-purpose type
Transformers (oil-filled), Sect. 502-2(b)(1)	Not permitted
Transformers (askarel), Sect. 502-2(b)(2)	May be general-purpose type Over 25 kVA must have pressure-relief vents
Transformers (dry type), Sect. 502-2(b)(3)	Over 600 volts not permitted; 600 volts or less permitted, must have tight-fitting enclosures
Wiring methods permitted, Sect. 502-4(b)	Rigid metal conduit EMT Type MI cable Type MC cable Intermediate metal conduit Type SNM cable Dust-tight wireways

ARTICLE 503 — CLASS III LOCATIONS

503-1 General

(See Section 500-1 for definition of Class III hazardous locations.)

This Section (503-1) sets down the maximum operating temperatures permitted for equipment installed in Class III hazardous locations. Equipment that is UL-approved for Class III locations will meet these requirements.

503-2. Transformers and Capacitors, Class III, Divisions 1 and 2

(1) Oil-filled transformers or capacitors are not permitted in Class III locations.

(2) Askarel-filled transformers with general-purpose enclosures, rated 25 kVA or less, may be installed in Class III locations.

Askarel-filled transformers with general-purpose enclosures, rated over 25 kVA, may be installed in Class III locations, but only if:

1. They have pressure-relief vents to relieve the pressure that may be built up by gases generated within the transformer. (Askarel generates gases when subjected to an arc.) If the pressure-relief vent exhausts direct to the room, the Code requires that, in addition, a gas absorber be provided inside the transformer. If the pressure-relief vent exhausts to the outside (this could be through a pipe flue), no absorber is required.

2. The transformer is kept at least 6 in. clear of any combustible material.

(3) Dry-type transformers of 600 volts or less may be installed in Class III locations, provided the transformer case is a tight metal housing without openings of any kind. Dry-type transformers of over 600 volts are not permitted in Class III locations.

503-3. Wiring Methods

(a) Class III, Division 1

In Class III, Division 1 locations the following wiring methods are permitted:

Rigid *metal* conduit.

Type MI cable (mineral-insulated).

Type MC cable (metal-clad power cable).

Threaded steel intermediate conduit.

(1) *Boxes and Fittings*

Boxes and fittings must have close-fitting enclosures with no openings (such as screw holes) that might transmit sparks to the outside of the box or fitting.

(2) *Flexible Connections*

In Class III, Division 1 locations, liquidtight flexible metal conduit or Type S, SO, ST, or STO cord may be used. Cord must have a grounding conductor, and be provided with bushed fittings.

(b) Class III, Division 2

Same requirements as for Division 1, except that in Division 2 locations open wiring on insulators is permitted in compartments used only for storage and containing no machinery.

503-4. Switches, Circuit Breakers, Motor Controllers, and Fuses, Class III, Divisions 1 and 2

These must have close-fitting enclosures with no openings that might transmit sparks to the outside, or that might allow fibers or flyings to enter the enclosure.

503-5. Control Transformers and Resistors, Class III, Divisions 1 and 2

This Section is for *control* transformers and resistors.

Resistors must have dust-ignition-proof enclosures, except that, where the operating temperature of a *fixed* resistor will not exceed 248°F, the enclosure need not be dust-ignition-proof, or when the resistor is part of an automatically-timed starting sequence, it need not be dust-ignition-proof.

Control transformers, solenoids, and impedance coils need not be dust-ignition-proof, but must have tight-fitting enclosures without any kind of opening. This applies also for any associated switches.

503-6. Motors and Generators

(a) Class III, Division 1

In Class III, Division 1 locations, motors and generators must be either

Totally enclosed, or

Totally enclosed, fan-cooled, or

Totally enclosed, pipe-ventilated.

A totally enclosed motor (or generator) is one so enclosed as to prevent exchange of air between the inside and outside. A totally enclosed, fan-cooled motor (or generator) contains a fan attached to the shaft of the motor. There are two housings, one within the other. The fan is in the space between the two housings. Air is drawn in through openings in the outer housing, passes over the inner housing, and discharges at the opposite end of the motor.

Totally enclosed, pipe-ventilated motors (or generators) are cooled by clean air forced through a pipe by a fan or blower. The clean air (from outside the hazardous area) is piped to the motor through an air intake in the motor housing, and exhausted through an exhaust pipe, which conducts the warm air to an area outside of the hazardous location. The vent pipes must be constructed according to the rules of Section 503-7, following.

By special permission, standard motors or generators may be installed in Class III, Division 1 locations if the authority having jurisdiction judges that conditions would permit the use of standard machines. Standard motors must be a type without brushes, make-and-break contacts, or thermal protectors. Open DC motors, wound-rotor motors, and capacitor-start motors are not permitted. DC motors and wound-rotor motors have sliding contacts, and a capacitor-start motor contains a make-and-break centrifugal switch, either of which could produce a spark. Open squirrel-cage motors or split-phase motors could be used, by special permission, but these must be without thermal protectors.

(If a sliding contact, make-and-break switch, or thermal protector is enclosed within a tight metal housing, the motor may be a standard open type.)

(b) Class III, Division 2

All motors and generators must be either

Totally enclosed, or

Totally enclosed, fan-cooled, or

Totally enclosed, pipe-ventilated.

(c) Types Not Permitted, Class III, Divisions 1 and 2

Splash-proof or partially enclosed motors or generators may not be installed in a Class III location.

503-7. Ventilating Piping, Class III, Divisions 1 and 2

Where pipe-ventilated motors or generators are used in Class III locations, the piping must be constructed according to the rules of this Section. Rules are listed below:

1. Vent pipes must be of metal not lighter than No. 24 MSG, or equal material.
2. The air intake and exhaust must be outside.
3. The intake air must be clean and unpolluted.
4. Vents must be screened at the intake and exhaust end.
5. Must be rustproof (galvanized sheet metal would meet this requirement).
6. Must be sufficiently tight to prevent the entrance of "appreciable quantities of fibers or flyings." This would indicate that the vents need not be entirely dust-tight.

503-8. Utilization Equipment, Class III, Divisions 1 and 2

"Utilization equipment" would be appliances.

(a) Heating appliances must be approved for Class III locations. Heating appliances would include water heaters and room heaters.

(b) For appliances having motors, the motor must be either totally enclosed; totally enclosed, fan cooled; or totally enclosed, pipe-ventilated.

(c) If an appliance has a switch, circuit breaker, or fuses, the switch, circuit breaker, or fuses must have a tight enclosure without openings that might allow sparks or burning material to escape, or might allow the entrance of fibers or flyings. (Holes for attachment screws would not be permitted.) The same requirement applies for motor controllers.

503-9. Lighting Fixtures, Class III, Divisions 1 and 2

(a) Fixed lighting fixtures must have tight enclosures, but need not be dust-ignition-proof. Maximum lamp wattage must be marked on the fixture.

(b) Any fixture exposed to physical damage must be suitably guarded. A "guarded-type" fixture (one furnished with a metal guard around the globe) would provide such protection.

(c) Pendant fixtures shall be suspended by rigid conduit or intermediate metal conduit.

If the length of conduit is over 12 in. the stem must be either braced at the lower end (the brace must be not further than 12 in. from the lower end) or, if the stem is not braced, a fitting or flexible connector must be provided within 12 in. of the upper end (see Fig. 513).

(d) Boxes used for supporting lighting fixtures must be approved for the purpose (provided with a fixture hanger).

(e) Portable lamps must be *unswitched,* guarded, and equipped with handles. Portable lamps with receptacles in the handle are not permitted. Exposed metal parts are not permitted. Must have a tight-fitting enclosure. Must be approved for Class III locations.

503-10. Flexible Cords, Class III, Divisions 1 and 2

Cords must be type S, SO, ST, or STO. All cords must have a grounding conductor. Clamps must be fitted at both ends to reduce pull on connections.

If a cord enters a dust-ignition-proof piece of equipment, a seal must be provided at the point of entry.

503-11. Receptacles and Attachment Plugs, Class III, Divisions 1 and 2

Receptacles and plugs must be the grounding type, and must be a type that will not allow a make or break "while live parts are exposed." A "twist-lock" type of receptacle and plug would meet this requirement, since with this type the plug must be inserted in the receptacle and then twisted before contact can be made. The plug cannot be withdrawn until contact is broken inside the receptacle. The conventional type of receptacle, with the conventional type of straight blade plug, would not be permitted.

503-12. Signaling, Alarm, Remote-Control and Local Loud-Speaker Intercommunication Systems, Class III, Divisions 1 and 2

Any equipment that has make-and-break contacts of any kind must have enclosures approved for Class III locations. This would include buzzers, bells, pushbuttons, and any other equipment having make-and-break contacts.

Motors and generators connected with signal and alarm equipment must be approved for Class III locations, or totally enclosed, pipe-ventilated.

Resistors, coils, and transformers must have enclosures approved for Class III locations.

503-13. Electric Cranes, Hoists, and Similar Equipment, Class III, Divisions 1 and 2

A crane with rolling or sliding current collectors and operating over combustible fibers would introduce the possibility of the combustible fibers being ignited, if there is arcing at the contact point.

There is also the danger of fibers and flyings collecting on the insulating supports of the bare conductor or rail, and forming a conducting path to ground. This danger would be increased if moisture is present.

To minimize these dangers, the Code requires that:

1. The power supply to the current collectors must be ungrounded. An accidental current to ground through the collected fibers or flyings would be less likely with an ungrounded system.

2. Current collectors must be so arranged that contact is always maintained. Each collector must have two rollers or contacts. With two paths for the current, there would be little likelihood of both being out of contact at the same time.

3. The collectors must be fitted with guards or barriers that will confine sparks or hot particles in case of arcing.

4. A ground detector is required in the supply circuit, which will give an alarm and automatically disconnect the circuit in case of a ground. Or, a ground-fault indicator, which will sound a continuous alarm in case of a ground, may be used.
5. Control equipment shall comply with Sections 503-4 and 503-5.

503-14. Storage-Battery Charging Equipment, Class III, Divisions 1 and 2

Charging of storage batteries is not permitted in Class III hazardous locations. This must be done outside the hazardous area, or in specially built rooms of brick, stone, or other noncombustible material.

503-15. Live Parts, Class III, Divisions 1 and 2

No exposed live parts are permitted in Class III hazardous locations, except the current collectors on electric cranes, hoists, and similar equipment.

503-16. Grounding, Class III, Divisions 1 and 2

Grounding requirements are the same as for Class II locations (see Section 502-16).

The Code requirements for equipment in Class III, Divisions 1 and 2 locations are listed in the accompanying table. Each equipment listing is followed by its Code reference section.

Summary of Equipment Requirements, Class III, Divisions I and II Locations

Equipment	Type Permitted
Appliances, Sect. 503-8(a)	Heating appliances must be approved for Class III locations
Sect. 503-8(b) Sect. 503-6(a)(b)	For appliances with motors, the motor must be totally enclosed
Sect. 503-8(c) Sect. 503-4	If an appliance has a switch, the switch must have a tight enclosure
	Other appliances may be the general-purpose type
Bells, buzzers, Sects. 503-12, 502-14(a)(2)	"Approved for Class III locations"
Boxes, fittings, Sect. 503-3(a)(1)	Must be tight enclosure, with no openings or screw holes
Circuit breakers, Sect. 503-4	Must have tight metal enclosure, without openings of any kind

Equipment	Type Permitted
Control transformers, Sects. 503-5, 502-7(b)(2)	Must have tight enclosure with no openings
Cords, Sects. 503-10, 502-12	Types S, SO, ST, and STO; must have grounding conductor; must be fitted with clamps to relieve pull on connections
Distribution Panels, Sect. 503-4	Switches, fuses, and circuit breakers must have tight enclosure with no openings
Fuses, Sect. 503-4	Must have tight enclosure with no openings
Generators, Sect. 503-6	Totally enclosed
Lighting fixtures, Sect. 503-9	Must have tight enclosure with no openings
Loudspeakers, Sects. 503-12, 502-14	May be general-purpose type
Motors, Sect. 503-6	Totally enclosed
Motor controllers, Sect. 503-4	Must have tight enclosure with no openings
Portable lamps, Sect. 503-9(e)	Must have tight enclosure with no openings; must be unswitched type, with no exposed metal, or plug-in; guard required
Pushbuttons, Sect. 503-4	Must have tight enclosure with no openings
Receptacles, Sects. 503-11, 502-13(b)	Twist-lock, grounding type
Resistors, Sects. 503-5, 502-7(b)	Dust-ignition-proof enclosures *Note: fixed* resistors with operating temperature of 248°F or less need not have dust-ignition-proof enclosures
Switches, Sect. 503-4	Must have tight enclosure with no openings
Telephones, Sects. 503-12, 502-14(a)(2)	"Approved for Class III locations"
Transformers (oil-filled), Sects. 503-2, 502-2(b)(1)	Not permitted
Transformers (askarel), Sects. 503-2, 502-2(b)(2)	May be general-purpose type; over 25 kVA must have pressure-relief vents
Transformers (dry type), Sects. 503-2, 502-2(b)(3)	600 volts or less permitted; must have tight enclosure; over 600 volts not permitted
Wiring methods permitted, Sect. 503-3	Rigid metal conduit Type MI cable Type MC cable Intermediate metal conduit

ARTICLE 510 — HAZARDOUS (CLASSIFIED) LOCATIONS—SPECIFIC

510-1. Scope

Occupancies such as commercial garages, aircraft hangars, and service stations are part nonhazardous, part hazardous, and would be subject to the rules of Articles 501 through 503 only in certain areas. The Code treats such occupancies individually in the following Articles 511 through 517.

510-2. General

The Code rules for general wiring, as well as the rules of Articles 511 through 517, apply for these occupancies.

ARTICLE 511 — COMMERCIAL GARAGES, REPAIR AND STORAGE

511-1. Scope

Article 511 applies for commercial garages in which repair and service work is done on automobiles, trucks, buses, and tractors.

Garages used *only* for parking or storage are not considered hazardous areas. The rules of Article 511 do not apply to garages in which no repair or service work is done, but the Code does require that indoor storage and parking spaces be adequately ventilated to remove exhaust fumes.

511-2. Hazardous Areas

The different areas of a commercial garage are classified as follows:

(a) The entire area above the floor up to a height of 18 in. is Class I, Division 2 [Fig. 515(a)]. (Where ventilation facilities warrant, the enforcing agency has the authority to classify this area as nonhazardous.)

(b) A pit below floor level is Class I, Division 1, up to floor level [Fig. 515(b)]. (Where ventilation facilities warrant, the enforcing agency has the authority to classify this area as Class I, Division 2.)

(c) Areas adjacent to the garage (stock rooms, switchboard rooms, etc.) and separated by partitions are not considered hazardous areas.

(d) Adjacent areas not separated by partitions are to be classified by the enforcing agency. Such areas may or may not be classified as hazardous.

(e) If fuel pumps are located inside, the rules of Article 514 (Service Stations) shall apply.

Portable lamps used in garages shall

1. Be of hard rubber or other nonmetallic material.

2. Be equipped with a handle.

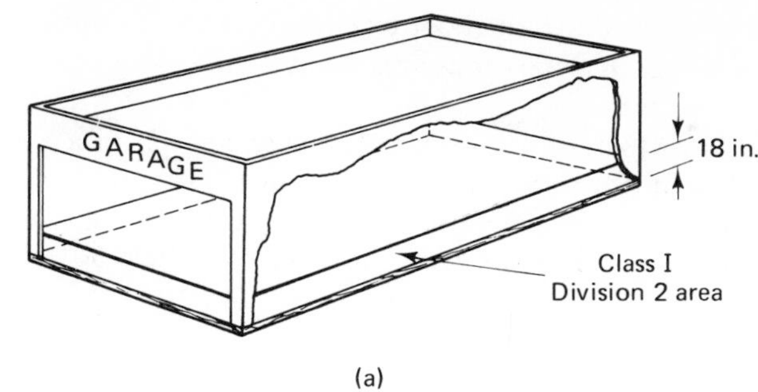

(a)

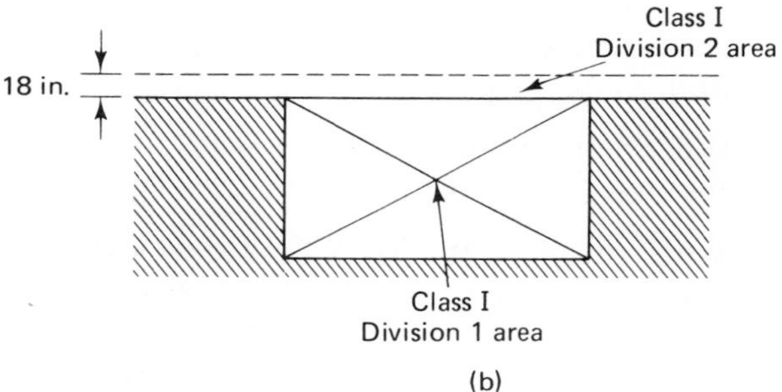

(b)

Fig. 515

Hazardous areas in a commercial garage (Sect. 511-2).

(a) The area from floor level up to a height of 18 in. above the floor is Class I, Division 2.

(b) Any pit or depression in a commercial garage is Class I, Division 1 up to floor level.

3. Have a guard and hook.
4. Be the unswitched type.
5. Have no plug-in.

If the portable lamp is to be used in a hazardous area (near the floor for instance), it must be a type approved for hazardous areas.

If the cord is connected in such a way that the lamp could not reach a hazardous level, a portable lamp may be the general-purpose type.

511-3. Wiring and Equipment in Hazardous Areas

Hazardous vapors in a garage are concentrated in low areas within a short distance above the floor. The Code sets the distance as 18 in., and the area below an imaginary plane 18 in. above the floor is classified as a hazardous area. Raceways beneath the floor or embedded in a masonry wall are considered to be within the hazardous area if any connections or extensions lead into the hazardous area.

Since hazardous vapors seek a low level, any pit in a garage floor would be hazardous down to the bottom of the pit.

All wiring and equipment in the space below the hazardous level must be suited for a Class I location, and the rules of Article 501 must be followed.

511-4. Sealing

The area between floor level and the 18-in. plane is Class I, Division 2. Wiring methods permitted for Class I, Division 2 locations are rigid metal conduit, enclosed gasketed busways, and type MI, MC, MV, TC, or SNM cable [Section 501-4(b)].

1. If conduit is used, a vertical run, unless unbroken, must be sealed at the hazardous plane level (18 in. above the floor). See Fig. 512(c) and (d).
2. Or, for a horizontal run, if the run leaves the area at a height below the hazardous plane level (less than 18 in. from the floor), the conduit must be sealed at the point where it leaves the hazardous area.
3. Seals must be placed in each conduit run entering the enclosures for switches, circuit breakers, fuses, relays resistors, or any other device that could produce arcing, sparking, *or high temperature,* if the enclosure is located beneath the hazardous level.
4. In each conduit run of *2-in.* or *larger* conduit, seals must be placed also at junction boxes and fittings if the box or fitting contains splices, taps, or connections and is located beneath the hazardous level. The seal must be within 18 in. of the box or fitting.

511-5. Wiring in Spaces Above Hazardous Areas

(a) Above the 18-in. level, the following wiring methods are permitted:

1. Rigid metal conduit.
2. EMT.
3. Type MC cable (metal clad).
4. Type MI cable (mineral-insulated).
5. Intermediate metal conduit.
6. Type TC cable (power and control tray).

7. Type SNM cable (shielded nonmetallic).

8. Rigid nonmetallic conduit.

Cellular metal floor raceways are a part of the building structure. The entire floor consists of sheet metal cells, or tubes, laid side by side to form the floor structure, and afterward covered with a layer of concrete.

In a garage, if the floor has cellular metal floor raceways, the raceway may be used to supply equipment in the room below the garage, but it may not be used to supply equipment in the garage.

If the cellular raceway is in the floor above, it may be used for ceiling outlets or extensions in the garage (see Section 356-2.)

(b) Flexible cord used for pendants may be one of the following types of cord: SJ, SJO. SJT, SJTO, S, SO, ST, or STO.

(c) Receptacles and plugs must be the *polarized* type. With a polarized plug and receptacle, the plug can be inserted in the receptacle in only one way; i.e., the same conductor of the cord always connects to the same slot in the receptacle. The Code requires that the neutral must always connect to the "identified" (white) terminal of an appliance or lamp. With a polarized plug and receptacle, this can be accomplished, since the plug connection to the receptacle cannot be reversed. The parallel-blade type of receptacle and plug is not permitted in the space above the hazardous area (except for *ungrounded* circuits).

(d) Receptacles should be located above the 18-in. hazardous level if possible.

511-6. Equipment Above Hazardous Locations

(a) Any equipment that might produce an arc or spark, and which is less than 12 ft above floor level, must have a tight enclosure that will prevent the escape of any arc or spark. Charging panels, motors, generators, if installed less than 12 ft above the floor, should be the totally enclosed type. (Lamps and lampholders are subject to the rule of Subsection (b) following.)

(b) If located less than 12 ft above lanes where vehicles are commonly driven, or if located where exposed to physical damage, lighting fixtures are required to be the totally enclosed type, or of a construction that does not permit the escape of arcs or sparks. Fluorescent and incandescent fixtures in these locations must be fitted with a lens or globe. Exposed tubes and light bulbs are not permitted.

511-7. Battery Charging Equipment

Battery-charging equipment must be located above the 18-in. level.

511-8. Electric Vehicle Charging

(a) Cord for battery charging must be one of the following types: S, SO, ST, or STO.

(b) Connectors must be of a type that will easily break apart. "Twist-lock" connectors would not be permitted. A connector may not be located below the 18-in. level.

(c) The plug-in on the vehicle may not be below the 18-in level.
A charging cord suspended from above may not touch the floor at any point; no part of the cord may be less than 6 in. above the floor.

ARTICLE 513 — AIRCRAFT HANGARS

513-1. Definition

The rules of Article 513 apply for hangars that store aircraft containing gasoline or other hazardous liquids or gases. Aircraft hangars are a Class I hazardous location, except that, if all aircraft have been drained and purged before entering the hangar, the hangar is not considered hazardous.

513-2. Classification of Locations

(a) A pit is considered a Class I, Division 1 location from floor level down to the bottom of the pit.

(b) The entire hangar area up to a height of 18 in. above the floor is considered a Class I, Division 2 location. All wiring and equipment between the 18-in. level and the floor must meet the requirements for Class I, Division 2 locations.

(c) The space around the aircraft engine compartment and aircraft fuel tank compartment are Class I, Division 2 locations. The hazardous area extends horizontally outward to a distance of 5 ft in all directions, and from floor level up to 5 ft above the wings or engine compartment (whichever is higher). All wiring and equipment within these boundaries must meet the requirements for Class I, Division 2 locations, as per Article 501 (see Fig. 516).

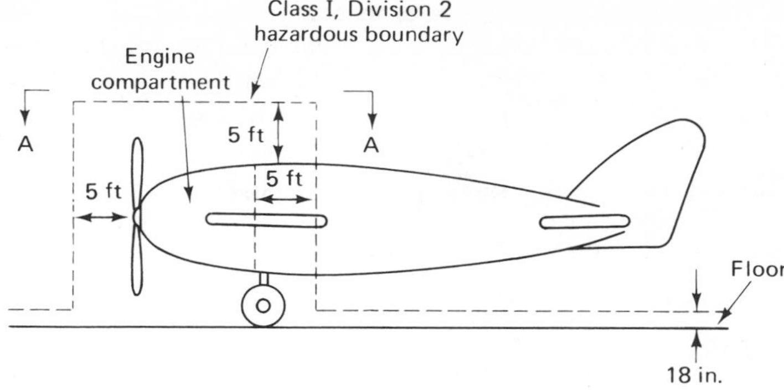

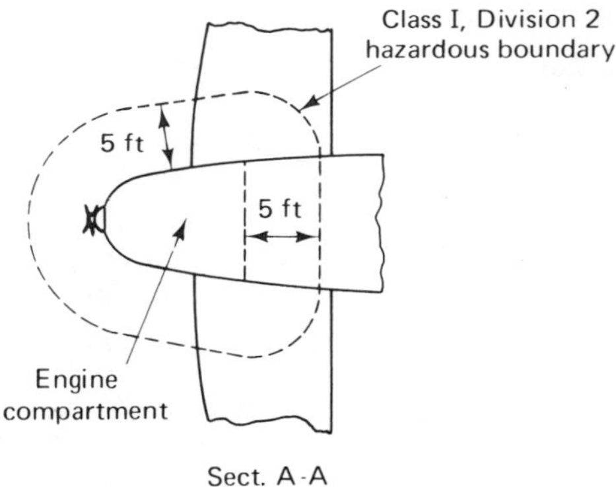

Fig. 516

Hazardous area around an aircraft engine compartment (power plant) [Sect. 513-2(c)]. The hazardous area around a fuel tank has the same extent: 5 ft outward from, and up to 5 ft above the tank.

(d) Adjacent areas, such as stock rooms, that are separated from the above spaces by walls or partitions, are not considered hazardous if properly ventilated.

513-3. Wiring and Equipment in Hazardous Locations

Section 513-2 gives the classification of different areas within a hangar—whether Class I, Division 1 or Class I, Division 2. All wiring and equipment within a hazardous area in a hangar shall meet the requirements for either a Class I, Division 1, or Class I, Division 2 location, according to the classification of the area in which the wiring and equipment is located. Note that wiring in or under the hangar floor is classified as Class I, Division 1.

Attachment plugs and receptacles in hazardous areas are subject to an option. They may be either approved for Class I locations, or, as an alternative, may be of a type so designed that they cannot be plugged or unplugged unless the circuit is "off." Plugs and receptacles must be the polarized type.

513-4. Wiring Not Within Hazardous Locations

(a) Wiring that is outside the hazardous areas in a hangar may be:

1. Rigid *metal* conduit.
2. EMT.
3. Type MI cable (mineral-insulated).
4. Intermediate metal conduit.
5. Type TC cable (power and control tray cable).
6. Type SNM cable (shielded nonmetallic).
7. Type MC cable (metal-clad).

This requirement is for nonhazardous areas in the room where the aircraft are stored, such as areas above the 18-in. level. In adjoining nonhazardous rooms, the wiring may be any approved type.

(b) Cords for pendants may be one of the following types: S, SO, ST, STO, SJ, SJO, SJT, or SJTO. The cord must have a grounding conductor.

(c) Cords for portable lamps and portable appliances are limited to type S, SO, ST, or STO. The cord must have a grounding conductor.

(d) Receptacles and plugs must be the grounding polarized type. The same circuit wire in the cord that connects to the "identified" (white) terminal in the appliance must connect to the "neutral" slot of the receptacle.

Appliances must be grounded. The green grounding conductor in the cord would be used for this purpose.

513-5. Equipment Not Within Hazardous Locations

(a) Any equipment that might produce an arc or spark, and which is less than 10 ft above wings and engine of aircraft, must have a tight enclosure that will prevent the escape of the arc or spark. An open-type lighting fixture would not be permitted in this area. A fluorescent tube or light bulb must be protected by a globe or by a lens in the fixture.

(b) Metal light sockets are not permitted in the nonhazardous areas in a hangar, for fixed incandescent lighting. Sockets must be of bakelite, porcelain, rubber, or other nonmetallic material.

(c) Portable lamps must be "approved for Class I locations" [see Section 501-9(a)(1) and (b)(1)].

(d) Portable heating appliances must be "approved for Class I locations" [see Section 501-10(b)(1)].

Portable appliances having motors with brushes, or capacitor start motors, or motors with a thermal protector, must be "approved for Class I locations" [see Sections 501-10(b)(2) and 501-8(b)]. If an appliance has a switch, the switch enclosure must be "approved for Class I locations."

Other portable appliances may be the general-purpose type.

The above requirements are for nonhazardous areas in the room where the aircraft is stored, such as areas above the 18-in. level. In adjoining nonhazardous rooms, equipment may be any approved type.

513-6. Stanchions, Rostrums, and Docks

(a) If these are located, or likely to be located, in a hazardous area of the hangar, the entire stanchion, rostrum, or dock is considered a hazardous location, and all wiring and equipment must meet the requirements for Class I, Division 2 locations.

(b) If they are not located, or not likely to be located, in a hazardous area, they are considered hazardous only up to a height of 18 in. above the floor. Above the 18-in. level, wiring and equipment may be according to Sections 513-4 and 513-5. Wiring and equipment below the 18-in. level must meet the requirements for Class I, Division 2 locations.

(c) The Code requires a warning sign for mobile stanchions having attached electrical equipment: WARNING—KEEP 5 FEET CLEAR OF AIRCRAFT ENGINES AND FUEL TANK AREAS.

513-7. Sealing

A seal is required at every point where a conduit run passes from a hazardous area to a nonhazardous area, or from a Division 1 to a Division 2 location. Note that conduit beneath the hangar floor is considered to be Class I, Division 1. If such conduit emerges from the floor, however, it is considered to be passing from a Division 2 area to a Division 2 area.

513-8. Aircraft Electrical Systems

When an aircraft is stored in a hangar, the battery should be disconnected. It should also be disconnected, if possible, when the aircraft is brought into the hangar for repairs or maintenance.

513-9. Aircraft Battery-Charging and Equipment

Aircraft batteries shall not be charged when the aircraft is in a hangar. The charging must be done when the aircraft is entirely outside the hangar.

It is recommended that battery chargers be kept in a separate building when not in use.

Mobile chargers must carry a warning sign, with the same wording as in Section 513-6(c).

513-10. External Power Sources for Energizing Aircraft

(a) Electrical equipment on energizers must be kept at least 5 ft clear of aircraft engines and fuel tank areas, and must be at least 18 in. above the floor.

(b) Mobile energizers must carry a warning sign, with the same wording as in Section 513-6(c).

(c) Cords used with energizers must be type S, SO, ST, or STO. Cords must have a grounding conductor.

513-11. Mobile Servicing Equipment with Electric Components

(a) "Servicing equipment" would include vacuum cleaners, air compressors, etc. Unless such equipment is approved for Class I, Division 2 locations, the electrical equipment connected with them must be kept at least 5 ft clear of aircraft engines and fuel tank areas, and must be at least 18 in. above the floor.

Such equipment must carry a warning sign, with the same wording as in Section 513-6(c).

(b) Cords used with servicing equipment must be type S, SO, ST, or STO. Cords must have a grounding conductor.

(c) Unless the equipment is approved for Class I, Division 2 locations, it must not be used where hazardous vapors are likely to be released.

513-12. Grounding

All electrical equipment, both fixed and portable, must be grounded.

ARTICLE 514 — GASOLINE DISPENSING AND SERVICE STATIONS

514-1. Definitions

The most common application of the rules of Article 514 would be for the gasoline service station.

Offices, repair rooms, compressor rooms, and other spaces outside the hazardous areas of a service station are subject to the rules of Article 511, Commercial Garages. Hazardous areas in service stations are defined in Section 514-2.

Gasoline service stations are not the only areas coming under the rules of Article 514. Any location having a gasoline dispensing pump, whether in a service station or elsewhere, would be subject to the rules of this Article.

Note that the rules apply not only for gasoline, but for any "volatile flammable liquid." See definition of "volatile flammable liquid," p. 70-14 of the Code.

514-2. Hazardous Locations

(a) The space surrounding a gasoline pump 18 in. out from the pump and 4 ft up from its base is a hazardous location (Fig. 517). The space within the pump and immediately beneath the pump is likewise a hazardous location. These are considered Class I, Division 1 locations, and all electrical equipment and wiring within this space must meet the requirements for Class I, Division 1 locations as set forth in Article 501.

(b) In addition to the above, the circular outside area surrounding the gasoline pump $18\frac{1}{2}$ ft out from the 18-in. circle is considered a Class I, Division 2 location up to a height of 18 in. above ground. A building, or any part of a building, within this circle is Class I, Division 2, if not suitably cut off (Fig. 517). (A solid wall or an 18-in. elevation above grade would in most cases constitute a suitable cutoff.)

(c) The circular outside area surrounding a fill pipe, 10 ft out from the pipe, is considered a Class I, Division 2 location up to a height of 18 in. above ground (Fig. 517). The space within a building that is within the 10-ft circle is Class I, Division 2, if not suitably cut off. (A wall or an 18-in. elevation above grade would in most cases constitute a suitable cutoff.)

(d) Wiring and equipment underneath the foregoing hazardous spaces (buried cable or conduit, for instance) is a Class I, Division 1 location *up to the point of emergence from the ground.*

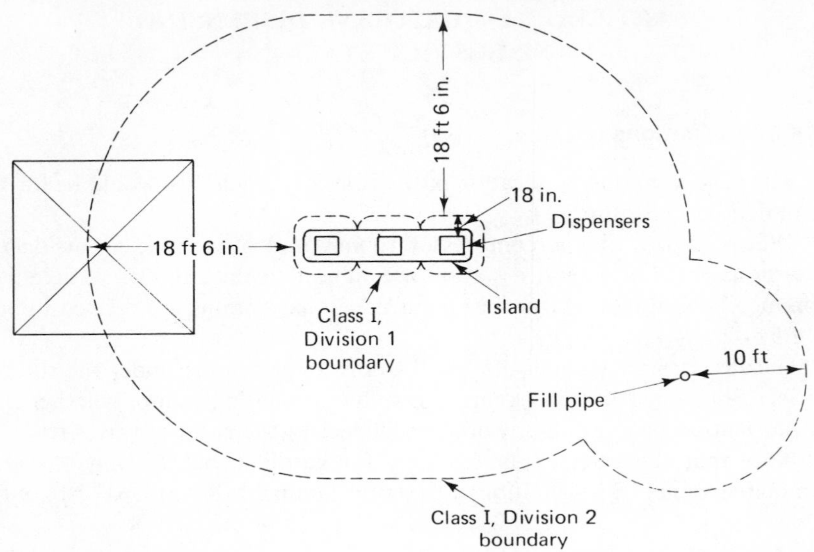

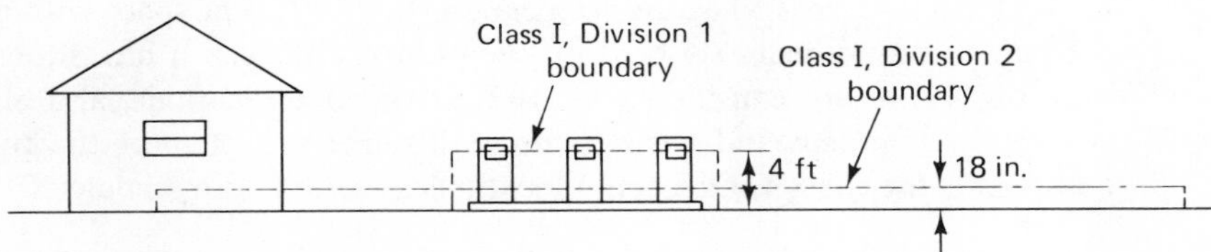

Fig. 517
Hazardous locations in service stations (Sect. 514-2).

(e) When a gasoline pump is suspended from a canopy, the entire area within the enclosure and 18 in. out from the enclosure in all directions is considered Class I, Division 1. The space 2 ft beyond the 18-in. limit and down to grade is Class I, Division 2.

The surrounding space out to a distance of 20 ft, measured from a point vertically below the edge of the dispenser enclosure, is Class I, Division 2 up to a height of 18 in. above grade. If a building or part of a building falls within this space, it is nonhazardous *if suitably cut off* by a ceiling or wall.

(f) The area 3 ft in all directions from the discharge ends of a vent pipe is Class I, Division 1. The area 2 ft beyond the 3-ft range is Class I, Division 2.

(g) A lubrication room is Class I, Division 2 up to a height of 18 in. above the floor. A pit in a lubrication room is Class I, Division 1 from the floor down to the bottom of the pit.

514-3. Wiring and Equipment Within Hazardous Locations

Wiring and equipment within the hazardous areas of a service station must meet the requirements of Article 501 for a Class I, Division 1, or Class I, Division 2 location, as the case may be.

There is one exception. Article 501 does not permit rigid nonmetallic conduit to be used in Class I hazardous locations, but for service stations this conduit may be run underground, as per Section 514-8. [Underground runs in some locations are classified Class I, Division 1; see Section 514-2(d)].

The use of rigid nonmetallic conduit in a Class I location of a service station is the only deviation permitted from the rules of Article 501.

514-4. Wiring and Equipment Above Hazardous Locations

The rules for wiring and equipment above hazardous areas (above the 18-in. level, for instance) are the same as for commercial garages (see Sections 511-5 and 511-6).

514-5. Circuit Disconnects

Circuits leading to a gasoline pump or through a gasoline pump must have a switch, with a pole for *each conductor,* including the neutral. The switch may be located within, or away from the pump.

514-6. Sealing

1. A seal is required where conduit enters a gasoline pump.

2. Seals must be placed in each conduit run entering the enclosure for switches, circuit breakers, fuses, relays, resistors, or any other device that could produce arcing, sparking, *or high temperature,* and located within a hazardous area. The seal must be no further than 18 in. from the enclosure.

   In each run of 2-in. or larger conduit, seals must be placed also at junction boxes or fittings if the box or fitting contains a splice, tap, or connection and is located in a hazardous area. The seal must be within 18 in. of the box or fitting.

3. A seal is required where a conduit run leaves a hazardous area and passes into a nonhazardous area. (Exception: If a conduit run simply "passes through" a hazardous area, seals are not required, provided the

run through, and 12 in. beyond the hazardous area, is without fittings of any kind.)

An example of an application of this rule would be an underground conduit run from within the service station house to a light standard on the premises. Assume that the light standard is in a nonhazardous location, but the conduit passes under a 20-ft circle, which makes the entire underground run Class I, Division 1 [Section 514-2(d)]. The run passes from a Class I, Division 1 location to nonhazardous areas at the light standard and at the service station house. If there is a box, fitting, union, or coupling anywhere in the underground run, seals are required at the light standard and at the service station house where the conduit leaves the ground (Fig. 518).

If the entire run is a single unbroken length of conduit, the seals may be omitted.

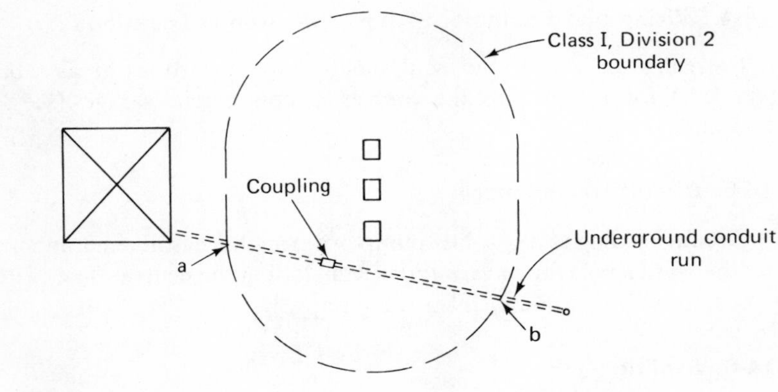

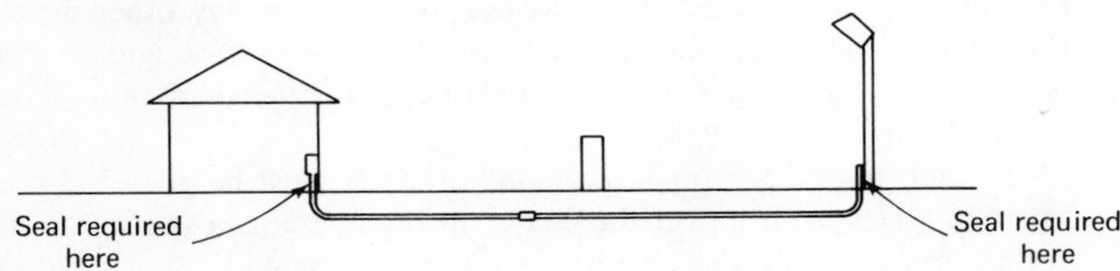

Fig. 518

Sealing (Sect. 514-6). Any conduit fitting located beneath a hazardous area requires sealing of the conduit.

514-7. Grounding

All electrical equipment must be grounded. Gasoline pumps must be grounded.

514-8. Underground Wiring

Underground wiring buried less than 2 ft below the surface must be rigid metal conduit or threaded steel intermediate conduit. If buried 2 ft or more below the surface, nonmetallic conduit may be used.

Type MI cable is also permitted for underground wiring.

ARTICLE 515 — BULK-STORAGE PLANTS

515-1. Definition

Article 515 deals with bulk-storage plants for gasoline or other "volatile flammable liquids."

515-2. Hazardous Locations

(a) Pumps, Bleeders, Withdrawal Fittings, Meters, and Similar Devices

Devices such as these in a gasoline pipeline could be subject to leakage, and therefore present a hazard. When such devices are located *indoors,* the hazardous area around the devices extends:

1. 5 feet in all directions. This boundary would be an imaginary sphere around the device.

2. 25 feet out horizontally and 3 ft up from the floor grade. This boundary would be an imaginary circular area around the device.

For adequately ventilated rooms, the above areas are considered Class I, Division 2 areas. For inadequately ventilated rooms, they are Class I, Division 1 areas (Fig. 519).

All wiring and equipment in these areas must meet the requirements for a Class I, Division 1 or Class I, Division 2 location as the case may be.

For a device located outdoors, the hazardous area (Class I, Division 2) around the device would extend:

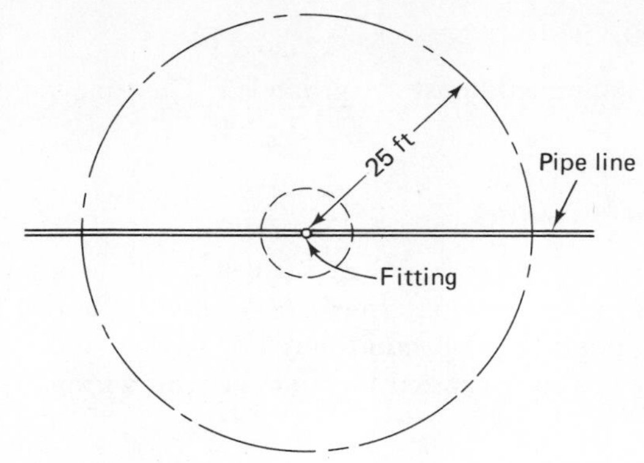

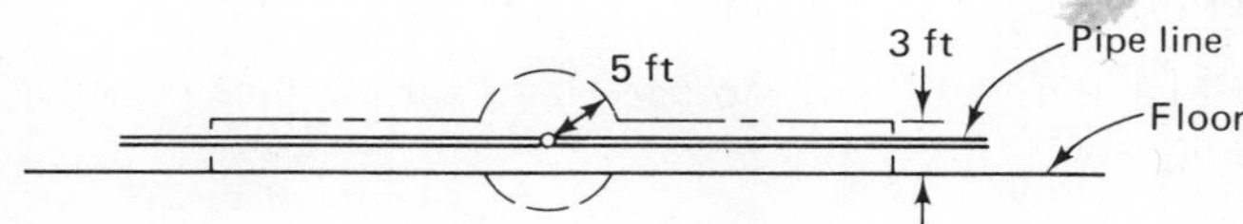

Fig. 519

Hazardous area around pumps, bleeders, withdrawal fittings, meters, and similar devices located indoors [Sect. 515-2(a)]. The hazardous area is Class I, Division 1 for locations with inadequate ventilation, and Class I, Division 2 for locations adequately ventilated.

1. 3 feet in all directions (an imaginary sphere).
2. 10 feet out along the ground and 18 in. up from the ground (an imaginary circular area).

(b) Transfer of Flammable Liquids to Individual Containers

For vent and fill pipe openings located outdoors, the hazardous area around the vent or pipe opening extends:

1. 5 feet in all directions.
2. To a 10-ft radius around the vent or pipe opening and 18 in. up from the ground.

The 5-ft sphere is Class I, Division 1 up to 3 ft out. The rest of the sphere is

Class I, Division 2. The 10-ft circular area is Class I, Division 2 from the 3-ft radius outward.

The same rule applies for vent and fill pipes in indoor areas *with adequate ventilation.*

For vent and fill pipes in indoor areas *without* adequate ventilation, the 10-ft circular area and the entire 5-ft spherical area are Class I, Division 1.

(c) Loading and Unloading of Tank Vehicles and Tank Cars in Outside Locations

The hazardous area extends 15 ft in all directions around an open dome or vent. The 15-ft sphere is Class I, Division 1 up to 3 ft out. The rest is Class I, Division 2.

For bottom loading or unloading, the hazardous area extends 3 ft in all directions from the fixed connection, and within a 10-ft radius and 18 in. up from the ground. This is all Class I, Division 2.

The above areas are considered hazardous only during loading and unloading operations.

(d) Aboveground Tanks

The space above the roof and within the shell of a floating roof type tank is a Class I, Division 1 location.

For other tanks, the area within 10 ft in all directions is considered Class I, Division 2, except that the area within 5 ft in all directions from a vent is considered Class I, Division 1; between 5 and 10 ft it is Class I, Division 2.

(e) Pits

A pit located anywhere in the 10- or 25-ft circle around pumps, bleeders, meters, etc. is a Class I, Division 1 location.

A pit located anywhere in the 10-ft circle around a vent or fill pipe opening is a Class I, Division 1 location.

A pit located in a nonhazardous area is considered nonhazardous if there are no piping, valves, or fittings in the pit. If the pit has piping, valves or fittings, it is Class I, Division 2.

(f) Garages for Tank Vehicles

Storage and repair garages for tank vehicles are Class I, Division 2 up to a height of 18 in. above the floor, but this area could be classified Class I, Division 1, if the authority having jurisdiction so judges.

(g) Adjacent Locations

Office buildings, boiler rooms, etc., are not considered hazardous locations (if not used for handling and storage of gasoline).

515-3. Wiring and Equipment Within Hazardous Locations

All wiring and equipment in a hazardous area must meet the requirements for a Class I, Division 1 or Class I, Division 2 location, as the case may be. See Article 501 for requirements.

515-4. Wiring and Equipment Above Hazardous Locations

This refers to wiring and equipment above any hazardous level, such as the 3-ft and 18-in. levels specified in the foregoing sections.

1. Wiring methods permitted are:

   Metal conduit.

   EMT.

   Type MI cable.

   Type TC cable.

   Type SNM cable.

   Type MC cable.

2. Equipment that might produce an arc or spark (such as lighting fixtures, switches, or receptacles) must be totally enclosed or have tight enclosures that will prevent the escape of arcs or sparks.

   DC motors, wound-rotor motors, capacitor-start motors must be the totally enclosed type. Squirrel-cage motors, split-phase motors (provided they do not have a built-in thermal protector) may be the general-purpose type, since these motors have no brushes or contacts that might produce a spark or arc. Any motor with a built-in thermal protector must be totally enclosed, regardless of the type of motor.

   Appliances and portable lamps used in the area above the hazardous level must meet the requirements for the class of hazardous location *underneath* them. This would be either Class I, Division 1, or Class I, Division 2.

515-5. Underground Wiring

If buried less than 2 ft, rigid or intermediate *metal* conduit must be used.

If buried 2 ft or more, nonmetallic conduit or underground cable may be used.

If nonmetallic conduit is used, a grounding conductor must be run with the circuit conductors.

If underground cable without a metal sheath is used, the cable must have a grounding conductor.

Conductor insulation must be of a type "approved for the location." (Lead-covered conductors are suitable for any location.)

If cable is used, it must be protected by rigid metal conduit at points where it emerges from the earth.

515-6. Sealing

1. Seals must be placed in each conduit run entering the enclosure for switches, circuit breakers, fuses, relays, resistors, or any other device that could produce arcing, sparking, *or high temperature,* and which is located in a hazardous area. The seal must be no further than 18 in. from the enclosure.

2. A seal is required at the point in a conduit run where the conduit leaves a hazardous area and passes into a nonhazardous area. The seal does not have to be at the exact boundary of the hazardous area. It may be at a convenient point in the run, on either side, but it is advisable to place the seal as near to the boundary as is practicable.

   A vertical run must be sealed where it enters or leaves the hazardous level (18 in., or 36 in. above the floor or ground). Or, for a horizontal run, if the run leaves the area at a height below the hazardous level, the conduit must be sealed at the point where it leaves the hazardous area.

   Exception: When a conduit run simply "passes through" a hazardous area, with *no fitting* within or 12 in. beyond the hazardous area, seals are not required.

3. For 2-in. and larger conduit, seals are required at the entry to a box or fitting if the box or fitting contains a splice, tap, or connection and is located within a hazardous area. The seal must be within 18 in. of the box or fitting.

   Conduit buried *underneath* a hazardous area is considered to be in the hazardous area beneath which it is buried.

515-7. Gasoline Dispensing

If there are gasoline pumps on the premises, the pump area must conform to the rules for service stations (Article 514).

515-8. Grounding

All metal enclosures of electrical equipment must be grounded. This applies for nonhazardous as well as hazardous areas.

ARTICLE 516 — FINISHING PROCESSES

516-1. Definition

Article 516 applies for locations where paint, lacquer, or powdered finishing materials are frequently applied by brushing, spraying, or dipping.

516-2. Hazardous Locations

If the brushing, spraying, or dipping is *not* done in a spray booth, the hazardous areas are as follows:

1. The space around a spraying operation which would contain a dangerous quantity of spray vapor is a Class I, Division 1 location. The Code does not set a definite boundary for this space. The extent of the hazardous area would be subject to the judgment of the "authority having jurisdiction."
2. The space beyond the Class I, Division 1 space is Class I, Division 2 up to 20 ft beyond, and up from the floor to a height of 10 ft above the spraying area.
3. For dipping operations, all space within 5 ft in any direction from the liquid—whether the liquid is in the tank or as a wet coating on the drain board or on the dipped object—is a Class I, Division 1 location.

If the brushing, spraying, or dipping is done in a spray booth, the entire spray booth is Class I, Division 1. Exhaust ducts for the spray booth are also Class I, Division 1.

If the spray booth has an open front, the space outside the booth is Class I, Division 2 as follows:

1. For spray booths with an interlocked vent system so arranged that no spraying can be done except when the vent system is operating, the space outside the booth is Class I, Division 2 to the extent shown in Fig. 521.
2. For spray booths without an interlocked vent system, the space outside the spray booth is Class I, Division 2 to the extent shown in Fig. 522.

For open-top spray booths, the hazardous areas are as shown in Fig. 522, except that the Class I, Division 2 hazardous area extends to 5 ft above the booth, instead of the 3 ft shown in the diagram.

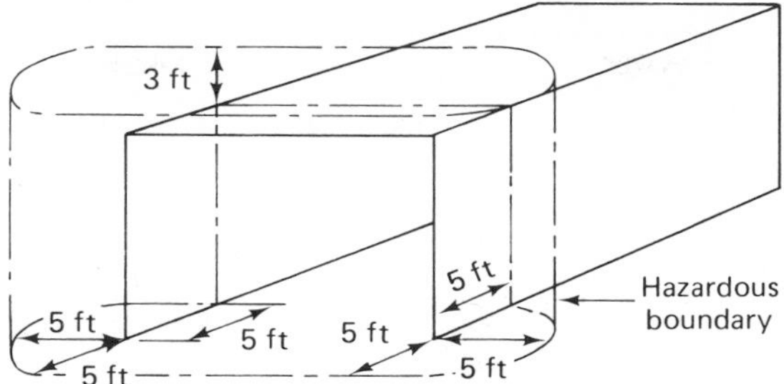

Fig. 521
Hazardous area outside an open-front spray booth with interlocked ventilation system [Sect. 516-2(b)]. The hazardous area is Class I, Division 2.

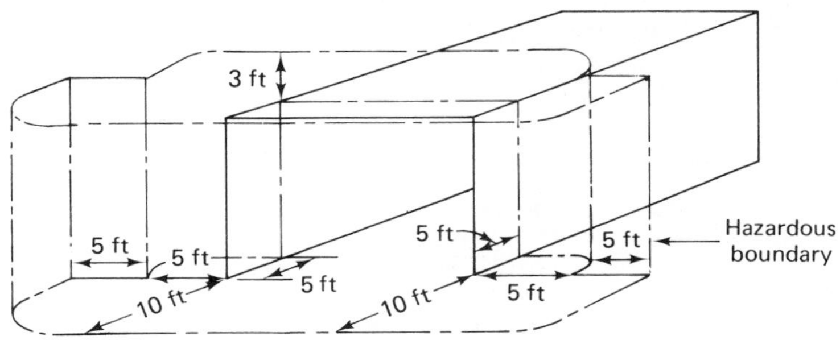

Fig. 522
Hazardous area outside an open-front spray booth having a ventilation system *not* interlocked with spraying equipment [Sect. 516-2(b)]. The hazardous area is Class I, Division 2.

516-3. Wiring and Equipment in Hazardous Locations

(a) All wiring and equipment in the hazardous areas must meet Code requirements for a Class I, Division 1 or Class I, Division 2 location, as the case may be. See Article 501 for requirements.

(b) Any equipment installed in a location where paint or lacquer might accumulate on the equipment to such an extent as to be hazardous must be approved for such service.

(c) Lighting fixtures within a spray booth are required to be "approved for Class I, Division 1 locations"—usually explosion-proof. To avoid use of these expensive fixtures, lighting is sometimes accomplished through glass panels in the wall or ceiling of the spray booth. In this way, the lighting fixture proper is outside of the Class I, Division 1 location, and a less expensive fixture can be used.

This arrangement is permissible if the panel is substantial and not likely to be broken, if the panel completely seals the lighting fixture from the hazardous area, and the size (wattage) of the light bulb (or tube) is such that the panel will not reach a dangerously high temperature.

(d) Portable lamps must be of a type "approved for Class I, Group D, Division 1 locations." Even so, portable lamps may be used in a spray booth only when no spraying, brushing, or dipping is being carried on.

516-4. Fixed Electrostatic Equipment

Fixed electrostatic spraying consists of atomizers and high-voltage grids. The high-voltage grids attract any excess spray material left in the air after the goods have been coated by the atomizer.

(a) Transformers and control equipment must be either located outside the spray booth in a nonhazardous area, or approved for Class I locations.

(b) Atomizers must be supported on insulators.

(c) Exposed high-voltage elements must be supported on suitable insulators. Means must be provided for automatic grounding of the electrode system when the primary of the voltage supply is de-energized.

(d) Goods being painted must be kept a distance from grids and atomizers equal to at least twice sparking distance.

(e) Goods being coated must be supported on conveyors or hangers. Goods must be grounded (may be grounded through the conveyor or hanger).

(f) Automatic controls must be provided, that will shut off the power to the grids (1) if ventilation stops, (2) if the conveyor stops, (3) in case of a ground, and (4) if clearance of the goods from grids or atomizers is reduced below twice sparking distance.

(g) All objects within the charging influence of the electrodes must be grounded. This includes paint containers and wash cans.

(h) A fence, railing, or other guard is required around the equipment.

516-5. Electrostatic Hand-Spraying Equipment

(a) High-voltage circuits shall be so designed or arranged as to prevent sparks.

(b) Transformers and control equipment must be either located outside the spray booth in a nonhazardous area, or approved for Class I locations.

(c) The spray gun handle must be grounded.

(d) All metal objects in the spray booth must be grounded. This includes paint containers and wash cans.

(e) Goods to be painted must be grounded (may be grounded through the hook and conveyor).

(f) Adequate ventilation must be provided for the spray booth. Electric equipment must be interlocked with the vent system so that equipment can be operated only when vents are in operation.

516-6. Powder Coating

Electrical equipment must be approved for Class II locations.

Transformers and control equipment must be either located outside the booth in a nonhazardous area, or approved for Class II locations.

All metal objects in the powder-coating area must be grounded.

Goods to be powdered must be grounded (may be grounded through the hook and conveyor).

Ventilation must be interlocked with the powder-coating equipment so that the equipment cannot be operated unless the ventilating fans are operating.

516-7. Wiring and Equipment Above Hazardous Locations

(a) Above hazardous areas, the following wiring methods are permitted:

1. Metal conduit.
2. EMT.
3. Type MI cable.
4. Type TC cable.
5. Type SNM cable.
6. Type MC cable.
7. Rigid nonmetallic conduit.

Leads without seals may be brought out of a cellular metal raceway in the ceiling, but leads may be brought out of a cellular metal raceway in the floor only if seals are provided.

(b) All equipment that might produce an arc or spark, such as lighting fixtures, switches or receptacles, must have tight enclosures without openings of any kind. DC motors, wound-rotor motors, capacitor-start motors, and all motors with built-in thermal protectors, must be the totally enclosed type.

516-8. Grounding

All equipment within hazardous areas must be grounded.

ARTICLE 517 — HEALTH-CARE FACILITIES

A. General

517-1. Scope

Article 517 sets down the special rules that apply to hospitals, sanitariums, and other occupancies where persons are treated for ailments or infirmities.

B. Wiring Systems—General

517-10. Wiring Methods

For hospitals with an emergency electrical system, the emergency system wiring must be "run in metal raceway" (Section 517-61). This would limit the type of wiring for emergency systems to metal conduit, EMT, cellular metal floor raceways or metal wireways.

For wiring other than for the emergency system, any approved wiring method suitable for the location is permitted.

517-11. Grounding

All metal electrical equipment in areas that are or may be occupied by patients, and which are subject to contact by persons, must be grounded by an insulated copper conductor sized in accordance with Table 250-95 of the Code. The copper grounding conductor must be run with the circuit conductors.

517-13. Ground-Fault Protection

When ground-fault protection is provided in the service disconnect for the "normal" supply, ground-fault protection shall be provided also in each feeder. Feeder ground-fault protection shall be designed to open before the main ground-fault device in the service disconnect opens should a ground occur in a feeder.

D. Nursing Homes and Residential Custodial Care Facilities

517-41. Facilities Limited to Specific Services

The following are requirements for nursing homes and custodial care facilities which do *not* provide life-support apparatus or surgery for patients. [Nursing homes and custodial care facilities having hospital facilities are treated as hospitals, and the alternate power source must comply with the requirements applying to hospitals. Note that, for hospitals, the only alternate power source permitted is a generator (Sect. 517-65).]

In addition to the regular power supply, an alternate source of power is required. The alternate power source may be any one of the following:

1. A generator.

2. A bank of storage batteries.

3. A second service.

The alternate source need not be sized to take over the entire electrical load. When the normal supply fails, the alternate source is required to take over only the emergency circuits. "Nonessential" circuits would be without power until the normal power supply is restored.

Generators must be provided with automatic starting, so arranged that the generator will automatically start up, attain full voltage, and deliver power to the emergency circuits within 10 seconds after a power failure.

Batteries must be capable of supplying the total emergency load at not less that $87\frac{1}{2}\%$ of full voltage, for a period of at least $1\frac{1}{2}$ hours; or of supplying emergency lighting (corridor lighting, exit signs, etc.) and alarm systems for a period of not less than 4 hours. An automatic battery charging means must be provided for the battery bank.

When a separate service is used as an alternate power supply, it must be completely separated from the normal service—with a separate drop or lateral, and separate service equipment.

The following Sections 517-44 through 517-46 apply specifically to nursing homes and custodial care facilities that provide life-support apparatus for residents (electric respirators, suction apparatus, etc.). Nursing homes without such patient-care facilities need not comply with the requirements of these Sections.

517-44. Emergency System

For nursing homes and residential custodial care facilities, the emergency system consists of:

1. The Life Safety Branch.
2. The Critical Branch.

517-45. Life Safety Branch

The life safety branch shall serve *only* the following:

1. Lighting for corridors and stairways.
2. Exit signs and directional signs.
3. Sufficient lighting in dining and recreational areas to provide illumination for exit of persons. (Not all of the lighting in these areas need be connected to the life safety branch, only enough to provide a safe exit of persons.)
4. Alarm systems.
5. Communication systems intended for use during emergencies.
6. Lighting and selected receptacles in the generator room.

Night Transfer of Corridor Lighting

In addition to ceiling lights, sometimes a corridor or passageway is equipped with lights set in the wall a foot or so off the floor. These are "night lights" and are intended to illuminate only the floor. At night the ceiling lights are turned off, and these lights are used instead, the purpose being to avoid the glare of ceiling lights. Where there are night lights, the Code permits a double throw switch that would allow an unauthorized person to change over from ceiling lighting to night lighting. The switch shall have no "off" position. A three-way toggle switch has no "off" position; it is on "make" in either position. Three-way *switching* is not permitted, but an *individual* three-way switch acting as a double throw switch would be permitted for this application.

517-46. Critical Branch

The following components of the Critical System shall be connected for automatic transfer to the alternate power source:

1. Task illumination and selected receptacles in

   Medication preparation areas.

   Pharmacy dispensing areas.

   Nurses' stations.

2. Sump pumps and other equipment required for major apparatus.
3. Elevator cab lighting and communication systems.

The following may be connected for either manual or automatic transfer to the alternate power source:

1. Heating equipment for patient rooms.
2. Elevator service (if provided) between patient rooms and ground floor, including elevator cab lighting, and control and signal systems.

Note: There are two exceptions for heating equipment:

(a) If the facility is located in a moderate or warm climate, this equipment may be connected to the normal supply system.

(b) If there are two separate normal services to the facility, connected to *two different distribution systems,* the equipment may be connected to the normal supply system, regardless of climate.

517-47. Inpatient Hospital Care Facilities

When a nursing home or a residential custodial care facility has inpatient hospital facilities, it is treated as a hospital, and must comply with the requirements for hospitals, as set forth in Part E, following.

E. Hospitals

517-61. Emergency System—Hospitals

The emergency system in hospitals is divided into two parts:

1. Life Safety Branch.
2. Critical Branch.

Wiring for the two systems must be kept completely separate from other wiring, and the two systems must be kept separate from each other. Wiring must be run in *metal raceway* (conduit is raceway).

Wiring for either system may not enter a box or enclosure containing other wiring. Exceptions are made for:

1. Transfer switches.
2. Exit or emergency lights served by two sources of power.
3. Separately derived low-voltage signaling, alarm, and communication circuits.

517-62. Life Safety Branch—Hospitals

The life safety branch of the emergency system shall serve the following equipment:

1. Lighting for corridors and stairways.
2. Exit signs and directional signs.
3. Fire-alarm systems.
4. Sprinkler systems.
5. Smoke detection systems.
6. Alarms for medical gases.
7. Communication systems intended for use during emergencies.
8. Lighting and selected receptacles in the generator room.

Night Transfer of Corridor Lighting

In addition to ceiling lights, sometimes a corridor or passageway is equipped with lights set in the wall a foot or so off the floor. These are "night lights" and are intended to illuminate only the floor. At night the ceiling lights are turned off, and these lights are used instead, the purpose being to avoid the glare of ceiling lights. Where there are night lights, the Code permits a double throw switch that would allow an unauthorized person to change over from ceiling lighting to night lighting. The switch shall have no "off" position. A three-way toggle switch has no "off" position; it is on "make" in either position. Three-way switching is not permitted, but an *individual* three-way switch acting as a double throw switch would be permitted for this application.

517-63. Critical Branch—Hospitals

The critical branch of the emergency system shall serve *only* the following:

(1) Isolating transformers for anesthetizing locations.

(2) Selected receptacles and task illumination in:

1. Infant nurseries.
2. Medication preparation areas.
3. Pharmacy dispensing areas.
4. Selected acute nursing areas.
5. Psychiatric bed areas (task illumination only).
6. Nurses' stations.
7. Ward treatment rooms.
8. Surgical and obstetrical suites.
9. Angiographic labs.
10. Cardiac catheterization labs.
11. Coronary care units.
12. Delivery rooms.
13. Dialysis units.
14. Emergency room treatment areas.
15. Human physiology labs.
16. Intensive care units.
17. Operating rooms.
18. Post-operative recovery rooms.
19. Corridors in general patient care areas.

517-64. Equipment Systems—Hospitals

This system serves equipment that, while necessary and important to the operation of the hospital, is not equipment of a highly critical nature such as lights and equipment in an operating room. The Code permits a delay of no longer than 10 seconds in restoring power to the *emergency* system, but for the *equipment* system a longer delay is permitted between power failure and restoration of power. In fact the Code *requires* a longer delay so that the equipment system is put back in operation after the emergency system is restored to power. Wiring for the equipment system may be run with the general wiring and installed according to the general rules for wiring. Any approved method of wiring suitable for the location is permitted.

The equipment system is divided into two parts:

1. Circuits that must be restored to power *automatically* after a time delay.
2. Circuits that may be restored to power either manually or automatically after a time delay.

Equipment in the first group consists of:

1. Central vacuum and medical air systems serving medical and surgical functions.
2. Sump pumps and other equipment necessary for operation of essential apparatus.

Equipment in the second group consists of:

1. Heating equipment for heating operating, delivery, labor, recovery, and patient rooms, intensive care units, and nurseries. There are two exceptions for heating equipment:
   (a) If the hospital is located in a moderate or warm climate, this equipment may be connected to the "general power" circuits.
   (b) If there are two separate normal services to the hospital, connected to *two different distribution systems,* the equipment may be connected to the "general power" circuits, regardless of climate.
2. Elevator service to (1) patient floors, (2) ground floor, (3) surgical floors, (4) obstetrical delivery floors.
3. Vent systems for (1) laboratory fume hoods, (2) surgical suites, (3) obstetrical suites, (4) infant nurseries, and (5) emergency treatment spaces with no windows.

The following equipment may be connected to the "manual or automatic" circuits, if desired:

1. Selected autoclaving equipment.
2. Other selected equipment in locations such as kitchens and laundries.

517-65. Power Sources

The standby (alternate) source of power must be a generator. Batteries are not permitted as an alternate source.

The normal source would be the service (or services). The Code recommends, but does not require, that there be two separate services, each capable of carrying the entire load. Such an arrangement would provide three sources of power: the normal service, the alternate service, and the generator.

517-66. Switching and Overcurrent Protection

(a)(b) The emergency generator must be able to start up, attain full voltage, and deliver power to the essential circuits within 10 seconds after a power failure. This would be accomplished through double throw automatic "transfer" switches. Normally, the essential circuits are connected to the regular power source. When the normal power source fails, the transfer switch automatically disconnects the essential circuits from the normal source and connects to the alternate source, within 10 seconds after the emergency generator has started up. (The generator must be capable of attaining full voltage in 10 seconds.)

When normal-service voltage is restored, the essential load is transferred back to the normal power source. The Code requires a time delay of 15 minutes before reconnection to the normal source. A time-delay feature would have to be built into the transfer switches to prevent reconnection immediately after a short-time power failure.

(c) A switch for exit lighting in a health care facility must be located where only "authorized" persons can turn the lights off. The switch could be located in the office of the building superintendent, for instance, but may not be located in a corridor or in any location where unauthorized people would have access to it. In addition to a switch so located, the Code permits one or more switches in places where "unauthorized" persons may operate them, provided the switches operate in parallel. With the switches connected in parallel, when the "authorized" switch is "on," the other switches cannot turn the lights off, and this satisfies the intent of the Code that the exit lighting cannot be turned off except by an "authorized" person. The Code has no objection to an unauthorized person turning the lights "on" when they are "off," but will not permit unauthorized turning "off" when they are "on." Three- or four-way switching is *not* permitted for exit lights.

Exit lights would be lights in corridors and stairways, and also the lights for "exit" signs and direction signs.

In addition to ceiling lights, sometimes a corridor or passageway is equipped with lights set in the wall a foot or so off the floor. These are "night lights" and are intended to illuminate only the floor. At night the ceiling lights are turned off, and these lights are used instead, the purpose being to avoid the glare of ceiling lights. Where there are night lights, the Code permits a double throw switch that would allow an unauthorized person to change over from ceiling lighting to night lighting. The switch shall have no "off" position. A three-way toggle switch has no "off" position; it is on "make" in either position. Three-way *switching* is not permitted, but an *individual* three-way switch acting as a double throw switch would be permitted for this application.

(d) The foregoing rules also apply to other lighting in a care facility that is connected to the emergency system. Only "authorized" persons may have access to a switch that would turn the lights off.

(e) In case of a power failure, the emergency generator serves the following systems [see Diagram 517-60(2), p. 70-407 of the Code]:

1. Equipment System.
2. Life Safety Branch.
3. Critical Branch.

Overcurrent protection for each of these systems must be kept separate from the others. Each system must have a separate transfer switch.

F. Patient Care Areas

517-80. General

An "electrically susceptible" patient is one being treated with an electric probe connected to the heart. Special precautions must be taken in the electrical installation in the rooms where such treatment is being carried on.

517-81. Grounding Performance

Patient-care areas are divided into three classes:

1. General care areas. Areas where patients have only occasional contact with electrical devices.

2. Critical care areas, controlled. These are areas where patients ordinarily are intentionally exposed to electrical devices (as for treatment), and the governing body requires protection of externalized cardiac conductors from contact with conductive surfaces.

3. Critical care areas, uncontrolled. These are areas where patients ordinarily are intentionally exposed to electrical devices (as for treatment), and the governing body has no requirements for protection of externalized cardiac conductors from contact with conductive surfaces.

   "Externalized cardiac conductors" are the conductors that are connected to a probe in the patient's heart.

If a heart-probe patient should contact an object with a potential difference of only 500 millivolts between patient and object, a fatal shock could result. In critical-care areas, all exposed metal objects (except chairs) are required to be bonded together and connected to a common bonding point. The bonding maintains the difference in potential between metal objects that are within reach of the patient, at a low level.

The potential difference between metal objects in the patient vicinity shall not exceed the following:

(1) General-care areas: 500 mV under normal operation.

(2) Critical-care areas, controlled: 100 mV under normal operation.

(3) Critical-care areas, uncontrolled: 100 mV under normal operation or conditions of line-to-ground fault.

517-83. General Care Areas

Each patient bed location shall be provided with a minimum of (4) single or (2) duplex grounding-type receptacles. Receptacle grounding must be by a copper conductor.

Each bed location shall be served by at least (2) branch circuits.

Grounding bars in the normal and essential panels feeding the location shall be bonded together. Bonding connection must be at least No. 10 copper.

517-84. Critical Care Areas

Each patient bed location shall be provided with a "reference grounding point." This is a common ground to which all grounding conductors in the location are connected. One bed location may not be served by more than one reference grounding point.

Each patient bed location shall be provided with a "patient grounding point." One or more jacks must be provided for grounding portable metal objects used near the patient. The patient grounding point must be bonded to the reference grounding point by a copper conductor, minimum size No. 10.

One or more room bonding points shall be provided for grounding metal objects in the room. Metal objects must be bonded together by a No. 10 minimum copper conductor. The room grounding point must be connected to the reference grounding point by a No. 10 minimum copper conductor.

Each patient bed location shall be provided with a minimum of (6) single or (3) duplex grounding-type receptacles. Receptacles shall be grounded to the reference grounding point by a copper conductor.

Each patient bed location shall be served by at least (2) branch circuits, one of which must be an "individual" branch circuit (see definition of "individual branch circuit," p. 70-5 of the Code.)

517-85.

When the electrical system is a grounded system, grounding of the feeder conduit shall be by grounding bushings connected to the panelboard grounding bus by a copper conductor, minimum size No. 12.

517-86.

When the electrical system is an ungrounded isolated system, and limits first-fault current to a low value, the grounding conductor may be run outside of the power conductor raceway.

517-88.

The equipment grounding conductor for special purpose receptacles shall be bonded to the reference grounding points.

517-90. Additional Protective Techniques

(a) An isolated power system, served from an isolating transformer, is permitted for serving ungrounded circuits.

(b) 125-volt, single-phase 15- and 20-amp. receptacles in wet locations shall be provided with ground-fault protection.

517-92. Wet Locations

15 and 20-amp., 125-volt single-phase receptacles in wet locations must have ground-fault protection, except where the load is such that an uninterrupted power supply is essential. When uninterrupted power is required, the

Code permits ground-fault protection to be omitted, but when ground-fault protection is omitted for this reason, an *isolated* power supply must be provided for the receptacles.

G. Inhalation Anesthetizing Locations

517-100. Anesthetizing Location Classifications

Anesthetics may be "flammable" or "nonflammable." The Code makes a distinction between the two in this Section.

(a) Hazardous Location

Any room or space where *flammable* anesthetics are used or administered is Class I, Division 1, Group C up to a height of 5 ft above the floor.

Any room or space in which flammable anesthetics or volatile flammable disinfecting agents are *stored* is Class I, Division 1, Group C throughout.

(b) Other-Than-Hazardous Location

These are rooms or spaces in which only *nonflammable* anesthetics are used.

All of the following Sections 517-61 through 517-80 apply to flammable anesthetics locations.

Nonflammable anesthetics locations are exempted from the rules of Sections 517-61, 517-62, 517-63(f)(2), and 517-63(f)(3) as applied to X-ray systems. All other requirements apply.

517-101. Wiring and Equipment Within Hazardous Anesthetizing Locations

All wiring and equipment installed below the 5-ft level in a room where flammable anesthetics are administered or used must meet the requirements of Article 501 for Class I, Division 1, Group C locations, if the voltage is over 8 volts.

The rule also applies to equipment of over 8 volts installed *anywhere* in a room where flammable anesthetics are stored.

Cords used in these locations must be type S, SO, ST, or STO when voltage is over 8 volts.

517-102, 517-103. Wiring and Equipment in Nonhazardous or Above Hazardous Anesthetizing Locations

(1) In rooms where flammable anesthetics are used or administered, the wiring method above the 5-ft level must be one of the following:

Rigid metal conduit.

Intermediate metal conduit.

Type MI cable.

EMT.

Type MC cable with impervious sheath.

These wiring methods are also approved for wiring *nonflammable* anesthetics locations both above and below the 5-ft level.

(2) Equipment that might produce arcs or sparks, such as lamps, receptacles, and switches, must be the totally enclosed type.

DC motors, wound-rotor motors, capacitor-start motors must be the totally enclosed type. Wound-rotor motors have slip rings, DC motors have brushes, capacitor-start motors have a built-in starting switch. Any of these devices could produce an arc or spark. Squirrel-cage motors, single-value capacitor motors, and split-phase motors may be the general-purpose type, unless fitted with a thermal protector. Motors with thermal protectors must be totally enclosed regardless of type, since the thermal protector contacts could produce an arc or spark.

(3) Lighting fixtures shall conform to Section 501-9(b), except that (1) the temperature limitations of 501-9(b)(2) do not apply, and (2) permanent fixtures with switches need not be approved for Class I locations.

(4) Seals must be provided as per Section 501-5.

(5) 125-volt AC receptacles and plugs used in anesthetizing locations must be approved for hospital use. Must have a grounding terminal.

(6) This rule is for 250-volt, 50- and 60-amp. AC plugs and receptacles used (1) above the 5-ft. level in flammable anesthetic locations, and (2) throughout nonflammable anesthetic locations. Receptacles shall be so designed that:

1. A 60-amp. receptacle will take both a 50- and 60-amp. plug.

2. A 50-amp. receptacle will not take a 60-amp. plug.

Plugs must have a grounding terminal.

517-104. Circuits in Anesthetizing Locations

(a) Switches must have a pole for each conductor, including the neutral. Single-pole switches are not permitted.

Except as in (f) and (g), following, circuits in anesthetizing locations must be "isolated" and ungrounded. This would require the use of an isolating transformer at the point where a circuit enters the location. Or the location may be served by batteries or a motor-generator set.

(b) Primary or secondary voltage of isolating transformers is limited to 300 volts maximum. Secondary circuits must be *ungrounded* and have overcurrent protection in each conductor.

Circuits supplied from batteries or from generators must also have overcurrent protection in each conductor.

(c) Transformers, motor generators, batteries, battery chargers are not permitted below the 5-ft level in rooms where flammable anesthetics are administered, nor anywhere in a room where flammable anesthetics are stored.

(d) Ground-detection lamps must be provided for isolated-type circuits in an anesthetizing location. A warning bell or buzzer must also be provided, which will sound a warning in case of a ground. An ammeter shall be provided for monitoring of fault currents.

(e) A circuit for an anesthetizing room may serve only outlets within the room. No outlet outside the room may be connected to an anesthetizing room circuit.

(f) A grounded circuit may be used for (1) fixed lighting or (2) fixed X-ray equipment provided:

1. The lighting fixtures or X-ray equipment are at least 8 ft above the floor.
2. The fixtures are not surgical lighting fixtures.
3. Switches are located outside the anesthetizing room.
4. The grounded circuit is run separately from the ungrounded circuit for the room.

(g) Components of an isolated grounded power center may be located above the 5-ft level.

517-105. Low-Voltage Equipment and Instruments

(a) In anesthetizing rooms, any equipment operating at more than 8 volts that might come in contact with persons shall be double-insulated. If not double-insulated, voltage is limited to 8 volts maximum. This rule would apply principally for portable equipment.

(b) Power for anesthetizing room equipment must be supplied by isolating transformers or batteries.

(c) Both the core and case of isolating transformers must be grounded.

(d) A resistance or impedance may be used to vary current to low-voltage equipment, but must be so connected as not to limit maximum voltage to the equipment.

(e) If batteries are used to supply power for the low-voltage equipment, the charging circuit for the batteries should be through an isolating transformer. If not, a double throw switch must be provided that will disconnect the low-voltage circuits when the batteries are being charged. The purpose of these precautions is to "isolate" the low-voltage circuits from any possible direct contact with a higher-voltage charging circuit.

(f) Receptacles and plugs for the low-voltage circuits must be of a type distinct from those used on 120-volt circuits, so that a 120-volt receptacle will not take a low-voltage plug.

517-106. Other Equipment

(a) Suction, pressure, and insufflation equipment having electrical elements is considered electrical equipment. If installed below the 5-ft level in a flammable anesthetizing room, or anywhere in a room where flammable anesthetics or disinfecting agents are stored, such equipment must be approved for Class I locations. This applies for all voltages.

(b) X-ray equipment installed in the above locations must be approved for Class I, Group C locations. This applies for all voltages.

(c) High-frequency equipment used in the hazardous areas must be approved for Class I, Division 1 locations if the voltage is over 8.

517-107. Grounding

All electrical equipment must be grounded if the voltage is above 8 volts. This applies for equipment located anywhere in a room where flammable *or* nonflammable anesthetics are administered, or anywhere in a room in which flammable anesthetics or disinfecting agents are stored. If the floor is of metal, it too must be grounded.

ARTICLE 518 — PLACES OF ASSEMBLY

518-1. Scope

The requirements of Article 518 apply to all places of assembly (except theaters) with a capacity of 100 or more persons. Examples are:

Dining rooms

Meeting rooms

Lecture halls

Armories

Mortuaries

Skating rinks

Auditoriums

Nightclubs.

518-2. Other Articles

(a) Wiring and equipment in any hazardous areas within these occupancies must meet the requirements of Article 500.

(b) Where temporary wiring is required, it shall meet the requirements of Article 305 (except that, in places of assembly, approved portable cords or cables are permitted on the floor).

518-3. Wiring Methods

Fixed wiring methods permitted are:

Metal conduit.

EMT.

Metal wireways.

Type MI cable (mineral-insulated).

Type MC cable (metal-clad).

(Rigid nonmetallic conduit may also be used if encased in at least 2 in. of concrete.)

For buildings not required to be of fire-resistive construction, Romex and BX may also be used.

ARTICLE 520 — THEATERS AND SIMILAR LOCATIONS

A. General

520-1. Scope

Note that Article 520 applies for theaters, but does not apply for other "places of assembly" such as those listed in Article 518 above.

520-2. Motion-Picture Projectors

520-3. Sound Reproduction

These must comply with Articles 540 and 640, respectively.

520-4. Wiring Methods

The following wiring methods are permitted in theaters:

Metal conduit.

EMT.

Metal wireways.

Type MI cable (mineral-insulated).

Type MC cable (metal-clad).

Rigid nonmetallic conduit may also be used if encased in at least 2 in. of concrete.

(There are exceptions for sound reproduction, communication circuits, Class 2 and 3 remote-control and signal systems, and fire-protective signaling circuits. For these systems, other types of wiring may be used. Refer to applicable Articles 640, 800, 725, 760, respectively.)

520-5. Number of Conductors in Raceway

The rules of Articles 362 and 374 limit the number of conductors allowed in any wireway or auxiliary gutter to 30, regardless of the wireway or gutter size.

When used for border or stage pocket circuits, or for remote-control circuits, this rule is waived, and the wireway or gutter may contain any number of conductors, as long as the total area of all conductors does not exceed 20% of the cross-sectional area of the wireway or gutter.

520-6. Enclosing and Guarding Live Parts

Exposed live parts are not permitted.

B. Fixed Stage Switchboard

520-21. Dead Front

Stage switchboards must be the "dead-front" type. Dead-front switchboards have no exposed live parts on the front of the board. "Live-front" switchboards have exposed live parts on the front, such as exposed knife switches. Live-front switchboards may not be used as stage switchboards.

520-22. Guarding Back of Switchboard

If the back of the switchboard is not enclosed, an enclosure must be provided. The enclosure in back of the board may be a wire mesh enclosure. Or the building walls may provide the enclosure. The enclosure back of the switchboard must be fitted with a *self-closing* door. A suitable spring on the door would meet this requirement.

520-23. Control and Overcurrent Protection of Receptacle Circuits

Circuits for stage and gallery receptacles would necessarily be controlled from the same location where other stage lighting is controlled. This would be at the switchboard, and the fuse or circuit-breaker protection shall also be at the switchboard. "Gallery receptacles" would include all receptacles, wherever located, that are intended for stage lighting equipment.

520-24. Metal Hood

A switchboard that is not completely enclosed, front and rear, must be provided with a metal hood. (If the switchboard is recessed into a wall, the hood is not required.)

520-25. Dimmers

(a) A resistance or series-reactor-type dimmer may be placed in either the neutral or hot wire side of a circuit *provided* it has no "off" position

[Fig. 524(a)]. If placed in the hot wire, overcurrent protection is required. The rating of the fuse or circuit breaker may be not more than 125% of the dimmer rating. If the dimmer is placed in the neutral, individual protection is not required for the dimmer.

(b) If the dimmer has an "off" position, it must be placed in the hot wire, since the Code does not permit breaking the neutral only [Fig. 524(b)(c)].

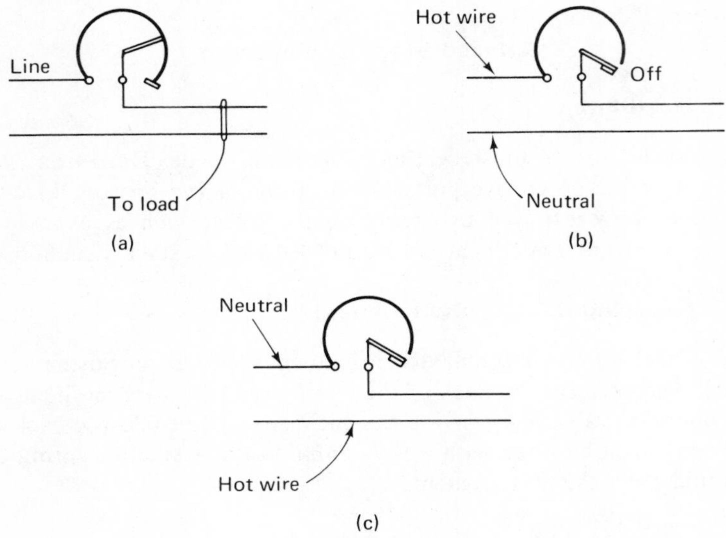

Fig. 524
Resistor-type dimmer connected in series [Sect. 520-25(b)].
(a) No "off" position: resistor may be placed in either the hot wire or the neutral.
(b) With "off" position: resistor must be placed in the hot wire.
(c) Violation: resistors with an "off" position may not be placed in the neutral.

(c)(d) With an autotransformer-type dimmer or a solid-state-type dimmer, one conductor goes "straight through" to the load. The Code requires that the "straight-through" conductor must be the neutral, not the hot wire (Fig. 525). Autotransformer-type and solid-state dimmers are limited to 150 volts maximum (between conductors).

520-26. Type of Switchboard

Stage switchboards may be the manually controlled or electrically controlled type.

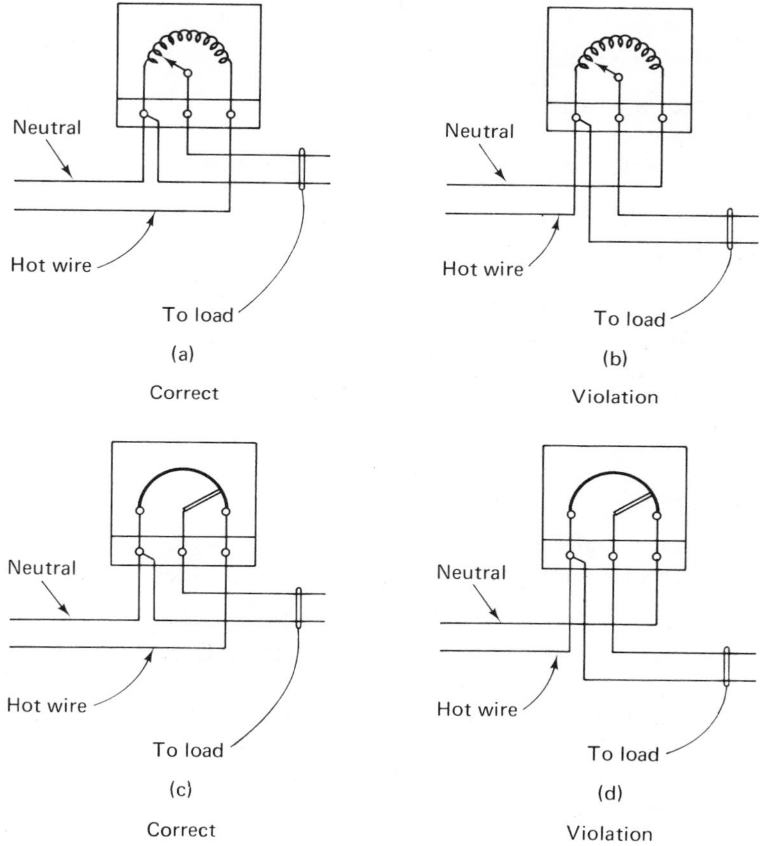

Fig. 525

(a)(b) Connections for autotransformer-type dimmer [Sect. 520-25(c)]. The neutral must be common to line and load, as in (a).

(c)(d) Connections for resistor-type dimmer connected across the line [Sect. 520-25(d)]. The neutral must be common to line and load, as in (c).

520-27. Stage Switchboard Feeders

Stage switchboards may be fed by either a single feeder or two or more feeders in parallel. When two or more feeders are used, all must be *the same length.* (This is to keep the voltage drops equal.) One neutral may serve for several parallel feeders. When two or more feeders are used, all must be fed from the same electrical system.

C. Stage Equipment—Fixed

520-41. Circuit Loads

When mogul-base lamps (lights) are used for stage lighting, a circuit may be loaded up to 50 amps.

When the lights are other than mogul base, the circuit load is limited to 20 amps.

520-42. Conductor Insulation

Conductors used for wiring footlights, border lights, and proscenium lights must have insulation suitable for high temperatures (257°F). Referring to Table 310-13 of the Code, the only type of insulation that would meet the requirements for this service would be an asbestos, mineral-insulated, poly-tetra-fluorethylene, or silicon type insulation.

520-43. Footlights

(a) If metal troughs are used, the metal must be No. 20 MSG or heavier. Circuit conductors must be *soldered* to lampholder terminals.

(b) Individual outlets are not often used for footlights, but when used they must be wired with either rigid metal conduit, Greenfield, Type MI or MC cable, or intermediate metal conduit.

Disappearing footlights would constitute a fire hazard if the lights should be left burning when in the recessed position. The Code requires a shut-off switch that will automatically disconnect the lights when they are in the recessed position.

520-44. Borders and Proscenium Sidelights

Borders are lighting fixtures for lighting the stage area. They are usually steel troughs, often hung from steel cables, so that the height may be adjusted. Cord may be used for wiring *adjustable* borders, but it must be an extra-hard usage type: Type S, SO, ST, or STO.

If the border is a fixed type, cord may not be used for wiring. A permanent type wiring method must be used.

520-45. Receptacles

Receptacles for arc lamps shall be no less than 50-amp. rating. Circuit conductors must be at least No. 6.

Receptacles for incandescent lamps must have at least a 20-amp. rating. Circuit conductors must be at least No. 12.

Plugs for arc lamps must be a different type than the plugs for the incandescent lamps, so that it would be impossible to plug an arc lamp into an incandescent lamp receptacle, or vice versa. Polarized type plugs and receptacles for arc lamps and conventional type plugs and receptacles for incandescent lamps would fulfill the requirement of this rule.

520-46. Stage Pockets

The Code requires special enclosures for stage receptacles. These are called "pockets."

Stage pockets are manufactured for either wall or floor service. They are sheet-metal boxes intended for use on a stage, for housing receptacles.

520-47. Lamps in Scene Docks

Lamps installed in scene docks must be kept at least 2 in. clear of combustible material.

520-48. Curtain Motors

This rule applies for motors having brushes or sliding contacts. It would apply for motors such as DC motors and wound-rotor AC motors.

When a motor with brushes or sliding contacts is used as a curtain motor it must be either:

1. A totally enclosed motor, or
2. Enclosed on the brush end by a sheet-metal housing, or
3. Have the upper half of the brush end enclosed by a screen and the lower half by a sheet-metal housing.

520-49. Flue Damper Control

Electrically operated flue dampers must have two control switches: one at the electrician's station and the other at a spot chosen by the "authority having jurisdiction."

In case of fire, a completely reliable means of closing off the stage flues could be of vital importance. The Code requires that "where stage flue dampers are released by an electrical device, the circuit operating the device shall be normally closed." The "electrical device" could be a solenoid wired so that, when the solenoid is energized, the flue dampers are held open; when the solenoid is deenergized, the dampers are released and the flues close. The switch at the electrician's station and the second switch would be wired in series so that opening of either switch closes the flues.

A "normally open" method of control is not permitted for damper operation. With a normally open circuit, the stage flues would close when the closing "device" is energized. With this arrangement, a blown fuse in the circuit would prevent closing of the flues. With the "normally closed" method, the danger of the control circuit being inoperative when needed is eliminated (see Fig. 526).

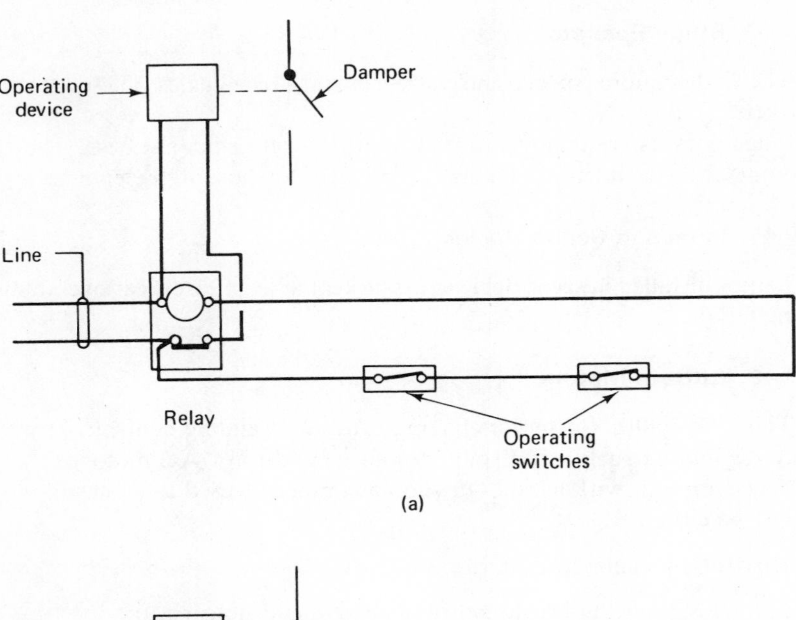

(a)

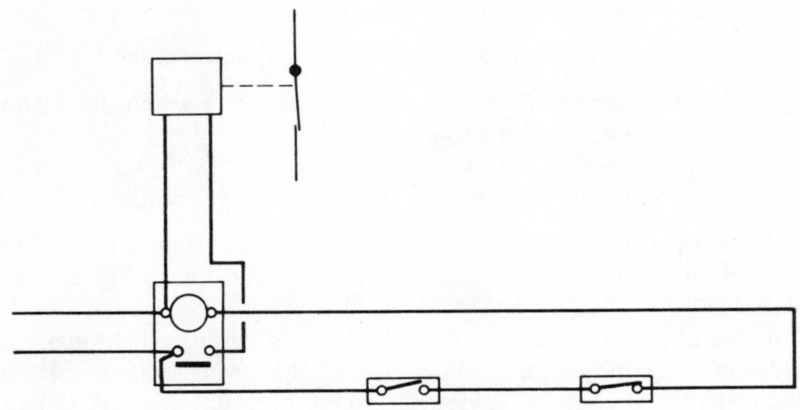

Fig. 526
Flue damper control (Sect. 520-49).

(a) Operating device energized, damper open.
(b) Operating device de-energized, damper released.

D. Portable Switchboards on Stage

520-51. Supply

Portable switchboards must be protected by a fused switch or a circuit breaker. The switch or circuit breaker may be mounted on the stage wall, or it may be in the main switchboard if the main switchboard is "readily accessible."

520-52. Overcurrent Protection

If the portable switchboard serves equipment with medium-base incandescent lamps, the fuse size or circuit breaker setting for the circuit to the equipment is limited to 20 amps.

If the portable switchboard serves mogul-base incandescent lamps, the fuse size or circuit-breaker setting may be as high as 50 amps.

For types of load other than lighting, the fuse size or circuit-breaker setting shall be no higher than that required to carry the load.

520-53. Construction

(a) Enclosure

Portable switchboards must be of sheet metal or, if of wood, must have a sheet-metal lining. The sheet metal must be corrosion-proofed and at least No. 24 gauge. Galvanized sheet metal would meet the requirement for corrosion-proofing.

(b) Live Parts

There shall be no exposed live parts, except for dimmer faceplates.

(c) Switches and Circuit Breakers

Switches and circuit breakers must be the externally operable type.

(d) Circuit Protection

Each circuit fed by the board must have individual protection in the hot wire(s) only.

(e) Dimmers

Dimmer terminals must be enclosed. The faceplate may be exposed.

(f) Interior Conductors

Switchboard wiring conductors must be asbestos-covered, Type AA, or equal.

(g) Pilot Light

A pilot light must be provided. The pilot light must be connected to the supply side, not the load side, of the main switch for the switchboard. With this arrangement the pilot light will stay "on" with the main switch open. It will go "off" only on power failure to the main switch.

(h) Supply Connections

The switchboard, being portable, would be connected by a cord. The cord must be an extra-hard usage type, Type S, SO, ST, or STO.

(i) Cable Arrangement

A bushing must be provided, where a cord or cable enters the switchboard.

(j) Terminals

Terminals for stage cables must permit convenient access.

E. Stage Equipment—Portable

520-61. Arc Lamps

Arc lamps must be approved types.

520-62. Portable Plugging Boxes

Plugging boxes are metal boxes containing a number of receptacles. The following rules apply to these boxes:

1. There shall be no exposed live parts.
2. Receptacles shall be at least 30 amp. rating.
3. Overcurrent protection must be provided as part of the assembly.
4. A bus bar and lugs must be provided for connecting the supply cable.

520-63. Bracket Fixture Wiring

Bracket fixtures are lights mounted near the top of movable scenery. Brackets may be either internally wired or fitted with a cord. Both types are provided with a connector on the rear side of the scenery for connection to the circuit.

520-64. Portable Strips

1. Sheet metal for conductor troughs must be at least No. 20 MSG.
2. A bushing must be provided where the supply cable enters the portable strip.

3. Supply cable must be arranged to take tension off the connections. An Underwriters knot in the conductors, where they enter the portable strip, would satisfy this rule.

520-65. Festoons

The lampholders for festoons have built-in leads, which are spliced to the circuit wires. The splices should not be side by side, but should be staggered where practicable. Lamps enclosed in combustible lanterns or other combustible enclosures shall be fitted with guards.

520-66. Special Effects

Special effects devices may produce arcs or sparks. Care must be taken to prevent any arc or spark from coming in contact with any combustible material.

520-67. Cable Connectors

Cable and cord connectors shall be arranged to take tension off the connections. An Underwriters knot in the conductors would satisfy this rule.

If a cord is to be plugged into an appliance, the female part of the plug connector must be on the cord, with the prongs on the appliance.

520-68. Conductors for Portables

Cord must be an extra-hard usage type, S, SO, ST, or STO, except that reinforced cord may be used on circuits of not over 20 amps., used to supply stand lamps.

F. Dressing Rooms

520-71. Pendant Lampholders

Pendant lampholders are not permitted in dressing rooms.

520-72. Lamp Guards

Guards are required for incandescent lights less than 8 ft above the floor. The guard must be a permanent type, one that cannot be removed. The guard must be open at the bottom for changing of light bulbs (Fig. 527).

520-73. Switches Required

Fixtures with switches are not permitted in dressing rooms. All lights must be controlled by wall switches.

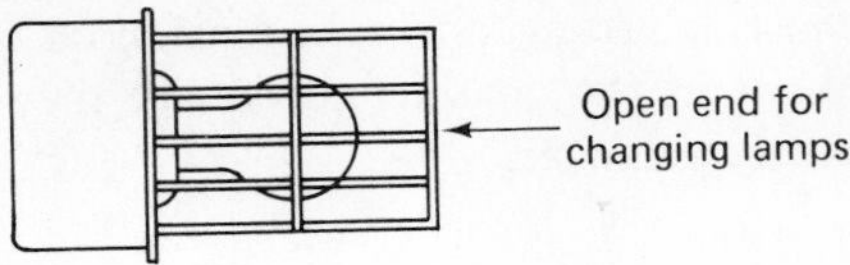

Fig. 527
Lamp guard for dressing room light.

All receptacles in dressing rooms must be controlled by wall switches with pilot lights.

G. Grounding

All fixed equipment and all raceways must be grounded.

Portable equipment need not be grounded unless operating at over 150 volts to ground or, for any voltage, within reach of a grounded object.

ARTICLE 530 — MOTION-PICTURE AND TELEVISION STUDIOS AND SIMILAR LOCATIONS

A. General

530-1. Scope

Article 530 applies for all parts of motion-picture studios and television studios, except for areas that incorporate assembly areas (see Section 520-1).

B. Stage or Set

530-11. Permanent Wiring

Wiring methods permitted are:

Metal conduit.

Metal wireways.

Nonmetallic conduit.

Type MI cable.

Type MC cable.

(This does not apply for communication and sound recording circuits, which may be wired as per Articles 640 and 800.)

530-12. Portable Wiring

Cord for portable wiring should be a hard-usage type: SJ, SJO, SJT, SJTO, S, SO, ST, or STO. (The Code requires "cord approved for the purpose.")

530-13. Stage Lighting and Effects Control

Switches or contactors may be used for stage lighting and effects control. When contactors are used, they must have a disconnect. Either of the following arrangements is permitted for contactors:

1. An individual toggle switch can be installed for each contactor. This switch must be within 6 ft of its contactor.
2. One switch may serve as a single disconnect for all contactors on the board. The single disconnect must be located not more than 6 ft from the board.

If there are remote-control switches or remote-control pushbuttons for operation of the contactor, the toggle switch could be in the supply line to the switches or pushbuttons, and within 6 ft of the contactor. See Fig. 528.

530-14. Plugging Boxes

Receptacles in plugging boxes must have at least a 30-amp. rating.

530-15. Enclosing and Guarding Live Parts

(a) All live parts must be enclosed or guarded.

(b) All switches must be the externally operable type.

(c) All live parts of rheostats must be enclosed.

(d) Current-carrying parts of bull switches, location boards, spiders, and plugging boxes must be either enclosed or placed out of reach.

530-16. Portable Lamps

Portable lamps must be equipped with guards.

530-17. Portable Arc Lamps

Portable arc lamps must be fitted with enclosures to contain arcs or sparks. Enclosures shall be ventilated.

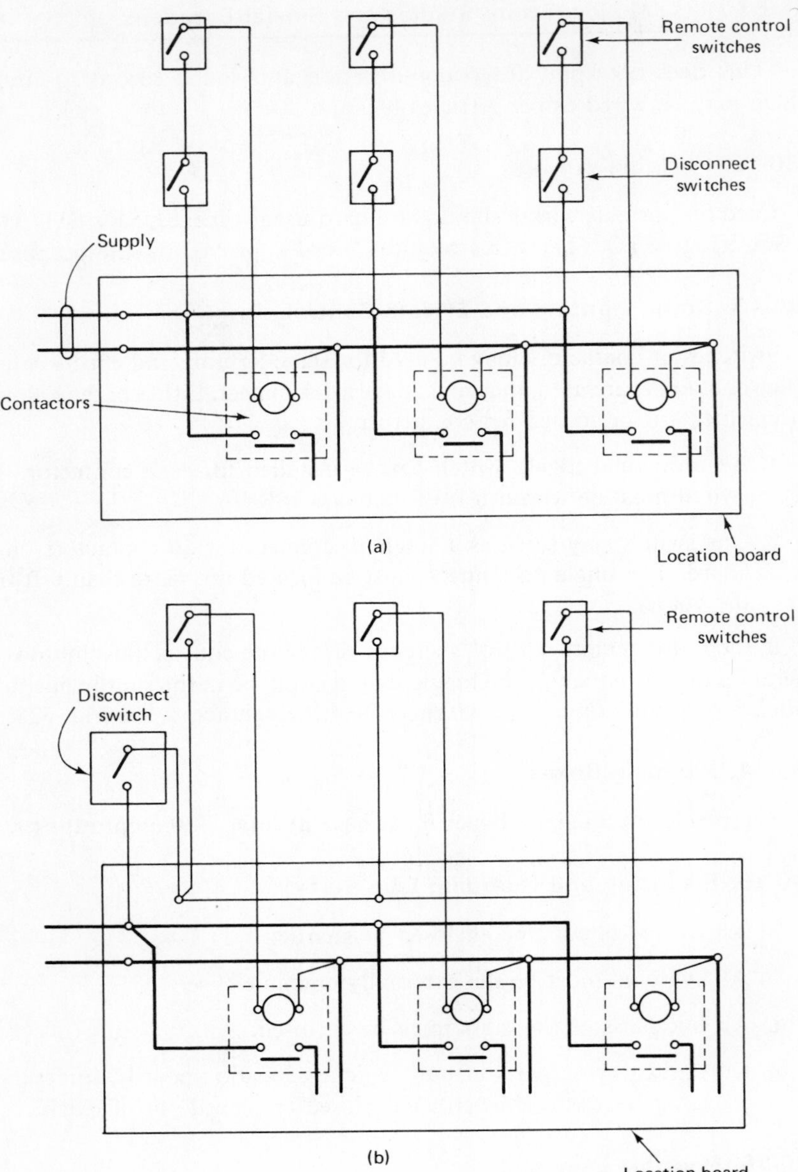

Fig. 528

Stage lighting and effects control (Sect. 530-13).

(a) An individual disconnect is provided for each contactor. Disconnects shall be located not more than 6 ft from contactors.

(b) A single disconnect is provided for all contactors on the location board. Disconnect shall be located not more than 6 ft from the board.

530-18. Overcurrent Protection—Short-Time Rating

Because circuits and cables in motion-picture studios are used only for short periods, the Code allows higher fusing than would be permitted in other locations.

Stage cable, stage cords, feeders may be fused at 400% of the current-carrying capacity of the cable, cord, or feeder. For example, referring to Table 400-5, p. 70-239 of the Code, a No. 10, three-conductor, rubber-covered cord has an ampacity of 25 amps. This cord may be protected by a fuse or circuit breaker setting of 100 amps.

If a plugging box does not have built-in overcurrent protection, cords and cables smaller than No. 8 that are plugged into the box must have individual protection. The protection shall be by two *cartridge* fuses or a circuit breaker contained in the plug. Fuse size or breaker setting may be up to 400% of the cord or cable ampacity, except that, where work lights, stand lamps, or fixtures are served by the cord or cable, fuses only are permitted in the plug, fuse rating 20 amps. maximum.

530-19. Sizing of Feeder Conductors for Television Studio Sets

Note that the demand factors given in this Section of the Code are for *television* studio sets. No mention is made of motion-picture studios.

(a) Referring to the Table of demand factors, as given in this Section, suppose that the total load on a feeder were 90,000 watts. The computed feeder load would be figured as follows:

1st 50,000 at 100%	50,000 watts
40,000 at 75%	30,000 watts
Computed load	80,000 watts

A permanent feeder may be sized to carry an 80,000-watt load.

(b) For portable feeder cords or cables, an ampacity of only one-half that of the load is permitted.

Referring to Table 400-5, p. 70-239 of the Code, a three-conductor No. 8 cord has an ampacity of 35 amps. This cord may be used to carry a 70-amp. load.

Note that the above rules are for *feeders.* The rules do *not* apply to branch circuits.

530-20. Grounding

Grounding is required for all equipment *except:*

1. Pendants and portable lamps.

2. Portable stage equipment.

3. Stage lighting and sound equipment.

This equipment need not be grounded unless operating at over 150 volts to ground. If the voltage is over 150 to ground, grounding is required.

C. Dressing Rooms

530-31. Dressing Rooms

For dressing rooms, wiring may be any of the wiring methods of Chapter 3, except those specified as "not permitted" in motion-picture studios.

D. Viewing, Cutting and Patching Tables

530-41. Lamps at Tables

There would necessarily be a good deal of exposed film around a cutting and patching table or a viewing table. Lamps must be guarded to prevent contact with the highly combustible film, and must be a composition or metal-sheathed porcelain keyless type.

E. Film Storage Vaults

530-51. Lamps in Cellulose Nitrate Film Storage Vaults

Film storage vaults are dangerous fire hazards. All lighting fixtures in such locations must be glass-enclosed and gasketed. No switches of any kind are permitted in film storage vaults. Vault light switches must be outside the vault and must have a pilot light. The switch must be wired to disconnect not only the lights, but also all other outlets contained within the vault. Switching is required only for the "hot" wires. The neutral may be unswitched.

530-52. Motors and Other Electrical Equipment in Cellulose Nitrate Film Storage Vaults

Motors, heaters, portable lamps, and portable appliances are *not* permitted in a film storage vault. No receptacles are permitted.

F. Substations

530-61. Substations

Wiring and equipment for circuits above 600 volts are subject to the special rules for high voltages as set down in Article 710 of the Code.

530-62. Low-Voltage Switchboards

Rules for low-voltage switchboards (600 volts or less), the requirements for clearances, grounding, overcurrent protection, etc., are given in Article 384.

530-63. Overcurrent Protection of DC Generators

The percentage rating of the overcurrent protection for a three-wire DC generator is not specified—whether 100%, 125%, 150%, etc. of the generator current rating. The overcurrent protection would be sized not higher than that specified by the manufacturer. No overcurrent protection is required for the neutral of a three-wire generator, whether grounded or ungrounded.

530-64. Working Space and Guarding

Section 110-16 gives minimum clearances required around live parts, such as live parts on a switchboard. Minimum clearance, generally, would be 36 in. between live parts and a wall, and 48 in. between live parts on both sides of a working space. These are minimums and should be increased if at all possible (see Fig. 354).

Section 110-17 sets down the rules for guarding of live parts.

Section 430-11 requires suitable protection for motors exposed to dripping or spraying liquids.

Section 430-14 requires that motors be located so as to have adequate ventilation to prevent overheating.

530-65. Portable Substations

Unauthorized persons would have access to portable substations, and these should be completely enclosed, with no live parts exposed.

530-66. Grounding at Substations

All metal equipment shall be grounded, except the frames of *DC* circuit breakers installed on switchboards.

ARTICLE 540 — MOTION-PICTURE PROJECTORS

A. General

540-1. Scope

Article 540 applies for professional and nonprofessional projectors having light sources that produce hazardous dusts, gas or radiation.

B. Definitions

540-2. Professional Projector

540-3. Nonprofessional Projector

A professional projector is defined as one using 35- or 70-millimeter film (about $1\frac{3}{8}$, $2\frac{3}{4}$ in.) and having 5.4 perforations per inch, on each edge of the film, and which produces hazardous dusts, gases, or radiation.

Any other projector is a nonprofessional projector.

C. Equipment and Projectors of the Professional Type

540-10. Motion Picture Projection Room

A projection room is required for all professional projectors. Projection rooms must be permanent, and completely enclosed. Projection rooms are *not* considered hazardous locations.

540-11. Location of Associated Electrical Equipment

For motor-generator sets, rectifiers, and rheostats, the preferred location is outside the projection room. If such equipment, for practical reasons, must be located inside the projection room, all such equipment must be suitably guarded or enclosed to prevent escape of arcs or sparks. The commutator end of motor-generator sets must have a metal guard, either completely solid, or solid on the bottom half, with wire mesh over the upper half.

Switches, fuses, and circuit breakers that are not used for the projectors or for sound reproduction, floodlights, or special effect lights must be installed outside the projection room. This would include light switches and distribution panels.

Exceptions to this rule are switches for auditorium lights, and for operation of the curtain. These may be located in the projection room.

540-12. Work Space

A 30-inch minimum working space must be provided on each side, and rear, of motion picture projectors, floodlights, spotlights and similar equipment. (A 30-inch space *between* two adjacent pieces of equipment is permitted.)

540-13. Conductor Size

Conductors feeding professional-type projectors must be at least No. 8.

540-14. Conductors on Lamps and Hot Equipment

Conductors for this service must have insulation suitable for 392°F. Type A or AA conductors would satisfy this rule.

540-15. Flexible Cords

Cords for portable equipment must be one of the following types: SJ, SJO, SJT, SJTO, S, SO, ST, or STO.

540-20. Approval

540-21. Marking

Professional projectors must be an approved type. They must be marked to show voltage, current, and maker's name or trademark.

D. Nonprofessional Projectors

Nonprofessional projectors using "safety" film may be operated without a projection room.

Nonprofessional projectors must be "listed." (See definition of "Listed," p. 70-10 of the Code.)

E. Sound Recording and Reproduction

Sound recording and reproduction equipment shall be as required by Article 640 of the Code.

ARTICLE 545 — MANUFACTURED BUILDING

A. General

545-1. Scope

545-2. Other Articles

545-3. Definitions

A "manufactured building" is one manufactured in sections, the sections being erected and joined together on the building site. A prefabricated home would be an example.

The manufactured sections may contain plumbing or wiring that is joined together when the sections are erected. The plumbing or wiring are "building components."

545-4. Wiring Methods

Wiring method may be any method approved by Chapter 3 for the type of building in question.

545-5. Service-Entrance Conductors

545-6. Installation of Service-Entrance Conductors

Service equipment could be furnished by the manufacturer as part of the assembly. When this is done, provision must be made for routing the service-entrance conductors from the entrance panel to the point on the outside where connection will be made to the drop or lateral.

The service-entrance *conductors* shall not be installed by the manufacturer, but shall be installed after erection of the building.

Exception.

If it is known in advance to which point on the building the drop or lateral will be attached, the service-entrance conductors may be installed by the manufacturer.

The rules of Article 230 (Services) must be complied with. Types of service entrances permitted are listed in Section 230-43; required size of conductors is stipulated in Section 230-41; types of insulation permitted are listed in Section 230-40.

545-7. Service Equipment Location

As with other buildings, service equipment must be located where "readily accessible," and as close as practicable to the point where the service-entrance conductors enter the building.

545-8. Protection of Conductors and Equipment

Proper protection of conductors and electrical equipment shall be provided by the manufacturer to prevent damage during transit and erection of the building sections.

545-9. Outlet Boxes

For manufactured buildings, the Code permits smaller boxes than required for other buildings, provided the boxes are "tested and approved" by the proper authorities.

545-10. Receptacle or Switch with Integral Enclosure

Receptacles and switches of a type that are furnished together with boxes as a complete assembly are permitted for use in manufactured buildings, provided they are "tested and approved" by the proper authorities.

545-11. Bonding and Grounding

Provision shall be made by the manufacturer for bonding together sections of metal conduit or raceway, and for grounding of exposed metal parts of electrical equipment, if furnished with the building.

545-12. Grounding Electrode Conductor

The "grounding electrode conductor" is the conductor that grounds the entrance panel enclosure to the grounding electrode (e.g., water pipe, etc.). Requirements are the same as for any other installation. See Article 250, Part J.

545-13. Component Interconnections

The manufacturer is permitted to include fittings and connectors of a type intended to be concealed, provided the fittings and connectors are "tested and approved" by the proper authorities.

ARTICLE 547 — AGRICULTURAL BUILDINGS

547-1. Scope

Article 547 covers rules for the wiring of certain "agricultural" buildings. If a building, or part of a building, is used for housing poultry, livestock, or products associated with agriculture, and conditions are such that "excessive" dust accumulates, Article 547 would apply. If conditions are such that "corrosive conditions" exist, or if the location is damp and wet, Article 547 applies. For agricultural buildings free from excessive dust or damp conditions, it is evidently the intent of the Code that the special rules of Article 547 need not be followed.

547-2. General

Electrical equipment shall be so installed that safe operating temperatures will not be exceeded. Special precautions may be necessary when "excessive dust" is present.

547-3. Wiring Methods

The Code specifies the following wiring methods:

1. Type UF (underground feeder and branch-circuit) cable.
2. Type NMC cable (Romex).
3. Type SNM (shielded nonmetallic-sheathed) cable.
4. Other cables or raceways "suitable for the location."

For buildings subject to dust accumulation, open wiring on insulators is also permitted.

Boxes containing splices or connections must be corrosion-resistant, dust-tight, water-tight.

Boxes containing "devices" must be corrosion-resistant, dust-tight, water-tight.

Cords used for flexible connections must be one of the following types: S, SO, ST, STO, SJ, SJO, SJT, SJTO. Liquid-tight flexible metal conduit is also approved for flexible connections.

547-4. Switches, Circuit Breakers, Motor Controllers, and Fuses

All make-and-break devices, including pushbuttons, are required to have weatherproof, corrosion-resistant enclosures. They must be provided with close-fitting or telescoping covers. (See definition of "Weatherproof," p. 70-14 of the Code.)

547-5. Motors

Motors must be totally enclosed, or designed so as to "minimize entrance of dust or moisture."

547-6. Lighting Fixtures

Where exposed to water or condensation, lighting fixtures must be watertight.

Where exposed to damage, they must be equipped with a guard.

547-7. Grounding

Grounding shall comply with Article 250.

ARTICLE 550 — MOBILE HOMES AND MOBILE HOME PARKS

550-1. Scope

(a) Article 550 stipulates rules for wiring and electrical equipment in mobile homes, and the rules for wiring and equipment in the mobile home park. If a mobile home park has a private distribution system for feeding the individual mobile homes, such a distribution system would also come under the rules of Article 550.

Certain rules of Article 550 may conflict with the Code rules for general wiring. In such cases, the rules of Article 550 shall prevail.

(b) Mobile homes used for purposes other than as dwellings are not required to meet the requirements of Article 550, as far as *number* and *size* of circuits is concerned. All other requirements must be complied with for 115-volt or 115/230-volt AC systems.

(c) The rules of Article 550 apply to mobile homes located anywhere—in mobile home parks or elsewhere.

(d) Article 550 applies to mobile homes intended for connection to 115/230 volt, three-wire AC systems.

(e) All electrical equipment must be "listed." See definition of "Listed," p. 70-10 of the Code.

550-2. Definitions

Note that a mobile home is defined as a structure made so as to be *readily movable on its own running gear,* and designed for use without a permanent foundation.

Mobile homes should not be confused with "recreational vehicles" and "travel trailers." A recreational vehicle is one intended for temporary camping or travel use. A recreational vehicle may have its own generator, or batteries for furnishing power, and may be parked anywhere, whereas a mobile home gets its power from an outside source furnished usually by a mobile home park. The function of travel trailers is similar to that of recreational vehicles, but travel trailers are not self-propelled. Mobile homes are intended for use as dwellings. Recreational vehicles and travel trailers are intended for recreational, camping, or travel use.

Mobile homes and recreational vehicles are customarily wired by the manufacturer.

A. Mobile Homes

550-3. Power Supply

The Code requires that service equipment for a mobile home be located *outside* the mobile home. Service equipment would consist of a disconnect, overcurrent protection, and meter. These are located adjacent to the mobile home. For loads of 50 amps. or less, a cord is used to connect to the built-in distribution panel in the mobile home. The cord is not a service; it is a feeder cord.

The following rules apply to the feeder cord:

1. The cord must be an approved mobile home supply cord, labeled for mobile home use.

2. It must be a four-conductor cord, with three circuit conductors, one grounding conductor.

3. It must be rated 50 amps.

   (There is an exception for mobile homes with factory-equipped gas or oil heating and cooking equipment, in which case a 40 amp. cord is permitted.)

4. It must be at least 21 ft long, but no longer than $36\frac{1}{2}$ ft.

5. It must enter the mobile home through the rear third section. If the mobile home is 30 ft long, the cord entrance must be at least 20 ft back from the front. (The cord may enter through the floor, wall, or roof.)

6. If the load is over 50 amps., a masthead must be installed, or the fixed supply entrance may be through the underside of the mobile home.

550-4. Disconnecting Means and Branch-Circuit Protective Equipment

(a) A main disconnect is required inside the mobile home. The main disconnect may be in the distribution panel. It may be either a circuit breaker or a switch and fuses.

The circuit breaker setting must be 50 amps. for 50 amp. cords and 40 amps. for 40 amp. cords.

For 40 and 50 amp. cords, a switch must be rated 60 amps. The fuse must be a 50 amp. fuse for 50 amp. cords, 40 amps. for 40 amp. cords.

If a permanent type feeder is used for the power supply (underground conduit or overhead feeder to a masthead), the main disconnect must have a rating at least equal to the load.

The disconnect must be in a readily accessible location near the point of entry of the power supply.

(b) Branch-Circuit Protective Equipment

(c) Two-Pole Circuit Breakers

Branch-circuit protection may be in the form of either fuses or circuit breakers. For 115-volt circuits, the circuit breakers would be single-pole; for 230-volt circuits, two-pole.

For general-purpose branch circuits wired with No. 14, the fuse size or circuit breaker setting is limited to 15 amps. maximum. For general-purpose branch circuits wired with No. 12, the rating may be 20 amps.

When a fuse size is marked on a motor-operated appliance, the circuit fuse size or circuit-breaker setting must be no greater than the size marked on the appliance.

(d) Electrical Nameplates

A metal nameplate is required on the outside of the mobile home near the feeder assembly entrance. Nameplate shall read: This connection for 120/240-volt, 3-pole, 4-wire, 60-Hertz, ——-ampere supply. (Correct amperage shall be inserted.)

550-5. Branch Circuits

(a) Lighting

Lighting load is figured at 3 watts per square foot.

(b) Small Appliances

At least two 20-amp. small appliance circuits are required, with receptacles in kitchen, pantry, family room, dining room, and breakfast room. Small appliances circuits shall serve these rooms *only,* and receptacles only in these rooms.

"General-purpose" receptacles are not permitted in a room served by a small appliance circuit.

(c) General Appliances

1. Total rating of *fixed* appliances on lighting circuits may not exceed 50% of the branch-circuit rating. For a 15-amp. circuit, this would be $7\frac{1}{2}$ amps. $7\frac{1}{2} \times 115 = 862$ watts.
2. When only fixed appliances are on a circuit, the circuit may be loaded to 80% of the branch circuit rating.
3. For a circuit serving only one portable appliance, conductors must have an ampacity at least 125% of the appliance current rating.
4. Range circuits may be sized smaller than would be required for the full nameplate rating. See the Table on p. 70-448 of the Code.

550-6. Receptacle Outlets

(a) Except where supplying special appliances (such as a range), all receptacles must be 15-amp., 125-volt, parallel-blade, grounding type (may be single or duplex), and if located outside, or in a washroom, must have ground-fault protection.

(b) All 15- and 20-amp., 120-volt single-phase receptacles installed in bathrooms (including receptacles in light fixtures), or adjacent to a lavatory, must have ground-fault protection.

(c) An individual grounding-type receptacle shall be installed for each cord-connected fixed appliance.

(d) A sufficient number of receptacles must be installed in each room so that no point along the wall (at the floor line) will be more than 6 ft from a receptacle. In addition, a receptacle must be installed in any wall space 2 ft or more in width. These rules do not apply for hallways or baths. If receptacles are installed in a hallway, they may be installed as desired. (Receptacles are not permitted in or adjacent to shower or bathtub spaces, but may be installed in a washroom.)

In addition, receptacles are required at these locations:

1. At each kitchen counter-top measuring 12 in. or more in width.
2. Near the refrigerator and free-standing gas-range space.
3. At counter-top space of built-in vanities.
4. At counter-top spaces under wall-mounted cabinets.

(e) At least one receptacle must be installed outdoors.

(f) Receptacles are not permitted in or *adjacent to* a shower or bathtub space, but may be installed in a washroom.

550-7. Fixtures and Appliances

Lighting fixtures in showers or over a bathtub must be a vaportight gasketed type. Switches for shower and bathtub spaces must be located *outside* the room.

550-8. Wiring Methods and Materials

Any wiring method suitable for a residence may be used in a mobile home. There is one difference: in a mobile home, Romex may not be used for *direct* wiring of a range or clothes dryer. (Romex may be used for wiring the *receptacle* for a range or dryer.)

Other rules applying to mobile homes are as follows:

(a) Nonmetallic outlet boxes may be used only with nonmetallic conduit or cable. (This rule is also stated in Section 370-3.) You can use nonmetallic boxes with Romex, but not with BX or metal conduit.

(b) Nonmetallic cable, such as Romex, if exposed and 15 in. or less above the floor, must have protection in the form of conduit or guard strips.

(c) Cables passing through studs must have protection if less than $1\frac{1}{2}$ in. from the inside or outside wall. A metal tube or steel plates are required for protection.

(d) Metallic faceplates such as metal switch and receptacle plates must be grounded. (They may be grounded through the box and attachment screws.)

(e) When a range or clothes dryer is wired direct with BX or Greenfield, a minimum 3-ft free length of BX or Greenfield must be provided to allow for moving of the range or dryer. The free length should be secured to the wall. [BX or Greenfield are the only wiring methods permitted for wiring a 115/230-volt range or clothes dryer direct. See Section 550-9(a)(2).]

Romex or type SE cable may *not* be used to wire a range or clothes dryer *direct,* but may be used to wire to a range or dryer *receptacle.*

(f) Rigid metal conduit requires two locknuts at boxes, one inside and one outside. In addition, a bushing is required on the inside.

(g) Switch ratings must be as follows:

1. For lighting, at least 10 amp, 125-volt.
2. Section 430-83 allows a general-use snap switch to be used as a controller for AC motors of 2 hp or less. When so used, the ampere rating of the switch must be at least 125% of the motor full-load current rating. (Full-load current ratings for single-phase AC motors are given in Table 430-148, p. 70-316 of the Code.)

(h) At least 4 in. of free conductor is required at boxes for making connections.

(i) Outdoor wiring exposed to damage or moisture must be protected by metal conduit. (EMT may be used if it "hugs" the surface.)

(j) All fixed equipment must be solidly secured in place.

(k) Circuit conductors to certain appliances such as heaters and the like must have insulation suitable for high temperatures (above 140°F). Rubber and thermoplastic-covered conductors (Types RUW, T, TW), customarily used for general wiring, are suitable for temperatures only up to 140°F. Types RH, RUH are suitable for temperatures up to 167°F; type RHH for 194°F. See Table 310-13, p. 70-124 of the Code.

When a high-temperature type of conductor is required, there are two ways of connecting to the appliance:

1. Using high-temperature conductors, such as RHH, for the entire branch circuit.
2. Running regular rubber or thermoplastic conductors to a box near the appliance, with high-temperature conductors from box to appliance in the form of cable or in Greenfield. The box must be at least 1 ft from the appliance, and the run from box to appliance must be

at least 4 ft long. (When a box is less than 4 ft from the appliance, a loop would have to be made in the run to get the minimum 4-ft length.) See Fig. 419.

550-9. Grounding

(a) Insulated Neutral

The neutral may never be used to ground any type of equipment in a mobile home.

All metal parts to be grounded must be connected either to the grounding terminal in the distribution panelboard or to the panelboard enclosure. (The panelboard enclosure is bonded to the grounding terminal.)

The grounding terminal is connected to the green grounding conductor in the feeder cable, which is grounded at the service equipment located outside the mobile home.

(1) Bonding screws, straps, or buses in the distribution panel or in appliances must be removed and discarded.

(2) If a 115/230 volt clothes dryer or range is wired direct, the only wiring methods permitted are BX and Greenfield. The metal sheath of the BX or Greenfield may serve as the grounding path back to the distribution panel. If nonmetallic cable (such as Romex) is used, it must be four-conductor cable, one conductor serving as a ground wire. The nonmetallic cable would be wired to a three-pole, four-wire grounding-type receptacle, with cord and plug connection to the range or dryer. Nonmetallic sheathed cable is not permitted for direct wiring of a range or clothes dryer.

(b) Equipment Grounding Means

(1) The green grounding conductor in the supply feeder to the mobile home must be connected to the grounding bus in the distribution panel.

(2) All exposed metal parts of electrical equipment must be connected to the grounding bus. This includes metal lighting fixtures, metal switchplates, washing machines, dryers, dishwashers, refrigerators, ranges, motor frames, and any other exposed metal parts.

(3) For cord-connected equipment, a cord with grounding conductor must be used, with a grounding-type plug and receptacle.

(c) Bonding of Noncurrent-Carrying Parts

Water pipes, sewer pipes, gas pipes, and metal vent ducts must be grounded to the grounding bus in the distribution panel or to the chassis grounding terminal.

The chassis of the mobile home shall be bonded to the distribution panel. The Code requires that the bonding jumper be a "No. 8 AWG copper minimum, or equal." If an aluminum conductor is used, it would have to be No. 6 minimum to equal a No. 8 copper for grounding purposes (see Table 250-95, p. 70-102 of the Code). Connection to the chassis must be made to an "accessible" terminal on the chassis. Solder is not permitted for making grounding connections; approved pressure-terminal connectors must be used.

550-10. Testing

After the wiring is completed, the wiring system must be subjected to a dielectric test. A dielectric test shows up any weakness in insulation.

The test may be either at 900 volts for 1 minute, or at 1,080 volts for 1 second.

550-11. Calculations

This Section gives an example of how to figure the load for a mobile home. The load is calculated in amps., to determine the proper size of feeder cable required (see example on p. 70-448 of the Code).

The method is as follows:

1. Figure the lighting load in watts. This is figured at 3 watts per sq. ft. To the lighting load add 1,500 watts for each small appliance circuit. The first 3,000 watts of the total is figured at 100%, the remainder at 35%.

2. Divide watts obtained by 230. This gives the lighting and small-appliance load in amps.

3. Figure the range load in watts. You don't have to use the full nameplate wattage but only a percentage of this, as listed in the Table on p. 70-448 of the Code.

4. Divide the range watts by 230. This gives the range load in amps.

5. For 230-volt appliances and motors, use nameplate amps.

6. For 115 volt appliances and motors, use nameplate amps. Balance this load as nearly as possible, half for each leg. Use the higher of the two amperages. Disregard the smaller amperage.

7. To the sum of the amps. obtained in steps 2, 4, 5, and 6, add 25% of the amps. of the largest motor. Size feeder for the total amps.

550-12. Wiring of Expandable Units and Dual Units

Expandable and dual-unit mobile homes shall be connected together by a fixed wiring method. Expandable and dual-unit mobile homes having cord feeders, and which are moved from one location to another, may have a distribution panel and disconnect in each unit.

550-13. Outdoor Outlets, Fixtures, Air-Cooling Equipment, Etc.

(a) Fixtures and equipment installed outdoors must be raintight. Receptacles must be fitted with gasketed covers.

(b) Outdoor receptacles for heating and air-conditioning equipment must carry a metal tag showing correct voltage and amperage for the equipment.

B. Mobile Home Parks

550-21. Distribution System

The park distribution system is required to be 115/230-volt, single phase. Note that a three-phase distribution system is not permitted for serving mobile homes.

550-22. Calculated Load

This Section gives the rules for figuring power requirements for the entire mobile home park.

550-23. Mobile Home Service Equipment

The equipment outside of, and adjacent to, each mobile home unit is the service equipment. The mobile home feeder is connected to this equipment. Rating of the service equipment must be at least 100 amps. There must be provisions for connecting a permanent type supply feeder as well as a supply cord. Receptacles for supply cords must be rated 50 amps., and conform to ANSI-C73, 17-1972.

Provisions must be made for connecting by fixed wiring to a mobile-home accessory building or additional electrical equipment located outside a mobile home.

ARTICLE 551 — RECREATIONAL VEHICLES AND RECREATIONAL VEHICLE PARKS

A. Recreational Vehicles

551-1. Scope

(a) Certain rules of Article 551 may conflict with the Code rules for general wiring. In such cases the rules of Article 551 shall be followed.

(b) A recreational vehicle is defined as one "primarily designed as temporary living quarters for recreational, camping, or travel use." Vehicles used primarily for other purposes (as an office, for example) need not meet the requirements of this Part (A) of the Code as far as *number* and *size* of circuits is concerned. All other requirements must be complied with for 115-volt, or 115/230-volt AC power systems.

(c) Part A applies for battery systems and for low-voltage DC power systems, as well as for 115-volt or 115/230-volt systems.

551-2. Definitions

Recreational vehicles should not be confused with mobile homes. A recreational vehicle is one intended for temporary camping or travel use. A recreational vehicle may have its own generator or batteries for furnishing power, and is most often used for traveling, whereas a mobile home gets its power from an outside source furnished by a mobile home park and usually remains fixed for long periods of time.

Recreational vehicles and mobile homes are customarily wired by the manufacturer.

551-3. Low-Voltage Systems

(a) Low-Voltage Circuits

Low-voltage circuits installed by the manufacturer must meet any applicable federal or state regulations, and must also comply with Code rules.

(b) Low-Voltage Wiring Materials

(1) Conductors must be copper. Conductors of aluminum or other material are not permitted.

(2) Conductor insulation must be suitable for at least 60°C (140°F). Any standard insulation is suitable for this temperature (see Table 310-13 of the Code).

(3) Single-wire, low-voltage conductors must be the stranded type.

(4) All insulated conductors must be marked with name or trademark of the manufacturer.

(c) Low-Voltage Wiring Methods

(1) Conductors must be protected against physical damage.

(2) Splices and connections shall be made with approved splicing devices, or by brazing, welding, or soldering.

(3) DC circuits must be separated at least $\frac{1}{2}$ in. from AC circuits.

(d) Battery Installations

Batteries must be vented directly to the outside.

(e) Overcurrent Protection

The Table in this subsection of the Code lists maximum fusing permitted for conductors of different sizes. Note that, for recreational vehicles, No. 18 and No. 16 conductors may be used. Circuit breakers shall be of an approved type. Overcurrent protection must be installed as close as practicable to the power supply entrance.

(f) Switches

Switches shall be rated at not less than the connected load.

551-4. Combination Electrical Systems

(a) General

A recreational vehicle wired for a battery or DC power supply may be connected to a 115-volt power supply, provided *all* wiring and equipment are suitable for 115 volts.

(b) Voltage Converters (115-Volt Alternating Current to Low-Voltage Direct Current)

Converters shall be of an approved type.

(c) Dual-Voltage Fixtures or Appliances

Fixtures with both 115-volt and low-voltage connections shall be an approved type.

(d) Autotransformers

Autotransformers may not be used in a recreational vehicle, nor for the power supply to the vehicle.

(e) Receptacles and Plug Caps

When a recreational vehicle is equipped for both AC and DC power, the receptacles for AC power must be a different type than the DC receptacles, so that DC appliances cannot be plugged into an AC receptacle, or vice versa. One way of doing this would be to have polarized receptacles and plugs for one system, and straight-blade receptacles and plugs for the other system.

551-5. Generator Installations

Generators must be bonded to the recreational vehicle chassis. Means must be provided to ensure that, when the vehicle is connected to an outside power source, the generator will be disconnected from the line. A double throw switch would accomplish this purpose. Appropriate ventilation shall be provided for the generator compartment.

Storage batteries must be secured in place in such a way as to prevent shifting.

An engine driving a generator in the vehicle is not permitted to exhaust in the vicinity of the gasoline fill spout inlet.

Supply conductors between a generator and the junction box must be stranded type conductors run in flexible metal conduit.

551-6. 115- or 115/230-Volt Nominal Systems

(a) General Requirements

Equipment and material shall be installed in accordance with the requirements of Article 551. Power supply may be two-wire, 115-volt (one wire grounded) or three-wire, 115/230 volt (one wire grounded).

(b) Materials and Equipment

All materials and equipment shall be approved for use in recreational vehicles.

551-7. Receptacle Outlets Required

A sufficient number of receptacles must be installed so that no point along the wall (at the floor line) will be more than 6 ft from a receptacle. In addition, a receptacle must be installed in any wall space 2 ft or more in width.

The rule does not apply for hallways. If receptacles are installed in hallways, they may be installed as desired. Receptacles are not permitted in a bathtub or shower compartment, but may be installed in a washroom.

In addition to the above, receptacles are required at these locations:

1. At each kitchen counter top measuring 12 in. or more in width.

2. Near the refrigerator and gas range space.

3. Adjacent to built-in vanities.

Bathroom cabinets having a built-in receptacle are permitted in washrooms. When a separate receptacle is installed in the wall adjacent to the lavatory, it shall be at least 30 in. above the floor.

All receptacles must be the grounding type (Section 551-19).

Ground-fault protection is required for 15- or 20-amp. 120-volt receptacles installed:

1. Adjacent to a lavatory.

2. In a toilet.

3. On the outside of the vehicle.

551-8. Branch Circuits Required

(a) *For Recreational Vehicles Without Electric Heating or Cooking*

If the total of lighting and receptacle outlets is 8 or less, only one 15-amp. or 20-amp. branch circuit is required.

The total of fixed appliances connected to the one circuit is limited to 600 watts for a 15-amp. circuit and 1,000 watts for a 20-amp. circuit.

(If there are more than 1,000 watts of fixed appliances, more than one circuit would be required.)

(b) *For Recreational Units With or Without Electric Heating or Cooking*

If the total of lights and receptacle outlets is more than 8, two circuits are a minimum requirement.

(c) If the feeder is rated 30 amps. or more, the following circuits are permitted:

(1) one 20-amp. circuit for the air conditioner.

(2) One or two 15- or 20-amp. circuits.

(d) Refer to this subsection of the Code for an example of load calculation.

551-9. Branch-Circuit Protection

(a) Branch circuit fuse rating or circuit breaker setting may be no higher than the ampacity of the circuit conductors.

When only one appliance, rated 13.3 amps. or more, is served by a branch circuit, the fuse or circuit breaker setting may be no higher than 150% of the appliance rating.

If a fuse size is marked on a motor-operated appliance, the branch circuit protection may be rated no higher than this.

Fixture wire and cords are considered to be protected by a fuse or circuit-breaker setting of 20 amps. or less.

15-amp. receptacles may be used on a 20-amp. branch circuit, provided there are two or more outlets on the circuit.

551-10. Power-Supply Assembly

(a) For recreational vehicles having only one 15-amp. general-purpose branch circuit, the power supply assembly may be 115-volt, two-pole, three-wire (two circuit wires, one grounding wire) with a 15-amp. rating.

(b) For recreational vehicles having only one 20-amp. general-purpose branch circuit, the power supply assembly may be 115-volt, two-pole three-wire (two circuit wires, one grounding wire) with a 20-amp. rating.

(c) For recreational vehicles having more than one general-purpose branch circuit, the power supply may be 115-volt, two-pole, three-wire (two circuit wires, one grounding wire) with a 30-amp. rating.

(d) For calculated loads of more than 30 amps., a 40- or 50-amp. 115/230 volt, three-pole, four-wire (three circuit wires, one grounding wire) power-supply assembly is required.

Exception: for (d).

If there are only 115-volt outlets in the vehicle, two 30-amp. cords may be used, provided that each cord serves its own load. The circuit wires of the cords may not be paralleled, but the *grounding* conductors of the cords *must* be connected together.

551-11. Distribution Panelboard

(a) The distribution panelboard shall be an approved type, and shall be the *insulated neutral type.*

551-12. Dual-Supply Source

(a) Where there is a generator supply, and in addition a power supply cord, means must be provided to ensure that, when the recreational vehicle is connected to the outside power source, the generator will be disconnected from the line. A double throw switch would accomplish this purpose.

(b) When there is a dual supply source, the load for the vehicle must be calculated, as per Section 551-8(d).

(c) The two power sources need not be of the same capacity.

(d) An AC generator source exceeding 30 amps. 115 volts may be wired either as a 115-volt, or 115/230-volt system.

(e) External power supply may be less than the calculated load, but in no case less than 30-amps. capacity.

551-13. Means for Connecting to Power Supply

(a)(b) Permanently connected power-supply assemblies shall be factory-supplied or factory-installed.

(1) Where the power-supply assembly is a separate cord, a permanent, male type receptacle shall be installed wired directly to the distribution panel. The feeder cord to the vehicle would plug into this receptacle. This feeder cord shall be not less than 20 nor more than $26\frac{1}{2}$ ft in length.

(2) When the power-supply assembly is a permanent feeder cord furnished with the vehicle, no power supply receptacle is required. Where the cord passes through the wall or floor, it must be protected by conduit and bushings. The cord shall be not less than 20 nor more than $26\frac{1}{2}$ ft in length, measured from the point of entrance to the vehicle.

(c) Attachment Plugs

(1) For recreational vehicles having only one 15-amp. general-purpose branch circuit, the attachment plug must be two-pole, three-wire grounding type, rated at 15 amps., 125 V.

(2) For recreational vehicles having only one 20-amp. general-purpose branch circuit, the attachment plug must be two-pole, three-wire grounding type, rated at 20 amps., 125 V.

(3) For recreational vehicles having one appliance branch circuit and one general-purpose branch circuit, the attachment plug must be two-pole, three-wire grounding type, rated at 30 amps., 125 V.

(4) For recreational vehicles having a 40- or 50-amp. power-supply assembly, the attachment plug must be three-pole, four-wire grounding type, rated at 50 amps., 125/250 V.

15, 20, 30, and 50-amp. plugs must conform to Fig. 551-13(c), p. 70-461 of the Code.

(d) Labeling at Electrical Entrance

A label must be provided near the power supply entrance, showing the correct voltage for the power supply.

(e) Location

A power supply entering on the side must enter the vehicle within 25 ft of the rear on the left (road) side. Or the power supply may enter the rear end not over 18 in. from the left (road) side.

An exception is made for camping trailers of 1,500 lb or less. For these, the power supply entrance need not be on the road side. It may be on either side, provided the drain outlet is on the same side.

551-14. Wiring Methods

(1) For interior wiring, rigid metal conduit, EMT, BX, Greenfield, or Romex with a grounding conductor are approved wiring methods. Greenfield may be used as a grounding conductor for equipment.

(2) Where conduit enters a box, two locknuts are required, one inside and one outside. In addition, a bushing is required on the inside.

(3) Nonmetallic boxes may be used only with nonmetallic-sheathed cable (such as Romex).

(4) In walls and ceilings of wood or other combustible material, boxes must be flush or projecting from the surface. Wall and ceiling outlets shall be mounted as per Article 370.

(5) Cable sheath of Romex and BX must be continuous between outlets. Splices are not permitted between boxes or other enclosures.

(6) Romex or BX may pass through holes in studs. Where the width of the stud is such that the cable would be less than $1\frac{1}{2}$ in. from either side of the stud, the cable must be protected by steel plates or tubes at each stud. If the cable is kept $1\frac{1}{2}$ in. or more from either side, no protection is required.

(7) Bends shall have a radius of at least five times the cable diameter.

(8) Cable shall be strapped within 12 in. of entrance to a box or other enclosure. Elsewhere, straps are required every $4\frac{1}{2}$ ft.

(9) If a nonmetallic box is without clamps, the cable shall be strapped within 8 in. of the box.

(10) Where subject to damage, Romex or other nonmetallic cable must be protected. Covering boards, guard strips, or conduit may be used for protection.

(11) Metallic faceplates shall be grounded.

(12) Outdoor wiring exposed to damage or moisture shall be metal conduit (or EMT may be used if it "hugs" the surface).

551-15. Conductors and Outlet Boxes

At least 4 in. of free conductor shall be left at each outlet.

551-16. Grounded Conductors

See Section 200-6.

551-17. Connection of Terminals and Splices

See Section 110-14.

551-18. Switches

(a) Light switches shall be rated at least 10 amps., 120-125 volts.

(b) For motor switches, see Section 430-83.

551-19. Receptacles

All receptacles must be the grounding type.

551-20. Lighting Fixtures

(a) General

Combustible material under a fixture canopy must be covered with noncombustible material. Sheet metal or asbestos paper may be used for this purpose.

(b) Shower Fixtures

Lighting fixtures in a bathtub or shower compartment must be an enclosed, gasketed type. Switches may not be installed in a bathtub or shower compartment.

(c) Outdoor Equipment

Must be approved for outdoor use.

551-21. Grounding

(a) Power-Supply Grounding

The grounding conductor of the power supply must be connected to the grounding bus in the distribution panel.

(b) Distribution Panelboard

The distribution panel must be provided with a suitable grounding bus.

(c) The neutral is not to be connected to the distribution panel enclosure, nor to any other equipment enclosure. Bonding screws, straps, or buses in the distribution panelboard or in appliances shall be removed and discarded.

Grounding of cord-connected 115/230 volt ranges and clothes dryers must be made by four-conductor cord (3 circuit conductors, 1 grounding wire) and a three-pole, four-wire grounding type plug and receptacle.

551-22. Interior Equipment Grounding

All exposed metal parts of electrical equipment must be grounded.

A green insulated wire or a bare wire may be used for grounding, with the grounding wire attached to the equipment by means of a grounding screw. Or conduit, EMT, or the sheath of metal-clad cable (such as BX) may be the grounding path. The equipment would be metallically bonded to the conduit, EMT, or BX by the locknuts or cable connector.

When a circuit with a grounding conductor feeds a number of receptacles, a box serving a receptacle could have "more than one grounding conductor," one entering and one leaving the box. The Code requires that the two grounding conductors be connected together in such a way that removing the receptacle would not break the grounding circuit. Both grounding conductors could not be connected to the grounding terminal on the receptacle, because, if this were done, removing the receptacle could result in opening the grounding circuit.

In metal boxes, the two conductors should be connected to the grounding screw in the box, with the connection to the receptacle made from the screw. In nonmetallic boxes, the two grounding conductors could be joined together, and the connection to the receptacle made from the joint. With either of these methods, removal of a receptacle would not break the grounding circuit. The same precaution should be taken in all cases where grounding conductors enter and leave any other box or enclosure.

Cord-connected appliances must be grounded through the green grounding wire in the cord, using a grounding-type plug and receptacle.

551-23. Bonding of Noncurrent-Carrying Metal Parts

All metal parts to be grounded must be connected either to the grounding terminal in the distribution panelboard or to the panelboard enclosure. A green grounding conductor run with the circuit conductors or the metal sheath of rigid conduit, EMT, or BX may provide the grounding path from the equipment to the panelboard.

The grounding terminal in the panelboard is connected to the green grounding conductor in the feeder cable.

The recreational vehicle chassis must be grounded. This may be by a bonding jumper between the chassis and the grounding terminal. The Code requires that the bonding jumper be a "No. 8 AWG copper minimum, or equal." If an aluminum conductor is used, it would have to be No. 6 minimum to equal a No. 8 copper for grounding purposes. See Table 250-95, p. 70-102 of the Code. (If the vehicle has a unitized metal chassis-frame type construction, and the panelboard is bolted, riveted, or welded to the chassis, a jumper is not required.)

Gas, water, and waste piping must be grounded or bonded to the chassis.

Air ducts must be grounded.

Soldering is not permitted for connecting a grounding conductor to a piece of equipment. Pressure connectors shall be used.

551-24. Appliance Accessibility

Appliances shall be accessible without removal of permanent construction.

551-25. Factory Tests (Electrical)

(a) Circuits of 115 or 115/230 Volts

The wiring system must pass a dielectric test of either 900 volts for one minute, or 1,080 volts for one second.

(b) Battery and Low-Voltage Circuits

The dielectric test required is 500 volts for one minute or 600 volts for one second.

B. Recreational Vehicle Parks

551-40. Application and Scope

In some cases the rules of this Part (B) may differ from the rules of other articles of the Code. In such cases, the rules of Part B shall prevail.

551-41. Definitions

Note that, for recreational vehicles, the service equipment is located outside the vehicle. The conductors or cord from the service equipment to the vehicle is a "power supply," not a service.

551-42. Receptacles Required

A minimum of 75% of the lots in the park must be equipped with at least one 30-amp. receptacle. The remaining lots may be equipped with only one 20-amp. receptacle.

Receptacles must conform to Figure 551-13(c), p. 70-461 of the Code.

551-43. Distribution System

The Code requires that the secondary distribution system in a recreational-vehicle park be single-phase, 120/240 volts, three-wire.

551-44. Calculated Load

This Section sets down the rules for figuring the load on the park distribution system.

Each lot is figured at either 2,400 or 3,600 watts, depending on number of receptacles per lot. A demand factor may be applied to the total load, according to Table 551-44 of the Code.

Example.

Thirty lots each equipped with 20- and 30-amp. receptacles.

Lots with both 20- and 30-amp. receptacles are figured at 3,600 watts each.

$$3{,}600 \times 30 = 108{,}000 \text{ watts, total load}$$

From Table 551-44, for 30 lots a 25% demand factor may be applied.

$$25\% \text{ of } 108{,}000 = 27{,}000 \text{ watts, calculated load for the park}$$

551-45. Overcurrent Protection

Overcurrent protection for the distribution system must be provided in accordance with Article 240.

551-46. Grounding

The distribution system and all electrical equipment must be grounded as required by Article 250.

551-47. Recreational Vehicle Lot Electric Supply Equipment

(a) A disconnect must be provided for each lot.

(b) Lot service equipment must be accessible by an unobstructed passageway not less than 2 ft wide and $6\frac{1}{2}$ ft high.

(c) Service equipment must be mounted at least 2 ft and not more than $6\frac{1}{2}$ ft above ground.

(d) Sufficient working space must be provided around electrical equipment. See Section 110-16 for minimum clearances.

The electrical supply equipment for a site is required to be located on a line between 8 and 10 ft to the left of the longitudinal center line of the stand, and not over 15 ft forward of the rear of the stand.

551-48. Grounding, Recreational Vehicle Lot Supply Equipment

(a) Exposed metal parts of fixed electrical equipment are required to be grounded by a continuous grounding conductor run with the circuit conductors.

(b) The neutral of the secondary distribution system must be grounded at the transformer.

(c) In no case may the neutral be used for grounding equipment in the park.

(d) The neutral may not be grounded on the load side of a service disconnect.

551-49. Protection of Outdoor Equipment

(a) Equipment located outdoors, or in wet places inside, must be the rainproof type. See definition of Wet Location, p. 70-10 of the Code.

(b) When a secondary meter is removed from its socket, the socket must be blanked off (covered with a blanking plate).

551-50. Overhead Conductors

(a) For areas where there is recreational vehicle traffic, overhead conductors of 600 volts or less must be at least 18 ft above ground. For other areas, minimum clearance for voltages of 600 or less is:

1. Over sidewalks or other pedestrian areas: 10 ft.

2. Over parking lots or areas subject to truck traffic: 15 ft.

3. Over public streets, roads, alleys: 18 ft.

(b) Minimum horizontal clearance from any object is 3 ft for conductors of 600 volts or less.

For clearance of high voltage conductors, see *National Electrical Safety Code* ANSI C2-1976.

551-51. Underground Service, Feeder, Branch-Circuit, and Recreational-Vehicle Lot Feeder Circuit Conductors

(a) Underground conductors buried directly in the earth must be insulated. Insulation must be a type suitable for direct burial. The equipment grounding conductor, if copper, may be bare. If aluminum, it must be insulated.

(b) Where underground conductors emerge from a trench, protection is required. Conduit or EMT may be used for this purpose, and must extend at least 18 in. into the trench. The same rule applies for underground conductors entering a building.

551-52. Receptacles

The type of receptacle used for furnishing power to a recreational vehicle is restricted by the Code, as follows:

1. 20-amp. receptacles: 125 V two-pole, three-wire grounding type, for 115-volt systems.
2. 30-amp. receptacles: 125 V two-pole, three-wire grounding type, for 115-volt systems.
3. 50-amp. receptacles: 125/230 V three-pole, four-wire grounding type, for 115/230-volt systems.

ARTICLE 555 — MARINAS AND BOATYARDS

555-1. Scope

Article 555 applies for marinas, boat-storage spaces, and boatyards. A "boatyard" would be distinguished from a "shipyard" in the usual sense, in that a "boatyard" builds or repairs only small craft, whereas a "shipyard" builds or repairs large vessels. The rules of Article 555 are not intended to apply generally to shipyards.

555-2. Application of Other Articles

Wiring and equipment in marinas and boatyards shall comply with applicable Code rules for general wiring, as well as the rules of Article 555.

555-3. Receptacles

All 15- and 20-amp., 120-volt single-phase receptacles, other than shore power receptacles, must have ground-fault protection.

Receptacles for *shore power for boats* must conform to the following requirements:

1. Must be rated at least 20 amps.
2. Must be single receptacles; duplex receptacles are not permitted.
3. Must be the locking type (such as twist-lock).
4. Must be grounding type.

(Receptacles other than shore power receptacles need not conform to all of these requirements.)

555-4. Branch Circuits

A separate individual branch circuit is required for each receptacle for shore power for boats. The branch-circuit conductors would be sized to carry the full amperage of the receptacle: No. 12 for a 20-amp. receptacle, No. 10 for a 30-amp. receptacle, etc.

555-5. Feeders and Services

For a feeder supplying less than five branch circuits for boat receptacles, the load on the feeder is figured at 100% of the sum of the receptacle ratings.

For a feeder supplying five or more receptacle circuits, a demand factor may be applied, as follows:

For 5 to 8 receptacles	90% of total receptacle rating
For 9 to 13 receptacles	80% of total receptacle rating
For 14 to 30 receptacles	70% of total receptacle rating
For 31 to 50 receptacles	50% of total receptacle rating
For 51 to 100 receptacles	40% of total receptacle rating

Examples.

A feeder supplying (4) 30-amp. receptacle circuits must have a minimum ampacity of $4 \times 30 = 120$ amps.

A feeder supplying (5) 30-amp. receptacle circuits must have a minimum ampacity of 90% of 5 $\times$ 30 amps. or $\frac{9}{10} \times 150 = 135$ amps.

555-6. Wiring Methods

Where exposed to the weather, the types of wiring permitted are:

1. Corrosion-resistant rigid metal conduit approved for the purpose.
2. Rigid nonmetallic conduit approved for the purpose.
3. Type MI cable.
4. Nonmetallic cable approved for the purpose.
5. Corrosion-resistant intermediate metal conduit approved for the purpose.
6. Type MC cable approved for the purpose.

Note that the Code specifies that metal conduit be "corrosion-resistant conduit" approved for the purpose. Galvanized conduit is corrosion-resistant, and would be approved for most applications in marinas and boatyards. However, under certain severe corrosive conditions, such as burial in cinder fill, galvanized conduit would not be approved. A special type of metal conduit, made especially for such conditions, would be required. See Section 346-3.

In addition to the six wiring methods listed above, open wiring may be installed *by special permission.*

An exception is also made for conditions where flexibility is required, in which case an approved flexible wiring method may be used.

Underground wiring may be a type other than the four listed above.

555-7. Grounding

All exposed metal parts of equipment, including conduit and metal sheath of cable, must be grounded.

Grounding must be by an *insulated* copper conductor run with the circuit conductors. The grounding conductor must be sized according to Table 250-95, p. 70-102 of the Code, on the basis of fuse size or circuit-breaker setting protecting the circuit. The Table applies for all circuits except for a 15-amp. circuit, for which the Table lists a No. 14 grounding conductor. This should be changed to No. 12, since for marinas and boatyards a No. 12 is the smallest size grounding conductor permitted.

If the equipment is wired from the service cabinet, the grounding conductors are carried back to the service cabinet along with the branch circuits. If wired from a panel, the grounding conductors are carried back as far as the panel, and a single grounding conductor for the panel is carried back to the service cabinet along with the feeder.

555-8. Wiring Over and Under Navigable Water

Shall be subject to the authority having jurisdiction.

555-9. Gasoline-Dispensing Stations—Hazardous (Classified) Locations

(a) The following spaces are Class I, Division 1:

(1) The space *within* the dispenser up to a height of 4 ft above the base.

(2) The space 4 ft out from the dispenser in all directions, and up to a height of 18 in. above the dispenser base level.

(3) For dispensers near and above the water, the space 4 ft out in all directions from the dispenser base and down to water level.

(b) The following spaces are Class I, Division 2:

The space 16 ft out in all directions from the 4-ft circle, and up to a height of 18 in. above the dispenser base level, and from the 18 in. level down to water level.

555-11. Sealing

A seal shall be provided in each conduit run entering or leaving a dispenser. Additional seals shall be provided in accordance with Section 501-5.

All wiring and equipment within the Class I locations described above shall meet the requirements of Article 501.

Chapter 6. Special Equipment

ARTICLE 600 — ELECTRIC SIGNS AND OUTLINE LIGHTING

A. General

600-1. Scope

An electric sign, according to Code definition, is a "fixed, stationary or portable self-contained electrically illuminated utilization equipment with words or symbols designed to convey information or attract attention."

Outline lighting is "an arrangement of incandescent lamps or electric discharge tubing to outline or call attention to certain features such as the shape of a building or the decoration of a window."

Article 600 applies for both of these equipments.

The provisions of Sections 600-1 through 600-10 apply for all voltages. Low- and high-voltage installations are treated separately in Parts B and C, respectively.

600-2. Disconnect Required

(a) All outline lighting and all signs except portable signs must have a disconnect, which may be a switch or circuit breaker.

The disconnect must be within sight of the sign or outline lighting.

Exception.

For signs having automatic controllers, the disconnect need not be within sight of the sign or outline lighting, but must be within sight from the controller. The disconnect must be equipped with a lock for locking in the open position.

(b) A transformer is an inductive load. Certain types of switches are made for inductive loads; for such switches, when used as a transformer disconnect, the switch rating need be no higher than the amperage of the load. If the switch is a general-use switch not rated for inductive loads, the ampere rating of the switch must be at least *twice* the ampere rating of the transformer.

The disconnect for a transformer may be an AC general-use snap switch. The ampere rating of this type of switch need be no higher than the ampere rating of the transformer. If an AC-DC general-use snap switch is used, the switch ampere rating must be twice the current rating of the transformer, since the AC-DC general-use switch is not rated for inductive loads. "General-use" knife switches used as transformer disconnects must also have a current rating twice that of the transformer current. Flashers controlling transformers should be specially designed for the service, or should have a current rating at least twice that of the transformer controlled.

600-3. Enclosures as Pull Boxes

The wiring methods required by this Article of the Code for signs and outline lighting would extend to the transformer or to the sign or outline lighting, but not beyond these limits.

Exception.

The wiring may pass through a sign or outline lighting system to other signs (and outline lighting) that are a part of the same sign, provided the extension is protected at 20 amps. or less.

600-4. Listing Required

All electric signs must be listed. For a definition of "Listed," see p. 70-10 of the Code.

600-5. Grounding

Metal parts of signs and non-current-carrying metal parts of the wiring within the sign (such as tube terminal boxes) must be grounded. Grounding may be through a grounding wire run with the circuit conductors (may be insulated or bare), or, if metal-clad wiring is used (such as conduit, tubing, or BX), the conduit, tubing, or BX sheath may serve as the grounding path.

The different metal parts of a sign may be bonded together by No. 14. The grounding conductor for the entire sign must be sized according to Table 250-95, p. 70-102, according to the size of the circuit protection.

There are two exceptions where grounding is not required:

1. If a sign is insulated from ground and not accessible to unauthorized persons, grounding is not required.

2. Portable incandescent or fluorescent signs need not be grounded if voltage is 150 or less to ground. For higher voltages, portable signs must be grounded.

600-6. Branch Circuits

(1) Circuits feeding transformers *and* lamps or ballasts are limited to 20-amps. rating. This means that the fuse size or circuit-breaker setting protecting such a circuit may not exceed 20 amps., and the circuit should be loaded accordingly.

(2) Circuits feeding *only* electric-discharge lighting transformers are limited to 30 amps. Electric-discharge lighting would include fluorescent and neon tubes.

Each commercial occupancy with ground floor footage *accessible to pedestrians* shall be provided with at least one outdoor receptacle for sign or outline lighting use. The circuit to each receptacle shall be a 20-amp. circuit, and shall supply no other outlets.

600-7. Marking

(a) Signs must be marked by the manufacturer with maker's name. Electric-discharge signs must be marked with full load amps. and input voltage. For incandescent lamp signs, the number of lampholders must be indicated.

(b) Transformers must be marked by the manufacturer with input amps. (or volt-amperes), input (primary) voltage, output (secondary) open-circuit voltage, and maker's name.

600-8. Enclosures

(a) Conductors and terminals (except supply leads) must be enclosed.

(b) Cutouts, flashers, etc., must be enclosed in metal boxes.

(c) Enclosures shall have adequate strength.

(d) Except for indoor portable signs, all signs must be constructed of metal or other material that will not burn. Wood may be used for external decoration if kept at least 2 in. clear of current-carrying parts.

(e) For outline lighting and for electric-discharge signs, sheet steel must be at least No. 24 gauge or, if ribbed or corrugated, No. 26 gauge.

For other than electric-discharge signs, sheet steel must be at least No. 28 gauge.

Sheet copper for signs and outline lighting must be at least 20 ounce weight.

(f) All metal enclosures shall be corrosion-proof. Galvanized metal would meet this requirement.

(g) Enclosures for outside use must be of weatherproof construction, and fitted with drain holes at least $\frac{1}{4}$ in. diameter, but not larger than $\frac{1}{2}$ in.

600-9. Portable Letters

The following rules apply to *portable outdoor* letters, symbols, and signs:

(a) A weatherproof grounding-type receptacle shall be provided for each letter, fixture, or sign.

(b) Cord shall be Type S, SJO, SO, ST, SJT or SJTO with grounding conductor.

(c) Cords must be at least 10 ft above ground level.

600-10. Clearances

(a) For clearances of open conductors, see Article 225.

(b) The bottom of sign and outline lighting enclosures shall be at least 16 ft above areas accessible to vehicles.

Exception:

If the enclosure is suitably protected, the clearance may be reduced.

B. 600 Volts Nominal or Less

600-21. Installation of Conductors

(a) Wiring Method

The following wiring methods are permitted for wiring to signs or outline lighting when the voltage is 600 or less:

1. Rigid metal conduit.
2. EMT.
3. Type MC cable.
4. Metal troughing.
5. Rigid nonmetallic conduit.

6. Type MI (mineral-insulated) cable.

7. Liquidtight flexible metal conduit.

8. Flexible metal conduit.

9. Intermediate metal conduit.

(b) Insulation and Size

No. 14 is the smallest size conductor permitted. (There are exceptions for conductors within a sign and for certain control conductors, where No. 16, 18, or 20 is permitted.)

(c) Exposed to Weather

Where exposed to the weather, BX must be the leaded type or other type specially approved for the conditions. Conductors in conduit, EMT, or other metal raceway need not be lead-covered, provided the conduit, EMT, or raceway is *raintight* and *arranged to drain.* Otherwise, they must be leaded.

(d) Number of Conductors in Raceway

For sign flashers, any number of conductors may be carried in a conduit or raceway, as long as the percentage of "fill" does not exceed that specified in Table I, p. 70-577 of the Code.

(e) Conductors Soldered to Terminals

When lampholders are other than the pin type, conductors must be *soldered* to the terminals.

600-22. Lampholders

Lampholders must be the unswitched type. Miniature type lampholders are not permitted.

600-23. Conductors Within Signs and Troughs

Wires within sign and outline lighting troughs shall be mechanically secured.

600-24. Protection of Leads

Bushings shall be employed where wires pass through enclosures.

C. Over 600 Volts Nominal

600-31. Installation of Conductors

The following wiring methods are permitted:

1. Concealed conductors on insulators.

2. Rigid and intermediate metal conduit.

3. Flexible metal conduit.

4. Liquidtight flexible metal conduit.

5. EMT.

6. Type MC cable.

(b) Insulation and Size

It should be remembered that conductors for general wiring have insulation suitable for voltages only to 600, and may not be used for voltages above this. Conductors used for high voltages must have high voltage insulation approved for the voltage of the circuit.

No. 14 is the smallest size conductor permitted. (There are exceptions for leads permanently attached to electric-discharge lampholders, and for show window and portable signs, where No. 16 and No. 18 are permitted.)

(c) Bends in Conductors

Sharp bends in conductors shall be avoided.

(d) Concealed Conductors on Insulators—Indoors

Shall be installed in channels on glazed insulators suitable for the voltage.

The conductors must be separated at least 1 in. for voltages of 10,000 or less, and $1\frac{1}{2}$ in. for voltages above 10,000. The same separation is required between conductors and nearby objects.

(e) Conductors in Raceways

In damp or wet locations, conductor insulation must extend beyond the raceway at least

2 inches for voltages of 5,000 or less.

3 inches for voltages of 5,001 to 10,000.

4 inches for voltages above 10,000.

In dry locations, conductor insulation must extend beyond the raceway at least

$1\frac{1}{2}$ inches for voltages of 5,000 or less.

2 inches for voltages of 5,001 to 10,000.

$2\frac{1}{2}$ inches for voltages above 10,000.

The purpose of these rules is to prevent arcing between the high voltage conductor and the raceway.

If a single conductor is run in a raceway, the length is limited to 20 ft. The purpose of this rule is to prevent a capacitive voltage from being established between the high voltage conductor and the raceway. An excessive voltage between conductor and raceway could result in damage to the conductor insulation. Such a condition is not likely to exist when the length of the raceway is 20 ft or less.

(f) Show Windows and Similar Locations

Conductors hanging in the air away from combustible material need not be guarded or protected.

(g) Conductors in Tubing

Conductors may be run from the ends of tubing to the grounded midpoint of transformers.

600-32. Transformers

The voltage rating given for transformers for signs and outline lighting is the open-circuit secondary voltage. A transformer rated at 15,000 volts has 15,000 volts at the secondary terminals only when there is no load on the transformer. When a load is connected to the secondaries, the secondary voltage drops abruptly. The greater the amperage, the less is the secondary voltage. Secondary current is rated in milliamps. A milliamp is 1/1,000 amps.

The volt-ampere rating is equal to secondary amps. × volts. For a transformer with a current rating of 50 milliamps. at 9,000 volts, the volt-ampere rating would be 50/1,000 × 9,000 = 450 volt-amperes.

(a) Voltage

Transformer secondary open-circuit voltage is limited to 15,000 volts (with a 1,000-volt additional test allowance).

For transformers with one end grounded, the secondary open-circuit voltage is limited to 7,500 volts (with a 500-volt additional test allowance).

The open-circuit voltage is the voltage at the high-voltage terminals when there is no load on the transformer.

(b) Type

Transformer rating is limited to 4,500 volt-amperes.

For outline lighting, transformer secondary current rating is limited to 30 milliamps. (If the installation complies with all the rules of Article 410, larger ratings are permitted, as per Section 410-83.)

Open core and coil type transformers may be used only in small portable signs *indoors.* Voltage is limited to 5,000 volts, with a test allowance of 500 volts.

(c) Exposed to Weather

Transformers exposed to the weather shall be the weatherproof type, or shall be installed in a weatherproof enclosure (which may be a weatherproof sign).

(d) Transformer Secondary Connections

The high-voltage (secondary) windings of transformers shall not be connected in parallel.

The high-voltage (secondary) windings of transformers shall not be connected in series, except as follows:

1. The secondary windings of two transformers may be connected in series, provided that the midpoint connection between the secondaries is grounded and connected to the transformer case. The grounding wire need not have high voltage insulation. A standard conductor may be used for this purpose, since the voltage at this point is at ground potential (see Fig. 420).
2. Transformers for small portable signs, or show windows, having permanently attached secondary leads not more than 8 ft long may be connected in series on the secondary side.

(e) Accessibility

Transformers shall be accessible. According to Code definition, "accessible" means "admitting close approach beecause not guarded by locked doors, elevation, or other effective means."

(f) Working Space

A work space of at least 3 ft shall be provided on all sides around a transformer (except for a transformer in a sign).

(g) Attic Locations

Transformers may be located in attics, provided there is a passageway at least 3 ft high and 2 ft wide to the transformer.

600-33. Electric-Discharge Tubing

(a) Design

The length of tubing served by a transformer should be no more than the length of tubing for which the transformer is designed. The length of tubing will depend upon the tube diameter. For larger tube diameters, the length of tubing may be greater. For smaller tube diameters, the length will be less. Each transformer has its specified tubing length.

If too much tubing is connected to a transformer or if the tube diameter is too small, the transformer secondary voltage will be excessive. Transformers for gaseous tubes are built to operate at a certain load voltage. Proper load voltage can be maintained by keeping tubing length within the recommended limit.

(b) Support

Tubing must be mounted on glazed insulators.

(c) Contact with Flammable Material and Other Surfaces

Tubing must be kept clear of flammable material. For tubing operating at more than 7,500 volts, a $\frac{1}{4}$-in. minimum spacing is required between tubing and *any* surface or object.

600-34. Terminals and Electrode Receptacles for Electric-Discharge Tubing

Tubing terminals must be "inaccessible to unqualified persons." Tubing terminals operate at a high potential, and must be either located so as not to be within reach, or must be enclosed. When enclosed, they must be on glazed insulators, or separated at least $1\frac{1}{2}$ in. from grounded metal or combustible material.

When signs or outline lighting are provided with electrode receptacles, the tubing terminates at the receptacle.

If receptacles are not provided, conductors must be separated at least $1\frac{1}{2}$ in. between conductors and $1\frac{1}{2}$ in. from grounded metal. Bushings must be used on all outdoor signs, and on indoor signs operating at over 7,500 volts.

For exposed-type show-window signs, the terminals must be enclosed by receptacles.

A flexible seal shall be used to close an opening between tubing and a receptacle or bushing.

600-35. Switches on Doors

For an indoor sign of over 600 volts, having a door or cover that is accessible to the general public, an interlocking switch must be provided, and wired to open the circuit on opening of the door or cover. Or, as an alternative, the door or cover may be fastened in such a way as to require special tools for opening. If this is done, an interlocking switch is not required.

600-36. Fixed Outline Lighting and Skeleton-Type Signs for Interior Use

(a) Gas tubing shall be supported independently of conductors.

(b) Transformers shall be in metal enclosures, and located as close as practicable to the gas tubing system.

(c) Supply conductors for transformers shall be in metal raceway or non-metallic conduit. Metal raceway shall be grounded.

(d) High tension conductors shall be in metal raceway. Raceway shall be grounded.

Exception: Conductors not over 4 ft in length may be in insulating sleeves.

600-37. Portable Gas Tube Signs for Show Windows and Interior Use

(a) Portable gas tube signs may be used indoors only.

(b) Transformer shall be the window type or in a metal enclosure.

(c) Cord shall be one of the following types: SJ, SJO, SJT, SJTO, S, SO, ST, or STO. Cord shall not be longer than 10 ft and must have a grounding conductor.

(d) High-voltage conductors shall be not more than 6 ft long and protected by sleeves or tubing.

(e) Transformers and other exposed metal enclosures shall be grounded.

(f) Portable indoor signs shall be held in place by *not more* than two hooks attached to the transformer case.

Index*

*Note: Except in a few instances, the references in this index are by section number, not by page number.